The World in 1800

The World in 1800

OLIVIER BERNIER

A ROBERT L. BERNSTEIN BOOK

John Wiley & Sons, Inc.
New York • Chichester • Weinheim • Brisbane • Singapore • Toronto

Published by John Wiley & Sons, Inc.
Published simultaneously in Canada

This publication is designed to provide accurate and authoritative information in regard to the subject matter covered. It is sold with the understanding that the publisher is not engaged in rendering professional services. If professional advice or other expert assistance is required, the services of a competent professional person should be sought.

Library of Congress Cataloging-in-Publication Data:

Bernier, Olivier.
    The world in 1800 / Olivier Bernier.
        p.   cm.
    Includes bibliographical references and index.
    ISBN 0-471-30371-2 (alk. paper)
    1. Civilization, Modern — 19th century. 2. Eighteen hundred, A.D.
I. Title.
CB417.B45   2000
909.81 — dc21   99-32208

TO ROSAMOND BERNIER RUSSELL,

whose knowledge, wit, and joie de vivre have been a lifelong inspiration, and for whose unfailing support I can never be sufficiently grateful.

Contents

Preface

THE WORLD IN 1800: why, two hundred years later, should it deserve our attention? Today, the different parts of the globe are so closely interlinked that we hear about an African civil war, a flood in Asia, or an election in South America almost as they are happening. The world, we often feel, is no further away than a television channel or the Internet; but, in fact, we tend to know very little about countries other than our own. At best, we extend ourselves to western Europe. News flashes, the occasional war, famine, or massacre refer to places and cultures that are utterly strange to us, even when they impinge significantly on our way of life. We understood very little about the Soviet Union; China remains, in many ways, a mystery. Much of the rest of the world is just as puzzling.

This lack of knowledge is one of the origins of *The World in 1800*. As we look across the globe, we find that it was far more closely connected than we might have thought possible in that long-ago era before satellites. Why 1800 in particular? Because, in many ways, 1800 is the beginning of our own era. The first real democracy proved itself in the United States when the presidency passed peacefully from one man to another, all because the people had spoken. In Europe, the principles of the French Revolution, Napoléon notwithstanding, gained increasingly wide acceptance: within a very few years, it had become all but impossible to run a country without a constitution.

The rest of the world was changing as well, in ways that still affect people today. Latin America ceased being a group of colonies and became independent. Great Britain conquered an empire in India and set the stage for the massive colonial expansion that occupied the rest of the century. China embarked on the path which made it a prey, first to the Europeans, then to Japan. The Ottoman Empire, decaying and powerless, prepared the Middle East of our time. Today, across the world, we are still dealing with the consequences of these events. Our world, in fact, was born in 1800.

Still, things were very different in 1800. The first Industrial Revolution was barely under way, steam had yet to be mastered, transportation was agonizingly slow. Social structures, too, remained very much what they had been for centuries. Except in the United States and revolutionary France, people mostly stayed in the place and in the class to which they had been born.

It is precisely the contrast between the survival of the old and the appearance of the new that makes 1800 so fascinating. Although we can see how far we have come, that world has lessons for us even today. *The World in 1800* is an excursion into a past that matters because it is close enough to affect us and distant enough to be seen clearly. And as we learn about what other places were like then, and how people behaved, we will perhaps understand better why things are what they are today.

Acknowledgments

I owe my thanks, for their comments and suggestions, to: Professor Andrew Shankman, of Princeton University, for the section on North America; Professor Frank Gibney, of the Pacific Basin Institute, for the section on China and Japan; Llewellyn Smith, the producer of the WGBH series *Americans in Africa*, and Her Royal Highness Princess Prudence of Swaziland, for the section on Africa. Any remaining mistakes are solely the author's responsibility.

My gratitude goes to Rui Lopes, who was of immeasurable help in gathering the illustrations.

I also wish to thank Hana Umlauf Lane, the editor of this book. Her patience, understanding, and acute sense of the English language have been a comfort and an inspiration. Her overall view of the vast subject of this book gave me immeasurable help in shaping it; and her consistent good humor has made the process a pleasure.

The New York Public Library, as always, is beyond praise. The depth and width of its collections, the working conditions it offers researchers, and the unfailing knowledge and helpfulness of its librarians have lightened my task.

Finally, this book owes its very existence to Robert Bernstein, who first saw that this was a worthwhile topic and asked me to write it.

INTRODUCTION

Two Worlds, One World

I

Two CENTURIES, TWO WORLDS: in 1700, people everywhere were prepared to obey their hereditary rulers; in 1776, the U.S. Declaration of Independence claimed freedoms that came to be seen as everyone's birthright. In 1789, for the first time in Europe, the French Revolution asserted that the basic necessities of civilized life included equality before the law, liberty, and the right for every people to choose its government. By 1800, the United States had a constitution that guaranteed this. France was just entering an era of dictatorship, but the way of life that had prevailed in the old European monarchies was clearly seen to be doomed.

That sense of progress, of the superiority of the modern age, was widespread throughout Europe and the Americas. Science, freed at last from the shackles of religion, had begun to explore and explain the world. Manufactures were giving way to industries in which new, advanced techniques prevailed. The middle class was expanding rapidly, and education was spreading. Wars, of course, continued, and so did the slave trade: the world, in 1800, was no paradise, but there was a new hope for change and improvement. Even the most reactionary rulers knew it. They hardly liked it, but they could not fail to understand the difference between the recent past and the present.

There was still a radical separation between the well-to-do and the rest of the population. Those without capital or significant property were the overwhelming mass of the population—from about 97 percent in Central Europe to about 80 percent in Great Britain, but only 10 or 15 percent in the United States. The United States was seen as the land of hope. Elsewhere, the rich, the noble, the powerful were highly visible: they ruled countries, built palaces, and were patrons of the arts. Because of that, they have remained visible. The poor tend to be almost invisible: they wrote no letters and left no memoirs.

For everyone, life was radically different from what we know at the end of the twentieth century. Many women died in childbirth—rich as well as poor, of course, but the poor had greater chances of infection; and, for them, medical care was nonexistent. Wounds, most often, did not heal; broken bones were set, usually badly. Pain was an everyday presence.

For the poor, or nearly poor, the world was a small place. They knew about their village or small town; they heard the local gossip, and rumors about the great events from the world outside. Some, perhaps a third, were literate in France and in England; in the rest of Europe, most were not. In those years, on the Continent, or in India, China, or Africa, the world often intruded suddenly into their lives as armies marched back and forth. Set against this, however, was their sense of belonging to the village community, to an extended family. Comfort was available when things went badly, rejoicing was often collective. As the world changed, and the poor began to understand that they could be free, they were still sustained by the traditional structures on which they had always relied, but they were also able to look forward to a time when they would be in charge of their own lives.

The world was still a simple place. Except in the big cities, only basic consumer goods were available: cloth, needles, thread, some instruments with which to work wood or metal, pottery, knives, and not much else. Food was grown locally; many villages still functioned as almost closed economic units. Houses had no plumbing, no services built in. That made them less comfortable than they are today, but it also meant that they were cheaper and easier to build and to buy. There were very few machines, of even the simplest kind. Transport was by horse or sailing ship. There was no machine a reasonably intelligent person could not understand with a little effort.

Still, there were signs of impending change in the structure of this simple, well-ordered world: when, in the 1790s, Babeuf preached that all property should be held in common, he began stirring aspirations that eventually produced cataclysmic change. When the French armies appeared, they often brought with them new ideas about the structure of society—and the rich began to worry. Revolution was thought to be catching; and that, in the end, brings the world of 1800 closest to that of today: dimly, fearfully, the poor began to see that they might one day claim a better standard of living.

II

Just as much of life in Europe was primitive, so it was in the rest of the world. There was not a great deal of difference between peasants in France, in Mexico, or in India. That sort of similarity, though, tends to divide rather than unite:

it creates small, closed-in communities, distrustful of their neighbors and uninterested in anything far away.

It took, often, as much as six months to go from London to Calcutta, more than six weeks to go from Le Havre to Boston. If you were rich, and could afford your own traveling carriage, the fees of the postilions, and the charges for the horses, you might get to Saint Petersburg from Paris in ten to twelve days; but that rate of speed was thought to be remarkable. And, of course, letters went no faster—and postage was expensive. How then, without phones, faxes, computers, and television, could the world have become one?

In many ways, it was not. Indeed, some of it was utterly unknown to any given group of people. The Europeans knew nothing about the interior of Africa, and very little about the islands in the Pacific; the Chinese and the Japanese knew very little about Europe and almost nothing about the Americas. Africans, kidnapped from their continent by the slave traders, did not even suspect the existence of the countries to which they were taken; and so it went.

In spite of all this, for the first time ever, the world was becoming one, united by war and by the survival of that most ancient of evils, slavery. Already during the Seven Years' War, from 1756 to 1763, fighting had ranged across the continents and across the oceans; but it had been disorganized and relatively brief, a series of spasms rather than a new sense of connection. The wars of the French Revolution, from 1792 to 1815, changed all that. Now the leading nations—France and Great Britain particularly—had worldwide strategies. What happened in Rio, Cairo, Calcutta, or Cape Town mattered to the governments in Paris and London; and each movement of the adversaries caused consequences thousands of miles away.

Sometimes these consequences were utterly unexpected: when Napoléon invaded Spain, he did not think that he was bringing about the independence of her American colonies; when the British government decided to conquer most of India, it did not know it was founding an empire. Most of the time, however, these interventions were meant to further an immediate goal. Communications might be slow; but in Whitehall or at the Tuileries Palace, they thought in terms of the entire world. Thus, it may be a coincidence, but it is no wonder, that Lord Macartney, the first British Ambassador to China, was appointed governor of the Cape Colony just a few years after his return from Peking. Even more striking, Waterloo, the battle that ended the era, was won by Wellington, who had learned his skills fifteen years earlier on the plains of India.

The world was one because of the war. It was one also because of an institution which seems, in retrospect, both paradoxical and anachronistic. Slavery has been a part of most primitive societies, but we expect it to disappear as a consequence of progress. Then there is Christianity, the religion professed, in one form or another, by most Europeans and Americans in 1800: given its doctrine about the equality of souls, it cannot easily accommodate itself to the tenets of slavery. A slave, after all, is held to be less than human, a creature not entitled to the basic rights shared by the rest of humankind. And yet, at the beginning of the nineteenth century, slavery was the norm in most of the world.

In Europe itself, most Russian peasants were serfs. In the Americas, slaves were held from Maine to Tierra del Fuego. The Ottoman Empire had its own slaves. So did Africa, both within the continent and for export. Many Chinese peasants were, in effect, also serfs. And four European countries, France, Great Britain, Spain, and Portugal, which did not practice slavery on their own soil, traded in slaves and allowed slavery in their colonies. There were slaves in the Dutch Cape Colony; there were slaves, in fact, almost everywhere.

This seems all the more extraordinary in that the world in 1800 prided itself (except, perhaps, for China and Japan) on its modernity, on its ability to transcend the customs and practices of earlier centuries. Much of it also emphasized its morality; and the United States, a major slaveholder and importer, had been recently founded on the premise that all men were entitled to life, liberty, and the pursuit of happiness. What remained true in so many parts of the world, though, was that the economy was based on slavery: a planter in the southern United States, a Russian nobleman, or a South African Boer would all have said that it was impossible to free the slaves without ruining the nation.

III

Finally, there was yet another phenomenon that united widely separated parts of the world. Today, we have grown accustomed to seeing, and sometimes lamenting, the Americanization of the world. In 1800, people were watching the Europeanization of the world. Paris fashions were copied from Moscow to Bombay, from Lima to Istanbul. European artifacts could be found in Peking as well as in the capital of the Kongo. English dining-room tables, French porcelain, German clocks circulated everywhere. Of course, you would not have found the latest fashionable novel in the middle of China, or an enameled snuffbox in Benin, but the connections were there. Already, in that sense, the world was one; and the trend, having just begun, was accelerating rapidly.

Soon, this European domination took the form of colonial expansion: the nineteenth century was the age of colonial empires in Asia and Africa. European civilization was held to be superior, the white man to be an *Übermensch*. All that was emerging in 1800, and much of it started in France.

The French Revolution changed more than the political geography of Europe: it also introduced new ways of establishing governments, new methods of administering the populations. The contemporaries were clear about it:

after 1789, nothing was ever going to be the same, and that sense of unstoppable change was widely shared. That is why *The World in 1800* begins with France. What started there affected, in one way or another, and sometimes by ricochet, the rest of the world. For a while, after 1789, kings everywhere hoped that the French Revolution would be contained and, eventually, reversed. They were mistaken. The military might of France could be broken—it was eventually in 1814—but the ideas of the Revolution could not be ignored or defeated. One law for all, the end of class and clerical privileges, consent to taxation, and, ultimately, the people's right to choose their government: those were immortal, undefeatable principles. They were applied in the United States first; but it was only when France adopted them that they became really universal. Eventually, Napoléon went into exile and the Bourbons returned to France, but even they, who were said to have forgotten nothing and learned nothing, were forced to grant a constitution. Here was another way the world became bound together: slowly, the ideals of democracy moved across continents and oceans. There was, in 1800, really one world.

PART ONE

Europe

CHAPTER ONE

A Very Great Change

The Center of the World

Europe, in 1800, had just met the future. Throughout the preceding century, its people—the educated part, at least—had felt that progress was constant, rational, and gentle. Then, in one great explosion, everything changed. The French Revolution, which began in 1789, created a new, fierce, often bloody world. No king, no church, no aristocracy; these were such shocking novelties that the other European Powers—Prussia, Austria, Great Britain—banded together to restore the old order. By 1800, it was clear that they had failed. They still had their own churches and monarchies, but all their leaders, political and intellectual, understood that they were facing not just a new century but a new world. Whatever happened, Europe was leading the way.

Because of these changes, and because they owned much of the rest of the globe, the Europeans were convinced that they were the only people who really mattered. Those parts they did not control were either too wild or too strange to be really desirable. All of North and South America, together with their assorted islands, had long been colonized, even if the United States was now independent; Great Britain had spawned cities on the edge of India and, from them, armed expeditions were conquering an empire; as for Africa, all that was wanted was the occasional trading port to tap the resources of that continent—slaves, gold, and ivory.

That, to be sure, left out a few major powers: Asia, the Europeans thought, consisted essentially of China, which was seen mainly as a source of porcelain, exotic silks, and lacquerwork; Japan, fiercely closed on itself; a few spice islands; and Siam, a funny kingdom where desirable tropical woods were easily found.

9

Then there was Turkey. Its sultan still ruled over a vast empire that included the entire Middle East, Turkey itself, Armenia, Georgia, most of the shores of the Black Sea, almost all the Balkan peninsula (today's Rumania, Bulgaria, and former Yugoslavia), as well as Greece. Only a century earlier, in 1684, Vienna had been besieged (and nearly taken) by a Turkish army; but by the 1780s, this once mighty giant was in full decadence. Russia ate steadily at its Black Sea possessions; Egypt had become semi-independent. The question now was a simple one: what to do with the Turkish empire's many possessions when it finally collapsed.

Indeed, the non-European world was seen mainly as a source of tropical goods—slaves, sugar, spices, coffee, tea, ivory, rare woods, gold, silver. There was a fierce rivalry between Spain, France, and England when it came to this kind of trade, with each country either defending its possessions (Spain) or trying to extend them (England). As a result, the Seven Years' War (1756–1763), in a haphazard and disorganized way, had become the first of the world wars. Fighting took place not just on the traditional European battlefields, but as far away as the South Indian coast and the frozen wastes of Canada, and so it was a rehearsal of sorts for the real world war that followed, the conflict which had begun in 1792 between revolutionary France and the rest of Europe and became the Napoleonic Wars before it finally ended in 1815. In 1800, armies and navies were fighting from the Netherlands to the southern tip of Africa, from Italy to India.

Of course, other peoples, on other continents, felt very differently about their relative importance. The emperor of China, for instance, knew very well that he ruled the only worthwhile portion of the earth, and the Koreans, next door, never forgot it; the shah of Persia, although he had to acknowledge that the sultan was a worthy rival, still considered himself a mighty potentate, as did the sultan himself. And inside Africa, local kings reigned in the full enjoyment of their own importance.

Was Europe, then, really the center of the world? Yes, in that it was entering a second period in which its power expanded throughout the known world (the first had seen the conquest of the Americas in the sixteenth century). There were a number of reasons for this, not the least of which was the development of the new technologies that had brought about the Industrial Revolution. Mechanical looms; faster, more destructive guns; more complex metallurgical techniques; the mass production of consumer goods; all these were new and unequaled elsewhere in the world. Just as important, these changes were financed by the development of banking and credit. As a result, Europe, economically and militarily, had become much the most powerful of all the continents.

It also mattered that the Europeans saw themselves as the most civilized people in the history of the planet. The Greeks and the Romans, they felt, had made a good beginning; Alexander and Caesar, Aristotle and Cicero were household names among the middle and upper classes; but then the Dark Ages had come, those times of superstition and ignorance. By the end of the eighteenth century, though, reason ruled once again. This was the Enlightenment: the light of intelligence, logic, and knowledge had dispelled the darkness.

For the first time, intellectuals, scientists, and those who read them felt sure that they could, eventually, understand the world because it was ruled by unchangeable principles, not the whim of a deity or the power of magic. Many laws of nature had yet to be discovered—science was, after all, still young—but the ultimate result was hardly in doubt. In the same way, the many species of animals and plants were being rapidly cataloged. No one believed any longer in the existence, somewhere far away, of strange, unlikely creatures. There was, in fact, nothing that could not be ascertained by rational inquiry.

Nor could people be prevented, any longer, from exploring subjects rejected by religious dogma. The history of the world was one of these subjects; virtually no educated person, at the end of the eighteenth century, believed either that the world had been created in seven days or that Adam and Eve had ever existed. That same attitude applied to sciences like physics and chemistry. Although the Catholic Church had reluctantly admitted that the earth was round and that it circled the sun, it held firm to quite a number of other strange beliefs, which none but the very pious still respected. At the same time, religious tolerance was rapidly gaining ground, despite the opposition of the various established churches. In Prussia, Frederick the Great (1740–1786) had allowed both Catholic and Protestant cathedrals to be built in Berlin—no doubt, it helped that he cared nothing for religion. Even in France, a country from which Protestantism had been banned in 1684, toleration was appearing; finally, in 1788, the French had been allowed to worship as they pleased.

Even more striking, great numbers of educated people felt able to reject all religious teaching—a few because they were atheists; most because, like Voltaire, George Washington, or Thomas Jefferson, they were deists. They thought that there must be a Supreme Being, but were unwilling to let themselves be hemmed in by a specific theology.

All this made for more freedom of thought than ever before; it also convinced the Europeans that, in this area as well, they led the world. And indeed, this new openness, this thirst for scientific knowledge, resulted in new techniques that gave Europe an even bigger lead over the other continents. The Europeans themselves never doubted what they saw as their intrinsic superiority. Little was known about Asian or African gods; but everyone agreed that the rankest superstition ruled those continents. Equally, no one thought that any of those distant cultures might be as rich, as advanced as the European; there was only one right way of doing things—and many wrong ways. It was

not the least shocking part of the Marquis de Sade's books that he was a cultural relativist, a man who thought that since the very same act could be
praiseworthy in one place, and a dreadful sin in another, there was no superior
civilization: the only thing that mattered in the end was to do precisely what
one pleased.

Those who viewed change with distaste clung firmly to the old standards
and had absolute values. They believed that God (the deity was either Catholic
or Protestant, depending on the location) had created a perfectly ordered hierarchy, in which the king was on top, the royal family next, the aristocracy
a small step lower, and the rest of humanity below notice. These conservatives formed a sizable group all over Europe; they could be found at the various courts, and in most government ministries, and they still owned much of
the land.

The reformers also disagreed with the Marquis de Sade. Although, of
course, they advocated change, they believed in the importance of virtue, usually as expounded by Jean-Jacques Rousseau. Kindness to others, a yearning
for the equality of mankind, a hefty dose of sentimentality, and a need to create
a morally sound world motivated them. On occasion that last need outweighed
any possible kindness; it was in order to build a more equal society that the
French revolutionaries sent a significant number of people to the guillotine.

Perhaps because his fellowmen made him so uncomfortable, Rousseau
had come up with a startling notion, that of the "noble savage." Civilization,
Rousseau said, was corrupt by definition. Only in a state of nature did mankind live virtuously; with organized societies came greed, tyranny, inequality,
and afflictions of all kinds. And so the very people who felt, with a degree of
justification, that they had reached an unparalleled degree of civilization, also
fantasized about life in a state of nature. This in no sense diminished their
sense of superiority over the rest of the world. Since no "noble savages" were
actually known, and since, in any event, no one really intended to trade gilded
carriages and sumptuous mansions for a cave, the yearning for a state of nature
could be understood as a sign of sophistication that simply confirmed a well-
understood fact: Europe was vastly superior to the rest of the world.

"Those who have not lived before the Revolution do not understand how
sweet life can be,"[1] Talleyrand wrote. He was right. Throughout the eighteenth
century, and culminating in the 1770s and 1780s, all across Europe, a new culture had been established in which pleasure was the key. Naturally, there were
all sorts of pleasures. Some could be found in a witty, far-ranging conversation;
and so, before 1789, people came from all over just to attend the Paris salons.
Other enjoyments were more sensual, ranging from an appreciation of the
nouvelle cuisine to the understanding of interior decoration: even today, the
great furniture makers of that time remain unequaled. And then, there had
been other, even more compelling, ways to enjoy oneself. Men and women alike

had felt free to love whom they chose; fidelity to a spouse was considered stodgy; and kept women had flourished. Here, in fact, choice had been everywhere, even if not many hosts went to the same lengths as one particular Neapolitan prince. Depending on his guests' preferences, they were greeted by ravishing young women or handsome young men—or both—standing naked around a pool and ready to do whatever the guests wanted.

That had been a time when refinement was everything. Manners, tastes, sensibilities, everything seemed to reject crudeness. As for sentimentality, it was everywhere. When, in 1782, Marie Antoinette was spotted sitting in the Garden of the Tuileries eating strawberries and cream, all the spectators burst into tears at her adorable simplicity. If your little dog had the sniffles, you announced to all your friends that your anguish was excruciating, and that, indeed, you would not sleep a wink that night.

In this endlessly refined world, it was understood that catastrophes (other than those due to nature) were impossible. There might still be a few local wars, but they would be minor and conducted with becoming humanness. There could be no great social upheaval: change would come gradually and without tears.

Of course, not all Europeans thought alike. The English aristocracy might love visiting Paris; it might think the French set the right standards when it came to culture, decor, and food; but the British government prided itself on its unique way of operating, and it was intent on securing trading posts around the world, an activity the French found deeply uninteresting. France had wanted no more conquests; Catherine the Great, empress of Russia, had been eager to expand her already enormous realm, and in order to do so, she had appropriated about half of Poland (the other half was split between Austria and Prussia) and a great swatch of territory in the Caucasus and along the Black Sea. Still, in the 1780s, the Europeans, for all their differences, had shared some certainties. Chief of them was that, in this most civilized, most superior continent, violent change was unthinkable.

THE WORLD UPSIDE DOWN

This wholly mistaken belief had survived for an amazingly long time. When, in 1789, the Revolution began in France with the election of the Estates-General, everyone (except a few die-hard reactionaries) felt sure that this was the first step in a process of peaceful reform. When, on July 14 of that year, the Parisians stormed and took the Bastille, it was seen as a positive step, even though it had involved the odd lynching. What mattered, though, was the final end of arbitrary government. Not to worry, well-informed people said, the Revolution was now over. And they repeated that statement when, on October 4, a mob dragged the king, the queen, and the royal family from Versailles back to Paris.

Of course, they were wrong; these events were merely the beginning of astonishingly violent and radical changes. Within three years, the monarchy had ended, the new constitution had been discarded, and massacres had taken place in the Paris prisons. In September 1792, the Republic was proclaimed. On January 21, 1793, King Louis XVI was guillotined and so, nine months later, was Marie Antoinette. A new revolutionary government took over, and the Terror began. France, that most refined, that most sophisticated of countries, had become unrecognizable.

The officially proclaimed Terror was, however, no random savagery. The approximately ten thousand men and women who were killed were selected quite carefully: if the new national assembly, the Convention, demanded such bloodthirsty policies, if its all-powerful committees sent cartfuls of aristocrats, priests, and assorted opponents to the guillotine, it was, they considered, for a good reason, and no one was more coldly logical, or more blood-chillingly threatening, than Robespierre. The Republic, he explained, was the hope of mankind; if it disappeared, tyranny would prevail forever; thus, in order to pre-serve liberty, it was necessary to suppress it temporarily. That line of reasoning, for all its self-evident fallacy, has continued to have enormous appeal. The Soviets used it in our own century, and so do dictators all over the world.

War as a Way of Life

The threat from outside also helped to sustain the Terror. France was at war with Prussia, Austria, and Great Britain, and they had all announced that they would restore the monarchy when they won. Many excesses, therefore, were passed off as needed for the defense of the Republic. By 1800, everybody understood that this was no longer a possibility, but between 1792 and 1795, France was in real danger. It should, by all normal standards, have been defeated; briefly, it even looked as if it would be. Just how wars were won, after all, seemed very clear: the side with the most powerful allies, the best officer corps, the greater firepower, and the best drilled troops obviously could not lose. The French army, by those standards, was woefully inferior: it had no allies; it was grievously undersupplied; the men were raw recruits; and most of the officers had emigrated because they were aristocrats who hated the Repub-lic. The Allies, therefore, expected to win quickly and easily. Then, having occu-pied Paris and shot a good many people, they would restore the monarchy, help themselves to some territory, and go home triumphant. In fact, to their horror, precisely the opposite happened.

In part because so many of the French now felt the country really belonged to them, in part because the economy was ruthlessly regulated so as to produce the necessary resources, the revolutionary army went on to win battle after battle. By the beginning of 1795, it had conquered the Austrian Netherlands (today's Belgium) and Holland, much of the left bank of the Rhine, and much of northern Italy. And while it was at it, it invented modern warfare.

The most important of these innovations was the adoption of universal conscription. Until then, troops had been recruited in one of two ways: by offering boons upon enlistment, or simply by force. Now, in France, it was the entire nation (or at least its young males) that came together to form the army; and those soldiers were not only numerous, they were highly patriotic, and cheered on by most of their compatriots. Thus, a relatively small professional army was replaced by the nation itself and, as a result, wars that, until then, had seemed mostly an aristocratic game had come to be supported by much of the population.

There was still more. Until the Revolution, wars had been fought for precise, limited reasons: to defend a country's honor, or to conquer territory. Now the Allies made it clear that they intended, when victorious, to restore the ancien régime; in response, the French fought a new, ideological kind of war. Having themselves become free, they announced, they would bring liberty with them wherever they conquered. Indeed, they said, they were in conflict only with the kings, not with the peoples, who were themselves oppressed and thus the natural allies of France; and French armies came, therefore, not to gain new provinces, but to spread the benefits of freedom and a republican form of government.

War had thus become not just unavoidable but, seemingly, the normal state of things. Years passed, and the war continued. Politics were defined by the necessities of the conflict; states were reorganized, the better to deal with it; and it spread throughout the world, linking areas as far apart as Europe, India, the Americas, and southern Africa. By 1800, it had already lasted for eight years; what no one knew was that it still had fifteen years to go.

A corollary of this vast, apparently endless struggle was that the monarchs of Europe, from Naples to Madrid, from London to Saint Petersburg, worried that their continued rule might be in danger. Many of them, at first, had been secretly delighted by the Revolution: because it weakened one of the great powers, it meant, they thought, that the others would prosper accordingly. Now they were faced with a hideous choice: they could continue the war, and risk complete defeat and the toppling of their thrones, or negotiate a peace and recognize the legitimacy of the French republic; and then, might not a taste for freedom spread to their own subjects?

So it was that, by 1800, France had become the most important country in Europe. It acted, everyone else reacted; and its army, with amazing speed, was changing the boundaries of states as far apart as Holland and Italy. That was not all, though: by reinventing itself, its system of holding property, the way it educated its children, the process through which it promulgated its laws, France was also creating a new world, one which forced change everywhere else as well.

Of course, another country had done much of that even before the French. The United States, having gained its independence in 1783, had added a Bill of Rights to its constitution. It, too, was a republic; it was governed by an elected Congress and president. Its government guaranteed freedom of thought, of expression, of worship; it was based on the consent of the governed, not on their enforced obedience. The very Declaration of the Rights of Man, which had begun the French Revolution, was a mere adaptation of the U.S. Declaration of Independence; but the example of the United States still remained unconvincing for the Europeans. It was too far away, too primitive, too small—its population barely reached 4 million. It had never had an established church, a feudal system of land tenure, an aristocracy, a resident king. No one in Europe worried about the United States; everyone worried about France.

And in fact, as the Revolution quieted down, the elites throughout Europe saw that the Republic was often formidably effective. The new pattern of land ownership was a case in point. Before the Revolution, the land, still by a very wide margin the most important source of wealth, had belonged mostly to the church and the nobility. Farmers were few, and the mass of the population consisted of peasants who had to pay rent, tithes to the church, feudal rights to their lord, and taxes to the king. Then, in late 1789, the lands of the church were taken over by the state, which proceeded to resell them at prices that grew progressively cheaper as the currency depreciated. To this vast ensemble—nearly one-third of all the land in France—were soon added the estates forfeited by the emigrating nobles. The result was agrarian reform on a vast scale. From a nation of peasants, France became a nation of farmers, people with a real stake in the country because they owned a small part of it.

The end of legal privilege was just as startling. Before the Revolution, the church had been tax-exempt, and this was a major cause of its unpopularity; but so had a large part of the nobility. Certain professions were closed to commoners; you had to be noble in order to become an army officer, for instance. Finally, the court system, to a startling degree, favored the rich and powerful. This was in part because the courts of last resort, the *Parlements*, were composed of men who had bought their offices, usually for a very large sum. This had two consequences: not only did the judges tend to favor their social equals, they also expected to garner more from their position than merely the salary paid to them by the government. If you wanted to win your suit, you bribed the judge; it was a fully recognized part of the way the system functioned.

Thus, for all the French to be equal before the law, and free from arbitrary arrest, was a major change in the way people lived their lives. So was the possibility of entering any profession to which you might feel suited; so was a system of courts dispensing free and fair justice; so was the principle of no taxation without representation. All these were such dearly loved conquests, in fact, that Napoléon at his most tyrannical never tried to abrogate them: he knew too well that any attempt to do so would provoke an instant, general, and violent revolt.

There were smaller changes as well. The metric system was one. Before 1789, the French had had to cope with a confusing series of measurements: a foot in Amiens was a little longer than a foot in Arles, a pound in Paris lighter than a pound in Tours. Now, throughout the country, distances were measured in meters, liquids in liters, weights in grams and kilos—a system now practiced everywhere except England and the United States.

This made life simpler. So did another innovation. Before the Revolution, the Catholic Church held the registries of births, marriages, and deaths. That meant all must live and die according to that church's precepts. If you died without its last rites, or if you were an actor, you could not be buried in a proper cemetery. Now the state took over these registries and the regulations of burials, and suddenly people were significantly freer. Far more startling still, divorce, for the very first time, was made legal. Of course, the church, when it was allowed back, refused to recognize people's right to divorce and remarry; but it found, in most cases, that they went ahead anyway.

All this was very startling to most Europeans, although less, perhaps, to the English than to anyone else. But in England, too, there were many legal inequalities. Catholics, for instance, could not hold any of the offices of state or be elected to Parliament; only a minute fraction of the male population—some three hundred thousand people altogether—was allowed to vote. The result was a House of Commons composed mostly of landlords, seldom a very representative group. The other house of Parliament, the House of Lords, was composed of hereditary aristocrats who never forgot to defend their own interests. All that hardly made for a democratic system: Great Britain was a limited monarchy that allowed the aristocracy to rule. This could be seen in many ways: only the rich and well-connected could get a divorce, for instance, since it required a special (and very costly) act of Parliament. As for the land, some 60 percent of it was owned by less than 5 percent of the population. There was also another, in some ways more shocking, tradition, that of making a great deal of money from the slave trade. France, on the other hand, had abolished slavery in all its possessions by 1791.

The abolition of slavery aside, the reforms carried out in France attracted many of the most intelligent people in Europe, from that brilliant English politician, Charles James Fox, to La Harpe, tutor to the future czar Alexander I of Russia. For them, as well as for much humbler people, France had shown the way. Unfortunately, much of that achievement was disfigured by the violence that had accompanied it; but if the killings were to stop, then the attraction might become well-nigh irresistible.

The series of military triumphs which accompanied the Revolution also dazzled people throughout Europe. That France had been reenergized was undeniable. That it had produced a large group of brilliant, nonaristocratic generals was equally obvious: the great upheaval had actually strengthened the country that a very few years before had seemed ripe for conquest. By the middle of 1794, though, it was also becoming clear that the Terror was out of control, and that it must be stopped.

War Continued: France after Thermidor

Robespierre: to this day, in Europe, the name has kept its potency. He was either a cold monster or a selfless patriot, depending on your point of view. He either saved France by so organizing it as to defeat both the enemy outside and the royalists inside; or he was a vain, ruthless, self-infatuated dictator whose rule caused France untold sufferings. Both these summaries of his rule are true. This slender, nattily dressed man, with curled, powdered hair, a sallow complexion, and weak eyes hidden behind green glasses, brought forth immense energies; he also sent thousands of innocent people to die by beheading, shooting, or drowning. And he finally made a terrible mistake: he frightened Tallien, Barras, and his colleagues at the Convention as badly as he had frightened the rest of the French.

By the summer of 1794, the Convention was not quite two years old; yet it had already several times turned against its own members. Starting with the more moderate Girondins, going on to the charismatic Danton, it had sent dozens of its own members to the guillotine. Now, it was largely controlled by its own permanent committees, chief among them the Committee of Public Safety; it was through them that Robespierre ruled, until July 27, 1794, the day when, in a speech to the full assembly, he announced that there were more traitors in its midst.

Had he named those traitors, he might well have prevailed; instead, he delayed, and in an agony of fright, all the remaining deputies, each of whom dreaded being among those on Robespierre's list, finally turned against him. Led by Tallien, whose mistress, already imprisoned, was due to be executed within the next few days, and by Barras, a bold and hungry former aristocrat, the Convention outlawed the dictator. That night, under confused circumstances, Barras arrested him; and a day later, he was guillotined together with a few followers.

The next step was to renew the membership of the key committees; and then the Convention settled down to govern France. It relied on a few basic principles: there was to be no more Terror, and the guillotine was dismantled; equally, there was to be no return to a non-Republican regime; the war must still be fought; and power must return to the bourgeoisie. In order to husband the country's resources, a system of rationing and rigidly enforced price controls was in effect; this was soon ended because it inconvenienced the middle classes, but the war continued to be fought successfully.

"With its insane laws, the Committee of Public Safety had taken the mad decision of providing all the Parisians with bread and meat, and all the civil servants with other foodstuffs like sugar, oil, rice, etc.,"[2] wrote one of the most influential deputies, though, actually, all the committee had done was to ensure food was available at a reasonable price. Now, the Convention thought it was better to let the Parisians starve, and to allow the civil servants to survive however they might on a salary paid in highly depreciated paper money. The many non-noble rich who had passed through the Revolution unscathed, and who were now reasserting control, always had enough to eat.

By December 1794, in a frenzy of what would today be called privatization, the state had given up its monopoly of foreign trade; it had stopped owning the weapons manufactures; it had outlawed forced seizures of goods in order to supply the armies. Trade and industry were free again; and firm police measures prevented the poor from rising again. Scarcity and inflation reinforced each other: the gold louis had gone in value from 24 paper livres in 1789 to 130 in 1794. By 1795 it reached 1,200 livres. Far more important to the poor, the standard measure of flour, which cost 2 livres in 1790, reached 225 livres in 1795, while a liter of olive oil went from 1.16 to 62 livres, and shoes from 5 to 200.

The remaining deputies were, most of them, men of property: they wanted to enjoy their wealth without annoying restrictions, and they no longer wanted to hear from the poorer part of the population. So they decided to create a new regime. Thus began a balancing act that was to last until the end of 1799: neither the extreme left, which wanted a return to economic regulation and the Terror, nor the right, which was waiting to restore the monarchy, would be allowed to prevail. And every time either party appeared threatening, it was ruthlessly crushed: when the poorer Parisians rose on April 1, 1795, they were mowed down by the troops. When the royalists did the same on October 5, they, too, were gunned down—by a young general named Napoléon Bonaparte, who was following Barras's orders. That had, in fact, been far the more dangerous of the two risings: most of the French, by the fall of 1795, liked neither the Convention nor the Republic. As Tallien noted: "If the country were allowed to fulfill its aspirations, we would have a constitutional Counter-revolution within the next three months."[3]

It was in part to avoid a restoration that the Convention had settled down to write a new constitution; in part, also, because France was a state without law. The constitution of 1791 had been abrogated in 1792; the constitution of 1793, although endorsed in a nationwide vote, had been suspended until the end of the war, and thus never applied. France, in late 1794, had neither an institutional framework nor, indeed, a valid legal code. Clearly something had to be done.

As it happened, the deputies knew just what they wanted: first came the preservation of their own power; second, the safety of all those who had voted the king's death in 1793; and third, a system that would guarantee and preserve property while ensuring that no new dictator could take over. The result was the constitution of the year III, which was adopted by the Convention on August 23, 1795, and by the electorate in September. At first glance, it met with almost universal approval: 914,853 votes for, a mere 41,892 against; but these figures were not what they seemed since, at the same time, over 4 million voters had abstained.

Most of the French, in fact, did not care about abstract things. For them, the constitution was hardly real: what defined their lives was the war and the lack of a reliable currency. The paper money created at the beginning of the Revolution, the assignat, was depreciating faster every day; there were virtually no gold or silver coins to be seen, largely because those who had them hoarded them. As for shortages—of food, of clothes, even of nails with which to shoe horses—they were universal. It wasn't just that no one could tell what would happen next: many people did not know whether they would eat the next day.

Still, it was in many ways a good constitution. Its authors tried to strike a balance between tyranny and anarchy, and they almost succeeded. All individual freedoms, including that of the press, were guaranteed; all the French were equal before the law. There was an attempt at separating the legislative and the executive, which had been one when the Convention ruled.

Just as important, none of the deputies could hold an executive function. Because everyone remembered Robespierre, the Republic did not have a president. Instead, the executive consisted of a five-member Directoire elected by the legislature. The directors were forbidden to appear before either house; they could only send messages. They had no veto; they could ask the councils to take appropriate measures but not send in a bill; they controlled the civil and foreign services, and the armed forces, and they appointed (and fired) the ministers, the generals, the ambassadors, and the top administrators.

This was, in many ways, a sound system: neither branch of government could oppress the other; on the other hand, neither had much leverage over the other, and conflicts were accordingly difficult to resolve, as the following years were to prove again and again. As for the judiciary, for the first time in French history, it was independent, and there were to be juries. Finally, the treasury was run by five commissioners, elected by the legislature, and thus wholly independent from the executive. They were to refuse all disbursements that had not been properly authorized by a law. So far, there was much to be said for the constitution: it was, on the whole, workable, moderate, and reasonably democratic; but then came two dangerous provisions. The legislature was to be renewed by a third annually, and the result was a virtually uninterrupted electoral campaign. Then there was the electorate itself.

Only men over twenty-one who paid taxes and had been resident for a full year in the same place were considered to be citizens. Even then, not all citizens could vote equally: the electoral college elected the deputies, and its members, who were elected by the regular citizens, had to own property producing an income worth 200 days of work in the cities, 150 in the country: there were only some thirty thousand such men in France. Thus, under an appearance of democracy, the suffrage was highly restrictive and made sure that only the well-to-do could, in the end, be elected.

This struck many of the deputies as entirely normal. "We should be governed by the best men," one of the authors of the constitution explained. "The best men are the best educated, those with the greatest interest in maintaining the laws; and, aside from a few exceptions, you will only find such men among those who, owning an estate, care about the country in which that estate is located. . . . If you give political rights to men without property, . . . they will throw us back into the convulsions from which we have only just emerged."[4] Now the country could be run by the bourgeoisie.

Even so, the deputies, who knew that they were generally loathed, decided something more had to be done, and so they came up with the Decree of the Two Thirds: of the 750 new deputies to be chosen, two-thirds would have to be members of the Convention. This, obviously, was both simple and effective: it meant that as the Convention finally dissolved itself, its members would automatically pass into the new legislature.

Indeed, no one was taking any chances. When the new councils met, their first task was to elect the five directors. To no one's surprise, they all turned out to be men who had voted for the execution of Louis XVI, all men of the center, and all backers of the new economic dispensation. On October 27, 1795, at the Palace of the Luxembourg, they met and assumed their new office. And just in case anyone still failed to understand why they were there, Barras made it plain: their task, he said, was "to save the men of the Revolution."[5]

The Beginnings of the Directoire

Still, none of the politicians could expect to be saved if the country itself perished; and there was a chance it might do so. The very installation of the directors was symptomatic. Their palace had been the residence of Louis XVI's brother until 1791. Now, when the Kings of the Republic, as they were soon called, moved in, they found cavernous, empty rooms—not a table, not a chair, not a log for the fireplace; and in order to certify that they had just taken office, they were forced to borrow five chairs, a kitchen table, paper, and ink from the concierge.

Eventually, they furnished the palace; but finding money to run the government and pay the armies was more difficult still. "The Treasury was completely empty, the assignats [the paper currency] valueless, the little they were worth vanished from day to day as their value fell to nothing . . . There were no revenues, . . . no financial plan . . . The credit of the State was dead,"[6] noted Louis-Marie de la Révellière-Lépeaux, one of the new directors. He knew what he was talking about.

Because the government had no metallic currency, it paid salaries and supplies in paper money; and since that was depreciating rapidly, it printed more and more of it. In August 1794, assignats of a nominal value of 7.5 billion livres were in circulation; by November 1795, that amount had risen to 20 billion, and to 39 billion by January 1796. In 1795, 1 gold franc was worth 50 paper francs. A year later, it was worth 1,000 francs, and all the prices continued to rise. Before the Revolution, a Parisian worker could live modestly on 2,000 livres a year. Now, coffee cost 210 livres a pound, a turkey 250 livres, meat 120 livres, bread 60 livres, a dress 2,500 livres—and the salaries for those who were still employed signally failed to keep up. At the same time, because the rich had either fled or gone into hiding, many Parisians found themselves unemployed: hairdressers and furniture makers, servants and jewelers, all were out of a job.

As, in late October 1795, the Directoire was installed, impoverishment was general. The aristocracy had fled or died, the rich bourgeoisie was in hiding. The small, mercantile bourgeoisie was ruined by the cessation of trade; and the urban proletariat was both unemployed and destitute. Paris itself, once the capital of all the pleasures, all the refinements, looked like a city half-dead. "Posters everywhere . . . tricolor rags fluttering from the windows—rivers of mud, urine and soap scum [running down the streets]—dried-up fountains—cheap restaurants by the hundred, wine and liquor vendors by the thousands . . .—the grandest private houses become shops for candy-makers, cooks, food-sellers, or dirty hotels . . . nameless streets, and everywhere, on the palaces, on the walls of the once-private gardens, these words: National Property For Sale . . . What a spectacle! Half of Paris was selling the other half!"[7]

Sometimes it seemed as if a good part of Paris was selling itself as well: prostitutes were everywhere, boldly soliciting. Some walked the streets, offering themselves to the passersby; others, the more successful ones, hid their activities in the back rooms of shops selling anything from a cold supper to perfume, dresses, even sealing wax. Yet others rented rooms in the Palais-Royal, the former residence of the duc d'Orléans, and hung erotic images on their doors to offer a preview of what they were willing to do.

Still, the killing had stopped, and the capital, impoverished, unkempt, gave itself to a whirl of pleasure. Suddenly, there were public balls everywhere: in a former Jesuit school, in a former convent of Carmelites, in the cemetery of Saint Sulpice, in the Élysée Palace. There were Victim's Balls, which the surviving relatives of the guillotined attended, wearing a red ribbon around their necks as a reminder of these executions. Everywhere, every day, Paris danced, and the fashions worn by the dancers seemed as astonishing as the fact that it was possible to have fun.

Abandon was the fashion and the women embraced it: tall, powdered coiffures, corsets, hooped skirts, silks, and velvets were all gone. Now a "Roman" look was in vogue: there were Vestal dresses, Ceres, Minerva, and Galatea tunics. High waists, or no waist at all, short sleeves, freely floating tunics prevailed; and they were made of the lightest, most transparent fabrics, worn sometimes over a flesh-colored body stocking, sometimes over nothing at all. The Citizeness Hamelin, one of the queens of the new regime, was seen on the Champs Élysées clad solely in a shift of pink transparent gauze. Mme Tallien, one of her rivals, could be observed, at the Ranelagh Gardens, dressed in a tunic split high on the side, flesh-colored panties, her bare feet shining with toe rings, her breasts uncovered, and her arms laden with diamond bracelets. And every day, she wore a different wig, blonde, brunette, red, blue, green.

There were other extravagantly dressed people—some of them officials. Louis David, the great painter, had been asked to design costumes for the new regime. He came up with toga-like cloaks for the deputies, and an ensemble for the directors that made them look dazzling, certainly, but also a little comical: it consisted of a purple cloak, draped in ancient Roman style; a blue jacket, lavishly embroidered in gold and closed in front; tight breeches; a tricolor sash set diagonally across the chest; an abundant lace cravat; an azure blue belt supporting a straight saber; shoes with silk puffs on top; and crowning it all, a hat lavishly adorned with blue, white, and red plumes.

Soon after the new regime's installation it became clear that in essence the Revolution was over. Once again, there was an upper class eager to spend its money. Houses were redone; brand-new, gilded carriages reappeared in the streets; dress designers, hairdressers, embroiderers, silversmiths, and furniture makers prospered again. The main difference was that Paris remained shabby, and that the new rich had earned their money by taking advantage of the government: they were bankers who lent money at incredibly high rates, purveyors who sent half-rotten food to the armies and charged enormous prices for it, speculators of all kinds, and, soon, generals who helped themselves from the treasuries of the countries they conquered.

The war, in fact, had served many people well, and it continued to do so. Holland, now controlled by France, gave itself a government modeled on the

French, lost its South African colony—and sent money to Paris. Prussia signed a peace treaty on April 5, 1795; Spain followed suit on July 4. That left two enemies: Austria on the Continent; Great Britain on the seas. As a result, there was no longer any danger of a real disaster; instead, the government, the generals, and many businessmen lived off the contributions imposed on the conquered lands and the seizures and sales of church lands, especially in Belgium. And there was yet another highly convenient aspect of the war: troops were always ready for use (so were generals) when civil disorders threatened.

From the very beginning of the Directoire, in fact, the army was given tasks that would have belonged to a properly constituted police force, had there been one. When, for instance, the directors feared that the left was preparing a new rising, Bonaparte was sent to close its main center, the Pantheon Club. It was no coincidence that the young, still unknown officer was made general in chief of the French army in Italy just ten days later: he had proved his reliability. Once in Italy, he continued to prove it by sending back gold and paintings. Of course, there was a serious danger in using the army in this way: neither generals nor soldiers were worried about violating the constitution; and they showed it within a year.

Still, laws could also be passed. In the first half of 1796, the directors were worried about the stability of the regime, and Barras, the cleverest, most energetic of them, decided to take action. The danger still came from the left, so on April 16, 1796, at the request of the directors, the councils voted a law punishing with death all those who advocated either the restoration of the monarchy or a return to the constitution of 1793, which had given all power to the Convention. Since at this point no one was foolish enough to be openly royalist, this, in spite of its appearance of evenhandedness, was directed against those who wanted to bring back the days of the Terror. It had, in any event, been balanced by another law requiring all government employees to swear they hated all monarchies; and as a corollary, the directors were given the power to remove names from the list of émigrés.

This was a key measure. Any person who had emigrated had their name placed on the list. The consequences were dire: their property was forfeited to the state, and they could be executed on sight if they ever returned to France. With the Revolution ended, however, many of the nearly quarter million émigrés wanted to return and, if possible, reclaim their property. Most of them had been royalist: by giving the directors the power to take names off the list, therefore, the councils also put them in a position to pressure the right.

A DELICATE BALANCE

It was the left that now seemed about to end the directors' balancing act. Happily for them, they had just the right enemy. His name was Gracchus Babeuf, and he was the first communist. He wanted all property to be held in common and shared out equally: no one was to own anything. To achieve this, he favored a return of the Terror. "All the evils are at their apogee . . . They can be remedied only by a complete upheaval . . . Let chaos therefore rule and from chaos, let there emerge a new and better world,"[8] he wrote in the newspaper he published.

Extremism is always easy to attack because it upsets so many people; so, naturally, Babeuf was the ideal ogre, no matter how small his actual following. The Terror, after all, was still fresh in people's minds. There were very few Parisians who did not feel that they would have something to lose if all private property were shared out; as for the new farmers, who now actually owned their land, they would have died rather than give it up. Finally, Barras himself was firmly committed to the Republic, and everyone knew it. He could therefore dispose of Babeuf without making people worry that it might be the preliminary to a restoration.

On May 10, 1796, Babeuf and 245 of his followers were arrested; a year later, Babeuf was executed. The Directoire was now firmly established as the defender of those of the French who were in a position to speak out. By beheading that fearsome (if largely imaginary) monster, Barras had shown that to a significant extent, he was the only director who mattered.

What was quickly happening, in fact, was a change in the regime itself. Far from being equal with the councils, the directors were seizing powers which made them almost supreme. The use of the police, to which they were entitled, proved far more potent than expected because no magistrate was willing to obey the law barring arbitrary arrests. There is nothing like the prospect of detention or deportation to encourage cooperation with the government.

The government badly needed this weapon: the financial situation, disastrous in 1795, was even worse in 1796. At the end of January, it was decided to do away with the now worthless assignats. This was fine except for one little fact: there was no alternative currency available, and specie failed to reappear; so, in March, a new paper money, the mandat territorial, was created. Its rate was fixed by law at 1 mandat territorial for 100 assignats, and it could be used to buy the many nationalized properties still held by the state.

No more than 2.4 billion's worth of mandats was printed. Within two weeks, though, it took only 35.5 gold francs to buy 100 francs in the new paper. By mid April, the rate was down to 20 gold francs, to 13.5 by May. And in February 1797, less than a year after their creation, the mandats were withdrawn. As for the assignats, which were in fact still circulating, they were not much better: France, in essence, was a country without a currency.

That, however, did not force the Directoire to sue for peace. Most governments raise money to pay their troops; this government kept the war going to raise money, because it expected repeated infusions of cash seized from those it conquered. Victorious generals were thus even more necessary than usual, and away in northern Italy, one such general was beginning to reach celebrity: Napoléon Bonaparte.

LOVE AND WAR

The Austrian armies, in Italy, had been doing quite well, but Bonaparte's arrival changed everything. This was partly because the new general in chief knew how to concentrate his army and strike a series of devastating blows, partly because he had invented a new way of massing his men in deep columns that punctured the line disposition of the Austrians. No one had realized yet, except for Bonaparte himself, that he was also one of the greatest generals in recorded history. He won again and again—at Arcole in mid-November 1796, at Rivoli two months later; then, early in February, having already conquered Bologna and Ferrara, he took Mantua and forced a peace upon the pope that gave France 15 million francs in gold and many works of art.

All these victories pleased the government, of course, but what made the real difference were those hefty war damages that the vanquished kept having to pay. The French, in 1796, had almost given up paying taxes: it was a good thing somebody else was doing it for them, and, not unnaturally, Bonaparte's popularity began to soar. Before leaving Paris, however, he had taken precautions—not even he, after all, could know that things would go so well. He had tried, therefore, to make very sure Barras would back him, partly by courting him assiduously, partly by marrying Joséphine de Beauharnais, Barras's discarded mistress and a woman of considerable charm.

It was a wise political move—Barras was often generous to his former mistresses—but there was more to it: Napoléon had also fallen passionately in love with Joséphine, not least, possibly, because she had had a great deal of experience in pleasing men. As for Joséphine, although she was much less enthusiastic, she was in need of a new husband (the last had been guillotined), was penniless, and had just been left by the notoriously fickle Barras. A general who could make his fortune by looting seemed as good a bet as any. At any rate, Joséphine did not bother to remain faithful; no sooner had Bonaparte left Paris than she started an affair with a charming young man; and she took the charming young man, one Hyppolite Charles, with her when she joined her new husband in Italy.

This was not as obvious a complication as it might seem. Bonaparte was quite busy pursuing and beating the Austrians; so, while never very far away, he was also seldom actually present; and when he was away from Joséphine, he wrote her. The result was a series of burning love letters in which the General revealed himself as unexpectedly human.

"I have felt sad ever since leaving you," he wrote her on July 17, 1796. "All my happiness is in being near you. I keep remembering, over and over, your kisses, your tears, your charming jealousy; and the beauties of the incomparable Joséphine constantly light a bright and burning flame in my heart and in my desire. . . . A few days ago, I thought that I loved you; but, since seeing you, I have felt that I love you a thousand times more still! . . . Ah! I beg you, let me see a few of your faults; be less beautiful, less graceful, less kind above all."[9]

It is a touching letter—but also a comical one. Joséphine, clearly, had decided to play her role to the hilt: for her to have pretended jealousy when she was in the middle of an affair with another man was, to say the least, management of a high order. As for Napoléon, just two days later he was writing: "I have not had a letter from you for two days. . . . Why, you wicked, ugly, tyrannical, pretty little monster! You laugh at my menaces, at my silliness. Ah! if only I could lock you up in my heart . . . I would keep you imprisoned there."[10] The happily free Joséphine, meanwhile, was enjoying herself in Milan, and Barras was congratulating himself on having, at one stroke, disposed of an unwanted mistress and earned the gratitude of that stiff, awkward, but very useful little general.

Eventually, Joséphine sent young M. Charles home—he had really been making himself too conspicuous—and Napoléon went on writing her almost every day. "Your letters are as cold as if you were fifty," he told her on October 17, "they look like a fifteen year old marriage. One sees there friendship and the other feelings of that winter of life. What, Joséphine! That is very cruel, very wicked, very treacherous of you! What more can you do to make me thoroughly miserable? Stop loving me? But you've already done that. Start hating me? Well, I wish you would, everything is humiliating except hatred; but Indifference, with its steady pulse, its unwavering eye, its monotonous pace! . . . A thousand, thousand kisses as loving as my heart."[11]

And since, as usual, Joséphine had not bothered to write him, he went on, a few days later: "I don't love you at all any more; on the contrary, I hate you. You are wicked, clumsy, stupid and plain. You never write me, you don't love your husband."[12] Happily for Napoléon, he did occasionally come together with the lazy Joséphine; and when he did, she taught him just how enjoyable sex could be—something he remembered to the end of his life.

Passion, whether unrequited or not, was not, however, the general's main occupation. Greatly to the directors' satisfaction, he was busy conquering northern Italy; and as he got closer to Rome a hitherto unexpected opportunity opened up. When, in 1790, the National Assembly had decided to have bishops elected by the faithful, Pope Pius VI had denounced the new laws, and many priests had followed him. The result was an immediate break between the Revolution and the church. When the monarchy fell, virtually all bishops and most priests remained attached to the ancien régime. All was now clear, and the Convention had proceeded to outlaw church and clergy.

The new constitution was more tolerant: it merely stated that the state neither supported nor endorsed any church, and that all ceremonies must remain private; but, in fact, the government continued to think of the Catholic Church as the enemy, and it was not wrong. Now, with the French army at the gates of Rome, it might be possible to destroy the church by seizing the pope and preventing the holding of a conclave when he died. "Romanism will always be the irreconcilable enemy of the Revolution," Barras wrote Bonaparte. "The Directoire thus requests that you do whatever you can to destroy the pontifical government."[13]

Had that order been followed, Barras would have reaped two major benefits from it: the church would, presumably, have presented less of a problem, and, far more important, the director would have earned the undying gratitude of the left just at a moment when the right was beginning to worry him. Unfortunately for him, however, Bonaparte was a general who never hesitated to disregard inconvenient orders. He was already looking forward to a future in politics: it would not look well if he were the man who seized the pope. Besides, hard cash was needed; so, instead, he signed the Peace of Tolentino, which included a large financial indemnity from Pius. Part of the money was then sent to Paris, a major sop to the directors; and, as was becoming usual, a very substantial sum was retained by the general for his own use. Indeed, the money was flowing in: 20 million livres from Milan, 15 from the Pope, 7.5 from Modena, 2 from Parma, without counting the odd bits of loot. Bonaparte, who had started the campaign as a poor man, was now wealthy.

There was another good reason to leave Rome alone: having settled his conquests in northern Italy, and created local republics, Bonaparte meant to use them as a staging ground for his next campaign, across the Alps and directly into Austria, thus winning the war in the enemy's heartland. An expedition to the south, therefore, would have been seriously counterproductive.

The fact that things were going so well in Italy did certainly ease the Directoire's financial position: by the middle of the year, for the first time, the army in Italy was being paid half in metallic currency, instead of merely receiving worthless assignats. The political situation in Paris was far more worrisome: because the constitution enfranchised the prosperous and only them, it looked as if the coming legislative elections might produce a right-wing, monarchist majority.

The directors did what they could. On January 27, 1797, they issued an executive order disenfranchising all those who, although back in France, were still on the list of émigrés—altogether a significant number of potential voters, men who were expecting shortly to have their names crossed off the list and so had already returned. Even so, most of the newly elected deputies were intent on restoring the monarchy.

This naturally alarmed the directors, and it affected their plans in two ways: Barras began scheming toward a coup to undo the elections; and Bonaparte was free to make peace. This last may seem an odd consequence of the election, but it worked out in this way: Barras began to think he would soon need a willing general right there in Paris to force the issue; he also thought that Bonaparte would be that general. It would have been impolitic, therefore, to annoy Bonaparte, and although the general had just signed a preliminary treaty with Austria at Leoben against the government's explicit orders, Barras did not feel he could disavow him.

As for Bonaparte, his reasons for wanting to make peace were simple: his troops were exhausted and too far from their base; he therefore needed a pause. Conveniently, the Austrians were in no position to argue; after taking Venice, which had been an independent state for over a thousand years, Bonaparte had moved through the Alps as far as Klagenfurt in the Tyrol. The Austrian government rightly felt that this was too close for comfort; and so the Preliminaries of Leoben were signed. They gave France Lombardy, much of northern Italy, Belgium, and the left bank of the Rhine subject to a later congress; Austria, in compensation, received Istria and Dalmatia, on the coast of the Adriatic. Bonaparte was pleased; and the French government acquiesced.

There still remained the threat from the right. Happily for the Directoire, though, its members were as flamboyant as they were lacking in seriousness. Encouraged by the election, the royalists were everywhere, recognizable by the fashions they sported. A contemporary pamphlet made fun of it all: "Come, fair youth; with your black velvet lapels, your victim-style collars [cut especially low to simulate those of people about to be guillotined], your tied and perfumed hair, your huge cravats, your pointy shoes and your square-cut coats."[14]

True enough, the fashionable places in Paris were full of these young men, many of them holding a cudgel as a symbol of their eagerness to put down the populace. Of far greater consequence, the new majority in the councils began to act. The laws directed against the émigrés' relatives were abrogated, as were those directed against the left (this was just a way of taking power away from the government). Even more inconvenient, the councils now set about refusing to vote the necessary appropriations, thus dealing the executive an almost crippling blow. That also threatened government employees, purveyors, and bond holders, however, and they rallied to the support of the Directoire.

Adding to the problem was the fact that by now the directors thoroughly loathed one another. Talleyrand, who had just been appointed foreign minister, was the witness of a typical scene. "Carnot and Barras had begun to quarrel, the latter accusing the former of having taken a letter which should have been seen by his fellow directors. Both were standing. Carnot, raising his hand, said: 'I swear on my word of honor that this is not true.'

"'Don't raise your hand,' Barras answered [referring to Carnot's part in the Terror], 'blood would start to drip from it.'"[15]

Finally, with the election of a new director, in late May–early June 1797, the Directoire was able to act. Now it was the conservatives who were in a minority of two.

DIRECTORS AND GENERALS

A good deal of planning was needed before the proposed coup to undo the elections could be carried out. The directors were, after all, preparing to violate the constitution; and to do that, they needed a compliant general. Bonaparte, always cautious, sent 3 million in gold and Augereau, his main aide, to Paris, but he remained in Italy. Then, on July 16, the directors dismissed two conservative ministers—the ministers were responsible to them alone—thus causing great alarm among the newly elected deputies. On August 26, things became clearer still. In a well-publicized speech, the director La Révellière-Lépeaux told the Parisians: "The Directoire will face any danger in order to assure the French their liberty, their constitution, their possessions, their peace and their glory."[16] Given the fact that the government was about to violate the very constitution it was claiming to defend, this had a certain involuntary humor about it; but it was, at any rate, clear.

Indeed, at 11:30 P.M. on September 3, troops were posted about the city and moved to occupy the bridges and the buildings where the councils met. At the same time, posters were put up everywhere denouncing the royalist plot—though, in fact, the royalists had not yet begun to plan their own coup. Immediately after these moves, Barras announced that anyone trying to restore the monarchy would be shot on sight. In the meantime, many conservatives were arrested, so that, not surprisingly, very few of them were present when the councils met the next day. The remaining deputies promptly did just what they were told.

They began by annulling nearly half of the elections; altogether, 177 deputies were dismissed, while 53 of them were sent to the French colony of Guiana, a hellhole that had been nicknamed "the dry guillotine" because tropical fevers usually dispatched its residents. There followed, still on September 4, a law ordering all the émigrés to leave the country within fourteen days or be shot on sight, another canceling all local elections and giving the Directoire the power to appoint mayors and judges, and still another giving the police the power to suspend publications for a year. Two innocuous but safe men were elected director; and everyone understood that Barras was now firmly in control.

This was a major turning point: the regime, in its first period, had been mostly liberal and democratic; it had expressed the will, at any rate, of its limited electorate. Henceforth, it canceled any election whose result was inconvenient and arrested people whose only crime was to have the wrong political views. In doing that, it lost whatever popular support it had had, and came to depend on compliant generals and the use of force. Its very strength, however, was its fragility: what one general had done, another could undo. As for the lack of popular reaction, it simply showed how cynical people had become. Too much had happened in just eight years: all they cared about now was being allowed to go about their business. It was a lesson of which Bonaparte took due notice. So, for that matter, did the Austrians. Having given up the hope that a royalist takeover would improve their negotiating position, they signed, on October 18, the peace of Campo Formio, which confirmed the Preliminaries of Leoben and gave France northern Italy, Belgium, and the left bank of the Rhine subject to further compensation, while Austria received Venice and its mainland possessions.

State-organized coups being now an accepted method of government, they began to multiply in the French-controlled territories. They also underlined the instability that had become one of the Directoire's essential weaknesses. Talleyrand saw it well: "The words: Republic, Liberty, Equality, Fraternity were written on every wall, but these concepts were nowhere a reality. From the highest of authorities to the lowest, there was hardly one which was not arbitrary, either in the way it had been installed or composed, or by its actions. All was violent; nothing, in consequence, was lasting."[17]

MONEY, THE GOVERNMENT, AND THE PEOPLE

The economy was another problem. At the end of September 1797, the government forcibly converted two-thirds of the national debt into coupons that could be used to purchase nationalized properties, thus impoverishing a great many people. Then, in 1798–1799, a shortage of currency provoked yet another crisis. The mandats had been withdrawn; the assignats were worthless; and specie was extremely scarce. In spite of this shortage of currency, however, the abundant crops harvested in 1796, 1797, and 1798 forced a dramatic drop in prices. Because of the war, France could not export its surplus production, and there was a glut at the very time when in England shortages resulted in dramatically higher prices. Once again, the war defined the world: because commerce was impeded, almost everyone suffered.

For the poorer French, peasants and workers alike, life had become almost impossible. There were shortages of every kind of manufactured products. Unemployment in urban areas continued to be high, so that, in the cities, the lower price of bread hardly helped the many who were utterly destitute. And in the country, the farmers, who still made up most of the French population, found themselves just as badly off. Rapidly, the price of a standard measure of wheat fell to twenty livres, then to fifteen. As the break-even price was between twenty-two and twenty-six livres, this was nothing short of a catastrophe. By 1799, the great majority of the French were desperate. After all the turmoil of the Revolution, after many years of war and the great effort all that entailed, many people were significantly worse off than they had been in 1789. More farmers, it is true, owned their land; but because the government had so mismanaged the economy, that was not yet doing them any good. The consequences of all this were clear: the Directoire was universally detested.

Still, the situation, in 1798, was not entirely bleak. There were a few fruitful conquests. In February and March, Switzerland was taken over. Geneva was annexed to France, the rest of the country was given a French-style constitution, and all public moneys were sent to Paris; the Swiss being what they are, it turned out to be quite a significant sum. Rome, too, and the Pontifical States were soon taken over; the pope was deported, first to Siena, then to France; Rome was proclaimed a republic; and the new government was promptly made to pay France 35 million in gold. Then, in January 1799, as the result of a foolish provocation by King Ferdinand of Naples, a man of quite extraordinary stupidity, the French army invaded and occupied the Kingdom of Naples, which became the Parthenopean Republic.

In France itself, however, these conquests changed nothing. The Directoire, lurching desperately from left to right, arrested those on whom it had recently relied. Indeed, violating the constitution, and using violence to oppose the will of the people, had become such a standard method that it began to be praised as the right way to govern. "The Revolution," a deputy explained, "has not ended; it will only do so when a general and sincere peace takes away from our neighbors any reason to create troubles within our country, when all the parties are finally convinced that the Republic will never perish."[18] And since revolutionary law always superseded regular laws, then, by definition, nothing the government ever did *could* be illegal. A newspaper article made things clearer still. "The unconstitutional acts committed by the government," *Le Conservateur* explained, "are in response to the will or the consent, expressed or tacit, of the best Republicans. Today, the *directorial* power is also a *dictatorial* power; that is what the circumstances demand."[19] It could not be clearer: since the will or the consent of the people was tacit, that is, unexpressed, anything the directors did was, by definition, praiseworthy.

Then, in June 1799, came a major change. As a result of that year's elections, it was the councils who prevailed: they forced the resignation of two of the directors, thus taking away Barras's majority within the Directoire. It hardly mattered, though, except as a sign that the end of the regime was in sight. No one, in the summer of 1799, believed the situation could last—least of all Barras, who was busy negotiating with royalist agents. How the regime would end was obvious: a general would stage a coup and, instead of leaving power in the directors' hands, take it over for himself. The question thus was: which general? And the answer was anything but obvious.

That was because one key general was away, so far away that he might well never come back: in May 1798, Bonaparte had left for Egypt, taking an army with him. On August 1 of that year, the British admiral Lord Nelson destroyed the French fleet at Aboukir. No one knew, therefore, whether Bonaparte would ever be able to sail back; and he was counted out—until, that is, October 1799, when the startling news that he had landed at Marseilles on the ninth spread rapidly through Paris. It was soon known that he had left his army behind; but far from blaming him, almost everyone turned to him as a savior.

An Unlikely Recourse

It is not easy, at first, to understand just what it was about Bonaparte that so fascinated people. A brusque and often rude Corsican, he had had a checkered career, veering from the extreme left during the Terror to faithful support of Barras to muted opposition to the Directoire. Certainly, no one had any particular reason to trust him or to think he could govern France. And yet, in spite of all that, his genius was manifest. There was something convincing, even fascinating, about him. To see him was to believe he could do anything.

This was true even of the man least likely to be fascinated by an uneducated, unpolished general. Talleyrand, the foreign minister, was the most civilized of men. The scion of one of France's great aristocratic families, he had been a fashionable young man before the Revolution—as well as a bishop. Then he had sat in the National Assembly among the liberal monarchists, left the church, emigrated just in time, and returned to become, after a short interval, an outstandingly successful foreign minister. He was enormously intelligent, completely amoral, a man for whom manners counted greatly. He should have loathed Bonaparte. Instead, he was dazzled.

Talleyrand and Bonaparte first met just before the general's departure for Egypt. "At first glance," Talleyrand noted, "I thought him full of charm; twenty victorious battles add greatly to youth [Bonaparte was twenty-nine], beautiful eyes, pallor and a kind of exhaustion."[20] In no time, Bonaparte showed just how quickly he could judge someone. Talleyrand was not only a great foreign minister, he could be of immense political help; and so the general proceeded to make him a friend: "He spoke with much good grace of my appointment to the Foreign ministry, and insisted on the pleasure it had been to correspond with a person of a very different sort from the Directors."[21]

This was typical of Bonaparte: perhaps because he was so sure of his own genius, he quickly recognized other men of merit, and made clear that he appreciated their true worth. In a world where mediocrity and envy ruled, it was a great attraction; so was the general's ability to go straight to the crux of the matter.

Having such a man back in Paris was thus a major event. The Directoire was tottering; the question was not whether it would survive, but when it would be replaced. A coup was expected every day; and, suddenly, the perfect man to lead it had appeared. The revolution had started as a claim for liberty, equality, and fraternity. The Directoire had suppressed most of the people's liberties; fraternity had never been even a remote possibility. Equality before the law applied to everyone, except for the government, which had been violating it with impunity. There remained one great success: the conduct of the war. And just as the conflict changed the other European regimes, so it determined what was to come next in France.

It was no wonder Barras had begun to worry. Still, it is easier to carry out a coup than to organize a government, a fact of which Bonaparte was fully aware. Thus the question as he reached Paris on October 16, 1799, was whether enough talented men were ready to follow him in changing, yet again, the way France was ruled.

CHAPTER TWO

All the Pleasures of Life

WAR AND PEACE: as much as the Revolution, they defined what was happening in France. The war, with Austria and England, then with England alone, then once more with the rest of Europe, shaped what the government could do, where it found its resources, and how it employed them. It made armies important and generals the arbiters of the political world. It defined the economy, created a new class of young, successful men—officers and purveyors. It also defined the way France saw itself, as the most powerful, most rapidly expanding nation on the continent.

Paradoxically, peace with the Continental powers was just as important. As Spaniards, Italians, and Germans returned to Paris, they brought with them the cosmopolitanism that had been a chief characteristic of the city before the Revolution. They provided eager clients for the reviving luxury trades; they made the Parisians feel, once again, that it was their taste, their sophistication, which set the standards for everyone else. Just as important, the arrival of the foreign visitors affirmed, yet again, that the world was closely interconnected.

THE OLD AND THE NEW

Paris, before 1790, had been the capital of Europe. Whether you were English, Austrian, Russian, or Portuguese, you went there when you wanted to have a good time. Of course, there were many kinds of good times: some people were interested in food and wine, others in painting. You might come because the conversation in the Paris salons had practically become an art, and you wanted to hear that extraordinary blend of intelligence, wit, and humor. You might be there in order to visit Mlle Bertin's establishment: it was, after all, that gifted woman who invented the French couture, and her designs were unparalleled when it came to sheer, dazzling chic.

35

Many people, from Grand Duke Paul, the heir to the Russian throne, to that darling of the English liberals, the Duchess of Devonshire, and on to Thomas Jefferson, came to see, and stayed because the famously polite French made them feel so comfortable. Most of them also wanted to do a little serious shopping. The best furniture makers—men like Georges Jacob, Riesener, Sené, Foliot—were in Paris; the most elegant silks could be bought there, and so could the most stylish silver. Of course, there was always wine: Jefferson placed many orders. Sèvres porcelain was the best in Europe; tapestries from the Gobelins were unequaled. The prettiest watches, fobs, and seals could be found at the Petit Dunkerque, and the most spectacular jewels at Böhmer et Bassange. You could, like the Polish count Stanislas Potocki, have your portrait painted by Louis David, the greatest painter of the time, or you could go instead to the greatest woman artist of the century, the immensely famous Mme Vigée-Lebrun.

And if Paris wasn't enough, there was always Versailles. The most sumptuous court in Europe displaying itself in its grandest palace was an unforgettable sight. Even if you were a nobody, you could still come and watch, every Sunday, the king and the queen processing to Mass and eating their lunch in public. If you were noble, or famous, then you could get your ambassador to introduce you to Their Majesties, and you would enjoy at first hand Marie Antoinette's inimitable grace.

Having done that, you need not give up splendor just because you returned to Paris. Many of its mansions were open to well-dressed visitors; and so you could see the baron de Besenval's new Roman bathroom, or the comte d'Artois's Turkish-style interior. Then, at the right season, there was the *Salon*, the gathering of the year's best paintings in one of the halls of the Louvre. There was the opera, of course, where Gluck's work was all the rage. The many theaters offered everything from highly controversial plays like Beaumarchais's *Marriage of Figaro* to the justly famous seventeenth-century tragedies of Racine and Corneille. Molière's comedies were as popular as ever; Voltaire's dramas were eagerly attended. There were gambling dens, of course, and brothels of every kind; but if that seemed a little coarse, many pretty and vivacious actresses and singers were to be had for the right sum.

All that had gone. The Revolution had swept away the pleasures of Paris along with the monarchy. Unkempt buildings, empty mansions, closed theaters, shuttered shops: by 1795, no one would have thought of going to France in order to have fun—indeed, it was a dangerous place for foreigners. You could hardly come if you were Prussian, Austrian, English, or Russian, or if you were an aristocrat. Wherever the center of pleasure might be, it was not Paris.

It took just five years to change all that. Already, under the Directoire, parts, at least, of Parisian life had revived. There were no salons, certainly, and Versailles was empty and deserted; but fashionable dress designers were already hard at work, and so were the makers of furniture, carriages, even silver (for the nouveaux riches). By 1798, whether to wear a turban or a vast straw hat topped with immense white flowers had become a serious issue for fashionable women. By 1800, operas were performed in three different theaters; all kinds of fascinating new books were published; new great houses were opening, to which it was easy to get an introduction. Slowly, Paris was becoming itself again; and so, as peace with most of Europe returned, foreigners came back. What they found was very different from what they remembered. They often made fun of the new manners (coarse and middle-class), of the newly rich (abysmally ignorant of everything except money), even of the new fashions — until, suddenly, they were wearing them. But they came, and wrote home, and their friends came in turn. They discovered an embryo court at the Tuileries Palace, the residence of the new First Consul, General Bonaparte, and of his wife, the endlessly charming and seductive Joséphine. They even found that the French had invented a whole new way to get great food by going to that recent invention, the *grand restaurant.*

THE PLEASURES OF THE TABLE

Restaurants themselves were a new invention; the first ones had been opened by a few bold entrepreneurs in the 1780s, but they were neither expensive nor fashionable. The Revolution changed all that. As the nobles fled, their suddenly unemployed chefs, desperate for work, opened their own places. Suddenly the best cuisine in Paris could be had outside the home; and when the gold standard was reestablished in 1800, and prices became stable, these new establishments prospered. There were all kinds of restaurants, of course. In the very simple ones, everyone sat around a big table and ate the same menu — plain but adequate food, which cost (with wine) between one and two livres. Others were more luxurious; none was as grand as Véry. "Nothing can surpass the sumptuousness of the rooms at M. Véry's," wrote Grimod de La Reynière, a man to whom eating was the purpose of life. "And here, the excellence of the cuisine corresponds to the beauty of the setting. . . . The prices are high, but not excessively so. . . . The wine cellar is always admirably complete."[1] A German composer, Johann Friedrich Reichardt, who visited Paris in 1802, fully agreed. "[Véry's] reputation," he wrote, "is fully justified."[2] It was not just the quality but the variety: the menu listed eight soups, fourteen appetizers, eleven main courses made with beef, ten with lamb, sixteen with veal, twenty-seven with poultry, sixteen kinds of fish, fifteen roasts, ten pastries, twenty-nine sweets and salads, twenty-five desserts, fruit, cheeses, fifty-five different wines, twenty-five liqueurs. As for the prices, they varied from two to eleven livres for the meats, from one to six livres for the poultry and game; turbot was three livres, champagne from three and a half livres to seven livres. This was not cheap: given the abundance expected of a dinner at this time, dining at Véry's probably cost an average of thirty to forty livres a person—about three times a workingman's daily wage.

Dinner was, in fact, the main meal of the day. An elegant Parisian would have a cup of chocolate upon rising, eggs and grilled or cold meats around eleven, a huge meal around five or six, and, occasionally, a late supper around eleven. Things were changing, though. "Since we now dine . . . at five, six or seven, lunch has become a real meal,"[3] Grimod explained in his *Manuel des Amphitryons,* a sizable "how-to" book for would-be hosts; and he thoughtfully went on to provide a model menu for twenty five—it was hardly worth bothering if you invited fewer people.

Set in the middle of the table was a calf's head. Then came four cold dishes, a Mainz ham, a paté of chicken, a stuffed beef tongue, and a paté of game. All this was put down before the guests came in, and they were meant to help themselves as they pleased. As they sat down, eight appetizers were brought in: sausages, little patés, kidneys in champagne sauce, grilled tripe, pig's feet with truffles, scallops au gratin, sautéed oysters, and eels. Then came the main courses: a saddle of lamb with turnips, poultry thighs baked in parchment, sautéed veal with greens, two ducks with olives, a veal roast, squabs in spicy sauce, a stuffed breast of veal, and German-style boiled meats. All this time, plates had been set on the table with pickles, fresh butter, anchovies on toast, tuna in oil, radishes, oysters, and olives stuffed with anchovies, while at each end of the table a melon was waiting. Finally came the desserts: pears, brioches, grapes, walnuts, cookies, a compote of pears, apples, a compote of apples, and a variety of pastries. Naturally, all that needed to be washed down, so the host provided twelve bottles of Macon (a burgundy), four of Bordeaux, four of Beaune (another burgundy), twelve of Chablis, four of Clos-Vougeot, four of Saint-Péray, two of Malaga, two of Cyprus wine, and two of French sweet wines—a total of one and three-quarter bottles per guest. We know that such meals were in fact served: how the guests then spent the afternoon (other than sleeping it all off) is hard to imagine.

Lunch was new and exciting, but real gourmets never quite took to it. Dinner, they felt, was the only serious meal, and that could only be planned by thoroughly knowledgeable hosts—who then expected their efforts to be appreciated. Cambacérès, the Second Consul, was such a man. The proud inventor of a special recipe for partridges (they were roasted on one side and broiled on the other), he made it quite clear that his guests were to pay attention to what was on their plates. "Please speak lower!" he exclaimed one evening. "We will hardly know what we're eating at this rate."[4]

It was not enough, however, to provide huge quantities of superb food. "One might compare a host who did not know how to carve or serve to the owner of a fine library who did not know how to read,"[5] Grimod explained.

And, equally, a man who knew the fine points of carving was an eagerly sought guest. Skill and knowledge of the bone structures of birds and animals were the beginning; but the way the host offered pieces of what he had carved to his guests also mattered greatly. Talleyrand, who was famous for his grand manners and his ancien régime courtesy, was held to be a model of what a host should be. Not only did he carve superbly, he also knew just what to say, so that the scale would run something like this: Will your Highness do me the great favor of taking a little beef; M. le duc, may I have the honor of giving you some beef; Excellency, will you allow me to give you some beef; Count, you'll have beef; Durand, beef.

Beef, indeed, was important, and when it came to the superiority of French beef, Grimod did not mince his words. "It is quite justly," he wrote, "that beef is called the king of the kitchen, and it is especially in Paris that it deserves this title for nowhere else in the world is it as fleshy, as flavorful, as succulent; English beef is . . . a mass of swollen flesh. The beef we eat here has a thousand times more spirit and juiciness."[6] But then, it was generally agreed (except by the English) that everything tasted better in Paris. At one famous restaurant, Le Rocher de Cancale, diners could order extraordinary oysters, as well as first-rate game and fowl; at many food stores they could get everything from the dewiest peaches to the most complex pastries.

Still, much as people enjoyed all these tidbits, it was dinner that counted for munificent hosts and serious eaters. Naturally, there was a precise etiquette: if your letter of invitation said four o'clock, you were meant to arrive at five; if it said four o'clock precisely, then you were expected at four-thirty; but if it read four o'clock very precisely you had to be there at four. Whatever the time, you would be shown, upon arriving, into a salon where you would expect to find newspapers, chess and checker boards so that you could while the time away without having to speak to your fellow guests, whom you might well not know. Conscientious hosts came in and introduced the guests to each other—it would have been a frightful faux pas to introduce yourself—but usually only just before going in to the dining room; and throughout this period, vermouth was served.

Naturally, table placement was crucially important. The host sat in the center of the table, his wife opposite; the guests were then arranged in order of importance, starting on the host's and hostess's right and left; and there were place cards. Wine and water, in carafes, were set on the table, ready for the guests: virtually no one drank their wine straight. As for the multitude of dishes offered, it was proper to ask the servant standing behind your chair to give you a helping of whichever one you wanted; then, at the end of the meal, everybody moved on to a salon where coffee was served.

Happily, unlike at the house of the Second Consul, the meal was not consumed in silence: conversation—light, witty, animated—was one of the expected pleasures. It was thus essential to choose the guests carefully: a table had to be composed with the same care as a menu; and one sure sign that Napoléon, for all his genius, lacked a proper regard for the decencies of life was that he bolted down his meals in a half hour or less, instead of eating at leisure, talking all the while. Indeed the emperor signally lacked several of the qualities which Grimod asserts any good host must have: "wealth, taste, an inborn feeling for good food, a penchant for magnificence, a love of order, a graceful manner, a kind heart and a lively mind."[7]

Grimod pointedly mentions wealth as the first in his list of qualities, and no wonder. Having a dinner party was enormously expensive. It wasn't just that huge quantities of food were served, but a good host needed a first-rate cook helped by several assistants, at least one butler, and a significant number of footmen. And the dining room (not to mention the rest of the house) had to look properly elegant. Then, at table, only the finest crystal, the best porcelain, and great quantities of silver would do: tureens, platters, servers of all kinds were the rule. That, indeed, is how it was at the house of the Second Consul. While the hushed silence may on occasion have proved a little oppressive, the rest of the dinner amply made up for it. As a foreign visitor noted:

> We were invited for six o'clock, and I counted thirty six guests. . . . At seven, we sat down around a sumptuously decorated table. . . . It was very big and laden with silver warming dishes on which the rarest foods . . . were successively placed. For the dessert, which was just as handsome and varied, everything on the table was replaced. The wines were perhaps even rarer and better chosen than the menu, which is not saying little!
>
> The Consul did the honors with all the amiability imaginable. . . . There is not a single guest whom he did not address several times, offering him some delicacy. . . . The exquisitely perfumed ices were served in the salon."[8]

Splendor and rareness were the keynotes here. No dinner at the Second Consul was ever less than exquisite; but for all that, it was limited, that night, to two services. For a really grand dinner, a full four services were required: the first was composed of soups, appetizers, and the main dishes except for the roasts; the second of the roasts, the cold meat placed in the center of the table (a ham, for instance), and the salads; the third of patés, vegetables, and pastries; and the fourth of fruit, compotes, cheeses, cookies, candies, petits fours, jellies, and ice creams.

Of course, no one ate of every dish. Rather, you chose among them, and took only very small amounts of any one; even so, the amount of food placed on a well-served table was nothing short of gargantuan. The menu for a relatively simple dinner in spring for fifteen—by no means a large group—consisted of twenty-eight dishes plus the desserts. "It will easily be seen," Grimod comments, "that this menu is rather simple and may be made by a not very skilled cook."[9]

Of course, not everyone in the upper classes ate this well. The lower bourgeoisie made do with soup, a stew, a roast, vegetables, and dessert, while working-class families (who ate their main meal around two o'clock) had meat no more than once or twice a week, and lived on a mostly bread diet. Even the emperor ate more simply than most. A typical dinner served at the Palace of the Tuileries consisted of two soups, one with macaroni, the other with chestnuts, followed by stewed beef and a pike, then partridge fillets, wild duck fillets, a fricassee of chickens, and lamb chops in onion sauce. The roasts were a capon and a leg of lamb; the dessert a coffee custard, a lamb jelly, a cake, and wafers. Given Napoléon's legendary speed, however, most of these dishes passed him untouched (and it was hungry work to be asked to dine with him). One of his officials saw it all.

"Bonaparte," he wrote in 1803, "only spends a quarter of an hour at table when he dines with just a few people. Even at State dinners, he does not sit for more than half an hour. All the dishes, roasts, stews, vegetables are served together; then comes the dessert. A few months after he had become Consul, he was told that his dinners were too quick. He added a few minutes to them. I told him: 'General, you have become less speedy at table.'

"He answered: 'It is already the corruption of power.'"[10]

LIFE AND THE PEOPLE

Those immense meals, those formal receptions, required both time and money. For the small bourgeoisie, both were scarce; the lower class, working endless hours and living from day to day, had neither. Paris was thus composed of two radically different groups. At the top was the new aristocracy—generals, ministers, financiers, with, usually a step below in terms of ability to spend, the old nobility, which was welcomed back by the first consul. Large private houses, staffs of many servants, horses, carriages, splendid clothes, diamonds—all the luxuries were theirs. And, no matter how recent their fortunes, they never doubted their superiority.

Most Parisians lived in a very different world, one in which both income and expenses were carefully watched. Among the middle class, it was understood that saving was better than spending. A dowry for the daughter, a small capital sum for the son, the purchase of a small house somewhere—those were the things that mattered. And the stability established by the new government made all the difference. The new gold franc was absolutely stable—its value remained unchanged from 1802 to 1918. The new state bonds were a famously safe investment, so anyone who could thought it worthwhile to save. For a notoriously industrious nation, this was the ideal situation: from lawyers to shopkeepers, and middle-level civil servants (of whom there were many) to university professors, men worked long hours, six days a week, with almost no holidays, and they prospered.

Women, ideally, were not supposed to have jobs; but starting at the shop-keeper level, they all did. Many stores were run by husband and wife, as were most of the fruit and vegetable stands at the central market. All seamstresses were women, as were the hatmakers, embroiderers, laundresses; their days usually stretched to fourteen hours, and they were paid a pittance. So were most domestics: grand houses had butlers and footmen as well as maids, but, below that level, it was women who did the domestic work, and they had a hard life. Domestic staffs had to be available at any time, all the time, from before breakfast to late in the evening. A lady's maid was expected to be pres-ent when her mistress awoke, and when she went to bed after coming home from a ball; in the meantime, there was the endless care required by fashion-able clothes. Servants lived in small, unheated rooms under the roof; they worked 364 days a year; a day out was the rarest of favors. Their salary remained somewhere between twenty and forty francs a month—barely enough to accu-mulate a little money to live on in old age. As for maids of all work employed by the lower bourgeoisie, their lives were notoriously the hardest of all.

In a world where any employee could be fired at will, and where there was no social safety net of any kind, the life of the poor was terrifying. If a maid was dismissed, she might, or she might not, get a new place. If she did not, she would be homeless and starving; the prettier ones then became prostitutes. The same was true of workingmen. Skilled craftsmen had a measure of secu-rity; all others lived from day to day, on the edge of absolute poverty. They, too, were expected to work twelve to fifteen hours, six days a week. With luck, they made just enough to eat, dress very plainly, and pay the rent for a small room. If they fell ill, or were wounded on the job, they were entitled to nothing. Many of them were illiterate; most of them had started to work almost as soon as they could walk. They did not very often live past their fifties.

Because the Revolution had been largely the work of the bourgeoisie, there were laws strictly banning the formation of unions, making the employer an absolute master in his establishment—far more absolute than the kings of France had ever been. Wages were what the employers thought they should be—as low as possible, just enough to keep the workers from starving. Of course, men remembered the days of the Terror when it was the workers who ruled the streets; but they knew that the government would not hesitate to repress any disorder; and so, hopelessly, they worked on.

THE PLEASURES OF THE CITY

All that remained invisible to the upper classes and foreign visitors alike. "As long as you know how to take on the tone of good temper usual to the French, you can always get along with the people of Paris,"[11] wrote a foreign visitor. He was right: after the great uprisings of the Revolution, the Parisians had once again become the most amiable, best-tempered people in Europe. They made travelers feel welcome; and the multitude of amusements to be found everywhere added greatly to the pleasures of any stay. There was, in 1800, a plethora of theaters—but by 1807, Napoléon allowed only eight to remain open, and they offered mostly weighty tragedies that took place in ancient Greece or Rome. Their justly forgotten authors, men like Carrion-Nisas, Arnault Aignan, or Lemercier, simply recycled the classics in ponderous alexandrine verse. Worse yet, after 1804 vigilant censors excised anything that might conceivably be interpreted as a criticism of the emperor, or his family, or his court, or the regime, and so these plays were as bland as they were full of improbably noble sentiments. Still, there were the actors, and the great ones were worshipped, chiefly Talma among the men—Napoléon was his most famous fan—and Mlle George among the women. Both strutted, ranted, and raved, and the thrilled audiences obligingly burst into sobs. Of course, both could also be seen in the classical French repertory—Corneille, Racine, Molière, Voltaire. Corneille was the emperor's favorite, probably because he was the most heroic. Content, in fact, was supposed to be noble, elevating, a lesson to all. The purpose of theater, Napoléon felt, was to educate: it must help to create yet more generations of young men ready to give their all on the battlefield, and in that sense the emperor, though he was born and educated in the eighteenth century, very much belonged to the nineteenth: for him, as for Queen Victoria, art was meant to be didactic.

Still, no one seemed to mind, except, perhaps, the authors whose plays were banned. Parisians and visitors alike eagerly attended the theater, argued about the merit of new plays, and went home content. They also argued, even more vigorously, about music, and there was a great deal of it to be talked over. The repertories of the three theaters where operas were performed were not only diverse but controversial. People, who of course were forbidden to discuss politics, debated opera passionately: should the French style as represented, ironically, by the German Gluck prevail over the Italian as heard in, for instance, Cimarosa's work? The Italians were more lyrical—it was the beginning of bel canto—the French more emotional. And there were the productions: the sets, usually splendid, and the costumes were eagerly discussed.

Happily for the Parisians, there was a good deal to be heard besides Le Sueur, a singularly untalented composer. Mozart was in vogue, as was Gluck; Cimarosa still being played; and new composers had just come from Italy, chief among them Paisiello and Spontini. Haydn's great choral pieces were also sung, not, a German visitor thought, particularly well; and there were also many concerts.

Music could, of course, be heard in the other great European capitals, and, in places like Vienna, it was often better than in Paris; but there was no museum like the Louvre anywhere—indeed most cities did not have a museum at all. Open daily from nine to five, and called the Musée Central des Arts, the Louvre was a brand-new concept. Elsewhere, royal collections remained in royal palaces, and were seen only by courtiers and royalty. In France, the Revolution had changed all that; and to the already huge royal collection, paintings seized from convents, churches, and émigrés had been added. Then, with the French conquests, yet more works of art had been sent to Paris; the result was incomparably the greatest accumulation of masterpieces in Europe.

The Louvre itself had not been lived in by the royal family since the 1660s, but it was quite big enough even for an immense collection. Before the Revolution, it had housed the yearly *Salon* of painting—as well as parts of the royal collection that were visible on appointment—and artists' apartments and studios. During the Revolution, there had been much debate over what was to be done with all the art works that had become the property of the nation, but no firm conclusion had been reached. Then Dominique Vivant-Denon, a connoisseur and art historian, had suggested the idea of a central repository, open to the public, where all these diversely acquired works of art could be displayed; and in 1800, for the first time, the Louvre museum opened its doors.

Immediately, people were dazzled. From Leonardo da Vinci, Raphael, and Michelangelo to Corregio and Guercino, from Clouet to Poussin, Fragonard, and David, without forgetting van Eyck, Hals, Rubens, Rembrandt, and Vermeer, countless masterpieces hanging in row upon row literally covered the walls. And from the very beginning, visitors crowded in, Parisians and foreigners alike. Of course, there was too much to be seen at one time—like today, you had to return, again and again, visit a few halls, a few galleries—but one thing was clear: the Louvre had become the center of Paris.

Visiting the museum was serious business, and so was going (by previous appointment) to see an artist's studio, but there was also a more frivolous side to Paris: more than ever, it was the capital of fashion. That, of course, could mean many things: when the king of Bavaria decided he needed a new, and very grand, silver-gilt service, complete with table decorations, countless tureens, platters, and serving utensils, he ordered it from the Paris silversmith Odiot, because it was a fashionable thing to do. He was, in any event, following precedent: in the eighteenth century, the king of Portugal and the empress of Russia, among others, had ordered their silver services from Germain, then the fashionable silversmith. Equally, Sèvres porcelain had been popular throughout Europe before the Revolution; now it was again, and foreigners could rely on its urns and its vases, its plates, platters, and covered dishes, being in the currently desirable neoclassical style.

More than anything, though, it was fashion itself everyone wanted: from Petersburg to Naples, it was well understood that there was nothing more elegant than French clothes. This was a relatively recent development. While the silks from Lyons had long been in demand, it was only when Mlle Bertin opened the first couture house in the early 1770s that fashion and Paris became synonymous. Now that hoops, bustles, and corsets were gone, there was a new fashionable designer—Leroy. His prices were high; so high, in fact, that Napoléon once sent him to jail for a few days after seeing one of his bills, and in an average year Joséphine would spend nearly 150,000 francs on Leroy's dresses. By comparison, workingmen made less than 5,000 francs a year; 50,000 francs was enough for a very stylish way of life. Of course, the empress liked quantity as well as quality: in 1809, she owned 676 winter dresses, 230 summer dresses, and 60 of the huge, ruinously expensive Indian shawls then so much in fashion.

Naturally, what had seemed desirable under the Directoire was hopelessly passé in 1800. Waists were still high, and sleeves short (but now they were puffed out); gauzes and muslins were thought dated: heavily embroidered silks, brocades, and velvets were the fabrics of choice. And the dress itself multiplied: to the bodice and skirt was added an overdress, starting at the shoulders in back and the waist in front, with a wide slit before and a train behind. Jewelry was naturally essential: the more belts, necklaces, and bracelets the better, while, for dressy occasions, elaborate tiaras were essential. Shoes were still as thin as could be, though: when a lady complained to the fashionable maker that her soles had worn out in a single afternoon, he asked her, superciliously, whether she had by any chance been actually walking.

For the men, too, the fashion was changing. The wrinkled look, which had been just right in 1797, was gone three years later. Breeches (as opposed to trousers) were in again; they were worn with a tailcoat, usually blue or black during the day; hair was still short, though many middle-aged men wore it long and powdered. For dressy occasions, embroidered velvet coats and vests were required; and in short order, Napoléon decided precisely who could wear what color and with what embroidery.

All this mattered greatly to the middle and upper classes; but fashion was not just what you wore, it was also how you spent your time. When, one evening, Reichardt, the German composer who visited Paris in 1802, was asked by one of the reigning beauties to play some Gluck duets with her the next morning, he was already Parisian enough to know that "Come in the morning" meant "Come at two in the afternoon." Even so, that proved still too much like dawn. Reichardt later recalled:

> I found the "beauty" resting in her splendid Greek-style bed, under sheets of the finest linen among a mountain of cushions covered in pale violet silk. To the right and left were some fine Greek [style] vases; on the platform of the bed, the little dancing shoes from the evening before! Her hair loosely tied, her head leaning on her right arm, her left knee slightly bent under the soft cover, the lazy beauty smiled and asked me to sit near her. We spoke of the latest ball, we mentioned a few of the new books . . . I then went in to the salon

while she rose. It only took a moment: Mme X reappeared wearing a charming negligee. Finally, we sat down at the piano-forte, but hardly had we sung a single scene but a very smartly dressed man came in: it was a jeweler who wanted to show her some ornaments. The piano-forte was abandoned so that the jewels could be looked at. Having handled them, turned them about again and again, it was decided that they were not right . . .

We returned to the piano-forte and launched into a duo. I was just playing the last chord when the maid brought Madame's lunch: a roast chicken and some [sweet] Syracuse wine. She ate a wing, drank a drop of the wine. . . . We then went back to the music but two fashionable ladies came in. Their dress was scrutinized, judged, criticized and Mme X became very angry at the designer who took it upon herself not to send her a hat like the one which looked so well on one of her visitors. Just at that moment, the guilty milliner appeared with her hat box and was immediately scolded for having neglected a faithful client. The accused one justified herself as best she could and . . . blamed the owner of the new hat for having played a dirty trick on her by wearing a coiffure that had been delivered to her barely an hour earlier. . . .

New visitors arrived, the salon filled up. Mme X was playfully reproached for her laziness; she herself laughed about the stupidity of her doorman who thought that she was seeing "everyone."[12]

And soon, no doubt, the "beauty" was dressing for that night's ball.

In 1800, the more opulent houses in Paris tended to be those of the bankers, speculators, and purveyors who had done well out of the Directoire; but with the advent of the consulate, everything changed. A new hierarchy appeared, and the various dignitaries—the First, Second, and Third Consuls, the senators, the deputies, the ministers—all began receiving people. The Bonapartes themselves, having begun modestly, surrounded themselves with something very like a court; and then there were all Napoléon's relatives: his brothers Lucien, Joseph, and Louis (Jerôme was still an adolescent), his sisters Caroline, Elisa, and Pauline, as well as Joséphine's two children, Eugène and Hortense de Beauharnais. Great houses multiplied, and so did the balls and fetes of every sort. Year by year, Paris became a busier place, although not always a more amusing one: if there was one thing Napoléon did not understand, it was having fun.

In 1802, most well-to-do Parisians were still lighthearted, and one of the queens of the city, Mme Récamier, was the very emblem of it all. Like so many people who had survived the Revolution, she was not quite what she seemed. Apparently, this ravishing young woman, with her dark hair, huge eyes, and dazzling complexion, was just that: a beauty. Her little feet were famous throughout Europe for their perfection; so was the simplicity of her dress: always in white, often barefoot, she hardly wore any jewelry, and yet she seemed, invariably, to outshine her rivals. As if great beauty weren't enough, she was also smart, a gifted listener to whose salon interesting people flocked.

She was admired, and eagerly courted, by men ranging from the Bonaparte brothers to great nobles freshly returned from exile and virtually every intellectual; but she, alone of all Parisians of her class, remained faithful to her husband. And most amazing of all, she had devoted women friends.

To make everything better yet, M. Récamier was a very rich banker who delighted in giving his wife everything she wanted, first and foremost what may well have been the most fashionably appointed house in Paris. It was all like a fairy tale without an evil witch. In fact, although Mme Récamier, in 1802, had been married for almost nine years, she was a virgin—not because her husband was impotent but because he was her father. He had been her mother's lover, and when, in 1793, he began to fear for his life, he married the young woman, whose official father was someone altogether different, so that she could inherit his property if he should be guillotined. Mme Récamier was told all this; she conceived a lifelong affection for her real father, and an enduring aversion to sex; and so, this apparently adoring and faithful wife, this dazzling beauty whom all men wanted, was in fact living like a secular nun.

Of course, she had certain compensations: it is not unpleasant to be generally adored; she knew all the most interesting people in Europe; and her house was a masterpiece of fashionable decor. To this day, it has remained, in memory, the epitome of that fugitive moment when neoclassicism reached its apex before declining into the more pompous, heavier Empire style.

Unlike the residences of the dignitaries of the new regime, the Récamier house was not huge. Like all sizable private residences, it was shielded from the street by a vast doorway leading into a front courtyard flanked by stables and carriage house; on the other side, there was a large, wall-enclosed garden. On those frequent evenings when the Récamiers were having a reception, the front courtyard was brilliantly lit, while the four steps leading into the house and the vestibule were covered with Persian carpets and filled with rare plants and flowers.

In most houses, it was the grand reception rooms that mattered; here, it was the beautiful Juliette's bedroom, boudoir, and bathroom—a suite of rooms so famous that the hostess would courteously ask any new guest if they would like to see it; and none ever refused. Many mirrors, sumptuous curtains of white silk voile, gold satin, purple silk, motifs inspired by the paintings recently rediscovered in the ruins of Pompeii and Herculaneum, it was all there. The fashion, in Paris, was for ancient Rome made new. Even the bed looked a little like the banquet couches used by the ancient Romans. Richly adorned with gilt-bronze palms, laurel crowns, and nymphs, it was flanked by Roman-style vases and Roman-style candelabras.

This, everyone agreed, was as beautiful a room as could well be imagined—and the watercolors that represent it are, in fact, stunning. Still there was more. Grand bathrooms were a recent invention: Marie Antoinette had them in her palaces (but they could not be visited); in the middle 1780s the baron de Besenval had had one installed in his Paris house, and immediately everyone wanted to see it. Had it not been for the Revolution, bathrooms would no doubt have multiplied. As it was, Mme Récamier's was the talk of Paris. More mirrors, walls covered with finely pleated green silk and red leather chairs: it was the perfect setting for a great beauty—and people admired both the decor and its owner.

The Récamier house was in Paris, the Récamiers were French; yet, like many of their compatriots, Napoléon first and foremost, their lives seemed to have universal value—for other Europeans, at least. People came from all over to see, to hear, to envy what was being done in Paris; then they went home and tried to replicate it. Because Juliette had a draped bathroom, draped bathrooms appeared from Naples to Saint Petersburg; because Malmaison, the Bonapartes' country house, had a tentlike room, tents became an inescapable leitmotif.

Napoléon is perhaps best known for having been a military genius; he also had an amazing ability to see how France should be organized; more unexpectedly perhaps, he could also have had a great career as an interior decorator; and this was first seen at Malmaison.

SETTING THE TREND

War or no war, it was France that determined what was seen elsewhere. The contemporary trends in decor were yet another affirmation that the world in 1800 was united in more ways than one, and Malmaison was famous the world over. It was (and, happily, still is) a small country château just a few miles outside Paris. Bought by Joséphine in April 1799, while Bonaparte was still in Egypt, the house, which had been built in the early eighteenth century, was gloomy and run-down, but, considering that the new owner had gone deep into debt to buy it, there was not much she could do to refurbish it. This annoying situation was, however, soon ended: in October, Bonaparte returned and discovered that his wife had been abundantly unfaithful. Frightful scenes followed. Joséphine was heard to sob spectacularly for hours on end (crying on cue was one of her talents) and Napoléon, vanquished as always by a beautiful woman's tears, forgave her. There remained the unpaid-for Malmaison, so Bonaparte showed he could be generous: he discharged all the debts connected to it, and then hired Charles Percier and Pierre Fontaine, the two most fashionable architects of the day, to redecorate it.

The result was an appealing blend of the classical and the warlike. Percier and Fontaine were devoted to the styles of ancient Rome: nymphs, columns, noble spaces, straight-legged furniture with bronze rams' heads and rams' feet,

Malmaison, the country home bought by Joséphine and lavishly redecorated for Napoléon by Percier and Fontaine. (*General Research Division, The New York Public Library, Astor, Lenox and Tilden Foundations*)

all were meant to make early nineteenth century Paris look like the capital of the Caesars. This was an attempt of which Napoléon thoroughly approved: although he soon thought of himself as the second Charlemagne, that did not prevent him from finding most of his references in the achievements of the first and second century emperors. As for the military look, it was so obviously appropriate as to need no comment. Still, there were many crises: Napoléon complained again and again about Percier and Fontaine's designs, and objected violently to their bills, which probably came to well over 3 million francs. In the end, however, he invariably allowed the work to proceed, and the result is an enchanting blend of the grand and the cozy.

Because Malmaison is not a large house, and because Bonaparte, as First Consul, ran the French government, it quickly became obvious that an extra room was needed where officials could wait for their audience. A stone excrescence would have looked unsightly; and so Percier and Fontaine came up with a bold, and highly successful, solution: a little pavilion of cast iron and glass in the shape of a tent. On the outside, it was painted to look as if it were made of striped fabric, while on the inside the windows and walls were draped with actual material. The result is light, cheerful, and just right for the residence of a general.

That theme is picked up again indoors. The Council Room, where the First Consul met with his ministers, had its walls and tent-shaped ceiling covered with a yellow, off-white, and black striped fabric. A black and gold faux-bronze balustrade with lions' heads ran around the lower part of the walls, and the doors were flanked with mahogany and gilt bronze poles topped with eagles. As for the door panels, they were painted with trophies on a dark ground. The extraordinary thing about the room, though, is its very conception: tents, after all, are for the outdoors, and yet the idea worked so well that it was immediately imitated throughout Europe.

The other rooms looked very different. The vestibule, which was also sometimes used as a salon, was a grandly austere composition with four majestic faux-marble columns defining an atrium-like space.

The antique look was continued in the dining room and in the library. No one, however, could have been less solemn than Joséphine, or more voluptuous—and those are indeed the characteristics of her round bedroom. It, too, is tentlike—but what a tent! The top opens in a circle to reveal a painted sky; the lushly draped red silk is held up by gilt-wood poles that lead the eye up to a frieze with gold decorative motifs on a red ground. The carpet, too, is red and gold; but the most amazing part of the room is the bed. It has a canopy topped with a great golden eagle and bordered in red and gold, and is draped with a double layer of curtains, cream colored with gold border embroidery on the outside, white with gold flowers on the inside. As for the great golden bed itself, it is flanked at the head by swans (Joséphine's favorite bird) and at the foot by brimming cornucopias. Nothing could be warmer or richer. In its splendor, this is certainly the right bedroom for an empress; but it is also a reminder that for a number of years, Joséphine's talents in bed helped earn her a living.

The house, naturally, was much visited and much copied; but there was also a good deal more to Malmaison. The fashion for English gardens had reached France in the 1780s. Nature, far too dull if unimproved, was rearranged to look more dramatic, yet untouched: hills, apparently random plantings, and occasional lakes were part of the look, as were carefully placed pavilions and grottoes. Naturally, Joséphine had all this at Malmaison, together with a bevy of swans; and then she went a step further. Because she loved flowers, she gathered the rarest and most exotic plants in existence—the British navy was courteous enough to let them pass. Because she loved roses, she had almost every known species growing in her gardens, so that Malmaison was known throughout Europe for the richness and quality of its plantings. Still, Joséphine decided that was not enough: flowers fade and die, images don't; so she commissioned Redouté, a flower painter of extraordinary talent, to record it all. The results were three books of watercolors that were made into engravings: *The Lilies,* with 486 plates; *The Roses,* with 168 plates; and *The Gardens of Malmaison,* with 120 plates. Today, all three are still eagerly sought collector's items.

THE DRAMA OF CLASSICAL ART

Redouté was talented; his work was much appreciated; but he scarcely belonged on the same level as Jacques-Louis David, that universally recognized genius. In 1800, David was the best-known painter in Europe, and that year, his *Portrait of Mme Récamier* confirmed his fame. Nothing could be simpler, nothing could be more artful. The background is a mottled dark gray-green, the ground is a beige mottled with gray; and in this absolutely plain space, the famous beauty sits on a plain wooden couch. There is a plain wooden footstool at one end of the couch, an oil lamp on a tall bronze stand at the other. Mme Récamier herself is sitting, her legs extended before her on the couch, an arm resting on her thigh; she turns away from us, yet the head turns back to look at us in a gesture at once shy and appealing. Except for the black band around her forehead, the only colors are those of her skin and plain white dress, which drapes down to the ground, revealing her famous feet. Here, as usual, David has brought his model most vividly to life: Juliette's charm, her beauty, her reserve, her fascination, are all depicted here.

By 1800, David had already had a long and dramatic career. A brilliant student, he had been sent to Italy, where the ruins of ancient Rome and the newly excavated remains of Pompeii transformed his understanding of art. He had started as a rococo artist; he brought back with him a style based on the most austere vision of the ancient world, and he was immediately recognized as the greatest painter of the age.

David did not limit himself to subjects taken from the antique, though. When a great cause came along, he embraced it with fervor. It is to him we owe a moving image of the Oath of the Tennis Court, that defining moment in 1789 when the deputies swore they would not separate until they had given France a constitution. In many ways, in fact, David was the artist of the Revolution. He was, himself, directly involved in politics, sitting in the Convention, friendly with Robespierre. He belonged to the more extreme left; and he helped to give the Revolution its look by designing the sets and costumes for the principal celebrations.

Those are, of course, long forgotten; but when a passionately royalist (and singularly unintelligent) young woman, Charlotte Corday, assassinated Jean-Paul Marat, the great journalist, David's painting celebrating his dead friend turned out to be one of the most striking in the history of painting.

Naturally, David organized Marat's memorial ceremony; just as naturally, when the Directoire was installed, it was David who was asked to design costumes for the various officials; but he also got into considerable political trouble. As a prominent member of the extreme left, he was twice sent to jail; by 1799, he had, in consequence, largely given up politics. Happily, he was painting better than ever; so, sensibly, he concentrated on producing masterpieces.

Bonaparte was now in charge; and it is through David we know him best. It started in 1801: *Bonaparte Crossing the Alps* is all movement and drama. Set against a tormented sky, with snowy peaks in the background, Bonaparte sits on a rearing horse, its tail and mane streaming forward in the furious wind. The general, his head turned to look at us, points imperiously forward with one hand while the other clutches the reins. He is draped in a vivid yellow cloak, which also streams forward, and his whole body, from the bent leg to the pointing hand, forms a dramatic zigzag. Here are energy and power made palpable: not an accurate representation of the crossing of the Alps, perhaps, but the kind of dramatization that is truer than mere accuracy.

Indeed, from the very beginning, David gave his allegiance to Bonaparte; as for the general, David's classicism, his taste for heroic subjects taken from ancient Rome, all seemed just right. Naturally, David was commissioned to paint him; but most of the portraits, both of Napoléon and of his family, are the work of younger, less expensive artists, men like Ingres and Gérard, who did a workmanlike job. When, however, it came to the defining moment of the new regime, the crowning of Napoléon as emperor of the French, only David would do.

The result is yet another famous image—and one that is singularly less accurate than it appears. Of course, David was present at the coronation; he made sketches and used them later; but the painting itself is the result of long conversations with Napoléon. The emperor wanted a perfect piece of propaganda; David gave it to him. The fact that it has proved completely convincing for nearly two hundred years is yet another proof of the artist's genius.

There are two kinds of "improved reality" in this vast painting: the physical arrangement of throne, altar, and attendants has been modified to create greater drama; and the emperor's mother, who was, at that moment, quarreling with him, and had consequently retreated to Rome, is depicted as present. The very moment chosen by the emperor is a curious one: although the painting is usually called *The Coronation of Napoléon*, because that is the event it is meant to celebrate, what we actually see is the crowning of Joséphine. There is a good reason for this.

Although Napoléon had been most anxious to have the pope himself present at the coronation, he was not willing to seem indebted to him (or, worse, controlled by him). At the actual ceremony, greatly to Pius VII's surprise, Napoléon crowned himself; in David's painting, we see him already crowned, with the pope sitting behind him, to show that he owed his title to no man—and that it was he, alone, who was making Joséphine an empress. This also allowed David to focus the painting on the dramatic figure of Napoléon, standing with his arms raised, and that of Joséphine kneeling before him: it is not the pope, or even God, who is worshiped here, but the emperor.

In comparison, the grouping of pope and bishops sinks into the background; they are present but not important. As for the many attendants, everyone from Napoléon's sisters to the great dignitaries of the empire (and the added-on Madame Mère, the absent mother), they are all behaving with just the right blend of awe and decorum—another serious rearrangement of reality. In spite of all that, however, David has painted a masterpiece. Set against very tall arches, we see a pageant of red, white, and gold, the graceful figure of Joséphine set off by her gold-embroidered velvet cloak and the curtseying princesses behind, while Napoléon is at the center of a circle of sumptuously dressed men. Each figure is clearly recognizable: David had all those present sit for him individually. Gold and jewels glitter throughout the vast composition; and Napoléon has been enshrined for all time. David was paid a hundred thousand francs for the painting—an immense sum. As it turned out, this was also the best bargain the emperor ever made.

The Triumph of the Germans

The emperor and the Parisians felt quite sure that when it came to another of the arts, music, they were living in the musical capital of Europe, but they were completely mistaken. Great music, in 1800, came from Germany; and the two most important composers of the age were unquestionably the old Joseph Haydn and the young Ludwig van Beethoven.

Haydn, who was born in 1732, had reached fame in the 1760s; since then he had produced an abundance of operas (today happily revived); but more than anything he transformed the symphony. He was the first to break the connection of music and theater (outside religious music), not in order to express torrential emotions but to create a world all of whose references were musical. It was a rationally ordered architecture of sound he cared about: as he chose a modulation or a crescendo, he did not try to paint a picture; he was, instead, bringing order out of chaos. Often his music is made of a juxtaposition of short melodic and rhythmical elements; his motifs are often built on two elements of which the second is the first, inverted.

As it was, Haydn triumphed wherever he went, whether it was London, with its fiercely competitive atmosphere and demanding audiences, or the musical Prince Joseph Esterházy's palace, where he was composer in residence for many years. He was also an inspired teacher, something for which his student Beethoven could vouch.

A quick look at his schedule tells a great deal. In 1794, he organized, wrote music for, and conducted fourteen concerts in London to universal acclaim; in the first half of 1795, he wrote his last three London symphonies, which were much admired by King George III and the Prince of Wales; then, in August, he returned to Vienna. There, he went on composing—among other works *Gott erhalte den Kaiser,* which became the Austrian national anthem, and that vast and splendid oratorio, *The Creation.* Its premiere, at Prince Schwarzenberg's, with Antonio Salieri at the piano, was a triumph. This creativity continued until 1803, when age caught up with him; he died in 1809, to universal regret.

It is not easy to convey the merit of music in another medium; but occasionally a genius has a try. Happily, Johann Wolfgang von Goethe decided to explain just why he liked Haydn, and, as he did so, he spoke for everyone who has heard that glorious music.

> For more than fifty years, the playing and hearing of [Haydn's] works have invariably given me a feeling of plenitude. When I come into contact with them, I experience an involuntary tendency to do what seems right to me, and likely to please God. . . .
>
> Haydn . . . does what he does without exaltation. . . . Temperament, sensitivity, wit, humor, spontaneity, sweetness, strength, even the two very signs of genius, naivete and irony, all this already belongs to him. . . . Let us recognize his art as ancient in the best sense of the word. At the same time, its modern character has been doubted by no one . . .: all of modern music is indebted to him . . .
>
> The perfect chord which expresses his genius is nothing less than the tranquil resonance of a free-born, clear and chaste soul. . . . His works are the ideal language of truth.[13]

There was nothing so serene about Beethoven. Just as Haydn, in his quest for order and balance, was typical of the eighteenth century, so Beethoven, that impetuous, tormented genius, was the very incarnation of the new romanticism. Permanently short of money, living in a world where nothing was quite as it should be, he struggled with everyone about everything—and most of all with himself. Unhappy love affairs seemed to go with a life that never quite settled down; torrential emotions poured into his music, and, often, his audiences were not sure what to make of them. In a final paradox, this composer of genius, still only in his forties, soon grew deaf: already well known in 1800, he was writing a friend: "The humming in my ears continues day and night without ceasing. I may truly say that my life is a wretched one. For the last two years, I have avoided all society, for it is impossible for me to say to people: 'I am deaf.' Were my profession any other, it would not so much matter, but in my profession it is a terrible thing. And my enemies, of which there are not a few, what would they say to this? . . . Often, I can scarcely hear anyone speaking to me."[14] Soon, he could hear no one at all.

It is impossible to imagine a blind painter; a deaf composer, as Beethoven proved abundantly, can create masterpieces. Reinventing the symphony, whose structure he had mastered when studying with Haydn, he gave it new amplitude; the orchestra received an increased, dramatic role. Themes, built on long melodic lines, run through the movements, reflecting emotions that, far from being reduced to a precise order, go on instead to redefine the world. Music, before Beethoven, had tended to be abstract. Even when it tried to reflect emotions directly, as was the case in some of Gluck's operas, they were grand, noble emotions. Beethoven changed all that: his music reflects, describes, and reshapes our whole experience, from a sunlit morning in the country to the march of a conqueror; and as it creates its own universe, it sweeps the listener into it.

As for the emotions which he so passionately expresses, there is nothing grand or elegiacal about them: they are fierce, immediate responses to the vagaries of life, and range from quiet happiness to majestic rejoicing, from gentle melancholy to devastating pain and rage. It is typical that when he wrote his only opera, *Fidelio*, he placed it in just the kind of vaguely earlier time and exotic place that allowed romantic feeling all the room it needed. Influenced, to a small degree, by Luigi Cherubini's *Lodoïska*, he substituted a mythical Spain for a mythical Poland and a persecuted hero for a persecuted heroine, but the themes are very similar: both operas tell the story of the struggle of true love against a tyrannical and cruel world.

Here, indeed, is the new nineteenth-century ethos. Elegance, remoteness, cleverness have been replaced by a focus on individual passions—everything from love to a craving for political freedom. Eighteenth-century music had concerned itself, when it left abstraction at all, either with the courtly or with the grand. For Beethoven, power, and the way of the world, are mere impediments preventing men and women from fulfilling their emotional needs. The composer was antisocial because he was deaf; but he also took a very bleak view of the effect of organized society on humankind.

That did not suppose that everyone was the same, however: the existence of genius is one of the key tenets of romanticism, and Beethoven knew genius when he saw it. Sometimes, though, the genius in question proved untrue to itself; that was the case of Bonaparte. Although Beethoven lived in Vienna, the capital of the firmly reactionary Habsburg dynasty, he admired the many achievements of the French Revolution and of the young general who presented himself as its latest incarnation. So it was that in August 1804, Beethoven wrote to the music publishers Breitkopf und Hartel announcing "a new grand symphony . . . entitled Bonaparte."[15]

Then the general turned emperor, and Beethoven was disgusted: the man he had seen as a revolutionary hero was, after all, hungry for the stalest titles, the most conventional return to the ancien régime. (That view was not, in fact, wholly accurate, even if Napoléon plainly relished being called Your Majesty.) The title of the still grand symphony was changed to *Eroica*.

Not all geniuses disappointed, though. Napoléon might have proved to be just an ambitious politician, but there was always the great, the august Goethe, and Beethoven did not try to hide how he felt about him. "I am only in a position to approach you with the deepest reverence, with an inexpressibly deep feeling for your noble creations," he wrote the master. "You will shortly receive . . . the music to *Egmont*, this glorious *Egmont*, with which I, with the same warmth with which I read it, was again through you impressed by it and set it to music. I should much like to know your opinion of it; even blame would be profitable for me and for my art, and will be as willingly received as the greatest praise."[16] The very confusion of the grammar is eloquent. As it was, Beethoven need not have worried: Goethe thought his music wholly admirable.

Music: The Foreigners in Paris

Napoléon, who was more Italian than he liked to admit, was fond of opera. German music held no great appeal for him: not surprisingly, perhaps, he preferred the new bel canto mode, in which melody, sung by a great voice, was everything. Still, he was an opinionated critic. Here, as everywhere, he made the law—only, he usually forgot what he had objected to, thus giving his court composers a great deal of freedom in the end.

He was not alone in caring about opera: it was the art form that gave rise to the most impassioned discussions; and Paris, naturally, flocked to hear the new works. That they should be mostly by foreigners apparently bothered no one, not even Étienne Méhul, the only really well-known French composer. Even then, Méhul's great success had come in 1790: his *Euphrosine et Coradin* had been a huge and instant hit, with even the dourest people humming its arias. Then came *Le chant du départ*, the greatest revolutionary song after *La Marseillaise*.

In style, Méhul owed much to Gluck. Like that great master, he tried to express believable emotions and create a realistic atmosphere, and in this combination of psychological description and well-motivated development, he can be considered an early romantic. That is true also of his choice of subjects: his operas take place in a wide variety of exotic settings very unlike the classical themes that had prevailed until the end of the eighteenth century. Some of his subjects are biblical, others Nordic (the setting of one opera is a mythical Scandinavia), others still medieval—and that eclecticism announced the future.

Méhul's strength, however, was not opera: he was the best French symphonic composer before Hector Berlioz. His symphonies respect the Haydn-like traditional forms, but the intensity of their rhythmic drive, the polyphonic use of the orchestra, and the emotionality of the content are reminiscent of Beethoven. Even so, the dominant figure in French musical life was an Italian, Luigi Cherubini. In 1800, he was famous for the huge success, three years earlier, of his best work, one that is still performed today—*Médée*.

There was much to be said for Cherubini. His vivid orchestration, much influenced by Haydn's symphonies, and his large-scale scenes, varied by strong ensemble and choral writing, give his work a strong emotional appeal, while providing the listener with a great deal of beautiful music. Just as important, the characters are often realistic: although, in *Médée*, Cherubini used a mythological theme, the opera is about real psychological conflict. The tragic figure of Medea dominates the stage, while her torments are expressed by the vividly colored and symphonically elaborate orchestral texture; and, just as important, the music reaches a degree of passionate intensity that was unusual for the time.

Cherubini, for all his Italian origins, was understood to be writing in the French style. Gaspare Spontini, who arrived in Paris just after the turn of the century, was also Italian, and like Cherubini, he felt that an opera required more than beautiful melodies. He also had a taste for vast, dramatic ensembles. He liked scenes to have spectacular sets and very large casts of choristers and extras. As a result, his operas were complicated and expensive to produce, and it took Joséphine's steadfast patronage to get his first major work, *La Vestale*, onto the stage of the Paris Opéra. A dark and dismal tale of fidelity and betrayal, politics and religion, with very villainous villains and very holy heroes, *La Vestale* is full of triumphant processions, large-scale religious rituals, and marching hymns. There are sudden and unexpected dramatic strokes, strong musical contrasts, and tense confrontations. The scene shifts from a vast plaza to the underground cells of a temple; and all is held together by Spontini's sense of musical and dramatic continuity and pacing. As it was, *La Vestale*, which is very seldom played nowadays, was a runaway hit. Méhul himself greatly admired it. "This opera has obtained a brilliant and lasting success," he wrote. "[It has] an interesting and truly tragic subject. His music has verve, energy, but also grace."[17] It also pointed to the future: Giacomo Meyerbeer, that most successful of mid-century composers, got many of his ideas from Spontini.

LITERATURE AND THE STORMS OF PASSION

When it came to both passion and being Parisian, though, no one could outdo Mme de Staël. She might have been the daughter of Swiss parents, the wife of a Swedish diplomat; but she had been raised in Paris and often explained that she found the gutter of the rue du Bac, where she lived, vastly preferable to the finest landscape. She was also, in her own way, one of the best representatives of the new century, because she stood, first and always, for freedom. She detested emotional and sexual repression as much as political tyranny; she was a brilliant advocate for the equality of women; she knew that a free press is the best protection of a free people. It was no wonder, therefore, that Napoléon detested her.

Her father, Jacques Necker, had been a hugely successful banker who tried to turn statesman and was twice finance minister under Louis XVI. Her mother, Suzanne, single-handedly had invented the art of public relations in order to advance her husband's career. She had one of the most influential salons in Paris; and Germaine, the couple's only child, was brought up with all the people who mattered, socially or intellectually, in the city.

As everyone quickly realized, the Neckers' daughter was intelligent and talented. Constantly indulged by her parents, she had developed an unbreakable self-assurance and gone on to play a major role in the early part of the Revolution. Her marriage, to Baron Erik de Staël-Holstein, had been carefully arranged: he was well born enough and poor; she was rich. Marrying gave her a noble name and complete freedom. This she used abundantly, taking one lover after the other; but unlike so many of the great French ladies, she limited her choice to men whose minds she respected.

By 1800, she was a well-known author, still very rich, still very free. She also had well-defined and loudly proclaimed political views: like the marquis de Lafayette, she believed in liberty, a constitution, and a very fair measure of parliamentary democracy. As she quickly discovered, those were the views best calculated to infuriate Bonaparte. He was not the man to conceal this, she was not the woman to give up her principles. The immediate result was a series of attacks in the press. "It is not your fault that you are ugly," wrote the government-controlled *Journal des Hommes Libres,* "but it is your fault that you are an intriguer."[18]

In 1802, Mme de Staël's new novel, *Delphine,* was published, and no one was surprised to find that the French press attacked it. Bonaparte himself denounced the book—anonymously—for "its completely wrong, anti-social, dangerous principles and its total lack of a moral aim."[19] Given the First Consul's already well-established taste for dictatorial power, and the repression of anything he considered unconventional, one can imagine no finer compliment. Indeed, the Parisians took it as such. "For the last eight days, *Delphine* has been the universal subject of conversation," a visitor noted. "I myself took great pleasure in reading it; I found in it the result of a deep observation and a thorough experience of life, all written in an energetic, abundant and refined style."[20]

Delphine is no masterpiece, but it is a lively and engaging novel, with a slightly creaky plot. The heroine is, naturally, traduced and betrayed: in literature as in life, Mme de Staël was an ardent romantic: after many a tribulation, the heroine takes poison and dies just as her émigré lover is shot by a French army squad. Because the Revolution is the background of the book, the events are dramatic. In 1802, they seemed very real; today, they still make for eager page turning. *Delphine* is also peopled with characters closely patterned after real-life models: Léonce, the hero, is quite obviously the comte de Narbonne, who had been the author's lover in 1791 and 1792, and war minister to Louis XVI. Mme de Vernon, her gender changed, is clearly Talleyrand—a fact that contemporaries duly noted. All that made for entertaining reading. What infuriated Bonaparte, though, was the overtly political content of the book.

To begin with, it is a ferocious attack on marriage unsanctified by love—at just the time when Bonaparte was busy arranging the marriages of all around him who were as yet single; and the very last thing he wanted said was that this process was immoral. As if that was not bad enough, the book is also a satire on Catholic bigotry—just when the Concordat of 1801 had reestablished the French Church and the consul was forcing his often reluctant fellow generals to attend Mass. Further, it defends divorce, which the Revolution had made easily available, and which the new Civil Code was restricting so severely as virtually to abolish it; and finally, it pleads for the rights of women, which, in the same code, were utterly eradicated. Bonaparte himself occasionally fell in love and he had many mistresses, but for all that he despised women. They had, he said, neither sense nor intelligence and ought to be treated like chattels.

All in all, Mme de Staël, both in person and as an author, was everything Bonaparte most detested. She talked and wrote. He, alas, could act, and did: the police were sent to inform Germaine that she would be wise to take a long trip somewhere outside the ever-expanding borders of France. It was not possible to ignore such a hint: complete with current lover, French-speaking servants, and a great deal of luggage, Mme de Staël set off for Germany. What she found there was nothing less than the new literature.

De l'Allemagne (*On Germany*) described her experiences. Because she was famous, and expected to meet everyone, she did in fact see everyone who mattered; she had read a great deal; and more than anything she had found a place where people could express themselves freely. Compared to the perfect stillness in France, where Napoléon's censorship was both effective and extreme, this struck her as almost miraculous; and to a significant extent, she praised what she saw for the wrong reasons.

In most ways Mme de Staël was still a daughter of the Enlightenment; she believed in rationalism and progress. The Germans she met were already romantics: dark passions, tumultuous souls, a radical refusal of modern life coupled with a yearning for a largely imaginary medieval past, all that was very foreign to her. Still, for all her French reason, her own tempestuous emotional and sexual life helped her to feel what the Germans were all about. Just as important, in an age when French was still the language of civilization, when being accepted in Paris meant almost everything, Germaine brought to the attention of the French a largely unsuspected body of literature. If, after that, she misunderstood some of Goethe's verse, if she misrepresented, in part at least, some of Immanuel Kant's thought, it really hardly mattered. By opposing the urbane, polished, and now sterile French to the inspired, natural, creative Germans, Mme de Staël was changing the shape of European culture. She also understood the spirit of the new age when, in the book's last chapter, "On the Influence of Enthusiasm," she described and praised the vivifying, generous emotions which led Schiller to write his "Ode to Joy" and Beethoven to set it to music in his Ninth Symphony.

Indeed, by 1810, much of what happened in music, in poetry, and in philosophy was happening in Germany. Even Napoléon, that most Gallocentric of men, understood he ought to meet the grand old man of German letters, so he arranged to have Goethe introduced to him. It was not a fruitful meeting; neither really knew what to say to the other. Still, those who watched felt they were present at a historic moment: there, stiffly chatting, were the two most famous men in Europe.

Born in 1749, Goethe had proved himself a universal genius. He had reinvented the novel, and created a new worldview in his *Sorrows of Young Werther*. Leaving all tradition aside, he had focused on a domestic theme: there was no complicated plot, and the characters were ordinary people; but their tempestuous emotions were enough to make the book an instant and immense success. He had also proved himself to be a gifted poet, who could give a most immediate feeling for the charms and sufferings of daily life. He was a passionate and eloquent art critic who had helped to create a new aesthetic; but he could also write a convincing scientific account of the theory of color. He was a statesman as well, who had given much-prized advice to the duke of Weimar. The very richness of his talent, his ability to see different fields of human achievement, his famously vast culture also enabled him to be, in his own person, the key turning point for German culture. As an art critic, he was fiercely classical; as a novelist and poet, he was equally romantic. The one justified the other: through his classicism, Goethe drew on the great achievements of the past and linked himself with them, thus justifying his excursion into a new way of thinking, of feeling, of judging the world.

It was, after all, no wonder that Napoléon did not have much to say to him: although he was so much older than the emperor, Goethe was radically younger in his art. Napoléon, for all his military and political inventiveness, feared artistic, literary, and philosophical innovation. Goethe looked fearlessly ahead and created a new culture, one in which the classicizing, rationalist emperor felt utterly lost. By 1810, political change still came from Paris; but Napoléon's attempt at imposing his form of culture on France and Europe had already failed.

CHAPTER THREE

Unbeatable Bonaparte

France, under the Directoire, had hardly been an example to be followed, and yet it was too powerful to ignore. Disorganized and corrupt though its government might be, its armies won battles and conquered territories. Just as important, the Republic endured, and its ideas were likely to be all the more contagious in that its troops spread its doctrine wherever they went. Then, it was widely thought that a more stable, more conservative regime would, in all probability, be less aggressive. What happened in Paris, therefore, echoed in Naples, Saint Petersburg, Vienna, or London. It also mattered in Philadelphia, and shaped Spanish policies. As the war spread throughout the world, so, in this age of primitive communications, distances shrank.

A Useful General

The Directoire, in October 1799, was a ghost waiting to be laid. The most recent elections had produced an antidirectorial majority, and, this time, there was no convenient general to carry out the yearly coup. Almost worse, Emmanuel-Joseph Sieyès, that declared enemy of the government, had been elected a director. He was busy writing a new constitution, and made it clear that he expected an imminent change. The regime, menaced from both inside and outside, no longer knew where to turn. The ever-prudent Barras was beginning negotiations with Louis XVI's brother, the Pretender to the abolished throne, and everyone in Paris waited for the next significant event.

That turned out to be the return of Bonaparte. The general should have been met with disgrace and perhaps even arrest. After all, he had led a fully equipped army into Egypt, only to abandon it there. Running the British blockade, he had brought only a few aides with him; and if losing an entire army were not bad enough, the French navy had been virtually annihilated by

Nelson. Egypt, however, was far away. What people remembered was Bonaparte's string of victories in Italy, his popularity among the troops, and his extraordinary intelligence. Here, clearly, was the man who could end the prevailing chaos. Indeed, the leading Paris newspaper proclaimed it on October 15: "Victory which always accompanies Bonaparte has preceded him [this was an allusion to two recent minor victories] and he arrives in time to deal the Coalition a final blow."[1] And as the left remembered well, Bonaparte was also the man who had defeated the royalist insurrection in 1795; with him in power, there would be no question of a restoration.

It was also clear that the general had no friendly feeling toward the Directoire. Already before leaving for Egypt, he had announced, in a public speech, "When the French people's happiness is guaranteed by the best of organic laws, then all Europe will be free."[2] There could be no better way of saying that the current constitution was inadequate.

Still, Bonaparte needed to justify his return; so, the very day he reached Paris, he wrote the director Gohier: "The news I received in Egypt was so alarming that I did not hesitate to leave my army in order to come and share your peril."[3] The peril was neither that great nor that immediate, but the pretext was sufficient. Talleyrand put it succinctly: "As [Bonaparte] had expected, the several parties saw in him, not a man who needed to justify his actions, but one made necessary by the circumstances."[4]

Talleyrand himself was one of the general's early visitors. This immensely talented former bishop had two goals in life: to be foreign minister and to be very rich. He had, until recently, been foreign minister; he intended to resume that position, but with the sort of government that would allow him to develop long-range policies. As for money, no sum was ever enough: like the great noble he was, Talleyrand insisted on living splendidly; and that required the massive bribes that were frequently paid to a foreign minister who knew when and how much to ask.

Bonaparte, the former minister realized, was the very man to lead the sort of government he wanted. At the same time, Joseph Fouché, the minister of police, better aware than anyone that the current government was on the verge of collapse, had no intention of being the victim of any change; so he, too, visited the general and came to an understanding. It would not be enough, the three men agreed, to have Bonaparte elected director; a whole new regime was needed. Talleyrand then promptly arranged a meeting between Bonaparte and Sieyès. The director was vain; Bonaparte assured him of his admiration. They discussed the future constitution, and Bonaparte made it plain that it should be the one elaborated by Sieyès: by November 1, two weeks after his arrival in Paris, the general knew he could count on one of the directors to be his accomplice. Naturally, Barras, who could see that things were not going his way, also tried to recruit Bonaparte; but the general was too thoroughly convinced of the director's unpopularity to be interested.

There now remained only to choose the form and date of the coup. Preparations were begun by arranging to have Lucien Bonaparte elected president of the Five Hundred, but much remained uncertain. Barras had, after all, surmounted many an earlier crisis. An anecdote told by Talleyrand reveals just how nervous Bonaparte and he actually were.

"We were in a salon lit by a few candles, and engaged in a most animated conversation. It was one in the morning when we heard a great noise in the street outside: to that of carriage wheels was added that of an escort of cavalry. General Bonaparte turned pale and so, I believe, did I. We both thought that we were being arrested on the order of the Directoire." In fact, it was merely the police escorting the take of a gambling house to a nearby bank. "We laughed a great deal, the general and I," Talleyrand continued, "about our panic."[5]

What mattered more than these temporary fears was that the plotters had assured themselves of accomplices throughout the executive and legislative: many of the Elders favored Bonaparte; Lucien presided over the Five Hundred; Sieyès could make sure the Directoire was paralyzed; as for Barras, it seems very probable he was promised a very large sum of money to do nothing. Certainly he was very much less active than he might have been. Finally, there were the soldiers. Most of them were prepared to obey Bonaparte; and General Augereau, who commanded the Directors' Guard, was in on the plot.

All was ready. On November 9, Bonaparte made his move. "Think," he told the men of the Paris garrison, "of the state in which I left France and of the state in which I now find her! I had left you peace, I find war! I had left you conquered lands and the enemy is breaching our borders! . . . It is high time that the defenders of the Fatherland be given back the trust which they have so fully earned."[6] In the end, the troops were sent into the hall where the Five Hundred were meeting. The deputies escaped, and the coup was successful. Later that night, the rump of the councils appointed three temporary consuls to write a new constitution. They were Bonaparte, Sieyès, and Roger Ducos, the first director to resign at Sieyès's urging.

THE NEW ERA

The coup was hardly a surprise: everyone had known that the Directoire could not survive much longer. Its result seemed also very much as expected. Bonaparte, having led the soldiers, was the most powerful of the three consuls; Sieyès had helped paralyze his fellow directors and had a constitution all ready; and Roger Ducos was being rewarded for his compliance. What did startle everyone, from the general on down, was that Sieyès, in spite of his many hints, had never actually sat down to write his constitution; and the one he produced eventually was both confused and confusing. This suited Bonaparte,

BONAPARTE, Ier CONSUL DE LA RÉP. FRANÇ.

Bonaparte in 1800 as First Consul. Talleyrand said of him that he was "not a man who needed to justify his actions, but one made necessary by the circumstances." (*Portrait File, Miriam and Ira D. Wallach Division of Art, Prints and Photographs, The New York Public Library, Astor, Lenox and Tilden Foundations*)

who knew just what he wanted. The trick now was to convince Sieyès that the new constitution was really his idea. Bonaparte knew how to flatter when necessary; within a few days, his fellow consul was endorsing the new text. What mattered the most, however, was that its basic principle was fully in accord with that of Sieyès's draft: henceforth, confidence would come from the bottom, but power from the top.

This sounds obscure, but it is very simple. The constitutions of 1791, 1793, and 1795 had all assumed that sovereignty lay in the people, and that the institutions should reflect this. The new constitution, on the other hand, assumed that sovereignty resided in the executive; the people could only give or withhold their trust, and should they wish to do the latter, the way would be a hard one indeed.

Universal manhood suffrage was revived; but the voters could elect only lists of candidates from which the executive chose the members of the legislature. The latter was divided in three: the Senate was composed of eighty life members who saw to it that no law violated the constitution; they could also amend it. The Tribunat was composed of one hundred members who discussed the bills brought to it by the executive, but could not vote on them. The Corps Législatif had three hundred members who voted the bills into law, but could not discuss them. All in all, this was an ingenious scheme: it gave the appearance of democracy while ensuring that the voters and the legislature would remain powerless.

It was, of course, the executive that really mattered. There were to be three consuls. The First Consul was the head of state; the other two merely had a consultative voice. They were elected by the Senate for ten years and could be reelected; but for this time only, as a sop to Sieyès, he was asked to name the consuls: they were Bonaparte as First Consul, and two highly skilled bureaucrats, Cambacérès and Lebrun, as Second and Third Consuls.

The First Consul had all the power. He appointed, and dismissed, the ministers, civil servants, and judges. He proposed the laws; none of the three legislative bodies could initiate a bill. He could arrest presumed plotters against the state; he declared war and negotiated treaties, subject to the eventual endorsement of the Corps Législatif; and, on most matters of government, he could rule by decree.

Finally, there was a new body, the Council of State, composed of thirty to fifty members appointed by the First Consul. It was to help write the proposed new laws, while at the same time acting as an administrative tribunal judging between the citizens and the state—roles it has kept to this day.

This new constitution, which organized the dictatorship of the First Consul, was made public on December 13, together with a proclamation that announced: "The Revolution has come back to the principles with which it began; it is now ended."[7] On December 25, the constitution went into effect. On February 7, 1800, the results of the plebiscite held to approve or disapprove it were announced: over 3 million voted "yes," 1,562 "no"—and 4 million abstained. The controlled press, ignoring the abstentions, trumpeted the consul's triumph; clearly, many of the French were not so sure.

Still, the new government immediately made itself popular by taking the kind of measures for which everybody was longing. The forced loan was promptly ended; the Bank of France was set up, and given the task of stabilizing the currency. By the spring, the new gold franc had universal currency. The hidden metallic currency came out as confidence returned; and the value set for the franc in relation to gold remained unchanged until World War I.

Almost as important, the list of émigrés was closed for good, thus ending a major source of instability and lawlessness, while it was deliberately made easy for those on the list to be rehabilitated. On October 20, 1800, whole categories were deleted, thus bringing the list down from one hundred thousand names to fifty-two thousand; within another year, most of the remaining exiles were back.

What the First Consul was doing, in fact, was ending the Revolution and suppressing its democratic principles while protecting the revolutionaries and preserving the new forms of property they had created. "We must distinguish," the Consul explained, "between the *interests* of the revolution and the *theories* of the Revolution. The interests began during the night of August 4th [1789, when the nobility renounced its privileges]. I have kept the interests of the Revolution alive."[8] And just in case that was not clear, the old revolutionary fetes were ended: there would be no more celebration of the death of Louis XVI, for instance. Instead, setting a lasting precedent, the Consul decided the French would celebrate a single national holiday on July 14, the day the Bastille was taken, and that it would be called the Fete of Concord.

All this eased life considerably. People were now able to go about their business, pursue their ambitions, and make money; they were also expected to refrain from disagreeing with the new government. One small fact was highly significant: while in October 1799, seventy-three political newspapers were being published in Paris, six months later, only nine were left, of which five soon closed down. Naturally, the remaining papers all supported the Consul's policies. Still, for most people that was a small price to pay: after the endless crises of the last ten years, order and prosperity seemed to matter more than liberty.

The Parisians also loved another aspect of the new regime: pomp and splendor were back, enlivening the city and making work for its artisans. On February 19, 1800, the First Consul moved from the Palace of the Luxembourg, where the directors had lived, to that of the Tuileries, the former royal residence. Here was a major hint, as was the great military review which followed the move and then the banquet attended by the consuls, the ministers, and the presidents of the three legislative bodies (Sieyès was president of the Senate). By October, the old etiquette was back, at least in some of its aspects: foreign diplomats were formally presented to the head of state, after which they went to see Joséphine—just as, once, they had been to see the queen. And if anyone doubted that there was a Court once more, they only needed to look around. "There was an incredible profusion of feathers, of diamonds, of dazzling dresses," an eyewitness reported. "Mme Bonaparte . . . was wearing a white voile dress with short sleeves; she had a pearl necklace on; her hair unadorned except by a turtleshell comb was charmingly informal . . . The First Consul was dressed in a very simple uniform. . . . That plainness, in the midst of the embroidered costumes, laden with orders and jewels worn by . . . the foreign dignitaries, created a contrast just as imposing as that of Mme Bonaparte's dress with that of the other ladies."[9]

All this had been carefully planned: Bonaparte's own tastes were simple, but he understood the French and was therefore determined to give France a court as splendid as those of the old monarchies. This was to demonstrate both the greatness of the country and the stability of the government while creating an ever-larger, ever-richer group with a direct interest in the preservation of the regime. As for what the Consul thought of kings, he made it plain in a conversation with one of his aides. After surviving an attempt on his life, he had demanded the suspension of all civil liberties; the Tribunat had tried to resist the new measures and been rudely put down, upon which Bonaparte explained: "I am a soldier, a child of the Revolution who has come from the midst of the people: I will not allow them to insult me as if I were a king."[10]

The emphasis here should be on the word "soldier." No one doubted that Bonaparte was First Consul because he had been an outstandingly successful general, or that the regime would live or die by the outcome of the war. By the summer of 1800, that issue was settled. Boldly crossing the Alps, Bonaparte proceeded to trounce the Coalition forces in Italy. On June 2, he took Milan; on the ninth, Lannes, one of his aides, won the battle of Montebello; on the fourteenth, the First Consul smashed the enemy at Marengo, while the French army in Germany, under General Moreau, beat the Austrians at Hohenlinden. The result, in 1801, was the Peace of Lunéville, by which France kept the left bank of the Rhine, all of northern Italy, Belgium, and Holland. In short order, a treaty with Great Britain followed this. For the first time in ten years, France was at peace; and the First Consul's popularity soared accordingly.

Government Reinvented

Having won all those battles and ended the war was no mean achievement. Far more amazing, Bonaparte was proving, at the same time, that he was as capable of rebuilding a country as he was of leading an army to victory. France had emerged from the Revolution with no laws, no institutions, no system of education, even. Except for the understanding that the purchasers of nationalized estates were to be protected, there was no principle on which to build; and yet, in less than four years from his assumption of power, a new code of civil, criminal, and commercial law was in place; a new school and university system was created; and a stable currency, managed by a national bank, was set up. All these innovations lasted, virtually unchanged, for more than a century.

Property—the way it could be earned, preserved, passed on—was a central preoccupation of the regime. That was determined, in part, by the new code; but just as important was the economic system itself. Bonaparte understood that the prosperity of a nation depends on both production and commerce. He was well aware that Great Britain's vast wealth came from its trade; but he never understood the laissez-faire principles on which the British economy was based. By 1800, Adam Smith's *The Wealth of Nations* was already twenty-four years old, and its principles were fully accepted in Great Britain, both by the government and by the bankers and traders of the City of London. The natural balance of demand and supply, the invisible hand of market forces, all these were thought to be irresistible. It thus would have been both wrong and ineffective, everyone agreed, for the government to meddle with the economy: the freer the market, the greater the national prosperity. That an underclass of destitute men, women, and children developed rapidly in the meantime worried no one; indeed, it was felt by all those who were comfortably off that, probably, the poor *deserved* to be poor. As a result, many of the paternalist regulations dating back to the Tudors were abrogated, and with them went the last shreds of protection for the disadvantaged.

Things were very different in France. There, the tradition of state control of the economy went back to the early seventeenth century. When Bonaparte decided to revive the moribund silk weaving manufactures, for instance, he placed huge orders (some of them were still being filled in 1815) and told everyone to wear silk and velvet; he also regulated production and prices. As for trade, it, too, was supervised by the state. The war, which had ended in 1801 only to begin again the next year, was as much about opening and controlling markets as it was about territorial expansion. Within this centrally regulated economy, however, there remained a vast area of free markets: the state, in 1800, was simply not equipped to control more than very small segments of the economy. Still, in many ways, the system discouraged initiative. France had no equivalent of the new textile factories which were revolutionizing weaving in Britain, and so it slipped further back in relation to its great rival.

In one respect, however, Bonaparte copied the English. Public finance had long been a British specialty: a funded Government Debt; a Sinking Fund; a currency regulated by an independent central bank, the Bank of England; all these had been an essential part of Britain's financial strength. The recently ended French Revolution, on the other hand, had shown just what happens in a country with an unfunded debt and an unregulated currency. Bonaparte was determined to prevent a repeat of the monetary convulsions of the Directoire, so he instituted a central bank, the Bank of France, patterned in part after the Bank of England. It was privately owned by its stockholders, but its governor was appointed by the government, and it was given the privilege of regulating the currency and setting interest rates. By removing the power to print money from the government, the new system withheld a dangerous temptation from those in power; and it created one of the world's most stable currencies. Just as important, the debt was now funded; bonds paid interest, regularly and on time; and the government's credit soared.

All this was a huge step forward; but still there was no recognizable body of law. Now the new *Code Civil* organized both people and property. It established a new register of births, deaths, and marriages; defined how all goods and estates were to be held, transferred, and inherited; and generally gave the rich an enormous advantage over the lower classes. Article 1781 was typical: "In any dispute regarding a salary," it stated, "the Employer will be believed on his mere affirmation, which will determine what wages are due."[11] In the same way, men were given sway over women, and parents over children. Henceforth, all decisions belonged to the husband and father: he, alone, determined where and how the family would live and how the children were to be treated and educated; he controlled family finances, including the wife's fortune. He was restrained in only one instance: two-thirds of his estate had to be left equally to his children. And as a consequence of all this, divorce was virtually abolished.

Thus had the family been made to resemble an army command. The same thing happened to the court system. No longer were judges to be elected; they were appointed by the First Consul (as they are, today still, by the minister of justice). Still, it was easier to defend one's rights than ever before: the courts, from the lowest to the highest, belonged to a rational structure; procedures were greatly simplified; the judges, amazingly, were competent and honest. Justice was now expeditious, and everyone was grateful.

Education was just as important. Before the Revolution, virtually all schools had been run by the church. Now the Consul created 800 primary schools, 370 practical secondary schools, and 30 lycées, those schools combining high school and the first 2 years of college that flourish today still; and that was capped by the universities. The Consul knew just what he was doing. "Of all our institutions," he told one of his councillors of state, "public education is the most important. Everything depends on it, the present and the future. We must see that the morality and the political ideas of the rising generation no longer depend on the news of the day or the circumstance of the moment."[12]

All these admirable new schools, however, were reserved for the boys. Girls, the Consul thought, should not be educated: "All young girls have the same goal: marriage, and public education almost always makes for bad wives, light, frivolous and coquettish wives . . . Women are better off living in the privacy of their homes."[13] It was, perhaps, a just punishment for these singularly backward notions that the First Consul was surrounded by strong women—his mother, his wife, his sisters, many of the ladies of the court—who, far from hiding in the privacy of their homes, set about influencing public policy and, on occasion, succeeded in doing so.

Still, in most other matters, Bonaparte was open-minded and, often, eager to learn. This was most visible when he presided over the Council of State. There, he asked, he listened, he encouraged disagreement; and, most of the time, new, highly constructive laws emerged from these discussions. Just as important, in a country rent by political enmities, he understood that it was essential to bring together men of diverse opinions, and to rebuild France by blending the best of the ancien régime and the Revolution. Thus, the membership of the Council of State included men who had served Louis XVI and once-ardent revolutionaries, as well as a number of men in their twenties; and because the Consul knew what to ask, how to criticize—in a word, how to lead—these men who, singly, were no geniuses, managed, under his direction, to create a new France.

The way he chose the young comte Molé was typical. The scion of an old and leading family of the judiciary, which had been half ruined by the Revolution, Molé combined the strength of tradition with the possession of a lively intelligence. Bonaparte met him and recognized talent. "When you saw him alone," Molé remembered,

> he was interested only in understanding the person he wanted to know, in seducing or amazing him. Above all, he knew, better than anyone, how to vary his way of speaking, how to change his appearance, the way he looked at you, the expression on his face, according to the effect he wanted to give. . . . I saw right away that he wanted to reassure my youth and know how far I would be of use to him. I wish I could adequately describe how simple, in such cases, was his greeting, how he obviously feared he might frighten the man he wanted to encourage into being open. He looked at me seldom and almost sideways so I would not feel he was watching me.[14]

This ability to choose the right men for the job was, in fact, an essential part of the Consul's genius. In this case, Molé was duly recruited for the Council of State. Bonaparte had been right, as usual: Molé eventually became prime minister in the 1830s; and he has left a striking account of the sessions of the council.

> Sitting deep in the armchair from which he presided . . . , plunged so far in thought that he sometimes forgot where he was, and even those who were listening to him, his eyes vague and unfocussed, the little gold snuffbox which he was constantly and automatically opening to take pinches of tobacco which he breathed in noiselessly and most of which fell back on the white lapels of his uniform which were soon covered with it, finally the mechanical movement of his arm to hand the snuffbox to the chamberlain standing behind him who filled it and gave it back to him, all that defined him so strongly as a man meditating in solitude that all eyes were on him but the silence was unbroken . . .

As his thoughts were born, he spoke them aloud without concern for form or phrasing. . . . He never feared he might contradict himself . . . but he was sometimes carried by the liveliness of the discussion, which he usually wanted to be free and complete, to defend opposite positions.[15]

That, of course, was only the preliminary phase. Once a decision had been taken, the Consul expected it to be codified and carried out exactly, and in that process (together with the winning of battles) lay the secret of the new regime. Bonaparte was, by nature, an autocrat, and the constitution gave him the legal basis from which to rule absolutely; but he was also intensely intelligent, eager to learn and open to ideas and measures. His decisions, when they came, were final; but they were so thoroughly informed, so carefully weighed that they most often met with general approval. Indeed, that is the reason why the regime was so popular: after the years of anarchy, order was desirable, especially when it was a rational and progressive order. Year by year the French were better off; year by year they felt more convinced that they could enjoy what they earned without having to fear a new convulsion.

There was another good reason for Bonaparte's popularity: taxes were low, in part because every victory meant a war contribution from the defeated enemy, in part because the government had stopped being wasteful. Under the Directoire, huge sums had gone to the army purveyors, with healthy kickbacks to the members of the administration. All that had stopped in November 1799. At the same time, because people actually paid their taxes—which had not been the case under the Directoire—the rates could remain low; so the French could feel that here, too, the government was doing well.

One extraordinary step backward, however, was almost unnoticed. France, at the beginning of the Revolution, had ended slavery in all its overseas possessions—mostly Caribbean islands. Now, in spite of the loudly proclaimed principle that all men were equal before the law, the First Consul brought it back. There were no slaves in metropolitan France, of course, and by 1803, Haiti had won its independence; but in Martinique, Guadeloupe, and Saint Martin, as well as in other scattered islands, black people were enslaved again, and the slave traders once more sold their captives to the French planters. Coming from someone who prided himself on being the son of the Revolution, it was an extraordinary and shameful move with a simple rationale: Bonaparte was always eager to conciliate the property owners. This was an easy way to do it.

A New Stability

By December 1800, it had thus become clear that the First Consul was able to ensure the welfare of France. That was just the point at which an attempted assassination took place, making him, if possible, even more popular. On

December 24, as the Bonapartes were driving to the Opéra, where they were to hear a premiere of Haydn's *Creation,* a barrel full of bullets and gunpowder exploded just as their carriage was passing. Both were unharmed, although a number of pedestrians were killed or hurt; and that perfectly genuine attempt on their lives was used by the Consul to nudge the regime still further away from the Revolution. "Amongst the men arrested by the police," the official newspaper explained, "not all were seized with a poniard in hand, but all are universally known as capable of sharpening it and using it. The point today is not to punish past actions but to guarantee the social order."[16]

Within the month, 130 known (but perfectly innocent) extreme leftists had been deported to Guiana; most died there, and the rest of the country applauded. Once again, Bonaparte was seen as the barrier to anarchy; and the fact that his life was threatened allowed him to hint that a mere ten-year term was, after all, a little niggardly: more was needed, at the very least the right to appoint his successor, so that the regime would continue unchanged in the event of his death.

That amendment to the constitution waited until the next summer. In the meantime, the foreign ambassadors, like the Parisians themselves, noticed that the originally informal gatherings at the Tuileries were beginning to take on the look of a real court. There was, to start, the official costume of the consuls: it was made of scarlet velvet, lavishly embroidered with gold palms; and it was worn with breeches (a return to prerevolutionary fashion), silk stockings, and a plumed hat. Just as important, a Household was being created. There was a governor of the palace, and under him prefects, whose costume was of scarlet cloth with silver embroidery, a white waistcoat also embroidered in silver, a sash of blue taffeta with silver embroidery and fringes, silver garters, and an embroidered hat. Helping them was a growing platoon of messengers, ushers, and footmen, all in brand-new liveries.

Just as important as all this new formality was the personality of Mme Bonaparte: it was she, far more than her husband, who knew how to give the feeling that the French were civilized again, that good manners mattered. She also knew how to spend money on herself—she loved jewels, clothes, houses. "[Joséphine] was pretty and kind," her husband remembered, "but a thorough liar and spendthrift. Her first answer to the simplest question was: 'no' because she feared it might be a trap; when she saw it was not, she changed."[17] As it was, she was just the right wife for the Consul: politics bored her, so she did not interfere; she looked endlessly appealing; and her eagerness to help brought over many of the returning émigrés. If you wanted to be crossed off the list, it was usually wise to ask Mme Bonaparte; and so those who remembered just what a court could be soon surrounded her. That, in turn, added to the feeling that old wounds were being healed.

One of the consequences of this evolution was that most evenings at the Tuileries were extremely dull. "The First Consul worked in his study. In order to kill time, Mme Bonaparte went to the theater every evening. . . . After the play, which most often she left before the end, she came back and ended the evening with a game of whist. . . . It was, every day, the same people, the same games."[18] It was also the height of respectability: Marie Antoinette had been endlessly traduced for her way of life. No one could say that Mme Bonaparte was anything but the perfect First Lady.

Although Joséphine, after her agitated early career, was now virtuous by necessity, she was anything but religious; but when the Consul signed a Concordat with the pope, she continued to play her role and duly went to church — as did Bonaparte, who was also completely nonreligious. For him, the reopening of the churches was merely a wise political act, and he made it quite clear in a conversation with Molé: "Why does a poor man find it natural that ten of the chimneys in my palace should be smoking while he is freezing," the Consul asked, "or that I should have ten suits in my wardrobe when he is naked, or that I should be served, at each meal, enough to feed a whole family for a week? It is religion which tells him that in the next life he will be my equal, that he even has more chances of being happy then than I do."[19]

What Bonaparte was saying, in essence, is what Marx was to repeat some sixty years later: religion has its chief use in making sure that the proletariat suffers patiently. Indeed, when on April 18, 1802, the Concordat, the agreement with the pope making Catholicism legal again, was promulgated, Lucien Bonaparte made this official: "Religion," he explained to the Tribunat, "is essential to the maintenance of our economy . . . It is useful, necessary for the State."[20] The Concordat itself was weighted in favor of state control. The pope agreed to give up the estates of the church, which had been confiscated by the state; he also agreed to seek the resignation of most of the bishops, who had been appointed by earlier regimes. In exchange, Catholicism became, once again, the state religion, although all other religions could be practiced as well — a clause to which the church had strongly objected. As Cardinal Consalvi, the pope's secretary of state, wrote the legate in Paris: "Intolerance is part of the very essence of the Catholic religion."[21] The state was to pay the stipends of priests and bishops; but the latter were to be chosen by the First Consul, with the pope then merely conferring the proper religious orders. It could not have been more simple: the bishops were now civil servants who were expected to carry out the Consul's orders just like their colleagues, the prefects or the generals; and, for the most part, that is precisely what they did. Indeed, Fouché, the police minister, made it clear to them in a circular letter. "The faithful," he wrote the bishops three years later, "will learn from you that they serve God by serving the ruler whom He has chosen and crowned. . . . The people in your sees will be eager to pay their taxes and to take in our armies the places to which they are called by our laws, our Emperor and victory."[22]

All was now in order. The French who read the praise of the government in the newspapers also heard it in church on Sunday. It is no wonder the promulgation of the Concordat was celebrated with great pomp: the consuls wore their red velvet suits, the ladies were covered with diamonds, and Joséphine wore a particularly noticeable pink satin hat topped with pink feathers, while music was played under the direction of Méhul and Cherubini.

This was followed by a Te Deum at Notre Dame; it was noticed that Mme Bonaparte looked appropriately pious and that some of the generals were gnashing their teeth and muttering imprecations. As for the brightest young writer in France, Chateaubriand, he dedicated his newly published book, *The Genius of Christianity,* to the First Consul, alluding to the hand of Providence as the author of Bonaparte's many successes. The book itself is unreadable (Chateaubriand was soon to do a great deal better); and the author soon disavowed the dedication.

The signing of the Concordat added greatly to Bonaparte's popularity; but what made him almost worshiped, in that same month of April 1802, was the Treaty of Amiens, which ended the war with England. Great Britain, now isolated, had begun to realize that it could no longer afford to fight alone a war it was unlikely to win; France wanted peace as well. The treaty gave Britain what it needed, an end to an enormously costly conflict. It confirmed France in the possession of the left bank of the Rhine, Holland, Switzerland, and northern Italy, with the exception of Piedmont, held in trust for its king, who had taken refuge in Sardinia. Tuscany, renamed the Kingdom of Etruria, went to a Spanish Bourbon; and English tourists came pouring in to Paris.

FROM REPUBLIC TO EMPIRE

It was a triumph. Peace, prosperity, and the unanimous admiration of Europe: by the end of 1802, Bonaparte had made France the leading nation on the Continent. A lesser man might have been content with things as they were; the First Consul had higher ambitions. He had long felt that a ten-year tenure of office was not enough, and so he arranged for an extension. That required amending the constitution, something only the Senate could do. The senators were willing enough—they had, after all, been appointed by the Consul—but even they failed to understand the extent of Bonaparte's ambitions. On May 5, 1802, they had offered him a second ten-year term, but the way he received their offer was so cool that the senators understood their blunder; and so, in July, after a plebiscite, Napoléon Bonaparte was made Consul for life with the right to name his successor. This was, in effect, a monarchy.

There was more. In imitation of the ancien régime, a Privy Council was created. The First Consul's yearly stipend became a Civil List of 6 million francs a year—less, admittedly, than Louis XVI, but vastly more than any other officeholder of the Republic. There was also to be a Consular Guard, on the model of the royal Bodyguard; coins were to bear the Consul's profile. Henceforth, the Consul could summon or suspend the sessions of the Senate and the Corps Législatif; he could also dissolve the latter as well as the Tribunat—whose membership was halved so as to get rid of its few dissenters. The First Consul also recovered the monarchical right to give pardons; and he could promulgate treaties without consulting the legislature. The Senate, having just shown its docility, was enlarged to 120 members, and estates with a yearly income ranging from 20,000 to 25,000 francs could be given to the senators of the Consul's choice—a convenient way to keep them in line.

Finally, elections were virtually eliminated. The electoral colleges were chosen by local assemblies, themselves elected by universal manhood suffrage; but the electoral colleges were composed of the six hundred most heavily taxed citizens in each area, and they were elected for life—thus, in effect, giving the voters no choice. To these, the First Consul could add any number of members, and he also appointed the president of each college. Further, the colleges only met when called into session by the First Consul.

This was, in many ways, a new constitution, and it contained at least one very remarkable article, the one that read: "The Senate will bring to the First Consul the expression of the trust, the love and the admiration of the French people."[23] As most people realized, in fact, the Republic had become a monarchy in all but name.

It took another two years for the fact to be acknowledged. On May 31, 1804, the now properly subservient Tribunat asked that Napoléon Bonaparte be proclaimed hereditary Emperor of the French. To no one's surprise, the Senate agreed, and a plebiscite confirmed it all. There were a few other changes as well: the new emperor could now legislate by decree and interpret all laws. Thus, whatever limits had existed on his power were gone, and he was more absolute than Louis XIV, that most promptly obeyed of French kings.

Together with the new imperial title, there were bonuses: the Civil List went up to 25 million francs, 5 million more than for Louis XVI, and the emperor was given the use of all the former royal palaces—the Tuileries, Saint Cloud (just outside Paris), Versailles (which he never used), Rambouillet, Fontainebleau, and Compiègne; Napoléon's heir was to be either his son or any male member of his family he selected; such of his brothers and sisters as he chose became princes and princesses (Lucien, with whom he had quarreled, was left out); and Grand Dignitaries of the Empire were created, as well as a new order, the Legion of Honor, and, soon after, a new nobility. Clearly, the Revolution was well and truly over. Once again, an all-powerful monarch sat on the throne of France, and the rest of Europe watched and wondered. Certainly, it was reassuring to have France become a monarchy again; but the new emperor frightened and disgusted most of his fellow rulers, not least because of his treatment of the duc d'Enghien.

Those foreign monarchs were right to be upset. When Napoléon decided that being consul for life was not enough, he faced the resistance of all those who had taken huge risks to abolish the monarchy in the first place. He decided to reassure them by proving that the new empire would be no restoration; and he did that by ordering the murder of a Bourbon prince.

The duc d'Enghien, a distant cousin of the Bourbon Pretender to the throne, was a bright young man in his twenties. He had imprudently settled in Baden, near the French border, and it was there a troop of cavalry was sent to kidnap him. That it did so outside French territory, in the fullest illegality, did not bother Bonaparte. Having been brought to the fortress of Vincennes, at the edge of Paris, the duc was summarily tried, convicted, and shot, all in the night of March 21, 1804.

The effect, in France, was precisely what Napoléon had expected: the assassination smoothed the way to his assumption of the imperial title. Everywhere else, it was greeted with horror, in Russia most of all — so much so, in fact, that the murder led directly to its joining the new anti-French coalition.

Splendor and Vanity

The French, however, soon forgot the duc d'Enghien. There was the new imperial court to think about, and it was far more interesting. "It is very convenient to govern the French through their vanity,"[24] Napoléon remarked at this time — and there could be no greater satisfaction for the vain than the myriad titles of the new system.

Already in 1802, Joséphine had been given ladies-in-waiting, chosen, of course, by her husband: that was made plain to the elect, who received a letter beginning: "Madame, the First Consul has chosen you to help Mme Bonaparte do the honors of the palace."[25] Very quickly, the etiquette surrounding the consular couple grew more complex; Mme de Rémusat, one of Joséphine's ladies, saw it clearly: "Every day [Bonaparte] invented something new in his way of life so that his abode soon greatly resembled the palace of a sovereign. He rather liked a kind of formality so long as it did not cramp his own habits; and so it was those who surrounded him who bore the weight of the etiquette. Besides, he was convinced that the French are seduced by the dazzle of pomp. Very simple for himself, he demanded of his officers that they wear the most luxurious uniforms."[26]

It was not just the officers. Surrounding the emperor was a vast Household: in order of importance, a great chamberlain, a first chamberlain, a master of the wardrobe, a cloud of chamberlains, a grand equerry, a first equerry, a commanding equerry, 20 ordinary equerries, a first aide-de-camp, 26 ADCs, and numerous pages. Then there was the staff under the grand marshal of the palace: a first prefect, 2 prefects, 2 marshals of the house, a secretary general, a quartermaster, a first maître d'hotel, 4 aides, the emperor's maître d'hotel, 4 ordinary maîtres d'hotel, and 192 other employees, including the 64 footmen.

The servants wore the emperor's livery of dark green and gold; each of the higher officials had a specially designed uniform: this was a military court where almost every man was told what he must wear. The emperor himself dressed simply, usually in his uniform of a colonel of cavalry: green coat with red lapels, white vest and breeches. Everybody else was expected to shine. This applied to the princes, who wore a white coat richly embroidered in gold, a short white cloak embroidered with gold bees, white breeches and silk stockings, white silk shoes with a gold ribbon, the gold and enamel collar of the Legion of Honor, and a black hat with floating white plumes. And so it went, rank by rank, color by color, with varying widths and motifs for the embroidery.

Even the ladies were told what to wear: admittedly, they could choose their color; but only the empress and the princesses were allowed a gown with a lace collar, a cloak with a gold-embroidered velvet train, a sash with hanging ribbons in front, and plumes on their heads, while the ladies-in-waiting had to make do with silver embroidery and no plumes. As for ordinary ladies, the fringes and embroidery at the bottom of their skirt was not to exceed ten centimeters in height. There was no limit, however, to the amount or splendor of the jewels which might be worn; and all observers agreed that the ladies were indeed glittering.

All this was admirably disciplined. One could tell, by looking at a man, just what his rank was; but the general effect, while undoubtedly colorful, must have looked a little like the kind of Hollywood movie in which huge casts of extras, splendidly dressed, parade in the background. And just as extras spend incredibly boring hours waiting for their scene to be filmed, so Napoléon's courtiers found themselves standing hour after hour wishing they could be elsewhere. The emperor himself, going round the circle, and addressing often rude remarks to his courtiers, was no help; the lack of manners of many of those who had risen to a high position from humble beginnings was felt by those who were more polished; and for all its splendor, the scene at the imperial palaces was marked by awkwardness and boredom. There was one saving grace, though: because the emperor worked so hard, the full court usually met on Sundays only.

This dullness was made still worse by Napoléon's firm determination to have a respectable court. Remembering the pamphlets against Marie Antoinette, he saw to it that no one could gossip about the empress. Aside from the servants (and the emperor himself), only women could enter her private apartments on the ground floor of the Tuileries. Her equerry, knight of honor, and pages were allowed only into her state apartment, and she was never alone with them. Her ladies-in-waiting were instructed never to leave her.

Joséphine complied with all these rules, but the emperor's own sisters signally failed to do so. It wasn't just that all had lovers; at first, when their brother became emperor, they were furious because they were not immediately made Imperial Highnesses. "When their complaints reached the Emperor's ears," his stepdaughter remembered, "he said, one day, 'In truth, to hear my sisters, wouldn't you think I had robbed my family of the inheritance of the king our father?'"[27] As it turned out, Caroline, Élisa, and Pauline did not have long to wait: Napoléon was incapable of resisting his siblings' demands; so the three sisters duly became Imperial Highnesses, complete with a Household and an income of a million francs a year. Eventually, two of them were given actual states to rule: Caroline's husband, Murat, became king of Naples, while Élisa was made grand duchess of Lucca in her own right. Naturally, the brothers were also found kingdoms: Louis was given Holland; Jerôme, Westphalia; and Joseph, first Naples and then Spain.

Even when it came to having fun, the emperor saw to it that life was organized with military precision. In 1807, for instance, he decided that, throughout the Season, Hortense, his stepdaughter and the wife of his brother Louis, would give a ball every Monday, Pauline every Wednesday, Caroline every Friday. At least those evenings were a little less stiff than the ones at the imperial palaces.

Of course, there were balls at court as well, and they often featured elaborately choreographed quadrilles. On one evening in 1806, for instance, the first quadrille was led by Hortense, and consisted of sixteen ladies dressed in white, crowned with flowers, with more flowers on their gowns and diamond ornaments on their heads, while the men wore white satin with sashes the color of their partner's flowers.

All this was very grand, but, of course, the most splendid fete of the reign was the coronation on December 2, 1804. By dint of promises, which were never carried out, Napoléon had convinced Pope Pius VII to come and crown him, though, in the event, the forlorn-looking pope simply sat while the emperor crowned himself.

There was a golden carriage for the pope, and another, much bigger golden carriage, topped with crown and eagle, for the imperial couple, and dozens of ornate carriages for the court. Notre Dame's unfashionable Gothic interior disappeared behind a neoclassical decor in white and gold. The costumes, designed by the painter Jean-Baptiste Isabey, were of great splendor—satin, silk, velvet, acres of gold embroidery—while Joséphine wore a gown of gold satin embroidered with gold bees, the symbols of the busy and productive empire; a red velvet train of immense length, lined with hermine and embroidered in gold; and diamond necklaces, earrings, and tiara.

Then there was Napoléon himself. His throne, facing the main altar, was much larger, and placed much higher, than that of the pope, which had been set up near the crossing. As for his own costume, it had been invented for the occasion and consisted of a white satin tunic topped by a gold dalmatic, with white satin gloves and booties. The crown he chose was, in fact, a gold laurel wreath—a reference to that worn by the Caesars—and a vast scepter and hand of justice completed the outfit. If you were in a properly reverential mood, it looked dazzling. If you were not, the figure of this small man swathed in yards of white satin looked nothing short of comical.

There was, however, nothing funny about Napoléon's achievements. By 1805, France was, once again, at war with most of Europe. In the end, neither France nor England had trusted the other enough to carry out the provisions of the peace treaty, and the emperor went on to win victory after victory. By 1805, it had become clear that he could reorganize the Continent as he saw fit: some German states, like Bavaria and Württemberg, were enlarged; others, like Prussia and Austria, shrank. Hanover was seized from the king of England, given to Prussia, and taken away again. Dalmatia, once part of the Venetian Republic, went to Austria, then became an actual part of France. Some of the tinier German states disappeared altogether, while those bordering the Rhine on the right bank were regrouped in a confederation whose mediator was Napoléon himself. North and central Italy were united into a single kingdom, with the Austrians, the king of Piedmont, the king of Etruria, the king of Naples, and the pope being dispossessed, and Napoléon himself becoming king. On the Iberian Peninsula, first Portugal, then Spain, were conquered. As far afield as Poland, the Grand Duchy of Warsaw was created, under Napoléon as grand duke, while a new kingdom, Westphalia, was put together specifically for Napoléon's youngest brother, Jerôme. Holland, nominally independent but in fact ruled by France, became a kingdom, and Louis Bonaparte became its king. Even stranger, odd chunks of Europe were incorporated into France, which now stretched from Hamburg, in northern Germany, to Split, on the coast of the Adriatic.

The alliance with Russia, which was established in 1807, was the confirmation that, henceforth, France would rule Europe. Then, after divorcing Joséphine, Napoléon married a Habsburg archduchess, and it seemed as if there would never be any stopping him; but it was not all just battles and conquests.

Although there was a very natural measure of resentment because French armies tended to appear in all kinds of odd corners of Europe, what they often brought with them was quite welcome. The Code Napoléon, the metric system, a more efficient way to govern—all these were prized acquisitions; and even when the emperor himself was resented, the lessons he taught were remembered. To a significant extent, nineteenth-century Europe (always excluding Great Britain) was what Napoléon had made it. Even in Prussia, the country where France was most hated, the ministers learned from the new French

The Napoleonic Empire, about 1812

Ruled directly by Napoléon

Ruled by a family member of Napoléon's

Dependent state

NORWAY

SWEDEN   Stockholm

St. Petersburg

North Sea   DENMARK

RUSSIAN

Copenhagen

EMPIRE

UNITED KINGDOM

PRUSSIA

London

Hannover   Berlin   Warsaw

WESTPHALIA   GRAND DUCHY OF WARSAW

Frankfurt

Paris

CONFEDERATION OF THE RHINE   Vienna

AUSTRIAN

Atlantic Ocean

FRANCE

ITALY   Milan

ILLYRIAN PROVINCES

Buda ●● Pest

EMPIRE

OTTOMAN EMPIRE

PAPAL STATES   Rome

CORSICA

Madrid

SARDINIA

Naples   NAPLES

SPAIN

Mediterranean

Palermo   SICILY

Sea

Algiers

MOROCCO   ALGERIA   TUNISIA

©1999 by D. L. McElhannon

institutions. Just as important, perhaps, much though Napoléon now disliked the Revolution, its ideas followed the movements of his troops. "After me, the Revolution, or rather the ideas which brought it about, will start their work with renewed strength," the emperor once remarked. "It will be like a book which one resumes reading just where one had left off."[28] He was right, of course: the nineteenth century was to be the century of revolutions.

Still, the sovereigns, even more than their people, did not like being chased out of their capitals and their palaces. Lisbon, Madrid, Rome, Naples, Turin, Florence, Berlin, Vienna, Warsaw, Brussels, The Hague, and Moscow—not to mention a long list of small German capitals—were all entered (and sometimes retained) by the French. Then there were the satellite states: Bavaria, Saxony, Württemberg, Baden, and a host of others. It was all more than enough to make a king nervous.

"The system adopted by Napoléon . . . must be counted among the causes of his fall,"[29] Talleyrand wrote in his memoirs. As others had discovered before him, as the Germans were to find out in our own century, no one nation can rule Europe for long. Had the emperor been more reasonable, he might well have stayed on the throne; but then, he would not have been the man he was. "Impossible," he once told Molé, "is a word whose meaning is purely relative; every man has his own *impossible* according to whether he is able to do more or less. Impossibility is the phantom of the fearful and the refuge of cowards."[30] It is a noble thought; but in pursuing it, Napoléon took the possible to such extremes as to defeat himself in the end.

CHAPTER FOUR

Great Britain and France

F<small>RANCE ALONE</small>, however great its power, however new its principles, would have remained a purely European power without its great rival. Great Britain, chastened by the loss of its thirteen North American colonies, was anything but eager to start expanding again. Its prime minister, William Pitt, was convinced that colonies cost more in money and trouble than they were worth. Without France, therefore, Great Britain would probably have concentrated on its traditional trading routes; without Great Britain, France would not have looked beyond the Continent. As it was, they fought each other all over the world for almost twenty-three years (from 1792 to 1815); the unexpected result was to make the whole world a single unit, one in which South America and South Africa became an integral part of the conflict.

ARMY AND NAVY

The whale and the elephant, they were sometimes called: one, Great Britain, ruled the seas; the other, France, was the most powerful of the Continental Powers; and each was intent on defeating the other. For England, the very existence of the French Republic was unacceptable—as was the fact that France now occupied the Belgian and Dutch ports. For France, Great Britain was the malign plotter who organized coalition after coalition.

That Great Britain was France's most determined foe no one doubted. That it, alone, could afford to fight for twenty-three consecutive years—with the brief interruption of the Peace of Amiens—was equally sure. Its worldwide trading empire and the soundness of its financial and credit structure enabled it to spend sums about which other governments could only dream.

Part of that prosperity was due to normal trade, part to the development of an industrial economy well ahead of the rest of Europe; but another element of that rise in wealth was due to an infamous practice, the buying of slaves in

Africa. The slaves were then shipped to North America and the Caribbean, where they were resold at enormous profit. In the English colonies themselves (although not in the British Isles), slavery was legal. More money came from the sugar plantations in the Caribbean, and from the famous Triangular Trade—slaves, sugar, rum. Because the last was considered an essential part of life—soldiers and sailors alike were allotted daily rations; the upper classes made punch from it—many of the English prospered on the backs of African men, women, and children. There were, it is true, a few people who denounced the immorality of it all, but, in 1800, they were thought to be unpractical idealists, to whose moans it was not worth listening.

Some of that money, through taxation, financed the Royal Navy. Because Great Britain was an island, it had a long tradition of seafaring. Already in the sixteenth century, its navy had defeated the Armada; in the seventeenth, it beat the Dutch, who were until then thought to be the greatest sea power in Europe. Now the British navy stood between France and a complete victory, since it prevented any possible invasion. There were obvious reasons for the power of the navy: it was unstintingly allotted the credits it needed, and its ships had the benefit of superior design. It was also a highly profitable service for its officers because they shared the resale value of the ships they captured. Younger sons of important families were therefore likely to join the navy, and they made its needs clear to cabinet ministers whose relatives they were. As for the sailors, they, too, could be recruited easily enough—through the barbaric custom of impressment. The authorities simply kidnapped, in and around the ports, the necessary number of men. Of course, some tried to desert when the ships came into port; they were promptly pursued, though, and usually caught.

The Royal Army was a very different organization. The British had feared standing armies ever since Cromwell. Their custom had therefore been to hire foreign mercenaries whenever needed, and to finance the armies of their allies: this had been the case, most recently, in the Seven Years' War and the American War of Independence. The result was an utter lack of everything a major army needed, from guns to horses, from food to powder and uniforms. Even worse, commissions were venal: anyone who wanted to be an officer could buy his position. Some control over promotions was still exerted by the commander in chief; but, by and large, the officer corps displayed the most thoroughgoing incompetence. It was therefore clear that Great Britain could not expect its army to win a war.

Great Britain in 1800

That hardly seemed to matter, though. Although the coalition with Russia and Prussia had collapsed a year earlier, leaving England alone in its fight against France, the king, the government, and the great mass of the people refused to contemplate peace. Monarchies and republics, it was felt, could not coexist: the latter form of government, complete with massacres and widespread dispossession, was too catching. Besides, France was the hereditary enemy; it seemed very natural to be fighting against it. Added to that feeling of intense patriotism was the deep-seated belief that Great Britain, alone, stood for liberty, and that it must therefore defend it to the last—a position akin to that adopted in 1940.

From the outside, therefore, it looked as if the British were united in their determination to reverse the French Revolution, especially since, in 1800, it was still hoped that Bonaparte would prove to be a second Monk and, like his seventeenth-century predecessor, restore the monarchy in France. In that goal of reversing the events of the previous eight years (back to a constitutional monarchy) the king, the prime minister, a part of the aristocracy, and an important section of the public were firmly united.

There was the opposition, though. It could be found in Parliament and among the great Whig aristocratic families; it also included many Londoners and some, at least, of the rest of the people. A few years earlier, it had denounced the American war; it had rejoiced when those colonies became independent; it had approved of the early phases, at least, of the French Revolution; and, finally, it wanted a lasting peace with France and its government.

In Parliament itself, Pitt had, ever since the 1770s, faced a talented and determined adversary. The Whig leader Charles James Fox, the most charismatic politician of the age, was also a great orator, and this counted for much with his contemporaries. He was a man of principle who spent his life fighting the power of the Crown and trying to bring a measure of democracy to what was still a political system controlled by the aristocracy. He believed in the right of peoples to choose their own governments, so he had naturally backed the Americans all through their struggle for independence. Now the idea of a French Republic appealed to him. He saw Bonaparte as the perfect example of talent succeeding in a country where the destruction of an oppressive establishment had at last removed the force of privilege. The Consul, in fact, struck him as a Gallic version of himself.

The King, the Government, and the Constitution

Although, in the 1790s, the two-party system as we know it had yet to develop, the government and the opposition were recognizably different, but the majority was made of groups whose allegiances shifted with what they perceived as their interests. As a result, the followers of a particular politician might move from one side to the other with stunning rapidity. Still, there were a number of great issues. The war with France soon outranked the others, but a close second was the role of the king.

King George III. Episodically sane, always obstinate and
close-mouthed, the king disliked the French and the Irish
Catholics almost equally. *(Portrait File, Miriam and Ira D. Wallach
Division of Art, Prints and Photographs, The New York Public Library,
Astor, Lenox and Tilden Foundations)*

George III, when he was sane, was fully aware of the contempt with which
Fox regarded him, and he naturally resented it. He was also convinced that Fox
was disloyal, not just to the person of the king, but to the very concept of
monarchy. Then there were the Whig leader's policies: George III never really
got over the loss of the American colonies, and was more than half convinced
that the fault lay with the opposition in Westminster. He governed, or sustained
his governments, through the judicious use of patronage, and Fox wanted to

abolish all sinecures. He was aware that the Crown's actual power had declined sharply since the days of his grandfather, George II, and Fox wanted to restrict these powers still more. All this, when added to the king's mental slowness and obstinacy, combined to make him think of the opposition as actually criminal: in his nightmares, George III could see himself walking up the steps of the guillotine with Fox applauding loudly.

Fox's view of the world was the exact opposite. He believed that the Crown was daily increasing in power and would soon turn Great Britain into an absolute monarchy. He was also aware (though a beneficiary himself) that the political system was thoroughly unrepresentative. The House of Commons, far from being an image of the country, was elected by a very few voters, many of whom could be bought or controlled by the great landlords. In some constituencies, there were as few as ten voters, while vast new cities like Manchester or Birmingham were not represented at all. Fox therefore favored a reform of the system; as it grew more representative, it would also resist and reverse royal encroachment. Fox himself proved willing to act on his beliefs. One of the few parliamentary boroughs with a significant number of voters was the City of London; he contested it and won it, thus earning the right to represent himself as the champion of the people.

The king was a dangerous and powerful enemy, because he still had real power. He alone chose the prime minister, who then had to have the backing of a majority in Parliament; he could also confer favors, both financial and honorific. There were sinecures to be handed out, bishops to be made, peers to be created. These considerable advantages, however, required skill and intelligence—sometimes even flexibility—to make them effective. George III, even when he was sane, was anything but bright. Alone, he would undoubtedly have been beaten. Luckily for him, the prime minister, William Pitt, was the smartest politician of the age, a man of acute intelligence who understood exactly how to control the House of Commons. And Pitt was entirely prepared to defend the powers of the Crown—after all, he largely exercised them. He was also an enlightened conservative, willing to reform in order to preserve—the restructuring of the government of India, for instance, was one of his great successes. Finally, he loathed the French Revolution and the leaders who had come out of it. He was sure that it was Great Britain's fate to be the first among the Great Powers, and that France was a threat, not merely to this goal, but to the very survival of the country.

Fox and Pitt were thus prepared to fight on every possible issue; they agreed only on the supremacy of the House of Commons, and their conflict was bound by its rules. There was a great difference, though: Fox counted on achieving mastery of the Commons as the only way to power. Pitt knew that much of his strength came from the unwavering support of George III; and indeed, when he eventually resigned, it was not because of a hostile vote in the House of Commons, but because he and the king no longer agreed.

William Pitt, the youngest British prime minister in the history of Great Britain. Clever, effective, undaunted, he was the principal enemy of France and its Revolution. (*Portrait File, Miriam and Ira D. Wallach Division of Art, Prints and Photographs, The New York Public Library, Astor, Lenox and Tilden Foundations*)

There were many questions on which Pitt and Fox differed; amazingly, however, they were at first substantially agreed on the excellence of the French Revolution. Pitt, who was a passionate Gallophobe, thought the events would weaken France; Fox, who was an equally passionate Gallophile, trusted that as France grew more democratic, it would also grow stronger. Both agreed that having a constitutional monarchy across the Channel was a good thing; both felt that the French were following the example of Britain, where many freedoms had long been part of life.

As the Revolution had begun to speed up, however, George III and Pitt grew progressively more alarmed—partly because, in Britain itself, there were increasingly loud demands for a reform of the system. Fox, on the other hand, was not fond of kings, and he watched events in France with delight—until the execution of Louis XVI, which shocked him deeply. Still, he defended the Revolution and explained just why to a friend, citing Thomas Paine, that champion of revolution. "*You* seem to dread the prevalence of Paine's opinions (which in most part I detest as much as you do)," he wrote in 1792, "while I am much more afraid of the total annihilation of all principles of liberty and resistance [to royal despotism]."[1] This was an extreme position for a party of antiroyalist grandees who watched with horror as their brethren across the Channel were either beheaded or forced into exile. In his enthusiasm, Fox forgot that in Great Britain, it was the aristocracy who ruled far more than the king; and so, with an ever-smaller group of followers, he drifted into political impotence.

When it came to the events in France, though, Fox's position was more moderate than it often sounded. He disapproved of the executions of Louis XVI and Marie Antoinette, and of the Terror, but he also held that these events were France's sole concern, and that Great Britain had no business waging a war to restore the ancien régime. At first, Pitt concurred and, resisting some of his own followers, advocated a policy of neutrality. As time passed, however, it seemed increasingly possible that the example of France might prove catching. Political clubs emerged, demanding the end of heredity—that is, no king—and the full granting of humankind's natural rights. This, obviously, was not something either George III or Pitt was willing to contemplate; but before they could start a war (they lost no time in putting down their domestic foes) the Convention obliged them by declaring it in 1792.

A POPULAR WAR

The result was immediate: anti-French hysteria became the order of the day. There was fear of secret Jacobins financed by French gold, or even of a possible invasion; there were said to be plans for a wide-scale insurrection that would make Britain a republic. It was all nonsense, of course; but the result was all that the king and Pitt could have wished. The country rallied behind them; an important group in the House of Commons, led by the Duke of Portland, joined the government majority; and Fox found himself completely isolated.

The war itself was a new kind of conflict. The French and the English had fought often before, most recently during the American War of Independence; but that was simply a question of political and commercial rivalry. Now, on both sides, the war turned into a crusade. For the French, the alliance of Great Britain and Austria, embodied by Pitt and by the Austrian commander, the Prince of Coburg, represented the forces of the counterrevolution. For the English, France—apparently intent on spreading the Revolution to the rest of Europe—meant chaos, devastation, and ruin. The British government said it was fighting to check aggression and restore traditional borders, but this, in fact, was the first ideological war of modern times.

It was not lost on many of the Whigs (or on Fox, their leader) that the immediate consequence of the war within Great Britain itself was a sharp curtailment of civil liberties. Here, for the first time, was an example of the often-repeated phenomenon in which a nation fighting for liberty begins by restricting it sharply within its borders. From 1793 on, Fox had vigorously denounced the "euthanasia" of the constitution; and because the Pittite majority in Parliament was so huge, he found instead another venue and advocated "the union of great [Whig] families, considering this as absolutely necessary to maintain the popular cause against the Court."[2] It is a measure of the power of the aristocracy, and of its traditional distrust of the Crown, that the Dukes of Devonshire, Bedford, and Grafton; the Marquis of Lansdowne; the Earl Fitz-william; and many others promptly joined the Foxite opposition.

Indeed, the great Whig families had long felt that they mattered far more than a royal family whose origins were, after all, foreign. George I had been elector of Hanover, and became king of England because he was a Protestant and descended from James I. George I spoke no English—he communicated with his ministers in French or Latin; George II had had a heavy German accent. The current king, George III, was thoroughly English; but this dull man with a dowdy wife, popular as he was among the people, had utterly failed to earn the respect of the grandees who, among them, owned much of England.

A BRILLIANT SOCIETY

London, in the 1790s, was in many ways a brilliant city. Many of its great houses were brand new, and Robert Adam's architectural triumphs of the 1770s and 1780s—at Northumberland House, Coventry House, and so many others—still fascinated people. Forms inspired by ancient Rome; plaster reliefs on which Pompeian urns, wreaths, and tripods were reinvented to suit English houses; furniture with straight legs and rams' heads: all these neoclassical elements

A VIEW of LONDON from the THAMES,
TAKEN OPPOSITE THE ADELPHI.

London, Pub. Nov.r.1st 1804, at R. Ackermann's Repository of Arts 101 Strand

A view of London, the center of world trade and of opposition to France. *(Print Collection, Miriam and Ira D. Wallach Division of Art, Prints and Photographs, The New York Public Library, Astor, Lenox and Tilden Foundations)*

were part of the decor. So was the brilliant color—green, red, bright yellow—Adam used on walls and ceiling medallions, and his designing of identical motifs for the ceiling and the carpet. Here, the old was made new and antiquity became modern, all in such as way as to suit the kind of life led by the upper classes. At the same time, John Soane took the new style a step further in designs like that of the Bank of England. Sober forms and stark geometric massing were relieved by screens of columns, so that what might have been heavy at the hands of a lesser master became grand, majestic, sometimes even solemn.

Architecture had always been an English specialty, but now there was painting as well. Thomas Gainsborough's vaporous, almost transparent style combined the most immediate sense of the way people looked, stood, and walked with an almost melancholy remoteness. He understood the beauties of the English countryside and of the London parks; he knew how to place his sitters in the right setting so that each looked at his or her best. He also understood how to blend reality and fashion so that the young women he portrayed, swathed in veils and silks, looked both utterly recognizable and mysteriously sylphlike.

Sir Joshua Reynolds could not have been more different. His brilliant, dashing portraits allied solidity and a sense of the splendid. The assurance, the wealth, the pride of his sitters always came through, and that seemed just right in work produced by the president of the Royal Academy. Gainsborough showed the romantic aspect of the British; in Reynolds's work, we see the energy of the nation that had just begun to conquer an empire.

Gainsborough and Reynolds were not alone. Competent artists like George Romney painted the rich in a straightforward manner: today his sitters look out at us, aware of their status, confident that they will be remembered. Then there was Benjamin West, an American who lived in London, whose great protoromantic compositions were much admired; and at the opposite end of the spectrum, the Swiss painter Henry Fuseli produced strange, haunting images in which dream creatures and oddly distorted figures lived in a world of their own. Finally, there was the inimitably English John Constable, whose landscapes, complete with winding rivers, spreading trees, and distant spires, took on a golden immortality.

The works of all these painters could be seen on the walls of the great houses, in London and the country alike. This, after all, was a society for whom life outside the cities really mattered. Peers, rich commoners, and county squires all had imposing residences surrounded by vast parks. Most of these owners also looked after their estates. The connection with the countryside was strong, and manifested itself in many ways, from the frequent redesigning of house and garden to the passion for the hunt or the visits to the tenants.

This can all be seen in the novels of Jane Austen: although the first of these was published only in 1811, nothing had really changed. One of the greatest of English writers, this modest young woman started a new trend. Until then, few women had dared to be novelists; after her, the Brontës, George Eliot (the pseudonym of Mary Ann Evans), Elizabeth Gaskell, and many others proved that the female gender was no deterrent to talent. Written in the clearest style, full of wit and psychological penetration, Austen's novels bring to life the ways of the gentry and upper middle class. Their stories take place, mostly, in the country; the weather, the seasons, matter greatly; but so does the complex hierarchy that divided Great Britain into many well-defined classes. Marriages and dowries; the exact income of the characters; their degree of politeness and culture all play a role, so that it is the whole world of rural England we enter as we read her books.

Although most of Austen's characters lead well-regulated lives, some are wild and dangerous. Indeed, while some members of society at the time seemed both imprudent and unprincipled, most felt deeply rooted. And as industrialization progressed, as coal mines were found, as the demand for iron soared, as the cities expanded, the rich got steadily richer.

As a result, all the appurtenances of life increased in splendor. English silversmiths had long been skillful; now they equaled their French rivals. It all happened in the nick of time: throughout the 1790s the demand for silverware of every kind was growing rapidly, and no dinner party was complete without silver dishes, platters, tureens, epergnes, and candlesticks.

In London, grand parties filled every night during the Season. Entertainment of every kind was available. Haydn's concerts offered the best of contemporary music, beautifully played. For those with more brutal tastes, boxing matches were fought without gloves. The fighters bled and sometimes died; the young men of the ton applauded. More civilized people went instead to amusement parks, like Vauxhall and Ranelagh, where the fashionable (together with the rest of London) strolled, heard music, watched acrobats, and enjoyed balls and fireworks. Many amorous intrigues were begun there; but, in case of need, there was also every kind of brothel, from cheap to luxurious and with specialties to appeal to every taste. There were horse races as well, and carriage races; and, at the very top of society, elegant young men set the fashion for the rest of the world. As for the great ladies who ruled London, although they missed their French suppliers, they, too, paraded an endless array of new and spectacular costumes.

Society was largely Whig; the king was essentially Tory; the grandees flouted their wealth, the royal family lived modestly and dully, most of the time in suburban residences. The nobility, on the other hand, kept racing through the city in its splendid carriages. The men (and a number of the women) ate and drank to excess, mocked the court, and gambled, often losing huge sums of money. They were also endlessly unfaithful to their spouses, one great lady giving birth to a number of children by a number of fathers, not one of whom was her husband. And in this glittering world, the brilliant Fox, frequently drunk and a formidable gambler, was universally loved. At the same time, these were people who also went, again and again, to see Shakespeare's plays and followed passionately the careers of the leading actors and actresses. It therefore surprised no one when one of them, the beautiful Mrs. Robinson, engaged in a particularly glamorous liaison.

The Prince of Fashion

Her new lover, as everyone knew, was none other than the heir to the throne, George, Prince of Wales. A handsome, intelligent young man, finally set free from his governor in 1782, the prince was also a gambler, invariably losing more than he should, and a womanizer. He loved clothes so much that he seldom bought less than twelve dozen of anything. His horses and carriages were as numerous as they were ruinous. The parties he gave reached a new degree of splendor—and cost enormous amounts of money. With all that, even a large income—over £90,000, or about $15 million in U.S. currency today—did not go very far. The prince accumulated huge debts, again and again. Throughout the 1790s, he repeatedly asked his father for help; with grim satisfaction, George III refused, and the spending went on.

That was more than enough to horrify the dull and dutiful royal pair. Just as bad, from their point of view, the prince also cared a great deal about decor, so that Carlton House, his London residence, became one of the most sophisticated, most luxurious palaces in Europe. It was not only that the house was almost completely redesigned by the architect Henry Holland in the late 1780s, or that the most expensive silks, velvets, and brocades were used in all its rooms. The prince also bought the best of everything, without regard to what it cost. That applied to silver, of course, or the specially woven carpets; but then, from 1793 on, the prince also took advantage of the French revolutionary sales to buy the very best French royal furniture and porcelain. He collected paintings, everything from Van Dyck and Gainsborough to Pieter de Hooch and François Boucher. The result was, and is, one of the greatest collections in the world.

That was in London; but the prince, ever aware of the latest fashion, also decided to build a house in that most chic of new resorts, Brighton. There, he sought the look of distant countries as a counterpoint to Carlton House. Because he wanted amusement even more than splendor, he looked to China. For several decades already, chinoiserie had been in fashion: embroidered silks, wallpapers, bronzes, and above all porcelain had come in great quantity from that still mysterious empire. It surprised no one, therefore, when, around 1800, the prince decided to redecorate his pavilion at Brighton, and switch from neoclassicism to a Chinese look. That, however, was a brief phase. Within five years, the prince and John Nash, his architect, decided to look farther south, to the India of the Mogul Empire; and so, under the gray English skies, an astonishing confection of onion domes and latticework was born. Inside, dragons held chandeliers in their mouths, ceilings were painted with nacreous scales, faux bamboo proliferated, and trompe l'oeil banana leaves decorated the walls.

Nothing could have been further from what was being done in the rest of Europe—where the strictest neoclassicism prevailed—and nothing could have been more pregnant with future developments. It was not only that the prince's pavilion reflected the fact that the British were in the process of establishing an empire in India: its bold juxtaposition of the proto-Indian and proto-Chinese with French Louis XVI and gilded, ornate English Regency furniture pointed to a radically new kind of eclecticism. In the decorative arts, in fact, the nineteenth century began at Brighton: After its blend of Indian, Chinese, and Regency, everything became possible. From then on, no single style prevailed. Neo-Gothic went together with neo-Byzantine; Japanese vases sat on neo-Renaissance chests. This was an absolute transformation of European taste: until then, there had been only one newly invented, universally prevalent style. The nineteenth century was a time of longing for the styles of earlier eras; and it was the Prince of Wales who showed the way.

That was altogether appropriate, in part because Great Britain, isolated by the endless war against France, had become very different from the rest of Europe, in part because it was the mightiest trading nation in the world. When huge fortunes were made in India, and increasing quantities of British goods were sold there, when British ships reached almost every part of the globe, it became impossible for the country to remain self-contained; and what Britain began, the rest of Europe eventually continued.

That extravaganza at Brighton was, from the king's point of view, bad enough. What angered George III even more was that the prince's closest friend was Charles James Fox, and that the house he frequented most often was that of Georgiana, Duchess of Devonshire. The duchess was not only the most fashionable of women, but she had also shown her contempt for the dowdy and disagreeable Queen Charlotte. Worse still, she was an enthusiastic Whig. By thus allying himself with his father's political enemies, the prince was merely following a Hanoverian tradition. George I had detested George II, who, in turn, had loathed his heir, Frederick, Prince of Wales. This time, though, the prince's politics made a difference: like Fox, he wanted reform and peace.

WAR, GLORIOUS WAR

That hardly impressed the country members of Parliament, who were the backbone of the Commons. Lady Bessborough and the Duchess of Devonshire might make fun of Mr. Pitt and dull King George; but when, in 1794, the prime minister introduced sedition and treason bills curtailing civil liberties yet further, they were promptly and enthusiastically passed. Fox gloomily predicted that within a few years the king of England would be as absolute as any of his Continental colleagues. The following year, the new acts were completed by the Seditious Meetings and Treasonable Practices Act; once again, Parliament supported the government. France, which had once been just a competitor, had become the incarnation of evil.

Thus, there seemed to be no possible end to the conflict. Fox, who advocated fighting a limited war for well-defined, limited objectives, was ignored. Only the complete defeat of France would satisfy the government; but, as it happened, French armies were victorious everywhere. And even when the Terror ended, little changed. Negotiations were conducted with the Directoire in 1795 and 1796; they proved utterly fruitless.

For Fox, it was an unhappy time. He distrusted the Directoire because it was corrupt and unwilling to restore to its previous owners the property seized during the Revolution; on the other hand, he felt sure that George III and Pitt were deliberately fanning the war hysteria so as to create the conditions favorable to the suppression of liberty. And then the French themselves turned the situation around.

First, in 1795, Prussia made peace with France; Austria followed in 1797, and Great Britain was left without allies on the Continent: now there could be no prospect of her ever winning the war. Undiscouraged, however, Pitt set about constructing the Second Coalition together with Austria; but then, in 1799, it collapsed as well. Once again, no other power was willing to fight. It was as complete a failure of his policies as could be imagined; and at that point, Ireland, as it has so often in British political history, added a whole new range of complications.

A DIFFICULT UNION

Religion and politics tend to make for an explosive mixture. This had emphatically been the case in Ireland ever since the Reformation, the Irish being Catholic, and the English Protestants. Then, with the expulsion of James II in 1688, penalties against the Catholics had been considerably aggravated—they could, among other disabilities, not hold public office. The result was that although a Parliament sat in Dublin, it represented mostly the tiny minority of Protestant settlers. Naturally, the small electorate made for massive corruption. There was thus an argument for enfranchising more of the population, ending the Dublin Parliament and allowing the electorate to send members directly to Westminster.

This solution commended itself strongly to Pitt. The Dublin Parliament, although it was both English and Protestant, had opposed several of his policies because it was more conservative than the cabinet in London. Then, in 1797, the situation worsened considerably. Lord Fitzwilliam, whom Pitt appointed lord lieutenant (that is, the representative of the Crown), was a man of goodwill and liberal views who was known to be in favor of lifting many of the Catholic disabilities. Pitt, who could, on occasion, back progressive policies, was perfectly willing to do so. Unfortunately, George III was having one of his sane moments. He was thus able to make his narrowness of mind count for a great deal, for it was still the custom that no bill could be presented to Parliament by the government without the king's consent. When Pitt explained what he wanted to do, George simply refused to consider any change in the laws, because, he said, such a change would violate his coronation oath. At his best, the king, as obstinate as he was slow-minded, was not an easy man to argue with. Now, it was understood that if he became upset, he might well go mad again; and if that happened, the Prince of Wales would become regent. Given that the prince and Pitt loathed each other, this was a possibility Pitt was eager to avoid.

The Irish, however, hardly had the same reason for sparing the king's feelings. Fitzwilliam's appointment had led them to expect change; when nothing happened, their disappointment was all the sharper—and it extended to many young men of the aristocracy who were no longer willing to see the country deprived of civil and political rights. The Irish also had another major grievance. The Established Anglican Church, which served only a tiny proportion of the population, was financed by tithes payable even by the Catholics. This grotesque situation cried for redress; it became a part of the demands for reform.

Since the king blocked all movement, and the Irish were thus denied redress by the English, many of them looked to France instead, in part because of old ties, but mostly because no religious establishment existed there; and they decided that what they needed was a nonsectarian Irish Republic independent from England. They were not so naive, however, as to expect that the English would simply go away, so, in 1797, they started to plot a rising that they expected the French to support.

Unfortunately for them, these plans were soon discovered; and because the rebellion began prematurely, the British promptly and easily crushed it. Still, something had to be done to remedy the general disaffection, and Pitt plumped on a union between Ireland and England. Following the model of Scotland, the Irish were to elect members to the British House of Commons, and the two countries would enjoy the benefits of free trade. This, Pitt hoped, would bring greater prosperity to Ireland, while the presence of Irish MPs at Westminster would make the necessity of Catholic relief measures evident.

For the English, the abolition of the Dublin Parliament posed no problems; and so, in 1798, the House of Commons voted easily for the union, and the House of Lords did the same. In Dublin, however, it was very different: there, the Parliament not unfairly minded its own abolition. Since, however, its members were notoriously venal, there was an obvious way out. Pitt authorized the practice of bribery on a large scale. That, together with pressure applied to the more vulnerable members, and what seemed to be the prospect of Catholic emancipation, did the trick. Pitt got his majority, and Ireland lost its Parliament.

There now remained one last step to be taken: with so large a Catholic population represented in Westminster, Pitt again brought up the need to annul the act forbidding the election of Catholics. George III, however, refused to listen to his prime minister's arguments. The most obstinate of men, and the most unable to contemplate change or compromise, he had convinced himself once and for all that any measure of Catholic relief would violate his coronation oath and invalidate his title to the throne.

The king was all the more immovable because he was backed by members of Pitt's own cabinet, reactionaries who loathed and feared the Catholics. Sim-

ilar men sat, in significant numbers, as members of Parlia
was no way Pitt could prevail, and when George III told Pitt
his trust, the outcome was obvious. Pitt knew that without
could not keep his majority intact; and so, in February 1801,
years in office, he resigned.

PEACE AT LAST

If a major earthquake had struck London, it could not have had a greater
effect. It seemed unthinkable that Pitt was no longer in office, and at first, no
one could imagine who might succeed him. Fox, of course, was delighted,
although there was no prospect of his becoming prime minister: what mattered to him was that peace with France was at last possible. It was known that
the First Consul wanted it; there was, in any event, no one left on the Continent to fight France; and nearly eight years of enormously costly war had signally failed to end the French Republic.

Among the results of all that expense was economic distress. No one liked
the new income tax that, for the first time in British history, had been imposed
in 1799; indeed, it was viewed by many as an intolerable attack on the sanctity
of property. Since its only purpose was to finance the war, peace, it was
assumed, would bring about an end to the hated tax. As for George III, he, too,
was pleased: Pitt's resignation confirmed the king's right to choose the prime
minister and, even more important, to veto those of his policies he did not like.
As so often before, the king misunderstood the situation: had the Commons
backed Pitt, he would have remained prime minister in spite of the king. But
this hardly seemed to matter, since the monarch was not aware of it.

At the same time, George III had approved of Pitt's other policies; so he
chose the Pittite Henry Addington as the new prime minister. A man utterly
devoid of charisma, Addington was hardworking and conscientious; he was
also a good manager and immediately proved it. Asking Pitt for his protection,
he convinced many of his fellow Pittites to remain in the cabinet and proceeded to govern with the essential assurance that he could count on the
king's support.

The next step was to negotiate a peace. Although George III hardly liked
to recognize the French Republic, he understood that Britain had no alternative. It was, as the future foreign secretary George Canning explained, a peace
of which everybody was glad and no one proud. The Treaty of Amiens, when it
was concluded with France in April 1802, confirmed the status quo—a major
defeat for Great Britain. It was also based on the understanding that Britain
would withdraw from Malta and France from Piedmont, and that no one would
conquer anything more, a dubious proposition at the very least. Still, in France,

yone was pleased, Bonaparte included; and in Britain, Fox described the situation honestly: "It may be said that the peace we have made is glorious to the French Republic, and glorious to the First Consul. Ought it not to be so? Ought not glory to be the reward of such a glorious struggle? France stood against a confederacy composed of all the great kingdoms of Europe; she completely baffled the attempts of those who menaced her independence."[3]

The first and most visible result of the treaty was that Paris was flooded with British aristocrats—including, of course, Fox himself. They gaped at the new fashions (and placed large orders), went to the Louvre, got themselves introduced to the consular court, and generally made up for ten years away from the center of everything modish. They also saw what was going on: the controlled press, the powerful police, the absolute rule of the First Consul, and that France, while nominally a republic, was, in fact, a tyranny. It was clear that the despot was popular; it was equally clear that he allowed no disagreement. Fox, for one, was grievously disappointed.

It did not take long for the incompatibility of France and Britain to reassert itself. The British felt humiliated and resentful; even more important, they did not trust Bonaparte. They were not wrong. Piedmont was not evacuated by the French, so the British stayed in Malta; and when the First Consul announced that, henceforth, he would be mediator of the Swiss Confederation—thus, in effect, taking over that little country—it was clear that France would continue to conquer its neighbors. In May 1803, Bonaparte made a public scene in which he accused Great Britain of reneging on its treaty obligations and shouted at Lord Whitworth, the ambassador, who was promptly recalled. After less than a year of peace, the war was resumed. To the horror of everyone in Britain, some ten thousand British tourists, caught in France at the declaration of war, were interned. Today, we have grown used to concentration camps and massacres; in 1803, although internment simply meant the tourists could not leave the country (they were not imprisoned), the measure struck everyone as barbaric.

The Unending War

There was still, however, a peace party in Great Britain, partly because the war was, once again, so ruinously expensive, partly because a significant group led by Lord Grenville believed in Catholic relief—which meant a Whig government. Together with the Foxites, the Grenvilles, as they were called, commanded a very substantial minority in the House of Commons—large enough, in fact, to force Addington's resignation in May 1804. As it was, he had been fatally weakened by the failure of his peace policy; and now that the war was on again, George III recalled Pitt on the understanding that the new cabinet would not back Catholic relief.

This second Pitt Administration was brief and unhappy. Pitt had wanted to form a broad-based cabinet in which the Grenvilles would have been included with Fox as foreign secretary. George III, who hated Fox, vetoed this formula; and without Fox, the Grenvilles would not accept office. By 1805, after a series of incidents in which Pitt opposed Addington, it became clear that the cabinet's support in the Commons was anything but firm. Then there was yet another major policy failure.

Pitt's first priority, once back in office, had been to cobble a new anti-French coalition and, with some difficulty, he succeeded in doing so. Austria and Russia agreed to fight France; in December 1805, both were thoroughly beaten at Austerlitz. Once again, a British-led coalition had served only to speed up French expansion. It was thus perhaps just as well that Pitt died suddenly (probably of acute alcoholism) in January 1806: again, Great Britain was left to fight a war it could not win.

This time, George III had to give in: there could be no viable government without Fox. Most reluctantly, the king was forced to accept the inclusion of the man he most hated. In February, under Lord Grenville as premier, the Ministry of all the Talents—so called because of the eminence of its members—came into office, with Fox at the Foreign Office. It was understood that Catholic emancipation was still blocked by the king, but Fox hoped he could at least end the war.

He soon found out that he had been wrong. The negotiation he started with Talleyrand could not have been more civilized in tone: the two men were old friends and both had admirable manners, but that failed to make up for the lack of a common goal. Great Britain wanted a peace that would stop, and even reverse, French expansion. Napoléon wanted peace, all the better to conquer new chunks of Europe; and so, before his early death in September 1806, Fox was forced to admit that his policy had failed as dramatically as Pitt's. *Le Moniteur*, the official French newspaper, made it all very clear when it commented, in June 1806: "If the affairs of the Continent are now taking the right direction, it is no thanks to England, which has done everything it could to disarrange them. Who could mistake British policy? It is to create conflict and dissension among the continental Powers, and to reign tyrannically over the seas so as to monopolize all trade."[4]

Napoléon then proceeded to add insult to injury. As part of a new settlement in Germany, he took over Hanover, King George III's possession, and handed it to Prussia. It now looked as if nothing could stop the French. As for the war, it, too, was out of control: it could, apparently, not be won; because of the navy, it could not be lost. The conflict looked, instead, as if it would go on forever, with taxes rising and discontent growing. Once more, France had proved that it determined what happened in Europe.

CHAPTER FIVE

Eastern Europe: Dealing with France

Austria, Prussia, and Russia were uneasy neighbors in 1800. Austria still resented Frederick the Great's conquests, and thought of Prussia as a dangerous potential enemy. Prussia, always greedy, wanted more than it had. Russia was eager to expand; it also felt both distrust and contempt for Prussia and Austria. Yet the three countries were on occasion able to agree as long as all three stood to gain. They had recently partitioned Poland, leaving nothing of that unhappy country. They had also decided to fight the French because they feared that the Revolution might prove contagious.

That had not been a good idea. The famous Prussian army was defeated again and again, and so were the Austrians. The Russians did not do well, either in Holland or in Italy. Still, they kept trying, usually with the encouragement of Great Britain. By 1800, two successive coalitions had ended in defeat: France and its revolutionary ideas were clearly there to stay. Even when Bonaparte became emperor, the three countries kept trying, and the Third Coalition, as usual, was defeated. Eventually, it occurred to all of them that they needed to make changes. How extensive those changes should be, and how they were to be carried out, then became the main preoccupation of their governments. Once again, France set the agenda; and other countries reacted as best they could.

UNHAPPY AUSTRIA

Life, for the emperor Francis II, was not easy. Only twenty-four in 1792, when he inherited the many states that made up the Habsburg possessions, the prospect of ruling them had filled him with terror. Everywhere he looked, he faced just the sort of problems that he felt unable to solve: restlessness in his own states, a depleted treasury, an army that had made a habit of being defeated and, worst of all, the question of what he should do about the French Revolution.

This had been a particularly painful problem. Marie Antoinette was his aunt and although he had never met her, he objected in principle to the humiliations she was enduring. Other archduchesses had, on occasion, had unpleasant lives: what really worried the emperor was that revolution, like the plague, might spread across Europe. Containing this appalling novelty thus became his central goal. It was not just that he feared he might be as badly treated as Louis XVI; he loathed constitutions with all the deep, unreasoning faith of a true reactionary.

The emperor felt that it was entirely reasonable to dread reform: his uncle Joseph II, who died in 1790, had been a bold reformer who tried to modernize the Habsburg states, and serious disturbances had been the result. A well-intentioned man, Joseph had freed the serfs, thus gravely upsetting the aristocracy. He had closed many convents and monasteries. This made badly run estates more productive, but it infuriated the Catholic Church. Finally, he had tried to centralize the governments of his many realms, thus provoking an uprising in Belgium and great dissatisfaction in Hungary. Although the lives of the lower classes, and particularly that of the peasants, had improved during his reign, what mattered far more was the anger of the aristocratic landlords. Francis II understood this; and he was firmly determined never to carry out any reform whatever.

Still, Francis II was not stupid. A modest, parsimonious man who did not wish to enlarge his empire, he was also timid, suspicious, unimaginative, and unable to take in large ideas. He dreaded change, and made it clear that he would prevent it at all cost. It was his misfortune that he lived in an era when change occurred on a breathtaking scale. Even worse, some of the ideas spread about by the French were particularly dangerous for the amorphous, multinational Habsburg empire. France, Spain, and Great Britain were all nation-states. In contrast, Francis II ruled over a mosaic of people whose only link was loyalty to himself. Once devotion to the monarch went, so did his empire.

Even a seasoned statesman would have had good reason to feel apprehensive. Francis was terrified; but, on occasion, he could be quite shrewd. He knew himself well enough to realize that he was too limited to come up with a policy by himself—so he relied on a few chosen ministers to do it for him, while always reserving the right to approve, disapprove, or modify. Unfortunately, the ministers he chose for the first eighteen years of his reign were scarcely more competent than he. Count Colloredo, for instance, had been his tutor. He was certainly honorable, unselfish, and devoted to his former pupil— all admirable qualities in a private person, but hardly the ones required of a prime minister in this stormy era. Even worse, the count was not just unintelligent, but an ultraconservative and a bigot, a man who watched what was happening with a blend of horror and incomprehension. Thugut, the new chancellor, and Counts Johann Stadion and Ludwig Cobenzl, who eventually succeeded Thugut as principal minister, were all narrow-minded bureaucrats utterly unable to understand that dealing with the French Republic was not the same as negotiating with a fellow monarch. And as if that was not bad enough, the emperor, always avoiding innovation, and often distrusting intelligent people, chose as his other ministers reactionary aristocrats, men of limited talents, or, not infrequently, no talents at all, who had a gift for making the wrong decisions.

But one thing at least had been made easy for the young emperor: in 1792, France had declared war on Austria without waiting for Francis to do so. At this point, Count Colloredo had answered with a bold move: he engineered an alliance with Prussia, which had been Austria's worst enemy, on the grounds that stopping the French Revolution was more important than any territorial rivalry; and then he and his master sat back, safe in the knowledge that the allied armies would reach Paris within three months.

They were disappointed. To the stupefaction of all Europe, the French had won, again and again. Even worse, they soon invaded two of the emperor's states: Belgium in the northwest, Lombardy in the southeast. At the same time, the Austrian government, never very efficient, became almost completely paralyzed, because the emperor, suspicious as always, insisted on reviewing every decision, seeing every paper. This would have been an impossible task even for a competent, hardworking statesman; but the emperor was slow, and fond of his amusements—hunting, and having sex as often as possible. The results were catastrophic: decisions waited until it was too late, problems went unsolved, and Austria lost the war.

At least the fighting had taken place far away from Vienna, and Francis understood it was better to stop it before it got closer. As a result, in 1797, Austria, at the Treaty of Campo Formio, ceded Belgium and Lombardy to France, while secretly promising to support the cession of the west bank of the Rhine to the Republic. Because the Holy Roman Empire still survived, this was a matter for the Diet, rather than the emperor alone, to decide. Still, it could have been worse: much against the wishes of the Directoire, Bonaparte handed Venice and the Veneto to Austria. Given that in 1795, the rump of Poland had been partitioned, with Austria acquiring Galicia, and that Belgium was far away and often troublesome, the emperor felt that he had not done badly.

This was especially true since he and his ministers considered that the peace was not much more than an armistice. With a few more allies (Prussia had dropped out), France, the emperor and the chancellor agreed, could still be beaten; and so they had started working on a new coalition. The result looked startlingly like a parody of ancien régime diplomacy. Although, admittedly, Britain was an important ally in that it could be counted on to help finance the forthcoming war, it had virtually no army. Its navy ruled the seas; but that, in a Continental war, was not of much help. As for the other members of the coalition, they were, in order of ascending importance: Naples, a tiny kingdom whose army was known strongly to dislike fighting; Portugal, which was separated by Spain from the rest of Europe, and thus was quite unable to be of help; and Russia, whose emperor, Paul I, was unbalanced and unpredictable. At least Russia had an army; it even sent part of it to fight in Italy; but, unfortunately, the Russian commander, Aleksandr Suvorov, had nothing but contempt for the Austrians, while, at the same time, the Austrians were convinced that the Russians were useless savages. These feelings did not make for much unity of command; and so, in March 1799, when Austria declared war on France, the weight of the fighting rested largely on its own army.

Still, the Austrians had two essential pieces of luck: the Directoire, entering its death throes, was not a very formidable adversary; and Bonaparte was in Egypt. Unfortunately for both the Directoire and Austria, he returned. This was a blow from which neither recovered. Once again, the Austrian armies were defeated with perfect regularity—not only by Bonaparte in Italy, but also by Moreau in Germany. At the same time, the Russians, having decided that they had nothing to gain, made peace. Austria was now left to face the French armies alone. Francis II was not always very quick to understand a situation, but this time, he saw right away what he needed to do; so he sued for peace. On February 2, 1801, in the Treaty of Lunéville, Austria lost only Tuscany and Modena, keeping the rest of its possessions. What mattered more than those two small Italian states was the remodeling of the western part of Germany.

Traditionally, Austria had been the leader of the south and west German states—in part because they were predominantly Catholic. Now, those states that had been on the left bank of the Rhine were French, and the others, major units like Bavaria and Württemberg, realized that France, not Austria, could reward or punish them; so they turned away from their traditional connections. At the same time, the territorial changes made it clear that the hoary structures of the Holy Roman Empire were not likely to survive. Francis II also understood this: in 1804, he announced that instead of being Francis II of the Holy Roman Empire, he was now Francis I, emperor of Austria.

Francis had thus lost two major wars, a sign that even he recognized as indicating a need for change, so he sacked Thugut, replaced him with the equally incompetent Colloredo and Cobenzl, and consulted his brother, Archduke Charles. By some genetic miracle, the archduke, alone among his numerous relatives, was both intelligent and competent. That was more than enough to rouse the emperor's deepest apprehensions, but clearly, something had to be done if Austria was ever to become reasonably strong again; and so the archduke was allowed to modernize the army. Military service was brought down to ten years (it had been lifelong), the armies were reorganized so as to function more efficiently, and a major new program to equip them with modern weapons was begun. At the same time, Hungary was pushed into providing more men (the number went up from fifty-two thousand to sixty-four thousand) and more money; and it looked as if, for once, the government was doing something right.

None of these measures really interested the emperor, though. He concentrated on what really mattered to him—stopping any possible revolution by banning most forms of thought. There had always been censorship in Austria, but it had been relatively tolerant. That changed in 1801 when the police were put in charge. Then, in 1803, the rules became even stricter: the newspapers could print nothing that had not been first approved by a censor; reading rooms, circulating libraries, even book reviews were forbidden. The Freemasons, who were believed to think freely, were dissolved, along with most learned societies. Naturally, all public meetings were banned; police permission even had to be obtained for balls at which the orchestra would be composed of more than two musicians; and the numbers of the secret police were greatly augmented. Still, because this was Austria, there were very few arrests. It was merely that thinking was no longer permitted.

Glamorous Vienna

In most ways, though, life in Vienna remained unchanged. Still a small city, the capital of the Habsburgs was a place of narrow streets, splendid baroque palaces, and much animation. The great families lived sumptuously; the court presented an appealing blend of splendor on state occasions and relative simplicity the rest of the time; as for the emperor, he felt free to stroll unescorted about the city, cheerfully returning his subjects' bows.

There were many pleasures to be sampled throughout the city. Viennese cafés were famous for the quality of their drinks and pastries; first-rate music could be heard by all; the great park, the Prater, was still a semirural fastness much enjoyed by everyone; and then there was that great discovery, the waltz. Starting in Vienna, it soon spread through Europe, and that seemed just right: the Viennese had always known how to enjoy themselves.

There were more intellectual pleasures as well. Archduchess Maria Christina and her husband, Albert von Sachsen-Teschen, were voracious, highly competent collectors of drawings; they bought well and often, and opened their holdings to all qualified people. The same was true of the emperor's library, and of at least a part of his art collection. The aristocracy, whose palaces were often treasure troves, was just as welcoming to visitors: all in all, there was much to be seen in Vienna. That, however, did not preclude the strictest social divisions: there was a "First Society" to which all the great nobles belonged; a

Vienna with the tall spire of Saint Stephen's Cathedral. The city was still a densely built, wall-girt capital surrounded by appealing countryside. (*General Research Division, The New York Public Library, Astor, Lenox and Tilden Foundations*)

less glamorous "Second Society"; and so on down the line. Here, as in most of Europe, civilized people spoke French. That, however, did not make the French Republic popular; most Austrians were simply waiting for the day when their country would at last defeat France.

In this feeling, the emperor was at one with his people. Just as he had considered the Treaty of Campo Formio to be a mere armistice, so now he was waiting for the time when Austria could, once again, go to war against France. He knew that it might take a few years before the army was ready, especially since the financial situation was tight. Like France (and Russia), Austria had been using paper money that had lost much of its value; and the Peace of Amiens meant that Great Britain was no longer subsidizing the government. New allies and new money were needed. The question, however, was not whether Austria would go back to war, but when, and whether it would be the only German power to do so.

THE DESCENT OF PRUSSIA

Prussia, in 1800, was even more unhappy than Austria, and its king, Frederick William III, had no idea what to do about it. Austria was used to losing battles but somehow keeping most of its possessions. Prussia, throughout the eighteenth century, had been famous for winning. Its formidable army had been reorganized in the 1730s by King Frederick William I; his son, Frederick II, had been one of the greatest generals of the age as well as a predatory monarch who had significantly enlarged his territories. Thus, in 1792, when Prussia had joined Austria in the war against France, it was widely expected that it would make mincemeat of the disorganized French forces.

Unfortunately for Prussia, however, Frederick the Great had died six years earlier. His nephew and successor, Frederick William II, was a vague, well-meaning man who tried hard to refrain from thinking. Under his reign, everyone had parroted what had been done before, without understanding why it had been done in the first place. If the French army had followed exactly the same rules as in the 1750s, it would no doubt have been beaten; but, unfortunately for the Prussians, the revolutionary armies had developed quite different methods. Frederick had been the great theoretician of the line method of arranging regiments: if the first line was broken, the second would take over while allowing the first to regroup. This made for slow, but very precise, shooting, and had proved highly effective. The French, however, now used columns bolstered by heavy artillery, and they had the depth needed for punching through all the enemy's lines. Napoléon soon perfected this method by strengthening the central columns while coordinating the attack of lateral columns.

This was all more than the king or his generals could understand. What they saw, however, was that they were losing the war. This was both puzzling and alarming; so, in 1795, they had made peace with France, and, having done so, sunk into inactivity on the grounds that the less you did, the fewer mistakes you made. Then, in 1797, Frederick William III had succeeded to the throne, but he allowed only the most moderate changes. Propelled by an unfortunate blend of greed and deep stupidity, the new king was too afraid to act; and so Prussia sank into relative insignificance while the rest of Europe fought. Once a major player, Prussia was rapidly becoming a secondary power.

Still, the king had his good side. He yearned to be fair and tolerant. The French Revolution, he wrote, "provides a powerful, terrifying example to all bad rulers who, unlike good princes, do not live for the welfare of their country, but like leeches, suck it dry."[1] Amazingly, when it came to making the necessary reforms, Frederick William did his best. Unlike most countries, where the state has an army, Prussia had been an army which had a state. Composed of disparate and, in some cases, widely separated pieces of territory, Prussia had grown powerful by subjecting everything and everyone to the needs of the army. Frederick II had continued that tradition, while bringing a spirit of religious tolerance and greater intellectual openness to a country that had been widely considered as semibarbaric.

The nobility provided the officer corps, and it had enormous privileges. It enjoyed tariff exemptions, which allowed it to make huge profits on imported goods; it paid virtually no taxes; and it had been allowed to reduce the peasantry on its estates to a state of slavery. Frederick William thus started where the greatest disparities lay. He canceled some, at least, of the tariff exemptions and set a good, but not widely followed, example by freeing peasants from forced labor on the state domains, allowing them to pay rent instead. Then, a few years later, he went on to emancipate them completely and allow them to own the land they farmed; in this, however, he was merely following the example of the Habsburg emperor Joseph II, who, some twenty years earlier, had freed the serfs in his own states. Finally, in order to stimulate trade, he abolished the duties imposed on goods crossing provincial borders within Prussia.

Just as important, the king tried to modernize the army. He created a few light infantry battalions of skirmishers in imitation of the French, but the two most harmful practices continued. These were, naturally, the use of line, instead of column, dispositions on the battlefield; and, just as important, the practice of hiring large numbers of mercenaries. Hired soldiers had done very well in the wars of the eighteenth century, but when confronted by a nation in arms, they tended to flee the battlefield. This had already been seen, to some degree, in the American War of Independence. Now, with large, highly motivated French armies in the field, the mercenaries were hopelessly outclassed.

At least the king knew it; so, prudently, he kept Prussia neutral, and resisted several offers of alliance from Austria while busily digesting his share of Poland. Besides, he found himself in the odd position of ruling a military state while disliking wars himself. A mild man, and very much in love with his wife, the beautiful Queen Louise, he was fond, in moderation, of the good things of life—his palaces around Berlin, his parks, and cozy domestic evenings.

PRUSSIA, SOCIETY AND THE ARTS

Frederick William, unlike Frederick II, was no intellectual, but he understood architecture. He was also lucky to have Karl Friedrich Schinkel, an architect of genius, at his disposal. The results were altogether happy. Already in the second half of the eighteenth century, Berlin had been transformed. Imposing baroque and neoclassical churches and theaters were built on Frederick II's orders: for the first time, the capital of Prussia looked like a civilized, western European city. Austere, beautifully proportioned buildings now added even greater elegance to the center of town and to the parks of the royal palaces at Charlottenburg and Potsdam. With its great open boulevard, Unter den Linden, bordered by these handsome structures, its rather dour but imposing Royal Palace, and the meandering curves of the river Spree, Berlin, in 1800, struck just the right touch of civility.

The same could not be said of its aristocracy. The Prussian upper class was famously rude—although Prince August of Prussia proved his appreciation of civilization by falling in love with Mme Récamier. Culture, in Berlin, could be found in the middle class: Rahel Levin had a salon where artists, intellectuals, and composers met, but where the great nobles would not have been seen dead. That left the court—never a very lively place. No one, certainly, went to Berlin because it was interesting.

PRUSSIA AND NAPOLEON

Making decisions was never easy for Frederick William III, not least because he was aware of his own limitations. To make the situation even more difficult, he found himself not altogether free to determine his own foreign policy: to a significant extent, Prussia's geographical position did that for him, and so did the decisions of its huge neighbor to the east. One of the results of the partition of Poland had been the creation of a long, common border between Prussia and Russia. If Russia ever decided to intervene in a European war, the shortest route would take its troops through Prussia; and if Russia and Austria were allies, and fighting France, they were not likely to allow a neutral or, worse, pro-French Prussia to threaten their lines of communication and the rear of their armies. So it was that while wishing earnestly to be left alone, Frederick William found himself in an increasingly awkward position.

France also added to his difficulties. Napoléon, who was well aware that Austria intended to attack at some point, tried to make sure that Prussia would remain friendly. He was not a man to be ignored, so the king, eager to show that he was ready to cooperate, had appointed Count Haugwitz as foreign minister. As Metternich, then a brilliant young diplomat stationed in Berlin, explained to Colloredo, Haugwitz was not only devoted to the French, but so well paid by them that there was no point in trying to bribe him into reversing his policy. What remained to be seen was whether Russia, being closer, would prove more importunate, or, perhaps, more menacing than France.

Then there was Great Britain: it had long been a friend of Prussia. England was, after all, ruled by a German dynasty; the two countries had been allies in the Seven Years' War (1756–1763) and, until 1795, in the conflict with France. Further, Prussia was not rich; it badly needed the subsidies it could expect to receive if it joined a coalition of which Great Britain was a member. And so Frederick William found himself pressured by all the great European powers, each of whom displayed lures while scarcely hiding the contempt they felt for him. By dint of equivocating, lying, and outright confusion, however, he managed, year after year, to remain uncommitted, with Russia carefully watching him.

Convulsions in Russia

That, in 1800, did not yet mean much. Czar Paul I was unbalanced, neurotic, and given to reversing his policies on a whim. What Russia might do at any given time was thus unpredictable—and so was the time the emperor might remain on the throne. His guiding passion was hatred of his mother, the empress Catherine the Great. In his four years in power, he had tried to undo as many of her arrangements as possible, thus gravely offending much of the nobility. His foreign policy depended entirely on his mood of the moment: what might come next, no one knew.

An essential part of Pitt's coalition making had been the wooing of Russia. This immense country, made larger still by its share of Poland and Catherine the Great's conquests in the Crimea, could obviously make a difference in a European war; but no one quite knew how to handle its rulers. Catherine herself, while loathing the Revolution, had been very determined to stay out of any coalition; so, in 1792, she had refused to join Prussia and Austria while hoping they would win. Then, in 1796, she died, and her only legitimate son became Emperor Paul I.

It had not been a happy moment for Russia. Catherine had disliked her son and thought him thoroughly inadequate; Paul naturally hated his mother in return. Catherine had been open-minded, cosmopolitan, and calculating. The impulsive Paul, despising his mother's reforms, loathed foreigners and believed that the czar ought to be a tyrant. He also had very ambiguous feelings toward his eldest son, Grand Duke Alexander.

That was in part because Catherine had been so fond of Alexander. It was widely believed that she meant to hand the throne directly to him, bypassing Paul. The new emperor never forgot that; he also disapproved of the education Alexander had received because it reflected all the values of the Enlightenment. Catherine had even gone to the extraordinary length of hiring as his tutor a Swiss, Frédéric-César de La Harpe, who was a fervent republican and extolled the virtues of democracy and constitutional government to the future autocrat.

There were still other reasons why the czar distrusted his son: Paul was short, ugly, not very bright, widely disliked—and severely unbalanced. Alexander was tall and handsome, with blond hair and large blue eyes; charming; intelligent; and universally popular. In 1796, he was nineteen, married to an adoring wife, and appealing in every way. Still, he had also learned to dissemble. Caught between his grandmother and his father, he was able to change personalities to suit: enlightened and cosmopolitan for Catherine, narrow-minded, military, and obedient for Paul.

This was certainly convenient, indeed, after his father's accession, necessary for Alexander's survival; but it led to chronic indecision. The young prince had also acquired another bad habit from his father, the obsession with

Alexander I, czar of Russia. Well-intentioned but indecisive, eager to reform Russia, but afraid to take risks, the czar was Napoléon's main protagonist. (*Portrait File, Miriam and Ira D. Wallach Division of Art, Prints and Photographs, The New York Public Library, Astor, Lenox and Tilden Foundations*)

parade-ground details. "The minutia of the military service, and the habit of giving it the greatest importance harmed the Grand Duke's mind," a close friend noted. "He contracted at Gatchina [Paul's residence] a taste from which he was never able to free himself. All through his reign he suffered from parade-mania, and thus lost much precious time once he had reached the throne."[2]

In 1796, however, none of that had mattered. The problem, for Alexander as for all Russians, was how to avoid displeasing the new emperor, for it became immediately clear that Paul was easily displeased, and given to ordering the most brutal punishments. In just a few days, everything had changed. Because Paul had admired Frederick the Great, the army was given Prussian-looking uniforms and military parades became the emperor's principal occupation. Catherine's carefully maintained neutrality was jettisoned: Russia joined the Second Coalition, and Suvorov led an army to Italy, where it won a few victories while Bonaparte was in Egypt.

In Russia itself, life was militarized. The army was greatly enlarged; the administration was expected to function like the staff of a general; censorship was reinforced, and the importation of foreign books absolutely prohibited; the police were everywhere. At court, especially, the atmosphere was poisoned by the emperor's suspicion that he was about to be murdered. As Grand Duchess Elisabeth, Alexander's wife, told her parents (secretly, of course), everybody in Russia feared the new emperor.

They had good reason. It was bad enough that Paul expected immediate and unquestioning obedience, that he took offense at the strangest things, and that he frequently went off, for no visible reason, into terrifying rages. He also could change his mind from one second to the next, then blame those who were implementing the policies he himself had decreed. As Alexander wrote to his former tutor: "He orders something today only to order the opposite a month later . . . and the welfare of the State has nothing to do with it. . . . There is only an absolute power turning everything topsy-turvy. . . . My poor country is in an indefinable state."[3]

So was the grand duke. From the moment of Paul's accession to the throne, it had been clear that Alexander was the ultimate recourse. Russia, as one observer remarked, was a tyranny modified by assassination, and no one forgot that Paul's father, Peter III, after the briefest of reigns, had been murdered to make way for his wife. Of course, the emperor was fully aware of this, and he watched his son most carefully. Alexander promptly learned to avoid foreigners at court and to take no notice of the ministers, while, in public, endlessly praising the policy of the month. Even more unpleasant, he was expected to report to his father every morning and every night, and his fright, when doing so, was obvious to all.

From the British point of view, however, Catherine's death had been a good thing. Since Paul immediately turned all Russian positions around, the country was now eager to join the coalition. Paul offered the French Pretender a refuge at Mittau, and announced that he would not stop fighting until the Bourbons were back on the throne of France.

This stance lasted less than two years. First, Paul quarreled with Austria and recalled his army; then he quarreled with Great Britain because it had occupied Malta, which he wanted returned to the Knights of Saint John; then he decided that peace with Bonaparte was the right policy, and he expelled the Pretender; and finally, he ordered his Cossacks to go off and attack India, firmly disregarding both the enormous distance and the fact that Russia and India did not have a common border.

All this naturally caused great alarm in Saint Petersburg. Russia was now without allies, without a reasonable policy, and at the mercy of someone whose eccentricities began to look very much like madness. Paul's very personality amplified the problems usual to Russia: corruption, for instance, had always been endemic, but under Catherine, it had been relatively moderate. Since, under Paul, disgrace could come at any moment, people stole as much as they could, as quickly as they could, and the never very efficient administrative machine virtually ground to a halt. Then, as if the situation were not already dangerous enough, Paul set out to affront the two most powerful groups in the empire.

For all her relative liberalism, Catherine had been well aware that it would not do to offend the nobility. She had conciliated it, principally, by extending serfdom. In the mid seventeenth century, most Russian peasants had been free. Under Peter the Great, many of them, suddenly and without understanding why, found themselves enslaved; under Catherine, the process was notably speeded up. This enriched the nobles, of course: the workers on their estates now belonged to them. They could be worked, and punished, as long and as hard their owners saw fit. The first result was a marked decrease of agricultural yields: if you are working for someone who owns you, and who is the sole beneficiary of all your efforts, you naturally do as little as you can. By 1796, serfs were being bought and sold; there were farm serfs and domestic serfs, serfs who were chefs, or violinists, or decorators. Some serfs were used as miners (and usually did not live long); others were footmen or coachmen; most were peasants. Some owners were cruel, others relatively humane; all were clear that they owned other human beings. Indeed, like so many other places in the world, from Africa to the Americas, Russia had an economy based on slavery.

For all his personal brutality, Paul was not inhumane. To the nobles' fury, he now proceeded to restrict their power over the serfs. Sunday, he decreed, was to be a day of rest; and it became illegal for masters to kill their serfs or have them killed. He was, of course, right to try and protect the millions who were oppressed and without rights; but it helped set the nobility against him.

Even more imprudently, he showed, at every opportunity, that he despised the regiments of the Imperial Guard because they had been Catherine's favorites. This was particularly foolish: after all, there was a solid tradition of intervention by these very regiments. The empresses Elizabeth and Catherine had owed their throne to them, and there was no reason to think they would not be willing to repeat their earlier interventions.

By the end of 1800, even Paul's ministers wanted him gone; and it was the two men he most trusted, Count Panin, the vice chancellor, and Pahlen, the governor-general of Saint Petersburg, who began the plot to replace him. First, and logically, they approached Grand Duke Alexander and asked him for his approval. They merely wanted to dethrone the emperor, they explained; he would then be confined to his Gatchina estate, where he could live in comfort.

It would have taken an idiot to believe this: a dethroned czar was far too dangerous to have around. A coup against Paul naturally implied his murder, and so Alexander refused—at first. Eventually, he consented to the coup on the grounds that it was his duty to Russia to do so, and with the proviso (which he must have known to be futile) that his father not be killed.

Naturally, Paul himself was well aware that a coup was always possible. He trusted very few people and felt extremely unsafe at the Winter Palace, and so he had a fortresslike palace built in the heart of Saint Petersburg. There, with all access tightly controlled, he would at last be able to relax. In fact, his move to the new palace, in late February 1801, proved fatal. Because he felt protected, Paul sent the faithful Semenovsky Regiment away; and on March 10, the plotters, led by Pahlen, made their way into the emperor's bedroom where, ignoring his willingness to abdicate, they strangled him. Alexander I was now czar of all the Russias.

A LIBERAL EMPEROR

"I cannot refrain from admitting that, together with the whole of Russia, I feel I can at last breathe freely,"[4] the new empress wrote her parents a few days later. That feeling was universal. Alexander's accession was greeted all through the country with a burst of joy. The new emperor was young, handsome, affable; he was known to be intelligent, sensitive, open-minded; and all rejoiced, except, perhaps, for Alexander himself, who never quite recovered from having allowed his father to be assassinated.

As it has so often since, Russia confidently looked forward to an era of reform, to the end of the tyranny. The new emperor made it clear that unlike his father, he wanted to rule by consent; that he cared deeply about the welfare of his subjects; and that he intended to change the system. Immediately, the hardworking Alexander relaxed the censorship; he allowed foreign books in again, and encouraged discussion. He curbed the secret police. He published a decree forbidding the sale of serfs without the land they worked. He promised to reform the Senate, that body of appointed bureaucrats, and hinted he might even turn it into a proper legislature. Everything seemed possible.

No one rejoiced more than the cosmopolitan upper class, or at least the part of it that lived in Saint Petersburg. The seat of the court, the new capital founded a mere century earlier by Peter the Great, was thoroughly European. French was the language spoken by its society; French literature, painting, and fashion the model. Still a largely baroque city, Saint Petersburg itself, girt and crossed by canals, was one of the handsomest cities in Europe. The palaces of the czar and the nobility were both vast and sumptuous, and, outside the city,

The Admiralty, Saint Petersburg. The modern capital of Russia, it was here that Paul was murdered and Alexander reigned. (*General Research Division, The New York Public Library, Astor, Lenox and Tilden Foundations*)

splendid residences dotted the countryside. Luxury was everywhere, from the cascades of jewels worn by its great ladies to the carriages driving down its streets. There were theater, opera, concerts. Famous chefs provided extraordinary meals; and there were just enough French émigrés to add a delicious ancien régime flavor.

Moscow was different—far more conservative, more Russian, more Orthodox. It looked at Petersburg with distrust; but it, too, was deeply penetrated by the culture and standards of the West. As for the rest of the country, it stretched on endlessly. There was a tiny middle class of merchants, millions of serfs, a few backward rural noblemen. What mattered, though, was the czar and the court. Everyone felt it immediately. Having liberalized internal policies, Alexander did the same in foreign policy. He lifted the embargo on trade with Great Britain, and signed a trade convention. Since the English were buyers of wheat, other agricultural commodities, and wood, the chief Russian exports, this was excellent news for the merchant community. At the same time, the czar mended relations with Austria; and, although not friendly toward France, he made it clear that he intended to maintain the peace.

It was within Russia, however, that the most significant changes seemed possible. Alexander had made no secret to his friends that he thought Russia should become a constitutional monarchy. This could be done, he thought, without undue difficulty because it would be he, the czar, who would grant the constitution to his subjects; thus all the excesses of the French Revolution could be avoided.

Even with the best of intentions, however, it was not easy to decide precisely what to do, or how to do it; and so Alexander created his Unofficial Committee. This was a group of four men; two of them were trusted officials, the other two, Count Pavel Stroganov and Prince Adam Czartoryski, were close friends of the emperor. Together, the four were to report on the state of the country, prepare reform, and point the way to a constitution. Deliberately insulating the group from the always conservative government structure, Alexander ordered it to meet every evening in his private apartments; and on most nights, he attended their deliberations.

A number of results were soon visible. The Senate had virtually ceased functioning except as an advisory body that kept track of the laws. Now it was reformed. There was no question of electing its members, but Alexander appointed a number of competent men. He gave them the responsibility of maintaining the law and supervising the government departments, as well as the right to ask that Imperial decrees be reconsidered when they conflicted with existing laws. In a country where a state based on law had never existed, and where the rulers had expected unquestioned obedience to their every whim, this was almost a revolution: Alexander was now implying that the law might be more powerful than the czar. Unfortunately, absolute power is an almost irresistible temptation. Within two years, Alexander found even this weak restraint annoying; the right to question decrees was ended, and the Senate sank back into inaction.

The top administrative structure was also transformed: Peter the Great's inefficient Colleges were replaced by eight Western-style ministries, with the ministers answering directly to the emperor. A State Comptroller's Office was created to control the deficit, while, at the same time, the emperor sharply reduced the luxury and consequent cost of the court. Then, in 1803, against the opposition of the Senate, Alexander promulgated a decree that made it legal for landowners to free their serfs: until then, no serf could ever be freed. He then went on to give an example by himself freeing a great number of serfs on the imperial domains. Not much came of this: from 1803 to 1824, private landlords freed only thirty-seven thousand male serfs, one-tenth of 1 percent of the slave population.

This was unfortunately typical. The Unofficial Committee had quickly decided to advise the emperor against sharing his legislative power with the Senate because that conservative body was likely to hamper reform. Alexander agreed with them, and soon concluded that Russia was not ready for a constitution after all: its happiness would have to depend on his good intentions instead.

RUSSIA, FRANCE, AND THE WAR

So far, at least, Alexander had shown an ability to make some decisions; when it came to foreign affairs, however, he drove his advisers mad by his hesitations. Neither Count Kotchubey, who advocated closer ties to France, nor Czartoryski, who thought that Bonaparte should be stopped sooner rather than later, ever quite had the emperor's ear: he listened, said nothing, and refused to adopt any particular policy. Still, by 1803, the continuing French expansion had begun to alarm him; so, without consulting either his ministers or his private advisers, he arranged to meet Frederick William III of Prussia at Memel, in western Lithuania.

From a personal point of view, the meeting was a great success. The two men liked each other; Alexander, who was much taken by Queen Louise, behaved like an old friend; but when he proposed a Prusso-Russian alliance to guarantee northern Germany against further French inroads, Frederick William refused. For all the pleasant atmosphere of this first attempt at personal diplomacy, the meeting had come to nothing.

It was at this point that one of the emperor's friends, Adam Czartoryski, came up with his "system." What he proposed, in a long memorandum, was that Russia pursue an active foreign policy guided by moral principles; it was to be "benevolent, generous and great . . . [with regard] for the general good of all nations."[5] Part of this "general good," however, implied the regrouping of all Slav nations under Russian tutelage, hardly a benevolent policy, and one most likely to be resisted by Austria (not to mention Turkey). Even more important to Czartoryski, who was a Pole, Poland was to be reunited under Alexander's rule. Quite how Prussia and Austria were to be convinced that they ought to disgorge their shares was never made absolutely clear; but, obviously, the redistribution of land in eastern Europe and the Balkans, where Turkey still governed many Slavs, could not be achieved by negotiation alone. Finally, in order to stop the spread of the French Revolution, Russia was to take the lead in resisting Bonaparte.

That part, at least, of the memorandum impressed Alexander so deeply that he tried to implement it for the rest of his reign. Henceforth, he saw himself as a disinterested arbiter whose actions were motivated solely by the desire to bring about a lasting peace. As to the anti-French actions, it was another half a year before he made up his mind; but then he began to look around for allies against Napoléon.

This search was considerably speeded up by the execution of the duc d'Enghien. Like all Europe, Alexander was aghast at the murder of the young prince, so much so that he ordered his ambassador to make a strong protest. To this Talleyrand answered tartly by pointing out that before blaming France for ensuring its own safety, Russia might have done well to remember the end of the late emperor Paul. No doubt an irresistible gibe, it also infuriated Alexander. As a protest, the court went into mourning. Two hundred thousand troops were put on alert (a singularly meaningless gesture since Russia had no common border with France) and Czartoryski, who was now vice foreign minister, denounced the assassination as "an insult against the whole association of European States and even against humanity itself."[6]

Certainly, international law and the rules of morality had been violated; but as Russia promptly found out, no one cared. Only Turkey and Sweden bothered to join its protest. And when, within two months, Napoléon became emperor, Czartoryski reconsidered: now that France was once again a monarchy, it was bound to stop exporting revolutionary principles. On the other hand, Alexander saw Napoléon's assumption of his title as a cheapening of the imperial dignity. Worse, the new emperor's repeated references to Charlemagne hinted strongly at further French expansion.

In June 1804, Napoléon became emperor; that same month, Alexander made Czartoryski foreign minister. It was not a wise decision. Alexander was not sure just what he wanted, but thought that Czartoryski, as his friend, would help him to find out. Czartoryski, on the other hand, was primarily interested in resurrecting Poland. Having decided that an alliance with France would help him achieve his goal, he recommended approaching Napoléon. Alexander, at this point, began thinking about joining the new coalition that Great Britain was putting together; and Russian foreign policy wobbled back and forth.

Pitt's means and goals, unlike the czar's, were entirely clear. He undertook to finance the new coalition, and to have an army ready for debarkation in northern Germany; he wanted the rest of Europe to bring France back to its 1792 borders, with the left bank of the Rhine going to Prussia. Whether Alexander was prepared to fight France remained, however, very uncertain. "New arguments are necessary to convince the cabinet of St. Petersburg, that by arms only the independence of Europe can be recovered,"[7] Lord Gower, the British ambassador to Russia, wrote to the foreign secretary in February 1805, and he urged offering the czar more generous terms.

Pitt made the offer, and it was accepted. On April 11, Russia and Great Britain signed a convention providing for an allied army of half a million men. Britain was to pay £1,250,000 per hundred thousand men; Austria, Prussia, Sweden, Denmark, Portugal, and Spain were asked to join the coalition; and the war was to be waged against Napoléon, not the French per se. Indeed, the latter would be allowed to choose their government once Napoléon was dethroned. The British ratification of the convention, which had been negotiated by Lord Gower, arrived in Saint Petersburg on June 24, 1805; the formal ceremony took place at the end of July. Great Britain and Russia were now allies; the question was whether anyone would join them.

HOSTILITIES AT LAST

It was not much of a question. Unchastened by his previous defeats, Francis I of Austria was ready to fight again—or, at any rate, his advisers were. The fact that Archduke Charles begged for time in which to complete his reorganization of the army was, if anything, an incentive to do the opposite: Francis was getting rather jealous of his more intelligent brother. In mid July, Austria accepted the Russian war plan; on August 9, it acceded to the Anglo-Russian treaty; and in late August, Russian troops crossed into Galicia, now the Austrian part of Poland, so as to join with the Austrian forces. By November, a full Russian-Austrian alliance had been signed and ratified.

That left Prussia. As a quick look at the map will show, Galicia was a considerable detour if the Russian troops were to move toward the French army; it also seemed highly desirable to have the Prussian army join the coalition; and so Czartoryski applied as much pressure on Berlin as he could. All he got in return was a lot of wavering. It was at this point that Czartoryski had an inspiration: if Russia were to invade Prussia, it could keep for itself the Prussian part of Poland, thus furthering his great goal of Polish reunification. Firmly disregarding the fact that Napoléon was a sufficient enemy, and that fighting both Prussia and France at the same time might be imprudent, the minister asked the czar to invade Prussia. Now it was Alexander's turn to waver. First, he agreed to an invasion of Prussia, and a date was set—September 28; then it occurred to him that, after all, it was perhaps not a good idea to be fighting both France and Prussia, so he canceled the invasion (on September 17) and arranged a meeting with Frederick William III instead. Still, Russian troops were concentrated within ten miles of the Prussian border.

The meeting of the two monarchs, though full of amiabilities, was not likely to be fruitful; but then Napoléon sent his army across Anspach, a Prussian territory in the west of Germany, without Prussian authorization. This was, at the very least, an insulting gesture; it also risked provoking an Austro-Russian preemptive attack against Prussia. The result, on November 3, was the signature of the Convention of Potsdam by Alexander and Frederick William: Prussia undertook to join the coalition provided that it received British subsidies (hardly a problem) and was given Hanover as well. Whatever Alexander might hope, this last condition meant that Prussia intended to stay out of the coalition. Hanover was George III's private possession; and when informed of Prussia's condition, Pitt, who knew the old king well, did not even bother to discuss it with him.

As it turned out, the Prussians knew what they were doing. Just two weeks earlier, an Austrian army commanded by General Mack had been annihilated outside the southern German city of Ulm: it was not a promising sign for the coalition powers. As for Napoléon, he was quite pleased. "I have carried out my plan," he wrote Joséphine on October 19, "I have destroyed the Austrian army . . . I have taken sixty thousand prisoners, a hundred and twenty cannon, more than ninety flags and thirty generals. I will attack the Russians next, they will be crushed."[8]

THE BATTLE OF THE THREE EMPERORS

Napoléon, unlike Francis and Alexander, knew just what he was doing. On December 2, near the little Moravian village of Austerlitz, his army faced the combined forces of Austria and Russia, the latter led by the czar in person. At the end of that afternoon, he wrote Joséphine again:

> The battle of Austerlitz is the finest of all those I have ever fought: forty five flags, more than a hundred and fifty cannon, the ensigns of the Russian Imperial Guard, twenty generals, thirty thousand prisoners and, horrible sight, more than twenty thousand [of the enemy] killed!
>
> The Emperor Alexander, in despair, is returning to Russia. The Emperor of Austria visited my bivouac yesterday . . . We have agreed to make a rapid peace.[9]

Napoléon was not exaggerating. Talleyrand, who was waiting at a nearby castle, noted: "At every moment there came Austrian and Russian flags, messages from the Archdukes, messages from the Emperor of Austria and prisoners bearing the greatest names in that Empire."[10]

It was a huge victory. Austria was crushed; Russia, although it remained in the war, had been humiliatingly defeated; and it had all happened on the first anniversary of Napoléon's coronation. The consequences were immediate. Before the end of the month, Austria had signed the Treaty of Pressburg: it lost its Italian and Istrian territories, as well as some of its possessions in southern Germany. Bavaria and Württemberg, two allies of France, were enlarged and became kingdoms; and Joseph Bonaparte was made king of Naples.

All this from the British point of view was bad enough. Worse yet, Prussia stopped vacillating: it signed a treaty of alliance with France and was given Hanover as a bonus. In London, the fury knew no bounds. As for the rest of Europe, it experienced once again Napoléon's propensity to treat countries as if they were counters in a poker game; only this time, there was no stopping him.

All this left Alexander in a most awkward position. He was still at war with Napoléon, and knew neither how to fight nor how to make peace. Even his foreign minister turned against him. On March 22, 1806, Czartoryski wrote the czar a bitterly reproachful letter: "Your Majesty seems to want to assume alone not only the responsibility for each decision but even its execution down to the least details . . . and to do everything yourself in both military and civil matters. . . . Your Majesty's guiding principle seems to be to follow the first thought that occurs to you without consulting the judgment or the experience of others."[11] Czartoryski was right: what he disregarded, however, was that Alexander had caught on to his foreign minister's Polish obsession and that as a result, he had lost his trust in him.

Never one to give up easily, however, Czartoryski continued to berate his master. In April, he gave him the kind of memorandum that, under a less liberal emperor, would have resulted in the immediate imprisonment of the writer.

> [After the execution of the duc d'Enghien] you believed until the last moment that there would be no war, that Austria would be too fearful to start it and that this would give Russia an excuse to do nothing. . . . Your Majesty allowed your ministers to go ahead because you thought that their policy was based on an eventuality which would not occur. . . . This indecisiveness, which results in half-measures, is the most harmful and the most dangerous . . .
>
> Mankind's abilities are limited. The same person cannot be at the same time an officer, a colonel, a general, a secretary, a minister etc, and a sovereign. . . . If the sovereign wants to do everything and be involved in everything, he will of necessity neglect his own task.[12]

Again Czartoryski was right—which did not endear him to Alexander. He was also willfully disregarding his own part in the recent disasters. No one was surprised when, on June 20, he was dismissed. The czar's indecision continued, however. In a halfhearted attempt to make peace, he sent an envoy to Paris—ostensibly to arrange an exchange of prisoners; in fact, to negotiate—but the envoy failed utterly. Then, as if fighting Napoléon were not enough, Russian troops entered Moldavia, thus beginning a war with Turkey. So far, Alexander had not proved a wiser emperor than his father.

At last, in October, things looked up. Prussia, infuriated by Napoléon's redistribution of territory on the right bank of the Rhine, declared war on France: once again Russia had an ally. As the world quickly discovered, however, Frederick William was even more foolish than Alexander.

In 1805, it had taken Napoléon just over six weeks to defeat the Russians and the Austrians; in 1806, a bare two weeks passed between the Prussian ultimatum to the emperor and their crushing defeat, on October 14, at Jena. Ten days later, the French entered Berlin; on November 27, they were in Warsaw. Never in its history had Prussia been so thoroughly beaten. Still, Frederick William did not give up: on November 3, a Russian-Prussian alliance was signed; and as military operations slowed down during the bitter winter months, the new allies prepared for what they hoped would be their revenge in the spring.

They should have known better. In February, they were attacked by Napoléon near Eylau, in eastern Prussia, and beaten. Then in June, the Russians lost yet another major battle, at Friedland. This time, the consequences were clear: if the war continued, the French army would enter Russian Poland. The Poles could then be expected to rise and join the French; and after that, anything was possible. For Alexander, there was no choice; as for Frederick William, destitute of territory, money, and artillery, all depended on the czar; and so Russia sued for peace.

Although he would not admit it, Napoléon was just as eager for peace. The recent campaign had been exceptionally bloody; it had also failed to follow the usual pattern of a swift French victory followed by a rapid and triumphant treaty; and so Napoléon decided to offer Russia generous terms while at the same time crushing Prussia. On June 21, an armistice was signed, and, four days later, at Tilsit, Alexander, trailing the humiliated Frederick William after him, met Napoléon for the first time.

It was a scene that astonished Europe. On a flower-bedecked raft floating in the middle of the Nemen River, the two emperors met and embraced; then, for the next two weeks, parades, banquets, negotiations, even private conversations filled their time. By the time they were done, Europe had been reorganized. All of Prussian Poland, including Warsaw, became an independent grand duchy run by the French; Prussia lost Hanover and other pieces of territory; Russia recognized Napoléon as emperor and his three brothers as kings (of Naples, Holland, and Westphalia); even more important, it joined the Continental System, the aim of which was to ruin Great Britain by keeping all English goods from entering Europe. Once again, the British-led coalition had collapsed. France, having defeated every one of the major powers, was supreme in Europe.

EUROPEAN EMPIRES

The French empire did not last long. Having made the mistake of invading Russia in 1812, Napoléon was defeated at last, less by enemy forces than the cold of winter. In 1814, ten years after the proclamation of Napoléon as emperor, the Bourbon monarchy was restored and France was back to something very close to its prerevolutionary size. That winter, at the Congress of Vienna, all Europe was reorganized: nothing was left, apparently, of the Revolution's conquests.

Those appearances were deceptive. No matter how hard Alexander I and Metternich, the Austrian chancellor, tried to suppress all progress, they could not prevail. Napoléon had been right after all: the spirit of the Revolution lived on, and so did the demand for democratic reforms.

PART TWO

North America

CHAPTER SIX

Inventing Politics

The United States, in 1800, was very far away from the rest of the world. To the east, it took at least six weeks to cross the Atlantic; to the west, all across the landmass, lay unexplored territory. Politically, too, people in the United States were busy creating a government and a society utterly different from those of their European forebears; and yet there were strong ties to the other continents. The traditional friendship with France endured; commerce with the European nations and the Far East mattered, and so did the slave trade. All through the end of the eighteenth century and the beginning of the nineteenth, tens of thousands of slaves were brought from Africa in U.S., British, and, occasionally, French ships. Many of the states practiced slavery: that was the case, most importantly perhaps, of Virginia, the largest state and the one that gave the Republic two of its first three presidents.

The almost continuous war between France and England also made a difference. American commerce was hampered by the conflict, of course; but it also mattered that the two warring countries each seemed to offer a political model. English order or French democracy: in deciding which was to be adapted to the United States, its citizens found themselves thoroughly involved with Europe.

A Very New Country

The government itself was both soundly established—George Washington's two terms had seen to that—and thoroughly malleable. From 1789 to 1797, the formidably honorable first president had ruled by consensus: he was so popular, so overwhelmingly dedicated to the welfare of the new Union, that almost no one was prepared to criticize him in public. Now John Adams, the second president, veered anxiously from repression to a defense of liberty.

It seemed possible that the new Constitution would be interpreted as creating an aristocratic republic, an England without a king. Yet, at the same time, the most vigorous democratic impulses could be seen across the country, and they seemed to promise a new administration—1800 was an election year—and a shift to the left.

The preceding decade, in fact, had been one in which every precedent had to be set, and a new way of governing was being invented. Liberty, government by elected officials, freedom of speech and of religion, all guaranteed by a brand-new, still untested constitution: France and the United States, in 1791, appeared to have much in common. There were differences, of course: France was a monarchy, even if the king had lost all his power; while the United States was a republic. France was an old country with a tradition of absolute rule and religious intolerance; the United States was the world's most recent nation, and already had a solid tradition of resistance to the wrong kind of authority. Still, the two were allies—France had helped the United States win its independence; and both countries looked forward to the glorious dawn of a new age.

Both the United States and Europe soon discovered, however, that these appearances were deceptive. By 1793, France was engulfed in the Terror while, in Philadelphia, George Washington was beginning his second term. Liberty, it seemed, had taken hold in the United States—though, even there, it still sometimes appeared weak and endangered, dependent on the conscience, on the formidable sense of duty, of the first president of the United States, and on the zeal and virtue of the men who surrounded him.

Thomas Jefferson, then secretary of state, understood this. "It rests now with ourselves to enjoy in peace and concord the blessings of self-government so long denied to mankind," he had written in March 1790, "to shew by example the sufficiency of human reason for the care of human affairs and that the will of the majority . . . is the only sure guardian of the rights of man."[1] There could be disagreement on specific measures, but there was general agreement on some basic principles. Among them was that the will of the majority must be respected; that the powers of the executive must be limited by those of the legislature, and vice versa; that the judiciary must be free from interference by the government; and that the liberties enjoyed by all citizens under the Constitution must be held sacred. As for the men who actually ran the many governments—that of the Union, those of the states and the cities—it was hoped and expected that they would be educated, virtuous, and eager to promote the welfare of all.

Still, even at the beginning, different people had different views. No one quite knew what Washington really thought. The president invariably said as little as he could, but he had made it quite clear that he liked the Constitution, and, once in office, he scrupulously respected the powers of Congress while

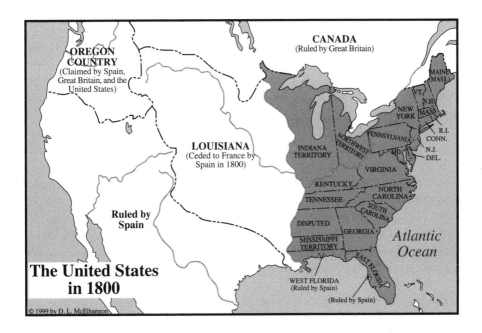

always refusing to suppress dissent. It was a remarkable performance. The president could have carried all before him if he had chosen to do so; instead, he practiced the most scrupulous self-denial and, in doing so, proved that the executive could be effective without being oppressive.

John Adams, his vice president, held quite different views. Because he believed that the British constitution, before it had become corrupted, was the best possible, he thought of the U.S. Constitution as its exact equivalent. The executive was the monarchical branch (and he was not at all sure it was a good idea to have such frequent elections for the presidency), the Senate was the equivalent of the House of Lords, and the House of Representatives that of the Commons. Even so, he, too, believed in the balance of powers, with the House and the Senate checking each other, and a strong, independent executive whose job was to control passions, encourage virtue, and make sure that the system worked.

Adams had explained some of this to Washington shortly after their joint inauguration. "The office [of President]," he had written, "by its legal authority defined in the Constitution, has no equal in the world, excepting those that are held by crowned heads; nor is the royal authority in all cases to be compared to it"; and because he believed in form and ceremony, he went on, "neither dignity nor authority can be supported in human minds . . . without a *splendor* and *majesty* in some degree proportioned to them."[2]

As it happened, Washington, who was in many ways deeply democratic, was enormously majestic in person. People quailed before him as if he had been a king; but he never forgot that he was the elected representative of his fellow citizens. So it was that he could conciliate views as different as those held by three of his principal officials: John Adams, his vice president; Thomas Jefferson, his secretary of state; and Alexander Hamilton, his secretary of the treasury. Invariably, the president sought the advice of his cabinet; invariably, he then decided for himself which policy should be adopted; and that decision was accepted even by those who might have been originally inclined to oppose it. In some ways, in fact, it was all too good to be true: under George Washington, the United States had almost lacked that essential ingredient of a democracy, politics as an integral part of government.

Almost, but not quite. The federal government was tiny: the State Department, whose jurisdiction embraced everything except the military, the Treasury, and the law, had a staff of five, and spent $8,000 a year (Jefferson's salary being $3,500). The Treasury, whose job was to collect indirect taxes throughout the United States (there was no income tax), was significantly larger—its staff was seventy. The War Department, in the 1790s, was sinking into insignificance; and the attorney general took care of the Government's legal cases almost by himself.

That struck Jefferson as just about right. For Hamilton, it was grotesquely insufficient. It must also be said in fairness that Hamilton faced what then seemed the government's knottiest problem: the funding of the debt left over from the War of Independence. Consequently, Hamilton favored a complex system through which the debt could be properly funded—a system not unlike that used in Great Britain, in which specific revenues ensured that interest was reliably paid. It would also tie the government to the banks. Jefferson opposed this, but Washington finally decided that it was necessary; and politics was born in the opposition of the secretaries of state and the treasury.

ALEXANDER HAMILTON: POWER AT THE CENTER

Hamilton and Jefferson disagreed radically over the way the federal government should be financed. The former believed that taxes knit the nation together, the latter that they were the source of corruption and eventual tyranny. In fact, the two men had radically different notions about the role of government in a free society. Jefferson believed in citizen control and a minimum of interference by both the executive and the legislature. The radically decentralized and weakened French government thus struck him as pointing the way. "I look with great anxiety for the firm establishment of the new government in France," he had written his friend George Mason in April 1791, "being perfectly convinced that if it takes place there, it will spread sooner or later all over Europe. . . . I consider the establishment and success of their government as necessary to stay up our own, and to prevent it from falling back to that kind of half-way house, the English constitution."[3]

A gentle movement toward the British constitution, on the other hand, was just what Hamilton had in mind: he liked the power of the aristocracy, of the great merchants and the bankers, and detested the lack of deference already seen in the United States. The son of unmarried parents, Hamilton had arrived in North America as a very young man. He was, a French visitor noted, "very small, and had a very formal manner, very small eyes and something uncertain in his glance . . . He had much wit, watched what he said carefully, but was . . . very brave, disinterested but devoured with ambition, and he admired the laws and government of England as well as its financial system."[4] What struck most people, in fact, was Hamilton's intelligence, his sophistication—and, of course, his ambition. That he felt better qualified than anyone except Washington to govern the United States was certain.

He was not inclined to hide that feeling, but he also had enormous charm. The duc de Liancourt, traveling through New York in 1797, had dinner with Hamilton at a time when the latter had apparently gone back to private life; like so many worldly people, the visitor was promptly charmed: "[Hamilton] united a powerful mind to much boldness and firmness of character. He is a most distinguished attorney, and is very generous. Born poor, he came out poor of his time as Secretary of the Treasury . . . This disinterestedness when it comes to money, rare everywhere, is one of the most universally recognized elements of Mr. Hamilton's character."[5] With all this, however, went a very sharp tongue. At a dinner two years earlier, when Washington was still president, Hamilton held nothing back. Washington, Hamilton explained astringently, "has little wit, knowledge or culture, but a good judgment, much wisdom, a prudence which seems the main element of his character and the guide of his political and private behavior. Secretive without being false, given to anger but thoroughly master of himself, devoted to the welfare and glory of his country, [he is] a faithful republican in all his actions."[6] Predictably, Hamilton added that the government lacked sufficient power to rule the United States properly.

What Hamilton had in mind was not a monarchy, but rather the kind of oligarchy in which property of all kinds has the decisive voice—very much on the English model. The people, he thought, were too ignorant to rule; elections could, to a significant degree, be managed; and those with a true stake in the country would thus, in essence, monopolize power. Because, in many ways, Hamilton was ahead of his time, he was acting on perceived reality instead of political theory. Power, he saw, follows money; but unlike Jefferson, he thought it should.

THE PEOPLE AND THE MOB

Hamilton was right in one respect, at least: money has spoken clearly throughout the history of the Republic. What he did not perceive, however, was that there was a strong opposition to the supremacy of the great interests. The people, he believed, were meant to obey; and when they refused to do so—or, even worse, when they rose against an act of the government—then they became a mob that must be put down, preferably with a little bloodshed. Washington, on the other hand, was extremely reluctant to use force. The law, he knew, must prevail, but the people's grievances should at least be heard; and the government's armed force should look imposing enough to avoid the need actually to use it.

These different positions had become clear in the summer of 1794, on the occasion of the Whiskey Rebellion. Three years earlier, Congress had created a series of excise taxes. They were to generate the revenue necessary for the service of the debt, and one of these taxes applied to whiskey distillers.

Although the liquor tax was small, it was calculated in a way that seemed to hit the small distillers of four counties in western Pennsylvania disproportionately hard. These small farmers found it profitable to sell their grain, after distillation, in the form of whiskey, and so they used their stills on a seasonal basis only. What upset them was that they were taxed on the same basis (the capacity of their stills) as the professional distillers who practiced their trade throughout the year. At the same time, because they lived in what was then the westernmost part of the United States, and because the major distillers tended to be on the East Coast, this new tax struck them as discriminatory both in terms of class and in terms of section. This is, in fact, one of the earliest examples of the poorer West rising against the richer Northeast.

To this was added the fact that many of these farmers were of Scottish origin; and there, the exciseman had been both familiar and hated. In Scotland, it had been a case of the men of the Highlands feeling themselves oppressed by the London government; in Pennsylvania, the farmers resented a system which they saw as serving the eastern moneyed interests. And this all came at a time when the Democratic-Republican Societies had been flourishing.

Partly because clubs had, from the beginning, played a key role in the French Revolution and seemed worth imitating, partly because there were many questions that suddenly seemed worth discussing, these societies had suddenly appeared. Their members were usually non-Federalists—that is to say, people who felt that the federal government should be weak and unobtrusive; they also included very few of the rich and powerful. It was at the meetings of these societies that for the first time, the unanimity of the small town communities no longer seemed like the most desirable good. Politics, in fact, were appearing at what later generations called the grassroots level. Here, all the issues of the day were discussed, and free thought was the rule. These meetings did much to dispel the deference that, at the end of the eighteenth century, was still often felt for the powers that be.

What the excise tax had done, in 1794, was to bring together old resentments, new anger at what was seen as an unfair tax, and the habit of political discussion. Added to all this was the extreme unpopularity of the chief collector; and soon, there was a rising in which several people were killed. Obviously, the federal government could not allow this kind of civil disturbance. Both Washington and Hamilton were agreed about that, but Hamilton thought that troops should be sent in and ordered to attack. Washington decided to gather enough soldiers to frighten the rebels while offering generous terms if the insurrection stopped. It was the right formula: the farmers went back to their fields before the troops had fired a single shot.

Still, the affair had one long-lasting effect: people everywhere in the United States began to think about the proper role of government, about the fairness of taxation and governance, and about the principles of men like Hamilton. None of this mattered while Washington was president: he was not only fair, but seen to be fair. Everyone also understood that he was not hungry for power; and he had the enormous prestige he has rightly kept to this day. What might happen under his successor, though, was an open question.

THE FEDERALISTS: PRO AND ANTI

Despite the many important people who supported Hamilton's financial system, the farmers of western Pennsylvania, and many others throughout the United States, detested it. The United States, in the 1790s, was still a nation without a proletariat; but it already had its share of those who felt no great respect for the upper classes, and said so. It was this group that most disturbed John Adams and his fellow Federalists, and not merely because they admired the English system: they resented and feared those they saw as feckless revolutionaries.

A bald and rotund little man, John Adams not infrequently looked ridiculous—in part because he could be extremely pompous, in part because he was thin-skinned and therefore reacted explosively when he thought he was being slighted. In fact, he was well-read, intelligent, and often fair; he could, on occasion, attain real wisdom. He was, after all, one of the earliest fighters for independence. Thus, despite his foibles, he remained an important figure, and, as such, a real help to Hamilton: together, they were unquestionably the heads of the emerging Federalist Party.

The Federalists, in the early nineties, were a very strong force, but, from the beginning, they were opposed by an equally strong resistance. For these Anti-Federalists, the Revolution had created a new tradition. The United States, far from being an England with a president instead of a king, was a place like no other on earth, the repository of all the best hopes of mankind, and these hopes were not going to be realized by kowtowing to a self-defined aristocracy. Their new republic, they believed, should belong to all the people, and be ruled by all the people. Thomas Jefferson was part of that group, and the paradox was that he was at the same time a populist by conviction and an aristocrat by birth and achievement.

Tall, elegant, with thinning red hair, Jefferson was one of the great masters of English prose. He had created that resounding document, the Declaration of Independence. His speeches, his letters, his state papers are models of style and content; and that was not all. He was also a competent scientist, able to exchange views with his more professional colleagues. He had read more, and better, than almost anyone; he was passionately interested in architecture—Monticello and the University of Virginia are proof of that; and at a time when eloquence was not rare, he dazzled listeners, whether they heard him give a speech or participate in an after-dinner conversation. Then there was the way he lived: although he cared little about dress and was the most informal of men, his house was filled with beautiful furniture and his table set with finely crafted silver; his cellar was full of the best French wines; and all that was done with a naturalness that was the very antithesis of pretension.

It might thus have seemed logical for this refined, cosmopolitan aristocrat, this owner of a great estate in Virginia, to share Hamilton's views; and, indeed, Hamilton reserved for Jefferson the kind of venom the Republicans spouted at Franklin Delano Roosevelt in the 1930s: had the expression been invented, Hamilton would no doubt have called him a traitor to his class. Instead, he contented himself with writing, in a New York newspaper: "There is always a first time when characters studious of artful disguises are unveiled; when the visor of stoicism is plucked from the brow of the epicurean; when the plain guard of Quaker simplicity is stripped from the concealed voluptuary; when Caesar, *coily refusing* the proffered diadem is seen to be Caesar rejecting the trappings but grasping the substance of imperial domination."[7]

Those, in 1793, were strong words. What Jefferson wrote about Hamilton was no more complimentary, even if it was more private. When he was thinking of resigning as secretary of state to return to Monticello, Jefferson wrote Washington: "I will not suffer my retirement to be clouded by the slanders of a man whose history, from the moment at which history can stoop to notice him, is a tissue of machinations against the liberty of the country which has not only received and given him bread, but heaped its honors on his head."[8] And this came just a week after another letter to the president in which Jefferson explained that Hamilton's system "flowed from principles adverse to liberty [and was] calculated to undermine and demolish the republic, by creating an influence of his department over the members of the legislature."[9]

There was the rub. Jefferson wanted as small a Treasury Department as possible. Hamilton, instead, had created a large organization and pushed through the bill creating the first Bank of the United States. Even worse, from Jefferson's point of view, the secretary of the treasury had spun a complex financial web connecting the Treasury to all the major moneyed interests. This, Jefferson felt, had a number of frightening consequences: one was that the government's financial arrangements were so intricate as to defy understanding by nonspecialists, and that made for a variety of potential abuses. Another was that the government (and the secretary of the treasury) were now in a position to affect the financial position of many members of Congress—or even to bribe them outright. And although, as far as we know, Hamilton bribed no one, there was obviously money to be made by remaining friendly to him.

Perhaps because Jefferson was so bad at handling money—he died deeply in debt—he distrusted those who understood how to make large profits based on financial maneuvers. Hamilton therefore struck him as far more dangerous than Adams, whose integrity he trusted. Hamilton believed in "the necessity of force or corruption to govern men,"[10] Jefferson eventually concluded; and as he tried to save the Republic from what he saw as a grave danger, he became one of the leaders of the Republican (or Democratic-Republican) Party. The name itself meant exactly the opposite of what it means today: the Republicans in 1800 were liberal and progressive, the left-wing party.

The very notion of party seemed, at this time, new and possibly reprehensible. In the small, tightly knit preindustrial society of the earlier eighteenth century, unanimity had seemed the only right way to run public affairs. The common good must rule, it was held, and it was easy to decide what the common good ought to be. Belonging to a party smacked of faction; it carried a denial of that all-desirable unanimity. For someone like Jefferson, therefore, belonging to a party was a very grave step. It was a step he took only because he felt that the Republic was in danger.

In 1792, the parties were still mere embryos; even so, their existence seemed worrisome. Happily, one man was unquestionably above party, and he thus seemed more needed than ever. When Washington considered retiring at the end of his first term, Jefferson had begged him to stay: "I consider your continuance at the head of affairs as of the last importance. The confidence of the whole union is centred in you. Your being at the helm, will be more than an answer to every argument which can be used to alarm and lead the people in any quarter into violence or secession. North and South will hang together if they have you to hang on."[11]

For Washington, who had a keen sense of duty, and no ambition left, remaining in office had meant a real sacrifice. To no one's surprise, he put country before self, and, having been begged to accept a second term by literally everyone, he stayed and was again elected unanimously. Then, greatly to his relief, Jefferson made the same effort and remained at the State Department. And John Adams, who had complained, in a phrase much quoted since then, that the vice presidency was "the most insignificant office that ever the invention of man contrived or his imagination conceived,"[12] also stayed where he was. Perhaps that was not as hard as he seemed to imply: there was, after all, the hope that four years hence he might succeed to the presidency.

Had the government been able to proceed as it had done in Washington's first term, concerning itself mostly with domestic matters, all would have been well; but from 1793 on, this had no longer been possible. Not even distance could shield the United States from the great events tearing Europe as a result of the French Revolution.

The first and most pressing matter was the safety of North American trade: the government, most of whose income consisted of customs duties, depended on it; so did the merchants, the bankers—all those newly rich and important citizens to whom Hamilton listened. There were, in fact, two radically different views of what the economic system should be. One, espoused by Jefferson and the Anti-Federalists, said that the soundest base for a free government was a large group of farmers owning their own land: they worked hard and created a modest, but sound, prosperity; they had a personal stake in the country and its government; and their very number made corruption virtually impossible. Hamilton and the Federalists, on the other hand, were convinced that prosperity depended on trade—the freer, the better. Merchants were, therefore, to be encouraged: as, by their dealings, they created capital, both they and the government grew richer. The other key need, according to Hamilton, was a properly funded public debt. By appropriating revenues produced by reliable sources of taxation, the government made it possible to trade the debt in the form of bonds; it thus mobilized the nation's capital and added to the general prosperity. Those taxes had, in fact, been enacted: they consisted principally of customs duties and, to a smaller extent, of excise taxes. The excise on liquor was, of course, the one that had caused the insurgency in western Pennsylvania.

The benefits of this system went, according to Hamilton, well beyond its economic results: it would unite the nation, and by enriching it, it would also make it powerful. The newly created Bank of the United States was a symptom of this new country-wide outlook, as was the close relationship between the Treasury and the new capitalist class of merchants, manufacturers, and bankers. Of course, there was an essential prerequisite: trade with the rest of the world must be free, that is, undisturbed by war or any sort of hostility with the principal trading partners of the United States. In 1800, the United States' principal trading partner was none other than Great Britain. Thus, Hamilton's economic and financial system had a major political consequence, a close friendship with France's principal enemy.

For Jefferson and his friends, indeed for all the Republicans, therefore, Hamilton, Adams, and the Federalists looked like a present danger to the Republic because they were in cahoots with a class of men able (and presumably willing) to corrupt officeholders; they wanted the government of the United States to favor rich, unprincipled traders at the expense of the hardworking, honest farmers; and they were friends of Great Britain, from whom the nation had recently, and at great cost, won its independence. Added to all this was a corollary: if you were pro-Britain, you must also be in favor of the aristocratic-authoritarian system that prevailed there.

The real situation was, however, not as simple as either party might have liked. Instead of happily trading with the United States, the British, as part of the war with France, began seizing neutral ships, their cargoes, and their crews, thus causing much damage to U.S. merchants. Happily, Great Britain was not eager to make war on the United States; on their side, the United States was aware that the new country lacked, among other things, an effective navy.

Consequently, a long and difficult negotiation started. Threats alternated with concessions, and much patience was needed—in particular by John Jay, the U.S. representative in London. Meanwhile in the United States, many were outraged because the government was talking instead of shooting. In 1795, Jay's Treaty was duly signed; it ended the hostilities without fully compensating the United States, thus giving each party some of what it wanted, and it proved, in the long run, to be reasonably fair and effective. It was, of course, strongly supported by Hamilton, who wanted to remain friends with Great Britain, and opposed by many Republicans, not least because it seem to invalidate some of the commercial clauses in the long-standing treaties with France, and to give away far too much to Britain. "An infamous act," the now-retired Jefferson called it, "which is nothing more than a treaty of alliance between England and the Anglomen of this country against the legislature and people of the United States."[13] Such as it was, however, it seemed satisfactory to the president, and, after much debate, it was duly passed by the Senate—more, perhaps, because a few senators trusted Washington than because they really approved of the treaty.

That left the other major power in Europe. The relationship between France and the United States was the result of their alliance during the War of Independence. The two countries had been bound by a treaty of friendship signed, on the French side, by Louis XVI; but then, in September 1792, France had become a republic. Should the United States recognize the new government? And were the treaties that bound the United States to France still valid? To these questions, both Washington and Jefferson had answered affirmatively. "We surely cannot deny to any nation," the latter wrote, "the right whereon our own government is founded, that every one may govern itself under whatever form it pleases, and change these forms at its own will, and that it may transact its business with foreign nations through whatever organ it thinks proper, whether king, convention, assembly. . . . The will of the nation is the only thing essential to be regarded."[14]

It is hard to realize, at the end of the twentieth century, how new these words sounded just two hundred years ago. In a world of monarchies by divine right, the notion that people might choose whatever form of government they liked, and that it would be legitimate just because they had chosen it, sounded terrifyingly new—everywhere, that is, except in the United States. Not a single European power recognized the French Republic; the United States did so promptly.

For a while, Jefferson had gone even further. Before the Terror was fully unleashed, but after many nobles and clerics had been massacred in the Paris prisons in September 1792, he commented: "In the struggle which was necessary, many guilty persons fell without the forms of trial, and with them some innocents. These I deplore as much as anybody, and shall deplore some of them to the day of my death. But I deplore them as I should have done had they fallen in battle . . . The liberty of the whole earth was depending on the issue of the contest, and was ever such a prize won with so little innocent blood?"[15] Soon after this was written, the innocent blood began to be shed far more abundantly; but already the implication seemed clear. What applied to France might also be true in the United States. Violent revolution there might encourage violent upheaval here; and as Adams and Hamilton, horror-stricken, had contemplated that possibility, they had become strongly anti-French.

Much as he had approved the coming of the republic in France, however, Jefferson had opposed any form of support to it. The war in Europe, he felt, should be no concern of the United States. He hoped that the French would win; he would have thought it catastrophic for his own country to join them. As for the Federalists, they came to the same conclusion even though they had very different sympathies: they hoped that England would win; many would have applauded the restoration of the constitutional monarchy in France, as it had existed in 1791 and 1792. None, however, at least before 1797, had wanted to declare war on the French.

By the time Jay's Treaty was in place, Jefferson had become a private citizen. Having postponed his resignation once, he had decided, in the course of 1793, that he would go by the end of the year. "The motion of my blood no longer keeps time with the tumult of the world," he wrote his friend James Madison in June. "It leads me to seek for happiness in the lap and love of my family, in the society of my neighbors and my books, in the wholesome occupation of my farms and my affairs, in an interest or affection in every bud that opens, in every breath that blows around me." In saying this, he was speaking the truth: he longed to go back to his building at Monticello; he wanted— and, for financial reasons, needed—to improve the cultivation of his lands.

Besides, he saw himself, perhaps with a little exaggeration, as "worn down by my labours from morning to night, and day to day; knowing them as fruitless to others as they are vexatious to myself, committed singly in desperate and eternal contest against a host [the Federalists] who are systematically undermining public liberty and prosperity."[16] And so, on December 31, 1793, he had resigned.

For quite a while, he let it be thought that he really meant to give up politics; in reality, he retained a passionate interest in what was happening, and even funded a Republican newspaper. By 1795, he was already telling his many friends just what he thought of people and events. We have seen how deeply he disapproved of Jay's Treaty; shortly before it passed the Senate, he wrote Madison: "Hamilton is really a colossus to the anti-republican [i.e., Federalist] party. Without numbers, he is a host unto himself. We have had only middling performance to oppose him. In truth when he comes forward, there is no one who can meet him."[17]

Of course, there was someone, none other than Jefferson himself, and he was fully aware of it: if Hamilton were not to win an easy victory, then Jefferson must drop his pretense of having renounced politics. Nor was he alone in thinking so. For many U.S. citizens, it seemed obvious that Jefferson was the right man to succeed Washington.

THE ANGUISH OF THE HEIR APPARENT

Presidential elections, in the early years of the Republic, were decidedly odd occasions, if only because the candidates steadfastly refused to admit that they were, in fact, candidates. Instead, they disclaimed all interest in the contest, said as little as possible, and left all the electioneering to their friends. Then there were the actual mechanics of the election. Before a constitutional amendment was finally passed to remedy the situation, there was no such thing as a ticket listing presidential and vice presidential candidates. Instead, whoever got the greatest number of votes in the electoral college was elected president; the runner-up, whether or not he belonged to the same party, became vice president. Finally, the electors themselves were chosen in ways that varied from state to state, thus making predictions extremely difficult. Not all states, for instance, had a presidential election as such: in New York and elsewhere, it was the state legislature that chose the electors; and that legislature, in turn, had often been elected as much as a year earlier.

None of that had really mattered in 1788 or in 1792: as long as Washington made himself available, everyone voted for him. Thus, in 1796, if the great man chose to retire, the first contested presidential election in the history of the United States would take place. But would Washington go? As John Adams had watched in anguish, all through the end of 1795 and the beginning of

1796, it seemed increasingly likely that he would. Even if he did, Adams kept wondering, would he really choose his vice president to succeed him? At least, from the latter's point of view, there was one favorable development. "The [cabinet] offices," he wrote Abigail, his wife, "are once more filled. [Washington had had great difficulty in finding replacements for Jefferson and Hamilton, who had also resigned.] But how differently filled than when Jefferson, Hamilton, Jay, &c were here! The present incumbents, not being much thought of, or at least talked of, for President, vice-president, or substitutes for both, the public may be less disposed to fight for or against them."[18]

That had no doubt been reassuring. Even more reassuring, if never mentioned, was the fact that Hamilton was not, at this point, a contender. Most reassuring of all, Washington, in the spring of 1796, announced that he would not accept a third term; after which he let it be understood that Adams would be a worthy successor. That, in fact, was essential: John Adams was not a popular man, except in Massachusetts and perhaps Connecticut. Without Washington's endorsement, he could hardly have been a viable candidate.

We know what Adams was thinking because of his constant communication with Abigail, who, for much of the time, remained at their farm in Quincy, Massachusetts, while he was in Philadelphia; and there was nothing Adams would not share with the woman whom he invariably addressed as "my dearest friend." Indeed, it is in his relationship with Abigail that John Adams was most truly himself. All his pride, his frequent vanity, his obstinacy, and his tendency to whine come through clearly in his letters to her; but so do his integrity, his genuine devotion to the country's welfare, his intelligence, his culture, and even, on occasion, a part of his personality that was utterly concealed from the rest of the world—his sense of humor.

Because so much about Adams was prissy and irritating, it is easy to forget that he could, on occasion, laugh at himself, as evidenced by a letter he wrote to Abigail in January 1796:

> Yesterday, I came to the Senate as usual on Monday morning pleasing my imagination and my heart with the hope and expectation of a letter from—my dearest friend. No letter for the Vice-President! says Matthew.
>
> All day in bad humor. Dirty weather—wet walking—nothing good—nothing right.
>
> The poor post-offices did not escape. It was some blunder—some carelessness of theirs—in Philadelphia, New York or Boston.
>
> Or perhaps Mam is sick—oh dear! Fever and ague! Thus peevishly, fretfully and unphilosophically was yesterday passed. Yet, to divert it, I read a number of books in Cowper's Homer and smoked I know not how many cigars.[19]

That endearing side of Adams's personality would have greatly startled most of those who thought they knew him. About his patriotism and his integrity, even his political opponents had no doubt. Jefferson and Adams were old, if not very close, friends; now they found themselves on different sides of most issues; yet Jefferson could write him, in February 1796: "I am sure from the honesty of your heart, you join me in detestation of the corruption of the English government, and that no man on earth is more incapable than yourself of seeing that copied among us, willingly."[20] In fact, Adams disliked Hamilton, and made a sharp distinction, as Hamilton did not, between the ideal English government (which had ceased existing some ninety years earlier) and its current, decadent form. And often though he might draw analogies between the British and U.S. constitutions, he was an ardent defender of the latter. Hamilton, on the other hand, had begun to find the Constitution inconvenient, and often mulled the possibility of transforming it so as to produce a more centralized, more authoritarian, less democratic system.

This represented a major problem for Adams. He could not be elected without the support of the Federalist Party, to which he belonged, or that of Hamilton, its brightest star. At the same time, Hamilton was eager to see Adams succeed Washington, largely because he thought so little of Adams, and since he was not himself ready to become president, the next best thing was to have a president who, willy-nilly, would follow Hamiltonian policies. This, Hamilton felt sure, he could induce Adams to do. There were three major reasons for this belief: first, Hamilton knew he could think and talk rings around Adams; second, he overestimated Adams's admiration for England; and third, he assumed (rightly, as it turned out) that Adams would retain the secretaries of state, treasury, and war currently in office. All three were staunch Hamiltonians, and they could be relied on to push whichever policies their leader favored. Further, Hamilton counted on two facts: Adams disliked Philadelphia and spent as little time there as possible, which would give his cabinet a far freer hand than it had had under Washington; and he could, on occasion, be rather lazy, thus again helping to transfer power away from himself.

For Adams, who had not yet realized how contemptuously Hamilton thought of him, the situation thus looked very promising. The Federalists then decided to have a southerner for vice president: Thomas Pinckney could be expected to rally votes in that section of the country. None of that became official until Washington delivered his Farewell Address on September 19. Just six days earlier, the most widely read of the Republican papers, the *Philadelphia Aurora,* had set the tone for the campaign: "It requires no talent at divination to decide who will be candidate for the chair," it announced. "THOMAS JEFFERSON and JOHN ADAMS will be the men and whether we shall have at the head of our executive a steadfast friend to the Rights of the People, or an advocate for hereditary power and distinctions, the people of the United States are soon to decide."[21]

This was certainly less than fair to Adams; but what about Jefferson? Was the man who had apparently renounced politics really a candidate? Of course, the Republicans pressured him for all they were worth, not least because, in their view, Jefferson was the only member of the party who could be elected. Madison, Monroe, and most of Jefferson's friends also begged him to run. More important, however, was what he saw as the danger to free institutions.

> In place of that noble love of liberty and republican government which carried us triumphantly thro' the war, an Anglican, monarchical and aristocratical party has sprung up . . . Against us are the Executive, the Judiciary, two out of three branches of the Legislature, all the officers of the government, all who want to be officers, all timid men who would prefer the calm of despotism to the boisterous sea of liberty, British merchants and Americans trading on British capital, speculators and holders in the banks and public funds.[22]

Clearly, this was an unbearable situation for the man who had crafted the Declaration of Independence. As for the corruption he described, all those people who wanted office, all those speculators, it was just what he had seen in France in the late 1780s, and he was determined that this new country would not repeat the errors of the old. All this was just enough to prevent him from withdrawing his name: he took no action, and that allowed his followers to campaign for him.

Even so, Jefferson had many reasons why he hoped he would not actually win. It was not just that he wanted to remain at Monticello; it seemed likely that the deteriorating relationship between France and the United States was about to produce an explosion, and this Francophile was not the man to lead a war against France, especially if it resulted in an alliance with Great Britain. "I know that no man will bring out of that office [of the president] the reputation which carries him into it," he wrote his friend Edward Rutledge. "The honey moon would be as short in that case as in any other, and its moments of ecstasy would be ransomed by years of torment and hatred."[23]

The French, or at least Adet, their minister to the United States, were in fact doing their best to influence the election, thus infuriating many voters. Convinced that the United States was on the verge of a second upheaval, Adet tried to strengthen what he saw as the rising revolutionary element: he announced that henceforth the French would treat U.S. merchant ships as the British had been treating them before Jay's Treaty. He then went on to denounce the treaty as a violation of the alliance of 1778, upon which he announced that he was suspending himself until the United States had adopted a policy more acceptable to France. Typically, however (Adet was not very bright), he did all this *after* the electors had been chosen; and there is no evidence that the latter were influenced one way or the other.

Indeed, the process by which the electors were chosen was such that until they actually met, no one could tell what was really happening. All voters had to list two candidates, one for president, one for vice president; and to complicate it all further, no one could vote for more than one candidate from his own state. All through this, both Jefferson and Adams preserved a dignified silence while attacks were made on them—they were, as Jefferson wrote Adams seventeen years later, "the passive objects of public discussion."[24]

As late as the middle of December 1796, it was still impossible to tell who (if anyone) had won. Adams had no doubt as to what he wanted, nor did Jefferson; but it was not the same thing. When it looked as if both he and Adams might have the same number of electoral votes so that the election would be thrown into the House of Representatives, Jefferson wrote Madison: "I pray you and authorize you fully to solicit on my behalf that Mr. Adams may be preferred. He has always been my senior from the commencement of our public life, and the expression of the public will being equal, this circumstance ought to give him the preference."[25] He meant it. Three weeks before, he had written Thomas Randolph, his son-in-law, to tell him just how much he hoped he would not become president.

It was only at the end of December that the last tallies came in, and, just barely, they made Jefferson's instructions redundant. The vote ran as follows: Adams: 71; Jefferson: 68; Pinckney: 59; Burr (whom the Republicans had chosen for the vice presidency): 30. Adams was president, Jefferson, vice president, an odd situation since they belonged to opposite parties and backed opposite policies. For Jefferson, it was all eminently bearable: he hoped that Adams would shed some of his Anglophilia, and that promises of support for the next election might wean him away from Hamilton. Adams himself took a very different view: he intended to remain civil to Jefferson, but mistrusted him utterly, and resented having him as vice president. As for Hamilton, he wrote Rufus King, the U.S. minister to Great Britain, and a High Federalist:

> Mr. Adams is President, Mr. Jefferson is Vice-President; our Jacobins [the word taken from the French to describe the extreme left] say they are well pleased, and that the *lion* and the *lamb* are to lie down together. Mr. Adams' *personal* friends talk a little in the same way. "Mr. Jefferson is not half so ill a man as we have been accustomed to think of him. There is to be a united, vigorous administration." Skeptics like me look forward to the event, willing to hope, but not prepared to believe. If Mr. Adams has *vanity*, 'tis plain a plot has been laid to take hold of it.[26]

There was, in fact, such a plot—but it was Hamilton's, not Jefferson's. For the next four years, the new vice president chaired the Senate, collected his salary of $5,000 a year, and remained utterly remote from the administration.

In the meantime, until March 4, 1797, Washington was still president; and Adams, whose most cherished ambition had just been fulfilled, proceeded to whine away the time. On December 30, he moaned:

> I have made some inquiries concerning horses and carriages and find that a common chariot of the plainest sort cannot be had under 1200 dollars, and if you go to a little more elegance and ornament, you must give 1500. The president has a pair of horses to sell, one nine, the other ten years old, for which he

asks a thousand dollars. . . . The plenty of paper [money] has unsettled everything. Nothing has a price. Everyone asks and everyone cheats as much as he
can, I think.[27]

He was right, at least in part: the United States was going through a period of
inflation, and Philadelphia was by far the most expensive of cities. Still, the
president's salary was $25,000—not worth as much as when Washington had
taken office, but a very considerable sum nonetheless.

Of course, the crux of the problem was that the president was provided
with neither house, nor carriage, nor servants, nor, indeed, a single secretary.
This had not mattered so much for Washington, who was a rich man and could
afford a considerable amount of display. The Adamses, who were land rich and
cash poor, would obviously not be able to duplicate Mrs. Washington's lavish
hospitality. John knew it. Their future, he informed Abigail in early in February
1797,

> appear[s] every day worse and worse. House rent at twenty seven hundred dol-
> lars a year, fifteen hundred dollars for a carriage, one thousand for one pair of
> horses, all the glasses, ornaments, kitchen furniture, the best chairs, settees,
> plateaus &c, to purchase, all the china, delph or wedgwood, glass and crockery
> of every sort to purchase and not a farthing probably will the House of Repre-
> sentatives allow, though the Senate have voted a small addition. All the linen
> besides. I shall not pretend to keep more than one pair of horses for a carriage,
> and one for a saddle. Secretaries, servants, wood, charities, which are demanded
> as rights, and the million dittos, present such a prospect as is enough to dis-
> gust anyone.[28]

It was all more than enough to upset His Rotundity, as he was being dubbed.
Still, not even the frightful difficulties facing him had made him contemplate
resigning the presidency.

As it turned out, the Adamses managed to find a house, furnish it, and
entertain in it—a little stiffly, perhaps, but adequately. Far more worrying was
the problem with France. Even before his inauguration, the president-elect
was trying to find a solution for it and, as usual, worrying a great deal.

The problem was as simple as it was intractable. The Directoire, which
paid attention to the United States rarely if at all, typically combined bombast
and inefficiency. As a punishment for Jay's Treaty, it abrogated, without prior
negotiation, the clause of the treaty of 1778 which provided that free ships
make free goods and that, therefore, neutral ships—those of the United States,
for instance—could carry whatever goods they chose, even those belonging to
a non-neutral nation. With the abrogation of that clause, British goods on U.S.
ships could now be seized; and since Great Britain was, far and away, the main
trading partner of the United States, this, in turn, subjected U.S. merchants to

ruinous losses. Then the Directoire went a major step further: it demanded that all American ships carry a certified list of the crew; without that list, the ship could be seized. And since, naturally, most U.S. ships had no such list, the French proceeded to seize a number of them.

Obviously something had to be done. "I have reflected . . . on the idea of an extraordinary mission to France," Hamilton wrote Washington on January 22, "and notwithstanding the objections, I rather incline to it under some shape or other. . . . The best form of the thing, in my view, is a commission including three persons."[29] What Hamilton did not know is that at just about this time, the Directoire proceeded to serve an expulsion order on Charles Pinckney, the U.S. minister to France: it was not only that the U.S. government had thus been insulted, there was not even any contact between the two countries.

Adams himself saw firm resistance as the only solution. "We have imprudently gone too far in our approbation of [the French Revolution]," he wrote Elbridge Gerry, one of the candidates for the three-man commission proposed by Hamilton and promptly confirmed by the president-elect, "and adopted by sympathy too much of her enthusiasm in it. . . . Our weak ideas and sensations of gratitude have led us into the fundamental error of taking too large a share of interest and sympathy in it."[30] Whether he was right or not, it still remained that the United States urgently needed to stop the depredations of French privateers, that it did not have an adequate navy, and that negotiations with the Directoire were the only way to end the crisis.

As February passed into March, Adams had continued to worry, and to listen to Hamilton's advice as passed through the secretary of state, Timothy Pickering. The attempted solution, therefore, was to be as much Hamilton's as his own.

CHAPTER SEVEN

Quasi-War and Dangerous Aliens

PARTY GOVERNMENT in the United States was an innovation. Until 1797 (and, indeed, for a while after that), the theory had been that all decent men would agree on what was good for the nation. Now, good men disagreed violently about the way the government should function, about its relationship to the electorate, and about most of its policies. This never stopped puzzling and horrifying John Adams, in part because he still believed in the theory, in part because he invariably saw dissent as factious. It was, however, during his presidency that most U.S. citizens learned that democracy means disagreement, that campaigns lend themselves to exaggeration, and that consensus is normally an unattainable ideal.

Thus, in the late nineties, as the bitterest of accusations were traded back and forth, and as predictions of doom multiplied, the citizens of the United States learned the practice of democracy. They also discovered that many of their choices were determined by outside events: here, too, the war between France and England forced the world to come together. As Jefferson pointed out, most U.S. citizens were either pro-French or pro-English.

A NEW ADMINISTRATION

At noon on March 4, 1797, in the crowded chamber of the House of Representatives in Philadelphia, an extraordinary event had taken place. For the first time in the history of the Republic, power was passed from an outgoing president to his successor. The atmosphere was solemn, made even more so by the majesty that, as usual, radiated from George Washington. Tall, solemn, dressed in black, his hair curled and powdered, the general handed his powers back to the nation that had chosen him as its leader in war and peace. Then, as he

John Adams, second president of the United States. His was not an easy period of office. *(Portrait File, Miriam and Ira D. Wallach Division of Art, Prints and Photographs, The New York Public Library, Astor, Lenox and Tilden Foundations)*

watched, John Adams took the oath of office. The new president had done his best to fit the part: wearing a pearl-colored suit, with powdered hair, sword, and cockaded hat, he looked and sounded solemn. As for the new vice president, the most fashionable of the three, he was wearing a long blue frock coat.

"A solemn scene it was indeed," John reported to Abigail, "and it was made more affecting to me by the presence of the General [Washington], whose countenance was as serene and unclouded as the day. He seemed to me to enjoy a triumph over me. Methought I heard him say: 'Ay! I am out and you fairly in! See which of us will be the happiest.' When the ceremony was over, he came and made me a visit, and cordially congratulated me."[1]

It was just like Adams to complain when he had achieved his highest ambition. Then, in his inaugural speech, he did more of the same. On the whole, it suited the solemnity of the occasion. It was long, vague, dignified; but even so, it did contain a few carefully pointed attacks on the Republicans. The new president declared,

> We should be unfaithful to ourselves if we should ever lose sight of the danger to our liberties, if anything partial or extraneous should infect the purity of our free, fair, virtuous and independent elections. If an election is to be determined by a majority of a single vote, and that can be procured by a party through artifice or corruption, the government may be the choice of a party, for its own ends, not of the nation, for the national good. If that solitary suffrage can be obtained by foreign nations, by flattery or by menaces . . . the government may not be the choice of the American people but of foreign nations.[2]

No one in the audience that day could doubt that Adams was referring to France or that his three-vote plurality rankled; and it was just as clear that he was vehemently anti-French. Frequently, however, Adams's behavior turned out to be more prudent than his words. An excitable, irritable little man, he often spoke sharply and went to verbal extremes; but then he usually cooled down and, having done so, found himself returning to the key principle of his political philosophy, that of balance.

It was this notion of balance that endeared the (uncorrupted) British constitution to him: a strong executive (the Crown) balanced by a strong legislature (Parliament); a strong aristocracy (in the House of Lords) balanced by a strong voice of the people (the House of Commons); a strong government balanced by a strong judiciary which would defend the common law and the people's liberties. This ideal applied also in the United States, to the way Adams expected the different branches of the government to function, but also to the kind of leadership due from the president. We in the twentieth century expect the presidency to be, in Theodore Roosevelt's words, a bully pulpit. This would have horrified Adams: he thought the president should hold the balance between extremes of policy, carefully preventing excesses on any side.

This mostly passive conception was not an easy one to implement. Parties usually want their man in office to be a clarion for their views; people want to see their ideas triumph. Having the president ensuring that this would not really happen is no recipe for popularity: it was, however, what Adams saw as patriotism. Unfortunately for him, he could hardly bear to be criticized; and so, from March 4 on, he had much misery in store. Indeed, he was already complaining to Abigail the very next day. "All the Federalists seem afraid to approve anybody but Washington," he moaned. "The Jacobin papers damn with faint praise, and undermine with misrepresentation and insinuation."[3] All this after exactly one day in office! And within two weeks, doom was clearly at hand: "I see a scene of ambition beyond all my former suspicions or imaginations; an emulation which will turn our government topsy-turvy," he wrote Abigail. "At the next election, England will set up for Jay or Hamilton, and France, Jefferson, and all the corruption of Poland will be introduced; unless the American spirit should rise and say, we will have neither John Bull nor Louis Baboon."[4]

When, however, he was not complaining, Adams tried to govern. There was, for instance, the three-man mission to France: everyone agreed that it should go, but who were the three men to be? The day before his inauguration, Adams asked Jefferson to take one of the places. Within twenty-four hours, Jefferson had turned him down—in part because he genuinely did not want to travel so far, in part because the job was below the dignity of a vice president, but mostly because he saw the offer as a trap: no matter what the results of the mission, he would be blamed for its shortcomings. In the end, all three men selected were Federalists: no Republican wanted to put himself in the position of having to defend Jay's Treaty to the French. And so Elbridge Gerry, John Marshall (the future Chief Justice), and Charles C. Pinckney were chosen.

CONFLICTS AND ALLIANCES

That was only a first step. On March 22, Hamilton issued his instructions to the secretaries of war and of state: "Increase the revenues vigorously," he wrote James McHenry, "and provide naval forces for *convoys* . . . Form a provisional army of 25,000 men . . . or do as much of all this as you can."[5] It is perhaps a little startling to find these orders coming, not from the president, but from an attorney resident in New York: now that Adams was safely in place, Hamilton clearly intended to set policy himself. As he explained patronizingly to his friend Rufus King: "I believe there is no danger of want of firmness in the Executive. If he is not ill-advised, he will not want prudence. I mean that he is himself disposed to a *prudently firm* course."[6] Since all the advice Adams was receiving from his cabinet was precisely what Hamilton wanted him to hear, there was little chance of his being "ill-advised." Indeed, by March 30, Adams informed his friend Henry Knox that war with France was becoming a real possibility.

That notion was far more startling than it might seem. Even if the United States had declared war on France, it is difficult to see just what it would have done next. The French had a navy, the United States really did not; the French were involved in a European war, and therefore highly unlikely to attempt a descent on the United States; and the United States was in no position to send an expeditionary force to invade France. That left the West Indies. But while

France had colonies there, garrisoned by a small armed force, their internal situation was so unsettled and the British navy so threatening that there was no possibility of attack from that quarter, either. As for the United States, it was in no position to conquer Martinique. What remained were the French depredations on U.S. shipping; and they could be stopped by means far short of all-out war.

Whatever he might say in his frequent moments of irritation, Adams knew all this: in the end, his policies were based on reality and what he perceived (often accurately) as the good of the country. For Hamilton, however, the situation was radically different. Of course, he wanted to restore the safety of U.S. shipping—that was the prime objective of many solid backers of his party. It was his own as well: only if commerce flourished would the United States become the strong nation ruled by men of fortune for which he yearned. Even more important, however, was what a war might bring about: an alliance with England and a reorganization of the government. With higher taxes and revenues, with a twenty-five-thousand-man army and a real navy, the power of the federal government would be greatly increased; its decisions would affect many more areas of the nation's life; and centralization would at last begin. Besides, the army could be used to repress dissent. Thus, from the start of the new administration, a gulf divided Adams and Hamilton; but Hamilton was clever enough to proceed incrementally and indirectly through the cabinet, men in whose loyalty Adams believed. What remained to be seen was how far Adams could be driven.

In the meantime, the president was discovering that having power meant making enemies. "The friends of my youth are generally gone," he lamented, "the friends of my political life are chiefly departed; of the few that remain, some have been found, on the late occasion, weak, envious, jealous and spiteful, humiliated and mortified and duped enough by French finesse and Jacobinical rascality, to show it to me and to the world."[7] The man Adams particularly had in mind was Jefferson, of course: a disagreement on policy was, he considered, the equivalent of a betrayal.

Jefferson, on his part, made an effort to be more positive toward Adams; but just as Adams was convinced that Jefferson had been duped by the French, so Jefferson was convinced (with every appearance of reason) that Adams was being co-opted by Hamilton's henchmen—that is, by his own cabinet. That being the case, what seemed to become increasingly clear, to Jefferson and to his fellow Republicans, was that they were watching an English plot unfold. By May 13, Jefferson was already explaining to Elbridge Gerry that the English had a virtual monopoly of trade and finance; that their agents were in positions of power; and that the takeover was well under way. He was wrong, of course: Hamilton was certainly both powerful and pro-English, but that was about as far as it went. Still, the Republicans, faced with what they saw as a kind of cancellation of the American Revolution, naturally decided to fight.

They had two problems, though: they lacked a majority in Congress, and the Directoire continued to insult the United States, thus making France highly unpopular.

For Adams, at least, the solution consisted in doing something, but not too much: that is what he recommended to Congress at the opening of its special session on May 18. After reporting the refusal of the French government to receive Pinckney, he recommended measures to protect commerce, strengthen the navy, and reorganize the militia—all mild enough, really. For Jefferson and his friends, this was nothing short of warmongering, and they said it loud and often. Adams heard all about it, of course, and was aware that Jefferson had called him vain and stubborn. Then Uriah Forrest, one of Jefferson's correspondents, sent Adams a greatly exaggerated summary of the contents of one of Jefferson's letters; and Adams exploded. "It is evidence," he wrote on June 20, "of a mind soured, yet seeking for popularity, and eaten to a honey comb with ambition, yet weak, confused, uninformed and ignorant."[8]

Mrs. Adams and the Presidency

By the middle of May, however, the president also had reason to be pleased: Abigail had at last arrived in Philadelphia. Traveling in winter was notoriously trying; even in the spring it was not easy. "We had very bad Roads," Mrs. Adams wrote her sister, Mary Cranch, "the Rains having washd all the stones bare, and the ruts were very deep. I was much fatigued."[9] And that was all before reaching New York. Then it got worse: "For 40 miles through the Jersies was the worst roads I ever travelld. The soil is all clay. The heavy rains and the constant run of six stages daily, had so cut them up, that the whole was like a ploughd feild, in furroughs of two feet in depth, and was very dangerous . . . so much so, as to confine me in my Room and Bed the greater part of two days."[10] For a woman no longer young, in frail health and wracked by rheumatism, it must indeed have been a painful journey. Still, she reached Philadelphia, and things began to look up.

As First Lady, Abigail was naturally expected to entertain, something she often did not enjoy much, perhaps because, unlike Mrs. Washington, she was not a natural hostess. She lacked her predecessor's easy (if always dignified) southern charm; she came from the solid middle class while the Washingtons were aristocrats; she could be, on occasion, less than amiable; but she managed anyway. On May 16, she described her first grand reception to her sister.

> Yesterday being Monday, from 12 to half past two, I received visits, 32 Ladies and near as many Gentlemen. I shall have the same ceremony to pass through today, and the rest part of the week. As I am not prepaird with furniture for a Regular drawing Room, I shall not commence one, I believe, as the Summer is too near at hand, and my Health very precarious. At the Winter sessions I shall

begin. Mrs. Tufts once stiled my situation, splendid misery. She was not far
from truth . . .

Evening 8 o'clock

The day is past, and a fatiguing one it has been. The Ladies of Foreign
Ministers, and the Ministers [actually, there were only four], with our own Secretaries and Ladies have visited me, and to add to them, the whole Levee
today of Senate and House. Strangers etc making near one Hundred asked
permission to visit me, so that from half past twelve to nearly 4, I was rising up
and sitting down.[11]

It is amusing to note that the Adamses kept the sort of etiquette that
might have been seen at the Court of Saint James's: there were levees, at which
the visitors remained standing and were each given only a few moments with
the First Lady; there would be drawing rooms in the winter when, with the
new furniture in place, smaller groups of visitors might expect cake, wine,
and coffee, and would actually be allowed to sit down. Of course, the Washingtons had set the precedent, but it seemed to come more naturally from
them; and there were mocking comments about the Adamses' stiffness and
pompousness.

Etiquette or no, it was hard work. Abigail promptly found that the only
free time she had was between dawn and breakfast at eight. Then her morning,
until eleven, was spent looking after the house and the family: unlike the
Washingtons, the Adamses had very few servants. Then, from eleven to twelve,
she dressed. From twelve to two or three was the time to receive visits, after
which came dinner—except for Tuesdays and Thursdays when, because there
were usually guests, it was put off until later. After dinner, there was time for a
walk or a ride. And every day, there was that awful obligation, the levee—
which, in truth, must have been a terrible bore, as its format virtually precluded any but the most superficial conversation. And this being the United
States, there was none of the glamour that made European courts more
appealing. As for those official dinners, they, too, were proving a nuisance. It
was with the gloomiest feelings that Abigail anticipated, for instance, the dinner on May 25 at which she was receiving the secretary of state, Mrs. Pickering,
and all thirty-two senators.

All that was bad enough. What made it worse was that she hated to be
anywhere except at home in Quincy; and she particularly loathed Philadelphia.
"I believe this city is become as vile and debauched as the city of London, nay
more so, for in the lower classes, much more respect is had to character there,"
she wrote her sister. "Speculation in Property, in politicks and in Religion have
gone very far in depraving the morals of the higher classes of the people of our
Country."[12] And two weeks later she added: "I long for my rose Bush, my clover
Field, and the retirement of Quincy, and the conversation of my dear Sister
and Friends."[13]

The result of all this was that the Adamses spent less time in the capital (first Philadelphia, then, after November 1800, Washington) than any other presidential couple. Abigail could not wait to get away, and John hated to be away from Abigail, so that soon, the government became bicephalous: away in Quincy, at least half the year, was the president, while the cabinet, together with the bureaucracy, remained in Philadelphia. Since it took several days for the mail to get from one to the other, this seriously delayed business. It also isolated Adams: in Quincy, he was cut off from the advice and contacts that in Philadelphia were his for the asking.

To make it all worse yet, there was the press. John Adams was entirely clear about the proper role of the newspapers: they existed to praise him. Unfortunately for his peace of mind, however, there were a number of lively, critical, and, on occasion, satirical Republican papers, which the president found very hard to bear. The First Lady did not like it any better. When the *Philadelphia Chronicle* was bold enough to publish a few figures, she exploded. "The Chronical . . . not only collects the Billingsgate of all the Jacobin papers but he adds to it Lies, falsehoods, calimny and bitterness of his own," she raged to her sister. "For what other purpose could he design that paragraph, that the president was to receive one hundred and 14 thousand dollars for four years? The sallery everyone knows is the same Nominal sum granted to President Washington without half its value. . . . Every dollar [of the $14,000] is laid out for the use of the United States."[14] The $14,000, of course, was the "small addition" that the Senate had voted, and the House finally passed, which paid for horses, a carriage, and the long list of domestic necessities enumerated in that earlier letter from John to Abigail. The president's salary, $25,000 a year, accounted for the remaining $100,000. The *Chronicle*, after all, was reporting no more than the exact truth; but then, "one hundred and 14 thousand dollors" did sound like a very huge amount.

The American press, by 1797, had already had a good twenty years' worth of paying attention to the way public money was spent. When it came to politics, however, objectivity was not considered a virtue: papers were, and were expected to be, the voice of their party. Thus, if you were John Adams, reading the pro-Federalist papers proved, in 1797 and 1798, at least, highly soothing; reading their Republican counterparts was, in equal measure, infuriating. Of course, the same applied in reverse to Jefferson; but then, he was such a convinced libertarian that the situation struck him as normal. The Adamses, however, took a much more simplistic view of the world: it was divided between the good (themselves and their friends) and the evil (the Republicans); and since good should triumph over evil, it was an outrage that evil should be able to express itself freely and bitingly.

Many traditions were set in the early years of the Republic. All unknowing, the Adamses' reaction to press opposition was also creating a precedent:

from that day to this, presidents have resented the criticism that invariably
comes their way. Naturally, the public does not always hear the direct expression of their feelings, but with the Adamses we are lucky: when John was not
writing Abigail, Abigail was writing her sister, Mary Cranch.

"The Tone of the Jacobins is Turned," she thus explained on May 24,
"[because] the president has committed with them the unpardonable sin 'by
saying [to Congress] that he was convinced that the conduct of the Government had been just and impartial to foreign Nations.' [Benjamin Franklin]
Bache [Franklin's grandson and the editor of the *Aurora*, the chief Republican
paper] opened his batteries of abuse and scurility the next day, and has in every
paper continued them. . . . These degraded beings would still have their countrymen 'lick the Hand just raised to shed their Blood.'"[15]

This was strong stuff—indeed, it makes one suspect that Abigail would
have been a highly effective editorial writer, especially since she alternated
between fiery denunciation and contemptuous pity. At the beginning of June,
she was writing Mrs. Cranch:

> Bache has undertaken to abuse the appointment [of John Marshall to the
> three-man mission] . . . But I can read all with a true Philosophical contempt,
> and I could tell them what the president says, that their praise for a few weeks
> mortified him, much more than all their impudent abuse does.
>
> There is no terror, Jack Cuss, in your threats
> For I am arm'd so strong in honesty
> That they pass by me as the Idle wind.[16]

It is not every First Lady who has been able to quote Shakespeare, neatly replacing Cassius with Jack Cuss, when the press annoyed her. As for John Adams
being "mortified by their praise," he had in fact complained to Abigail, the day
after his inauguration, that he was being "damn[ed] with faint praise"—thereby
hinting that he would have liked a more enthusiastic endorsement.

Quite properly, from his point of view, Adams now restricted his appointments to good Federalists; Abigail confirmed it to her sister. After telling her
that the Republicans in Congress were complaining about this, she went on:
"This is not true in its full extent. . . . The President has said . . . that he will
appoint to office merit, virtue and Talents, and when Jacobins posses these,
they will stand a chance, but it will ever be an additional recommendation that
they are Friends to order and government."[17] The whole concept could not be
more neatly put: since, by definition, the "Jacobins" were devoid of virtue, and
since, on the other hand, there was an ample supply of virtuous and talented
"Friends to order," it would have been a singularly blind Republican who
expected to receive office from Adams.

Here, again, an important precedent was set: henceforth, presidents
appointed mostly men who belonged to their party. As for Adams, he went a

step further and practiced nepotism on a very large scale. Having the advantage (or bearing the burden) of belonging to a very large family, he proceeded to find federal jobs for great numbers of his relatives, while invariably protesting that he had merely chosen the best among the applicants for that particular office.

That, surely, was a consolation; but there were so many annoyances. Firmly disregarding the fact that John Adams could hardly compete with George Washington, both husband and wife were outraged when, in February 1798, the Philadelphians decided to give a ball in honor of the general's birthday. Of course, the Adamses were stunned: it was so obvious to them that the celebration should have been for the birthday of the current president. Then, adding insult to injury, the organizers of the ball had the effrontery of inviting the Adamses. It was more than John and Abigail could bear: "The President of the United States to attend the celebration of the birth day in his publick Character of a private Citizen!" Abigail exploded to her sister, "for in no other light can General Washington now be considered . . . I do not know when my feelings of contempt have been more called forth, in response to this invitation."[18] There was the rub: president though he certainly was, His Rotundity evoked not a tenth of the gratitude or respect the nation felt for Washington.

Even when people were paying the proper respects to the president, the Adamses complained. In June 1797, Abigail listed resentfully the dinners to which she had had to invite, in batches, all the members of Congress and their wives. Then, just a few days ahead, an even worse trial loomed, the Fourth of July, which, Abigail explained, "is a still more tedious day, as we must then have, not only all Congress, but all the Gentlemen of the city, the Governour [of Pennsylvania] and officers and companies, all of whom the late president used to treat with cake, punch and wine. . . . As we are here we cannot avoid the trouble nor the expence. I have been informed that they used to cost the late president 500 dollors. More than 200wt of cake used to be expended, and two quarter casks of wine besides spirit."[19] Happily, though, it was not all a dreary waste of cake: there was the time, in March 1798, when three Indian chiefs came by for a visit, ate cake, shook hands with Abigail, and told her they prayed to the Great Spirit to keep and preserve her. Some people, it seemed, still had a sense of decency.

An Earnest Attempt Rebuffed

Receptions, birthday balls, and other such celebrations were, in the end, minor events. What to do about France, and the attacks on U.S. shipping, mattered a great deal more; but, unfortunately, it had become purely a party matter. By June 1797, Jefferson had become the full-fledged leader of the Republicans, and he saw it as his task to turn back the encroachments of the executive, avert war, and revive the spirit of 1776. He was a Francophile, of course, but he could also see what the country needed, and he put it neatly in a letter to Edward Rutledge: "Our countrymen have divided themselves by such strong affection to the French and the English that nothing will secure us internally but a divorce from both nations; and this must be the object of every real American, and its attainment is practicable without much self-denial. But for this peace is necessary."[20]

Jefferson was right: the United States could not afford a war, and lacked the means to wage it; but, just as important, a war would have split the country, perhaps for good. Interestingly, Adams, too, saw this. Early in July 1797, he explained his position fully to Elbridge Gerry, one of the members of the three-man commission: "It is my sincere desire," he wrote, "that an accommodation [with France] may take place; but our national faith and the honor of our government cannot be sacrificed. . . . As to being a divided people, all nations are divided . . . but our people will support their government, and so will the French theirs. Not to expect division in a free country, would be an absurdity."[21]

It is at moments like this that Adams's full scope is revealed. There is no rancor here, no partisanship; a reasonable accommodation was unquestionably the only sane goal; and for the usually thin-skinned little man to see that free nations will always be divided was nothing less than a brilliant perception—as was the understanding that, in the end, people would rally around the flag. In 1797, the notion that a healthy country should also be unanimous was still very firmly entrenched. It is much to Adams's credit that he was able to look beyond it.

Whether a similar spirit prevailed in Paris was, however, most uncertain, and there lay the problem: being ready to accept a decent compromise will only work if the other party is also well disposed. The Directoire, characteristically, had given no sign that it was prepared to be reasonable. For the United States, resolving the conflict with France was essential. For Barras and his fellow directors, the United States was so distant, and so unimportant, as to be quite forgotten. As they lurched from coup to coup and crisis to crisis, it hardly mattered to them whether a few people scattered on the shores of North America were inconvenienced by French privateers. Indeed, from their point of view, the current policy (or to be more exact, the lack of it) had a decided advantage: now and again, fresh money, made by seizing U.S. ships, actually reached the perennially empty treasury. In the United States, people debated and worried; at the Luxembourg Palace, the whole question seemed scarcely worth considering.

That left it all up to the United States, and, more specifically, to the three-man commission. Because communications between Europe and America were so slow—ships often took six weeks one way—much depended on the sort of men they were. Once in Paris, they would often have to tread in areas not covered by their instructions. How far they were prepared to do so, and in what manner, mattered a great deal. John Adams knew this, and it was not by accident that he chose Elbridge Gerry.

A small, nervous, birdlike man, Gerry was one of the fighters of '76—that, in fact, was when Adams had met him—and he was a devoted patriot. He was also full of odd, quirky ideas: he advocated the creation of two capitals and a legislature that would move back and forth between them, for instance. He was firmly against giving the federal government the right to levy taxes or have a standing army, and he had retired from the House of Representatives because he was disgusted by the rise of party spirit. That, however, had not prevented him from being an elector pledged to Adams in 1796.

What mattered most, however, was how Gerry felt about the current crisis, and here his position was as clear as could be: he thought a war with France would be a catastrophe of such magnitude that it must be avoided by virtually any means. He thus went off resolved to bring back an accommodation of some sort; and because he was himself honorable but a little naive, it might be wondered how well he would do when he had to deal with wily and unscrupulous opponents.

Adams was aware of all this. Gerry was his bid to avoid war; the next appointee to the commission, John Marshall, was to be Gerry's counterweight. Indeed, the two men could hardly have been more different. Marshall was tall, relaxed, powerful, and enormously intelligent. A devoted Federalist, a strong advocate of the Constitution, he had served in the Virginia legislature and headed his party in the state. He had enthusiastically backed Jay's Treaty, and generally took the view that the federal government ought to extend its powers. He was thus likely to take a very different position from Gerry's, and he had better means to make himself heard: an accomplished and wily lawyer, he was a powerful debater, a man who knew how to win an argument. He also trusted people no more than was absolutely necessary, and could be relied on to point out—not without amusement—that the French were trying to fool Gerry.

As for the third man, Charles Cotesworth Pinckney, he was to be the bridge between the two. A South Carolina aristocrat of enormous integrity, he was reasonable, dependable, generous—not unlike his British counterparts, in fact. He understood that his station in life conferred certain obligations upon him; he expected his country to call on him and was always ready to respond to that call. He had done so often, fighting in the army during the War of Independence, attending the Constitutional Convention, and then ensuring that South Carolina ratified the Constitution. That was no surprise: his influence in the state was immense; and he was a firm believer in the supremacy of the federal government. Although he had supported Jay's Treaty, he was at best a lukewarm Federalist, mostly because he considered himself far too grand to be constrained by party, but also because he understood that his duty was to the nation itself. Taken together, these were the qualities of a statesman — or they would have been if only the ever-dignified Pinckney had not been so lacking in intelligence. As it was, his benevolence was often mixed with puzzlement.

It was thus a rather odd threesome who sailed for France. By October 1797, they were in Paris, and they met briefly with Talleyrand, the French foreign minister, on the eighth. For what happened next, we must rely on John Marshall, who wrote the dispatches; but since neither of his colleagues disagreed with their overall content, it seems probable that, in spite of their anti-French slant, they are reasonably accurate.

Not surprisingly, given their very different personalities, Gerry, Marshall, and Pinckney reacted very differently to the situation in Paris; but it was immediately clear to all of them that they were being very badly treated. What happened, in fact, was that nobody cared much about settling with the United States — unless massive bribes made the settlement worthwhile. These bribes, as the three envoys soon discovered, were to be of two kinds. First there was to be an outright cash payment to Talleyrand, the foreign minister; then there was to be a massive loan to the French Republic; and as a sweetener, assorted — and highly humiliating — apologies from the U.S. government to the French.

Even to obtain these bribes, however, the French did not think it necessary to treat the envoys with a minimum of courtesy. The appointment with the foreign minister, on October 8, lasted a bare fifteen minutes. After that, there was no more official contact: the Directoire would not receive the envoys, the minister was otherwise busy. What the three U.S. representatives were yet to learn was that when it came to keeping his distances, Talleyrand was a true master; nor did they (or, as yet, anyone else) know that they were facing one of the greatest diplomats and foreign ministers in all French history.

All in all, Talleyrand was not the sort of man with whom the commissioners were accustomed to deal. His distance, his aristocratic hauteur, scared Gerry, offended Marshall, and puzzled Pinckney, who expected to be treated like a great aristocrat himself. As for the bribes that were soon demanded, they stunned the three men, who, for all their differences, were models of integrity.

Of course, Talleyrand was not so careless as to ask for the bribes directly. Instead, he sent his emissaries to see the envoys. Because there were three of these intermediaries, and because Marshall, in his dispatches, thought it best not to name names, he referred to them successively as X, Y, and Z.

The first visit, the one from X (his name was actually J. C. Hottinguer), took place on October 18, and that was when the full extent of the French demands became clear. John Adams's speech to Congress in which he had complained about French depredations was to be disavowed; the debts due by the French to U.S. suppliers were to be assumed by the U.S. government; the indemnities due U.S. citizens for the ships and cargoes seized by the French were also to be paid by the U.S. government; the United States was to make a large "loan" to France; and there was to be a substantial gift to Talleyrand himself.

All that was shocking enough. Since, however, most details had been left vague, the commission agreed to ask for further precisions. These were brought two days later by Y (Pierre Bellamy), who explained that the minimum amount of the "loan" would be 32 million Dutch guilders, and that of the bribe to Talleyrand $150,000. The stunned commission answered that it had no power to negotiate the loan and proposed to send Marshall home for further instructions, provided the French stopped attacking U.S. shipping.

This was not at all what Talleyrand wanted. The whole point of having the commissioners in Paris was that they could be browbeaten into accepting these extortionate terms; so silence fell for a few days and then Z (Lucien Hauteval) appeared, merely to explain that these were nonnegotiable terms. In fact, there was no reason for Talleyrand to be concerned: he was willing enough to take the bribe, the loan, and the treaty, but none of the three was important enough to make a substantial difference to him. He was also the greatest exponent alive of masterly inactivity, so he simply sat back and did nothing. When, on November 11, the envoys reminded the minister that they were still waiting to be officially received, he did not even bother to acknowledge receiving their letter.

There the negotiation stuck until March. By then, Talleyrand had decided that Gerry was the most naive and the most pliable of the three envoys, so he announced that henceforth he refused to see the other two; and when told it was all three or none, he proceeded to expel Pinckney and Marshall. Gerry stayed on for another five months, and made it clear that he longed for an agreement; but all the while he steadfastly refused to negotiate any of the substantive issues.

In the meantime, of course, John Marshall's dispatches had reached the United States and caused angry reactions in the cabinet. Attorney General Charles Lee wanted to declare war forthwith; Pickering was not opposed to a declaration of war, but he first wanted to sign a treaty of alliance with England; and Secretary of the Treasury Oliver Wolcott and McHenry, who leaned toward war, were opposed to the English connection; so no decision was taken, either by these four men or by Adams. For a few days, these discussions remained confidential, but everybody knew that the Directoire had issued another decree empowering French privateers yet again to seize U.S. ships carrying English goods—a clear act of hostility. And, of course, there was no news of progress from the commission.

This was all too much for Congress. The Federalists assumed that the French were behaving badly, and demanded detailed information; the Republicans assumed that the administration, being hostile to France, had given the commissioners secret instructions that prevented any sort of agreement with France; and both sides demanded to see all relevant papers. On April 3, 1798, after some hesitation, John Adams agreed to hand them over.

THE XYZ AFFAIR

The effect of the XYZ Papers, as they were universally called, was nothing short of explosive. In mid February, Abigail had complained to her sister that the president had been worn down by "continual opposition and by constant exertions," and that they were both "sick, sick, sick of publicke life."[22] Within three months, and for the first time in his life, John Adams was the most popular man in America—a position he relished. Addresses came from all over the country, praising his steadfastness; the Republican opposition collapsed; and, after two years of mostly ignoring him, Congress gave him just what he wanted.

It was no wonder: that sordid tale of intrigue and deception, the insults heaped on the country and its envoys, the very refusal to receive the latter officially, while, all the time, the French were strangling U.S. trade, was more than either the people or their representatives were prepared to accept. The XYZ Papers became a huge publishing success, and war with France loomed ever closer.

That it did not actually break out was due in large part to the president's good sense; but then, Hamilton was not quite ready for war, either. On March 17, after he had read Marshall's dispatches, he issued his instructions to Pickering: "I wish," he explained, "to see a *temperate,* but *grave, solemn* and *firm* communication from the president to the two Houses . . . to review summarily the course of our affairs with the French, . . . to allude to the dangerous and vast projects of the French government. . . . Our duty, our honor and safety, require that we shall take vigorous and comprehensive measures of defense."[23] He then went on to enumerate and describe the measures in question—the very measures that were actually taken. Although Adams did not know it yet, Hamilton was, in fact, setting his policies.

On March 19, therefore, Adams told Congress that there was "no ground of expectation that the object of [the commissioners'] mission can be accomplished on terms compatible with the safety, the honor or the essential interests of the nation." He asked that American trading ships be protected, that the arsenals be replenished, that military manufactures be established, and that new revenues be created to pay for all this; and he finished by asking Congress to show "zeal [and vigor]"[24]—a truly Hamiltonian touch. In fact, Hamilton had every reason to be pleased: not only had the president said precisely what he wanted him to say, the new policies were also the ones he longed for: more taxation, more centralization, and a greatly enhanced military establishment.

The first step was to strengthen the virtually nonexistent navy. A Department of the Navy was created; ships were bought and reconditioned, sailors taken on, cannons and cannonballs manufactured. Then, in May, Congress approved an even more drastic step: it authorized the creation of a new, ten-thousand-man standing army. This was a grave step in a country many of whose citizens thought that standing armies were dangerous because they led to government tyranny. It was also just what Hamilton wanted—partly because he confidently expected to be in actual command under Washington's distant leadership, partly because he was planning to use the army to repress dissent when and where necessary.

That both Adams and Congress should have concurred in the creation of this new army showed hysteria rather than need. Not even Hamilton could say just what the army would be *for;* there was no more real prospect of a French invasion than before, but the mass indignation caused by the XYZ Papers had turned into a great wave of unreasoning fear. Hamilton himself did his best to sustain it, even writing the ever-composed Washington:

> There is certainly great probability that we may have to enter into a very serious struggle with France; and it is more and more evident that the powerful faction which has for years opposed the government, is determined to go every length with France . . . They are ready to *new-model* our Constitution under the *influence* or *coercion* of France, to form with her a perpetual alliance, *offensive* and *defensive*, and to give her a monopoly of our trade by *peculiar* and *exclusive* privileges. That would be in substance . . . to make this country a province of France.[25]

He urged Washington to make a tour through the southern states in order to influence public opinion.

Washington, of course, kept his calm; he stayed in Mount Vernon and made no public statements. The general was exceptional, however, in refusing to panic. John Adams was busy denouncing "a spirit of party which scruples not to go all lengths of profligacy, falsehood and malignity in defaming our government,"[26] while Abigail refused to be satisfied until all criticism was suppressed. "We are now wonderfully popular," she informed her sister, "except with Bache and Co. who in his paper calls the President old, querilous, Bald, blind, cripled, Toothless Adams. Thus in Scripture are the Prophets mocked."[27] In her indignation, Abigail was perhaps going a little far: the picture of John Adams as a prophet from the Scriptures is more comic than convincing.

If to call John Adams bald was almost treason, there were now no words to describe Jefferson. "At this moment," he wrote James Monroe on April 5, "my name is running through all the city as detected in a criminal correspondence with the French directory, and fixed upon me by the documents from our envoys now before the two houses. The detection of this by the publication of the papers, should they be published, will not relieve all the effects of the lie."[28] Here, again, a precedent was being set: this was the first of the great waves of fear or indignation that, at periodic intervals, have swept through the United States.

By June, all these indignant words were beginning to be accompanied by action. The infuriated Pickering sent Gerry a letter ordering him to return home forthwith, upon which Talleyrand, urging him to stay on, announced that France no longer required either an apology or a loan. This was at least in part because the French press had been reprinting the XYZ Papers, thus giving rise to an annoying blend of mirth and indignation; but the concession made no difference. Gerry, still saying he was not empowered to negotiate alone, finally left in August.

In Philadelphia itself, the new Department of the Navy now came into being. Adams chose Benjamin Stoddert as its secretary; he could not have picked a better man. With the help of five clerks, with no naval staff, no trained officers, no procurement organization, and only a single warship, Stoddert created a new navy from scratch. By the middle of 1800, there were 54 naval ships in operation; and that did more than anything else to resolve the crisis with France. It was just in time: in the years 1797 and 1798, 330 U.S. ships had been seized by French privateers, while insurance rates rose from 6 percent of the value of the cargo to a ruinous 33 percent, and French ships hovered just outside the ports, waiting for their prey. It was Stoddert's great achievement that even while he was re-creating the navy, he saw to the armament of U.S. merchant ships. French privateers tended to behave very differently when they discovered that their prey was able to defend itself.

Indeed, the tone of the day was decidedly martial. John Marshall, whose return was nothing short of triumphant, made his famous comment about the United States being prepared to spend millions for defense but not a cent for tribute. Congress, for its part, unilaterally abrogated all treaties with France, while addresses from towns and universities, clubs and legislatures, urged the president to declare war. John Adams himself, almost giddy from his new popularity, gave them answers which became daily more warlike; and then there was the announcement of the administration's policy. No minister would henceforth be sent to France, Adams announced, without assurances that he would be "received, respected, and honored as the representative of a great, free, powerful and independent nation."[29] It sounded impressive, even if "great" and "powerful" were, at this point, a bit of an exaggeration. As for "free," that was about to be called into question by the actions of the Federalists.

LIBERTIES CURTAILED

It is never comfortable to oppose a wave of political hysteria. Just how dangerous it actually becomes depends on the laws guaranteeing an individual's civil rights, and whether they are carried out. In the early summer of 1798, the Federalist majority in Congress, urged on by its party press, decided to expel or imprison those who were rash enough to disagree with them.

This first attempt at creating an authoritarian society in the United States—again, it set a precedent—took the form of four acts of Congress, duly passed by both houses and signed by the president. The first, the Alien Enemies Act, which was voted with full Republican cooperation, provided that in the event of war or invasion only, the president had the authority to designate as enemy aliens the citizens of the hostile nation residing in the United States whose presence he regarded as dangerous. In order to do so, he was empowered to make regulations for their apprehension, restraint, or removal, with the arrests proceeding according to law and under the supervision of federal and state courts. Since, in fact, the United States did not go to war, and since it was not invaded, the law was never applied; but it remained on the books.

The second of the measures was the Naturalization Act, which was designed to get rid of a great mass of potential Republican voters. Because many new citizens had originally emigrated from Ireland, they tended to be very anti-British and therefore anti-Federalist. The bill therefore provided that no foreign-born person would be allowed to vote or hold office. Because the United States still prided itself on its openness to immigration, this was a little extreme; consequently, that provision of the bill was defeated. Another provision became law, however: henceforth, it took fourteen years of residence, instead of five, to become a citizen; and even this passed both House and Senate by a single vote.

The third of the repressive laws, the Alien Act, was also directed at the Irish. This empowered the president to expel all persons he deemed dangerous to the peace and safety of the United States without a hearing and without specifying a reason. Any expelled person who failed to depart was to be jailed, without a judgment or other court procedure, for three years. The rationale for this was clear enough: first, prevent the Irish from becoming citizens; then expel them for not being citizens. It was ingenious, certainly; it was also appalling, so much so that under color of restricting use of the act to its strictest interpretation, Adams never invoked it; and the law, which had been voted for two years only, expired in June of 1800.

Finally came the Sedition Act, which seemed tailor-made for all the resentments felt by the Adamses. It made it a crime, punishable by jail and a fine, to bring any member of the government or the Congress into contempt or disrepute; so if you said that the president understood nothing, or that a senator was a model of obduracy, you could be prosecuted; indeed, if you hinted that a policy defended by either was not for the greater good of the country, that was enough. Of course, the authorities had to find a jury ready to convict, not always a very easy thing to do; but it happened. Before the law expired on March 3, 1801, a number of men were imprisoned because they had criticized the government.

Of all the four acts, this last was the most bitterly opposed by the Republicans, Jefferson first and foremost. Oddly enough, it was, in its own way, less repressive than it might have been: British acts had gone even further, and the Federalists thus claimed they were being moderate. What might have been true in Britain, however, was not in the United States. There it embodied a clear violation of the Bill of Rights; it tried to make political dissent a virtual impossibility, and had it been applied more often, it would have become impossible ever to have a genuinely free election. That Adams should have signed, then used, such an act, says a great deal for the thinness of his skin, and very little for his understanding of what freedom really was. Even so, not many prosecutions were begun; not many people went to jail; and the half dozen who were still incarcerated on March 4, 1801, were promptly pardoned by the new president.

Legislation was one way to curtail civil rights. Force was another, and that was where the new army came in. For several years, Hamilton had wanted the United States to have a real army—something more effective than the few regiments fighting American Indian tribes in various odd corners. These new troops might, Hamilton hoped, eventually conquer an empire to the south; but, far more important, they could be used to quell civil disorders provoked by widely unpopular policies, or even to constrain various states. As a result, it was of the first importance that the commander of the new army be thoroughly reliable; and when it came right down to it, Hamilton could think of no one more trustworthy than himself.

Of course, there could be no question of his being appointed commander in chief. That position obviously belonged to Washington, but the general was old; he was willing to serve because his country called, but he could be expected to take a rather detached attitude to the new army; and so it was the second in command who mattered most. That, Hamilton had decided, would be his job, and, on June 2, he made it clear to Washington: "If I am invited to *a station in which the service I may render may be proportionate to the sacrifice I am to make,* I shall be willing to go into the army. If you command, the place in which I should hope to be most useful is that of Inspector General [i.e., second in command], with a command in the line. This I would accept."[30]

As for Washington, who exhibited little enthusiasm for the new army, his position was exactly what might have been expected: he wanted his officers to be the ones who had performed best during the War of Independence, men he felt he could trust. The three at the top of his list were Hamilton, Henry Knox, and C. C. Pinckney. All three were thus to be commissioned as major generals. The trick was the order in which this happened: whoever had seniority, even if only by five minutes, would be second in command.

Only Congress can confirm a military rank, but only the president can deliver commissions; and so John Adams was immediately involved in the matter. It did not make him happy. He had no objection to the making of the three major generals; their claims were justified by their service during the war. Having Hamilton as inspector general, however, was a different matter. Adams had never much liked Hamilton—the two men were too different to get along easily, and Adams was aware that Hamilton preferred to run things. He had very little doubt, therefore, that having him as second to Washington would entail a serious loss of power for the president.

It was a while, however, before Adams realized what was going on. "[Washington's] advice in the formation of a list of officers would be extremely desirable to me," he wrote McHenry, the war secretary, on July 6. "Particularly I wish to have his opinion of the man most suitable for Inspector General."[31] Indeed, he could hardly have bypassed the general; but the result of the consultation struck him as wholly unpalatable. Under much pressure from Hamilton, who demanded the position of inspector general, and announced that he would serve in no other capacity, Washington decided to back his claims—which went a good deal further than being a mere second in command. As Hamilton explained to his chief, "My friend McHenry is wholly insufficient for his place, with the added misfortune of not having himself the least suspicion of that fact."[32] The implication was clear: Hamilton was to be de facto secretary of war, as well as officially inspector general. And since, until now, McHenry had obediently carried out all of Hamilton's suggestions, there was every reason to think he would continue to do so.

There was a major drawback to Hamilton's position, however: it was rapidly making Adams into an enemy. Such was Hamilton's contempt for Adams, though, that he never thought it worth his while to shade his attitudes in order not to offend the president. As it was, Washington nominated Hamilton as second in command, and Adams tried hard not to listen. "In my opinion," he wrote McHenry on August 14, "Gen. Knox is legally entitled to rank next to Gen. Washington, and no other arrangement will give satisfaction. . . . The consequence of this will be that Pinckney must rank before Hamilton."[33] And as late as August 29, he was still trying hard: "The officers appointed on the same day, in whatever order, have a right to rank according to precedent services," he explained to McHenry. "I made the nomination . . . believing at the time that [it] . . . would give them no command at all." He added, pathetically, "The power and authority are in the President. I am willing to exercise this authority at this moment."[34] It was no good, though. Hamilton would only serve as inspector general, and Washington was determined to have Hamilton. Adams could not face the possibility that Washington would resign his command because he had been denied the aide of his choice. With intense feelings of humiliation, therefore, he gave Hamilton his coveted title.

This defeat changed Adams in a number of ways. First, there was his attitude to his party. Even as the Federalists, carried by the hysteria of the XYZ affair, were winning a solid majority in the congressional elections, Adams felt cut off from all those who followed Hamilton: this was a serious and lasting split. Then there was his policy toward France, the bugbear of the Federalists: suddenly, the enemy at home—Hamilton—began to seem more dangerous to the president than the enemy abroad; perhaps, after all, some accommodation could be reached with Paris. Finally, any army that was run by Hamilton was, in Adams's view, an army not worth having. There, the president was well served by the slowness and incompetence of the war secretary: somehow, over the next year, nothing much happened. Supplies failed to come in; recruits did not appear in sufficient numbers; and that powerful army urged by Hamilton, funded by Congress, and headed by the Father of the Nation, simply failed to materialize. By September 1799, the United States was as poorly armed on land as it had been a year earlier.

In the meantime, Adams showed plainly that he resented Hamilton. It was not just that he refused to appoint Hamilton's nephew inspector of artillery, he did so in the words best calculated to annoy: "As his native country is France, and his speech betrays his origin, I am very apprehensive that in a French war neither the army nor the people would be without their jealousies and suspicions, which might be very injurious to the service."[35] Given Hamilton's known detestation of France, and the fact that no one really believed in a land war with France, this was the most transparent of pretexts.

To a friend, however, Adams needed no veil. "This man [Hamilton] is stark mad, or I am," he wrote. "He knows nothing of the character, the principles, the feelings, the opinions and prejudices of this nation."[36] And although Hamilton favored a war with France, Adams thought of reopening negotiations. By November 23, when the president at last returned to Philadelphia, he was thinking of the possibility seriously enough to mention it to his cabinet. This could hardly prove acceptable to Hamilton's friends. Instead, they urged the president to let it be known that it was up to the French: if they wanted to resume communications, let them send a minister to the United States. Safe in the knowledge that this would not happen, they sat back and relaxed.

They and their leader soon had reason to worry again, though. The president's message to Congress, on December 8, was, from their point of view, all wrong. Far from asking for a declaration of war (which Hamilton wanted), Adams announced only that he would not send another minister to France without assurances that he would be received. This was as good as a guarantee: let the French say only that they would behave normally by receiving the new envoy and negotiations could begin.

With this message, the great rift among the Federalists came out in the open. The party was well aware that it had won the elections on the strength of the anti-French feeling generated by the XYZ affair, and it hoped to keep on using Francophobia for a very long period. It saw, therefore, any attempt at reconciliation with France as a dastardly attack on its future prospects; and, of course, there was always Hamilton, whose disdain for Adams was becoming more public every day.

By January 1799, a variety of reports indicated that the Directoire actually did wish to open negotiations; and so, to the Federalists' horror, the president announced that he was appointing William Vans Murray, the U.S. minister to Holland, as minister to France. Murray was known to believe in the possibility of a successful negotiation with France, which annoyed the High Federalists even more; and Hamilton was the most furious of all. He had (successfully until now) relied on the cabinet to ensure that Adams would behave as desired, but Adams had made his announcement without even consulting the cabinet. Aside from going against Hamilton's own policy, the presidential announcement hinted at something equally disturbing: if Adams had caught on to the fact that the cabinet's loyalty belonged, not to himself, but to Hamilton, he was not likely to heed its future advice.

For Adams, however, there really was no choice: as he saw it, his constitutional authority was at stake. He had already been forced to appoint Hamilton inspector general; a step more, and he would become nothing but his master's voice. Even so, he was far too prudent to rush anything: it took him until March to request that Talleyrand guarantee Murray's reception. These assurances were not received until July 30, a time at which Adams was already in Quincy; and Murray's instructions were not sent out until the late fall. As Adams remarked to Washington in a letter criticizing the Republicans' demand for peace, "In elective governments, peace and war are alike embraced by parties, when they think they can employ either for electioneering purposes."[37] What was true of the despised Republicans was, as he had discovered, also true of his former Federalist friends.

All this naturally had an effect on the stillborn army. The dislike Adams already felt for it was greatly increased in February 1799, because Hamilton suggested that it be used for an attack on the Spanish possessions in Louisiana and Florida—supposedly to prevent the French from invading them. Another possibility was to foment a movement for independence in South America, which would then be backed by the U.S. army. Finally, if neither of the above were possible, the army was, Hamilton suggested, to be used to force the cancellation of the Kentucky and Virginia Resolutions.

The resolutions in question were the direct outcome of the repressive laws, most particularly the Sedition Act, and they raised a fundamental question. The first of them, passed by Kentucky on November 3, 1798, had been secretly drawn up by Jefferson. It pointed out that the Constitution was a compact between sovereign states (which was then a widely held view), and that the states therefore did not owe unlimited obedience to the federal government. So far, this was a principle with which almost everyone could agree, but then the resolution went on to say that the Sedition Act fell within none of the powers delegated to the government; that, furthermore, it violated the First Amendment; and that, in consequence, it was automatically void.

Nullification, as it was called, was something the Federalists could view only with horror: it meant that every time a state felt that Congress and the president had gone too far, it could nullify the actions of the Federal government. There would then be no more United States, and the Union would revert to being a confederation, as had been the case before 1789. This point was not lost on Jefferson: while Kentucky adopted the resolution, it refrained from taking the next logical step, that of actually nullifying the act: thus, the legislature's action remained merely a warning shot.

Then, on December 24, Virginia followed suit. There, James Madison, in full accord with Jefferson, was the author. "The authority of constitutions over governments," he wrote, "and of the sovereignty of the people over constitutions, are truths which are at all times necessary to be kept in mind, and at no time, perhaps, more necessary than the present."[38] Here, too, was a blend of the obvious—the authority of constitutions over governments—and of the revolutionary: while certainly the constitution derived its authority from the consent of the people, the sovereignty of the people over the constitution had implications that were familiar to everyone. It was the very principle invoked by the French revolutionaries when they decreed the Terror.

Naturally, the Federalists made the most of these exaggerations: they promptly described the resolutions as treason, and hinted darkly that since Virginia was believed to be arming, it might well have to be subdued by force. That, of course, was where Hamilton's New Army came in, and the inspector general was fully prepared to lead the attack. Suddenly, there seemed to be a real possibility that civil war would break out; but, in fact, all the angry words were more hysteria than true menace. Neither Jefferson nor Madison wanted the United States to break apart, and so, as already noted, actual nullification of the act was never carried through. As for John Adams, he loved his country far too well, and disliked Hamilton far too much, to allow any military intervention. Thus, except for the usual political rhetoric, nothing more happened.

These nonevents were not without consequence, though. Jefferson, by the beginning of 1799, felt sure that the whole XYZ Affair had been a Federalist plot, that the U.S. envoys and the French as described by Marshall were, respectively, improbably good and improbably corrupt. He called it "the X.Y.Z. dish cooked up by Marshall"[39] in a letter to jurist Edmund Pendleton, and he became genuinely convinced that there was an organized effort to abridge the liberties enshrined in the Constitution. Even worse, he feared the Constitution itself might well be in danger of being, as he put it, "monarchised" through the creation of a Senate and president for life; and in a long letter to Elbridge Gerry, he explained that in his view, the best government was the least and cheapest—views that changed significantly within the next two years.

Jefferson and Madison were not alone in their fears: all through 1799, a marked change was noticed in the electorate. The alarm resulting from the XYZ Affair had faded, and many ordinary U.S. citizens were coming to feel, as did Jefferson, that the story was a little too perfect, and that the Federalists were being too extreme. The plans for a standing army added to these apprehensions. Before the XYZ affair, the Democratic-Republican Societies had been debating the rights of the people. Now that the patriotic excitement had died down, the Federalists' possible encroachments on the rights and liberties of the citizens became a widespread subject of concern.

Naturally, the circle around Hamilton reacted to this with alarm. "I am almost afraid to write you about the state of our political affairs," Robert Troup, a close friend of Hamilton's, announced to Rufus King, the arch-Federalist minister to Great Britain. "We have experienced a sad reverse in the temper, ardor and zeal of our fellow citizens. . . . The army is progressing like a wounded snake. Last year its progress was obstructed by the President's retiring to Braintree [Quincy]." That, of course, was bad enough, but there was worse, much worse. "The late nomination of the president for the purpose of renewing negotiations with France has given almost universal disgust [within the party] . . . There certainly will be serious difficulties in supporting Mr. Adams at the next election if he should be a candidate."[40] Here was the key remark: because the Hamiltonian Federalists blamed Adams for their unpopularity, and because Hamilton himself so disliked the president, there would be the utmost reluctance to support him for reelection. That he would stand, however, seemed highly probable; and in that case the result would be a radically split party. Interestingly, this dislike of Adams was based on the assumption that a *true* Federalist would be prepared to adopt policies that might result in the coercion of the people: it was less a question of attracting votes than of imposing the government's authority.

By the end of the year, the split among Federalists had become almost a reality. On July 30, Talleyrand's assurances that a U.S. envoy would be properly received reached Philadelphia and were sent on to Quincy, where the president had moved for the summer. On August 6, Adams asked Pickering promptly to finalize the mission's instructions. He received this document on September 2, but the cabinet asked him to suspend the mission. Adams hesitated for five weeks: the French defeats at Aboukir and in Italy made it seem likely the Directoire would fall, and the Federalists were arguing that this was the perfect time to declare war on France so as to join in the eventual spoils.

He failed to be convinced, though. He approved the instructions on October 15 and ordered the envoys to leave by November 1.

That, in turn, seemed to prove that the danger from France had just been carefully provoked political hysteria. It was, after all, a Federalist president who was ordering the negotiations; and so, unfairly perhaps, Adams, by doing his duty, jeopardized both his standing within his party and that of his party among the voters. As if that were not enough, he reinforced his image as a would-be monarch by urging more prosecutions under the Alien and Sedition Acts. On July 24, for instance, Pickering wrote him: "There is in the *Aurora* of this city [Philadelphia] an uninterrupted stream of slander on the American government. . . . It is not the first time that the editor has suggested, that you had asserted the influence of the British government in affairs of our own, and insinuated that it was obtained by bribery. I shall give the paper to Mr. Rawls, and if he thinks it libelous, desire him to prosecute the editor."[41]

Of course, it was infuriating to the ever thin-skinned president to be so accused, but then the Federalists hardly hesitated to claim that Jefferson was in the pay of the French: unpleasant—and unjustified—as the article may have been, it was only a case of politics as usual. To prosecute was thus to invite an accusation of tyranny, and that accusation would not be unfounded. Still, by return mail, Adams answered: "If Mr. Rawls does not think this paper libelous, he is not fit for his office; and if he does not prosecute it, he will not do his duty. The matchless effrontery of this Duane [William Duane, the editor, who, though born in New York, was raised in Ireland] merits the execution of the alien law. I'm very willing to try its strength upon him."[42] In the end, Duane was not expelled, but the administration looked, yet again, as if it were trying to restrict the liberty of speech.

It is, however, not surprising if John Adams felt as if he were being attacked from every side: the Republicans made fun of his looks, his abilities, and his opinions at the very time when he was finally on the way to ending the conflict with France, while the Federalists were deserting him in droves. This last, of course, was the most painful: the very men he had promoted and favored were daily turning against him. In December 1799, for instance, John Marshall wrote his brother: "The Eastern people [i.e., those living in the northeastern states] are very much dissatisfied with the president on account of the late mission with France. They are strongly disposed to desert him and to push some other candidate."[43] He went on to outline a probable strategy: if there was an Adams-Pinckney ticket, then there would be no need to dump the president. Adams would get the northeastern vote and so would Pinckney; but the latter would also get some of the southern vote, thus outpolling Adams. That was precisely the conclusion Hamilton had already reached; and Adams was quite smart enough to know what it meant.

Hamilton himself felt less and less need for restraint. Virtually everyone who knew him, or even met him, knew of his contempt for Adams. On January 5, 1800, for instance, he wrote Rufus King: "At home, everything is in the main well, except as to the perverseness and capriciousness of one [Adams] and the spirit of faction of many [the Republicans]. Our measures from the first cause are too much the effect of momentary impulse. Vanity and jealousy exclude all counsel."[44] Hamilton was right, although perhaps not in the way he thought. Adams was indeed no longer willing to be advised by him or his surrogates in the cabinet; but it took Hamilton's unbounded vanity not to understand that any president would resent being controlled by an outsider. As for the Republicans, it was a normal political slur to refer to them as a "faction," the implication being, of course, that Hamilton and his friends alone cared for the welfare of the country; but he should have looked more carefully: the "faction" was rapidly becoming the majority.

None of this affected the majestic course of the president's official life, though. During those brief periods when Abigail Adams resided in Philadelphia, her receptions continued to be as formal, as grand as ever, and she observed it all as sharply as ever. On December 30, 1799, she wrote her sister:

> Last Friday's drawing Room was the most crowded of any I ever had. Upwards of a hundred Ladies and near as many Gentlemen attended, all in mourning [for the recently deceased George Washington]. The Ladies's Grief did not deprive them of taste in ornamenting their white dresses: two yards of black mode in length, of the narrow kind pleated upon one shoulder, crossd the Back in the form of a Military sash tyed at the side, crossd the petticoat and hung at the bottom of it, were worn by many. Others wore Epaulets of Black silk trimmed with fringe upon each shoulder, black Ribbon in points upon the Gown and Coat, some plain ribbon, some black [chenille] etc. Their caps were crape with black plumes or black flowers. Black gloves and fans.[45]

Clearly, the standards of elegance at the presidential receptions were rising. Indeed, at the dawn of the new century, the United States was fast catching up with all sorts of modernity. Soon the President's House in Washington would be ready; and already observers from abroad looked with fascination at the new nation that, as they saw it, was on the verge of becoming an economic power.

CHAPTER EIGHT

A Vast New Country

THE UNITED STATES was new, unexplored, different. It was, many Europeans thought, a place that corruption had not yet spoiled; and yet it had one essential political and economic feature in common with Russia and Africa, with the Ottoman Empire and the Spanish colonies. In all these places, slavery was considered a necessary part of the system. Just as the world, in 1800, was united by the effects of the war between England and France, so it was bound together by the slave trade—from Africa to the Americas, the Caribbean, and the Ottoman Empire—and by the practice of slavery. Slaves might, in one place or another, be treated a little better, or a little more harshly. It remains that in the United States, the newest, freest country anywhere, many men, women, and children were still considered merchandise.

SLAVES IN THE LAND OF LIBERTY

North America, throughout the eighteenth century, was as much a mental construct as an actual continent. The home of Rousseau's virtuous savages, a place where nature could be seen in all its extreme manifestations, these vast, still largely unknown lands seemed to many Europeans more fantasy than reality. Then the War of Independence brought a great wave of visitors from Europe; the French Revolution sent another; and by 1800, the United States, together with its immediate northern and southern neighbors, had become at the same time less romantic and more real.

That was in part because it occurred to many Europeans that a country capable of defeating Great Britain (admittedly with a little help from France) was worth knowing about; but it was also because so much about the United States seemed both strange and fascinating. First, of course, came nature itself. Most European countries had one climate, but from the long, snowbound winters of upper New York State to the tropical summers of Georgia, from the relative sophistication of cities like Boston and Philadelphia to the vast spaces where Indian tribes roamed, the range of landscapes, customs, and populations was immense. The Charles River looked nothing like the Mississippi, the swamps near Savannah were utterly unlike the mountain ridges of western Virginia.

Naturally, many different ways of life prevailed in all these dissimilar places: different crops were grown, different foods eaten. The very look of the houses changed utterly as one went from Massachusetts to South Carolina. And then there was that great divider, slavery. By 1800, slavery no longer existed in Massachusetts or Rhode Island; it was almost extinct in Connecticut, where it was officially scheduled to end in 1816. Delaware had slaves, but prohibited bringing new slaves into the state, and decreed that henceforth all persons would be born free, even if their parents were slaves; the same was true in Pennsylvania. In New York, on the other hand, slavery still flourished, as, of course, it did throughout the South: the two Carolinas between them had over seventy thousand slaves—and Albany, New York, over two thousand. By 1800, many slaves were native-born, but many still came every year from Africa, to be sold on the U.S. markets.

Already slavery was an issue with the potential to divide the new nation. John Adams, taking a principled stand, boasted that he had never bought or hired a slave: even in the North, an owner would sometimes offer a slave for employment. George Washington, of course, had slaves, and, belonging as he did to an older generation, never worried about it. Thomas Jefferson, who also had slaves, found himself in a quandary: although he thought that owning human beings was ethically wrong, he believed that freeing the slaves would ruin the landholders of the southern states. He was also aware that general emancipation was not a practical possibility, so he compromised by refusing to split families and by treating his slaves like valued employees instead of human cattle. No doubt, his slaves had reason to be grateful. Nonetheless, they were still considered property, to be bought, sold, and valued like any other asset. And the arguments given for not ending slavery were, in the United States, remarkably similar to what they were in Russia.

This great difference between the states struck most European visitors as decidedly odd. Either slavery was wrong or it was not (and they had no doubt that it was wrong). If it was wrong, it should be abolished everywhere; if it was not, it should be allowed everywhere; but then those visitors were accustomed to relatively centralized countries where the laws were uniform within the national boundaries, and they were fascinated by the fact that in the United States, what was legal in one state was utterly prohibited in another.

What seemed strangest, and most shocking of all, was the way slaves were traded in the South. In all the major cities, slave markets were held at frequent intervals. There, men, women, and children were on display, much like horses or cattle. Like these animals, they were examined, poked, prodded, and made to display their teeth; and there was a well-established range of prices. In Charleston, in the middle 1790s, a hardworking man was worth between $300 and $350, an ordinary man would cost about $200, and a woman, depending on her skills, between $100 and $150—all significant sums of money. In that same city, people might have as few as two or three slaves, and as many as two thousand: that was the case of its richest citizen, a Mr. Bligh. In some places, like Baltimore, the slaves comprised 10 percent of the population—fifteen hundred to fifteen thousand; in New York City in the late 1780s, there were only twenty-five hundred slaves in a total population of forty thousand. There were cities where slaves were hired out and allowed to retain a large percentage of their earnings—that was the case in Philadelphia; in others, every penny they were paid went to their owners. And, of course, slaves were conveyed, in all slave-owning states, like any other form of property.

Just how inhumanely they were treated also depended on the laws of each individual state and the principles of their owners. They were far more likely to be found automatically guilty of real or imaginary crimes in South Carolina than in Pennsylvania; they were punished far more harshly in the South than an equally (and more surely) guilty white man. In the middle and late nineties, the duc de Liancourt traveled all through the United States. He was a man of sound and enlightened ideas, charitable both by nature and by principle, a man who loved liberty. He found the country and its citizens appealing in a great variety of ways; but, like most visitors, he was shocked at the cruel treatment of the slaves. In Charleston, he noted, blacks were severely whipped or executed for the slightest trespass, and that was true in most of the South. From Pennsylvania northward, on the other hand, slaves were treated like human beings.

The Size of America

Liancourt, and the other European visitors to the United States, made a point of traveling widely, and so they were able to note all these differences. Most U.S. citizens, however, tended to avoid moving, in large part because travel was still difficult, expensive, and highly uncomfortable. The roads, as Mrs. Adams knew all too well, were deep in mud when it rained, covered with dust when it was dry. Their deeply rutted surfaces kept carriages jolting and bumping until people became roadsick, just as they would have been seasick on the ocean. Wheels broke, horses were often hard to find; and it took even the president of the United States three and a half days to go the 120 miles from Monticello to Washington.

Naturally, if you traveled by stagecoach, you went even more slowly: if you left New York one morning, for instance, you would reach Philadelphia at 1:30 the next day, having spent a short night in Princeton, New Jersey, although in the summer, with fast horses, you could cover the distance in eighteen hours. As for the coaches, they were pulled by four horses, usually had from nine to twelve seats, with leather side curtains and an open front; and they were extremely uncomfortable. That, perhaps, was to be expected: after all, the United States was a brand-new country. What really startled European travelers, though, was that on public conveyances, the coachman was treated as an equal and allowed to eat at the same table as his passengers.

Still, if your destination was along a navigable river, like the Hudson, or along the coast, you could avoid the dreadful roads. Everywhere, entrepreneurs of all kinds were offering accommodations on board their ships. Schedules were published, prices publicized. In 1794, it cost $1.25 to go from Philadelphia to Baltimore by sea, and that included meals. From New York to Baltimore, it was $8.50 with meals; from New York to Norfolk, $12 with meals, $8 without. By comparison, a skilled sail maker earned $1.75 a day, an unskilled laborer $0.75 a day. There were no cabins, and very few beds, though. You stretched out wherever you could and slept little and badly. It was also incomparably easier, faster, and cheaper to transport goods by water. As a result, all the major cities were river or sea ports.

The new industries struck all the travelers: in the North, at least, they were appearing where none had been before; sometimes, they were being created to produce all kinds of manufactured goods which, just a few years earlier, had been imported from England. And they were all prospering. All along a tributary of the Schuylkill, for instance, mills were grinding tobacco (for snuff), mustard, chocolate, paper paste, plaster, and wheat, while one enterprising citizen, a Mr. Nicholson, was building factories to manufacture glass objects and metal buttons, which employed over a hundred workers.

That was all near Philadelphia, the largest city in the country; but the new industry was everywhere. In Albany, New York, already a well-established town since it had been founded in 1660 and incorporated in 1686, there were major glass manufactures that produced windowpanes, bottles, and various useful objects like glasses and pitchers; but there were also many tobacco mills that paid their adult workers $100 a year and their child workers $1 a week. In a country where, astonishingly, at least half the population was literate (a far higher rate than in France or England), it still seemed in order to send poor children out to work from the age of eight.

Nor was this all. Albany exported grains, wood, potash; and to keep all this moving, more than ninety ships plied the New York–Albany route from mid April to mid November. The rest of the year, the river was frozen, and goods accumulated until the spring thaw. Land prices reflected all this prosperity:

they could go as high as $75 an acre in the center of the city, three-quarters of the yearly salary of an adult workingman. By comparison, it is perhaps useful to know that at this same time, the tuition at Harvard College was $16 a year, plus $6 a month for food and lodging—but then, Harvard was cheap. At the incomparably more glamorous Princeton (then called the College of New Jersey), tuition was $100 a year, food and lodging the same, and laundry was extra.

City Life North and South

New York, in 1800, was the largest, and the handsomest, city after Philadelphia. Already, its population had reached fifty thousand inhabitants, but, as the duc de Liancourt observed, "this is an area that is growing so fast that whatever is true today concerning its population, its establishments, its prices, its trade was different six months ago and will be different six months from now."[1] Liancourt was right: in the five years from 1791 to 1796, for instance, the value of goods exported from the harbor of New York had risen from $2.5 million to $12.75 million. It was a busy, prosperous place, full of lively, ambitious people, and it was ideally situated. "There is probably not a more beautiful street than Broadway anywhere in the world," Liancourt wrote. "It is nearly a mile in length and about to be made longer still; it is over a hundred feet wide . . . Most of the houses are built of brick and many are very beautiful."[2] The mile in question started, as it does today, at the Battery, and ended a little past City Hall; and those brick houses belonged mostly to prosperous merchants.

Of course, if you came from south or west of the city, you first had to cross the Hudson. Naturally, there were no bridges: the river was far too broad to span with the contemporary technology, so travelers took one of the many ferries. They cost seven cents a person, fourteen cents for a horse, thirty cents for a carriage; sums that were considered to be reasonable. Once you got to the city, which covered the southern tip of Manhattan Island, though, you were entitled to wonder whether this could really be the place described by the duc de Liancourt. Except for Broadway, the streets were narrow, twisting, and crowded. Pigs roamed amid heaps of garbage, which stank to high heaven. As for water, the only way to get it was from the carts, which went up and down the streets, and sold it for one cent a pail. Clearly, this was no way to live, and the New Yorkers knew it: by the late nineties, lead pipes were being installed and pig owners were asked to move their beasts to the countryside higher up on the island.

For all its apparent disorder, New York was clearly prospering: between 1790 and 1797, its population increased from a little over thirty thousand to a little over fifty thousand, and, to serve the spiritual needs of all these people, there were twenty churches. At the same time great civic institutions were created. The poor, when ill, could be treated for free in a city hospital with a

New York City: view of Wall Street, Broad Street, and City Hall in 1797. Already a thriving metropolis, New York was on its way to becoming the largest city in the United States. (*General Research Division, The New York Public Library, Astor, Lenox and Tilden Foundations*)

capacity that grew from 60 to 120 beds—though if you could afford it, you paid $2 a day. At the hospital, one surgeon and twenty-four nurses were salaried, while four physicians gave their services free, each working for three months of the year. The whole operation cost the city some $3,000 a year.

That was charity; and so was the foundlings' home. The churches, too, looked after the poor, but they were not heavily burdened. There was a lot of work to be had in New York, so much so that it was very difficult to find domestic servants; and when you did hire one, people complained, he, or more likely she, was often lazy, demanding, and capricious. Still, that did not stop the rich: there were a great many merchants making a great deal of money, and for them England still provided the standard. Here, English furniture, English objects, and English habits prevailed, although, by the middle nineties, local creations were rapidly replacing imports. Furniture makers were a typical case: Walter McBride's Windsor chairs were selling briskly by 1795, and Duncan Phyfe was prospering. Although hardly original in his designs, Phyfe knew just how to adapt English and French styles to please his customers. He had several dozen employees working in his shop, much the largest establishment of that type in the United States, and produced great quantities of finely carved neo-classical furniture, complete with acanthus leaves, columns, lyre-back chairs (his great specialty), and the occasional Egyptian motif. Like the French, he often used mounts of gilded bronze; like the English, he produced severe-looking tables and straight-legged, unadorned chairs. And he was not alone. The French-born Honoré Lannuier naturally favored Paris styles and made very convincing Directoire and Empire pieces, in which sphinxes and assorted winged creatures served as the supports, while the highly successful Michael Allison stuck close to the Phyfe look. In one respect, though, New Yorkers looked firmly backward: their social customs remained thoroughly English. Ladies left the table at the end of dinner while the gentlemen passed the claret or the port around; ladies called on one another just as they did in London; and the food served in the great houses was far more English than French.

Still, all these grand occasions were only a small part of life in the city. Before anything else, New York was a busy harbor, so the streets were full of sometimes rowdy sailors; and naturally, there were prostitutes to serve them. For those interested, there were two choices: they could either walk along the several streets on which long lines of women were waiting for customers, or go to one of the several brothels that functioned quite openly. All this gave New York a rather raffish quality: it was busy, jostling, and by the standards of the time, rather dangerous. The crime rate was one for every 129 inhabitants; upstate, the ratio was only one in 2,633.

You could find almost everything in New York, but everything was expensive, and workers knew it. A washerwoman, for instance, was paid $0.50 a day, plus meals, coffee or tea, and a tot of rum. A laborer received $0.75 a day if unskilled, $1.25 if skilled; sail makers received as much as $1.75 a day, the workday being from 6:00 to 8:00, 9:00 to 12:00 and 2:00 to 6:00 for a total of 9 hours of actual labor. A skilled laborer, working 6 days a week, and taking no holidays, as was usually the case, could thus earn about $370 a year—as compared, for instance, with the laborers in Lancaster, England who only made $100; but then, in New York, the wages were not supplemented by food and lodging, and prices were incomparably higher.

Milk was $0.07 a pint, as much as it cost to cross the Hudson. Meat—poor quality beef—cost only $0.10 a pound, but the kind of veal that was served in the great houses fetched as much as $1.50 a pound, more than a laborer earned in a day. Butter was expensive too, at $0.25 a pound, and so were eggs at $0.12 the dozen. Shoes, though, were only $2.00 a pair; but boots, worn only by the wealthy, could go as high as $7.00. You could get a cheap chair for $1.00, or pay as much as $15.00 at one of the better makers. And if you had money to invest, you could buy a draught horse—for $75.00—and rent it out; or, if you had real capital, you could have a ship built to order: new, it would cost you the immense sum of $11,000, but if you were smart, you could recover your investment in as few as four or five years.

New York was rich, forward-looking, and increasingly open to new ideas and new techniques. Other U.S. cities, though prosperous, were much quieter, much more conservative, far less able to take advantage of the changes in shipping, commerce, and industrial techniques. Many also had serious health hazards: in Baltimore, as in Charleston, yellow fever and malaria were rife, and often deadly. Charleston had reason to fear the hurricane season. Even Philadelphia was given to epidemics so devastating that in 1799 the federal government had to move out, for a time, to Trenton, New Jersey. New York, on the other hand, was messy: most other cities were models of neatness and order, safe places where you never need lock your door. In Baltimore, tidy two-story brick houses were separated from the horses, carts, and carriages by swept and washed sidewalks; all streets were paved, many were broad, and all lined with birdhouses (a resident swallow was believed to bring luck). More important perhaps, the garbage was removed every day.

Of course, not all these orderly cities were fun to live in. A French traveler who spent time in Norfolk, Virginia (it had a population of three thousand), complained about the paucity of entertainment; but, being French, he praised the food. The fish, he noted, was fresh, delicious, and cheap: you could buy a twenty-pound weakfish for $0.90, while beef was $0.12 a pound, though pork was only $0.06 a pound. You could have a good dinner for $0.50, a full day's food, at an inn, for $1.00.

Once you had finished eating, though, there were few distractions, as the French traveler noted:

> Norfolk has two printers and two newspapers but these are used almost only to publish the announcement of Negroes for sale, lease or rent, to list the runaway Negroes and the names of those who citizens who are temporarily going out of town.
>
> The furniture [in people's houses] is simple; there are no mirrors or tapestries. The tables, desks and mahogany dressers are always in the English style. . . . Those who like cleanliness wash their floors.[3]

He then goes on to complain about the dreadful mosquitoes and the prevalent fevers.

Norfolk was small, Charleston was big. It was hot in Norfolk. In Charleston, everybody agreed, it was torrid, so much so that no lady would ever walk anywhere; as a result, carriages were numerous. "It is in relationship to the excessive heat of the summers that all architecture is designed," Liancourt noted. "The windows are open, the doors latticed, the possibility of having a perpetual draft always sought for. Wide outside galleries shield the houses from the sun . . . People in Charleston do not brag about owning the handsomest house, but the coolest."[4] That also meant bare floors, as little upholstery as possible, many fans, and many slaves to work them.

Slaves were in fact far more numerous than the white citizens, 55,000 to 30,000; but then the city was the major center for trade and luxury: in the whole of South Carolina, the white population was only 140,000. As for the government, it was kept cheap and unimportant. The only taxes were 0.5 percent on the value of land and other capital holdings, plus a head tax on blacks, $2.00 on males between sixteen and fifty, $1.00 on all others, and that was, of course, paid by the slaves' owners; and there was also a carriage tax, $0.75 per wheel per year (gigs had only two wheels). All that together produced $120,388.00. As for the government, it gave its officials modest salaries: the governor was paid $2,725.00 a year, the chief justice $3,300.00, thus firmly establishing the order of priorities. The courts mattered, and were busy protecting property: stealing a horse was a capital offense, stealing an ox was punished with thirty-nine lashes. The administration was far less important. As for the prices, they were as high as you would expect in a major center. You could rent a sizable house in Charleston for $300.00 a year and buy a cord of wood for $5.00; meat of indifferent quality was more expensive than in New York.

PHILADELPHIA, INCOMPARABLE PHILADELPHIA

Both New York City and Charleston were cheap compared to Philadelphia, though. There a large house downtown rented for as much as $2,500 a year, and land was just as outrageous: plots 150 feet deep cost $200 per foot of frontage, although in the suburbs the price dropped to $30 a foot. If you stayed at an inn, you had to pay $12 a week for your meals, and that did not include wine, candles, or a fire in your bedroom. A pair of good chickens, at the market, could fetch as much as $1. Travelers, whether American or foreign, complained bitterly about the prices. Still, all were amazed at the assessment of the taxable land within the city: in 1797, its value reached $102 million. By contrast, the state of Pennsylvania spent only $130,000 a year.

It was no wonder, really, that land was worth so much: in the late nineties, Philadelphia was still the richest, busiest city in America. The population had reached 60,000; 1,600 ships came yearly in and out of its harbor, and exports were up to $17.5 million, a third more than New York. As a result, the collector of customs was paid $8,500 a year, a huge salary at a time when the secretary of the treasury received a mere $5,000 and the chief justice of the United States $4,000. For that matter, even the local postmaster did better than the chief justice: he had $4,500 a year. Indeed, there was more here of everything: 33 churches; a 15,000-volume public library open 6 days a week; over 1,000 carriages, 600 of them gigs. Even the women, it seems, were more beautiful, no mean achievement since U.S. women were notoriously attractive; but then,

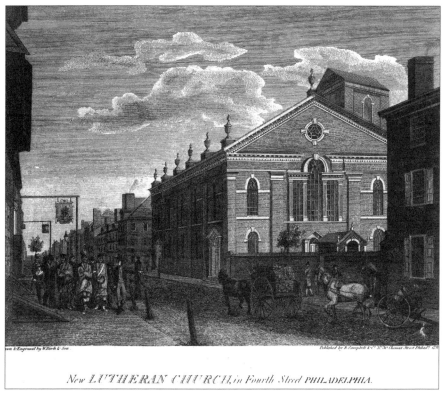

New *LUTHERAN CHURCH, in Fourth Street PHILADELPHIA.*

Philadelphia: The New Lutheran Church in 1799. Palladian architecture and a group of visiting American Indians: this most prosperous of U.S. cities had it all. *(General Research Division, The New York Public Library, Astor, Lenox and Tilden Foundations)*

complained one of the French visitors, Moreau de Saint-Méry, they were faded at 23, old at 35, and decrepit at 40.

Young beauties aside, Philadelphia had two other major attractions: scientific and philosophic societies of a caliber such as to excite the admiration of all European visitors. Papers were read, great questions discussed, and no one forgot that it was Benjamin Franklin who had invented the lightning rod. Discussions of a very different sort also added interest to life in the city: as the (temporary) capital, it was home to the president and Congress, at least until the fall of 1800. Although Congress was a much smaller institution than it is today—there were only sixteen states—it was nonetheless busy. The Republicans denounced the Federalists, and vice versa, on the floors of the House and the Senate and in their newspapers. There were impassioned debates, sharp attacks, and, on occasion, doses of negative campaigning—at least for the three to four months of the session. Still, you did not become rich by being a member of Congress: senators and representatives alike received $6 per day during the sessions, nothing the rest of the time; but they were also given an extra day's salary for each twenty miles of travel to and from their constituencies. As for the president, who resided in a large brick house and earned that measly $25,000 about which John Adams complained so bitterly, he remained the center of attention; and, of course, foreign envoys (the French, the British, the Dutch) added to the animation of the city.

Then there were the many printers and booksellers: the city was the center of the book trade, and you could find not only the latest U.S. books, journals, and pamphlets, but also a great variety of imported works in foreign languages. As for the avidly read newspapers, they were all frankly partisan: each sheet defended a party with more zeal than truth, and the most popular were those that were also the most violent.

The duc de Liancourt, who spent several months in Philadelphia, did not approve of this; but, otherwise, he could not praise the city too highly. "It is not only the most beautiful city in the United States," he wrote, "but one of the most beautiful in the world. It is true that it has none of the great and ancient monuments which we can admire in many European cities . . . but the houses are all sturdily built of brick; their facades reflect an unassuming simplicity and great cleanliness. Many have white veined marble ornaments on their lower floors, their stoops and around their windows . . . The streets are wide, almost all lined with trees, the sidewalks are wide and convenient."[5] And almost everywhere there were streetlights, which burned over thirty thousand gallons of oil a year.

For shopping, it was also, by far, the best provided city in the country. The shops stocked not just everyday needs, but all kinds of rare and luxurious objects, often imported from Europe. The shopkeepers were notoriously polite and, as long as the purchaser's credit was good, willing to wait for payment. The artisans' skills were equally well known, the only problem being that they earned so much money that they kept relatively short working hours; thus you were likely to wait quite a while for whatever you had ordered.

Money was indeed the key word: because Philadelphia was still the major banking center, because the traders grew richer every year, what mattered most was how rich you were. Liancourt, who was, after all, a duke, was invited to all the great houses, and he observed it all.

> The vanity of one's luxury is everywhere. People like to show off to the newly arrived European travelers their fine furniture, their English glass, their porcelain. But once that visitor has seen it all displayed in the course of a formal dinner, the hosts would rather invite some one else, a newcomer who has not yet been shown the magnificence of the house . . .
> Sumptuous dinners and teas are given for those who have just arrived from anywhere in Europe, whatever their social standing or their achievements: philosophers, priests, literary men, princes, tooth pullers, be they witty

or dull; and the next day this honored guest of the night before is barely greeted in the street unless he is thought to be rich, for this homage to wealth is the universal standard.

To these normal conditions of Philadelphia society, the circumstances of the moment bring the heat and intolerance of politics. In its first circles, Anglophilia dominates.[6]

And needless to say, these same circles were firm Federalists.

It was naturally annoying to be virtually ignored by your host of yesterday or of the week before; still, there were many of these grand houses, many dinners, many balls, and they were indeed glittering: just like in Europe, silver, crystal, porcelain, and flowers made the tables splendid. The jewels worn by the ladies were equally glittering, so much so that the balls were thought to be the equals of those at any European court, with the further advantage that the ladies in question were widely considered to surpass their old-world rivals in beauty. And unlike Boston, where old families still mattered a great deal, here it was enough to be rich: society was defined by income, not by birth, and consisted largely of traders and successful lawyers.

All that might perhaps have been expected. Far more surprising, these lavish displays, suitably diminished, reached down into the lower classes: they could be found, astounded observers noted, even among the black population. It, too, gave balls at which the food and drink were excellent, and the costumes sumptuous.

The luxury was almost as great in the better lodging houses: large rooms, good furniture, good service, all that could safely be expected at a time when country inns tended to be primitive in the extreme. Even better, there were chamber pots under every bed—a most useful convenience, as one of the hosts pointed out, since it obviated the necessity for a trip to the window during the night. Even so, it was perhaps a good thing that stoops and sidewalks were thoroughly scrubbed twice a week, a custom that also had an inconvenient aspect: the streets in winter tended to be covered with sheets of ice.

In this civilized, luxurious city, many habits had remained European; meals were a case in point. Just like in England, a solid breakfast complete with ham or fish, buttered toast, and tea or coffee would be eaten at nine. Dinner, at two o'clock, was the big meal of the day; it was the time at which all the silver was displayed on the sideboard, the time for guests. The meal itself was invariably plentiful; in a well-to-do house, it might consist of broth or a soup, several roasts (meat or poultry) with potatoes, peas, or another seasonal vegetable in butter or a spicy sauce, boiled or fried fish, salad (cabbage in the winter) for which each diner mixed his own dressing, pastries, fruit, cheese, and a pudding. Cider, beer, and light wines were served with the meal, Bordeaux or Madeira with dessert, at which point the ladies left, cigars were passed around, and so was a chamber pot. Then, at eight o'clock, tea was served with a light meal which often included oysters. All in all, it was enough to get through the day.

In this money-centered city, people looked to the future. There were brand-new model prisons, for instance, in which the inmates were kept in separate cells instead of vast holding pens; but then, the laws were very lenient. Capital punishment was for murder only; for most other offenses the prison sentences were shorter than in many states, and thought to be rehabilitative rather than merely punitive. There was also a possible escape from what some people considered a form of prison: divorce, while not very easy, was possible, and that, too, was considered most advanced. As for the most painful social issue of the day, slavery, Pennsylvania was, not surprisingly, liberal and enlightened. Any slave entering the state from elsewhere automatically became free; all slave children born after 1780 were also free, but bound to serve their former master until they were twenty-eight; and no citizen of the commonwealth was allowed to engage in the slave trade.

All this modernity, all the street cleaning, did not preserve the city from epidemics, though, the worst being those of yellow fever. In 1798, for instance, a traveling Englishman found himself in what had become virtually a ghost town. He described its horrors in vivid terms.

> Nothing was seen, but coffins carried through the streets unattended by mourners . . . Philadelphia which in the spring was a scene of mirth and riot, was in the summer converted to a sepulchre for the inhabitants. The courts of law were shut . . . The door of the tavern was closed . . . Every house was deserted by those who had strength to seek a less baneful atmosphere . . . Nothing was heard but the groans of the dying, the lamentations of the survivors, the hammers of the coffin-makers or the howling of the domestic animals which those who had fled from the pestilence had left behind, in the precipitancy of their flight. A poor cat came to the porch where I was sitting and demonstrated her joy by the caresses of fondness. An old negro-woman was passing at the same moment with some [tripe stew] on her head. With this we fed the cat that was nearly reduced to a skeleton; and . . . we asked her the news. God help us, cried the poor creature, very bad news. Buckra die in heaps. Bye and bye, nobody live to buy tripe stew and old black woman die too.[7]

Still, the epidemic eventually ended, and the city went back to its usual cheer. It thus seemed perfectly typical that the first balloon flight in the country should take place there. J. P. Blanchard, who made the ascent in 1793, charged the spectators the stiff fee of $5 a head, but Thomas Jefferson, who was there, thought it was well worth it. "The security of the thing appeared so great," he wrote his daughter Martha, "that everybody is wishing for a balloon to travel in. I wish for one sincerely, as instead of ten days I should be within five hours of home."[8]

Balloons and grand dinners were spectacular in different ways; the many carriages driving through the streets (including, of course, that of the president) clearly spoke of the city's importance; but all through the late nineties, its citizens knew that a severe loss was on the horizon. Because Congress had decided to build a federal capital on land given by Virginia and Maryland, which had also offered, respectively, $180,000 and $72,000, the government was bound by law to move to the District of Columbia in 1800. In many ways, that was a startling idea: from the most sophisticated city in the United States, the president, the legislature, and the central administration were to move to a hilly waste. At first, most people refused to believe that anything would be ready to receive them. They were wrong, though. On the date appointed, the federal establishment left Philadelphia, never to return.

A Brand-new Capital

It was a wilderness centered on a very small town; untamed forests, the odd torrent, and inconvenient hills hardly seemed to make the environs of Georgetown the right place for the capital of a new country. There was, however, nothing untrained about George Washington when it came to surveying a site and its possibilities. Hills from which, eventually and after a good deal of tree-cutting, the majestic Potomac River could be seen; potential for vistas; solid ground for building; and perhaps also a decent proximity to Mount Vernon— all these helped to determine the first president's choice. It had been generally agreed that the new city must be close to the Potomac; but when the first surveyors selected what Washington considered to be the wrong area, he promptly put them straight.

As it turned out, the new capital, originally called Federal City, was shaped by two great men: Washington and Jefferson. When, in 1790, Congress decided to go ahead with the building of a new capital, and accepted the offer of land and money from Virginia and Maryland, it was those two men, working closely together, who made it all happen. By the standards of the time, indeed, the work progressed remarkably quickly.

Congress had determined that the government would move ten years after the passage of the act creating the District of Columbia: amazingly, on November 1, 1800, President Adams did in fact take up residence at the still-unfinished President's House. That could not have happened if the president and his secretary of state had not been such determined and practical men. First, Jefferson interpreted the act as allowing the government to acquire enough land to create a real town, complete with public parks, instead of restricting its scope to the space needed just for government buildings; and then he made the decisions that shaped the city: the streets were to be straight and wide; the buildings were to be limited in height.

From then on, it all went very fast. Early in 1791, a presidential proclamation defined the boundaries of the district and appointed the commissioners who were to oversee the work of laying out and building the new city. In March, Washington, who admired the splendid neoclassicism, complete with gilded stars and eagles, of Federal Hall in New York City, commissioned its architect, Major Pierre Charles L'Enfant, to create a plan which was to include not just the streets and avenues but also the placement of all major buildings; and the next month, the president told L'Enfant he wanted the plan centered on the tallest hill—the one where the Capitol now stands. Of course, Jefferson also took the greatest interest in the project. He wrote L'Enfant on April 10:

> In compliance with your request, I have examined my papers and found the plans of Frankfurt-on-the-Mayne, Carlsruhe, Amsterdam, Strasburg, Paris, Or- léans, Bordeaux, Lyons, Montpelier, Marseilles, Turin and Milan, which I send in a roll by the post. . . . I am happy that the President has left the planning of the town in such good hands . . .
>
> Whenever it is proposed to prepare plans for the Capitol, I should prefer the adoption of some one of the models of antiquity, which have had the approbation of thousands of years; and for the President's House, I should prefer the celebrated fronts of modern buildings, which have already received the approbation of all good judges. Such are the Galerie du Louvre, the Garde Meuble [on the Place de la Concorde] and the two fronts of the Hotel de Salm.[9]

L'Enfant, who did not take advice well, largely ignored Jefferson's suggestions; but, by June, he had come up with his plan for radiating avenues superimposed on a grid pattern: the idea was to create diversity within order, unexpected views, and, most important, a whole series of plazas that would give the city a grand and spacious feel. Finally, on September 18, the commissioners decided that the area would be named the District of Columbia, and the city Washington; that height limits would be strictly enforced; that the streets would be 160 feet wide; and that all houses would be built of materials more permanent than wood. At the same time, the commissioners also decided to raise funds through the sale of the first lots, all of which were eagerly bought, some by people who really meant to live there, many more by speculators who expected to make a sizable profit.

So far, it had all been relatively easy. Nature had not exactly cooperated— between the vines, the occasional hidden gulch, and the mosquitoes, life on the site of the future city was a miracle of discomfort—but the plans were moving ahead and the funding was coming in. It was just then that most unwisely, L'Enfant, having first copiously insulted the commissioners who were, in fact, his employers, decided that he knew better than Washington, and told the president as much. The result came swiftly: on February 27, 1792, L'Enfant was fired. It was typical of Washington, however, that having dismissed that impossibly vain and disagreeable man, he then ordered that the plan was to remain unaltered.

Naturally, L'Enfant's departure created a void. In March, the government opened a competition, asking architects to submit plans for the Capitol and the President's House; the judge, it was understood, would be the president himself. Of course, there was, right at his side, a man who was deeply interested in architecture. Naturally, Jefferson submitted a proposal for the Executive Mansion—anonymously, because he did not want to trade on his position as secretary of state. He based his design on Andrea Palladio's Villa Rotonda in Vicenza, but it was rejected by Washington, who thought it looked too exotic. Instead, the commission went, in July, to James Hoban. The cornerstone was laid in the fall; and building proceeded, rather more slowly than wanted, but fast enough to keep reasonably within the preset schedule. As for the Capitol, the plan chosen was by Dr. William Thornton, an amateur architect; and Stephen Hallet was soon hired to rectify its many shortcomings. As a result, the first stone was only laid on September 18, 1793. Still, Jefferson had not lost out completely: to this day, much of official Washington remains shaped by the look of those "models of antiquity."

As for the President's House, even though work was proceeding, it posed something of a conundrum. Because L'Enfant had planned everything on a grand scale, he had also defined a space for that building that would have made it five times its present size: in fact, it was to be not the large mansion that was eventually built, but a palace worthy of Louis XIV—696 feet from east to west, 206 feet from north to south, with terraces, ponds, fountains, and a garden three-quarters of a mile in length. Before the architect was fired, the cellars of the proposed edifice were actually dug; but then Washington thought again. The work was stopped, and new specifications were issued.

As it turned out, however, Washington soon decided that the next plan, Hoban's, was not right either. He thought the mansion would now be too small and wanted it enlarged by a fifth; he also thought it was too plain, so the design kept changing until early in 1794. Even then, it remained austere—the North Portico, now the mansion's most recognizable feature, was yet to be imagined. As it was, work proceeded slowly: the walls were made of brick covered with stone, and while the brick could be made locally, the stone had to be brought in, and stoneworkers were hard to find. The basement was completed in September 1793, but it was not until the spring of 1799 that plastering began inside the house; wallpapering, in a few ground-floor rooms, was only begun a year after that.

Thus, when John Adams moved in, much still remained to be done. Only half of the mansion's thirty-six rooms had yet been plastered; where the grand staircase was to be, there was just a gaping hole. Indeed, only one of the two

PRESIDENT'S HOUSE.

Published by Bly J. Stow, Washington, 1826.

The President's House. The White House, without the portico, which was added later, had this facade when Adams and Jefferson lived there. (*General Research Division, The New York Public Library, Astor, Lenox and Tilden Foundations*)

backstairs was finished; the other was not completed until January 1801. The furniture was worn, inadequate, and sparse; the only painting was the Gilbert Stuart portrait of Washington. As for the grounds, they were a sea of mud from which emerged the shanties of the construction workers. Under these circumstances, it took both optimism and vision to write, as John Adams did, "I pray Heaven to bestow the best of blessings on this house, and on all that shall thereafter inhabit it. May none but honest and wise men ever rule under this roof."[10]

In the meantime, life in the President's House was anything but easy. For one thing, the building was freezing; for another, it was huge, requiring long walks to get anything done. Abigail Adams, when she finally came, was less than pleased. First, she had trouble finding the city: "I arrived on the 16th ult.," she wrote her sister on November 21. "Having lost my way in the woods on Saturday in going from Baltimore, we took the road to Frederick, and got nine miles out of our road. You find nothing but a Forrest and woods on the way, for sixteen and eighteen miles not a village."[11] Nor did things improve much when finally she reached the capital. "As I expected to find [Washington] a new Country, with Houses scattered over a space of ten miles, and trees and stumps in plenty, with a castle of a House—so I found it. The President's House is in a beautiful situation in front of which is the Potomac with a view of

Alexandria. The country around is romantic but wild, a wilderness at present." Then, after complaining of the size of the house, she went on: "The establishment necessary is a tax which cannot be borne by the present sallery. . . . I had much rather live in the House at Philadelphia. Not one room or chamber is finished of the whole. It is habitable by fires in every part, thirteen of which we are obliged to keep daily or sleep in wet and damp places."[12]

To keep this huge mansion up properly would have needed thirty servants, Mrs. Adams went on to complain, and she had only four. Congress had yet to decide that the expenses of running the mansion should be assumed by the government, so all depended on the occupant's means; and the Adamses, who were certainly not rich, hated to spend money. At least the unfinished state of the building offered one unexpected convenience: the East Room, which had yet to be plastered, was strung up with lines on which the laundry was hung to dry.

For the remainder of John Adams's presidency, in fact, only the western half of the mansion was actually lived in. Upstairs, the president had his office and his private quarters; downstairs, the house was turned around: instead of entering, as planned, on the north side, visitors came in through the rotunda on the south, via a wooden staircase and balcony. The oval drawing room was used as an entrance hall, and the other rooms as reception and state dining rooms. None of this made for comfort; furious though she was at her husband's defeat, Abigail was delighted to leave. The next occupant looked at things very differently, but then Jefferson enjoyed building and decorating. He never hesitated to spend money, and he saw the problems of the house not as a burden, but as an opportunity.

As for the city, it, too, was struggling to be born. Two brick buildings had been put up, one for the Treasury, the other for the State, War, and Navy Departments. There was a chamber in the north wing of the Capitol, but the south wing had yet to be started, so a cheap and temporary brick chamber for the House had to be put up in a hurry. The few residences still seemed lost in a wilderness; the streets were unpaved, rutted, and muddy, so that going from the President's House to the Capitol turned into a major expedition. Even on the Hill, the most settled part of the city, the rooming houses were so few that the members of Congress had real difficulty finding accommodation. There were neither public buildings nor churches: Washington, in 1800, was still more dream than reality.

It remained important nonetheless because the United States was a country in search of its center. With such dissimilar states being melded into one nation, a single focus was essentially needed, and people knew it. Diversity could be taken for granted, but it had to be tempered with a measure of uniformity—a capital placed outside any single state, a single currency, laws that applied alike to citizens of Vermont and Georgia. Just as important, because the House of Representatives was apportioned according to population, the citizens of all the different states needed to be counted by the central government; and so the census was born, at a time when most European countries had only the vaguest ideas about the numbers of their population. The meaning of that was clear: in the United States, democracy meant progress.

It also meant a growing population: in 1790, there had been slightly fewer than 4 million people in the United States, of whom about 700,000 were slaves. Ten years later, there were 5,308,473. Thus, by the time the third president was elected, the United States, having already invented itself, was ready for greater changes still. Whether in Washington or in the nation at large, and no matter how violent the political disagreements, one thing at least was sure: the next few years were likely to transform the city and the country.

CHAPTER NINE

The Spirit of 1800

BUILDING DEMOCRACY and expanding the United States: those were to be the two great themes of Thomas Jefferson's first term. Liberty mattered more to the president than any convenience of state. John Adams had felt that it was for him to speak and for the people to obey; Jefferson was never afraid to lead, but he also never forgot that in this new country, the people were sovereign. That, and the treaty signed with France, helped to reverse the relationship of the United States to the rest of the world. Now it was no longer France and Great Britain who set the terms of the political debate; it was instead the United States who hoped, by its example, to export the spirit of freedom.

At the same time, it was under Jefferson that the United States undertook its first major expansion. The Louisiana Purchase added a vast territory that was eventually divided into six states. It removed a potentially dangerous neighbor; and it made the United States into the major power on the North American continent.

CHANGES EVERYWHERE

"The spirit of 1776 is not dead. It has only been slumbering,"[1] Thomas Jefferson told a correspondent in 1799. Within eighteen months, he had been proved right, less perhaps because of its resurgence in America than because of its extinction in France. Paradoxically, it was General Bonaparte's coup that ensured the conclusion of an accord between France and the United States; and no one could accuse the ambitious Corsican of being too fond of liberty.

If there was anything the new First Consul understood, apart from winning battles, it was how to set priorities. The Directoire had left him defeated armies, a bankrupt treasury, and a nation in turmoil. The last thing he needed was an unnecessary dispute with the United States; and so negotiations could proceed meaningfully. Talleyrand, now foreign minister again, agreed. With astonishing prescience, he wrote: "[The Americans] will achieve a destiny that we can no longer prevent."[2] Naturally, he did not mean to give away anything unnecessarily; but this time, his tactics were the mirror image of what they had been during the XYZ episode. He saw the U.S. envoys frequently and was invariably pleasant and forthcoming. He insisted that he wanted to achieve a settlement, provided it took due account of French interests; and together with the First Consul, he decided to organize a period of solemn mourning for George Washington, who had died in December 1799. There were speeches eulogizing Washington as the Father of the Country and the Bringer of Liberty. The U.S. envoys were given the place of honor; and, thereafter, they found themselves frequently invited to the Tuileries and the houses of the other Bonaparte brothers.

Even so, every inch had to be fought over; and it was not until September that the convention was signed between the two countries, at the cost of $12 million in claims, which the United States agreed to forego. Whether a better bargain could have been struck must remain a moot point: what is sure is that the peace was advantageous to both sides. As for Adams, he had been proved right; but that hardly endeared him to the many Federalists who longed to be rid of him.

Of course, it also made a difference that France had a new government. Whatever Bonaparte might turn out to be like, it seemed clear that the French Revolution was finally over. By the spring of 1800, the Consulate was understood to be more stable, more responsible than the Directoire, and therefore France was no longer seen as a threat. Still, even so ardent a Francophile as Jefferson had his doubts. "A great revolution has taken place at Paris," he wrote John Breckinridge. "The people of that country having never been in the habit of self-government, are not yet in the habit of acknowledging that fundamental law of nature, by which alone self government can be exercised by a society, I mean the lex majoris partis [majority rule] . . . Perhaps it is now to be wished that Buonaparte may be spared as, according to his protestations, he is for liberty, equality and a representative government, and he is more able to keep the nation together, and to ride out the storm than any other."[3] In 1800, it was a view that was widely shared. France was no longer exporting revolution, and that contributed to the disappearance of the Federalists' best issue.

That naturally helped the Republicans, as did that resurgence of the spirit of '76 caused, at least in part, by the excesses of the Alien and Sedition Acts. Unfairly, however, Adams received almost no credit for his bold and selfless decision to resume the negotiations with France; and as winter passed into the spring of 1800, it became clear that the Republicans were immensely more popular than the Federalists. There were many reasons for this. Among them, certainly, was the work of the Democratic-Republican Societies, the lingering memory of the Whiskey Rebellion and the growing suspicion that the Federalists were no friends to liberty. Two more factors added to the plight of the Federalists: one, that Jefferson would certainly be the Republican nominee; and the second, that no one would fight the sitting president harder than the leaders of his own party. That, in doing so, they created deep unease in the northeastern states, where Adams was still liked, bothered them not at all.

HAMILTON VERSUS ADAMS

Hamilton, for one, knew precisely where he stood. "*Most* of the *most influential* men of the party consider [Adams] as a very *unfit* and *incapable* character," he wrote his friend Theodore Sedgwick. "I will never more be responsible for him by my direct support even though the consequence shall be the election of *Jefferson*. If we must have an enemy at the head of the government, let it be one we can oppose . . . The only way to prevent a fatal schism in the Federal party is to support General Pinckney."[4] It is in many ways a typical letter: Hamilton knew just how to rationalize what had become an unreasoning hatred for Adams, even going so far as to prefer Jefferson; but as any New Englander could have told him, the best way to create that "fatal schism" was precisely to support Pinckney.

Naturally, Adams detested Hamilton equally, but with better reason. Until the spring of 1800, he had tried to hide his feelings; but then in May he exploded. Fully aware that Hamilton was trying to replace him with Pinckney, he finally burst out in the course of a conversation with James McHenry, his secretary of war. Adams had long been aware that McHenry was merely Hamilton's tool; and he knew therefore that his every word would be promptly passed on. After first storming for a while, he went on to say that Hamilton was "the greatest intriguer in the world—a man devoid of every moral principle—a bastard and as much a foreigner as Gallatin [Albert Gallatin, the Republican congressman from Pennsylvania, who was Swiss-born]. Mr. Jefferson is an infinitely better man." He then turned on the secretary of war. "You are subservient to Hamilton, who ruled Washington, and would still rule if he could."[5] Upon that, he fired McHenry. The painful truth was, however, that Hamilton had ruled Adams indirectly as well, at least for the first two years of his presidency.

It was bad enough, from the president's point of view, that McHenry should have been essentially his master's voice; but his very incompetence meant that he was not dangerous. Far worse, as he slowly found out, the two key men in his cabinet, Oliver Wolcott and Timothy Pickering, were also followers of Hamilton. This was particularly painful, in part because Adams had really trusted them, in part because they were smart and influential; but as the spring passed into summer, the president finally understood that he had been betrayed by the very men who should have supported him, and he denounced them accordingly.

He had good reason to be angry, especially since he understood that putting Pinckney on the ticket was simply a stratagem to ensure his own defeat; but he was also an honorable man. Much as he despised the Republicans, he did not think it right to steal the election from them; and that was precisely what a Senate bill introduced by the Federalists had proposed to do. The means were extremely simple: Congress was to set up a committee of federal officeholders to count the votes in the electoral college. The officeholders in question, eager to perpetuate their rule, would then adjust the count as necessary.

That was too much even for the Federalist majority. The Senate bill never passed, but the attempt made it clear to all that this was likely to be a particularly dirty election. At the same time, the Republican feeling in the country was unmistakable; it owed a great deal to the Federalists' arrogance, and to their conviction that it was the people's duty to obey its betters. This they had proceeded to demonstrate again in 1799, during the course of the Fries's Rebellion.

FRIES, THE FEDERALISTS, AND CIVIL RIGHTS DENIED

The events had been simple enough. During the period of war hysteria, the Federalist Congress had passed a number of new taxes to fund the military effort. These new taxes were seen as illegitimate, particularly by the farmers of German origin who lived in some half dozen counties of central and western Pennsylvania. These people were further upset by the Alien Act, because it seemed to make it possible that under the new, narrow definition of who was entitled to stay in the United States, some of them at least would be forced to leave the country.

By January and February 1799, these people had prevented the assessors for the new taxes from carrying out their work. Some 18 men were arrested; and, on March 7, an armed group of some 140 men led by John Fries compelled their release. There the rising ended; within days, the rebels let it be known that they had reconsidered and would pay the new taxes.

Hamilton, however, thought he had found the ideal pretext for showing the military might of the federal government. The Federalist newspapers screamed about a Jacobin uprising, and Adams was persuaded to send in troops. It then took the army four weeks to reach the rural area around Bethlehem; and there it proceeded to behave as if it were in some subdued enemy area, thus earning itself and the government the deepest hatred.

In the meantime, John Fries had been arrested; in the course of two successive trials, at the urging of High Federalist judges, he was convicted of treason, and would indeed have been executed if the president, horrified at what he finally understood to be a most reckless and unjust verdict, had not pardoned him. All in all, Fries's Rebellion was just a minor episode in a remote rural area; but it had a powerful effect. If the Federalists were prepared to be so tyrannical under a president who was, after all, a moderate, what might they not do if Hamilton's candidate were elected?

The result was a Republican tide. In March, elections in New York State gave the legislature a Republican majority; and because the legislature chose the electors, it was a certainty that the state would be in the Republican column at the presidential election. The nomination of Aaron Burr for vice president strengthened the ticket still further: with Jefferson bringing in the South, and Burr a good deal of the North, the Federalists seemed very likely to lose. What then was that once-dominant party to do? Dumping Adams would mean losing New England, so they duly nominated an Adams-Pinckney ticket in the hope that Pinckney would win; but then Pinckney, having finally understood Hamilton's stratagem, announced that he would accept no vote that Adams did not also receive. That was the end of Hamilton's hopes. As for Adams, who was not mollified by this development, he went on to denounce Hamilton and his friends as being part of an English faction. Two years earlier, the majority of the people had been anti-French; now they were prepared to be just as anti-English—a distinctly awkward development for Hamilton.

Indeed, he was well aware of it. "It is plain that, unless we give our reasons in some form or other, Mr. Adams' personal friends, seconded by the Jacobins, will completely *run us down in the public opinion*," Hamilton wrote Wolcott in early October. "Your name, in company with mine, that of T. Pickering, etc, is in full circulation as one of the *British faction* of which Mr. Adams has talked so much." He added, menacingly, "I have serious thought of giving to the public my opinion respecting Mr. Adams."[6]

That was just what the Federalists dreaded. Already, Hamilton had told—privately—anyone who would listen just what he thought of John Adams, and, of course, these "private" conversations were widely repeated. If Hamilton were now to attack Adams openly, the Federalists would not stand a chance; but, given the tone of the campaign so far, it would hardly be a surprise. In 1788 and in 1792, there had been no campaign for the presidency; in 1796, because Adams was Washington's chosen successor, the campaign had been brief and dignified. Now, for the first time, the United States experienced what was to be called, at the end of the twentieth century, negative campaigning. The religious right, in a striking preview of its role in the 1980s and 1990s, took a leading part in the campaign. Its ministers denounced the Republicans in terms both scurrilous and grossly slanderous while presenting themselves as radiant with virtue. Following their lead, the Federalists described Jefferson as a Jacobin atheist. "Do you believe in the strangest of paradoxes—that a spendthrift, a libertine or an atheist is qualified to make your laws and govern you and your posterity?"[7] one of the party's pamphlets asked. That, in fact, was one of the key accusations against Jefferson: as an atheist, he was not entitled to govern a Christian country.

Atheism, at the end of the eighteenth century, was rare, and Jefferson himself was a deist: like most of the enlightened men of the period, from Voltaire to Franklin, he believed in a god who was an immanent abstraction and who required neither a particular creed nor a particular rite. That, for a fundamentalist, was almost worse than atheism; so the sects were enlisted in the anti-Republican fight. As for Jefferson, his reaction was, as usual, rational and eloquent. "The returning good sense of our country threatens abortion to their hopes," he wrote, "and they believe that any portion of power confided to me will be exerted in opposition to their schemes. And they believe truly. For I have sworn upon the altar of God eternal hostility against every form of tyranny over the mind of man."[8]

It was also during the campaign that the Sally Hemings story began. Jefferson was supposed to be the lover of one of his slaves, to have fathered children from her, even secretly to have married her—something that could diminish him only in the mind of a confirmed racist. That questionable story has been taken up again recently—hardly a surprise in a period that combines a passion for gossip with the desire to tear down great men. Misleading DNA tests have been held to prove Jefferson's guilt, when it seems far more likely that Sally Hemings's lover was in fact Jefferson's profligate nephew Roger. Obviously, nothing can ever be proved one way or the other; but it is seldom wise to believe scurrilous campaign literature. A look at the character of James Thompson Callender, the author of the accusation, may also be edifying. A recent defector to the Federalists, Callender was a habitual drunk who died by drowning, facedown, in a Washington puddle—killed, it is tempting to point out, by the mud he was so fond of slinging.

While Republicans and Federalists were busy attacking one another, the candidates remained silent; to indicate any sort of desire for office was still considered highly improper. At most, friends might circulate the occasional letter: the fiction remained that the presidency could be accepted, but never sought. It could, however, be snatched away; and that is just what Hamilton proceeded to do next.

As it was, Hamilton had written to all the important men of his party to denounce Adams. He was aware that what he called "the leaders of the second class"—that is, the local leaders who did not have a statewide following—were mostly in favor of Adams, so he wrote Oliver Wolcott, urging him "to inform them . . . of the facts which denote the unfitness of Mr. Adams."[9] Coming from

Adams's own secretary of the treasury, the campaign would, he hoped, prove convincing; but then he decided even that might not be quite enough. So it was that on October 24, to the horror of most of his fellow Federalists, there appeared a pamphlet entitled *Letter from Alexander Hamilton Concerning the Public Conduct and Character of John Adams, Esq., President of the United States.* The rationale of the pamphlet was simple: Hamilton, having been slandered, was forced to defend himself, and could only do so by pointing to the slanderer's shortcomings.

"There are," he explained, "great and intrinsic defects in [Adams's] character, which unfit him for the office of Chief Magistrate . . . [He] is a man of an imagination sublimated and eccentric; propitious neither to the display of sound judgment, nor to steady perseverance in a systematic plan of conduct. . . . To this defect are added the unfortunate foibles of a vanity without bounds, and a jealousy capable of discoloring every object."[10]

It was a strong beginning. From there, Hamilton went on to criticize Adams's whole career, which, according to him, had been a succession of blunders, inconsistencies, and foolishness. Adams was blamed, naturally, for not consulting his advisors (i.e., not doing what Hamilton wanted done), for sending the mission to France, and for his abrupt dismissal of McHenry and Pickering, in order to replace them with men more attached to Adams himself. Then, changing the focus, Hamilton defended his honor against the accusations that he was unprincipled and that he had formed a British faction; and, finally, he concluded that he was "still . . . resolved not to advise the withholding from [Adams] of a single vote."[11]

That last was hardly convincing. If indeed Hamilton's description of Adams was accurate, none but a fool would vote for the president; and that was what the Republicans gleefully concluded. The *Letter* was circulated, less by Hamilton's friends than by Jefferson's supporters. The reaction of the foremost Republican newspaper, the *Aurora*, was typical: "The pulsation given to the body politic by *Hamilton's* precious letter, is felt from one end of the Union to the other," the editor wrote. "It has displayed the treachery not only of the *writer*, but of his *adherents* in public counsels; and while it has thrown much false glare on the character of Mr. Adams, it has given some new and faithful traits also."[12]

It was almost too good to be true: the Republicans could now shower Adams with faint praise, saying that he really was not as bad as Hamilton said; Hamilton and his friends could be made to look like a nest of vipers; and the result of the election was less in doubt than ever. As for poor John Adams, now installed in the echoing, unfinished President's House, he maintained as dignified an appearance as his justified rage would allow. Perhaps it was just as well after all that George Washington had died: the man whom a contemporary Revolutionary leader, Light-Horse Harry Lee, described as first in war, first in peace, first in the hearts of his countrymen, would have been both puzzled and offended by this new kind of politics.

UNEXPECTED RESULTS

It was Hamilton's last hope that his *Letter* would, after all, elect Pinckney; it did no such thing, but for a long time, the results remained uncertain. Communications were slow, and the methods of voting varied from state to state. By early December, it was known that in the House the Republicans would have a 65 to 41 majority; but the electoral votes of the presidential election remained very much in doubt—though the general assumption was that Jefferson must have won. It was not until December 28 that the news could finally be confirmed, and then it was a shock: Jefferson and Burr were tied with 73 votes each; Adams trailed with 65, and Pinckney came last with 64.

As John Adams wrote Elbridge Gerry, "In the case of Mr. Jefferson there is nothing wonderful; but Mr. Burr's good fortune surpasses all ordinary rules and exceeds that of Bonaparte. All the old patriots, all the splendid talents, the long experience, both of Federalists and Antifederalists, must be subjected to the humiliation of seeing this dexterous gentleman rise, like a balloon, filled with inflammable air, over their heads."[13]

Indeed, it seemed all but impossible. Adams was beaten, of course, but the tie between Jefferson and Burr reflected both poor organization in the Republican party and a gap in the electoral system. Since there were no tickets on which candidates were listed together with the office they sought, simple numbers prevailed: whoever received the most votes became president; the runner-up was vice president. In 1796, the system had produced a president and vice president of opposite parties. Now it had brought about a real crisis. A simple way out of it, of course, would have been for Burr to encourage at least one of the electors pledged to him to vote for Jefferson instead; and on December 23 he wrote Jefferson: "My personal friends are perfectly informed of my wishes on the subject and can never think of diverting a single vote from you."[14] So far, so good; only Burr signally failed to act on his promise, and the deadlock remained unaltered.

At least some of the Federalists had an idea: the Constitution called for the House to make the choice; but if the House were to be deadlocked as well, could the government not devolve on the chief justice, the secretary of state, or the president pro tem of the Senate, good Federalists all? It seemed like so strong a possibility that Jefferson was seriously worried, but Hamilton knew better: playing with the voters in that way simply would not do. So it was that he wrote James A. Bayard, the sole representative of Delaware, a letter that, for all its backhanded compliments, actually endorsed Jefferson:

I admit that [Jefferson's] politics are tinctured with fanaticism, that he is too much in earnest in his democracy, that he has been a mischievous enemy to the principal measures of our past administration, and that he is a contemptible hypocrite, but it is not true as is alleged that he is an enemy to the power of the Executive. He is as likely as any man I know to temporize—to calculate what will be likely to promote his own reputation and advantage; and the probable result of such a temper is the preservation of systems, though originally opposed.[15]

This was a key letter. The hitherto obscure Bayard had suddenly become a very important man because of the constitutional provision that in case of a tie the House would decide the election, with each state delegation voting as a unit. Many of these delegations were split; but Bayard, as the sole representative of Delaware, had a full vote—and a single vote was likely to make all the difference. Then, to complicate things further, it was the House elected in 1798, with its Federalist majority, which was to do the voting; the new House would only come into office on March 4, 1801. Still, the vote by state weakened the Federalist advantage: a deadlock was by no means impossible.

In the meantime, except for assorted intrigues, everything stopped. Nothing could be done until the electoral college met on the second Wednesday in February—only three weeks before the inauguration of the new president. The tensions ran high, and the Federalists tried one last bold maneuver. Burr, it was generally assumed, was capable of being flexible in order to earn the presidency; thus, if the Federalists voted for him, and elected him, he would, although originally a Republican, probably do what he was told. This was, on the face of it, a dangerous assumption, and Hamilton would have nothing to do with it. Given the choice, he thought Jefferson infinitely preferable to the man he called "the Catiline of America," a reference to a notably treacherous politician in ancient Rome. Burr, as he explained to his friend Gouverneur Morris, "in my judgment has no principle public or private—could be bound by no agreement—will listen to no monitor but his ambition."[16]

On February 11, at a joint session of Congress, the results of the vote in the electoral college were proclaimed; and attention passed to the House of Representatives. It took nine states to make a majority; by early February, it was clear that the Republicans would support Jefferson, and the Federalists Burr. As for the latter, he had clearly given up all thought of helping Jefferson to win. Now it was time to make a president; and in order to do so, the House decided not to adjourn until it had chosen the man.

On that one day alone, there were nineteen ballots; there were sixteen more over the next five days. The result was always the same: Jefferson eight (one less than the constitutional majority); Burr six; and two delegations equally divided and therefore unable to vote. By the time the House was ready to cast its thirty-sixth vote, the situation looked desperate; but in fact, the pressures exerted by Hamilton, by local potentates, and by the fear of the voters caused a change. The Federalists in the two divided states, Vermont and Maryland, abstained, thus propelling them into Jefferson's column; but Delaware and South Carolina also abstained, thus restoring the deadlock. It was all up to James Bayard: having heard abundantly from Hamilton, having reached the conclusion that Burr absolutely could not be elected, and feeling that the deadlock was, in effect, flouting the spirit of the Constitution, the sole representative of Delaware voted for Jefferson, thus bringing him the ninth and decisive state. At last, on February 17, 1801, the United States had a new president.

THE SPIRIT OF JEFFERSON

When, on the morning of March 4, Jefferson walked over, unescorted, to the Capitol, it was at once clear that there had been a great change. Both Washington and Adams had maintained a semimonarchical state; all that seemed wrong and silly to the third president. He saw himself less as the ruler than as the servant of the people; he detested pomp and pretension, and wanted neither guards nor an entourage. Indeed, he had been staying at the same rooming house as always. Even after his election, he neither required nor accepted treatment that would set him apart from his fellow boarders, going so far as to refuse the place at table that was the nearest to the fire and thus the most comfortable.

In other ways, too, this inauguration was different from the three earlier ones: it was the first to take place in Washington; it was also the first not to be attended by the outgoing president. At four o'clock that morning, John Adams, in high dudgeon, had left for Massachusetts. The most important precedent set that day, however, may well have been the coming into office of a president of the opposition party: when that happened, democracy was proved to work in the United States.

Much was expected, therefore, of the new president's inaugural address. What policies would he proclaim? What methods of government would he advocate? How was the country going to change? And there was also the curiosity to hear a man with a notable talent for expressing himself. First, of course, Jefferson had to be sworn in by the new chief justice, the High Federalist John Marshall; and then he spoke to the crowd packed into the Senate chamber.

> During the contest through which we have passed, the animation of discussions and of exertions has sometimes worn an aspect which might impose on strangers unused to think freely and to write what they think; but this being now decided by the voice of the nation, announced according to the rules of the Constitution, all will, of course, arrange themselves under the will of the law, and unite in common efforts for the common good. All, too, will bear in

Thomas Jefferson, third president of the United States. This brilliant and cultivated man believed in freedom, equality, and the sovereignty of the people. *(Portrait File, Miriam and Ira D. Wallach Division of Art, Prints and Photographs, The New York Public Library, Astor, Lenox and Tilden Foundations)*

mind this sacred principle, that though the will of the majority is in all cases to prevail, that will, to be rightful, must be reasonable; that the minority possess their equal rights which equal law must protect; and to violate which would be oppression . . . We have called by different names brethren of the same principle. We are all Republicans, all Federalists . . .

Let us reflect that having banished from our land that religious intolerance under which mankind so long bled and suffered, we have yet gained little if we countenance a political intolerance as despotic, as wicked and capable of as bitter and bloody persecutions.

I know, indeed, that some honest men fear that a republican government cannot be strong, that this Government is not strong enough. . . . I believe this, on the contrary, [to be] the strongest government on earth. I believe it is the only one where every man, at the calling of the law, would fly to the standard of the law, and would meet invasions of the public order as his own personal concern.[17]

Here was a noble voice. In affirming the rights of the minority, as well as the principle of majority rule, Jefferson was setting a course that can still be followed two centuries later. Indeed, the denunciation of political extremism has lost no relevance, nor has the reliance on a law equal for all. Perhaps the most famous sentence of the address was "We are all Republicans, all Federalists." This was not meant to deny the differences between the parties, but to reaffirm the common republican ground on which all U.S. citizens stood; and that, in the early days of the Republic, needed to be said.

In 1801, it was also crucially important to reaffirm the respect owed the defeated party—that minority whose rights must be preserved. In this first really disputed presidential election, one party had really won, the other had really lost. This was new. Very different consequences might have been deduced from the event: it is Jefferson's great achievement that he saw and emphasized the common ground. There was to be no persecution—or prosecution—of the Federalists; but that did not imply that Jefferson was reaching for bipartisanship: he promptly fired as many officeholders as he could, and replaced them with Republicans.

Still the great political lesson went on. The "essential principles" of the U.S. system of government, Jefferson said,

[are] equal and exact justice to all men . . . ; peace, commerce and honest friendship with all nations, entangling alliances with none; the support of the state governments in all their rights . . . ; the preservation of the general Government in its whole constitutional vigor . . . ; a jealous care of the right of election by the people . . . ; absolute acquiescence in the decisions of the majority . . . ; the supremacy of the civil over the military authority; economy in the public expense . . . ; the diffusion of all information . . . ; freedom of religion; freedom of the press and freedom of person under the protection of the habeas corpus and trial by juries impartially selected.[18]

Here were all the great principles without which a democracy cannot exist. The miracle was that these lofty ideas were expressed so plainly: there was nothing here that every citizen of the United States could not understand. Clearly, since writing the Declaration of Independence, Jefferson had lost none of his political and literary genius.

That was so patently true that John Marshall, one of his greatest opponents, praised the address, in a letter to C. C. Pinckney, as "in general well judged and conciliatory. It is in direct terms giving the lie to the violent party declamation which has elected him, but it is strongly characteristic of the general cast of his political theory."[19] As for Jefferson, he took an even broader view than Marshall supposed: it was not just within the United States that the new administration hoped to create a new climate of liberty. "A just and solid republican government maintained here," he explained on March 6, "will be a standing monument and example for the aim and imitation of the people of other countries."[20]

A New Government

Admirable though these principles were, it remained necessary to apply them. As soon as he had been inaugurated, Jefferson found himself faced with three urgent issues. One, the legacy of the previous administration, was that a number of people who had been convicted under the Sedition Act were still in jail. Until the act itself could be repealed—and Congress did not meet until December—Jefferson settled the issue by pardoning all those who had suffered fines or imprisonment. The next of these issues was the appointment of a cabinet. Adams had simply kept Washington's appointees; now there was to be a clean sweep, and Jefferson began to show his talent for governing by picking outstanding men.

The most important office, that of secretary of state, went to James Madison. It made every kind of sense. Madison was highly competent—eight years later his talents carried him to the presidency; he and Jefferson were old friends; and Madison, as coleader of the Republicans, was responsible for much of the party's electoral triumph. At the Treasury, Jefferson put Albert Gallatin, a former congressman of Swiss origins and enormous competence, famous for his trenchant critique of Hamilton's financial schemes. Here was a man who could be relied on to run the government as economically as possible. The new war secretary, Henry Dearborn, brought both administrative know-how and geographic balance to the cabinet: Madison was from Virginia, Dearborn from Massachusetts—as was the attorney general, Levi Lincoln, a man who understood the claims of liberty. Finally, Robert Smith, of Baltimore, was made secretary of the navy. Each of those men was, individually, a good choice. Just as important, they formed a harmonious and loyal cabinet: Jefferson knew that he could count on them, and they trusted one another. It was quite a contrast to the Hamilton-controlled Adams cabinet. Jefferson then completed this first round by appointing Robert Livingston as minister to France. Once again, he had chosen well: the near future was to prove it.

All through the president's term, the cabinet met on an average of once a month. There were real discussions between its members, but on every occasion a consensus was reached. Still, Jefferson worked most often with individual cabinet members. Although he was scrupulous in never exceeding his

powers, he understood clearly that he was in charge, that the ultimate responsibility was his, and that therefore the great decisions must also be his. Here,
indeed, was no weak government.

The third of the three urgent issues was that of actual governance. No matter how talented a president may be, he must govern through his appointees.
In 1801 there were 316 officers subject to direct appointment and removal—
mostly collectors, federal attorneys, and U.S. marshals; the postmasters were
chosen by the postmaster general who was, himself, a presidential appointee.
What Jefferson found, however, was that Adams had made a mass of appointments after becoming aware of his defeat; the last of these were the 42 justices
of the peace for the District of Columbia whom Adams had appointed on
March 2. These had been duly confirmed by the Senate on the very last day
of its term, but the commissions had not yet been sent out. Finally, although
many of those appointed to the various offices were removable, the judges
were not; and Adams had seen to it that the judiciary was solidly Federalist.

This struck Jefferson as very much less than fair. Three years later, in June
1804, he wrote his old friend Abigail Adams and told her so:

> I can say with truth, that one act of Mr. Adams' life, and one only, ever gave me
> a moment's personal displeasure. I did consider his last appointments to
> office as personally unkind. They were from among my most ardent political
> enemies, from whom no faithful co-operation could ever be expected, and laid
> me under the embarrassment of acting thro' men whose views were to defeat
> mine; or to encounter the odium of putting others in their places. It seemed
> but common justice to have a successor free to act by instruments of his own
> choice.[21]

Unquestionably, John Adams had allowed himself to be carried away by
his anger at his defeat: there was something both mean and childish in
attempting to deny his successor the means of governing, in a spirit of "If I
can't have it, he won't, either." The fact that the outgoing president should have
known better, however, did nothing to resolve the problem; and it was one Jefferson was forced to tackle immediately.

He tried to do so in a fair and reasonable spirit: there must, he felt, be an
equilibrium between the two parties in the staffing of the government, but, on
the other hand, he was resolved not to fire competent men merely because
their opinion differed from his. He thus defined two categories. The first was
comprised of the appointments marred by "inherent disqualification"—those
made by Adams after his defeat was known. Naturally, the "midnight appointments" of the justices of the peace, those whose commissions had been signed
late on the evening of March 3, were included in these: Jefferson simply refused to send out the commissions, and made his own recess appointments
instead.

The second category included those whose official misconduct offered sufficient grounds for removal: customs officers who were delinquent in their accounts were a good example of this. That left all the Federalist judges in place—they were unremovable—so, in an effort to create a balance, Jefferson decided to replace all federal attorneys and marshals. All other federal (and Federalist) officers were to remain in place. Given the spirit and customs of the time, this was a singularly moderate policy.

A typical case of these guidelines could be found in Connecticut, a strongly Federalist state. There, John Adams had appointed Elizur Goodrich as collector of customs of New Haven late in February. Jefferson promptly removed him and replaced him with Samuel Bishop, the mayor of the city. Naturally, there was a good deal of local protest—but less on strictly political grounds than because Goodrich was competent and Bishop, at seventy-eight, too old for the job.

It would have been very unlike Jefferson to ignore these reactions. On March 27, he wrote to a local merchant, Elias Shipman. "If a due proportion of office is a matter of right," the president asked, "how are vacancies to be obtained? Those by death are few; by resignation, none. Can any other mode than that of removal be proposed?" Having then gone on to say that the total exclusion of Republicans from office called for prompt correction, he explained that once this had been done, he would "return with joy to that state of things, when the only questions concerning a candidate shall be, is he honest? Is he capable? Is he faithful to the Constitution?"[22]

All this was especially galling to the Federalists, who, considering themselves the natural party of government, utterly failed to see why any but themselves should run it. More, they failed to acknowledge that this one-party staffing was the invention of John Adams. Given this fact, his successor surely had the right to do at least half of what the former president had done; but that was an argument the Federalists refused to consider. Typically, the *New York Post* denounced "a deadly revenge, an inexorable rancour, a vindictive malice against all and every one who had dared to differ in sentiment from [the Republicans], however good, however virtuous, however meritorious he may be [which] marks and controuls the measures of those now in power."[23]

It was natural for the *Post* to rave; it was equally natural for Jefferson to state, quite openly, what he was doing. Adams had announced that he would base his appointments on competence alone, but then had gone on to disqualify all Republicans. Jefferson said he wanted to create a balance between politics and competence, and behaved accordingly. He also thought, and said, that it was important to get the best man for the job, whatever the job might be, because the citizens of a country administered by incompetent officials would soon become disaffected. If the Republic was to survive and prosper, then it must have honest and efficient administrators.

Just how fine a line he meant to tread he explained in a letter to Lincoln, his attorney general. "Every officer of the government may vote at elections according to his conscience," the president explained in October 1802, "but we would betray the cause committed to our care, were we to permit the influence of official patronage to be used to overthrow that cause."[24] It made perfect sense: Jefferson and his party had been elected to carry through measures and principles; they had a duty, therefore, to the majority that had brought them to office, but at the same time they must take care to respect the liberty of the individual. As the president wrote Elbridge Gerry: "The rights of opinion shall suffer no invasion from me."[25]

DEMOCRACY AND THE JUDICIARY

All this applied to removable appointees; but there were also the judges. In the judiciary, too, Adams and the Federalists had tried to nullify the results of the election by ensuring that the Federalists would remain in charge no matter what. The Judiciary Act of 1801, which had become effective only on February 13, authorized a great increase in the number of federal judges, six of whom were appointed on March 3, the very last day of Adams's term; and naturally all the judges chosen by Adams were fervent Federalists. At the same time the justices of the Supreme Court were reduced in number from six to five in an attempt to make sure Jefferson would never get a nomination to the High Court. Taken altogether, it was nothing less than an attempt to pack the judiciary in defiance of the voters' express will. The fact that many of the new judges promptly displayed an arrogant and domineering spirit only added insult to injury.

There was a remedy to at least some of this. In his first message to the new Congress, which met in December 1801, Jefferson said: "The judiciary system of the United States, and especially that portion of it recently erected, will of course present itself to the contemplation of Congress."[26] The president's meaning was entirely clear, and Congress did better than contemplate: it acted promptly. On January 6, 1802, two close friends of Jefferson, John Breckinridge of Kentucky and Stevens Thomson Mason of Virginia, introduced a motion before the Senate tending to repeal the Judiciary Act.

This action seemed particularly timely. The Supreme Court, in December, had taken its first step in what, two years later, turned out to be a test case, *Marbury v. Madison.* The Court granted a preliminary motion made by former attorney general Charles Lee to show cause why a writ of mandamus should not be issued against Secretary of State Madison requiring him to deliver commissions as justices of the peace to William Marbury and three others. These were the commissions that had been duly completed late on March 3, but which Jefferson had decided not to forward to their addressees. The constitutional question was whether a president had the power thus to annul an appointment that had been confirmed by the Senate. The Republican majority in Congress saw it simply as one more attempt to preserve the Federalist establishment.

The Court having acted, so did Congress. On February 3, the Senate, where the Republican majority was small, passed the repeal of the Judiciary Act by sixteen to fifteen, and in March the House did the same by a substantial majority. As the new judicial offices were abolished, so, to the rage of the Federalists, ended the tenure of Adams's midnight appointees.

Making the Country Well

"No more good must be attempted than the country can bear," Jefferson had written a friend on March 31, 1801. "[We must] reform the waste of public money and thus drive away the vultures who prey on it, and improve some little on old routines."[27] This was entirely consistent with his political philosophy: far from launching expensive programs, creating great armies, or interfering either within or without its borders, the government of the United States should spend as little as possible, and largely restrict itself to preventing and stopping evils. Today, this may seem an extraordinarily limited view, but the United States was then still a country of independent farmers with expanding markets. The new industries were small, poverty was exceedingly rare, the country very sparsely settled: there really was not very much to do. Hamilton had wanted to create an expensive army, and spend generally, as a way toward a strong centralized government. Jefferson saw that simply as a potential for oppression, and was determined to focus on liberty rather than expansion.

Still, in that first session of the Seventh Congress, there were things to be done besides the repeal of the Judiciary Act. In his first message, Jefferson was able to announce the signing of the agreement with France, and his consequent ability to cut down on military costs. He also told Congress that he had abolished a multitude of offices created by Adams, that he had reduced foreign missions to three (Paris, Madrid, London), that he had laid up five frigates and reduced the Naval List from fifteen captains to nine, so that expenditures would shrink from $2 million in 1801 to $915,000 in 1802. He now asked Congress to reduce the army, so that its expenses would be cut in half; and as a result of all this retrenchment, he recommended the immediate repeal of all internal taxes—including the hated excise—and the use of specific rather than general appropriations. Thus the government would derive its income exclusively from customs duties and no longer burden the citizens in any way.

Conveniently, however, these new arrangements did not mean that the government was short of money. With trade increasing every year, the customs dues brought in ever-larger sums, and so Jefferson was able to set about doing what he most wanted to do. In 1801, the national debt stood at $83 million, the result mostly of money spent during the War of Independence. Together, Jefferson and Gallatin decided that a little over $7 million of this would be repaid every year, so that, within sixteen years, taking interest payments into account, the government would owe no more money. In fact, these reimbursements did not proceed quite as fast as planned; but by the end of Jefferson's second term, the debt had been reduced by a third.

With the further repeal of the Alien and Sedition Acts, the president's program was pretty well exhausted—and that made perfect sense since he thought that there was no sense in burdening the people with unnecessary obligations. Of course, Hamilton was left fuming. "No army, no Navy, no *active* commerce," he wrote Rufus King in March 1802. "National defense not by arms, but by embargoes, prohibitions of trade, etc; as little government as possible within;— these are the pernicious dreams which, as far and as fast as possible, will be attempted to be realized."[28] He was exaggerating, of course—Jefferson did not do without a navy, but not by much.

While the new president certainly wanted to shrink the role of the federal government—in part also to keep from impinging on the rights of the states— he had every intention of being very much in charge as chief executive. Returning to Washington's practice, which Adams had abandoned, he insisted on seeing the significant correspondence of all the departments as it came in, and on defining the proper response. Once again, he was treading a fine line: he knew the dangers of being swamped by unimportant material, but he always managed to preserve the distinction between what was merely routine and what was really important. He was also willing to work hard. Adams had spent up to eight months a year in Massachusetts; Jefferson retreated to Monticello only for the two summer months, a wise precaution since, in Washington, the danger of malaria was always present; and unlike Adams, who always found himself overworked, Jefferson, even when he was away from the capital, spent twelve- to fourteen-hour days on the duties of his office.

A Most Attractive President

That the new president governed smoothly and effectively no one doubted— even the most extreme Federalists never accused him of laziness or incompetence—but it is only fair to add that he was also lucky. It was not just that his predecessor had, in effect, ended the crisis with France: the conclusion, in 1802, of the Peace of Amiens between France and Great Britain removed the one remaining foreign affairs problem. Temporarily, the United States was no longer forced to defend its right to sail and trade—although that happy state of affairs lasted only as long as the Peace of Amiens. There were no more pressures to favor one side or the other; and that also meant that the president could shrink the navy without endangering the country's commerce. As for the other change that eased his way, his unparalleled control of Congress, that was due both to popularity and good management. Like Adams, Jefferson could count on substantial majorities of his own party in both houses and the election of 1802 only strengthened them: as its result, the Republican majority was 25 to 9 in the Senate, and 103 to 39 in the House. Unlike Adams, however, Jefferson was the actual leader of the party. Partly because he had been its effective head before taking office, partly because he remained highly popular among the voters, the president found himself in the strongest of positions. He was also a man capable of being enormously charming; he made himself accessible to senators and representatives; he listened to them carefully; and the result was a degree of presidential ascendance very seldom duplicated in the course of the nineteenth century.

Jefferson's manner, in fact, was both an accurate reflection of his personality and an extraordinary tool of government. The president should, in theory, have been just the sort of man most U.S. citizens disliked: he was fascinated by Europe (France particularly) and its achievements; he liked French wine, French furniture, and French books; he was better read than just about any of his compatriots; far from being limited to politics, he was also an architect, an inventor, and an agronomist. He had learned in Paris that witty conversation is one of the pleasures of life, and had never forgotten it. All that should have put him far beyond the reach of most of his fellow politicians; but it came with an egalitarianism that was both natural and deliberate. Although Jefferson might be a superior man, he was never proud, impatient, or disdainful. Attending his daily dinner parties came to be seen as nothing less than a huge treat—one to which members of Congress were often invited. Finally, in a country that still distrusted pomp and ceremony, it seemed just right that the new president ended all the semimonarchical ceremony dear to his two predecessors: those levees of which Mrs. Adams complained were never seen again. Naturally, what pleased the people of the United States upset some foreigners. The president, the British minister reported, is "careful in every particular of his personal conduct to inculcate upon the people his attachment to a republican simplicity of manners and his unwillingness to admit the smallest distinction, that may separate him from the mass of his fellow citizens . . . [He will see any person at any time] with a perfect disregard to ceremony in his dress and manners."[29] It was just another paradox: this most European of Americans was also perfectly in tune with the country's disdain for artificial formality.

All in all, the president's combination of high intelligence and utter lack of pretension was hard to resist. Margaret Bayard Smith, who came to Washington in 1800, and remained to become one of the city's great hostesses, could testify to it. She was the wife of a newspaper owner close to the Republicans and met Jefferson, then president-elect, when he dropped by her house one day. He had business with her husband; while waiting for him to return, he entranced Mrs. Smith by the quality of his conversation. Far from frightening her, he immediately put her at her ease; he paid attention to her, made her feel interesting, and was himself interesting in return. From then on, she considered, rightly, that they had become friends. On May 28, 1801, for instance, she told her sister all about it. "Mr. Smith and I dined at the President's," she wrote. "He has company every day but his table is seldom laid for more than twelve. This prevents all form and makes the conversation general and unreserved. I happened to sit next to Mr. Jefferson and was confirmed in my prepossession in his favour, by his easy, gentle and candid manner."[30]

Soon the Fourth of July, that celebration so dreaded by the Adamses, came around. Naturally, Mrs. Smith went to the President's House. There, she noted,

> we found about twenty persons present in a room where sat Mr. J. [sic] surrounded by the five Cherokee chiefs. After a conversation of a few minutes, he invited his company into the usual dining-room, whose four large sideboards were covered with refreshments, such as cakes of various kinds, wine, punch, etc. Every citizen was invited to partake . . . and the invitation was most cheerfully accepted. . . . The company soon increased to near a hundred, including all the public officers and most of the respectable citizens, and strangers of distinction. Martial music soon announced the approach of the marine corps of Captain Burrows who, in due military form, saluted the president . . . After undergoing various military evolutions, the company returned to the dining-room, and the band from the adjacent room played a succession of fine patriotic airs . . . Mr J. mingled promiscuously with the citizens, and far from designating any particular friends for consultation, conversed for a short time with everyone who came his way.[31]

No doubt, it helped that unlike John Adams, Jefferson had great personal dignity; but his approachability was not just an affectation—it reflected his genuine interest in his fellow citizens.

The presence of the Cherokee chiefs was also not an accident. From the beginning of the Republic, a state of uneasy truce had prevailed between the American Indians and the white settlers. The settlers were still few enough, in most places, not to be a major threat to their predecessors on U.S. soil; but their numbers were growing, and it was becoming evident that some sort of policy would soon have to be devised. Naturally, Jefferson thought about this. Unfortunately, the solution he proposed, while eminently rational by his standards, took no account of the basic elements of the Indians' culture. Hunting, which the president saw only as a food-providing activity, was in fact essential to the American Indians' self-image and to the performance of their religious rites. It was not a case of switching jobs, so to speak, but of understanding that ethnicity is not based on reason; and that, for an eighteenth-century thinker, was utterly incomprehensible.

Unlike some of his compatriots, who simply wished that the American Indians would go away, Jefferson was concerned about the welfare of the men and women whom he saw, in a Rousseau-inspired view, as noble savages. The solution, therefore, seemed obvious: "The promotion of agriculture . . . and household manufacture are essential in their preservation," he wrote in 1803, "and I am disposed to aid and encourage it liberally. This will enable them to live on much smaller portions of land . . .

"While they are learning to do better on less land, our increasing numbers will be calling for more land, and thus a coincidence of interests will be produced between those who have lands to spare, and want other necessaries, and those who have such necessaries to spare, and want lands."[32] It seemed so logical. Alas, it was so wrong.

Washington Society

It was no wonder Mrs. Smith found the Fourth of July celebration so cheery: not only did Jefferson enjoy it himself, he was also rapidly improving the house itself. Although Monticello was as yet unfinished, the president knew just how to live in a mansion. The Adamses, for all their landholdings, were middle class in their habits, mean and stiff in their entertaining; the new president was an aristocrat who knew how to do things grandly. Of course, that had drawbacks: John Adams economized a substantial part of his salary, Jefferson spent every penny of his, and a good deal more besides. The yearly bill for wine alone came to $3,000, that for provisions and groceries to the enormous sum of $6,500, while the twelve servants were paid $2,700 and (the men, at least) given liveries. And then there was Meriwether Lewis, Jefferson's secretary, whose salary of $500 a year the president paid himself.

As for the mansion, it was transformed by its new tenant. The wooden stairs and balcony on the south facade were removed, and the entrance restored to the north front; the oval saloon was now used as the main drawing room, and there were two dining rooms—one official, one informal. The decoration everywhere was enriched by the addition of carved architraves and door cornices, new glass doors and transoms, chair rails, and fancy baseboards. Upstairs there were now two flush toilets, while wood was replaced by coal in all the fireplaces. Coal burned hotter and longer, but it was far more expensive, so the State reception rooms were heated only when actually in use. On the other hand, Jefferson opened them to the public on a daily basis, thus setting another precedent. He also had the garden cleaned up, the shacks demolished, and, in 1803, commissioned Benjamin Latrobe, the new surveyor of public buildings, to design two wings to the east and west, the smaller ancestors of today's structures. These were completed in 1808; but already by 1804, the grand staircase of the mansion had been finished. As for the East Room, it remained in its earlier raw state, except for the part that was walled off and served as a bedroom for Meriwether Lewis.

In this new, more elegant President's House, however, informality prevailed. There were, of course, large receptions for New Year's and the Fourth of July; but otherwise Jefferson invited people mostly to those small four o'clock dinners Mrs. Smith described. Guests numbered from four to fourteen; the servants, having once brought the food in, vanished. The guests served themselves so that they could talk freely without outside listeners; there were five dumbwaiters to ease the process. All at table were deemed equal: nothing interested the host less than the quarrels about precedence of which the Europeans were so fond. The result was an easy, relaxed atmosphere. The food was good, the wines superb; and conversation was the order of the day. All in all, having dinner with the president was more like visiting a well-managed private house, even if, most of the time, there was no hostess. Jefferson, after all, was a widower; but one of his daughters would occasionally visit, and then she would sit at the head of the table.

It was a good thing that Jefferson was so sociable because amusements were still few in Washington. So it was that the Sunday religious service held in the chamber of the House of Representatives became, improbably, a gathering for the city's elite, with the president himself in regular attendance. Mrs. Smith, naturally, was there, and described the scene to her sister.

> The gay company which thronged the House looked very little like a religious assembly. The occasion presented for display was . . . a favorite one for the youth, beauty and fashion of the city. . . . The members of Congress gladly gave up their seats for such fair auditors, and either lounged in the lobbies or round the fireplaces or stood behind the ladies of their acquaintance. This sabbath-day resort became so fashionable that the floor of the House offered insufficient space, the platform behind the Speaker's chair, and every spot where a spot could be wedged in was crowded by ladies in their gayest costume and their attendant beaux. . . . Smiles, nods, whispers . . . sometimes tittering marked their recognition of each other and beguiled the tedium of the service. Often, when cold, a lady would leave her seat and, led by her attending beau, would make her way through the crowd to one of the fireplaces where she could laugh and talk at her ease. . . . The musick was as little in union with devotional feelings as the place. The marine band were the performers. Their scarlet uniforms, their various instruments, made quite a dazzling appearance in the gallery.[33]

Happily, there were also more secular parties. Already a few hostesses kept open house—Mrs. Smith was one of them—so a pleasing mix of people would stop in: members of Congress, army and navy officers, physicians, landholders, ladies about town, and the young, all chatting, making music, and, of course, eating. All this was leavened by an occasional scandal. That, on a number of occasions, was caused by Maria Bingham, the divorced wife of a French émigré, Count de Tilly. Already, in the spring of 1800, Mrs. Adams had been exposed to her, and she promptly wrote her sister that Maria's dress was "an outrage upon all decency"; then, instead of drawing a veil upon the shameful exhibition, she went on to describe every detail with considerable gusto. The lady wore, she explained,

> a satin petticoat of certainly not more than three breadths [i.e., narrow and clinging] gored at the top, nothing beneath but a chemise. Over this a thin coat, a muslin sometimes, sometimes a crape made so straight as perfectly to show the whole form. The arm naked almost to the shoulder and without stays or bodice. A tight girdle around the waist and "the rich Luxurience of natur's charms" fully displayed without a [scarf]. The face, a la mode de Paris, red as a brick hearth. When this Lady has been led up to make her curtsey, which she does most gracefully, it is true, every Eye in the Room has been fixd upon her.[34]

The problem, from Mrs. Adams's point of view, was that though nearly naked, the former countess was so enchanting; and the lady obviously knew it. Four years later, still braving the gossip and censorious glances of the matrons, she gave Mrs. Smith a delicious shock, as the hostess breathlessly wrote her sister.

> Her appearance was such that it threw all the company into confusion and no one dared look at her but by stealth. The window shutters being left open, a crowd assembled around the windows to look at this beautiful little creature . . . Her dress was the thinnest sarcenet and white crepe without the least stiffening in it, made without a single pleat in the skirt, the width at the bottom being made of gores. There was scarcely any waist to it and no sleeves; her back, her bosom, part of her waist and her arms were uncovered and the rest of her form visible. She was engaged the next evening at Mdme P's; Mrs. R. Smith and several other ladies sent her word, if she wished to meet them there, she must promise to have more clothes on.[35]

Reading this, it is hard to know who had the better time: the near-naked former countess, the scandalized matrons, or the admiring crowd in the street outside.

Not all parties were so noteworthy: some were simply improvised get-togethers. Thus, when Mrs. Law, Martha Washington's granddaughter, saw Mrs. Smith walking by, she promptly invited her in.

> We had sat only a few minutes when she said: "Lay down your hat, Mrs. Smith, we have a fine roast turkey and you must stay and eat of it." Talking of

conveniences in cooking, "Come," said she, "you are young housekeepers, come and look at my kitchen." She has a contrivance, more convenient than any I ever heard of . . . The chimney is six feet in width, in this is placed a thing called the Ranger, in the center is a grate, about two feet wide, on one side a place to boil in, which contains 6 or 8 gallons of water, on the other side a place of the same dimensions for an oven, which opens in front, with a door, and has a shelf inside, so that two ranges of dishes can bake at the same time. Both the boiler and the oven are heated by the pine in the grate; which at the same time can roast anything placed before it, and as many pots as you please can hang over it. The kitchen is well heated, and the oven and boiler are always of a uniform heat. Here, with a small quantity of coal, she has often cooked dinner for large companies. They are to be had at Baltimore.[36]

Already, in the fall of 1800, the modern North American kitchen had been born.

Progress, however, often had a less pleasant aspect than that seen in the Ranger: as Washington grew, so was its natural beauty despoiled. Capitol Hill had been crowned with a fine stand of tall poplars, but, in 1801, they were cut down for fuel, and Jefferson did not like it. As Mrs. Smith observed:

Nothing afflicted Mr. Jefferson like the wanton destruction of the fine trees scattered over the city-grounds. I remember on one occasion . . . his exclaiming: "How I wish that I possessed the power of a despot." The company at table stared at a declaration so opposed to his disposition and principles. "Yes," continued he in reply to their inquiring looks, "I wish I was a despot that I might save the noble, the beautiful trees that are daily falling sacrifices to the cupidity of their owners, or the necessity of the poor."

"And have you no authority to save those on the public grounds?" asked one of the company.

"No," answered Mr J., "only an armed guard could save them. The unnecessary felling of a tree, perhaps the growth of centuries, seems to me a crime little short of murder."[37]

Here, too, fateful precedents were being set.

They were in other ways as well. Already, anything that was the largest of its kind attracted attention—the "mammoth cheese," for instance. This vast object, the size of the rear wheel of a wagon, was the homage of the farmers of Cheshire, Massachusetts, to the president. Shipped by sea from Boston to Baltimore, it was then brought to Washington and presented to Jefferson who, having expressed his thanks, proceeded to share it with a great number of people. The Federalists, at first, thought they had found the perfect pretext to mock: it was they who dubbed the cheese "mammoth"; but as many others were to learn over the next two centuries, in the United States, the biggest most often seems the best.

THE ARTS IN A NEW COUNTRY

Politics, in 1800, was part of the very being of the United States. It seemed the most important of subjects, one on which the greatest men in the country thought it worthwhile to write and dispute. The arts, on the other hand, often mattered a good deal less. Europe had an artistic tradition, the United States had nature. Of course, there had been many portrait painters over the previous century—most of them utterly devoid of talent, so that wooden figures stared glumly from many a canvas. And then, in the 1760s, with the appearance of Benjamin West, everything had changed. His vast depictions of heroic subjects—*Agrippina Landing at Brindisium with the Ashes of Germanicus* is a good example—proved that he was talented, as well as able to express himself fluently in the fashionable neoclassical style. There was a hitch, though: he moved to England and stayed there, and so did two other talented artists, John Trumbull and John Copley. The latter two returned, though, and went on to prove themselves competent men, able to turn out a pleasing portrait or the representation of an important historical scene. Both could paint large-scale canvases; both had a sense of the heroic with its inevitable romantic exaggeration. Trumbull's *Death of General Montgomery in the Attack on Quebec*, painted in 1786, with its dramatic smoke, its swirling flag, and the dying hero, is a good example of the mode.

The best of these painters, though, and unquestionably the greatest portraitist the United States had yet produced, was Gilbert Stuart. Born in Rhode Island in 1755, and trained in England, he returned to the United States in 1793 and painted portraits that have remained national icons. Concentrating on the faces, barely indicating the setting, or sometimes posing his figure against an absolutely plain background, he managed to combine aloofness with intense presence. We know Washington through the Stuart portraits; his Jefferson, now at Bowdoin College, is a striking representation of that most intelligent of men; but he was also capable of imbuing the women he painted with a soft, romantic charm that has never ceased to fascinate.

Stuart knew how to make great men look appropriately impressive. Charles Willson Peale was a much more down-to-earth painter. Instead of remote grandeur, he showed warmth, a cozy intimacy, as in the case of the *Peale Family Group*, in which men and women smile, converse, and hold one another while an amiable infant sprawls on the table. It was Peale from whom Congress commissioned a portrait of Washington in the spring of 1776; and he went on to have a long and fruitful career, opening a portrait gallery in 1782, a museum of natural history in 1786, and an art school in 1794. What was perhaps most remarkable about Peale, though—aside from his abundant family, all of whom were artists as well—was his ability to renew himself. His *Staircase Group* of 1795 is very different from the portraits. It is both a genre scene—a smartly dressed young painter holding brushes and palette is walking up a winding stair while another looks down from the upper corner—and a highly successful trompe l'oeil in which the top figure seems to stand in front of the canvas; but more than that, it has an almost dreamlike intensity that makes Peale an artist of the very first rank.

At the same time, painting in the United States stood at the threshold of a great era: the vastness of the landscape that had fascinated travelers and writers now became the subject of wide-scale compositions by Trumbull and Washington Allston. Whether it was Niagara Falls or a thunderstorm at sea, these canvases showed the immense vistas to be found in the New World, and they started a trend which flourished, in the 1840s, with the Hudson River School.

Important as these artists were, however, they could hardly compete in fame with a man whose main occupation was very different: when it comes to architecture in the United States at this period, the first name that comes to mind is invariably that of the third president.

From the first, Jefferson had found that architecture was one of his great passions; so, with characteristic thoroughness, he read up on it. From Vitruvius to Colen Campbell and Robert Adam via Palladio, classical building was utterly familiar to him. Of course, classical is the key word: in this era of neoclassicism, only that style would do. Very quickly, though, it occurred to him that Palladio was particularly suited to the United States because he had designed villas: these were headquarters of agricultural estates, not palaces; they were on a scale that suited the people of the United States; and they could readily be adapted to the building materials found, for instance, in Virginia.

It was therefore to Palladio that Jefferson looked when, having carefully chosen a hilltop site with a spectacular view, he decided to build Monticello. As his model, he chose the Villa Pisani, the only one of Palladio's houses to have a two-story portico. There were some major differences, though: whereas Palladio had an even roofline, Jefferson made the center much taller than the side pavilions; then, at the back, he gave the parlor a three-sided projecting bay— that was the influence of English architecture—and he also added octagonal projections in each corner, thus departing considerably from Palladio's austerely rectangular plan.

The building of this first Monticello was interrupted by the War of Independence; then Jefferson went to Paris, where he saw a whole series of architectural masterpieces—as he noted in his recommendations to L'Enfant—but the one which fascinated him the most deeply was the Hotel de Salm (today the Palace of the Legion of Honor). The work of Pierre Rousseau, it was built while Jefferson was minister to France; he often went to the construction site and watched the walls go up. Jefferson admired both the graceful colonnaded semicircular projection at the back and the grandly severe portico at the front; and when, just before he was elected president, he started on the second Monticello, he kept the Hotel de Salm firmly in mind.

The result was a house that is arguably still today the most charming in the United States. The two-story portico vanished, to be replaced by the four great columns, topped with a triangular pediment, which lead to the recessed entrance with its three elegant arches. The play between columns and arches opens up the house; inside, the majestic entrance hall leads into the parlor, thus giving the center of the house openness and transparence. The bay at the back of the house, with its screen of columns, has great dignity, but the stepped dome, which is hard to see from several angles, is really too low for the house. The combination of red brick with white columns and trim is at the same time warm and restrained, while the balustrade that crowns the roofline gives the house added unity. Then, inside, the famous arrangement of Jefferson's bed between study and dressing room reminds us vividly that the third president was an intellectual for whom quick access to books was an essential part of the good life.

A closer look soon reveals architectural errors, however. The dome, copied in part from that of the Hotel de Salm, is placed too close to the garden facade; it is also a little squat. The windows—made to look, from the outside, as if the house was a single-story building—are oddly placed inside—either too close to the ceiling or too near the floor. The stairs are so narrow—twelve to eighteen inches—as to make going up and down very difficult; and the round room placed immediately under the dome is thus scarcely usable. Still, all that adds an endearingly amateurish quality to the house: as one walks through it, it almost seems that Jefferson has never left it.

Naturally, Monticello was much imitated; but what matters more is that in the wilds of rural Virginia, Jefferson had created an architectural masterpiece. He had also firmly set the classical style as the one most appropriate for the new Republic; and that, too, was an enduring legacy.

Judges, Politics, and Territory

Jefferson's buildings were carefully planned; the reading of the Constitution that resulted from one of his actions surprised him as much as it did most of his contemporaries. Naturally, it all had to do with a political vendetta. When a party and its leaders decide that they are the natural rulers of a country, electoral defeat always seems particularly bitter. That certainly was the case of the Federalists in 1801 and 1802, a group Jefferson described as "rendered desperate and furious by despair."[38] The problem, of course, was that the Republican majority in Congress was solidly united behind the president, and that the cabinet was entirely loyal. That left only the judiciary. John Adams had nominated only Federalists to the federal bench; and now it was from this last refuge of the beaten party that an attack was made on Jefferson. Two centuries later, *Marbury v. Madison* is considered to be a landmark in constitutional history. At the time, it was seen simply as the Federalists' frantic effort to make up for their loss of the election.

The crux of the matter was that Jefferson had told the clerk in charge at the State Department not to deliver the commissions of the justices of the peace for the District of Columbia who were among John Adams's "midnight appointees" (Madison actually became secretary of state several weeks later). Could the president thus deny an office that had been given by his predecessor and confirmed by the Senate? Then, to complicate the question further, the bill creating the offices of the justices of the peace left it to the president to determine their number. Adams had decided on forty-two of these officers for the counties of Washington and Alexandria; Jefferson, using that same power, brought the number down to thirty. Of these, twenty-five had been appointed by Adams and confirmed by Jefferson; five were the new president's choices.

Not surprisingly, the president and the chief justice, that High Federalist John Marshall, took very different views of the situation. Jefferson held that only delivery of a commission makes it valid; Marshall replied that signing and sealing were enough. It was a nice piece of irony that the secretary of state who had forgotten to order the delivery of the commissions, on that busy last day of John Adams's term, was none other than Marshall himself.

As noted earlier, it was at the December 1801 session of the Supreme Court that Charles Lee, the former attorney general, made a motion requesting a writ of mandamus to compel Secretary of State Madison to deliver the commissions. The Court agreed to hear the argument and scheduled it for its next term, which was not until February 1803—and by that time William Marbury's term of office, if indeed he was entitled to it, would be half over; so Jefferson assumed, mistakenly, that the case was moot.

For Marshall, eager as he was to defeat Jefferson, *Marbury v. Madison* presented a very serious drawback: even if the Court were to issue a writ of mandamus, it had no way to enforce it; its writ was sure to be ignored by the executive and Marshall would look like a fool. At the same time, a rejection of the petition would have vindicated Jefferson, something which Marshall was determined to prevent. A lesser man might have been baffled, but not the chief justice.

His solution was to decide without deciding by asking three questions. Did the applicant have a right to the commission? Marshall asked, and promptly answered that he did. If he had the right, and that right had been violated, did the law afford him a remedy? Marshall asked next. The answer was that Marbury did have the right, and that the law indeed afforded him a remedy; but then came the third question, which allowed Marshall to wriggle out of his dilemma: Was the remedy, he asked, a writ of mandamus from the Supreme Court? No, he said, the Court did not have jurisdiction.

It was undoubtedly a smart maneuver. Jefferson said, some years later, that the justice, while disclaiming cognizance of the case, had stated what his opinion would have been, had he taken cognizance of it. In fact, Marshall had denied Marbury's petition after having elaborately argued its rightfulness, thus at the same time blaming the president and avoiding the certainty that the writ would be unenforced. The chief beauty of the whole maneuver lay in the legal reasoning: there was, the Court claimed, no legal proof that Jefferson had withheld the commission because there was no legal proof that it had ever existed. At the same time, Marshall clearly accused Jefferson of breaking the law, since the president's authority and discretion were held to end with the signing of a commission and its transmittal to the secretary of state for sealing. After that, argued Marshall, the officers of the government are subject to the laws governing the rights of individuals.

Then Marshall went a step further. The Court could not issue a writ because it had no jurisdiction, he said, and that was because the grant of authority to the Court by Congress in the act creating the justices of the peace was itself an unconstitutional action; and so it invalidated that section of the act. It was a fateful precedent: for the first time in the history of the United States, the Court had held that "a law repugnant to the Constitution is void and that courts, as well as other departments are bound by that instrument."[39] That day, a new understanding of constitutional law was born. Oddly enough, though, it was scarcely noticed at the time: what people cared about was the attack on Jefferson.

Thus *Marbury v. Madison* ended with a triple irony: the disputed commission would have gone to Marbury if Marshall, on March 3, 1801, had been a little more careful; the chief feature of the decision was the least noticed; and the president accused of flouting the law held, as he was proving at the same moment, a passionate respect for the Constitution. Did it afford the government the authority, Jefferson wondered, to add by treaty a vast tract of land to the Union as constituted?

THE LOUISIANA PURCHASE

The land in question was on the southern border of the United States, and it held the key to the prosperity of an important section of the country, since it controlled the rights of navigation on the Mississippi River. At a time when water transport was often the only one available, the great rivers were essential for trade and communication. The United States had begun to expand toward the west: if the Mississippi were to be blockaded, a fearful crisis would ensue; and that, in 1802, began to look as if it might be the case.

Up until then, the lands across the great river had been held by Spain. In 1795, the Pinckney Treaty had stipulated that the United States held the right of free navigation on the Mississippi, and that its merchants could deposit goods for export in New Orleans warehouses without paying the Spanish government custom duties, that city being then part of the Spanish colonies. As a result, U.S. traffic on the river grew from about twelve boats in 1792 to over five hundred in 1802. This in turn enriched U.S. merchants, not just in the West but also in mid-Atlantic cities.

Unfortunately, Spain, as part of the Treaty of San Ildefonso, which was signed in March 1801, ceded the province to France, and, in the autumn of 1802, the Spanish intendant at New Orleans proceeded to close the Deposit—as the tax-free warehouses were called—prior to the cession of the city. This was more than the frustrated merchants were willing to bear. As for Jefferson, he was a passionate advocate of orderly expansion. He saw the territories to the west as the reservoir for just the kind of self-sufficient and independent farmers whom he most respected, and was, from the first, in favor of admitting new states as soon as they became sufficiently populated. The coming to self-government of the West would, he thought, reinforce its ties with the rest of the country, a position that was well known and earned him great popularity.

Before 1800, there had been only two trans-Appalachian states, Kentucky and Tennessee; then, in 1798, Ohio became a territory (it was granted statehood five years later). That left a vast settled area south of Georgia and between the Mississippi and Chattahoochee Rivers: as a second-grade territory, it had an elected legislature but federally appointed officials; and it was augmented when Georgia sold it the land between its present western boundary and the Mississippi for $1.25 million.

France was the very last neighbor the United States wanted: whereas Spain was considered to be a declining power, too weak to interfere with the United States and certainly with no thought of expansion, France, under Bonaparte, was clearly intent on seizing what it could. As a result, Jefferson hinted, in his conversations with Pichon, the French minister in Washington, that he was not happy about the cession of the Spanish territories. To Robert Livingston, the new U.S. minister in Paris, he was much more forceful: New Orleans, he wrote, must be ceded to the United States. If it were not, then he would conclude an alliance with England, and, as soon as war resumed in Europe, the allies would take the city.

This was a credible threat. The English were very anxious to avoid a French presence on the Mississippi, because it would provide a base for the reconquest of Canada by its former owner; and no one, in Paris or London, thought the Peace of Amiens likely to endure. France had an invincible army, but virtually no fleet; and it was in no position to prevent a successful attack on its new American possession.

All through 1802, the situation was further confused by the fact that the extent of the territory ceded by Spain was far from clear. At one point, Jefferson suggested, in a letter to Livingston, that he might be prepared to accept a compromise through which Spain would sell the Floridas, and France New Orleans, to the United States, while allowing the rest of the territory to remain French, but the official policy was simply one of exploration: the government wanted to find out what the price of acquiring the territory was likely to be, without, however, being prepared to make an actual offer.

For Livingston in Paris, the situation was difficult. Bonaparte was not particularly interested in the fate of Louisiana, and the result was that no one in Paris knew what should be done; there was even talk of a French military expedition to New Orleans. On September 1, 1802, Livingston wrote despairingly to Madison: "There never was a government in which less could be done by negotiation than here. There is no people, no Legislature, no counsellors. One man is everything. He seldom asks advice, and never hears it unasked. . . . Though the sense of every reflecting man about him is against this wild expedition, no one dares to tell him so."[40] It was no wonder that Livingston was worried: Bonaparte had, quite recently, sent off his brother-in-law, General Leclerc, to reconquer the French possessions in the Caribbean.

Six weeks later, the Spanish intendant closed the Deposit. The assumption in Washington was that he had done so at the order of his government; and that Madrid, in turn, was following French instructions. Had that been the case, the United States might well have felt compelled to follow through with the British alliance—Hamilton's policy would thus have been carried out by Jefferson, as bitter an irony as can well be imagined. Happily, what looked like provocation turned out to be simply bad communications: the Spanish governor of Louisiana promptly informed the U.S. governor of the Mississippi territory that the closing of the Deposit had not been authorized by the Spanish government. This was promptly confirmed by Morales, the Spanish minister in Washington: the intendant, it seems, had merely misinterpreted a secret message from his government ordering him to end the smuggling that had been taking place. Morales himself was aware of the gravity of the situation, and in his letters to Madrid, he fully supported the policy of the U.S. government.

In the meantime, the tension rose. On January 7, 1803, the House of Representatives passed a resolution blaming the "unauthorized conduct of certain individuals";[41] on the eleventh, Jefferson nominated James Monroe as minister extraordinary to France with full powers to settle the question; and on the twelfth, Congress, in secret session, appropriated $2 million so that the president might start negotiations tending to the purchase of New Orleans and the Floridas, while at the same time a two-thousand-man militia was organized in the Mississippi territory.

War, it seemed, might not be far away. On January 13, Jefferson wrote Monroe: "The agitation of the public mind . . . is extreme. . . . All eyes, all hopes are now fixed on you . . . for on the event of this mission depend the future destinies of this republic. If we cannot by a purchase of the country insure to ourselves a course of perpetual peace and friendship with all nations, then as war cannot be distant, it behooves us immediately to be preparing for that course without, however, hastening it. . . . This can only be prevented by a successful issue to your mission."[42]

That was the very day on which Jefferson received a memorandum from Albert Gallatin, the secretary of the treasury, on the constitutionality of an eventual purchase. Gallatin made three essential points:

> 1st. That the United States as a nation have an inherent right to acquire territory.
> 2nd. That whenever that acquisition is by treaty, the same constituted authorities in whom the treaty-making power is vested have a constitutional right to sanction the acquisition.
> 3rd. That whenever the territory has been acquired, Congress has the power either of admitting it into the Union as a new state, or of annexing it to a state with the consent of that state, or of making regulations for the government of such territory.[43]

It was a sound argument; and as we have seen from his letter to Monroe, Jefferson was fully convinced.

Still, nothing was settled, and the delays involved in communicating with Europe did not help. At best, it took three weeks for a dispatch to come from Paris; but when the weather was bad, the three weeks could turn into six; and the public was little disposed to wait. Hamilton, writing as Pericles in the *New York Evening Post*, was more bellicose than most: he advocated first seizing New Orleans and the Floridas, and negotiating afterward. In Congress, meanwhile, the Breckinridge Resolution authorized the president, at his discretion, to raise an eighty-thousand-man militia. As for Jefferson, who was taking no chances, he ordered the removal of the American Indians from the border to avoid their falling under French influence, and he sent Meriwether Lewis and William Clark off to the Northwest with an appropriation of $2,500: their exploration, as well as increasing knowledge, was to ensure that the United States laid claim to whatever new lands might be discovered. In fact, it was the first major gesture toward creating a transcontinental nation.

By April 19, however, the clouds looked less dark. That was the day when it was known in Washington that the Spanish government had ordered the reopening of the Deposit, and certified that it would remain open even when New Orleans passed to the French. What made all the difference, though, was a development wholly unconnected with the United States: as war began again between France and Great Britain, and it became clear that France would not be able to protect its new possessions along the Mississippi, Bonaparte decided to make the best of a bad situation: rather than lose it to England, it was obviously better to sell the area to the United States. Further, it would have been unwise to help create an alliance between Great Britain and the United States; and so the official delays of which Livingston had complained suddenly ended.

On April 11, before Monroe had actually arrived, Talleyrand asked Livingston whether the United States wished to buy the entire Louisiana territory. When, within a few days, Monroe arrived, he and Livingston answered with a decided affirmative—an infringement of their instructions, since only New Orleans and the Floridas had been considered for purchase by the United States. They were right to be bold, of course, and Jefferson fully endorsed their action. In the event, it took barely more than a fortnight to reach an agreement: the United States promised to pay France $11.25 million in 6 percent bonds not redeemable for fifteen years, and it assumed responsibility for $3.75 million in claims made by U.S. citizens against France. It further agreed that for the next twelve years, French and Spanish ships would pay the same duty as U.S. ships in the acquired territory. On May 3, the treaty was signed. On July 3, the good news reached Jefferson.

It could not have been more timely: the Louisiana Purchase was announced to the public as part of the Fourth of July celebrations, and at the President's House, the mood was exalted. Mrs. Smith, naturally, was there. On July 5, she told her sister:

> Yesterday was a day of joy to our citizens and of pride to our President. It is a day which you know he always enjoys. How much more must he have enjoyed it on this occasion.... The news of the cession of Louisiana only arrived about 8 o'clock of the night preceding ...
>
> At the early hour the city was alive—a discharge of 18 guns saluted the dawn, the military assembled exhibiting a martial assurance, and at eleven o'clock an oration was delivered by Capt. Sprig (well written but poorly pronounced), at 12 company began to assemble at the President's; it was more numerous than I have before marked it, enlivened, too, by the presence of between 40 and 50 ladies clothed in their best attire, cakes, wine, punch etc in profusion.[44]

There was good reason to rejoice: the United States had not only ensured the freedom of its commerce and given itself room for expansion—eventually, six of its states emerged from the territories west and south of Georgia—it had also proved that in the fierce exchanges of international politics it could hold its own; and it had done so entirely by peaceful means. Still, Jefferson was not convinced that what he had done was fully legal.

On August 12, he wrote Senator Breckinridge a long letter about that: "The Executive in seizing the fugitive occurrence which so much advances the good of their country, have done an act beyond the Constitution. The Legislature, in casting behind them metaphysical subtleties and risking themselves like faithful servants, must ratify and pay for it, and throw themselves on their

country for doing for them unauthorized what we know they would have done
for themselves had they been in a situation to do it."[45] He was almost alone in
worrying, though. The purchase was immensely popular; even if it stretched
the Constitution a little, it did not infringe it. Jefferson himself, after having
first thought that an amendment might be necessary, decided that he could do
without one; and even that stickler for the law, that man most suspicious of
power, Thomas Paine, wrote the president:

> It appears to be one of those cases with which the Constitution has nothing to
> do, and which can be judged only by the circumstances of the times when
> such a case will occur. The Constitution could not foresee that Spain would
> cede Louisiana to France or to England, and therefore it could not determine
> what our conduct should be in consequence of such an event. The cession
> makes no alteration in the Constitution; it only extends the principle of it over
> a larger territory, and this is certainly within the morality of the Constitu-
> tion, and not contrary, nor beyond, the expression or intention of any of its
> articles.[46]

When, on October 17, Congress reassembled for an extraordinary session, it fully concurred. Within four days, the Senate approved the treaty by
twenty-four votes to seven, while, on its side, the House eagerly passed the
required financial legislation. The armed forces were then authorized to occupy
the territory; the president was empowered to nominate the officers constitut-
ing its government; and all agreed that they had remained well within the spirit
of the Constitution. As for the electorate, it made its feelings clear the following year when Jefferson was triumphantly elected to a second term.

All that mattered, of course. The United States, by 1804, had shown that it
could not only survive, but prosper. The government functioned smoothly; the
economy was expanding; new territories were being settled; taxes were down—
nonexistent, in fact, except for customs duties; revenue was up. The president
and Congress worked together harmoniously, and there was a sense that the
new nation had an assured future. There were problems, of course: the North
African pirates preying on U.S. ships finally necessitated sending the navy as
protection; the renewed war in Europe created new tensions and new problems that eventually led to the War of 1812—but there could be no disputing
that the first great experiment in democratic government was a success.

Jefferson saw it well. "No experiment can be more interesting than that
we are trying, and which we trust will end in establishing the fact, that man
may be governed by reason and truth," he wrote Judge John Tyler in June
1804. "Our first object should therefore be to leave open . . . all the avenues to
truth. The most effectual hitherto found is the freedom of the press."[47] He was
right, of course: the first thing General Bonaparte had done, as first consul,
was to assert control over the newspapers. Except for Great Britain—and there,

to a lesser extent—the United States was the only country in the world where the press was free and protected.

The fact that this great experiment in democracy was succeeding made the most enormous difference, not just within the boundaries of the United States, but on the rest of the North American continent and in Europe. By proving that men needed neither king, nor established church, nor censorship, nor institutionalized class privilege to prosper, this new country offered an example that fascinated people everywhere. The European monarchies might appear largely unchanged; France might be trading liberty for military glory; but there remained one place where reason and freedom combined to make life better.

PART THREE

Another America

CHAPTER TEN

New Spain, Old Habits

SKIN COLOR, in 1800, was crucially important. Whites were superior, blacks inferior and often enslaved. Asians remained merely exotic because they were so distant: there was not much occasion to discriminate against them. In Spanish America, though, the situation was unique: most of the population was American Indian. It belonged, therefore, to a conquered people whose land and freedom had been forfeited to the Spanish and Portuguese conquerors. Strictly speaking, the Indians were not slaves, but they could not leave one employer for another, and were required to give their labor for a variety of government-appointed tasks. As a result, although slavery had been outlawed, a form of slavery—indentured labor—remained. And, naturally, the ruling class was white.

Geographically, Spanish America was even farther away from Europe than the United States. Politically and economically, though, it was much closer. Its king was the king of Spain; its viceroys and governors came from Madrid; its economies were controlled by the mother country. In one way, it was distant and exotic; yet, in many of the ways that mattered, it was an essential part of that single world all of whose parts were tied together.

THE POWER OF WEALTH

The United States was the way of the future: its citizens were free—to speak, to worship, to vote. They had chosen their own government, they elected their representatives, and their economy was expanding as fast as their territory. There were significant carryovers from the colonial past, of course, but, by 1800, most people felt thoroughly at ease in their new and rapidly changing world.

The rest of the Americas could hardly have been more different. There, colonialism endured, but in the guise of direct monarchy. Catholicism, in its extreme Spanish form, was the only religion allowed. Censorship prevailed, and so did a strict class system complete with titled nobility. The ruler was an absolute king who ruled by divine right and lived in Spain. As for change, it was widely loathed: things were fine as they were and any novelty could only make them worse, most everyone agreed.

This other America was a much larger place. With the exception of Brazil and the Guianas, it all belonged to the king of Spain and stretched from the northern boundaries of present-day Texas, New Mexico, and California all the way to Tierra del Fuego at the bottom of the continent. Still, this immense geographical area was not a monolith. There were nine major governments—all, of course, appointed by the king of Spain and reporting to him: the kingdom of New Spain, or Mexico (the old name was just being revived), and those of Peru, Buenos Aires, and New Granada, ruled by viceroys; the *capitanias generales* of Guatemala, Puerto Rico, and Caracas; and the smaller *capitanias* of Chile and Havana (which took in the Floridas), ruled by governors.

As an observant visitor noted, New Spain, or Mexico, was the most important of these several states. "Mexico ranks first, both because of its territorial riches and because of its favorable position which allows it to trade with both Europe and Asia,"[1] Alexander von Humboldt wrote a little after 1800. Indeed, Mexico was Spain's prize possession. It had a good deal of fertile land, and the capital, with its 137,000 inhabitants, was the most populous city in the Americas. The country as a whole was prosperous. It grew more than it needed and exported the surplus; but from the Crown's point of view, its most important attribute was that its mines produced great quantities of precious metals. Every year, about 2 million silver pesos (a peso was worth about U.S. $50) were sent to Spain, a real help to the chronically impoverished treasury, while another 4.5 million went to subsidize the governments of Cuba, the Philippines, the Marianas, Louisiana, and Puerto Rico, thus sparing the Crown that same amount.

This really mattered: the rest of Spanish America contributed only another 1.5 million. And just as important, the mines enriched not only the treasury, but—most of the time—their owners and the rest of the country. Every year, their workers extracted 3,520 pounds of gold and 1,181,000 pounds of silver, for a total value of 23 million pesos, almost three-fourths of which remained in Mexico. Even better, there were other sources of wealth. Leather and textile manufacturers produced about 8 million pesos' worth of goods a year; on the haciendas, grains, potatoes, corn, bananas, manioc, agave, sugarcane, cocoa, indigo, and vanilla grew in abundance, and wax was a significant resource.

That had a lot to do with geography. New Spain, in 1800, stretched north from the border of Guatemala and included today's Texas, New Mexico, and

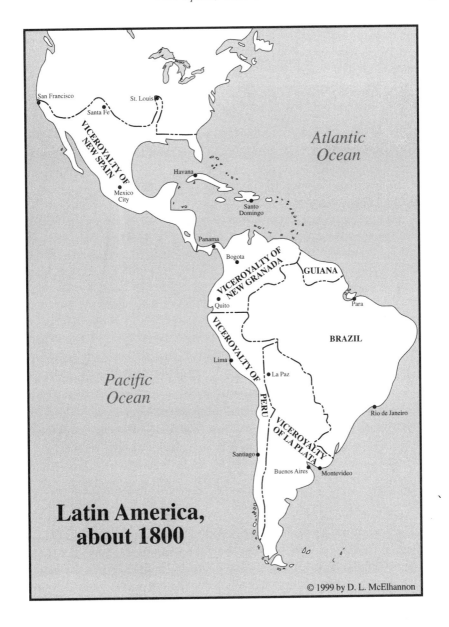

Latin America,
about 1800

© 1999 by D. L. McElhannon

California. It had cool highlands (the *terras frias*) and tropical lowlands (the *terras calientes*), so that a great variety of crops could be grown. In the mountains, there were mines; and because the country could also boast of good harbors on both oceans, trade flourished together with fishing. Because most of the exports were commodities, and most of the imports manufactured goods, the balance of trade suffered from a deficit of 14 million pesos; but that was more than made up by the export of bullion.

Still, in this rich country, there were shocking disparities. "Mexico is the land of inequality," Humboldt wrote. "The architecture of public and private buildings, the elegance of the dress of women, the tone of Society, all bespeak a refinement in sharp contrast with the nudity, the ignorance and the lack of civilization of the people. The Indians . . . offer a picture of terrible misery."[2] Indeed, the wealthiest had the greatest fortunes, by far, of anywhere in the Americas, North and South. The count of Valenciana, for instance, had an estate worth 5 million pesos, while from a single mine, near Guanajuato, he drew an annual income of 300,000 pesos. His was only one of the three branches of the family, at that: together, their income rose to 440,000 pesos, and so they spent fast and furiously.

Of course, the count was treated with the respect his millions deserved; but neither his title nor his wealth were enough to put him at the top of the upper class: that was reserved for an altogether different sort of people, and everyone knew it, for the Mexicans were divided into four unchangeable, unbreakable categories.

WHITES AND INDIANS

At the top were the *Gachupínes,* those born in Spain. They included the viceroy and vicereine, together with a number of officials, noblemen, investors, and traders. The Creoles, whose origins were Spanish, but who had been born in Mexico, came next. Some of them were born of *Gachupín* parents—to be born in Mexico made you a Creole—others could look back to many generations of Mexican-born ancestors. Many were officials, but they never reached the first rank. Some owned mines, like the count of Valenciana, or vast estates. Others were clerics, but they were rarely made bishops, and never archbishop of Mexico. Still others were clerks, shopkeepers, or craftsmen. A few were poor or even destitute; and all felt vastly superior to the next two categories, those of mixed blood (Indian/black, Indian/white, black/white) and the Indians. The people of mixed blood were few; but the Indians, about 82 percent of the population, were inferior to all others by law, custom, and, of course, income.

There was no mistaking who was who. The *Gachupínes* and the Creoles were obviously white. Not so the Indians, who were described by Humboldt, accurately, as being "a dark copper color, with smooth, flat hair, hardly any facial hair, a chunky body, long eyes with the corners rising toward the temples, prominent cheekbones, thick lips, and an expression of sweetness contrasting with the dark and severe look of their eyes."[3] These obviously non-European people still remained, in 1800, a conquered population. Slavery, instituted by the conquistadores, had indeed been officially abolished; but an effective system based on debt kept most rural Indians in peonage. It was very simple. They could be forced to work on a specific hacienda. There, the store charged such high prices that the workers were perpetually in debt, and therefore unable to leave. And while this was not true in the larger cities—Mexico, Puebla, Querétaro, Guanajuato, Vera Cruz—the work they were given was always the roughest and least well paid. In theory, the Crown tried to protect them, but its edicts were usually ignored; and there was no question of ending the Indians' unique status because they, and only they, paid a special head tax, which was one of the treasury's major sources of income (1.3 million pesos out of a total of 20 million). There were other disadvantages as well: Indians were not allowed to wear European clothes; they could not own horses or weapons; they were judged in separate courts, and these last were unlikely to be either open-minded or indulgent. In counterpart, however, they were exempt from tithes—but, in fact, they often gave what little they had to the church—and they did not have to serve in the militia.

Unlike Creoles who could rise, if not quite to the top, at least near it, Indians were stuck at the bottom and so, naturally, they worked as little as possible, and got very drunk any time they could. Indian laziness was a famous cliché. As Mme Calderón de la Barca, a North American married to a Spaniard, wrote in one of her letters:

> The badness of the servants is an unfailing source of complaint. We hear of their addiction to stealing, their laziness, drunkenness, dirtiness, with a host of other vices. . . . A girl will go to service merely sufficient to buy herself an embroidered chemise; and if in addition to this she can pick up a pair of small red satin shoes, she will tell you she is tired of working and is going to rest, *"para descansar."*
>
> A decent old woman . . . came to the house to [do the washing] . . . and left us at the end of the month, *"para descansar."* Soon after, she used to come with her six children, they and herself all in rags, and beg the gardener to give her any odds and ends of vegetables he could spare. My maid asked her why, being so poor, she had left a good place where she got twelve dollars a month. "Jesus!", said she, "if only you knew the pleasure of doing nothing."[4]

The anecdote, of course, is amusing and picturesque; but the "old woman" was right. She had no hope of ever being even reasonably well-off: why, then, should she have worked more than she absolutely needed? And there is another telling touch: if the washerwoman had six children, all obviously still too young to be earning, or scrounging, their own living, how old could she really be? That she looked old is easy to believe; but that look was due to hardship, not age.

A more observant visitor understood the situation better. "The Indians," Humboldt wrote, "suffer the indignities which are still frequently inflicted on them by the whites: their only defense is ruse hidden under the guise of apathy and stupidity."[5] Given the general hopelessness of life for most Indians, it should have surprised no one that the cities were full of beggars—demanding, obstinate beggars who would not leave you alone. Visitors and prosperous Mexicans often complained about this plague. Measures, each more ineffective than the last, were occasionally taken; and nothing changed, because nothing could.

Dispossessed and inferior, the Indians had very little reason to serve diligently. Humboldt, though a Prussian aristocrat, saw it clearly. "These Indians, stupefied by the despotism of their Aztec kings and the brutalities of the conquistadors, are protected by the generally wise and humane Spanish laws; but they hardly enjoy that protection because of their great distance from the supreme authority [i.e., the king]."[6] Withholding their work was, in fact, all the Indians could do: they were in no position to protest any more effectively.

CREOLES AND GACHUPINES

The opposite was true for the Creoles—or for some of them, at least. As a group, they included virtually all the non-Indian population: in 1810, a tax surveyor, basing his figures on the 1793 census, determined there were 1,082,928 Creoles and only 15,000 *Gachupínes.* The former were, however, not a homogeneous group. A tiny minority, the European Creoles, was firmly oriented toward Spain. Usually the children of *Gachupínes,* often noble, they were normally sent to Spain for their education. They tended to be passionate monarchists, firmly European, and averse to the local culture. Of course, they, too, sometimes resented their inability to reach the highest positions; but they kept quiet, and feared any disturbance, which might threaten their wealth.

The American Creoles, the vast majority, were beginning to be far more vocal. A few of them were rich and titled; most were petty government officials, lawyers, doctors, priests, small businessmen, artisans—and some were unemployed. They were all descended from Spanish settlers, but they felt far more Mexican than Spanish. This implied no disloyalty to the church or to the king, who was seen less as king of Spain than as king of New Spain. This was the group that was reviving the use of the name "Mexico," and it was because they thought of themselves not as a colony, but as one of the king's many realms. Theirs, they felt, was an ancient country (although their point of reference was the Spanish Conquest, not the civilizations which preceded it). They were perfectly content to be ruled by Charles IV of Spain, but they wanted him to appoint Creoles, not *Gachupínes,* to all the major command positions: it was typical, for instance, that in 1808, only one bishop in nine was a Creole.

The Creoles also resented being seen as generically inferior. Cornelius de Pauw, a Dutchman who lived in Berlin, came to Mexico in the 1760s, and his attitude was characteristic. "As it is principally to the climate of the New World that we have attributed the causes which have vitiated the essential qualities of man and have caused human nature to degenerate, it is, doubtless, correct to ask if any disturbance has been perceived in the faculties of the Creoles. . . .

The degeneration we had believed possible [is] real. . . . The Creoles of the fourth and fifth generation have less talent, less capacity for learning than the true Europeans."[7] This sort of racism, based on climate rather than ancestry—North is good, South is inferior—was widespread and helped give an apparently scientific gloss to the Crown's entirely selfish motives. In fact, the reasoning of generations of Spanish ministers was extremely simple: if Creoles were given the top jobs, they would learn to govern themselves and would demand their independence; and so the *Gachupínes* continued to rule both state and church in New Spain.

Although it had been going on for over two centuries, this method of government, from the 1770s on, rankled more every year. The Creoles now claimed that the Spanish administrators, provincial governors, generals, and bishops were incompetent to rule because the laws of Mexico differed from those of Spain, because they were unaware of local conditions, because they understood nothing about the Indians, and because, finally, they were surrounded by sycophants. Some of this was, no doubt, partly true. Against this, however, can be offset a major consideration. As new arrivals, the *Gachupínes* were outside local rivalries and intrigues; in consequence, they were more likely to be fair and impartial, thus providing a cheaper, more efficient, and more just administration. Of course, it also rankled that so many of these Spaniards came to Mexico firmly determined to make a fortune. Not infrequently, they did; and their methods were not always ethical.

Still, it must be said that the viceroys of the last quarter of the eighteenth century had been, on the whole, competent, open-minded, and conscientious men, some strikingly so. Why, then, did these resentments develop? One reason was certainly the behavior of the lesser *Gachupínes*. "The most miserable, uneducated, uncultured European thinks himself superior to the whites born in the New World . . . ," Humboldt noted. Nevertheless, he added, "One often hears people saying proudly: 'I am not *Spanish,* I am *American.*"[8] Here something new was emerging: after 1776, it actually meant something to have been born in the Americas. Certainly, in 1800, the Creoles had not even begun to think of independence—they remained devoted to Charles IV and the House of Bourbon—but autonomy, with perhaps a younger Spanish prince as their own king, was no longer quite unthinkable.

Still, that exceedingly faint possibility of autonomy was not what fueled the Creoles' resentment. Amazingly enough, what really upset them was the Crown's attempt at improvement and modernization.

CHANGE AND REACTION

The government of New Spain, in 1760, owed far more to chance than to design. Its way of functioning (or not functioning, as was often the case) was in large part the result of events thousands of miles away. The progressive decadence of Spain, starting in the 1640s under Philip IV, had greatly increased the distance between the two countries. Fewer orders were sent from Madrid, the Council of the Indies' decrees were enforced laxly at best, and while new viceroys kept arriving every four to five years, they, too, often cared mostly about enriching themselves and getting through their term without major trouble. It was only in 1759, when Charles III succeeded to the throne, that things began to change. A hardworking and conscientious monarch, Charles put in train a vast ensemble of reforms so as to bring Spain and its colonies into the modern world, and add to the power of the empire. Spain thus had a selfish reason to carry out reforms—and the Mexicans knew it—but Charles III also had a real wish to improve the government of all his kingdoms. A typical enlightened despot, he set about rationalizing government so that it could provide services more effectively, encourage trade, and raise the general level of prosperity. Naturally, that in turn tended to improve the tax yield. More revenue meant a more powerful navy; and this new might was to return Spain to the exalted status it had enjoyed in the sixteenth century.

None of this entailed political liberalization. The king still governed absolutely and expected to be obeyed promptly. Naturally, censorship remained in effect. As for the Catholic Church, it kept its exclusive position. Here, however, there was a good deal of ambiguity. Like other Catholic sovereigns, Charles III made a sharp distinction between the faith and the clergy. The faith was unquestioned, but the clergy was seen, accurately, as a very mixed blessing. It owned too much land and contributed too little tax; it often seemed to be almost a state within the state; and too many of its members were incompetent.

THE POWER OF THE CHURCH

Most offensive, perhaps, to the government was the Mexican church's sheer, massive wealth: in 1799, its income came to the huge sum of 4.5 million pesos. That, however, was unevenly distributed. The archbishop of Mexico, for instance, enjoyed yearly revenues of 130,000 pesos, and consequently led a life of great splendor, while many village priests almost starved on 100 pesos a year. Naturally, the church owned a good deal of land, worth about 3 million pesos, but the bulk of its capital, some 46 million, was invested in mortgages. Then there was its visible presence: in Mexico City alone, there were a hundred churches and chapels, twenty-three monasteries, and fifteen convents. Finally, all non-Indians had to pay tithes that, in 1789, came to nearly 2 million pesos a year, of which two-ninths was given to the Crown.

More than all that, the church had an array of privileges that made it virtually immune from the law. The clergy could be judged only by its own courts, no matter how grave the crime. These courts also had jurisdiction over all wills, probates, and disputed inheritances; decided the validity of marriages; dealt with accusations against priests; and had the power to seize and auction goods they deemed owed to the church. The church had its own police and its own jails, both used to enforce the decisions of its courts. Finally, individual priests could compel their parishioners to confess and take communion at Easter under threat of imprisonment.

And then there was the Inquisition. Although it no longer inspired the same terror as in the sixteenth century, it still ran the censorship and had jurisdiction over a long, oddly assorted list of offenses: heresy; sorcery; casting spells; bigamy; polygamy; writing anti-*Gachupín* texts; sacrilege; drunkenness; slander; sodomy; bestiality; suspicious declarations and acts; malpractice in confession; soliciting; owning, importing, or publishing pornography; insulting the pope; denying being a Catholic; perjury; reading or writing forbidden books; curing by superstitious devices; and on and on. People were arrested daily—the Inquisition had its own jails—and no one was exempt, from the poorest Indian to the bishops themselves and even the viceroy. When, however, on one occasion the Inquisition did try to summon that exalted official before its Mexico City tribunal, it found itself ringed by the Viceregal Guard and promptly changed its mind.

Although canons, and even a bishop, were among those condemned by the Inquisition, most of its victims belonged to the lower classes: Indians who did not go to church often enough, folk healers who were accused of witchcraft, prostitutes, and other small fry. Still, that gave the church a formidable power. In counterpart, though, the king was recognized by the pope as administrative head of the church in America, and he appointed all church officials, canons, vicar-generals, and bishops, as well as the Grand Inquisitor; and the viceroy often played a major role in settling disputes within the clergy.

All that sounds very grim, and, for the increasing number of the intellectually liberated, it was. The church also had another face, however: as much as anything, it was a provider of spectacle. The gold and precious stones worn by the statues of the Virgin and the saints, the gilded altars, the soaring domes were all a part of this. "The gold stand in which they carry the host is entirely encrusted with large diamonds, pearls, emeralds, amethysts, topazes and rubies," Mme Calderón reported after a visit to the cathedral in Puebla. "The chalices are equally rich. There are four sets of jewels for the bishop. One of his crosses is of emeralds and diamonds, another of topazes and diamonds, with great rings of the same belonging to each."[9] The many festivals were just as splendid. "It is not a dogma which has replaced another, but one set of ceremonies which has been substituted for another," Humboldt noted. "The natives know nothing of religion but the outward forms of worship. . . . The feast days of the Church, the fireworks that go with them, the processions interspersed with dances and oddly costumed marchers are for the poorer Indians a rich source of entertainment."[10] Indeed, processions were often so costly that the government tried to limit their splendor.

The Catholic Church, of course, had been imposed on the natives by the conquistadores; but by the end of the eighteenth century it had become an integral part of Mexican culture, and, to that repatriation of Catholicism, a single phenomenon contributed more than anything: the apparition of the Virgin of Guadalupe. Invariably depicted as a Creole, the Virgin had conveniently appeared in a village just outside of Mexico City. As a result, a church was built in her honor, and great processions made their way there. Even more important, most people now thought that the christianization of the country was due to her, that God had sent her specially to convert the Mexicans; and so devotion to the Virgin had a major nationalist component.

Thus, all in all, the church was a formidable institution, and one which, by its very nature, was resistant to change. In that, it was not alone. The *cabildos* and *ayuntamientos* that ran the cities—they were a blend of mayor and city council—were composed almost exclusively of Creoles. Far more important, their seats were hereditary. In Mexico City, for instance, the *ayuntamiento* was composed of three honorary perpetual *regidores* (city counselors) who were *Gachupínes* appointed by the viceroy, and fifteen hereditary *regidores* who owed their office solely to their being heads of ancient noble families. As a result, "[they] were generally very deficient in learning and the majority of them with ruined fortunes . . . Almost all the perpetual *regidores* were Americans, having inherited their jobs from their fathers who had bought them to give luster to their family."[11] Obviously, this group, and its equivalents throughout Mexico, was no friend of change. At least, it represented a measure of control by the Creoles, but even then not all was well. In 1771, and again in 1792, the Mexico City *ayuntamiento* complained to the king that the Spaniards who came to Mexico either did not bring their wives, or did not marry, so as not to father Creole children who could never attain the same exalted positions as their fathers.

The Crown naturally had a different point of view. It wanted to be able to appoint Spaniards to positions of honor and profit in what was seen, essentially, as a colony; and it also distrusted local officials who were likely to have vested interests within their own jurisdiction. Thus, both convenience and good government required the sending of Spanish appointees to Mexico. Still, until the 1760s, ad hoc arrangements, reciprocal rights and obligations, and the weight of old relationships were the key elements of a working compromise, but any change was likely to create grave conflict.

Added to that was an ambiguous relationship to the king. The reverence for His Majesty, who had, after all, been appointed by God, went together with a tradition of popular protests against abuses of power—due, supposedly, to wicked ministers. The Mexicans were often heard to shout: *"Viva el Rey, muera al mal Gobierno!"* (Long live the king, death to bad government). In the end, though, it all worked out: inefficiency, incapacity, and corruption made for great flexibility, some autonomy, and the beginnings of self-government.

Keeping the Creoles sufficiently satisfied was one thing, though; it was quite another fully to exploit the country's potential. The former precluded change; the latter made it necessary to reform both institutions and personnel. Still, as long as no one in Madrid really knew what was going on, the status quo could prevail; but, in 1765, Charles III sent José de Gálvez to view, report, and suggest reforms. Then, as if that were not already upsetting enough to the Creoles, the king, in 1767, ordered the expulsion of the Jesuits from Mexico. The two most powerful groups in the country were now under attack.

THE BEGINNINGS OF REFORM

The expulsion of the Jesuits actually had nothing to do with Mexico as such: it was part of a Europe-wide movement initiated by the (Catholic) king of Portugal joined by the (Catholic) kings of Spain and France that eventually resulted in the dissolution of the order by the pope. Still, because most major schools and colleges in Mexico were run by the Jesuits, this proved to be a major blow to the educational system. At the same time, the sight of often elderly Jesuits being arrested and dragged to the ships that were to deport them caused a great deal of anger. As a result, there were riots in Guanajuato and San Luis Potosí—which the viceroy brutally suppressed. This in turn confirmed Charles III's view of the church as an obstacle both to reform and to the revitalization of the powers of the Crown.

Four years later—the Spanish government was not exactly swift—came the next step. As chief administrator of the church, the king ordered a visitation. That meant closing down insufficiently occupied convents and monasteries, reforming those orders whose rule was either lax or poorly obeyed, and transferring the services in the churches from the regular to the secular clergy: priests (as opposed to friars) were supposed to be better educated and more amenable to the authority of the bishops. In fact, the Franciscans, in particular, were far closer to the Indians and their culture. They had published vocabularies, grammars, and catechisms in Nahuatl, Mazahua, and Otomí, while most priests spoke only Spanish; as a result, many Indians minded losing a cleric they could actually understand. The bishops cooperated happily, though, because the changes extended their power.

What they eventually discovered was that it had been only a first step. In 1786, the Crown tried to take over the collection and administration of tithes; the bishops resisted and the Crown backed down, in part because Charles III, rationalizer though he was, did not want to push them too far, in part because the takeover of tithes would not have made a major difference to the treasury.

As it was, other clerical privileges had also been abolished. In 1784, jurisdiction over wills, probates, and inheritances was transferred to the royal courts, and in 1795, these same courts were for the first time allowed to judge clerics committing "grave and atrocious crimes." It hardly mattered that these were extremely few: the principle of clerical immunity had been breached, and an institution that thought of its rights and possessions as sacred found itself being treated almost like everybody else. That, of course, was when it began to wonder whether it would not do better without interference from Madrid.

That sentiment was by no means reserved to the church. Gálvez, during his five-year visit, had seen a rich country badly run, a place capable of doing very much more to make itself really wealthy and Spain powerful. He was also offended by the administrators' frequent incompetence, by their collusion with the local powers, and by the endemic corruption. What he saw clearly was that the system was an offense to all rational thinkers and planners; but he failed to understand that these very shortcomings were the condition of Mexico's continued subjection to Spain.

His recommendations, therefore, were simple: the reforms that had been carried out in Spain were to be extended to Mexico, while corrupt Creole administrators were to be replaced by *Gachupínes*. And so it happened. Mexican provinces were divided into smaller units, each administered by an intendant (an administrator sent by the Crown and reporting directly to it, thus taking away the powers of the local magistrates), and by subdelegates and district officers. Until the 1780s, Spanish rule had been based on the active cooperation of the Crown and the local elite; the intendants ended all that, and the result was that the Creoles, feeling betrayed, became far more self-assertive. The central government was modernized and enlarged as well; and all these new positions were filled by *Gachupínes* who tended to be unaware of what people considered to be their rights. This was followed by a new, slightly more effective tax system; and all Mexicans found suddenly that they were united in denouncing Spanish tyranny while still affirming their loyalty to the king. As for Madrid, its view was simple: any resistance, it announced, would be considered treason. Still, there were more ways than one of opposing the new system: *cabildos* and *ayuntamientos,* not usually the most efficient of bodies, started claiming a variety of privileges, while cooperation with the administration almost vanished. This was passive resistance, not rebellion; and a resistance mitigated by the fact that the several provinces, each jealous of the others, did not attempt to unite against the reforms. Still, it made a great difference.

By 1786, the intendants were all in place, and they, together with their officials, were all *Gachupínes*. In 1750, for instance, the Creoles had held 55 percent of all positions in the *audiencias,* the judicial and administrative courts that ran much of the country. By 1785, they had only 23 percent of these positions and thus found themselves deprived of powers and salaries that had been theirs for centuries. This was a terrible blow, not just to the pride of the Creoles, but to their very livelihood. Large families and mismanaged estates had created a significant group of penniless younger sons of noble families who depended on government jobs. This group was obviously well able to make itself heard, and did so when it found itself frozen out.

It was easy enough to oppose these changes by claiming that all had been well in the past, that tradition was what mattered, and that breaking with age-old customs was simply wrong. To add that all the decisions came from Madrid, that the Mexicans themselves had never been consulted, only made the argument more effective. Emotionally, too, there was a sense of being abandoned, rejected, as the Crown moved from "authoritarian paternalism to bureaucratic authoritarianism."[12] This feeling that Mexico was being exploited by Spain was promptly made even more convincing by events far away. First there was the French Revolution: traditionalist, Catholic Mexicans watched with horror as church and monarchy were, one after the other, abolished. Europe, obviously, was a terrible place.

It rapidly got worse. To the horror of all Mexicans, Spain entered into an alliance with England. For the Mexicans, Great Britain was the hereditary enemy. It attacked Spanish fleets and American fortresses, it was Protestant, it was everything they had always feared. That the king of Spain could make such an alliance, even against revolutionary France, was almost beyond comprehension. And when, by the Treaty of Basel (1795), Spain made peace with the French Republic, the Mexicans were more horrified still. Their loyalty to Charles IV remained intact—a statue of the king was erected in Mexico City with much pomp and fanfare—but the argument that Mexico should have as little to do with Europe as possible became a compelling one.

Money, Splendor, and the Good Life

In spite of these tensions, life continued at an even pace, and formality was an essential part of it. Mexicans were a people among whom a certain kind of politeness had reached a quite astonishing degree.

Mme Calderón reported:

> I had a dispute this morning with an Englishman who complains bitterly of Mexican insincerity. I believe the chief cause of this complaint among foreigners consists in attaching the slightest value to the common phrase "Está à la disposicion de V." Everything is placed at your disposal—house, carriage, servants, horses, mules, etc.—the lady's earrings, the gentleman's diamond pin, the child's frock. You admire a ring—it is perfectly at your service; a horse—ditto. Letters are dated "from your house" (de la casa de V).[13]

Indeed, for the upper classes, much of life had become an elaborate ritual; people went through the motions, although they were wholly unconnected to reality. Simple visits, for instance, entailed the observance of the most elaborate protocol, as Mme Calderón noted:

> After [the hostess has] embraced each lady who enters . . . and seated the lady of most consequence on the right side of the sofa, a point of great importance, the following dialogue is *de rigueur.*
> "How are you, are you well?"
> "At your service, and you?"
> "Without novelty at your service."
> "I am rejoiced, and how are you, Señora?"
> "At your disposal, and you?"
> "A thousand thanks, and the Señor?"
> "At your service, without novelty," etc., etc., etc. Before sitting down, there is "Pray be seated."
> "Pass first, Señorita."
> "No, Madam, pray pass first."
> "Vaya, well, to oblige you, without further ceremony; I dislike compliments and etiquette."[14]

The men were no less ceremonious. Joel Poinsett, the first U.S. ambassador to Mexico, came to that country in 1822, at a time when manners were still what they had been at the end of the eighteenth century, and he, too, thought it worthwhile to record the scene.

> Remember, when you take leave of a . . . grandee, to bow as you leave the room, at the head of the stairs, where the host accompanies you, and after descending the first flight, turn around and you will see him expecting a third salutation, which he returns with great courtesy, and remains until you are out of sight; so that, as you wind down the stairs, if you catch a glimpse of him, kiss your hand, and he will think you a most accomplished cavalier. This is the only ceremony you have to undergo, for your reception will be cordial and friendly. The gentlemen of Mexico are not hospitable, in our sense of the word. They rarely invite you to dine with them; but they introduce you to their families, assure you of being welcome at all times, in a manner that convinces you of their sincerity, and, if you call in the evening, regale you with ices, chocolates and sweetmeats.[15]

Hospitality (albeit not at dinner) and formality: these were the keynotes of upper-class life in Mexico. As for the ceremoniousness described by the previous two authors, it had become so routine as to be unnoticed by the Mexicans; but this absurdity was not without reason. It helped to fill the time of an idle upper class; it was a way of distinguishing oneself from common mortals. And indeed, while the poor begged or led lives of hard labor, while the traders and artisans all worked long hours, most gentlemen and ladies had nothing but time on their hands. A few of the men, it is true, looked after their property, mines, and haciendas; but in Mexico City, the day was consumed by afternoon visits, slow drives on the Paseo de Bucareli, where Society congregated at the end of the day, and *tertulias* (evening parties). There was also the theater, of course, and bullfights, and occasional balls at which the women were covered with diamonds: show was an important part of life, so the Mexican ladies were famous for the magnificence of their jewels.

What struck observers as remarkable was that these idle, ceremonious people could have spent their time more profitably. "The gentlemen with whom I have associated are intelligent men," Poinsett reported. "The Creoles in general possess good natural talents, and great facility in acquiring knowledge. They are extremely mild and courteous in their manners, kind and benevolent toward each other, and hospitable to strangers. Their besetting sin is gambling."[16] "Besetting sin" is putting it mildly: betting on cards, dice, bullfights, cockfights, and anything else that interested people had become a devastating habit. Fortunes were lost in one night, families impoverished, estates ruined; and even when that happened, there were no complaints, at least on the part of the gambler. The beggar at the street corner might once have been a rich man; he would tell you his story if you asked, and apparently think that it was all part of the normal order of things.

It was, after all, no wonder: gambling has always been a favorite pastime of the idle rich. And working at almost anything (except, perhaps, in a high government position) was most definitely beneath a nobleman's dignity. "The titled nobility," Poinsett observed, "are white Creoles who, satisfied with the enjoyment of large estates, and with the consideration which their rank and wealth confer, seek no other distinction. They are not remarkable for their attainments or for the strictness of their morals. The lawyers who, in fact, exercise much more influence over the people, rank next to the nobles. They are the younger branches of noble houses, or the sons of Europeans, and are remarkably shrewd and intelligent."[17]

That lack of moral strictness naturally applied to upper-class men and women alike—much as it did in Madrid, Paris, or London. Affairs were condoned, provided they lasted a fair amount of time and remained relatively discreet. "The married women," Poinsett went on, " . . . are said to be faithful to the favored lover, and a liaison of that nature does not affect the lady's reputation."[18] It was no wonder, really: among the rich, marriages were invariably arranged. Girls were often married at fourteen or fifteen, and expected to provide a sufficiency of heirs by the time they were twenty. After that, it was only fair to let them enjoy life, especially since most of them had a great deal of charm. "The young women are lively and accomplished. They sing and play agreeably, dance well, and know all they have an opportunity of learning," Poinsett noted approvingly; but then he went on to complain: "If they would leave off the detestable practice of smoking, they would be very pleasing and amiable."[19] They would not leave it off, however: they all smoked cigars and gave every sign of enjoying it.

Charm was one thing, education was quite another. While many upper-class women indeed might know "all they have an opportunity of learning," that was very little. The convents where they were schooled taught religion, manners, and deportment—this last included music and dancing, as well as the rules of etiquette—but an intellectual, or even a person accustomed to the salons of eighteenth-century Europe, would not find much interesting conversation in the great houses of Mexico City.

Most of these grand establishments belonged to noblemen, or people who would, in all likelihood, soon be given a title: wealth, in Mexico, meant ennoblement. It was thus characteristic that of eighty titles given by the kings of Spain between 1529 and 1821, sixty were awarded in the eighteenth century to successful entrepreneurs, financiers, and landowners. These, however, did not come cheap: not only did they reward the possession of a large fortune, they also carried heavy costs—thus making them different from all European titles. First there was the tax of *media annata* to be paid on creation or succession to the title, which was equal to half a year's income of the entail supporting the title; then *lanzas* had to be paid yearly in lieu of military service. Altogether, the burden could prove too heavy for financially straitened noble families, who then found themselves compelled to give up their status. Still, there were advantages: social prestige, naturally, but also freedom from arrest for debt, exemption from the torture that was still a normal part of the criminal judicial process, and finally the privilege of being beheaded rather than hanged if it should come to that. More important, perhaps, the nobles were exempt from all taxes besides the *lanzas* and the *media annata*. All this would have been more desirable, though, if the same privileges and exemptions had not been shared by judges, lawyers, military officers, university graduates, and students: within the context of an ancien régime organization, Mexico came closer to being a society of equals than most European monarchies. Not only that, while there were only eighty, generally intermarried, titled families, nobles abounded: all Basques and their descendants, for instance, were automatically noble, so that, in 1800, in Guanajuato, a city with a population of thirty thousand, some eight hundred families identified themselves as noble, but only five had titles.

Shows and Spectacles

Naturally, not all those nobles were rich, although the titled aristocracy was the wealthiest in Spanish America. Many of them led quite modest lives, some on the borders of poverty, but all, from millionaires on down, shared the same love of spectacle. If you had the money, you could participate in all the grand entertainments of Society; if you did not, there were still the many splendid processions which made their way through the city. Although religion was the reason for all these—the feast of a saint or the Virgin of somewhere or other, Lent, Easter, Corpus Christ, and so on—the actual event could vary quite widely.

In 1805, for instance, a procession to solicit alms to obtain the canonization of the Blessed Felipe de Jesus, a Mexican-born Franciscan martyred in Japan, made its way from the Mexico City cathedral to the convent of San Francisco; and it was more like a vaudeville show than a religious event. First came fifteen images of the martyr, carried by the city guilds; they were followed by floats depicting scenes from his life, some of which were done in grotesque style, with a devil in horns and tail dressed in the most recent fashion, and a Chinese torturer wearing a Jacobin cap. Then came the religious communities, the university, the Cathedral Chapter (the governing body of the Cathedral) with its choir, the city council with three bands, all playing as loud as could be; and all along the route, huge crowds were watching.

As processions went, this one was relatively simple and highly respectable. Night processions, though, were a very different kind of event: they were likely to end in orgies of drinking, gambling, and sex, all impossible to stop because it was hidden in the darkness; as a result, the authorities and most of the bishops tried, unsuccessfully, to limit processions to the daytime hours. Even those, however, could sometimes prove a bit of an embarrassment; when they involved self-scourging with chains, the frenzy which they aroused also worried the church. The processions, in fact, were more like a wild fiesta than acts of devotion, a way for the Indians to take a little pleasure, and the bishop of Silao knew it: he promptly prohibited the holding of processions in several towns of his diocese because the crowds had converted "this devout act into a scandalous spectacle."[20]

Naturally, the greatest, most spectacular religious observances took place in Mexico City, with the viceroy in attendance and the archbishop saying Mass. Some merely entailed decorating the cathedral. On Palm Sunday, for instance,

> the whole cathedral presented the appearance of a forest of palm trees moved by a gentle wind; and under each tree, a half-naked Indian, his rags clinging together with wonderful pertinacity; long, matted dirty black hair both in men and women, bronze faces with mild, unspeaking eyes, or all with one expression of eagerness to see the approach of the priests. Many of them had probably traveled a long way and the palms were from *tierra caliente*, dried and plaited in all manner of ingenious ways. Each palm was about seven foot high, so as far to overshadow the head of the Indian who carried it; and whenever they are blessed, they are carried home to adorn the walls of their huts.[21]

That was just a single ceremony which took place within the cathedral; but during the whole week that followed, business came to a stop while the entire population indulged in one religious spectacle after the other. Naturally,

there were processions, best seen in the Zócalo, the great central square bordered by the cathedral and the Viceregal Palace. Mme Calderón, who was there,
recorded it all.

> It was dark when the procession made its appearance. . . . The Virgin, the
> saints, the Holy Trinity, the Saviour in different passages of his life, imprison-
> ment and crucifixion, were carried past in succession, represented by figures
> magnificently dressed, placed on lofty scaffoldings of immense weight, sup-
> ported by different bodies of men. One is carried by the coachmen, another
> by the water carriers, a third by the porters, a Herculean race.
>
> First arrived the favorite protectress of all classes, the Virgin of Dolores,
> surmounted by a velvet canopy, seated on a glittering throne, attired in her
> sable robes, her brow surmounted by glittering rays, and contracted with an
> expression of agony. . . . Then followed the Saviour bearing the cross, the Sav-
> iour crucified, the Virgin supporting the head of her dead son; the Trinity (the
> Holy Spirit represented by a dove); all the apostles, from Saint Peter with the
> keys to Judas with the money bag; and a long train of saints, all brilliantly illu-
> minated and attended by an amazing crowd of priests, monks and laymen.[22]

Gatherings and spectacles on that scale were relatively rare; but the animation of the city never stopped. There were markets every day, with abundant
provisions of flowers, fruit, vegetables, and poultry. There you could also buy
wild ducks, birds of various sorts, venison, and hares. As for the prices, Poinsett
recorded, they were very reasonable: "Beef, 28 ounces, 12 1/2 cents [about
$1.25 modern value]; mutton and veal, 12 1/2 cents a pound; eggs: 25 cents
a dozen—fowls from 50 to 75 cents a pair—turkeys from 75 cents to a dollar
each—peaches 50 cents a dozen, pineapples 12 1/2 cents each."[23] Equally
important, these markets were also quite splendid to look at, as Humboldt
noted.

> Indian merchants are seen sitting in a wall of greenery. A hedge three feet
> high and made of fresh grasses . . . surrounds like a semi-circular wall the fruit
> being sold to the public; the back, of a uniform green, is divided by flower gar-
> lands arranged so as to be parallel to one another; small bouquets, placed
> symmetrically between the festoons, give this wall the look of a carpet scat-
> tered with flowers . . . [and] the fruit are arranged with great care and elegance
> in small boxes made of a very light wood.[24]

This need for color and an appealing decor was typical. From the feathers
and lace on the hats of the children on Good Friday to the brilliantly colored
skirts and rebozos of the women, bright, intense color was everywhere, and it
was made more brilliant still by the clear air and brilliant sunlight. Life in the
streets of Mexico was an endless, often glittering spectacle: sumptuous carriages, horsemen with embroidered clothes and trappings, priests and monks

in their vestments all added to the animation of the streets; and then there were those key actors of the everyday, the vendors, whose cries and activities changed with the passing hours. "At dawn," Mme Calderón remembered,

> you are awakened by the shrill and despondent cry of the . . . coalmen, "Carbon, Señor?" . . . ; then the grease-man takes up the song, "Mantequilla! Lard! Lard! At one real and a half." "Salt beef! Good salt beef!" interrupts the butcher in a hoarse voice. . . . Then passes by the *cambista*, a sort of Indian she-trader or exchanger, who sings out "Tejocotes por vena de chile?", a small fruit which she proposes exchanging for hot peppers.
>
> A kind of ambulating peddler drowns the shrill treble of the Indian cry. He calls aloud upon the public to buy needles, pins, thimbles, shirt buttons, tape, cotton balls, small mirrors, etc . . . Behind him stands the Indian with his tempting baskets of fruit.
>
> A sharp note of interrogation is heard, indicating that something is hot and must be snapped up quickly before it cools. "Little fat cakes from the oven, hot?" This is in a female key, sharp and shrill. Follows the mat seller. "Who wants mats of Puebla, mats of five yards?"
>
> At midday, the beggars begin to be particularly importunate, and their cries and prayers and long recitations form a running accompaniment to the other noises. Then above all rises the cry of "Honey cakes?", "Cheese and honey?" . . . Then come . . . the sellers of sweetmeats, of meringues, which are very good, and of all sorts of candy. . . . Then the lottery men . . .
>
> Toward evening rises the cry of "Curd cakes?" or "Do you take nuts?" succeeded by the night cry of "Chestnuts, hot and roasted!" and by the affectionate vendors of ducks, "Ducks, oh my soul, hot ducks!", "Tortillas!", etc., etc. As the night wears away, the voices die off, to resume next morning in fresh vigor.[25]

There was also another street population: the beggars. It was hard being a beggar: because people were too used to them to give much, they had to depend on the church. There were monasteries that were both rich and charitable: once a day, they distributed soup and tortillas to all comers; but there were also great numbers of *pulquerias*, places where the poor could buy strong, cheap liquor and sleep it off in sheds. Drunkenness was indeed the Indians' great vice, and it is no wonder. Dispossessed of their land and their culture, unable to earn a decent living, they often drank the pittance they had just earned by occasional work: unconsciousness was better than any part of their ordinary lives.

The presence of vast numbers of the destitute and homeless—perhaps as many as 20,000 in a total population of some 130,000—did nothing to restrain the amusements of the rich, however. On most fine days (that is to say, most of the year) they congregated in the late afternoon on the Paseo Nuevo, the boulevard created by Viceroy Antonio Bucareli in the 1770s. It was "a broad road raised about three feet above the meadowland that surrounds the city and planted on both sides with willow trees," Poinsett recorded, adding:

> The Paseo was crowded with carriages, some whirling rapidly along, and others drawn up round the open circle in the middle of the road, where the ladies amuse themselves for hours examining the equipages that roll by, and nodding, smiling and shaking their fans at their acquaintances as they pass. . . . The bodies of their coaches are large, but of a very good form and well painted: a little too fine, as you will think, when I tell you that Guido's Aurora frequently adorns the middle panel.[26]

This sort of display was just as important to Society people as processions were to the Indian peasants. Compared to Europeans, the Mexicans usually overdressed. Ladies went to simple evening parties wearing highly elaborate dresses and a great deal of jewelry. As for the theater, people attended it, not for the performances, which were usually abysmal, and even less for the sets and costumes, but simply because it was another occasion to shine. On one such evening,

> the boxes at the theater were filled with well-dressed people; the front part of the pit, where there are seats, was occupied by gentlemen, and the back part was crowded with common people and soldiers, who are obliged to stand during the whole performance. The theater is shaped like a horseshoe, the stage being at the smallest end, so that very few of the spectators in the boxes can see the whole of it. A balcony projects from each box where the ladies display their persons and finery to great advantage.[27]

Of course, it hardly mattered that the view from the boxes was so poor: the reason to be there was not to see the play but what your friends were wearing.

At least, at the evening parties, life was a little more amusing. There was often music and dancing, food served before and after, and, of course, gambling. Card games were the staple entertainment; young and old loved them; but, in society houses at least, the stakes were not such as to ruin a loser in one night. All that was much as it might have been in Europe; but here there was a major difference: the mix of courtiers and intellectuals, pretty women and foreigners was nowhere to be found. Mexican society was rigidly stratified— which of course meant that you spent your life seeing the same small group of people. It is no wonder that the rare foreign visitor was so effusively greeted: he or she at least brought something new into what was, otherwise, a very monotonous round of pleasure.

Another missing element was the sophistication and variety of food to be found in the great European houses. Of course, there was an abundance of tropical fruit and fresh vegetables. Local specialties like *mole,* that spicy blend of spices and bitter chocolate used as a sauce for a variety of foods, were as good as they are today, and so were the fried bananas, the fried beans, and the stuffed peppers: Indian-inspired food was prized in the highest society. Game birds, turkey, and all kinds of fowls varied the menu. There were massive stews like the *puchero*, in which lamb, beef, slab bacon, chickens, chickpeas, gourds, potatoes, peas, and green vegetables were simmered together. A piece of each meat, together with a sampling of each vegetable, was then put on each plate, and the whole was served with a sauce of tomatoes and herbs. As for the desserts, they consisted of a wide variety of pastries, most of them very sweet, and ices: Mexico City, being so high up, had an easily available supply of snow and ice. All that made for very pleasant meals; and in between, or at breakfast, there was the justly famous Mexican hot chocolate, and delicious coffee: no one who could afford to eat had reason to complain. Still, there were no great chefs, no recondite dishes to surprise the palate, none of the kind of gourmet dinner parties that might have provided an element of the unexpected in what was otherwise a very predictable life: boredom, in fact, was never very far away.

Another possible source of interest, the decoration of houses, was also lacking. Of course, there were very grand residences, but the whole feel of them was different. Mme Calderón noticed it immediately. "It is a handsome new house," she wrote of one such,

> built in a square, like all Mexican houses. The ground floor, which has a stone-paved court with a fountain in the middle contains about twenty rooms besides out-houses, coach-house, stables, pigeon-house, garden-house, etc. the second story, where the principal apartments are, the first floor being chiefly occupied by servants, has the same number of rooms, with coal-room, wood-room, bathroom and water everywhere, in the court below, in the garden and on the azotea [the flat terrace roof] which is very spacious. . . . The great defect in all these houses is their want of finish. The great doors that will not shut properly, and the great windows down to the ground which in the rainy season will certainly admit water, making these residences appear like a cross-breed between a palace and a barn; the splendour of the one, the discomfort of the other.[28]

That was typical. There were many servants, but they wore soiled liveries; and beyond that, the effect was of accumulation, not planning. The interiors were rich, but haphazard, the silver at dinner massive and often beautiful while the tablecloth was likely to be dirty or torn. And so, unlike the European rich, who gave a great deal of time and care to the decoration of their houses and the gathering of a collection, the Mexican grandees failed to take a real interest in their surroundings.

There was one particular ceremony, though, in which no detail was neglected and the most thorough planning prevailed. It was the funeral: in 1800 as today, the Mexicans had a fascination with death. Already on the Day of the

Dead, sugar and papier-maché skulls and skeletons were sold everywhere, while ornaments and even costumes faithfully reproduced all its more macabre effects. For the funerals of the rich, therefore, nothing was too good, from the procession of black-draped carriages to the very toilette of the departed. "A lady of high rank having died [around 1805]," Mme Calderón recorded,

> her relatives undertook to commit her to her last resting place, inhabited according to the then prevailing fashion in her most magnificent dress, that which she had worn at her wedding. The dress was a wonder of luxury, even in Mexico. It was entirely composed of the finest lace, and the flounces were made of a special point which cost fifty dollars a vara (the Mexican yard). It was also ornamented and looped up at certain intervals with bows of ribbon very richly embroidered in gold.[29]

Not only that, the lady in question was buried in the same elaborate gold necklace she had worn at her wedding. A few weeks later, though, her relatives were startled to discover that same necklace for sale at a fashionable jeweler's. Inquiries were made, a dishonest sacristan discovered, and the custom changed: thereafter, the finery was removed after the service and before the entombment.

It almost seemed, in fact, as if life itself made for untidiness: death was more orderly, church services were better organized (and the churches themselves far more consistently decorated), and the convents the most stately of all. Of course, there were many different sorts of convents: a small house far away in a distant province was very unlike one of the more splendid establishments in the capital. There, the daughters of great families, when they were too numerous, would become nuns: a dowry for the convent was cheaper than the dowry demanded by a prospective husband. Mere residence in a convent did not have to entail deprivation, however—except, of course for two major areas: life in society, and sex. Priests and monks often had common-law wives, and there was really nothing the bishops could do about it, but nuns in aristocratic convents tended to remain chaste.

There were other pleasures, though. The Convent of the Encarnación was one of the most elegant in Mexico City, and its standards were correspondingly high. It was, as Mme Calderón noted,

> in fact a palace. The garden . . . is kept in good order, with its stone walks, stone benches and an ever-playing and sparkling fountain. The trees were bending with fruit and they pulled quantities of the most beautiful flowers for us: sweet peas, roses . . . , carnations, jasmine and heliotrope . . .
>
> Most of the halls in the convent are noble rooms . . . [We] admired the extreme cleanliness of everything, especially of the immense kitchen . . . each nun has a servant, and some have two . . .
>
> Having visited the whole building, and admired one Virgin's blue satin and pearls, and another's black velvet and diamonds, sleeping holy infants,

saints, paintings, shrines and confessionals . . . we came at length to a large hall . . . where a very elegant supper, lighted and ornamented, greeted our astonished eyes; cakes, chocolates, ices, creams, custards, tarts, jellies, blanc-manges [mousses], orange and lemonade.[30]

For all their wealth and neatness, these grand establishments were only tiny islands. Outside their high walls, life went on tumultuously: that was a characteristic that struck all visitors. There was an intensity, it seemed, in the very air, a theatrical quality to people, buildings, and events; it might make for untidiness, for unevenness in the standards of institutions and domestic life alike, but that was an unavoidable consequence. The official language of Mexico was Spanish; the people who ran the country, its trade, its mines, its manufactures, its schools, and its church were white, some newly arrived from Spain, others descended from earlier arrivals. The king was the king of Spain; the country's alignment in foreign affairs was entirely Spanish. In spite of all that, however, Mexico was not at all like Spain, and its people, in 1800, were just beginning to notice it. Never really a colony, not quite an extension of the mother country, Mexico was unlike any other place. It was also intensely conservative, and so it might well have remained just as it was if events in Europe had not shaken it out of its complacency.

CHAPTER ELEVEN

Autonomy or Independence?

THAT MEXICO should be closely linked to Europe was not surprising: its king was the king of Spain, its viceroys were Spanish, as was its archbishop. Much more startling is the fact that the severance of these ties was precipitated, not by a local yearning for independence, but by events that originated in France. In 1808, when Napoléon decided to replace the Spanish Bourbons with his brother Joseph, the crucial link that tied Spain to its colonies was severed, and the Mexicans began to think they might possibly be a self-sufficient nation.

Once again, it was all an effect of the world war. Napoléon conquered Spain and Portugal because he wanted to deny the British access to those markets, and to those ports. Here was another perverse effect of his policies: the independence of Spanish America, by opening its economy to British trade and investment, actually fortified Great Britain and provided one more proof that, no matter how great the distances, the world was really one.

A WELL-ORGANIZED COUNTRY

For all its apparent disorder, New Spain functioned surprisingly well. Of course, the viceroy's decrees were not obeyed as fast or as thoroughly on the edges of the country as they were in center—partly because of sheer distance, partly because the whites who carried the apparatus of government tended to avoid the frontier provinces. That was especially true in the north. In Texas, New Mexico, and California, the American Indian tribes were almost impossible to contain, let alone rule. But there, too, an effort was made: in August 1776, the viceroy created the *provincias internas.* Consisting of Coahuila, Texas, New Mexico, Nueva Vizcaya, Sinaloa, Sonora, and the Californias, these faraway and wild areas were henceforth ruled, not from Mexico City, but by a virtually independent *commandante general* with troops at his disposal; and the system did bring about a greater measure of order.

The rest of the country answered to orders from Mexico City. There, the bureaucrats ran everything—the government, the customs, the mint (and, by extension, the distribution of the ore from the mines of gold and silver), the post office, the organization of the guilds, and, of course, the police, the courts, and the army.

Each of these administrations required a substantial staff. Because Mexico was rich, they paid decent salaries. The viceroy's principal secretary, for instance, whose functions were clerical, not executive, was paid 2,000 pesos a year—a pittance compared to the income of a rich man, but more than enough for a big house, a carriage, and many servants. In contrast, the lowest category of clerk was paid 600 pesos—not enough for luxury, certainly, but enough for comfort. As for the principal executive assistant, he received 4,000 pesos a year, and the head of one of the secretariats, the equivalent of a ministry, received 6,000 pesos, something not far below what an official of that rank might be paid in Europe. The same was true of the superintendent of customs and of the superintendent of the mint, whose salaries were also 6,000 pesos.

Lower officials were also very fairly remunerated: 4,000 pesos for the administrator of the post office, 1,000 pesos for an archivist, 3,000 pesos for an inspector of customs, and 1,000 for an assessor. Even the lowliest clerk in the post office was given 600 pesos a year. As a result, there was very little corruption. Officials could live, and live well, on their salaries, something the younger sons of noble families never forgot.

Amazingly, these officials were often better informed than their European counterparts. In 1793, Viceroy Revillagigedo had a census taken; then, very much as in the United States today, allowances were made for undercounting (due, in this case, to the number of Indians trying to evade the head tax), and the result showed that the population must be around 5,200,000. It was growing rapidly, though: by 1803, it was probably up to 5,800,000. Part of the reason for that growth was progress. Inoculation against smallpox, a brand-new discovery, was general throughout the country and ended the hitherto periodic epidemics of that deadly disease. By comparison, the population of the United States, which was also expanding, came to 7,240,000.

The very idea of a census was highly modern; so was the understanding that encouraging the teaching and study of science also made for prosperity through the development of improved industrial techniques. In the universities, chemistry and the natural sciences received attention, their practitioners encouragement. In the capital itself, there was a School of Mining, where teaching and research went on concurrently. There was also an Academy of Fine Arts complete with a large collection of casts and a library. All that, of course, made Mexico City an exceptionally civilized place; and it was all paid for by the government.

The teaching and research at the School of Mining had an immediate effect, and so did the relaxation of trade restrictions. The great reforming ministers of Charles III understood that freeing the economy from still medieval regulations was likely to result in increased prosperity. This was a principle they applied first in Spain, then eventually in Mexico. The results were immediate: the total amount of tithes, one of the surest indicators, was 40 percent higher in 1789 than it had been ten years earlier, while the organization of the Mining Guild in 1777, by generalizing the use of improved methods and technology, stimulated production in Guanajuato, Zacatecas, and Pachuca. And in that same ten-year period, the landholders' income went up by 50 million pesos. By comparison, total government expenditure by 1803 was just under 8 million. Thus, despite the grumbling caused by the reforms, and the Creoles' fear that power and jobs were being taken away from them, the Mexicans had every reason to be loyal: they were, after all, more prosperous and no less free than in any other period in the country's history. At the same time, the king could congratulate himself. He was also getting a great deal more from Mexico: in 1712, the Mexican government had barely paid for itself; by the late 1790s, it was sending 6 million pesos a year to Madrid, a major sum considering that the whole budget of Spain came to about 30 million. And there was more: because Mexico imported all kinds of goods from Spain, and paid for them in gold and silver, the net bullion returns to Spain rose from 59.5 million pesos in 1776–1780 to 120.9 million in 1791–1795, all of which was taxed by the king.

Mining, of course, was the key to all this prosperity. The great mining centers provided the bullion that helped balance the budgets, Mexican and Spanish, right the balance of trade, and stimulate the economy. "The art of mining is being perfected more every day," Alexander von Humboldt noted. "The graduates of the School of Mining of Mexico are spreading precise knowledge about the circulation of air in the wells and [underground] galleries; machines are being installed which have rendered obsolete the old methods of having the ore and water carried by the men."[1] Just as important, the mines were in just the right part of the country. "The richest silver lodes, those of Guanajuato, Zacatecas, Taxco and the Real Monte are at altitudes of five to six thousand feet. The mines are surrounded by cultivated fields, towns and villages . . . and everything makes it easier to exploit the underground wealth."[2] Humboldt was right: food was readily available, there was work for the miners' wives and relatives, the necessities of life were all there. The only major element missing was a system of navigable rivers: water transport was easier, faster, and cheaper—and sadly lacking.

Still, for the owners, mining could be a dangerous business. It was a capital-intensive industry: expensive machines were required, and so was much digging. A good mine could make you rich—that, as noted earlier, was the case for the counts of Valenciana—but a significant proportion of that vast income had to be reinvested in order to keep the mine productive. It was calculated, in fact, that of ten newcomers to the industry, eight would be ruined, and among the failures were members of quite a few noble families.

A Traditional Agriculture

Those, of course, were the dangers of modern capitalism. The agricultural sector, on the other hand, was far more traditional in its structure: it had changed little since the sixteenth century. Most years, Mexico grew more food than it needed, although in a bad year there could still be an occasional local famine. Except for the market gardens at Xochimilco, just outside Mexico City, the main production units were vast haciendas, often employing up to six hundred people. Largely manned by Indians bound to the land by their debt, these huge domains were anything but efficient. Still, they produced sugar, tobacco, and coffee both for local consumption and for export.

The main building of the hacienda, a combination of residence and farming center, was usually a fortresslike, utilitarian building that might cost between 5,000 and 10,000 pesos to build and have some twenty rooms, along with the usual dependencies. Of course, conditions varied widely. In the northern provinces, the haciendas were actually fortified so as to withstand Indian raids. Nearer the capital, and along the coasts in the *terras calientes,* they were built to suit the tropical climate. Everywhere, though, the estate tended to be a little self-enclosed realm. The artisans produced most of the goods needed, a significant share of the crop was consumed on the spot, and the owner's will was law. This could be seen in a variety of ways: the single priest on the hacienda, for instance, was usually a man chosen by the owner and confirmed by the bishop; corporal punishment—flogging, mostly—was widespread and inflicted as the owner pleased; and, sadly, all those royal decrees protecting the Indians were generally ignored.

The hacendado himself could be quite a splendid figure, a traveler noted.

> We behold the proprietor of an hacienda decked in a style of the most costly, but awkward, grandeur. He has on a pair of country-made boots, which cost from fifty to a thousand dollars; large spurs inlaid with gold and silver; a superb horse with a bridle and saddle which cost a hundred and fifty to three hundred; a cloak . . . richly embroidered, and full of gold and silver buttons, laces and fringe. He lives in a spacious house, within whose walls every luxury is to be found that the country affords; but when he sallies forth, he is lost amid a group of half-naked, badly fed wretches, whose only dress is sheepskins.[3]

Here, too, conditions varied widely. Some hacendados felt a paternalistic responsibility for their workers. They were no less absolute, of course, but at least the Indians were likely to fare better. Other owners were tyrants, pure and simple. Some supervised the estate closely; others collected the income from several of these vast estates and lived in Mexico City. There were landholders who surrounded their houses with parks and every possible amenity while, next door, every acre of land would be used to increase production and income. Still, taken as a group, the hacendados were proud, independent, and unaware of improvements in agricultural technique.

That was hardly surprising: much the same conditions prevailed in Spain, where government regulations were also ignored, and where the peasants were not treated much better than the Indians in Mexico. Like their Spanish equivalents, the great landholders tended to be not just noble but titled. There was, however, a major difference: the Spanish aristocrats often served, for a while at least, in the army—as officers, naturally. Mexico, on the other hand, had virtually no defense establishment. Because there were no hostile neighbors, the land borders were safe; and the Spanish navy protected the coasts. There was a militia in the towns, but it was inactive; a few regiments of regular soldiers manned the coastal fortresses and, to both north and south, provided protection against the Indians.

This happy situation, however, was not allowed to continue unaltered. When Spain joined France and the United States in 1779, and thus found itself at war with England, Charles III began to think it was time Mexico defended itself, and provided both men and money for the purpose. To the intense annoyance of the Creole middle classes, the militia was reformed and put on a more active footing. Nevertheless, by 1800, Mexico was still incapable of defending itself against attack by a major power.

CENSORSHIP AND PROGRESS

There was one other aspect of Mexican society that remained at odds with the modernization of the country: the censorship as enforced by the Inquisition. It was very simple, really. Not only were antireligious books banned; so were compendiums of knowledge, including, naturally, the great French *Encyclopédie*, books on the events in France, books on constitutions and constitutional law, including those containing the U.S. or French constitutions—anything, in fact, which might cause people to think. Even so, books were smuggled in; but their owners were regularly denounced to the Inquisitors. In 1795, three prominent Creole families found themselves in considerable difficulty because they had sets of the *Encyclopédie*.

In Spain, under Charles III, new scientific and philosophical ideas had been allowed to circulate freely. It was only with the onset of the French Revolution that censorship was reimposed; and by then, it was too late. In Mexico, on the other hand, there had been no such relaxation. There, too, the French Revolution terrified the ruling classes, and it was typical that in 1800 Viceroy Berenguer de Marquina should tell the Inquisition, in a letter marked "top secret": "Warnings which have been communicated to me by anonymous messages and other observations . . . have made me decide that the Superior Government ought to move with the greatest care and precautions in the critical circumstances of the day, particularly since such suspicious liberties and occurrences have taken place for some time."[4] The letter is an unwilling tribute to the power of ideas and free thought; it also indicates the terror felt by the *Gachupín* officials at the possibility that ideas of self-government might begin to spread.

That, of course, was anathema to the authorities, lay and religious: there was, after all, the dreadful example of the United States, where the people elected their government and worshiped as they pleased. A degree of autonomy had been considered, though: in 1783, Charles III's chief minister, the count of Aranda, had come up with a plan for sending Spanish princes as kings to New Spain, Peru, and the rest of South America, while at the same time these countries would retain strong military, political, and economic ties to Spain. The king considered the possibility, then decided against it, perhaps because he was aware that most members of the Spanish royal family were perfect imbeciles. Then, in 1797, Prime Minister Manuel de Godoy suggested making Louisiana a federated kingdom with one of Charles IV's younger brothers on the throne; but again, nothing came of the idea. Still, the feeling that there were real nations in Spanish America was slowly gaining ground.

A Splendid Capital

There can be no respectable state without a large, well-organized capital, and there, too, Mexico did well. Just as Madrid was the most glamorous city in Spain, so Mexico City was incomparably larger, richer, and more fashionable than Puebla, its nearest runner-up. There was, it is true, no court to compete with that of Spain—the viceroy, when it came to display, just did not make the grade—but there was an aristocracy and a vast, well-laid-out city. Joel Poinsett, the U.S. Minister to Mexico, later wrote:

> The streets are sufficiently wide . . . , intersecting each other at right angles; they are all well-paved and have sidewalks of flat stones. The public squares are spacious and surrounded by buildings of hewed stone, and of very good architecture. The public edifices and churches are vast and splendid . . . and have an air of solidity and even magnificence. They are of three or four stories high, with flat terrace roofs, and many of them are ornamented with iron

balconies . . . Our large cities are many of them neater than Mexico, but . . . there is an air of grandeur in the aspect of this place . . . which [is] wanting in the United States.[5]

It was the grandeur that struck everyone. The Zócalo was as vast and majestic as any city square anywhere; the cathedral and the viceroy's palace, which bordered it, were both large and impressive; and everywhere there were great monuments. The Minería, the neoclassical School of Mining, for instance, was "a palace whose fine proportions would render it remarkable amongst the finest edifices of any European country. All is on a great scale, its noble rows of pillars, great staircases, large apartments and lofty roof."[6]

Mme Calderón was right. The Minería, with its 360-foot front, is the work of Francisco de Tresguerras, the greatest of the late-eighteenth-century Mexican architects. With its double pilasters on the upper facade, its windows topped by semicircular pediments, its triple-arched doorway, and its central triangular pediment, the main facade blends poise and majesty and looks like what it was, a great institution that was also a major civic monument. Just as important, like all great architects, Tresguerras understood the importance of proportion: size alone is not enough, it is what you do with it that matters.

Nor was the Minería an exception: today, the Zócalo still retains its impressiveness, but in 1800 there were also the Mint, the Academy of Fine Arts, hospices, more than a hundred churches, twenty-three monasteries, fifteen convents, the university, and one of the best botanical gardens in the world. Then, as if that was not enough, Mexico had excellent street lighting—and had had it, in fact, before both Paris and Madrid.

Naturally, there was an elegant part of town, which was defined by the streets which ended in the Zócalo. The grandest houses belonging to the greatest nobles, like the marqués de Guardiola, were on one of these, the Calle San Francisco. The conde del Valle de Orizaba's house was famous because its facade was covered with blue and white Puebla tiles; the conde de Borda had spent the immense sum of 300,000 pesos on his house, the marqués de Prada Alegre 37,000 pesos on his furniture. The most famous mansion of the street, though, was that of the marqués de Jaral, because it was a replica of the royal palace in Palermo. Then there was the conde de Santiago's house: it had turrets, battlements in the style of a medieval fortress, but made of rose-colored stone, with windows framed in cream-colored arches and drain spouts carved to resemble cannons.

The mock-military look given by crenellation was a popular one. Unlike the grand town houses in most of Europe, those in Mexico tended to be closed to the world—a last remnant of the Arabic influence on Spanish architecture. What mattered even more than the street facade was the patio, and much of the house opened onto it, or onto the back garden. At the conde de San Mateo de Valparaíso's home, for instance, the patio had broad, majestic arches on the ground floor and a gallery supported by columns on top. Outside, though, a

VUE DE MEXICO.

The Zócalo, Mexico City. The Viceregal Palace, to the left of the cathedral, was the center of power in Mexico. (*I. N. Phelps Stokes Collection, Miriam and Ira D. Wallach Division of Art, Prints and Photographs, The New York Public Library, Astor, Lenox and Tilden Foundations*)

deliberate toughness prevailed, with plain brown stone walls, a powerful corner tower rising one level higher than the rest of the house, and walls made of dark brown stone.

Even that was more ornamental than the facades of most of the aristocratic houses, many of which were just one story high, with plain walls and late baroque window and door frames. Sometimes, though, an element of animation was provided by shops on the ground floor: those noble families whose fortunes had been made in trade saw no reason why their houses should not bring in a profit. That, too, was very different from Spain, where trade was considered a non-noble occupation.

Architecturally, though, Mexico remained a little behind the times. Neoclassicism reached it some twenty-five years after it had begun to flourish in Europe: many of the grand houses of the capital seemed to belong more to the seventeenth century than to the end of the eighteenth. Still, there was Tresguerras. The Minería, which he designed, was one of the great public buildings of its time; but his most beautiful private house was not in Mexico City. The conde Rul owned mines in Guanajuato, which had made him very rich indeed, so when he commissioned a house from Tresguerras, he made it clear that only the best would do. The result was—and still is—a masterpiece.

Fully open to the street, the house has a relatively plain ground floor animated by rusticated piers that separate the doorway from the windows on either side. On the main floor, the central window is topped by a semicircular pediment and framed by double Ionic columns, while double Ionic pilasters separate the two windows on either side and are repeated at the right and left ends of the facade. Below the windows there is a cast-iron balcony; above them a frieze with a Greek key motif runs the length of the building; and, finally, the center is topped by a triangular pediment. The result is a building that gives a feeling of refined, yet stately elegance; and the hexagonal patio, with its colonnade on the main story, adds to that impression.

THE HARDSHIPS OF TRAVEL

Guanajuato itself is a handsome town. Because there were so many others in Mexico, and because they reflected a high degree of planning and maintenance, most people understood that this was indeed a real country, not just a colonial dependency. Still, reaching these towns and cities was not always easy. The roads were safe; but unless you had friends in whose strategically placed haciendas you could stay, travel was often rough. The carriages for rent were wretched vehicles, badly made and badly sprung, which, in any event, were useless on mountain roads, where they were replaced by primitive litters. As for the inns, they left almost everything to be desired. Poinsett stayed at two of these on his way from Vera Cruz to the capital. The first was a one-room house.

> On one side lay a traveler, stretched on a hurdle of canes; on the other, a child was sleeping on the floor. The bed of our hostess occupied the side opposite the door. This she insisted that we should take possession of . . .
>
> The laths that surrounded the bed and supported a tattered curtain to screen the lady from the view of her guests, and from the wind that entered through the chinks and crevices innumerable, served at the same time to hang *tasajo* on. *Tasajo* is beef cut into long strips and dried in the sun; while it is curing it must not be exposed either to rain or dew, and is always put under cover at night. The bedstead and all the rafters were festooned with it.[7]

Poinsett does have a point: meat, as a decor, is not really inviting.

Things were not much better the next night.

> [The bed] consisted only of canes laid lengthways and covered with a blanket. This, and even the smell of raw meat, might have been endured, but we were visited by such swarms of fleas, sancudos and mosquitoes, that we rejoiced when we saw the light of day. . . . It is impossible, without experience, to form an idea of the torments of the crawling, skipping and flying insects of this country. Bugs and worse than bugs, fleas, sancudos and mosquitoes at night,

and gnats and xixens in the day. The xixen . . . is a very small winged insect that draws blood from the face and hands the instant it alights on them.[8]

Because travel was so difficult, each province felt almost like a little country of its own; as for the viceroy, he tended to make the journey from Vera Cruz only when arriving and departing the country. Luckily, though, Puebla was on the way. Its cathedral was one of the most splendid in Mexico: marble, gilt bronze, sculpture, and paintings all made its interior one vast treasure house. All over the country there were splendid churches: in Querétaro, for instance, brightly colored ceramic tiles covered many domes; in Valladolid, the altar frontal was made of beaten silver; and so it went.

Closer by, just outside Mexico City, there was the most unforgettable of views, which was described by Poinsett:

> From the terrace that runs around the castle [of Chapultepec] . . . the whole valley of Mexico lies stretched out as in a map; the city itself, with its innumerable churches and convents; the two great aqueducts which cross the plain; the avenues of elms and poplars which lead to the city; the villages, lakes and plains which surround it. To the north, the magnificent cathedral of Our Lady of Guadalupe—to the south, the villages of San Agustin, San Angel and Tacubaya which . . . look like an immense garden . . . [and the] glorious enclosure of mountains above which tower the two mighty volcanoes, Popocatepetl and Iztaccihuatl.[9]

It was all, from landscape to churches to universities, more than enough to make the Mexicans proud. But in spite of the growing realization that Mexico was a real country, in spite of all the complaints generated by the government's reforms, it still occurred to no one in 1800 that they ought to be governed by someone other than Charles IV.

A MONARCHY WITHOUT A KING

This fidelity to the king was the proof that the complex system devised by Spain had been effective; but the independence of the United States should have had consequences in Mexico. In fact, the extreme Catholicism of the Mexicans, their apparently innate conservatism, and, in the upper classes, the desire for titles and orders all worked together to prevent significant discontent. So did the restraints on trade that had been in place ever since the sixteenth century. All Spanish possessions were required to trade only with the mother country: foreign ships were not allowed into American ports, and all convoys from the New World had to go to Cádiz or Seville. Thus, all those who were involved in trade—most of the middle and upper classes—were economically dependent on Spain.

By 1789, things had begun to change, however: ships were now free to trade with any Spanish port, and a wave of Spanish immigrants rushed to take advantage of these new opportunities. At the same time, intracolonial trade was allowed for the first time. These reforms were, in fact, little more than a bow to reality: despite official prohibitions, Mexico traded as much or more with the Americas as it did with Spain; and there was so much smuggling (on which, of course, no tax was collected) that it seemed wiser to legalize the situation. The first, and most immediate, consequence of all this was an inflow of European goods balanced by a compensating outflow of bullion, and greater prosperity all around.

That, in turn, made a great difference: Mexico was now behaving like a fully autonomous entity. From commercial freedom to independence was a very big step, but already the country was learning to think of itself as a state that responded to its own needs rather than to those of the colonizing power.

Then, beginning in 1797, a still more radical change took place. The decay of the Spanish navy under Charles IV, and the maritime wars between France, England, and the rest of Europe, meant that the trading fleets could no longer be protected from a variety of predators. The only way to ensure the continued flow of goods back and forth was to put them on the ships of neutral powers—neutral ships made neutral goods—so that they were not seized by the French or English navies. Thus, for the first time ever, the Spanish government allowed neutral trading vessels to enter Mexican ports. This revolutionary change ended in 1799, but it had to be reintroduced in 1801–1802, and again in 1804–1808. For the first time, the Mexicans were beginning to depend on countries other than Spain for an essential economic activity.

That was still not enough to change their loyalties—just enough, perhaps, to make a few people think about a wide range of possibilities. Far more important were the government's financial measures beginning in 1804. By then, the yearly tribute paid by Spain to France weighed so heavily on its treasury that Godoy, the Spanish prime minister, simply took whatever he could get, the assets of the church and the charitable institutions with the rest. This was an enormously unpopular move, partly because the mortgagees found that the Crown raised their interest rates while demanding gradual repayment of the borrowed capital. The church, for decades, had been content with low rates and no capital repayment. As a result, these sudden demands were, for quite a few landowners, nothing short of catastrophic. Forced sales were carried out by a special junta; and as if to make the whole process even more infuriating, the viceroy and other *Gachupín* officials were allowed to keep a percentage of the proceeds for themselves.

It was also a measure that touched a very wide public. By 1806, about a quarter of the total capital from the mortgages—a little over 10 million pesos—was going to the treasury. Even those Mexicans who did not have a mortgage resented having the money go out of the country. The regular surplus that went to the Spanish Crown was hardly noticed because the procedure was so ancient; these new demands, on the other hand, were seen as a crying injustice; and even worse, the money went to France, a country that most Creoles believed to be ruled (almost literally) by the Devil.

Godoy, however, was even more unpopular than the king, and so was Viceroy José de Iturrigaray, his friend and appointee. Still, nothing might have happened if it had not been for the stunning news that began reaching Mexico in June 1808. At first, indeed, all seemed well: Charles IV had abdicated, Godoy was under arrest, and the prince of Asturias, the king's eldest son, had become King Ferdinand VII. The fall of the hated Godoy was naturally greeted with joy, while Ferdinand himself was highly popular because he was known to be anti-French. Except for the viceroy, therefore, everyone approved of the change; and expressions of the most fervent loyalty to the new king abounded.

It was in this atmosphere that the next news arrived. Both Ferdinand and Charles had been ordered by Napoléon to join him in Bayonne, on the French side of the Pyrenees; both had been made to renounce the throne; and the new king of Spain was Napoléon's brother Joseph. Suddenly, the world was upside down. There was no question of recognizing Joseph as king of Mexico, of course. In any event, the union with the Crown of the various South American countries and provinces was a purely personal one: it was not that Spain owned Mexico, it was that the king of Spain was also the king of Mexico. Thus, by the end of June 1808, the Mexicans found themselves living in a monarchy without a king, while the government, which for three centuries had taken its orders from Madrid, was cut adrift. Never, in the history of colonial Mexico, had there been so fundamental a crisis.

There was, in simple legal fact, no legitimate government. The viceroy was merely the king's representative: he had no standing of his own. This was so evident that on July 19, the *ayuntamiento* of Mexico City, that Creole stronghold, passed a resolution demanding that henceforth power proceed from the governed: "In the absence or during the impediment [of the king], sovereignty lies represented in all the kingdom and all the classes that form it, and more particularly in those superior tribunals [the *audiencias*] that govern it and administer justice and in those corporations that represent the public."[10]

This was a radical claim: the upper classes, the *ayuntamiento* said in effect, had now replaced the king. The people were never mentioned, of course: it occurred to no one that the Indians might have a say in the country where they were an immense majority; but the Creoles, who had of late complained so bitterly about being excluded from power, now boldly demanded it all. Worst of all, from the *Gachupín* point of view, was that they had a very strong argument: all Mexicans owed loyalty to Ferdinand VII; but Ferdinand VII was imprisoned in a French castle.

The viceroy understood all that—and he was anxious to stay in office. Then, in August, the situation was made even worse by the arrival of Jáuregui and Jabat, the representatives of the Central Junta that sat, briefly, in Seville. Claiming that the junta governed Spain in the absence of the king, they demanded that New Spain transfer its loyalty to that body. This only the *Gachupínes* and a few ultraconservative Creoles were willing to do: to everyone else, it was clear that allegiance to a person, the king, could not be transferred to a self-appointed body. As for the viceroy, it was not just that he recognized the Creoles' claim: as a protégé of Godoy's, he had every reason to fear the junta; and so, all of a sudden, he was seen to distance himself from the *Gachupínes*.

The results came swiftly. On September 15, a coup led by Gabriel Yermo, a wealthy Spanish hacendado, deposed Iturrigaray and replaced him with Pedro de Garibay, a doddering octogenarian; then, when it became clear that the new viceroy was half senile, Yermo removed him and appointed the timid and naive archbishop of Mexico, Lizana y Beaumont. The purpose of that double operation was to maintain *Gachupín* control, and on the surface it did. The trouble was that the Creoles, grumble though they might, had recognized an ultimate loyalty to the king before 1808; now they simply evaded the orders of the new viceroy and plotted a change in government.

Even the archbishop, however, understood the fragility of his position; so he tried to placate the Creoles. On January 23, 1810, he issued a proclamation in which he announced: "A Gachupín is a Spaniard born in Europe; a Creole is a Spaniard born in America; the Gachupín is the father of the Creole; the Creole is the son of the Gachupín . . . They have both lived three centuries peacefully inhabiting this flourishing, rich and harmonious empire."[11] It was all true enough; the problem was that *Gachupínes* and Creoles both wanted the same positions of power and profit.

A FUNDAMENTAL CHANGE

In the meantime, however, things had changed in Spain. On September 25, 1808, the junta had recognized the equality of the Spanish American kingdoms: henceforth, although ruled by the king whenever he was restored, they would be treated exactly like Spain. Then, in 1809, the junta invited Mexico to elect representatives to the Cortes, the national assembly, the following year; and indeed, when the latter met at Cádiz in 1812, Mexican deputies were present and treated exactly as if they had been Spanish.

The existence of the Cortes was a revolutionary innovation. Spain, until 1808, had been an absolute monarchy. Now, the lack of any obvious legitimacy had driven the junta to call for an elected assembly which, in turn, would appoint another junta; this body would thus be seen as truly representing Spain. And so it was that when it appointed a new viceroy, Francisco Javier de Venagas, an honest, hardworking, and very competent soldier, he was accepted, in appearance at least, by both *Gachupínes* and Creoles. The reason for all this goodwill was, however, not what it seemed. By 1810, virtually the entire upper class of Mexico was terrified enough to take whatever help it could get against an insurrection led by a radical priest.

A Revolutionary Priest

Miguel Hidalgo was a Creole who differed from his kind because he cared about the sufferings of the peasants. Even worse, from the point of view of the propertied classes, he wanted to do something to help them. Still, before 1810, he had had just the sort of career that might be expected from a man of the upper middle class.

Hidalgo, who was fifty-seven in 1810, "was of medium height, round shouldered, of dark complexion and lively green eyes, his head drooping slightly over his chest, rather bald and white-haired, as if he were already past sixty, yet vigorous, although neither active nor quick in his movements; of few words in ordinary conversation, yet animated in argument like a collegian when he was in the heat of any dispute; conservative in his dress, he wore only what the priests of small villages were accustomed to wear."[12]

Having won the appropriate degrees, he had been ordained a priest in 1778, and had spent the next twelve years as one of the most distinguished professors at San Nicolas in Valladolid. During those years, he was given two benefices as a way of supplementing his income; but the duties resulting from them were carried out by his nominees. By 1790, when he was appointed rector of the college, he owned three haciendas. Then, in February 1792, he quite unexpectedly resigned all his positions: as it turned out, there were problems with his financial administration of the college, and he was asked to leave. He then moved on, first to one parish, then nine months later to another, richer one, San Felipe Torresmocha, west of Guanajuato, where he remained for ten years. In the meantime, he had had three children and at least two common-law wives—a not uncommon lifestyle for Mexican priests of the time.

As parish priest, Hidalgo had the leading position in the village—and the most imposing house in it. More, it was also the literary, musical, and social center: there were *tertulias*, those evenings of discussions that Hidalgo so enjoyed, but also concerts (with a full orchestra), readings, amateur theatricals, and even balls, as well as card and parlor games. It was not all just fun, though. Many of the conversations were informed by the new ideas developed in Europe at the end of the eighteenth century, both in philosophy and in theology; and several neighboring priests, alarmed by the radical content of Hidalgo's conversations, reported him to the Inquisition. Apparently they were not fully convincing: in 1800, the Inquisition started putting together a case that was then suspended.

That, however, did not prevent Hidalgo's next promotion: in 1803, he was transferred to Dolores, a sizable, prosperous town; and, in consequence, his income rose substantially. There he led much the same sort of life as before, but he also involved himself in the local industries—silk weaving, pottery, and tanning. He not only invested in them, but tried to develop improved methods and designs. Some of his ideas proved impractical; others succeeded, and, by 1810, pottery, in particular, was prospering.

In the meantime, of course, the Bourbons had fallen. A church council was called in 1808 to deal with the new situation, but it was canceled after the coup that deposed Iturrigaray. The coup, having succeeded, left the Creoles even more dissatisfied. In 1809, a Creole conspiracy, led by two officers, had been planned in Valladolid: the rising was to start on December 21 and call for the election of a congress empowered to govern in the name of Ferdinand VII. The plotters were denounced; but the authorities, besides stopping the rising, did very little—so little, in fact, that many participants were not even reprimanded.

One of those who came out of the affair unscathed was a rich, pleasure-loving officer named Ignacio Allende. A man of fiery disposition and strong physique, Allende was a perfect illustration of the kind of machismo for which Mexican men were famous; and like the good Creole he was, he hated the *Gachupínes*. None of these characteristics, of course, made for efficiency, or even efficacity: concurrently with the plot in Valladolid, Allende was involved in a plot in Querétaro, inspired, ironically enough, by loyalty to Iturrigaray, who was now seen as the defender of the Creoles. By September, he had met Hidalgo—they both spent time in Guanajuato and Allende's home town, San Miguel—and the two of them came up with the Plan of Querétaro. It was simple enough.

First, they were to establish secret revolutionary juntas in all the major cities; then, when the rebellion began, the juntas were to depose the authorities, seize all rich *Gachupínes*, and confiscate their assets to finance the movement; finally, all *Gachupínes* were to be expelled, and a junta composed of representatives chosen by the provinces was to govern in the name of Ferdinand VII while all allegiance to Spain was ended.

That was all simple enough—indeed, perhaps a little too simplistic. First, of course, the Creoles were hardly united; then the armed forces, such as they were, were still mostly loyal to the government. Something more was obviously needed; and that was when the plotters came up with the idea of using Indians to swell their numbers. That, in turn, had an immediate consequence: Hidalgo, throughout his years as a parish priest, had had notoriously good relations with the Indians. Now he was made head of the conspiracy on the assumption that the Indians would follow his lead.

All through the first eight months of 1810, the plotters met, planned, and raised money. Then, on September 14, Francisco Venegas, the new viceroy, took office. This was a blow, since he was likely to prove more effective in fighting an uprising than his predecessor, the archbishop. By then, of course, many people knew about the plot: neither Allende nor Hidalgo was good at keeping secrets. Thus, on the night of the 15th to the 16th, both men were awakened by a friend who had just arrived in Dolores from Mexico City with the news that the plot had been discovered. There were now two ways out of the situation: they could flee the city and hide; or they could start the revolt at once. It was this last they decided to do.

Before dawn, Hidalgo and Allende had gathered and armed their local supporters, many of them small shopkeepers and artisans; and Hidalgo issued his famous *Grito de Dolores,* his "Shout from Dolores" (today, Dolores Hidalgo): "Neither the King nor tributes [the head tax paid by Indians] exist for us any longer," he proclaimed. "The moment of our freedom has arrived, the moment of our liberty has struck; and if you recognize its great value, you will help me defend it from the ambitious grasp of the tyrants. . . . The cause is holy and God will protect it . . . long live, then, the Virgin of Guadalupe! Long live America for which we are going to fight!"[13] Although there were ambiguities and contradictions—Hidalgo then announced that he remained loyal to Ferdinand VII—his shout has echoed on to our day: almost two hundred years later, it is still seen by all Mexicans as the founding moment of their new nation.

Early that morning—it was a Sunday, market day, so the town was full of people—Dolores rallied to Hidalgo's banner, which bore the image of the Virgin of Guadalupe. That, in itself, was a highly significant choice. First, of course, it emphasized the fact that Hidalgo was a priest, and the Indians were nothing if not pious; then there was the widespread, often frantic, devotion to that particular manifestation of the Virgin who was seen as specifically Mexican. Thus, claiming her as patroness was at the same time a rejection of the *Gachupínes* and a claim to be doing her will.

Hidalgo was eloquent, Allende looked fierce and enthusiastic; and the people of Dolores followed them. They took control of the town that very day and moved on to San Miguel (today, San Miguel Allende), which they reached that evening. There, Allende had prepared everything. The militia promptly went over to the rebellion, the *Gachupínes* were seized and jailed, and a significant part of the Creole aristocracy trembled. By September 19, the neighboring town of Celaya had capitulated, but it was pillaged anyway on the 21st, and that was when alarm began to replace sympathy. Rising against the *Gachupíne*-run government was one thing; enrolling the Indians and allowing them to rob

Miguel Hidalgo, the leader of the fight for Mexican independence.
His Indian following alarmed both Creoles and *Gachupínes*.
*(Portrait File, Miriam and Ira D. Wallach Division of Art, Prints and Photographs,
The New York City Public Library, Astor, Lenox and Tilden Foundations)*

and murder was quite another. Within a very few days, all those who owned
property found themselves united against Hidalgo and his troops.

They had reason to be alarmed: most of the rebel army soon stopped dis-
criminating between *Gachupínes* and Creoles: government officials and the
prosperous had become the enemy. That was all too clear when, on September 28, Guanajuato was taken. The city was sacked, its defenders were massacred; and then many more of its citizens were killed in the disorders that
followed. For Hidalgo, who now called himself "Captain General of America,"
and Allende, the rapid progress of the rebellion was a dream come true. They

began to feel sure that the whole country would soon be conquered, and hardly cared about the massacres. Then, on October 17, they took Valladolid: clearly they were unstoppable, all the more that now their army was sixty thousand strong.

There is much to be said both for and against Hidalgo and Allende. If, today, they are still heroes for most Mexicans, it is because of their concern for the poorer peasants and the Indians, those very people who had been ignored and exploited for centuries. An essential part of the rebellion was a demand for social justice, and that deserves to be remembered. So does the claim to independence: although Ferdinand VII's name was used abundantly, there is no doubt that both leaders wanted a free Mexico governed by free Mexicans. Unfortunately, the movement was also unspeakably brutal: the rapes, the murders, the pillages, while they were certainly the consequence of three hundred years of repression, were crimes nonetheless. It is Hidalgo's real tragedy that the idealism of the beginning should have been so soon replaced by endless violence.

While all this was happening in the countryside, the new viceroy was hard at work in Mexico City. Troops were raised, measures taken to defend the capital; and the archbishop made his own contribution by declaring the rebels anathema. Amazingly, this had an effect: far fewer Indians joined the rebels after his declaration than before. Then, on October 29 and 30, the first real battle between the government troops and the rebels was fought at Toluca. Hidalgo won, but it was a Pyrrhic victory: not only were there many wounded, his soldiers began to desert in droves once they found themselves facing real resistance.

In fact, because neither Hidalgo nor, in spite of his being an officer, Allende understood much about armies, strategy, or even tactics, they relied on propaganda. If the whole country supported them, they reasoned, it would no longer matter whether the government had the better army. This was a startlingly innovative view: the power of propaganda is something with which we have become very familiar. Unfortunately for the rebellion, however, the more they publicized their goals, the more they alienated the most powerful section of the population. A crudely printed handbill released in September was typical. "Creoles of San Luis," it proclaimed, "it is right for you to seize all the Gachupínes. Do not oppose the Priest of Dolores. God raised him to castigate these tyrants. Soldiers of San Luis, it is necessary to banish these hypocritical robbers from the entire kingdom. Do not touch their lives because that would cover our nation with shame. But deliver them to the Priest of Dolores if you want to be happy."[14]

There were several things wrong with this exhortation. First, Hidalgo had already become the terror of all those Creoles who owned property: asking them to trust him was simply foolish. Calling out the soldiers was both self-defeating—the viceroy had the army well in hand—and frightening to everyone else: rogue soldiers were notoriously impossible to control. Finally, telling those soldiers to spare the lives of the *Gachupínes* was bound to be seen as mere rhetorical flourish: the record, at Guanajuato and elsewhere, was one of widespread massacres in which the entire upper and upper middle classes were exterminated; and there was nothing the Creoles feared more than a racial war.

Hidalgo, who was anything but stupid, quickly noticed that he was failing to attract the Creoles, so he added another theme: Unlike the Spanish, who had been conquered by Napoléon, the Mexicans would resist when attacked by the unlikely conjunction of France and England. To join the rebellion, therefore, was to be part of the forthcoming resistance to these God-hating nations. Again, that was hardly convincing: France and England were at war, France had no fleet, and the British navy was far too busy fighting Napoléon to bother with Mexico. So Hidalgo shifted once more: by the end of October he had renamed the rebellion the Reconquest and made full independence his goal.

That left Hidalgo with precisely the support most likely to alienate the Creoles: rebel Indians and parish priests with democratic views. The Indians could be won over by songs, slogans, banners, and the desire to throw off centuries of oppressions; the priests resented being so poor when the bishops were so rich. Of course, there were lots of Indians, but they had neither firearms nor any understanding of what it was like to face a properly constituted army; and, to make it all even worse, Allende never hesitated to show his contempt for them. The ultimate results were thus predictable.

On November 1, a large royalist army from San Luis Potosí, the very city at which the pamphlet was directed, reached and retook Querétaro. Two days later, Hidalgo, who had led his troops to the very edge of the suburbs of Mexico City, decided not to attack the city: his public motive was that he had insufficient support within the capital; his actual reason was that a royalist army was approaching. It was good thinking: on November 7, his troops suffered a major defeat at Aculco and lost most of their artillery and baggage, along with a portable brothel.

Even so, all was not lost. On November 11, Torres, one of the rebel generals, took Guadalajara. Hidalgo joined him there on the 26th, and promptly ordered the execution of the *Gachupínes* in all the cities he still controlled, thus further alienating the Creoles. At the same time, a new army was recruited and organized. It did not last long. On January 12, 1811, at the battle of Calderón Bridge, the government troops under Félix Calleja del Rey won another major victory. After that, the issue was certain. Hidalgo fled north, while central Mexico was reconquered by the viceroy; and on March 21, both Hidalgo and Allende were taken prisoner. The inevitable followed: they were brought back to the capital, swiftly tried, and executed.

The Road to Independence

The Hidalgo rebellion was thus, on the face of it, a complete failure. It lasted less than six months and was utterly crushed; and yet, nothing was ever again the same. Guerrilla warfare, though spotty and unorganized, continued throughout the next decade. Far more important, though, was the slowly spreading feeling that autonomy was possible, and that it might lead to independence. Spain itself encouraged these ideas. In 1812, the Cádiz junta put in place a liberal constitution that then applied to the rest of Spain when it was liberated in 1813–1814. It made Spain and its American possessions equal partners, abolished the Inquisition, guaranteed freedom of the press, and limited the powers of both government and church. Even more important, it created an electoral system; and most of the candidates elected in Mexico favored home rule.

The restoration of Ferdinand VII, in 1814, proved both a setback and a spur: he abolished the constitution of 1812, thus making the Mexicans even more eager for independence. By 1821, this was an accomplished fact. Briefly as an empire, then as a republic, Mexico would become its own country.

CHAPTER TWELVE

Peru and Brazil

Not all of Spanish America was eager to be free of the colonial yoke. In Peru, fidelity to Spain was such that it steadfastly adhered to whatever form the Spanish government might take. In Brazil, the presence of the Portuguese royal family evoked the most ardent loyalty. Both countries, therefore, remained closely tied to Europe. Peru considered itself essentially a distant province of Spain; Brazil was the only South American state ever to be ruled directly by a European monarch.

There were other links as well. Both countries had slaves, and were a part of the vast commercial network that bound Europe, America, and Africa. Both had long been economically tied to the mother country. The distances were great: they delayed communications, but they never separated the continents.

The Waning of Splendor

Peru: the very name suggested inexhaustible riches. When, at the beginning of the sixteenth century, the conquistadores had arrived, they found ton upon ton of gold and silver in the Incan king's treasury; just as important, vast quantities of the precious metals could be extracted from the mines in the mountains. And so, at the beginning of the Spanish Empire, Peru and Mexico were the two most important centers of power.

Almost three centuries later, the two viceroyalties still had much in common. The king of Spain ruled them both; they shared the same language, the same structure of government, the same currency, the same tax system, and, of course, the same religion. But there were also great differences. Economically, Peru was sinking rapidly; culturally, it was very far from being Mexico's equal; it had recently gone through a major Indian uprising; and, perhaps most important of all, it was very far away.

Getting to Mexico from Cádiz was relatively quick, a simple ocean crossing. Sailing to Peru was a much longer, more risky trip. First, ships went to the island of Madeira; from there, they continued to the Canary Islands, and on to the Cape Verde Islands; then they crossed the Atlantic over to Recife, stopped (but only to take on provisions) at Rio de Janeiro and at Buenos Aires; after that, they sailed through the Magellan Straits at the bottom of the continent and up the Pacific coast, stopping at Antofagasta and Arica in Chile before reaching Callao, the port for Lima. That all took a lot of time; the weather in the Magellan Straits was often rough; and the cost of shipping was greatly increased.

None of that had mattered in the sixteenth century, when Callao was the greatest port in South America. By 1800, Buenos Aires had taken over, and dealt the trade, and thus the prosperity, of Peru a mortal blow. In theory, the Spanish colonies could trade only with the mother country; thus a merchant could not legally send goods to Buenos Aires, then have them carted across to Lima. In fact, there was a great deal of smuggling, much to Peru's detriment.

The distance from Spain had another major consequence: because Peru was invariably the last to get the news from Madrid (it normally took at least five months to arrive), its viceroys were far more autonomous than those of Mexico. Thus a great deal depended on the talents and thoroughness of a single man: from 1808 on, this became even clearer than before. There was another major difference as well: Mexico thought of itself as a country; its borders were permanent; and within those borders it had developed a national identity. Peru, on the other hand, was a mere geographical entity, and a changing one at that: until 1776, for instance, it had included Upper Peru, today's Bolivia; but when the viceroyalty of Río de la Plata was created, it included this vast area as well as today's Argentina. This was a double loss: with the territory went highly productive silver mines.

Even the population was small. Lima, the capital, and much the most important city, had 52,547 people in 1790—less than half of the number in Mexico City. As for the entire viceroyalty, it was even further behind: in 1795, the population was only 1,115,207 to Mexico's 5,200,000. It was no wonder, really: the coast was mostly a narrow band of sandy waste; and apart from a few fertile valleys, the interior consisted mostly of mountains. That was where many of the Indians lived—the higher areas were not productive enough to interest the whites. Of course, there were also Indians working on the haciendas and in the mines: they were, after all, 60 percent of the population. The mestizos (part white, part Indian) were 22 percent, the whites a mere 12 percent; and unlike Mexico, Peru had a significant number of black slaves, some 40,000 in 1800.

It was, of course, that small minority of whites—mostly Creoles, with only a few Spaniards—who controlled the economic and political life. It was thus not surprising that Lima should be 32 percent white, with slaves making up 28 percent and the Indians only 16 percent of the population. And although Peru had far more titled families than Mexico—105 to 63—only two families had fortunes of over half a million pesos, against seventeen in Mexico. There was an easy explanation: the titles were old and dated back to the era of prosperity; now the wealth was largely gone. Indeed, while money in Mexico came from trading, mining, and land, in Peru it came mostly from government salaries: 41.7 percent of the Lima elite owned no real property within the city. As a result, the government was far more intrusive than in Mexico; and the elite who depended on their official salaries were not likely to back any form of independence.

This reliance on government jobs was a consequence of the shortage of capital. The country lacked everything, it seemed: money, men, and resources (except silver). Even that metal was no longer as plentiful as it had been, since the most fruitful mines were in Upper Peru. In 1811, the archbishop of Lima, Bartolomé de las Heras, lamented, "This kingdom is today a pallid shadow of what it was before being dismembered of the opulent provinces contiguous to Potosí,"[1] and he had a point. Because Spanish colonies were not supposed to trade with each other, the shift of Upper Peru had meant not only the loss of the silver mines but also that of a considerable market. Instead of coming to the mint in Lima, the bullion now went to Buenos Aires; even worse, the people of Upper Peru stopped buying industrial products from their former country, and that dealt a death blow to the Peruvian manufactures. Cloth, for instance, had been a major product. After 1776, Upper Peru bought its cloth from Río de la Plata, and manufacturing stopped in Peru. Upper Peru still bought some oil, grain, sugar, pimiento, and *aguardiente,* a liquor made from maize—but not enough to make a real difference. Further, the shift in borders encouraged smuggling: English manufactured goods made their way into Peru, and depressed domestic production even more. That left foodstuffs; but Peruvian agriculture was notoriously inefficient, in part because it lacked capital, in part because the Indians, who were forced to work on the farms, were slow and unproductive. By 1800, to the viceroy's shock, Peru had become unable to feed itself.

Still, there was the silver. One major mine, that of Cerro de Pasco, remained, and it had to pay for everything. In the period from 1785 to 1789, silver made up 88 percent of Peru's exports—some 22 million pesos. Unfortunately, this reliance on bullion was dangerous: production could fluctuate considerably. In 1792, silver exports reached 8 million pesos; in 1793, they sank to 1.5 million, rising the following year to 4 million. Even worse, beginning in the mid 1790s, the combined production of gold and silver declined steadily. In 1796, the mines gave 629,798 pesos' worth of gold, and 5,269,580 of silver, for a total of 5,899,378 pesos. In 1800, that went down to 4,778,005 pesos; by 1808, the total came to a bare 4.5 million.

That was just not enough. Every year, the balance of trade registered a 3 million peso deficit, so that in a country where silver was mined, there was a permanent shortage of coins. Equally, since Peru was paying for its consumption with silver, there was no capital accumulation; and that, in turn, meant less, and less effective, production.

This already bad situation was worsened by the lack of decent roads. Getting from one place to another in Peru was a major endeavor. Roads were virtually nonexistent, except for the one from Callao to Lima, which ran some eight miles and was highly unsafe at night. Although, admittedly, Mexican inns were bad, they still existed, as did passable highways. Peru was far more primitive. W. B. Stevenson, an Englishman who spent twenty years in South America, described the situation vividly:

> If a resident of Lima wishes to go any considerable distance from the capital, the best plan . . . is to inquire . . . for mules which are from the [part of the] country he intends to visit, and agree with the muleteer . . . for the number of mules he may want. With an eye to comfort, the traveler must provide himself with a mattress, bedding and a . . . leather bag . . . sufficiently large to hold, besides the bed, his wearing apparel. . . .
>
> I always formed another load with a trunk containing linen, books and writing materials; also a canteen, holding two or three small pans, oil, vinegar, salt, spices, coffee, tea, knives and forks, spoons, &c, and thus equipped, having a good poncho, saddle . . . bridle and spurs, a traveler has little to apprehend from the want of inns. The plan I usually followed was, to go to one of the principal houses in the town or village, and to ask if I could remain there during my stay in that place; this request was never denied me.[2]

The Economy and the Indians

The lack of the simplest staples—oil, salt—is striking. In fact, goods hardly moved within Peru. This hampered agriculture as well as industry: there is no sense in growing a surplus if you cannot get it to market. It also meant that it was impossible to accrue surplus capital from land, and hardly worth it to improve either tools or seeds. The economy was thus left to depend on trade—which had shrunk drastically—silver, and of course, the government. The latter, in turn, depended on taxes: the *alcabala*, a sales tax levied at the rate of 6.5 percent; the tribute, or head tax, paid by the Indians; the shipping tax—5 percent of the goods carried on entering, 2 percent on leaving a port; the usual one-ninth of the tithes; a fifth of all mined precious metals; 500 pesos yearly per title of nobility; the vacant income from ecclesiastical seats; and the *media annata*, half the first year's income of all government jobs. In an average year, all this together produced a little over 4.5 million pesos and left a surplus of 1 million; but in 1812, the military cost of maintaining Peru as a colony surrounded by neighbors in revolt brought expenditures up to 5.3 million, and by 1820, the government was bankrupt.

The economy was bad enough. Almost worse was the fear that the Indians would rise again, and more successfully. Unlike Mexico, where the Indians were peaceful and obedient, at least until the *Grito de Dolores,* there had been frequent risings in Peru. Here, the Incas remembered their great ancestors, and were far more inclined to resent their exploitation by the white colonizers. Indeed, unlike the revolt led by Hidalgo, the attempts in Peru combined a socioeconomic revolution with a racial war in which the mestizos and the Indians came together against the Creoles.

Most of these risings had been on a fairly small scale, but all that changed in 1780. It was no wonder, really: as Viceroy Amat himself admitted, the Indians were "as unhappy and humble a people as exist on earth, totally at the mercy of their Spanish masters."[3] Oddly enough, though, the leader of the rebellion, José Gabriel Condorcanqui, was not an Indian, but a mestizo, the cacique (native mayor) of a small town. Quickly, though, he changed his name to that of the last Inca emperor, Tupac Amarú.

In 1777, he had already protested against the corruption and brutality of the *corregidores,* the government appointees who governed outside the capital; but, characteristically, he had been ignored. Madrid was too far, the Creoles too near; and so the rising began in Cuzco. Its demands were moderate and fully consistent with loyalty to Crown and church: Tupac Amarú II made that very clear. All he wanted was the creation of a royal *audiencia,* that combination of tribunal and administrative body, in Cuzco, so as to end the power of the *corregidores;* the redress of the economic mistreatment of the Indians and mestizos by these same corrupt civil servants; the abolition of custom duties on trade between the several provinces of Peru; the abolition of *repartimiento,* the law that allowed the *corregidores* to seize all the possessions of an Indian who failed to pay the tribute, because it was often used unfairly; the abolition of forced labor drafts for the Indians; the improvement of working conditions in mines and factories; and the eventual end of slavery.

This was not an unreasonable program; most of it, in fact, was implemented after the crushing of the rebellion. In the meantime, however, the viceroy, with the full concurrence of the Creoles, decided on repression. The rising spread to most of the country and lasted for two years. By the time it was over, a hundred thousand Indians had been killed, including Tupac Amarú. The result, naturally, was an even greater hatred between the races; a country whose economy had been further set back; and a feeling that if ever Spanish rule were to end, it would be the signal for a massacre of the whites.

GLAMOUR IN THE CAPITAL

The revolt had been fought out in the provinces: Lima itself was never in danger, and, to a significant extent, Lima was Peru. The government was there, and so were the archbishop and the central office of the Inquisition. It was the place where jobs were to be had, and deals were made. In the sixteenth and seventeenth centuries, it had been a famously glittering city; but since then it had had to contend not just with the decline of the economy, but with devastating earthquakes: those of 1630, 1687, and 1746 had been particularly destructive, and so Lima was largely a new city. These cataclysms came roughly twice a century—there was another bad earthquake in 1806—but even in the more peaceful years in between, the ground shook frequently. "The native Peruvians, as well as the Spanish who have settled here, praise the country very highly," a Russian visitor, Vassilii Golovnin, noted. "They say that the only annoying features are the frequent earthquakes and the Spanish policies in dealing with their colonies, the latter being much the more intolerable of the two. The earthquakes occur once or twice weekly, but they are very weak and cause almost no damage; formerly they were much stronger and brought fearful devastation, reducing the best part of Lima to ruins several times."[4]

The city, he went on, "is filled with the poorest of structures. . . . The houses are mostly of one story . . . The buildings are generally made of wood, but are plastered and whitewashed so they appear made of stone, although actually only the foundations are stone. Strong earthquakes make it imperative that the inhabitants use lumber instead of brick or stone. The local Spanish are so clever in this type of construction that they erect huge buildings of lumber, for instance the Cathedral which does not in the least look like a wooden structure."[5] It is hard not to think that Francisco Pizarro, who founded Lima in 1535, had been a little careless; but for all the destruction, the city was full of charm.

Built on the grid pattern typical of Spanish colonial cities, Lima was cleaner than most because it was built on a gentle slope: the river could thus be canalized and its water used to sweep the streets. As for the houses, they were painted in bright, cheerful colors—blue, pink, yellow, or ocher—and, in the better areas, they had a feature seen nowhere else, the enclosed balcony. These were rectangular protrusions one story up, usually made of carved wood. Their lattice windows allowed the air to circulate, not perhaps the major consideration in what was, most of the year, a moderate climate. Far more important, they made it possible to look out without being seen, as did the ground floor *ventanas de rejo,* a kind of bow window adorned with elegant cast-iron latticework. All that looked very appealing. Even the critical Stevenson was charmed.

Vista de la Ciudad de Lima desde las inmediaciones de la Plaza de los Toros.

Lima, the capital of Peru. The cathedral is on the left; the bridge to the right was the site where evening walks and amorous encounters went together. (*I. N. Phelps Stokes Collection, Miriam and Ira D. Wallach Division of Art, Prints and Photographs, The New York Public Library, Astor, Lenox and Tilden Foundations*)

Some of the houses of the richer classes have simply the ground floor, but there is a patio before the house, and the entrance is through a heavy-arched doorway, with a coach-house on one side; over this is a small room with a balcony and trellis windows opening on to the street. Part of these houses have neat green balconies in front, but with few of the windows glazed. Having capacious patios, large doors and ornamented trellis windows, besides painted porticoes and walls, with neat corridors, their appearance from the street is exceedingly handsome. In some, there is a prospect of a garden through the small glazed folding doors of two or three apartments.[6]

Indoors, there could be a good deal of luxury: silk wall hangings and gilded furniture, large silver objects, and the occasional tapestry all spoke of wealth; but they tended to be very old-fashioned. In 1800, the rococo still largely prevailed in its Peruvian form. The carving of chairs, chests, and table legs was deeper, more exotic than its European counterpart: Lima was so far away that European fashions arrived very late, and were modified by local taste.

Outdoors, there was the expected bustle: carts, carriages, flocks of vicuñas, water carriers and their donkeys, street merchants selling bread, milk, and all kinds of merchandise, llamas, and beggars all mingled happily, raising clouds of dust and making a great deal of noise. At night, the streets were sluiced down, but the dirt came back quickly. At least it was never mud: one of the peculiarities of the local climate was that it never rained. Instead, for about eight months of the year, a heavy, very wet fog settled during the night and often lasted for much of the morning, giving the soil all the water it needed. The Lima market gardens that surrounded the city were famous for their fertility and the quality of their produce. As for the temperature, it, too, was ideal, never sinking in winter below nine degrees Celsius (about fifty degrees Fahrenheit), and seldom rising in summer above twenty-two degrees Celsius (eighty degrees Fahrenheit). As a result, the markets were dazzling in their abundance and quality.

Indeed, they were a spectacle in themselves, as Stevenson noted approvingly.

> The butcher's market is generally well supplied with excellent beef and mutton. Pork is sold in one part; in another, all kinds of dried and salted meats . . . , ham, bacon and frozen kid from the mountains, which last is most delicate eating; there are likewise many kinds of sausage; salt fish, principally *bacalao* [salt cod] [comes] from Europe. . . . The fish market is . . . abundantly supplied from the neighbouring coasts. . . .
>
> The vegetables are remarkably fine, in great abundance and generally cheap. The fruit market is splendid, furnishing the most delicious fruits of Europe—the grape of several varieties, the peach, apricot and nectarine, the apple, the pear, the pomegranate, the quince, the tomato and the strawberry; and an abundance of luscious tropical fruits—the pine[apple], the melon, badeas, granadillas, sapote, lucuma, nisperos, guavas, pattos [avocados], guanabanas, custard apples, the sweet and sour orange, lime and lemon, the shaddock, the citron, the plantain, the banana and, above all, the chirimoya, the queen of tropical fruits.[7]

Nor was that all: there was a spectacular flower market, where people met to flirt and drink iced lemonade, pineapple juice, almond milk, or pomegranate water.

Flirting was easy—and a major activity. The upper classes were idle, the ladies welcoming, and fidelity not at all the fashion. The Russian visitor Golovnin, although he came from a country where the nobility led very free lives, was struck by this. "I heard very little praise of the morals of local women, even those of the better classes," he wrote. "Both the Spanish and the foreigners living here laughed and called them 'weak and lenient' . . . I attribute this to the hot climate and the lazy life, which incidentally, makes them incredibly stout, but I was told that their behavior is governed more by mercenary motives than anything else."[8] Not exactly a charitable description; but not all Limenas were both fat and greedy. Indeed, Stevenson—who, after all, spent twenty years in Peru—took a distinctly more charitable view.

A Creole of Lima is lively, generous and careless of tomorrow; fond of dress and variety, slow to revenge injuries, and willing to forget them. Of all his vices, dissipation is certainly the greater; his conversation is quick and pointed—that of the fair sex is extremely gay and witty, giving them an open frankness which some foreigners have been pleased to term levity, or something a little more dishonourable, attaching the epithet immoral to their general character—an imputation they may deserve, if prudery and hypocrisy be the necessary companions of virtue; but they certainly deserve it not, if benevolence, confidence, unsuspecting conviviality, and honest intention be the true characteristics of morality.[9]

The truth probably lies somewhere in between: manners were unquestionably more relaxed and less ceremonious than in England, but it was normal for married women to have a lover. What made the difference was having no more than one at a time.

Dress itself was a contributing factor. In the evening, and for all formal occasions, the upper classes wore European fashions; but during the day—for those meetings at the flower market, for instance—the *saya y manto* was the norm. This consisted of a very tight (and therefore revealing) skirt, made of velvet, silk, or satin folded into very small pleats; for the lower classes, it was black or brown; for the upper classes, it came in a great variety of bright colors. The bottom was too narrow for a normal stride; the Limenas, therefore, took very small steps, a mode of walking which further emphasized those charms already revealed by the tightness of the skirt. Then, at ankle level, there was fringe, or lace, or pearls, or artificial flowers. The top, the *manto*, was a hood of thin black silk, tied around the waist and flung over the head so as to hide most of the face; thus, it was easy to flirt in public while retaining a great degree of privacy.

Of course, the market was only one possible meeting place; there were all kinds of promenades. Stevenson provided a description of one.

The wall which encloses Lima, except on the side bordering the river, is built of adobe . . . [and is] on average twelve feet high . . . , about ten feet thick at the bottom and eight at the top, forming a beautiful promenade round two thirds of the city. . . .

On the east side the water falls from an elevated stone base, and forms a species of cascade, the sound of the falling water adding much to the pleasure enjoyed during the cool evenings of a tropical climate.[10]

That sound also made it easier to whisper sweet nothings or make an assignation without being overheard, and that sensual dusk did nothing to cool ardors; but there were other, less discreet, resorts. There was an avenue on which carriages congregated, and the number of mules drawing each conveyance was strictly defined: one for a rich tradesman, two for a local noble, four for a noble with a Spanish title, six for the viceroy. The gentlemen usually rode, and flirted with the ladies as they were driven.

There were also special festival days on which Lima society ventured into the suburbs. "The *paseo de las lomas* . . . is a visit to the hills on the north side of Lima on the days of Saint John and Saint Peter . . . ," Stevenson wrote. "The *amancaes*, yellow daffodils, being then in flower, the hills are covered with them . . . The principal incitement is to drink milk, eat custards, rice milks &c. In the evening it is very amusing to see thousands of people in coaches, on horseback and on foot, returning to the city, almost covered with daffodils."[11]

Those were merely daylong excursions; but Lima was close to the coast, and so the prosperous thought themselves deprived unless they owned a seaside villa in the little resort town of Miraflores. There, too, flirting prospered and affairs multiplied. More surprising, perhaps, the Limenos actually went in for sea bathing, a pleasure that the Europeans only began discovering in the 1820s. Of course, the ladies wore long dresses even when in the ocean; still, it was both daring and healthy. It was also consonant with another startling habit, that of being habitually clean. A French visitor, used to his own country's less stringent standards, was startled.

"Word cannot describe [the Peruvians'] perfect cleanliness," he noted in amazement. "Cleanliness bordering even on refinement is generally noticeable amongst all women (nobles and poor, white ladies and black slaves alike). . . . That is also true of their houses which are the object of the most meticulous care."[12]

Unfortunately, life in Lima was not always pleasant. Because so many men derived their incomes from the government, the fight for place and emolument was ferocious. This was a society characterized by suspicion, name-calling, deep-seated personal feuds, and rapacious ambition. Simon Bolívar, the South American revolutionary leader, saw it clearly: "This country is afflicted with moral pestilence," he wrote. "Every scoundrel wants to be supreme."[13] And, naturally, endless denunciations to the authorities were commonplace.

Even the merchant class, which after all derived its income from business, not government jobs, behaved very much the same way. All the visitors noticed it. "It seemed that the people were much given to squabbling and slander," Golovnin reported.

> Once, accompanied by a large number of officers, I dropped by the house of Abadia, the chief factor of the Philippines Company, just before dinner. Not wishing to put him to the trouble of preparing a meal for all of us, I told him we had just stopped in for a moment and were on our way to do some sightseeing, and would have dinner at one of the cafes because we wanted to find out what they were like. However, he kept us, saying: "You do not know the local people and how they love to spread malicious gossip; they will

immediately spread the rumor all over town that I did not wish to extend my hospitality to Russian officers and sent them to eat at an inn."[14]

Perhaps the gossip was all the more malicious that it was the principal source of entertainment: there was not much else going on in Lima. The single theater put on plays that were as dull as they were poorly performed; there was very little culture; that left the bullring and the cockfights, both of which were particularly savage, and, of course, gambling, that last resort of the truly bored. There were no gambling houses as such, but most noblemen kept gambling tables to which all were admitted—and from which they sometimes derived a profit. The result, which amazed all foreign visitors, was that a workingman might sit next to a count, or a peddler next to a rich merchant.

Women did not gamble; but like men, they ate, and their food was anything but light. Meals were expected to be abundant, rather than refined. The cuisine, in Lima, was typically South American. There were tamales, for instance, made of ground maize; hot peppers; pork or chicken or hard-boiled eggs; raisins and almonds cooked in large banana leaves; and, of course, the universal *puchero*, made just as it was in Mexico. Because Lima was close to the sea, seviche, that combination of raw fish, onion, lemon juice, and hot pepper, was much in favor. Then there were the local specialties. *Lahua* was a thick, highly spiced maize flour porridge to which pork or turkey was added; *cazuela* was a light broth served with pieces of beef and chicken; *sancochado* was rare lamb cooked with yucca, yams, cabbage, and rice. There were oddities as well: guinea pigs, for instance, were thought to be a great delicacy.

As for the desserts, they tended to be very sweet. Custards of all kinds were popular; so was *zango de manjú,* a kind of sweet porridge made with maize flour and raisins, or empanada, a cake made with maize flour and anise. The sweetest dessert of all was the *turón de doña Pepa,* a pastry combining flour, eggs, and butter, which was then fried and served in syrup.

All that, of course, was for the prosperous. The poor were essentially vegetarian, and lived on a diet of beans, maize, pumpkins, and gourds.

Churches, Palaces, Processions

Unlike Mexico City, Lima was no cultural center. In the last twenty years of the eighteenth century, the university was indeed permeated by Enlightenment thought—but of a very limited sort. Its intellectuals criticized the inefficiency of the regime, not its philosophical basis; they found the plight of the Indians quite lacking in interest; and they, too, yearned for government jobs. As for the newly established School of Mines, it never came close to equaling its Mexican model. Still, Lima was not without its own kind of splendor.

That, as in every major Latin American capital, was concentrated on the Plaza Mayor. "On the north side," Stevenson noted,

> stands the viceroy's palace, having an ornamented gateway at the center where the horseguards are stationed; this front is 480 feet long: the lower part is divided into petty pedlars' shops, filled with all kinds of wares, open in front. . . . Over these runs a long gallery with seats rising one above the other, for the accommodation of the inhabitants when there is any fête in the square; on the top there is a railing carved in imitation of balustrades. At the northwest corner is a gallery for the family of the Viceroy, which on days of ceremony [is] fitted up with green velvet hangings, ornamented with gold lace and fringe.[15]

Inside, however, the palace was painfully plain. There were many large rooms, but they were hardly decorated and almost empty of furniture. The viceroy's salary was sixty thousand pesos, just as it was in Mexico; but there were fewer expense accounts, and the viceroys tended to be relatively poor. As a result, Captain Basil Hall, an English visitor, deprecated its "intermixture of meanness and magnificence," the blend of "the shabby and the gorgeous" so that "one was never sure that any thing pleasing would not be found contiguous to something offensive."[16]

In the center of the plaza, there was a large and beautiful brass fountain. Then, across the plaza, the archbishop's palace looked particularly appealing because of its green-painted, glazed balconies. The most impressive monuments, though, were the cathedral and the adjoining Sagrario, Lima's principal parish church—not because of their facades, which were relatively plain, but because their interiors were full of treasures. "The high altar [of the Cathedral]," Stevenson observed,

> has a most magnificent appearance; it is of the Corinthian order, the columns, cornices, mouldings, pedestals, &c. being encased in pure silver; it is also surmounted with a celestial crown of gilt silver; in the center is the sacrarium, richly ornamented with chased silverwork. The custodium is of gold, delicately wrought, and enriched with a profusion of diamonds and other precious stones; from the pedestal to the points of the rays it measures seven feet, and is more than any moderately-sized person can lift.[17]

Obviously, the current economic distress had not affected the church, in Lima at least: well into the new century, its splendor was undimmed; and so was its horror of all non-Catholics. A priest, "happening one day to visit a house where four or five Englishmen were dining," Hall reported, "joined in conversation with them; and was so much pleased with his company that he turned round to a friend and exclaimed: 'Oh! What a pity it is that such fine, rosy-looking, good young men should all necessarily and inevitably go to the Devil!'"[18]

The priest in question was unusually open-minded: most of his colleagues would have rejoiced at the dreadful fate awaiting the Englishmen after they died. Happily, though, there were few occasions for these displays of bigotry: everyone in Peru was Catholic (no other religion was allowed) and the Inquisition, which had been a fearful presence a century earlier, had become, if not inactive, at least mild in its punishments, which tended to be the local equivalent of a few months of community service. Indeed, when the Spanish Inquisition was suppressed by the Cádiz Cortes in 1813, its Lima headquarters were broken into by a large, exhilarated mob. There was, predictably, a torture chamber full of dreadful implements; but closer inspection showed that they had all been long disused.

Far more cheerful were the yearly religious processions. They were not as essential a part of life in Peru as they were in Mexico, but they could be spectacular nonetheless. The greatest of these celebrated the feast of Corpus Christi. As usual, Stevenson was watching it all.

> The procession leaves the Cathedral attended by all the civil and military authorities holding huge wax tapers, the different orders of friars, the dean and chapter, the Archbishop, under a splendid canopy, supported by twelve priests in their robes of ceremony, his Grace bearing the Host . . . which is deposited in a superbly rich hostiarium [monstrance]. The military force is drawn up in the square, and after kneeling and pointing their bayonets to the ground, the banners and flags being prostrated as the sacrament passes, they all join in the procession, falling in at its rear. . . . The most particular feature in this procession is the assistance of all the clubs or cofradias of the Africans: each separate company has its appropriate national music and songs, some of them carrying wooden idols on their heads and dancing about with them among those who belong to their confraternity.[19]

That was all very grand and formal; but in the countryside, the celebration was a good deal more cheerful. First, the day before, came the feasting, in the course of which a great deal of *chicha*, a liquor made from fermented cane juice, was drunk. On the day itself, the drinking resumed; and there was music to which groups of dancers performed. "One, called huancos, is composed of eight or ten men," Stevenson noted.

> They have large crowns of ostrich feathers . . . on their heads. The quills are fastened in a roll of red cloth, which contains more than five hundred long feathers dyed of various colours, but particularly red. They have small ponchos of brocade, tissue or satin; on their legs they wear leather buskins loaded with hawks' bells; their faces are partly covered by a handkerchief tied high above their mouths. . . . They dance along the streets to the sounds of a pipe or tabor, keeping pace to the tune, that the bells on their legs may beat time [to the music]. . . .

The chimbos are very gaily dressed: they have crowns ornamented with all the jewellery they can borrow: necklaces, earrings, bracelets and rosaries are fastened on them in abundance; and when these cannot be procured, they have drilled-in doubloons and new dollars with which they load them. I have seen fifty of each on one crown. Their dress is a gay poncho, with wide Moorish trousers; and their music consists of one or more harps or guitars.[20]

That, at least, was one day on which the Indians could forget the miserable condition of their life, and, indeed, the music and dancing were reminders of their pre-Hispanic past.

Peru and the Political Storms

As usual, Peru was the last to hear the news: five months passed before knowledge of the abdication of Charles IV reached Lima, and the same was true of Ferdinand VII's collapse at Bayonne. It took even longer—six months—before the viceroy found out that the Central Junta had come into being. Nevertheless, these successive earthquakes appeared to have no effect at all. When, on August 8, the authorities found out that they had a new king, they began arranging for the ceremonies marking his accession to the throne; when, on October 4, they discovered that the king in question was a prisoner of the French, they simply moved up the date of the oath taking, which was celebrated amid considerable pomp on October 13. Evidently, Peru did not feel that the end of the Bourbon dynasty was either permanent or a cause for serious worry. And on March 9, 1809, Lima equally promptly offered its loyalty to the Central Junta. It seemed, in fact, less a South American country than a faithful, if extremely distant, province of Spain.

Of all the vast Spanish empire in the Americas, Peru, parts of Central America, and the islands in the Caribbean were alone in their unbroken fidelity, joined only briefly by New Granada (today's Colombia, Panama, Venezuela, and Ecuador). The Peruvians, unlike the Mexicans, made no claims to sovereignty; no revolt broke out against the authorities. More surprising, this perfect calm remained unaltered even when the rest of the colonies exploded. In 1808, the Mexican viceroy had been deposed. In 1809, Ecuador was in revolt; in 1810, it was followed by Venezuela on April 19, the viceroyalty of Buenos Aires (today's Argentina) on May 22, New Granada on July 20, and Chile on September 18.

None of these rebellions either influenced or worried Peru. Quietly, the viceroy arranged to defend the country's borders; and his only reaction to the events in Buenos Aires was to reannex Upper Peru. That was not as difficult as it sounds: ever since the Tupac Amarú revolt, Peru had had the largest, most modern army in Spanish America; just as important, most of its officers were

Spanish, not Creole. Then, at the viceroy's orders, it was further enlarged so that it numbered seventy thousand men by 1812. Clearly, Peru could stand on its own.

Of course, the army would have been perfectly useless if the country had risen against the government; but, in fact, all was quiet. Firmly ranging themselves behind the viceroy, the authorities, followed by the upper classes, fully approved of what was being done. As far as Peru was concerned, none of the shattering events of 1808 made any difference: the only thing that mattered was the unchanging duty of allegiance to Spain. Even more amazing, in spite of the economic slump, Peru promptly sent off the largest contributions to the junta: 1.3 million pesos in 1809, 2.7 million pesos in 1810—very nearly one third of the total remissions from South America.

There were a number of reasons for this amazing fidelity. One was that unlike Mexico, Peru had never seen itself as a real nation: instead, it had remained very much what it had been ever since Pizarro's time, a place where the Spanish and the Creoles ruled a vast majority of resentful Indians—a typical colony, in fact. Terrified of another, more successful uprising, the whites relied on Spain to protect them; and that was far more important to them than the absence of the king or his replacement by the junta. Then, the fact that the army had been trained to repress rebellions, and had been successful in doing just that twenty-eight years earlier, meant that events like those at Dolores were simply not a possibility. Finally, because Peru was so far away, and so lacking in prosperity, there were (except in the officer corps) very few Spaniards—and hence no Creole resentment against those representatives of the mother country.

These were sufficient causes for continued allegiance to whatever free Spanish government there might be at any given time, especially since so many influential Limenos were eager to keep their government salaries. It was not easy for Peru to remain loyal to Spain, however: as its neighbors rebelled and claimed either autonomy or independence, they pressured Peru to do the same. Had the country been militarily weaker, or even poorly led, it might well have given in to these demands, but there was one man who made all the difference: Viceroy José de Abascal. Unlike José de Iturrigaray, who was made viceroy of New Spain simply because he was one of Prime Minister Manuel de Godoy's followers, Abascal was a professional whose career had taken place in the Americas. Typically for an upper-level civil servant, he had been an intendant, ruling Nueva Galicia, the area around Guadalajara, in Mexico, effectively and fairly. Then, in 1806, he was promoted to the viceroyalty of Peru, where his many qualities promptly made him popular.

Indeed, Abascal was that exceedingly rare creature, the model viceroy. Unlike most of his colleagues, he was scrupulously honest (and therefore anything but wealthy); he lived, as modestly as his position would allow, with his teenage daughter; and although widowed, was not known to have a mistress.

More important, perhaps, he was extremely hardworking and tried not just to obey Madrid, but to improve the lot of those he governed. It was typical, for instance, that he introduced vaccination against smallpox as soon as he arrived, with benefits that were obvious to see. Lima had become a dangerous, dirty city: he cleaned it up; he made it safer by increasing the number of night patrols; he made it healthier by forbidding burial in the churches and creating a new public cemetery just outside the city.

These innovations improved the daily life of the Limenos; but there was more. Science was stimulated by the creation of the first medical school and the first botanical garden. The mint was improved; steam engines were introduced in the mines; the powder factory destroyed in the last great earthquake was reopened; the forts were strengthened and the army enlarged by two divisions. All that helped to stimulate the economy and excited much gratitude.

A great deal therefore had depended on the viceroy when the news arrived from Spain; and, as usual, Abascal did his duty. He calmly proclaimed Ferdinand VII as king even after he had heard about his abdication; then, in April 1809, a commissioner from the junta arrived in Lima, and was able to report home that "this capital can glory with justice in the fact that nobody has vacillated for a minute."[21] The fidelity of Peru, uniquely, had never been in doubt; as for Abascal, when money was sent to Spain, it included his entire life savings. He went a good deal further than contributing money, though: he organized expeditions to help other royal governments under assault, defeating rebels in Quito, Santiago, and La Paz. It was no wonder, really, that in 1812 the Cortes of Cádiz granted him the somewhat unwieldy title of marqués de la Concordia Española del Peru, and equally unsurprising that until the end of his term as viceroy, Peru remained, from a Spanish point of view at least, a model colony.

AN AMERICAN DYNASTY?

The history of Spanish America might well have been different if the several viceroyalties had become kingdoms, each ruled by a Bourbon prince—assuming, of course, that the princes in question were not imbeciles. In the end, of course, they all became republics; but one very large area of South America became, in 1807, precisely that improbable compromise, a South American state governed by a resident European dynasty.

Brazil had been ruled by Portugal ever since the end of the fifteenth century and thus, naturally, by its king. Portugal being as distant as Spain, however, Brazil was just as loosely connected to Lisbon as Spanish America was to Madrid. Then, suddenly, to the thrill and surprise of the Brazilians, the royal House of Bragança was there.

The cause, as with so many of the great changes of this period, was Napoléon, who decided to conquer Portugal because it was Great Britain's closest

ally. In 1807, with the full consent of Charles IV and Godoy, he sent an army
across Spain into Portugal; and rather than be taken prisoner, the old, insane
Queen Maria I, her son Dom João (the prince regent), his family, his court,
his ministers, his counselors of state, his bishops, and most of the notables—
thousands of people in all—had taken ship for Brazil, Portugal's largest and
richest colony. The whole fleet sailed with them: eight ships of the line, four
frigates, twelve brigs, and a number of merchantmen, all accompanied by a
British squadron. It was not just the royal family that left: they brought anything of value that could be moved, from the crown jewels and the contents of
the treasury to the royal collections, the governmental archives, the royal horses
and even the royal library, complete with its two Gutenberg Bibles.

It was a surprisingly bold move: other royal families had simply allowed
themselves to be taken—Charles IV and Ferdinand VII would soon be examples of that. Brazil, after all, was very far away. Having left Lisbon on November
26, 1807, just ahead of the French, the fleet only reached Bahia on January 21.
Altogether, the stormy passage had taken fifty-seven days, toward the end of
which food, water, and soap had become very scarce; but when the ships
reached South America, it was indeed a great event: never before had a European monarch set foot on the continent or in the Southern Hemisphere.

Bahia itself was not unlike a Portuguese city, a sight which no doubt re-
assured the exiles. Far more important, they were greeted with ecstatic cheers:
the Brazilians, it turned out, were faithful and loving subjects; and the enthusiastic reception was repeated on March 7 when the fleet reached Rio de
Janeiro. Clearly, appearances failed to disturb the happy crowds: the old Queen
screamed that she was being murdered all the way off the ship and into the
monastery where she was taken. In fact, the House of Bragança was also a perfect example of the dangers of inbreeding. At every generation, the royal families of Spain and Portugal had intermarried: Queen Maria, the only child
of José I, was the daughter of first cousins; and she was, in turn, married to
her father's brother. As a result, her son, João, was a vast, ugly, awkward man
afflicted with a permanent erysipelas of the legs, a skin affliction as painful as
it was unsightly. Maria herself had always been strange; in 1792, her strange-
ness had changed to insanity and her son became regent.

In spite of his rather peculiar appearance, Dom João was quite intelligent. His wife, however, was as stupid as she was ugly. A witness described her,
in 1809, in realistic, if unflattering, terms: "Soured, with the features of a man,
mustaches on her lip, hairs on her face, hairs on her hands, hairs every other
place—this furry object was Dona Carlota Joaquina."[22] This less than feminine
appearance had not stopped her from having five daughters and two sons;
indeed, her sex life was as wild as it was abundant, her lovers being so numerous that she herself could not have named them all. Since she was also foul-
tempered and foulmouthed, extremely greedy, a fanatic racist—all Brazilians,

according to her, were the dregs of humanity because their blood was mixed—she quickly made herself unpopular. Nor did it help when she decided to claim the viceroyalty of the Spanish colony of La Plata on the slender grounds that she was Ferdinand VII's sister. That pretension quickly made her an object of fun. It did not diminish her amorousness, though, so, to her husband's great relief, she soon moved to her own palace, and left him to live in peace.

As for Dom João, with his children, he moved into the viceregal palace, a building he found dark, depressing, and too small for a European-sized court; but things soon improved. A rich merchant had built a house "fit for a king" in the suburb of São Christovão in the hope that the monarch might indeed come one day to Rio; this house he presented to the regent, and the royal family moved in. The huge park was filled with tropical flowers, and the palace itself was new, cheerful, and spacious. And so Dom João set about improving Brazil.

The colony itself was something of a novelty to him, but he was a quick learner. Of course, he knew that there was a viceroy, and that each province had a captain-general who governed it; that these dignitaries stayed in office for no more than three years, received their instructions from Lisbon, were forbidden to marry within their jurisdiction (so as to avoid potential favoritism), were barred from commercial transactions, and prohibited from accepting money other than their government salary.

The regent was also aware that the administration was directed by a Council of Finance, of which the captain-general was president; that all judges were appointed by Lisbon, except for municipal judges who had to have first held office in the town; that appeals could be taken to Lisbon; and that the code of laws was that of Portugal.

All this made Brazil completely dependent on the Portuguese Crown, especially since all army officers were appointed by Lisbon, and all church tithes were appropriated to the Crown, which then funded ecclesiastical salaries and the cost of public worship. The result was a totally submissive church, especially since the king also nominated the bishops; but being more enlightened than his Spanish colleagues, he chose only native Brazilians. The result was a money-poor Catholic church. The primate, the archbishop of Bahia, received only the equivalent of 10,000 pesos—a mere pittance compared to the income of the archbishop of Mexico; the bishop of Rio, the colony's largest city, only had the equivalent of 5,600 pesos; and many priests were desperately poor.

Nor was there a powerful aristocracy. Titled families were few, entails firmly discouraged. There was a small group of prosperous traders, and a few large landowners, but nothing like Mexico's upper class. The population of this immense country was also unduly small: 3.6 million people, of whom two-fifths were black slaves; the rest, a little over 2.0 million men, women, and children, were a mix of white, black, and Indian blood. As for educational or cultural institutions, there were none: no university, no school of mining (although there were fairly productive gold mines), no school of medicine, no library, not even a single printing press.

There was much to do, therefore, if Brazil were to be transformed from a backward colony into a thriving nation. Luckily, Dom João had both the desire and the intelligence to start making changes as soon as he arrived. Sensibly, his first act was to decree free trade. Until then, Brazil had been allowed to trade only with Portugal; by opening the ports, the regent brought instant prosperity. Other restrictions were also promptly ended: no manufacture except sugar had been permitted, since Brazil was expected to export commodities and gold, and buy all its finished goods from Portugal. Now Dom João not only permitted, but encouraged, the setting up of manufactures.

There was more. A new commercial code was created, along with organizations to help the new industries, and a printing press was set up. Education was improved as well, with the founding of a medical school and a military academy. The Royal Library, sixty-thousand volumes strong, was opened to the public, and a National Institute was created in which the best writers, historians, geographers, and scientists were enrolled—many of them, admittedly, recruited from abroad.

These were immense changes: not only did they make for a wave of economic growth, they also provided Brazil with the kind of institutions that transformed it from a colony to a real country. As a result, something very like patriotism appeared for the first time. Of course, it helped that the regent was there: easily accessible, simple, open, his awkward person soon came to represent the best kind of progress. Oddly enough, however, in spite of the simplicity of his own tastes (his idea of gastronomy ran to great quantities of fried chicken), Dom João felt the need to keep up the splendors of the Portuguese court, at a cost of over 1.5 million pesos a year. This caused some grumbling, as did the arrogance of the newly arrived Portuguese. Then, because money was short, the regent multiplied titles, so that, in the first two years, more distinctions were given than in the three previous centuries. That annoyed the old aristocracy, but it also created a new nobility based on success. Giving out offices as rewards, though, turned out to be a seriously flawed idea: because the salaries were so small, they made for corruption, an evil which, until then, Brazil had been spared. Still, overall, no one doubted that the presence of the royal family was a blessing.

This happy state of affairs might have continued indefinitely, had it not been for events in Europe. With the fall of Napoléon, Portugal became independent once more, a tiny country on the edge of Europe ruined by war and invasion. That was so clearly the case that it never occurred to Dom João that he should go home. All was going well in Brazil, and there he remained. The death of the old queen, on March 20, 1816, changed nothing: the new King

João VI stayed just where he was. A year earlier, it had become so clear that Brazil was no longer a colony governed from Lisbon that he had proclaimed it to be a separate kingdom. For the first time, Brazil was an actual country.

There were problems, however: it was impossible to govern Portugal from Rio; the ministers chosen by the faraway king were anything but popular; and neighboring Spain had a liberal constitution. The results were predictable: on August 24, 1820, the people of Oporto rose and demanded a constitution, and the convening of a Cortes; they were joined, three weeks later, by the population of Lisbon; and in January 1821, the newly elected Cortes met. Its first act was to blame the dire state of the economy on the absence of the royal family and the instauration of free trade in Brazil. Clearly, it was becoming imperative for a Bragança to go home.

Even then, the king did not think of moving; instead, on February 18, 1821, he issued a manifesto announcing that he was sending Dom Pedro, his eldest son, to Lisbon, where he would consult with the Cortes about the contents of the desired constitution; and that this constitution would apply to Brazil as well, with whatever modifications seemed suitable. This last clause was immediately opposed by much of the population, who wanted the whole, unmodified constitution—in spite of the fact that there existed, as yet, no such document. And when Dom Pedro and his younger brother Dom Miguel joined in the demand, the king had no choice but to give in.

It was then that more news reached Rio: the Lisbon Cortes were demanding the return of the king. So, in a direct reversal of his earlier manifesto, João VI announced he would indeed return to Portugal, leaving Dom Pedro as regent in Brazil. Chaos ensued. The electors meeting in Rio to choose their deputies to the Lisbon Cortes, quite unwarrantedly transforming themselves into a kind of constituent assembly, decided to prevent the king's departure and adopted the Spanish Constitution of 1812 instead of the one eventually to be written by the Lisbon Cortes. That was on April 21.

Late that afternoon, João agreed to these demands. Then, in the evening, he sent in the troops and dissolved the meeting. That enabled him, the next morning, to annul all the decrees of the previous day. Once again, he announced that he was leaving, and, five days later, he did so, leaving Dom Pedro as regent.

By then, it was clear that Portugal and Brazil were on a collision course. The Lisbon Cortes wanted to recolonize Brazil; the Brazilians were not about to give up their new prosperity or, indeed, their newfound sense of nationhood. As for the king, he had very little choice: on the very day he reached Lisbon, he was required to swear obedience to the as-yet-unwritten constitution, and it was clear thereafter that the Cortes were in charge. This they proceeded to show by abolishing all institutions—including the army—set up in Brazil since 1808, ordering Dom Pedro back to Lisbon, appointing a governor, and preparing to send Portuguese troops to enforce these orders. The results were predictable: as soon as the news of these developments reached America, São Paulo rose and demanded that the regent stay. It was just what Dom Pedro wanted to hear. Having arrived as a ten-year-old boy, he felt far more Brazilian than Portuguese and had no desire to visit the country he only dimly remembered.

From there, independence was the obvious next step. In June 1822, the Brazilian Constituent Assembly was called into being; it confirmed that Brazil was a separate country and settled the crown on Dom Pedro as emperor. Of course, the former regent felt compelled to apologize to his father, but the choice was clear: either a Brazilian empire with a Bragança as monarch, or a republic. There could be no hesitation: on December 1, Dom Pedro was crowned emperor of Brazil amid much pomp and rejoicing. For the first and only time, independence in America meant not the instauration of a republic, but the setting up of a full-fledged monarchy. More amazing still, the system lasted until 1889. The Bourbons had lost everything because it never occurred to them to visit their dominions. For a while at least the Braganças, with one branch ruling in Rio and the other in Lisbon, kept everything they had ever had.

PART FOUR

Asia

CHAPTER THIRTEEN

The Center of the World

CHINA, that vast, self-sufficient, and self-satisfied empire, seemed very far away from the Western world, and not just because of actual distance. Its civilization was both incomparably more ancient and utterly different. It sold silk, lacquer, porcelain, and tea to Western traders, but was hardly dependent upon them. Even more important, perhaps, at a time when the great European nations were absolutely sure of their superiority over the rest of the world, China was equally sure that it was the only power that really mattered.

By 1800, though, under the Chia-ch'ing Emperor, who had just succeeded his father, change was coming. The first non-Asian ambassador had been received by the Ch'ien-lung Emperor, in 1793, at precisely the time when the structure of empire and army were weakened by corruption. The conquest of much of India had brought the British closer. Even worse, the extraordinarily strong resistance to change meant that the country that had invented gunpowder was becoming more technologically backward with every passing year.

China, in 1800, still seemed as strong as ever; but the internal weaknesses that had appeared in the 1790s made it a potential prey. It was in that decade that all the events of its nineteenth century history found their source.

THE SON OF HEAVEN

He was, according to the Chinese, the most powerful man in the world, the richest, the wisest. As emperor, he stood halfway between humanity and the gods who had endowed him with the Mandate of Heaven. He wore a special color (yellow) that did not, however, preclude the use of gold, silver, and many other bright tints. He wrote in red ink, the only one in the empire to do so. All within his vast realm owed him not just obedience, but personal loyalty.

293

He made war, peace, and the laws; he regulated the economy, and controlled all appointments, civilian and military. He could order punishments of every kind, from a light flogging to the most prolonged and agonizing death. He even chose his own successor from among his many sons. As if that were not enough, he ruled over the most civilized people on earth: the emperor of China, the Son of Heaven, was indeed a sovereign like no other.

For the Chinese, there could be no doubt: their country was the largest, most powerful, most civilized in the world. On the borders were various half-primitive peoples. A little further away, in places like Korea and Annam (today's Vietnam), there were kingdoms that sent tribute and could be conquered when necessary. Japan, although useful as a copper producer, was a place of no great interest. At still greater distances were barbarians, populations devoid of both culture and manners, with whom it was mostly not worth bothering. China might trade with them, but since it grew and made practically everything it needed, these exchanges were at best nonessential. Indeed, these foreigners had little to offer, except for their silver coins, while China sold them its silks, porcelain, and lacquer.

In so great an empire, foreign relations were an almost abstract concept. On occasion, an embassy would come bearing tribute and a humble request. The ambassador, like all those who approached the emperor, would perform the kowtow—three kneelings, nine prostrations with the forehead striking the floor. And then, in 1793, there came a change. For the first time ever, a Western country—Great Britain—sent an embassy to China. Its purpose, which was not achieved, was to lower the trade barriers put up by the Chinese. Still, for the first time, a foreign envoy was allowed to kneel on one knee, rather than kow-tow, largely because after months of negotiations, it hardly seemed worthwhile to go on teaching proper manners to an uncouth barbarian from an enormously distant and unimportant country. So the embassy came, went, and made no lasting difference—to the Chinese, at least.

For George, Lord Macartney, the ambassador, however, the experience was both enlightening and riveting. Here was a form of civilization utterly different from his own; and yet, it worked. "Everything is at the instant command of the state," he noted in his diary,

> and . . . even the most laborious tasks are undertaken and executed with a readiness and even a cheerfulness which one could scarcely expect to meet with in so despotic a government. The Chinese seem able to lift and move almost any weight by multiplying the power; thus they fasten to the sides of the load two strong bamboos; if two are not sufficient, they cross them with two others, and so proceed quadrating and decussating the machine, and applying more bearers, till they can master it and carry it with ease.[1]

For an Englishman, accustomed to the most minimal sort of government, this was most extraordinary. "Indeed," he wrote, "the machine and authority of the Chinese government are so organized, and so powerful, as almost immediately to surmount every difficulty, and to produce every effect that human strength can accomplish."[2] That, and the fact that the emperor could command any piece of property, proved that here, indeed, was a very different world. It was noticeable in the houses put at the ambassador's disposition as he traveled from Tientsin to Peking and beyond to the emperor's hunting palace at Jehol. As for the Son of Heaven himself, he, like the civilization he headed, seemed both very old and very powerful. In 1793, the Ch'ien-lung emperor was eighty-two years old; he had been on the throne since 1736 and, according to Macartney, showed no sign of losing his grip.

> The Emperor . . . is of so jealous a nature, that no person as yet knows with certainty which [of his seventeen sons] he intends for his successor. He does not allow any of them to interfere in his government, but manages it in a great measure alone, reading all the dispatches himself, and often entering into the minutest detail of affairs. His principal minister is Ho-shen, a [Manchu] of obscure origin but considerable talents, whom he has raised by degrees from an inferior post in his guards to his present elevation, having been struck with the comeliness of his person at a review twenty years ago.[3]

When it came to detail mattering greatly, Macartney was right. As soon as the emperor was informed, by a memorial from the local governor, that an ambassador from Great Britain was asking to be received at court, he promptly sent back a decree.

> The English barbarians . . . presented a petition saying that the last year was the Great Emperor's birthday, but the king of their country had not sent his congratulations in time. Now he has especially sent [Macartney] . . . to go to Peking and present tribute.
>
> The original petition has been . . . presented to us. . . . Both its sentiment and its language are submissive and sincere. Thereupon We approved their petition to satisfy their desire to . . . turn toward Our civilization.[4]

That was only the beginning. A flurry of decrees followed, all dealing with the great kowtow controversy. At first, due allowances were made: after all, you could hardly expect an Englishman to have decent manners. It must be explained to Macartney, the decree stated, that "when Ambassadors of various vassal-states come to the Celestial empire to present tribute and look upon her brilliance, . . . they perform the rite of three kneelings and nine prostrations."[5] That was on August 14. Unfortunately, Macartney obdurately refused to do more for the emperor than he did for King George III—kneeling on one knee and kissing the sovereign's right hand. Kneeling, from the Chinese point of view, was at least a beginning; kissing the emperor's hand was too revolting to be contemplated. So time passed and on September 9, Macartney arrived in Jehol, where he was to be received by the emperor. That day, the Grand Council informed the ambassador's escort, Cheng-jui, of their annoyance. "The envoys who have come to Jehol are totally ignorant of the proper ceremonies," it thundered, "and we are deeply dissatisfied. . . . These are ignorant barbarians and it is not worth treating them with too much courtesy."[6] It was not ignorance, though, it was obstinacy; and so the question really was whether to receive Macartney after all. In the end, curiosity prevailed: the ambassador was allowed to forego the kowtow.

  Because Jehol, some 120 miles northwest of Peking, was a summer hunting retreat, the ambassador's reception was a good deal simpler than it would have been in the Forbidden City. Even so, there was enough ceremony to impress so a skeptical an Englishman as the ambassador.

> [Ch'ien-lung's] approach was announced by drums and music. He was seated in an open palanquin carried by sixteen bearers, attended by a number of officers bearing flags, standards and umbrellas, and as he passed we paid him our compliment by kneeling on one knee, whilst all the Chinese made their usual prostrations. As soon as he had ascended his throne, I came to the entrance of the tent and, holding in my hands a large gold box enriched with diamonds in which was enclosed the King's letter, I walked deliberately up and, ascending the side steps of the throne, delivered it into the emperor's own hands. He then gave me the first present from him to His Majesty, the jui-i as the symbol of peace and prosperity, and expressed his hope that my Sovereign and he should always live in good correspondence and amity.[7]

  Naturally, that was all through an interpreter—one of the very few foreigners who resided at the court. For Macartney, that introduction meant that the first step in a negotiation had been taken; for the emperor, the reception was a mere ceremony in which he accepted the tribute of a faraway barbarian for whom he cared nothing. It was made more interesting, though, by the exotic character of the embassy: the Englishmen were just as amusing as some strange-looking animal in a zoo, particularly since the wigs worn by Westerners were thought to be both weird and comic. Had Ch'ien-lung known that George III was a mere parliamentary king, dependent on a majority in the House of Commons, his contempt would have been unfathomable.

  Still, the ceremony was not over. As Macartney noted in his diary:

> We then descended from the steps of the throne, and sat down upon cushions at one of the tables on the Emperor's left hand; and at the other tables, according to their different ranks, the chief [Manchu] Princes and the Mandarins of the Court at the same time took their places, all dressed in the proper robes of their respective ranks. These tables were then uncovered and exhibited a sumptuous banquet. The Emperor sent us several dishes from his

own table, together with some liquors, which the Chinese call wine, not, however, expressed from the grape, but distilled or extracted from rice, herbs and
honey . . .

The Emperor's manner is dignified but affable and condescending [i.e.,
friendly] and his reception of us has been very gracious and satisfactory. He is
a very fine old gentleman, still healthy and vigorous, not having the appearance of a man of more than sixty.

The order and regularity in serving and removing the dinner was wonderfully exact, and every function of the ceremony performed with such silence
and solemnity as in some measure to resemble the celebration of a religious
mystery.[8]

Coming from an Englishman, that was no mean compliment. That the
court was impressive was certain. As for the emperor's majesty, no one could
doubt it: here, visible even to a foreigner, was the Ch'ing dynasty at its apogee.
What, under the Mings, the preceding dynasty, would have been all preening
eunuchs and confusion, was grave, ordered, awe-inspiring. As for the size and
wealth of the country, that, too, was obvious. But for Macartney, at least, and all
the other Westerners, China remained a mystery.

THREE HUNDRED MILLION CHINESE

In 1800, France, the most populous country in Europe, had a population of
about 20 million; Great Britain had only some 10 million inhabitants, and the
United States about 6 million. China had 300 million, of whom about a million
were Manchus, and that crucial fact, alone, made it unlike any other place
on earth.

To most people at the end of the eighteenth century, 300 million people
was an inconceivable number—too many to feed, to count, to govern. In an age
that still believed (except in the United States) that one man should rule, the
amount of work reaching the emperor would have seemed inhuman, impossible. China was the oldest civilized country on earth, however. The Empire,
which had gone through many dynasties, had been founded some two thousand years earlier; and ways to rule a great many people had been found, and
improved, and then refined still more.

Even in China, 300 million was a huge number. The population may have
reached 200 million in 1600, only to decline to some 150 million by 1650. By
1750, it was again well over 200 million; by 1770, it had reached 270 million; by
1800, it was up to 300 million and still growing rapidly.

The main cause for this was the success of the dynasty. All through the
late seventeenth and the eighteenth centuries, for the first time in a long time,
peace had prevailed. Trade expanded along with agricultural production, and

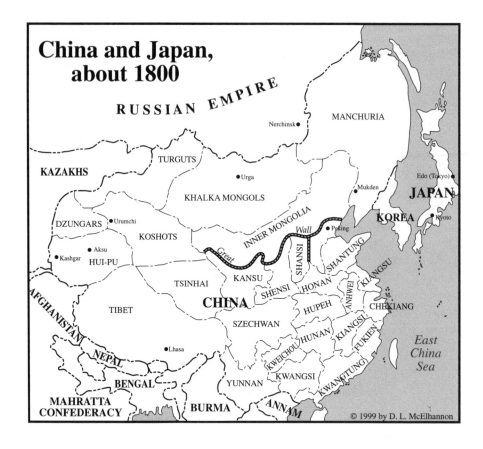

China and Japan, about 1800

people multiplied. That the dynasty was foreign—they were Manchus—made not the slightest difference. It was true, of course, that like the emperors and the princes, the empresses, the princesses, and the concubines were Manchus; that special schools for Manchus had been set up and were financed by the imperial bounty; that the president of every ministry (assisted, however, by a Chinese vice president) was a Manchu. In the provinces, while most governors were Chinese, most governors-general, who oversaw three or four provinces, were Manchu; and a few Chinese resented this. Most did not, though. The government, after all, kept essentially the same structure and methods as under the Mings—only it was more efficient, fairer, less corrupt. When the army was sent to conquer a border people, it did so successfully. China prospered; and so the emperor, foreigner or not, was seen as having the Mandate of Heaven.

A DIVINE ORDER

That mattered a great deal. China was a tyranny tempered by failure: if invasion, civil war, or natural catastrophes disrupted the natural order of things, or if a pretender to the throne seemed likely to be successful, then it was considered that the Mandate of Heaven had been withdrawn, an event usually accompanied by a great deal of violence and civil unrest. An emperor could also lose the mandate by ruling in an immoral way: a good ruler was considerate to his family, attentive to his ministers, a father to his subjects, and put his care of them before his own pleasures. This, it was held, would cause the empire to prosper as moral behavior spread from the top down. If, on the other hand, the emperor was immoral, then corruption would reign, the peasants would revolt, and, eventually, a new dynasty would take over. Because the emperor was the link between earth and heaven, the many complex ceremonies that surrounded him were very important: the proper rituals kept the two spheres in balance. Finally, the emperor's individual efforts mattered—it was rather a matter of God helping those emperors who helped themselves.

These ideas corresponded to a cyclical view of history. As dynasties came and went, there was no progress, merely a repetition of the inevitable process through which morality and energy decayed into immorality and sloth. In Europe, people assumed that the new was better, that civilization grew ever more perfect, that governments became more just and efficient: progress was the idea underlying everything. Progress, in China, was not a comprehensible notion. The result was not just immobility, but a constant yearning for those periods of the past that were seen as having been particularly successful.

Except when the dynasty was being replaced, the emperor was entitled to absolute obedience. Of course, the emperor, being human, could not control everything himself: there was a centralized, organized government to help him. Actually, as those in the know realized, there were *two* governments, one highly visible—the Outer Court—the other—the Inner Court—hidden behind the walls of the Forbidden City.

The visible government was nothing if not bureaucratic: there were methods, procedures, precedents; there was a table of ranks—from number 1 to number 18; all actions followed a well-established pattern; and paper multiplied. As a result, the emperor's rule was predictable, and, at least in Chinese terms, mostly fair. As for the civilian administration (there was a separate military establishment), it was divided into two great categories. In the first were the Six Boards or Ministries, each run by a Manchu president assisted by a Chinese vice president. Each had its special function—personnel, revenue, rites, war, public works, and punishments—none had anything to do with that key function of all European governments, foreign affairs, because China never thought of foreigners as anything but tribute bearers. In the second category

was the Censorate, whose task it was to keep the bureaucracy honest and efficient, and to review both policies and the way they were applied. The censors
denounced inefficient or corrupt bureaucrats, from the top ranks down, but
that was not all: they were also allowed to criticize the emperor's own decisions—although, not unnaturally perhaps, they tended to do this with extreme
caution. Finally, there was yet another way for the emperor to find out a truth
undiscovered by the Censorate: all major officials, and the people themselves,
could send him memorials directly, thus bypassing the normal bureaucratic
channels; and given the normal tendency bureaucrats have to cover for each
other, this provided an essential method for preventing ossification or corruption of the system.

Above these boards were the grand secretaries. Originally mere assistants
of the emperor, they had gradually gained status so as to become a Chinese
equivalent of a Western cabinet. By the end of the reign of the Ch'ien-lung
emperor, though, the grand secretaries functioned more like glorified supervi-
sors, having been essentially superseded by the Grand Council, a group of six
to ten officials, both Manchu and Chinese, some of whom might be grand secretaries as well. The Grand Council met solely at the call of the emperor, and
was part of the Inner Court. It had also largely become the creature of its most
influential member, Ho-shen, the emperor's favorite.

All these powerful people ran an empire divided into eighteen provinces
and some fifteen hundred counties, each of which was drawn so as to have a
population of about two hundred thousand people. Each province had its governor, each district had its magistrate, and within each government house (they
were all called *yamen*), whether at the provincial or at the district level, the
functions of the Six Boards were replicated. Within each district, there was
only one magistrate, who was at the same time a civil servant, a tax collector,
and a judge. Of course, he had assistants—secretaries in the *yamen*, runners
outside who functioned as tax collectors and policemen. All assistants and runners, though, were paid directly by the magistrate from the fees he received
locally. That, in fact, was one of the key features of the system: each district was
supposed to be fiscally self-sufficient, with the taxes going to fund the key
functions of the central government (mostly war and public works) and, of
course, its Peking bureaucracy. As a result, this vast empire was governed by a
mere handful of officials—fewer, certainly, than five thousand.

Even the judicial system was set up so as to keep disputes on the local
level whenever possible. In Confucian theory, the extended family (which might
number several hundred people, from the poorest to the richest) was the proper
venue for the resolution of disputes; so the judicial system was deliberately
kept small and expensive, and geared to the prosecution of criminals rather
than to the resolution of civil suits. Even so, it had six levels: there were 1,500
district courts, 180 prefecture courts, 18 provincial courts, the Board of Punish-

ments in Peking, the High Court, which could overrule the Board, and, finally, the emperor himself, who served as court of last resort. Only serious cases went beyond the district court, and, at every level, precedents were considered; but they were not binding. And if the gravity of the offense justified it, judicial torture was used.

There was also a code that listed some four thousand offenses, and a carefully graded series of punishments that ranged from a light caning with a bamboo stick to a heavy caning or penal servitude. This last was greatly feared: the families had to pay the notoriously corrupt jailers large fees to keep the inmate clothed and fed. After that, and more severe still, came exile, for a time or for life, to a distant province, or to service on the military frontier. And finally, there was death, the punishment for some eight hundred offenses. Even that came in varying degrees of horror, from decapitation (clean and fast), through strangling, to a slow death in which a man's flesh was slowly and carefully cut away, a process that could last many agonizing hours—the famous death of a thousand cuts. There were also more specialized penalties; a dishonest boatman was punished by being slapped in the face with a leather paddle, for instance. Still, judges had to be careful: if they inflicted a penalty on an innocent man, or if they ordered the wrong penalty, they were liable themselves to that same penalty.

In spite of all that, however, great areas of life were not covered by law at all, property being the most conspicuous. The state could at any time seize anyone's assets, whether land or movable property; and the only way to prevent that was to maintain the right relationship with the district magistrate. Happily, that was not difficult at all, because the landowners and the wealthy were normally members of the gentry, and magistrates were well aware they had no hope of discharging their many functions efficiently without the gentry's help.

A POWERFUL UPPER CLASS

The gentry were the backbone of China. The emperor, unless one lived in Peking, was far away; because the magistrates had to cope with an almost impossible workload, in the countryside, where at least four-fifths of the population lived, it was the gentry who actually ran things. There was no way around it, really: although the laws, the administrative system, and the taxes were the same throughout the empire, China was a patchwork of very different regions. Lifestyles, the crops, the transportation system varied widely from north to south and east to west. The southern provinces were flat and tropical; some of the western areas were all mountains; the north had severe winters and short, hot summers. There was cereal farming in the north, rice farming in the south. And because local conditions were different, so were the needs of the people. Even with a much larger bureaucracy, decisions appropriate to local problems could not have been made in Peking; but the gentry was there to keep everything in order.

Like the nobility in the West, the gentry had both privileges and duties; but while titles existed at court—there were princes and dukes—the gentry was not defined by its bloodlines. In that sense, its members were not noble per se: they were simply landowners, some belonging to families who had held their estates from time immemorial, others who had been rewarded, in the 1640s, by the new dynasty. There were even a very few landlords who had bought their estates after making money in that most despised of occupations, trade.

Like the justices of the peace in England, the gentry in China took on many of the functions of government. Its members superintended the upkeep of bridges, ferries, wells, and temples; they supported schools of different levels and managed their endowments; they organized disaster relief for refugees, the homeless, the aged, the destitute. Just as important, they sponsored local gazettes and paid for their printing; and finally, they played a key part in a variety of Confucian rituals. Once again, this was a function similar to that of a Church of England vicar: in a system where the state controlled the church, the rites made visible the morality endorsed by the government. Since Confucius had posited that prosperity and peace depended on morality, these rites were meant as a reminder of the proper way to behave. At the local level, and in a much less exalted manner, the gentry played a role not unlike that of the emperor.

In exchange for this, the members of the gentry were free from manual labor requirements—they could not, like the peasants, be drafted to build a dam, a bridge, or a road. They were also exempt from corporal punishment—but not exile or the death penalty. As a sign of their status, they wore long gowns and long fingernails, were literate—indeed, sometimes quite cultivated—and had the leisure to display polished manners, enjoy the arts, and think long and hard about the proper etiquette. Each extended family—grandparents, parents, children, aunts, uncles, cousins, and many servants—normally lived in the same great house, with each group having its own courtyard.

All those visible signs of status were naturally underpinned by a solid economic reality. Put simply, the gentry were rich because they owned the land and worked the peasants so hard. Rents were high, and had to be paid unfailingly. As the century came toward its end and the pressure for free land increased, it became ever easier to find new tenants. As for taxes, they tended to be as low as the rents were high: since the magistrates thoroughly understood the power of the gentry—which could easily, if it chose, provoke disorder in the countryside—they allowed it to define the incidence of taxes; so, on top of the rent, the peasants paid a high proportion of their income in taxes, while the landlords usually contributed at most 13 percent of theirs.

Thus, life was hard on the peasants. When it became unbearable, there would be an explosion, and it was up to the magistrates to keep these hardships just limited enough so that the peace would not be disturbed. By and large, the peasants died young, after having suffered most of their lives from a variety of epidemic eye and skin diseases, and also from intestinal parasites. They understood and respected the bonds of kinship: here, too, the extended family was a source of strength. Their religious worship consisted of a series of Taoist-Buddhist folk observances. Confucian rites were well beyond them; and they seldom ventured more than two or three miles away from their village. As a result, while they would occasionally see their landlord, they might not set eyes on an official more than half a dozen times in their entire lives.

The peasants could not hope for change: the world in which they lived was as eternal as their lives were brief; and what they did not realize was that their landlords' power was derived not just from their ownership of the land, but also from the fact that most officials, from the magistrates on up and down, belonged to gentry families. For that, as well, there was a good economic reason: the degrees required to enter the civil service needed many years of study, and the passing of many exams. With few exceptions, therefore, only the wealthy could afford to educate their children.

Naturally, the emperors had long been aware of this; and the Ch'ing dynasty, in particular, was eager to prevent collusion between magistrates and landlords. Consequently, there was an unbreakable rule that no official could serve in the province from which he came. That, no doubt, helped; still, there was real class solidarity throughout the empire. Although the magistrate might know no one when he arrived, although he might neither speak nor understand the local language, he was well aware that the landlords' economic needs were the same as those of his own family; he therefore satisfied them. That, and the fact that he could not run his district without the help of the gentry, meant that they, as much as the emperor, governed China.

In essential ways, in fact, the Mandate of Heaven depended on the gentry—although it would have been a sacrilege to say so. The emperor's claim to rule was based on his capacity to maintain a unified control, thus preventing civil strife, local disorders, and banditry. The gentry, so long as they remained loyal, could ensure that all would be well throughout the empire; and as long as they themselves prospered, it was in their interest to do so. For most of China, and much of the Ch'ien-lung emperor's reign, that was in fact the case. Thus, although the emperor's power was limitless, it was also extremely superficial. Most of China, ruled as it was by the gentry, never felt the weight of the imperial government. The consequence was twofold: first, as we have seen, the civil servants were extraordinarily few; second, civil peace was mostly guaranteed without much effort from Peking. That left two categories of threat to the government: invasion from abroad, which, in the 1790s, was not an issue; and subversion at court.

INNER COURT, SECRET GOVERNMENT

European kings had their palaces, where they surrounded themselves with courtiers and tried to dazzle the world. Theirs was an open display that all could come and admire. The emperor of China, on the other hand, lived in a separate world of his own, the Forbidden City. Access was severely restricted, and the population was quite unlike that of any other place in the empire—a mix of foreign princes (the Manchus), eunuchs, officials, bonded servants, great nobles, and soldiers. There were (and are) high walls all around the Forbidden City, and massive, well-guarded gates. Inside, there was the great ceremonial axis on which pavilion followed pavilion, each rising from a tall stone platform reached by majestic stairs, each crowned with a yellow-tiled roof curling at the edges. Then, to the sides, there were many complexes of smaller living pavilions separated by gardens, the odd theater, and many offices. The Ch'ien-lung emperor even added a large pleasure garden, complete with meandering stream, picturesque rocks (brought there at great expense), and a dining pavilion, crossed by a rivulet of its own whose gentle current floated cups of wine to the emperor's guests. And in the pavilions where the emperor, his empress, his concubines, his children, and his relatives lived, there was a great accumulation of treasures of all kinds, from silks and the most delicate of jewels to porcelain and bronzes of dazzling quality.

Much the same was true even when the emperor left Peking. The summer palace, the Yüan-ming Yüan, outside the city was also an enclosed world of its own, a separate universe of gardens and sumptuous pavilions. At Jehol, the summer hunting retreat, tents were the order of the day—but there was nothing austere about them. When Macartney was received by the emperor, for instance, he found himself in a tent

> about twenty five yards in diameter, . . . supported by a number of pillars, either gilded, painted or varnished according to their distance or position. . . .
>
> The materials and distribution of the furniture within at once displayed grandeur and elegance. The tapestry, the curtains, the carpets, the lanterns, the fringes, the tassels were disposed with such harmony, the colours so artfully varied, and the light and shades so judiciously managed that the whole assemblage filled the eye with delight and diffused over the mind a pleasing serenity and repose undisturbed by glitter or affected embellishments. The

commanding feature of the ceremony was that calm dignity, that sober pomp of Asiatic greatness, which European refinements have not yet attained.[9]

Nor was it just that the emperor was surrounded by the most refined splendor: everyone he could see was there to obey his orders, from the members of the Grand Council to the eunuchs sweeping the courtyard, from his guards to his concubines. European kings had mistresses, of course, usually one at a time. The emperor of China had as many concubines as he thought fitting—quite a number, usually, because he wanted to have the greatest possible number of sons. This was not merely self-indulgence (although, obviously, there was something to be said for the process of begetting them); the more sons an emperor had, the better the chance that one of them would be intelligent and industrious enough to be an adequate successor. It was the emperor, alone, who chose the son to succeed him; and that method eliminated the parade of the idiot, the lame, and the impotent who sat on many European thrones. Equally, there could be no reversionary interest, no crown prince setting himself up against his father. As long as he kept the Mandate of Heaven, the emperor was indeed absolute.

Even so, there was the weight of the institutions. Because successive emperors had understood any bureaucracy's tendency to resist change and look after itself, they had added new layers of control—first the grand secretaries, then the Grand Council—and they had also devised the system through which they could be memorialized directly. Thus, in theory at least, information, that key ingredient of power, flowed freely to them and enabled them to outwit and discharge lazy, corrupt, or obdurate officials. Still, one man, even if half-divine, can only do so much. In the last resort, the emperor had to depend on his close entourage. As long as he kept those few men up to the mark, all was well; if he allowed himself to be fooled by them, disaster eventually followed.

The emperor's power, and that of his closest advisers, was further multiplied by a single institution, the Imperial Household Department. Originally, the department's purpose had merely been to make sure that life at court ran smoothly, that the imperial family's needs were met, that the ceremonies followed the proper etiquette. Under the Ch'ing dynasty, it was still carrying out its original functions, but it also began to serve an altogether different purpose: it became, in fact, one more tool of direct imperial rule, a way to bypass the regular government and its bureaucracy. By 1796, it had 1,623 employees, about a third the number of the civil servants in the entire country.

The department had a number of strengths. One, of course, was its proximity to the person of the emperor. Its most important offices were in the Forbidden City, its officials had frequent access to the Son of Heaven; and as White House aides still freely admit, proximity is everything. Another was the reliability of its staff: because it was composed mainly of eunuchs and bond servants, it depended almost completely on the emperor's favor. Regular bureaucrats had careers; eunuchs were rejects in a society defined by lineage — and so, like bond servants, they could not hope ever to conquer the throne. Under the Ch'ings (who were anxious to avoid a repetition of the disasters that brought down the Mings), the eunuchs were firmly controlled, and kept in menial positions, while never being given control of any of the court's spending. Thus the emperor knew that he could absolutely depend on people whose only hope of comfort came from him. Finally, of course, the orders given by the department were seen as coming directly from the emperor, and so they were likely to be obeyed promptly and fully.

Some of the department's functions were self-evident. It looked after the emperor, providing him with food, clothing, shelter, and all the necessary surroundings. It organized his ceremonial duties as well as his entertainments. It ran manufactures that served the emperor. Some were for his exclusive use, like the Palace Printing Office and the bindery; others were prosperous industries, like the silk and porcelain manufactures, over which the emperor had a monopoly.

The Imperial Household Department also managed the great quantities of objects stored in the Forbidden City — everything from the bullion that was kept in the treasury, to the weapons, carpets, saddles, musical instruments, fur, silk, porcelain, or tea stores, keeping track of goods received and disbursed. There was, naturally, an imperial wardrobe, and also a chancery in charge of janitorial and other menial services. Nor was that all: the Imperial Household Department also ran the Bureau of Imperial Gardens and Hunting Parks, the Imperial Boats Office, the Imperial Construction Office, the imperial dispensary, the upkeep of the imperial mausoleums, and the palace stud and its stables. So far, it was not unlike its counterparts at the European courts, although on a very large scale. But then there was more, much more.

Some of the household institutions were a logical outcome of the way it was staffed: there was a Eunuch School, a Manchu School, even a Muslim School (in the Tibet campaigns, the Chinese had taken Muslim prisoners who became the emperor's bond servants). There was a subdepartment that managed the recruitment and promotion of personnel, and also exercised judicial and supervisory functions. The Privy Purse Office also looked after the imperial estates, which were mostly in the vicinity of Peking and covered half a million acres. These were supposed to provide both income and food. They did, but, being badly managed, not nearly as much as they should have — only 140,000 taels a year (an ordinary worker earned three taels a month), together with some forty-two thousand measures of grain.

Since, after all, the emperor was an absolute ruler, and could therefore command the Board of Revenue to disburse whatever he chose, it might have made sense for the Imperial Household Department to be financed out of general funds. That, however, was not the case. The emperor arrogated to himself several major sources of revenue, and the Privy Purse kept the surplus it generated. Thus, for instance, ginseng, then considered an essential medicinal plant, was an imperial monopoly that brought in over a million taels a year; the copper trade, which paid heavy dues, also remitted very large sums to the Privy Purse; from the salt monopoly came another half million taels; the custom dues taken in at Canton brought in yet another million; the silk and porcelain manufactures, also imperial monopolies, made very substantial profits. There were still more sources of income—the property of officials whose crimes were punished by confiscation, for instance, or the gifts and tributes received from within the empire or from the states on its borders. Taken together, all these sources brought in huge sums yearly, far more than was needed to run the Household Department or even build new palaces.

There were, of course, exceptional expenses: the Ch'ien-lung emperor's southern tours, for example, were terribly expensive, so much so that his successors remained within the vicinity of Peking. Most of all, though, the Privy Purse was a source of power: it controlled key sectors of the economy; it gave its officials reason to inquire and interfere everywhere, in every domain; and it accumulated the huge sums that made it possible for the emperor to finance, himself, whatever he saw as an essential need of the state. In 1765, for instance, the Privy Purse had spent 5 million taels building walls around the cities of the lower Yangtze as an insurance against possible rebellion; in 1768, 1.5 million was spent on a military expedition in Yunnan. In a huge empire, where local risings were always possible, these great reserves of bullion played an essential role in consolidating the emperor's rule.

CORRUPTION AT THE TOP

Corruption, in China, had always been a fact. When emperors were weak, it grew so vast that it led to the end of the dynasty. When emperors were strong, it was sufficiently contained so as not to harm seriously the country or its economy. Usually, the emperor, on mounting the throne, would start an anticorruption drive—but always with the understanding that it would only go so far. Jailers were corrupt, but that was considered a part of the penalty suffered by prisoners. Officials were corrupt: if you wanted a promotion, you were expected to give substantial gifts in all the right places; but, under good emperors, the official accepted gifts only from the person he meant to promote, anyway. It was the same with candidates for their first job in the administration: the right degrees were a necessity, but so were the "greetings" offered to powerful officials. Nepotism was also the rule: that was hardly surprising in a society based on lineage. Promoting one's relatives was a virtue—and one that was universally practiced. Good officials helped those relatives who were able to carry out their functions; bad officials helped their relatives indiscriminately.

Even ministers were corrupt—once again, it was a question of degree. It was always possible to gauge the integrity of a high official by the number of hangers-on waiting outside his door: the greater their numbers, the greater his corruption, so that one highly praiseworthy minister was described thus: "His doors were without private petitioners."[10] As for lower-level officials, it was understood that they would do nothing without a tip.

Into this highly ambiguous world there came, in 1775, a beautiful twenty-two-year-old man named Ho-shen. The Ch'ien-lung emperor, who was sixty-five that year, noticed him as he stood guard and, for all his wives, concubines, and many children, promptly fell for him. Within a year, Ho-shen had been made a grand councillor, a post that normally came at the end of a long and distinguished career, and showered with gifts and privileges—heady stuff for such a young man. The newly rich and powerful Ho-shen might have responded by displaying unflinching devotion to the emperor and to the state. Instead, he decided to use his position for everything it was worth, and then a good deal more.

It was an easy task. He placed his henchmen in key posts, and gave them a simple mission: to steal as much as possible and, after they had taken their cut, pass the rest on to him. By 1784, he controlled the boards of appointments and revenue, thus getting a stranglehold on the two most remunerative functions of the government: he could take a percentage of every tael that came in and get a bribe for every civil servant who was either hired or promoted. By that time, he also controlled the Grand Council, and thus the flow of memorials to the emperor, so that the besotted old man only heard what Ho-shen wanted him to hear; then, in 1790, he was given the emperor's favorite daughter in marriage.

Because of the inventory made at Ho-shen's death, the extent of the favorite's greed can be described precisely. By 1799, he had accumulated 60 million ounces of silver, 27,000 ounces of gold, 256 pearl necklaces, 456 rubies, and 4,070 sapphires—28,000 pieces of jewelry altogether. He also owned 1,417 sable robes, 4,000 other fur garments (it does get cold in Peking in the winter . . .) as well as 2 storehouses full of white jade and another 2 full of silk. In his principal residences, there were 11 bronze tripods of the Han dynasty (206 B.C.E.– 220 C.E.); 18 jade tripods; 711 antique ink slabs, some of the Sung dynasty (960–1279); 28 imperial jade gongs; 38 European clocks inlaid with gems; 140 gold and enamel watches; 18 solid gold statues over 2 feet high; 9,000 scepters of solid gold and 507 of white jade—all without counting the 500 pairs of ivory and gold chopsticks; the 4,288-piece gold table service or its replica in silver;

the gold screens; the lacquer screens; the 144 couches decorated with lacquer, gold, and gems; or the eight-foot-long solid piece of jade, carved and engraved with the poems of a Ming emperor, now at the Metropolitan Museum of Art in New York. All that was worth some 220 million taels, many times the reserves in the treasury; and to that must be added real estate and a variety of businesses the value of which was estimated as high as 900 million taels.[11]

Decay Everywhere

Repulsive though Ho-shen's greed and selfishness may have been, they would not have mattered all that much if it had not been for the system he had set up. By the time he fell, though, the administration had been corrupted throughout the empire. At every level, in every district capital, officials were busy pocketing money to which they were not entitled. Instead of doing their jobs, they sold exemptions from the rules, demanded more taxes from the already hard-pressed peasants, and took money for themselves when it should have been used to keep the country running.

The army was one case in point. Funds were assigned every year to pay salaries—for officers and soldiers—and buy clothing and weapons. Now the money stayed in the hands of a few generals, with Ho-shen taking his cut. The results were not long delayed: soldiers deserted, or augmented their nonexistent pay by taking on other jobs; weapons were rare, usually antiquated; and the soldiers lacked all training. Thus, when a serious rebellion broke out in 1793, it promptly became obvious that the army was unable and unwilling to fight. The rebellion was eventually put down by other means; and, happily, there was no major threat on the border; so very few people were aware that the once fierce and effective Manchu-led Chinese army was now nothing but a ghost. As for the emperor, reliant as ever on Ho-shen, he simply never knew: with his favorite controlling the flow of information, defeats were presented as victories.

An ineffective army was bad enough, but, at the moment at least, it affected relatively few people. The tax shortfalls, on the other hand, touched just about everybody. By 1790, there were widespread shortages in the central and provincial treasuries, which naturally meant that the government carried out its functions badly and late. These shortfalls, in turn, resulted from the universal demand for "squeeze." The district magistrates, at the bottom of the food chain, found themselves in an impossible position. Because the administration did less and less, they had to hire more help, and pay their salaries; then they had to bribe, year in, year out, their superiors in the administration because, if they did not, they risked being fired. Finally, they had to take for themselves what they needed to survive; and, of course, while they were at it, they kept rather more than their due. There was only one source for all this money:

the tax revenues they were supposed to forward to the treasury. Their employees and their patrons would not wait; the treasury did, and so, in many ways the government became irrelevant. As for the peasants, they were expected to pay more every year—until they finally ran away or rose in revolt.

That was exactly the process through which earlier dynasties had lost the Mandate of Heaven; but still the emperor failed to notice. That he should have remained so blind would be amazing if he had been himself. By the 1790s, though, he was declining into senility, and so he had ignored another alarm bell: the successive floods of the Yellow River.

These floods, in fact, should never have happened. Earlier dynasties had built a series of canals, dams, and catchment lakes with two purposes in mind: one was to prevent flooding; the other was to ease the transport of rice from the south, where it was grown, to Peking, where it was needed. For that purpose, a separate bureaucracy had been set up, the Grain Tribute Administration. Its job was to collect the rice tax from eight provinces in southern and central China, then load the vast quantities of grain on fleets of up to a hundred junks which made their way, via the Grand Canal, the Yellow River, and its tributaries, to an unloading point in northern China. There, the crop would be stored in granaries and distributed to the court and the population. To accomplish this massive job, there was a director in charge of provincial intendants, who supervised families of hereditary boatmen living in military colonies along the Grand Canal, inspectors, porters, and a special militia. Naturally, all these people had to be paid.

The first step in the corruption of the administration responsible for preventing both flood and famine was to look the other way when the regular employees stopped working—while, of course, still collecting their salaries. Then some forty to fifty thousand vagrant workers were hired to do the work of those who were idle, and since these new employees had to live, they exacted their own fees, while hundreds of perfectly useless deputy controllers were also appointed. The unsurprising result was an immediate rise in transportation costs, and therefore in the price of a measure of rice. In 1732, for instance, the fees per grain junk ranged from 130 to 200 taels; by 1800, they were up to 300 taels; and by 1810, in spite of the Chia-ch'ing emperor's best efforts, to 500 taels.

These rising prices affected everyone. The northern gentry, for instance, which bought its rice from the imperial granaries, found itself paying far more than before, so it negotiated with the magistrates for tax exemptions that would allow them to make this up; invariably, the magistrates gave in to their demands, thus causing an even greater shortfall in tax collections; and that, in turn, meant pressing the peasants even harder. Just as bad, local officials, unable to pay for the rice from the imperial granaries, were then forced to buy from private traders—who were cheaper. But no funds had been allocated for those payments; and, once again, money had to be taken from those least able to pay.

All that was bad enough; but the next step entailed death and devastation. Every year, a sum of 10 million taels was appropriated for the upkeep of the Grand Canal, the subsidiary canals, and the antiflood network of the Yellow River. As it was, the Yellow River, a notoriously eccentric body of water, which radically changed its course soon afterward, was never easy to control. What happened then was that the work on dams and canals almost stopped—of the 10 million taels a year, only 1 was actually spent as it should have been, the other 9 disappearing into the pockets of Ho-shen and his friends. The results were almost immediate: as the canals silted up, the junks could no longer get through; and when the yearly high water came, they were too shallow to convey it to the catchment lakes. The water had to go somewhere, so it flooded the countryside, drowning men and beasts and spreading its ravages all up and down its course. That, of course, damaged the canal system yet more, ensuring both that the next flood would be more destructive and that northern China would get even less rice.

For the latter problem, at least, there was a solution. The rice, instead of being shipped by land, could go by sea. One of the original justifications of the canal system had been that the coastal waters were infested by pirates, but that was no longer the case. Not only would shipping by sea have been faster, it would also have been vastly cheaper, because it entailed none of the fee-exacting checkpoints that existed on the land route. The coastal officials, who wanted the business, very properly memorialized the emperor to suggest the change; the Grain Tribute Administration, anxious to keep its bribes and its power, memorialized against it; and that left it up to the Son of Heaven.

This, in 1799, was the new Chia-ch'ing emperor. He received both sets of memorials and found himself sorely puzzled. On the one hand, he was anxious to end the corruption that had marred the latter part of his father's reign; on the other, he was aware that good emperors listened to their ministers—and the ministers were not in favor of the change, mostly on the grounds that any change was bad by definition. That, in turn, was a typical manifestation of the fossilized mind-set exhibited, among other places, in the Empire's relations to foreigners: China was superior to all other countries; it was more powerful, more righteous, more advanced; therefore, a patronizing tone could be used, while no effort was made to ascertain whether the foreign country in question was potentially dangerous. Together with the weakening of the army, that attitude led straight to the disasters of the nineteenth century; it also precluded interior change or reform, and so the rice continued to make its slow, costly, inefficient way through the silted-up canals.

Too Many People

Change, however, was everywhere: not because of the emperor, the Grand Council, or the ministers, not because of pressure or opportunity from outside, but simply because every day the population grew. By the 1790s, the demographic pressure had become tremendous: there were too many people for not enough land. As families expanded, therefore, they were forced to abandon the plot they farmed in the hope of finding either work or land elsewhere; and that, in turn, was enormously disruptive. Vagrants drifted from village to village, bringing lawlessness with them; others tried settling in marginal areas, often near the borders, where the soil was poor and the administration virtually nonexistent. Since Peking firmly refused to create more districts, appoint more magistrates, or modify the means of keeping the peace, these newly settled places often lived in a state of virtual anarchy; and the disorder had a tendency to spread to formerly quiet parts of the empire.

Indeed, no government structure was ever modified. A larger population should have meant an increase in the size of the bureaucracy—but it did not. In spite of this, more families had more children who took the exams, earned their degrees, and were thus—in theory at least—entitled to a place in the administration. There was no room for them either, though, so they bribed their way in, thus adding to the corruption of the system. Further, since the need for state employment grew more desperate as more gentry families tried living off the same amount of land, and also because state employment required degrees, a new practice sprang up, that of buying favorable examination results. This was far more dangerous than it appeared. The emperor relied on a corps of competent and relatively honest administrators; but the people who had bought their degrees, and then bribed their way into an official position, were not only incompetent—they were eager to recover the bribes they had paid, and so they, in turn, stole as much money as they possibly could. Everywhere one looked in China around 1800, in fact, money was changing hands in destructive ways.

Even those degree holders who had actually passed the exams contributed to the slow decay of the administrative system. There were three levels of degrees, the upper of which was never reached before the age of thirty-five. Unfortunately all that studying, which involved memorizing vast quantities of text, and doing endless textual criticism, positively discouraged thought. What mattered was knowing the important authors, some of whom had lived fifteen hundred years earlier; and that did not make for flexibility when the happy degree holder was finally given a government post. Once again, nothing was meant to change; and if the condition of China or of the outside world did, that was too bad.

An Expanding Economy

Of course, there were some positive consequences to this population growth: because the numbers of the consuming public increased every year, the domestic market economy expanded rapidly; interior trade grew as well, and as a consequence so, for the first time in Chinese history, did banking, credit, and the use of bills of exchange. That should have had a wholly positive outcome: prosperity, in theory at least, favors development of all kinds. In China, however, it did not work quite that way. Unlike England, or the Italian merchant city-states, the empire had no commercial law, no limited liability companies, no insurance of any kind, no guarantee that the government would not seize what it pleased when it pleased.

Just as bad, trade was thought to be the lowest possible occupation because it was neither physically productive (like working the land) or intellectually productive (like running the country, writing, painting, or teaching). Being a merchant, even a very rich one, was therefore neither safe nor honorable—until, that is, some of the capital was invested in land, and then the trader joined the gentry. Still, there was one way to buy relative safety, and that was to bribe enough important people. Thus, paradoxically, the growth of the economy that should have resulted in overall modernization had precisely the opposite effect. It worsened corruption and helped maintain that frozen status quo.

There was also a major discrepancy between the coastal areas and the interior regions—as, in fact, there is today. Every year, Chinese manufacturers (i.e., mostly the Imperial Household Departments) made enormous profits satisfying the ever-increasing European demand for tea, silk, porcelain, lacquer, and other luxury goods. That, in turn, fostered employment, but not where it was needed most, in the marginal areas; as a result, people there grew more and more dissatisfied. As for the gentry, once a stabilizer, it was now beginning to play a very different role. Because it, too, felt pressed both by the growth of the population and the decline of the administration's reliability and efficiency, it tended to take over more and more of the government's functions, thus gradually reducing its power.

The White Lotus

Although nothing was ever supposed to change, China, in the 1790s, had come into a state of flux. Because of population growth, massive migrations took place from the more populous areas—the plains, the valleys, and the deltas—to the mountain areas and the recently settled borders in Szechwan, the backcountry of Kwangsi, or the Hunan-Kweichow borders. These places were, in some ways, still wild: the administration was either absent or impotent, and groups of bandits ruled in place of the emperor. Further, because the earlier settled populations were most unwilling to make room for the newly arrived immigrants, a state of semiwarfare existed between the two groups. That, in turn, entailed a high degree of militarization. It was every man for himself; arms were numerous, and people knew how to fight.

If the local populations wished to resist the government, therefore, they had the necessary skills. There had already been rebellions in the seventeenth and early eighteenth centuries in Szechwan, Honan, Hupei, and Shantung. In that broad stretch of central China, fidelity to the fallen Ming dynasty had been used as the perfect pretext to resist the new Manchu rulers.

As so often before, it took a combination of circumstances to push people from habitual disobedience to actual rebellion. One, of course, was the lack of civil peace. As long as the emperor held the Mandate of Heaven, there was order and prosperity; when he lost it, strife, banditry, and corruption ravaged the land. In the 1790s, the people of the newly settled outlying areas of China had good reason to feel the time had come for a change of dynasty. The other circumstance was the sudden revival of the White Lotus Society. This was a network of devotional congregations which served as a principal vehicle for popular religion and practiced a blend of Buddhism, folk Taoism, and doom-laden doctrines. Perhaps the most important tenet of the White Lotus sect was the belief in the imminent ultimate reincarnation of the Buddha as Maitreya, who would usher in an age of peace and plenty.

This was not a doctrine that pleased the authorities; in the seventeenth century, the sect had been banned. By 1775, however, the White Lotus had shown clear signs of renewed influence. This was due in large part to its charismatic leader, Liu Chi-sieh, who was not only a gifted communicator, but also an able strategist, and who now made two key announcements: first, that Maitreya was incarnate in a son of his own master, Liu-sung, and second, that he had discovered a member of the Ming dynasty who was, therefore, the legitimate emperor. Both these ideas had a powerful resonance, since they promised the long-awaited era of peace and plenty under the rule of the right emperor, although they might not have spread so quickly without the unwitting help of the authorities. As the government forces persecuted the sect, they forced its masters to flee to new areas where they promptly began proselytizing; so what started as a local belief rapidly spread across the more lawless parts of central China.

Soon the government began to notice that all was not well; so, in 1793, it ordered an investigation of the White Lotus congregations. The local authorities, accustomed as they were to using strong-arm methods, promptly unleashed a reign of terror on the villages; and many communities, which had been fighting bandits and new arrivals for many years, armed themselves for defense against the government forces, thus, in effect, joining the rebellion. The next step was unavoidable: in February 1796, village after village rose in open revolt, starting on the mountain border of western Hupei, and spreading rapidly to the entire border area of Hupei, Szechwan, and Shensi. At first, the White Lotus's military tactics were simple: they would raid valley towns from the mountains, take them, sack them (and kill any remaining government representative), then disappear back up to their own well-fortified villages. At the same time, the sect allied itself to armed bands proficient in the martial arts, boxing, and cudgel fighting. These men soon became the military backbone of the rebellion and brought in well-armed bandits, as well as smugglers and counterfeiters, against whom the state had been carrying out an armed repression. These new allies made for further successes; and many separate local risings followed, since the authorities were no longer in a position to put them down.

The White Lotus had another piece of luck. The Miao aboriginal populations along the Hunan-Kweichow borders were finding themselves increasingly dispossessed by the flow of new, ethnically Chinese immigrants; and they were extremely averse to the new bureaucratic system the authorities were trying to impose in what had been essentially an autonomous region. And so, after a series of risings that were put down with great severity, the entire Miao population rose against the government, thus helping the White Lotus.

Earlier in his reign, the Ch'ien-lung Emperor had conducted campaigns against restive populations just outside the borders of the empire, and he had also reconquered Tibet; but strife within China itself was a novelty. Although not aware of the full gravity of the rebellion, he understood that it must be put down. He was, however, in his dotage, and as fond of Ho-shen as ever; so the leadership of the campaign against the White Lotus fell to Fu-k'ang-an, a Manchu prince related to the emperor, but who was also an associate of Ho-shen, and to Ho-shen's brother, Ho-lin.

Naturally these two, under Ho-shen's close supervision, assumed that it was business as usual, and that the rebellion simply gave them yet another way to fill their pockets. Once again, but on an even larger scale, funds that were to clothe, feed, arm, and pay the army found their way instead into the trio's pockets. The result, naturally, was a series of government defeats that Ho-shen presented to the emperor as victories. Still, reality caught up with him: late in 1796, Fu-k'ang-an and Ho-lin were actually killed in battle. Generals who had been fighting the Miao were now transferred to the area, but the undertrained, underarmed, and underpaid troops did no better. Only after the death of the Ch'ien-lung Emperor, and the dismissal of Ho-shen by his heir, did the situation improve. The government began a policy of fortifying the villages so that they could resist the White Lotus raids. Local administrators—all members of the gentry—set up their own well-trained militia; mercenaries were hired; and by 1805, the White Lotus Rebellion was finally over.

THE BEGINNING OF THE END

The consequences of the government's many failures endured, however. The first, and most obvious, was the shaming of the Manchu Banners, those famed army groups that had conquered China in the seventeenth century. The dynasty's power rested on that of the Banners; but now it was clear that the emperor could no longer depend on them. Just as bad, the militias that had defeated the White Lotus remained. They, not the emperor, guaranteed the peace, making government seem irrelevant. Then there was the heavy financial cost. Throughout his reign, the Ch'ien-lung Emperor had been accumulating a reserve to be used in emergencies. By 1795, it had reached 78 million taels; but 120 million was spent on fighting the White Lotus, thus leaving the government with a worrisome deficit at a time when the tax yield was shrinking due to the universal corruption. For Ho-shen, the rebellion had merely created one more source of income; for the dynasty, it was the first of the great disasters which led, a century later, to the semicolonization of China.

The Ch'ien-lung Emperor, fallen into dotage and blinded by his trust in Ho-shen, had remained unaware of all this. His son, who succeeded him in 1799 as the Chia-ch'ing Emperor, saw the situation far more clearly. On February 8, 1799, he gave forth the following decree:

> The commanders in chief do not seem in the least anxious to put down the rebellion, since they are able to enrich themselves and wax fat at the expense of the disturbed districts. They report mythic victories and are lost to all sense of shame. . . . Penniless officials come back from service at the front with amply lined pockets. . . . All this money comes ultimately from the unfortunate people, plundered to satisfy their insatiable greed. . . .
>
> These abuses cannot be allowed to continue. I insist that I be informed of the true state of affairs. What good can come of representing a disgraceful defeat as a glorious victory? I am Lord of the Empire and I require the truth above everything. . . . I shall show no mercy for misconduct in the field. . . . Do not imagine that your new sovereign can be hoodwinked.[12]

The emperor was right, of course. Ho-shen was arrested and forced to commit suicide; a few other officials were dismissed; but the habit of corruption had spread, undermining both the efficacy of the state and the legitimacy of the emperor. It was apparently too late for reform. By 1800, change was indeed in the air—not the kind of change the emperor wanted, but, instead, the decline for which China was to pay so huge a price throughout the rest of the nineteenth century.

CHAPTER FOURTEEN

A Civilized Empire

BOTH AMERICAS had strong cultural ties to Europe; India, because it was conquered by the British, was also Westernized. The Ottoman Empire understood that it must modernize—become more European—in order to survive. China, on the other hand, was content to be what it was. Except for clocks, it needed nothing from the West.

The richness and diversity of what they saw stunned the few Europeans who visited China around 1800. Everything, from food and clothes to the policing of the cities, reflected a high degree of sophistication. This, indeed, was a different world; and even if many peasants were, in effect, serfs, the economic system was very different from the slave economies elsewhere.

That was in 1800. Within forty years, the first Opium War was to show the West that China was an easy prey: all those differences, after all, mattered less than the technology of firearms and the corruption of the imperial government.

THE IMPORTANCE OF LITERATURE

Philosophy, history, and a fine writing style: all these matters were considered so important in China that they were a key part of the education of all the young men of the upper classes, from the imperial family to the lowest gentry. The greater the task, the more need there was for a full knowledge of the various components of civilization. Precedent was everything, innovation deeply feared—and that applied to the arts as well as to governance. The education of the princes, therefore, tended to be rigorous; and the one who showed the greatest intelligence, the deepest understanding, and the most impressive willingness to work hard normally became the heir to the throne. This had certainly been true of the Ch'ien-lung Emperor. His classes lasted every day from five A.M. to four P.M., with only five days off a year, and he was given a thorough grounding in the classics, history, and philosophy, so that he could easily cite precedents and use classical citations. He then went on to study the Confucian canon, moral science, and metaphysics, and was also given a grounding in mechanics and the sciences. At the same time he was taught calligraphy, painting, and poetry, and eventually considered himself a great connoisseur in all three fields.

The semiworship of parents and grandparents was a key element of the Confucianism taught to the young prince. It was typical of the Ch'ien-lung Emperor that when he set forth on his enormously costly southern tours, the reason given was not the real one—he wanted to see the country and hunt. Instead, it was announced that these were to be pleasure trips for the Empress Mother. Another essential achievement was the ability to write poetry. This, with mostly unfortunate results, the emperor did throughout his life. Like so many bad poets, he thought that following the rules was enough: what counted was the meter, not the spirit. That is the case of one example of his vast production, a poem written about the gardens of the Summer Palace:

> In my leisure after toil I have come for an outing . . .
> In the clean air after the rain the aspect of the mountains has
> Crystallized to blue-black.
> The wind blows on the water and turns it to wrinkled silk.[1]

The poem goes on at much greater length, but it does not improve. Still, except in his dotage, the Ch'ien-lung Emperor was a hardworking ruler: the fact that he cared enough to write a great deal of poetry shows how important literature seemed to all the Chinese.

It was just as well, however, that he never knew anything about the single most important literary achievement of his reign—not only because he would have hated it, but also because he would no doubt have seen to it that it was destroyed. Ts'ao Chan's *The Story of the Stone* flouted all the conventions: it is neither the recounting of a hoary historical episode nor the praise of a dead emperor, but the first true novel in Chinese history. The characters are ordinary people who struggle with the many problems of life, from unreciprocated love to the threat of poverty. More startling still, the story is based on a real event, the decline of the Cao family, which had prospered under the K'ang-hsi Emperor, and found itself out of favor in the reign of his successor. The loss of wealth, possessions, and privilege in the novel corresponds to Ts'ao Chan's actual experience and has the immediacy, the ability to reach us, that is characteristic of all great novels. Just as important as the fact that *The Story of the Stone* is based on reality, however, is the inner life of the principal character. This is one of the mainstays of the novel. His memories propel the plot and create the atmosphere, so that together with many descriptions of everything from a banquet to an illness or a business transaction, the reader is also offered a series of psychological truths.

Of course, *The Story of the Stone* remained unpublished during Ts'ao Chan's lifetime, and, indeed, well into the nineteenth century. The Ch'ien-lung Emperor would have considered it subversive in every possible way: the subject was inappropriate, the political content unacceptable. Real persons (as opposed to heroic figures), with their loves, hates, triumphs, and failures, would have struck him as intolerably commonplace; and so it was that what is arguably the greatest Chinese novel ever written remained totally unknown for decades.

PAINTING AND CONVENTION

Painting, of an equally conventional kind, was as important to the emperor as literature and poetry. He collected enthusiastically, commissioned abundantly, and painted himself. "I avidly studied the works in the palace collection of such masters as Lin ch'un, Pien luan, Huang Chüan . . . and applied myself to copying them," he wrote. "Yet I could merely imitate their form, not their grace or their elegance. Later, I came to realize that I had to look with my own eyes at the world of nature and not attempt copies of former artists."[2] The emperor was right, of course; but since he lacked real talent, even looking at the real world made very little difference.

He was, however, able to appreciate the art of his time. Kao Ch'i-p'ei's fingernail paintings or Ching-nung's nervous landscapes are the work of literati who revolted against the polished style of the Imperial Academy, but their witty, innovative distortions could only be appreciated by those already familiar with the brushwork techniques and calligraphic symbols of earlier schools. Thus, their originality was merely a reworking of convention, not a real break with the past, and served to amuse the jaded eye. There were also less sophisticated artists, who tried to paint just like their predecessors; indeed, the revival of earlier styles was an important element of their work. They painted landscapes of all sorts, some on a very large scale with distant mountains fading into the mist, others small and intimate with a tiny animal, a rabbit perhaps, in the foreground. Sometimes a cat is shown, sitting on a rocky ledge surrounded by small bamboos; a spiky, twisting branch with a flower or two can also be a sufficient subject. The skill of the artists involved in all this tends to be great; the subjects are both traditional and appealing, but there is a certain dryness to it all. What these conscientious men lacked was a feeling for the poetic.

As a result, the palace scenes have more life in them, while, at the same time, they remain fascinating documents. In these cheerfully colored works, the courtyards, gardens, and pavilions of luxurious compounds are depicted. Watercourses undulate, flowers give touches of brightness, splendidly dressed people stroll, recline, drink; and the whole enchanting world of the Chinese upper class spreads out, unchanged, before our eyes.

CENSORING THE PAST

Architecture, too, referred invariably to a model past. Visitors always found it impossible to date a palace or a temple because they were built to look as if they had always been there. There were no new purposes for the architects, no new types of construction, no new techniques, and no new ornaments. All was to be as it had always been. Thus, because the past was everywhere present, it mattered enormously, and so its culture was not only preserved, but manipulated to emphasize the legitimacy of the current dynasty. History was rewritten for propaganda purposes, not merely by commissioning new accounts, but by amending or suppressing older books that could, in the light of current politics, be considered subversive. Preservation thus went hand in hand with censorship, and when the Ch'ien-lung Emperor decided to save all the worthwhile books in existence—some thirty-six thousand volumes were to be copied and stored in the palace library—he quickly turned what had started out as an attempt to preserve the culture of the past into a literary inquisition.

Certain categories of books had always been banned in China: it was forbidden to write about magic, the supernatural, or sex; nor were philosophical texts allowed if they diverged from the official Confucian canon. Of course, people still wrote about these subjects, and books still circulated, but secretly. All this changed in 1772, when the order went out to collect for the imperial library all the texts that might otherwise be lost, copy them there, and return them to their place of origin. This vast collection, the emperor ordered, must include materials belonging to private owners as well as those to be found in libraries, administrations, and the shops of book dealers. By the end of August 1774, over ten thousand books had arrived in Peking. Because, however, the culture of the past was seen as having far greater weight than that of the present, the emperor also ordered that books thought inimical to the dynasty should be destroyed whenever they were found; and there were more of these than might be thought. Texts criticizing the Mongol dynasty (1279–1368), for instance, were subversive because, like the Manchus, the Mongols were foreigners who had seized the throne—even if these texts had been written well before the arrival of the Manchus. Equally, writings that praised the Ming dynasty were considered to be automatically anti-Manchu; and there were many other possibilities.

The emperor himself made it clear that his purpose was not only to save the culture of the past, but to sanitize it. "When the aforesaid officials received my previous edict," he announced in 1774, they should have sent meritorious books together with a list to the commission; had they noted [some containing] words or ideas of a seditious nature, they should have grouped them separately, wrapped them up carefully and submitted them to me with the suggestion that they be committed to the flames; or in their own precincts burned the books sending me a list for my information. Now, of the over ten thousand volumes submitted by the several provinces, none has been singled out as offensive. How is it possible that among such a quantity of books bequeathed by former generations, not one should contain a trace of sedition?[3]

And in case subversion was hard to recognize, there was a list of prohibited subjects. Books were to be seized and destroyed if they were anti-dynastic or rebellious; insulting to previous dynasties considered ancestral to the Ch'ing, or to the Mongol people; concerned with the north or northwest frontiers, the military, or general defense; if they contained quotes from prohibited authors; if they contained heterodox opinion on the Confucian canon; if they were written in an inferior or unliterary style; if the account they gave of the Manchu conquest was unfavorable to the Manchus; or if they concerned political parties which flourished at the end of the Ming dynasty.

That was quite a list of forbidden topics, and people who feared punishment suddenly developed a blind eye for the contents of their libraries. So the emperor took the process one step further. On December 11, 1774, he sent out a new decree. "Perhaps the families that collect books feared that penalties would be meted out and consequently did not submit any [subversive] volumes," he announced. "If certain people have volumes which should not be kept, they should hand them over . . . [and] no guilt will be attached to them."[4] And in case any doubt remained, by 1782 an index of proscribed titles was compiled and sent out to the provinces.

Even so, not everyone cooperated. Proclamations were posted everywhere, but still not enough subversive books were sent in. Clearly a house-to-house search, throughout China, was in order. "If we should merely order the local districts . . . to instruct the village headman to make an inquiry from house to house, we would perhaps be able to cover every place,"[5] the governor-general of Hukuang explained. This totalitarian attempt to control both the present and the past was largely successful: 2,320 books were listed for total suppression, 342 for partial suppression, and 476 were condemned but preserved.

By the end of the century, although the odd subversive volume remained unapprehended, the inquisition came to an end. The emperor had reason to be pleased, but much historical knowledge, particularly that concerning the fall of the Ming and the takeover of the Ch'ing, was lost, and so were many works of literature.

CIVILIZATION AND EMPIRE

Eradicating all possible sources of subversion also seemed important because China, being the center of civilization—indeed, being the only truly civilized country—must shine as a cultural beacon for the rest of the world. The letter sent by Ch'ien-lung to George III made it all very clear: "You, O King, from afar have yearned after the blessings of our civilization, and in your eagerness to come into touch with our converting influence, have sent an Embassy."[6] George III may have felt a little surprise when he read this; but had he known about the emperor's power to suppress subversive literature, he probably would have been envious.

That the king of England wanted to learn from China was an automatic assumption; that China had the right to invade and rule neighboring states seemed equally obvious. Tibet was a typical example of this. In 1792, after the Chinese army had invaded the country—in theory, to protect it from other invaders—the emperor issued a decree. "We are informed . . . that Ho-lin [Ho-shen's brother] is displaying great skill in the management of Tibetan affairs and does not kneel or kowtow to the Dalai Lama, who obeys every order that he may give. We are the more delighted to hear that Ho-lin is thus conscious of the dignity of the State because of late years Tibet has been steadily sinking into depths of barbarism and its government has degenerated into hopeless inefficacy."[7] China, happily, was there to set things in order, and while doing so, it took over the government. Obviously, a Tibet ruled by China must, by def-inition, be better off—a convenient justification for tyranny inside and aggres-sion outside, and one which, in Tibet particularly, is still in daily use by the Chinese government.

THE TRANSFER OF POWER

Early in 1796, the Ch'ien-lung Emperor, whose vigor, several years earlier, had so impressed Lord Macartney, decided to abdicate, not because he no longer wanted to rule, but in order to perform a spectacular act of filial piety. The K'ang-hsi Emperor had reigned exactly sixty years. His grandson now decided that by refusing to reign any longer he would prove his respect and devotion to the great ancestor. He therefore announced that he would abdicate in favor of his fifteenth son, shortly to become the Chia-ch'ing emperor. Of course, he was not running any real risk of losing power: a proper son would consult his father before acting, so the new emperor would be no more than a figurehead, while the senior emperor gained a reputation of extraordinary piety.

The Abdication Proclamation made this perfectly clear. "We have carried on our great heritage, pacified the entire realm, sought conscientiously to rule and been unsparingly diligent from day to day," the emperor announced. "The universe enjoys peace, the people enjoy happiness and abundance. . . . Meritorious accomplishments have exceeded expectation."[8] How then could his son fail properly to venerate so great and so meritorious a ruler? And indeed, until the Ch'ien-lung Emperor's death on February 7, 1799, it was he who actually ruled the empire. The Chia-ch'ing emperor performed the ceremonies, his father set policy and made appointments.

Still, the abdication ceremony was carried out with all the pomp characteristic of the Imperial Court, and the contemporary account runs to many pages. On the day itself, the imperial regalia was set before the Throne Hall, in which the abdication was to take place. The imperial palanquins and five state carriages were in readiness. They were to follow the parade of elephants, which wore caparisons in plaited yellow silk; bridles, halters, and cruppers set with jewels and hung with tassels and bells; and white leather saddle flaps painted with dragon and cloud motifs bordered with floral patterns. Other saddles were made of vermilion leather pointed in gold and surmounted by a gold-embossed bronze jewel casket. There were also ten splendidly outfitted processional horses bearing the imperial arms and insignia, while along the ceremonial route (entirely within the Forbidden City) the terraces had been decorated with ceremonial umbrellas. And naturally there were musicians playing ritual and processional airs.

In the Throne Hall itself, altar tables displayed the Abdication Proclamation, while a cushion had been placed in front of the throne, since the Chia-ch'ing Emperor was to kneel while accepting the succession. Naturally, there was a vast gathering of officials, each in the proper ceremonial costume. When, finally, the two emperors arrived, all those present went through the ritual kowtow—three kneelings, nine prostrations. The senior emperor sat on the throne, with his heir next to him. There was more music; then the princes and nobles took their place and kneeling officials read the proclamation, upon which the Chia-ch'ing Emperor knelt before the throne and was presented with the Great Seal by his father. He then left the hall, returned, kowtowed to his father along with the rest of the court, and went off to change into imperial robes, yellow with five dragons; upon which he returned yet again and received the kowtow. After that, came one more procession and a state banquet—strictly vegetarian, as was the Manchu style.

The next three years turned out to be a period of almost unbearable frustration for the new emperor. He could make no decision without first consulting his father, whom Ho-shen ruled more completely than ever. The Chia-ch'ing Emperor was thus forced to watch all the disasters of the White Lotus Rebellion without being able to do anything, a situation all the more painful in that he knew about the spread of corruption and the decadence of the state.

The death of the Ch'ien-lung Emperor must thus have come as a huge relief to his son; and once it happened, his successor wasted no time. Within six days, Ho-shen had been arrested, and an imperial proclamation explained exactly why.

> Ho-shen received extraordinary favors from His departed Majesty and was promoted from the low position of Imperial guardsman to the highest offices, which he has held for nigh on twenty years. His crimes are too grave to admit of possible pardon. . . . After the outbreak of the Hupei and Szechwan rebellion . . . my father used eagerly to await the news . . . sitting up until late into the night taking neither food nor sleep. But Ho-shen deceived him, deliberately suppressing and even falsifying reports from the field. . . .
>
> Ho-shen's property has just been examined. . . . Among his jewels and precious stones he has collected two hundred pearl necklaces, a number greatly exceeding those in the Imperial palace. He possesses one particular pearl far superior, both in size and lustre, to that worn by me in the Imperial hat of state. . . . Such a career of venality and corruption may be called unique . . . Ho-shen is a deep-dyed traitor, lost to all moral sense, who has betrayed his Sovereign and jeopardized the State.[9]

In its jumble of accusations, this proclamation is a fascinating document: owning a better pearl than the emperor is put on the same level as the failure of the campaign against the White Lotus; but that struck no one as odd. Lèse-majesté was an attack on the emperor's position as mediator between heaven and earth, and it disturbed the harmony, the cosmic balance considered essential for the well being of humankind. With his father gone, it was easy enough for the Chia-ch'ing Emperor to dispose of Ho-shen: in a magnanimous gesture, the new ruler allowed him to commit suicide instead of undergoing the punishment incurred by traitors, the death of a thousand cuts.

The next step was not so easy. Ho-shen had filled the bureaucracy, from top to bottom, with his followers. Dismissing them all would have utterly paralyzed the government; so the Chia-ch'ing Emperor replaced or downgraded a number of powerful administrators while retaining those of his father's advisers he trusted—his own former tutor, for instance, or the president of the Censorate. At the same time he called for open criticism of the way the administration functioned, and commanded officials to memorialize him directly and secretly so as to bypass the holdovers from the former regime; but it was already too late. Corruption had tainted not only the central government, but also the provincial administration—and those who were still busy taking bribes were not about to denounce themselves. Nor did the replacement and indictment of many high provincial officials really help. Even if their successors were, for a while, less dishonest, theft continued to be the rule at the subordinate levels.

The emperor also made reforms at his own court. The Ch'ien-lung Emperor's enormously costly southern trips were discontinued—but that had a drawback, as well. The emperor was now confined to the Forbidden City, the Summer Palace, and his hunting lodge at Jehol, and became so isolated from his own people as to be virtually unaware of their true condition. More successful was the attempt to cut the cost of the court; but even so, the support of the huge Imperial Household Department remained enormously expensive, and so did that of the now idle and useless Bannermen. To have dismissed these once elite troops would have been to admit that the military power of the Manchus was gone; so the pretense was kept up even though the state could hardly afford to do so. Effective reform would have required a complete reordering of the very bases of the imperial power, and only a genius—and a ruthless genius, at that—could have been expected to see the need and to provoke the enormous upheaval involved. The Chia-ch'ing Emperor was hardworking and conscientious, but he was no genius; and so China, in spite of all his good intentions, slipped deeper into the abyss of corruption and inefficiency.

The Radiance of the Dragon Throne

The Imperial Court in China had, for many centuries, been a place of dazzling splendor. Rituals mattered enormously, since they defined and preserved the emperor's unique status. The imperial family—the wives, concubines, siblings, cousins, and assorted relatives of the sovereign—stood, in varying degrees, within the sacred pale; the great nobles had their own status as did the officials, from grand councillors on down; and then there were the almost innumerable attendants, each performing his appointed function and kowtowing ceaselessly. Visitors naturally noticed this. John Barrow, who accompanied Lord Macartney as his secretary, and then wrote about what he had seen, naturally commented on it. "The incalculable numbers of the great officers of state, all robed in their richest silks, embroidered with the richest colors and tissued with gold and silver, the order, silence and solemnity with which they arrange and conduct themselves on public court days are the most commanding features on such occasions,"[10] he noted. The contrast with the noisy, often disorderly European courts was indeed striking, and Macartney felt it also. The ceremonies, Barrow added, were "performed with such silence and solemnity as in some measure to resemble the celebration of a religious mystery."[11] However odd Chinese customs might seem to visitors, there was no mistaking the aura of a twice-millenary civilization; and for the Chinese themselves, this was yet another proof that they were superior to the rest of the world.

This glamour did not stop with court rituals. Because of the month in which he reached the emperor, Macartney was received at the hunting park of Jehol instead of one of the palaces. Even so, the decor was anything but rough, Barrow noted.

The Emperor's tent or pavilion, which is circular . . . [is] about twenty five yards in diameter and is supported by a number of pillars, either gilded, painted or varnished according to their distance or position . . .

The materials and distribution of the furniture within at once displayed grandeur and elegance. The tapestry, the curtains, the carpets, the lanterns, the fringes, the tassels were disposed with such harmony, the colours so artfully varied, and the light and shade so judiciously managed, that the whole assemblage filled the eye with delight and diffused over the mind a pleasing serenity and repose undisturbed by glitter or affected embellishments.[12]

Although serene, the scene was anything but austere; and while among courtiers the greatest decorum prevailed, outside the tent acrobats, dancers, actors, and musicians were performing. And then, at night, came that ancient Chinese specialty, a display of fireworks.

A green chest five feet square was hoisted up by a pulley to the height of fifty or sixty feet above the ground. The bottom was so constructed as then suddenly to fall out and make way for twenty or thirty strings of lanterns inclosed in the box to descend from it, unfolding themselves from one another by degrees so as at last to form a collection of at least five hundred, each having a light of a beautifully coloured flame burning brightly within it. This devolution and development of lanterns (which appeared to me to be composed of gauze and paper) were several times repeated and every time exhibited a difference of colour and figure. On each side was a correspondence of smaller boxes, which opened in the like manner as the others, and let down an immense network of fire, with divisions and compartments of various forms and dimensions, round and square, hexagons, octagons and lozenges, which shone like the brightest burnished copper and flashed like prismatic lightening, with every impulse of the wind. The diversity of colours indeed with which the Chinese have the secret of clothing fire seems at least one of the chief merits of their pyrotechny. The whole concluded with a volcano, or general explosion and discharge of suns and stars, squibs, bouncers, crackers, rockets and grenadoes.[13]

A Luxury Trade

That spectacular display dazzled, but did not amaze, the English visitors. It seemed, after all, of a piece with what was already known about China: porcelain, lacquer, silks, furniture had already given the West a high idea of what might be expected from the emperor's realm. Although there were, by midcentury, a number of European porcelain manufactures, Chinese porcelain remained highly prized. This was true, of course, of the vases, plates, and platters of the earlier K'ang-hsi period, with their white ground and blue landscapes, architectural scenes, or vignettes from daily life. By the end of the eighteenth century, though, the polychrome porcelain, in which green (famille verte) or pink (famille rose) was the predominant color, had become particularly popular: more brilliant, if perhaps less refined, these lively and charming representations of life in China were just what people wanted to see. Then there was Chinese export porcelain, table services specially commissioned by rich Westerners and usually bearing their coats of arms. These tended to have a more European decor, since the buyers specified what they wanted, and most of them had a very limited imagination.

Lacquer was just as popular. It, too, was imitated in Europe, but the Chinese version was incomparably superior in clarity of color, refinement of decor, and perfection of surface. When the panels were big—often eight by three or four feet—they were made into screens, and were then extremely expensive. When they were smaller, they were used in furniture; and lacquer boxes were all the more desirable in that they were more affordable. In 1800, they were still as beautifully made as ever, but their decor had become even more complicated. Form crowded upon form, so that sometimes it would take a real effort to decipher the landscape or the clouds; but that was seen by the court as an improvement, as a proof of ever greater skill. Chinese silk, with its dragons, birds, butterflies, flowers, and clouds woven in bright, exotic colors, was also in great demand as a luxury fabric, either as a wall covering or for clothing worn by both sexes. The prince regent in England was an eager collector of all these beautiful things, and so were many other people.

A few pieces of furniture were also exported, but, being bulkier in an age of relatively small ships, they were not as much in demand. Nor, indeed, were they as beautiful as the porcelain, lacquer, or silk. Abandoning the harmonious forms and supremely elegant simplicity of the Ming period, Ch'ing furniture went in for curve upon curve, twist upon twist, endless tortured detail and very dark woods. While, unquestionably, these pieces could only have been made by highly skilled craftsmen, they now seem like attempts at proving just how many finicky complications can be contained by a few square inches of arm or leg.

A Dazzling Palace

Thus, when the British Embassy arrived in China, it discovered much that was strange—including a great deal of the architecture—but the decor, at least, seemed familiar. Since the emperor was away, the visitors did not see much of the Forbidden City, but they were taken on a tour of the Yüan-ming-yüan, the Garden of Perfect Brightness, as the Summer Palace was named. It was, of course, not a palace in the Western sense, but a series of pavilions with roofs covered in yellow, blue green, turquoise, or purple tiles and lavishly frescoed walls and galleries. All this was set in an immense park, complete with a lake,

View in the Eastern side of the Imperial Park at Gehol.

The Summer Palace outside Peking. Outdoors, its lakes, pavilions, bridges, and islands made it an idyllic spot; indoors, the most refined luxury prevailed. (*General Research Division, The New York Public Library, Astor, Lenox and Tilden Foundations*)

islands—one had the emperor's private apartments, together with those of the empress and the concubines—as well as a wide variety of gardens and a vast area carefully designed to look like untamed nature. There were bridges and gazebos, sports grounds and areas reserved to deer and other decorative animals. Some pavilions were used for official business—the Throne Hall, the courthouses, the offices of the ministries—while others were the residence of the imperial family. Some gardens were enclosed and could be viewed from a pavilion made just for sitting at a particular time of day. On the islands and the banks of the lakes, more pleasure pavilions could be used for anything from a banquet to the contemplation of the sunset reflected in the water. This array even included a vast baroque fountain designed by one of the three court Jesuits, and a (sort of) Western-style building where European objects (clocks, mostly) were kept.

The entrance to this huge compound was shielded by a masonry screen 137 feet long and 15 feet high, painted red with dragons and topped by a coping made of yellow tiles—these being used exclusively in the imperial palaces. Then came the great palace gate whose elaborate roof had the usual up-curved eaves and whose lacquered red doors were studded with gilt knobs. Large bronze lions stood guard at either side. The first buildings were all official—reception rooms, halls for the courts and ministries. They, in turn, led to a curved moat crossed by a white marble bridge. On the other side was the second principal gate, flanked by gilt dragons; and within the gate were several waiting rooms; and then, across a courtyard, stood the Throne Hall, with doors of red lacquer held by gilt hinges and columns carved, embossed, and lacquered with golden twisting dragons and multicolored, wavy clouds.

Like all visitors, Barrow was properly impressed.

> The principal hall of audience stood upon a platform of granite raised about four feet above the level of the court. A row of large wooden columns surrounding the building supported the projecting roof; and a second row within the first and corresponding with it . . . served for the walls of the room. The upper part of these walls was a kind of lattice-work, covered over with large sheets of oiled paper, and was capable of being thrown entirely open on public occasions. The wooden columns had no capitals, the only architrave was the horizontal beam that supported the rafters of the roof. This . . . was . . . a broad screen of wood fastened between the upper parts of the columns, painted with the most vivid colors of blue, green and red, and interlaced with gilding . . .
>
> The length of this room was a hundred and ten feet, the breadth forty two and the height twenty feet; the ceiling, painted with circles, squares and polygons, whimsically disposed and loaded with a great variety of colours. The floor was paved with gray marble flagstones, laid checker-wise. The throne, placed in a recess, was supported by rows of pillars painted red. . . . It consisted entirely of wood, not unlike mahogany, the carving of which was exquisitely fine. The only furniture was a pair of brass kettle-drums, two large paintings, two pairs of ancient blue porcelain vases, a few volumes of manuscripts and a table at the end of the room on which was placed an old English chiming.[14]

That old English clock was a typical oddity. It played, according to Macartney, "twelve old English tunes, the 'Black Joke,' 'Lillibullero' and other airs of the 'Beggar's Opera.' It was decorated in a wretched old taste, with ornaments of crystal and coloured stones, but had been, I dare say, very much admired in its time."[15] The "wretched old taste" was the rococo: in this neoclassical age it was considered both old-fashioned and hideous, but the Chinese, not being slaves to fashion, undoubtedly still thought it beautiful. Indeed, they loved clocks, and since they were unable to make them themselves, they cheerfully imported as many as possible.

The Throne Hall's relative paucity of furniture was suitable to its purpose as a gathering place. In the imperial apartments and the many pavilions scattered throughout the park, on the contrary, objects of all kinds were accumulated: not just porcelain and lacquer, but also huge vases made of jasper or agate, jade objects, jeweled boxes, screens of all kinds, gold, jade, as well as a variety of mechanical toys, music boxes, and scientific instruments—spheres, orreries, and others. As for the landscape, it, too, was infinitely varied. The lakes, which had been artificially created, were given highly complex, irregular shapes, with many bays and promontories, so as to provide the greatest possible variety of landscapes. Each of the islands was a world in itself—some hilly, some flat, some forested, others full of flowers; and on the water, a whole splendid fleet, complete with flags and streamers, awaited the emperor's pleasure. Then, on the mainland, many of the hundreds of pavilions were linked by arbors, passages cut through huge, fantastically shaped rocks or delicately designed galleries.

USEFUL FOREIGNERS

Except for the clocks, the baroque fountain and the semi-Western palace, all this had been designed by Chinese architects, painters, and designers; but just as the Europeans loved the exoticism of Chinese objects, so did the Chinese like the strange talents of Westerners, clock making and astronomy first and foremost. The emperor, therefore, usually had a few foreigners at his court— only a few, of course, since, for all their specialized knowledge, they remained barbarians. On occasion, though, when the supply looked like drying up, the Ch'ien-lung emperor ordered up more. In May 1781, for instance, he wrote the Viceroy of Kwangtung: "Previously, whenever the Westerners wished to come to Peking to serve us, the viceroy of Kwangtung accordingly memorialized us on their behalf. In recent years, very few [such] persons wish to serve us. . . . If there are men from Europe coming to Kwangtung, he should search them out, memorialize us and send them to Peking."[16]

Still, it was possible to have too much of a good thing. In January 1785, Ch'ien-lung made this quite clear. "Because Westerners in the Imperial capital were diminishing in numbers, we ordered the Viceroy of Liang-Kwang . . . to . . . send several Westerners to Peking. Last year, two Westerners . . . and another; this year, four Westerners . . . and two others came to Peking. Now we have enough Westerners in our service. Hereafter, they are no longer to be chosen and sent to Peking."[17] It is hard not to feel that for the emperor, Westerners were a commodity: you wanted a sufficient supply, but not so many of them that they would clutter up the place.

THE PROPER ORDER OF LIFE

The splendor achieved by the court, and many magnates, depended, as we have seen, on order. People knew their place and their role; there were none of the raucous disputes or the lack of discipline that made life in Europe so much less serene. Naturally, therefore, there were rules. Salutations were a case in point: far from leaving anything to chance, there were eight different grades of greetings, ranging from the one offered a not terribly important equal (hands joined before one's chest), moving on to the addition of a deep bow, to kneeling with one bent knee, to full kneeling, to kneeling and striking the ground with one's forehead, all the way to the full kowtow (three kneelings, nine full prostrations) that was due to the emperor alone. And, of course, everyone knew precisely which form of greeting was appropriate in any circumstance.

The same precise rules applied to clothes; they may not have made the man, but they certainly defined him. It started with the most universally visible sign of the Manchu conquest, the queue. "All the Chinese . . . have their heads close-shaved, except on the crown where the hair is left untouched by the razor for about a couple of inches in diameter and is suffered to grow to a great length," Macartney observed. "It is plaited in a tress and falls down the back. I have seen some of them a yard long."[18] This hairdo was not a matter of choice: it was the mark that distinguished the Manchus from the Chinese, and was enforced by imperial decree.

The Realm of the Golden Lotus

Another major difference between the two peoples was foot-binding. The Chinese did it, the Manchus never; so the Empresses, the princesses, and the concubines were able to walk normally. For most Chinese women, though, foot-binding was not a matter of choice. In a society where the family was everything and remaining unmarried was not a possibility, mothers knew that their daughters would not find a husband if their feet had not been bound.

This appalling custom had probably begun in the twelfth century, when girls' feet had been bound to make them look narrower and more elegant. By the eighteenth century, when a woman's foot—her "golden lotus"—was supposed to be no more than three inches in length, it had become a lifelong torture. The first six to eight years were the worst; after that, at least, the foot stopped growing so that the pain was less, although the deformation made it impossible for women to walk without help. Binding usually began at the age of five or six. The bandage was two inches wide and ten feet long. One of its ends was placed inside the instep and carried over the toes so as to force the toes inward and toward the sole, only the large toe being left unbound. The bandage was then wrapped around the heel so forcefully that heel and toes were drawn closely together. The process was then repeated until the entire bandage had been applied, the object being to make the toes bend under and into the sole.

The pain felt by the little girls on whom this barbaric practice was inflicted was so bad that, frequently, they were unable to sleep for nights on end. The flesh of the toes and foot often became putrescent during the process, so that portions of it sloughed off from the sole, and one or more toes frequently dropped off. At the best of times, the feet were one mass of infection, with pus oozing steadily out. After three years of this treatment, the feet, although still painful, were almost dead, but they usually went on growing, so it was not till the age of fourteen or so that the worst of the pain was over. Then, for the rest of their lives, women suffered at least grave discomfort. Infections were frequent, the lack of mobility permanent; and because the leg muscles were hardly used, Chinese women tended to have semi-atrophied, spindly legs.

The question, of course, was why all this was done. Mothers of every social class felt they had to bind their daughters' feet to preserve their desirability as wives; so that left the ultimate responsibility to the men, and they unquestionably wanted women to have bound feet. One explanation was that it was a way of ensuring fidelity: women could hardly be keeping assignations if they were unable to walk; they could not ask a lover home without being seen by the servants or the neighbors; and they could not go off in a litter without the bearers knowing about it.

On the face of it, the explanation makes a perverse sort of sense; but it is most likely not the real one. In fact, bound feet were considered to be the most sexually arousing part of a woman's body. Of course, there were other theories. "Foot-binding had a physical influence on a woman's body," a Taiwanese physician explained in the 1930s. "Her swaying walk attracted male attention. When the foot-bound woman went walking, the lower part of her body was in a state of tension. This caused the skin and flesh of her legs and also the skin and flesh of her vagina to become tighter."[19]

That is, at the least, a highly suspect explanation. The truth is that lotus feet were considered essential to the man's sexual enjoyment. Because they were always covered by bandages and shoes, unwrapping them and bathing them reputedly drove men wild; they were caressed, kissed, licked, sucked; their contact with a man's sexual organs was thought to be an indescribable pleasure, so that actual intercourse seemed rather less exciting; and, of course, there were (banned) books describing in detail just what you could do with a golden lotus. Indeed, it is difficult to think of a better way to reduce a woman to the status of a pure object: after all, no one has ever fallen in love with the spiritual qualities of a maimed foot.

Foot-binding, by 1800, was not limited to the upper classes. Merchants' wives, even some peasant women, had their feet bound; so did many daughters of very poor parents: it was the necessary requisite to life as a successful prostitute. All across China, women hobbled on burning, crippled feet—Chinese women, that is, but not Manchus. From the very beginning the emperors strictly forbade the practice for their own people; they tried forbidding it for the Chinese as well, but they were simply disobeyed. Even so, Manchu women longed for small feet, so they wore two-story shoes. The top level, well hidden under the robe or trousers, was the real shoe; then underneath, a fake small shoe that appeared below the hem gave the sought-for illusion.

Unchanging Fashion

There were rules about women's feet, there were rules about men's hair, and there were also rules about clothing—but these only applied at court. Elsewhere, people could wear what they pleased, and costumes ranged from wide trousers stopping at mid-calf, worn with a loose, hip-length coat slit at the sides and a straw hat for laborers, street vendors, and the poor to loose trousers and long brocade robes, lined with fur in winter, for the rich and the scholars. As for the women, they, too, wore trousers, with a three-quarter-length, fairly loose tunic opening in front to show a floor-length apron. What differed greatly, though, was the coiffure: men wore hats, usually black for the upper classes, and made, according to the season, of straw, silk, or fur. Women had highly elaborate headdresses with many jeweled ornaments set on little springs or pins so that their heads were crowned with precious, multicolored ornaments.

Outside the court, people were free to wear any color (except golden yellow, which was reserved for the emperor), any of a wide variety of designs, whether woven or embroidered, and coats of any shape and length they chose. At court, however, they had no choice at all. Men and women alike wore trousers; men topped them with a hip-length coat with very broad, very long sleeves that fully covered the hands (this was in part a precaution against assassination attempts: it was almost impossible to stab someone if your hands were entangled in your sleeves). Under the coat, two floor-length aprons overlapped at the sides, while the women's coat was floor length and sleeveless. Men and women alike wore the *p'i ling,* a wide triangular collar flowing over the shoulders with its point reaching up in the back of the neck; and for men, there was a black hat with a colored top and the prescribed stone as central ornament.

This uniformity of line did not make for a uniformity of appearance, however: there were many possible colors and designs, all strictly regulated, and all meaningful. Yellow, the imperial color, symbolized the center of the earth; green or blue and dragons stood for the east; red and the phoenix for the south; white and the tiger for the west; black and the tortoise for the north. As a result, red was worn for weddings, and white for funerals (the sun dies every evening in the west), while the coats of the imperial family were decorated with clouds of five colors (often pink, pale blue, light green, violet, and dark yellow).

Formal dress at court had always been carefully defined. Typically, the Ch'ien-lung Emperor, who loved order and magnificence, came forth with an elaborate new dress code. Rank was made visible by the insignia embroidered on the front of the coat. For the emperor, that meant four medallions with front-facing, four-clawed dragons as well as emblems of the sun and the moon; the background color was bright yellow and the front of his hat was adorned with a large pearl—hence, of course, the Chia-ch'ing Emperor's indignation when it turned out that Ho-shen owned a larger pearl. The Heir Apparent's coat was orange; he, too, was allowed four medallions, and he wore a ruby in his hat. A prince of the first degree wore brown; and so it went. Of course, there were other decorations as well. A Manchu prince's brown coat, for instance, could be embroidered not just with his regulation dragons in gold, white, and red, but also with multicolored clouds, mountains, waves, and little dragon friezes at the waist and bottom of the coat. Waves, symbolized by broad slanted lines, were a popular ornament; they often took up as much as a quarter of the coat (always the bottom) and were embroidered in a dazzling variety of shades—blue, green, purple, red, white.

A princess's costume was almost as formally regulated: she, too, was entitled to dragons, but she could choose her own colors. Thus a dark blue coat could be embroidered with gold dragons, red flames, light-blue and white clouds, with more gold at the hems, multicolored bats, and yellow, red, blue, and green waves at the bottom. The empress, of course, was entitled to wear yellow.

Formal court dress was necessary only for a few major rituals and the most important ceremonies. The rest of the time, the virtually unregulated semiformal costume prevailed, but it was just as sumptuous. An empress (probably Chia-ch'ing's) had a black coat decorated with circles, dragons, and bats in blue, red, green, white, and gold, with white, red, gold, and blue mountains and a wide bottom border of waves in blue, pink, orange, and green—altogether a dazzling sight. And, of course, for the emperor, even semiformal dress was yellow—in one case, with blue, white, and red dragons and clouds, blue mountains with white and yellow highlights, and, at the bottom, blue, white, and red waves. To this a good deal of jewelry could be added—pearl necklaces for the emperor, and precious ornaments for one and all.

Unlike the West, China simply did not have fashions. The court costume worn in 1800 could have been made in 1700 or 1900; the shape of the coats, trousers, aprons, and collars never changed, nor did the decoration: like architecture, clothing was meant to reflect an unalterable perfection. Perhaps more surprising, this was also true of informal clothing. Occasionally, for a celebration, a new decor might be designed, but its elements—dragons, clouds, bats, cranes, waves—were the same. And while Chinese silks, embroidery, and clothing struck Westerners as being sumptuous and beautiful, Western clothing was considered grotesque by the Chinese, who found both silk stockings and powdered wigs utterly comical. Since clothes, to a significant degree, defined their wearer, the Chinese thus found themselves confirmed in their opinion: Westerners were not merely barbarians, they were also grotesque.

PRIVATE LIVES, PUBLIC PLEASURES

It was, however, not very easy to see well-dressed people in China: unlike European palaces, which were open to all decently dressed persons, the Forbidden City and the other imperial residences were reserved to the court. Private ceremonies, from weddings to banquets, took place in the compounds of the wealthy, and richly dressed people did not walk in the streets. The litters in which they were conveyed were not such that people could look into them: for all the crowds, life remained essentially private. The streets might be teeming, the numerous poor might live in public, but anyone with any resources could enjoy the most complete privacy, just so long as the presence of numerous relatives continued to be taken for granted.

It was a poor family indeed whose house had only one courtyard. All through the better areas of Peking, blank walls, occasionally interrupted by closed gateways, stretched endlessly; and behind, just as in the Forbidden City, there were many pavilions separated by many courts and many gardens. Some of these buildings were service areas—kitchens, larders, toolsheds, servant quarters; others, usually in the second courtyard, were reception rooms, while farther away from the entrance came the family rooms and the gardens. Usually, these great compounds housed more than one generation and more than one branch of the family—everyone from the great-grandparents to the newest babies, uncles, aunts, cousins. And always the oldest member of the family was treated with the almost fawning respect deemed appropriate for the Ancestor.

Courtyards and pavilions: it was all much the same at court, except that sections of the Forbidden City were reserved for the Household Department's offices; but there, too, the great ceremonial lineup of central halls was sharply differentiated from the compounds of the several members of the imperial family. Today, after the inroads made by the bad taste of the late-nineteenth-century rulers and a variety of depredations, the area of the Forbidden City once reserved for the emperor and his immediate family has the dingy look of preserved Victoriana, dust and all; but a piece of the late eighteenth century at least has survived—the Ch'ien-lung Emperor's garden. Completely surrounded by walls, decorated with fantastically shaped rocks and rare trees, it looks just like one of those landscape paintings of which the emperor was so fond; and in the marble floor of the pavilion, a winding channel was filled with slow-moving water on which cups of wine floated gently to the emperor and his guests. Here, at the very center of power, was an idyllic retreat where every carefully contrived view was such that beauty was everywhere. Being enclosed, the garden is perfectly private and, being artfully designed, it seems very much larger and more spacious than it actually is.

Retreats like this were used for two essential activities: philosophical talk, and the composing and reciting of poetry. The discussion of Confucian precepts (always keeping within the limits of the strictest orthodoxy) was a key part of the life of any cultured person, from the emperor down to the local landowner. As for poetry, it was the very life breath of this group, and that meant both enjoying the delights of famous texts and composing on the spot. A theme would be set, and every member of the party was expected to improvise a poem that followed all the rules. Because this was so frequent an activity, there were special places for it: they had to be quiet, serenely beautiful if possible, and always removed from the bustle of court or family life. Paintings, too, might be shown at these sessions, the scrolls unrolled slowly to reveal scene after scene, each of which was then discussed at length. As for the women, they stayed among themselves—except, of course, for the occasional courtesan.

Not all entertainment was so private, however. The theater was public, except for the one in the Forbidden City, which was reserved for the emperor and his attendants. Many of the plays were good-natured farces in which mistaken identity was often a major factor; but there were also high-toned tragedies about historical subjects that appealed more to the numerous cognoscenti than to the regular audiences. As for the opera, it, too, prospered. Highly formalized, its performances often lasted for several hours, its characters and music following well-understood conventions. This was an art form for the educated who could distinguish often subtle nuances; and much attention was paid to the talent of the actors and singers, especially those (always men) who played women's parts. Grace, and a femininity so artful as to be more convincing than the real thing, were expected of them; and the spectacle was fascinating even for foreigners. Félix Sainte-Croix, a Frenchman who visited China in 1804, found "the costumes very rich and beautiful," and added: "The actors seemed highly talented but the music overwhelms the singing. . . . It accompanies both gesture and voice."[20]

There were also private theatricals, Sainte-Croix noted.

> It is the custom, among the rich to have a play during resting hours. Dinner . . . was served [at a rich merchant's house in Canton] and the actors began. [The actors were] children, all between ten and twelve years old . . . who performed with much intelligence. . . . The leaps and acrobatics of this little troupe are the most extraordinary I have ever seen. . . . Imagine twenty-four children standing on one another's shoulders and forming a pyramid with twelve of them at the base, one at the top. Then, at a sign, they all leap off while somersaulting backwards.

As the Chinese guests grew pleased with the performers, they threw on to the stage little red bags filled with money.[21]

Of course, "play" is hardly the word for this sort of entertainment—watching acrobatics hardly strained the spectators' intelligence—but then merchants, who could become very rich, and whose work was beginning to transform the economy of China, were never literati: they wanted tumblers, not classical verse.

The emphasis, when the arts proper were concerned, was on culture, not the pleasures of the flesh; but, of course, rich men had concubines as well as wives. Courtesans, ranging from simple streetwalkers (with normal feet) to the most refined foot-bound young women, abounded, and they did a thriving business. There was nothing shameful in resorting to the services of a prostitute, and men never hesitated to do so. As for the wives, most of whom were, in any event, quite unaware of what their husbands did outside the family compound, it never would have occurred to them that they ought to complain. Prostitutes, after all, were just temporary concubines.

REFINED GASTRONOMY

Almost as important as sex was eating. Food in China (rather like in France) mattered enormously. Inviting people to a meal was among the key social activities of the prosperous, and the meal reflected directly on both the taste and the resources of the host. Great banquets were an accepted way of consolidating one's position, whether in a provincial town or at court. Very occasionally, these spectacular displays might even arouse the emperor's displeasure because of their excess. Indeed, visible spending sometimes seemed almost more important than the actual food, so that a single one of these formal meals might cost hundreds of taels, especially if a delicacy like birds' nests was served. Naturally, there were also intimate parties where a few friends met, and if they were gourmets, the dishes were subtle and recherché. Finally for most of the population, food was what you ate to survive—rice and a few vegetables for most peasants and the urban poor, an occasional meat or fish dish for the lower middle class.

Food itself was not cheap. China was a world in which a poor peasant needed 50 cash a day to survive (there were 1,000 cash in a tael). A boatman earned 80 cash a day; a soldier 1,600 cash a month, plus 10 measures of rice each worth 130 cash, for a total of about 3 taels a month, or 100 cash a day. In contrast, the budget of Anhui Province ran to 180,000 taels a year, while the government in Peking took in about 35 million, Ho-shen had accumulated property worth nearly 80 million, and a frugal governor expected to get by

on 6,000 taels a year—though most of them spent many times that on conspicuous consumption and display. For rich and poor alike, though, rice, the most
basic, most universal staple, cost 1,300 cash per shish (133 pounds), or about 10
cash a pound. Millet, the essential ingredient in another basic dish, a kind of
porridge, was 1,050 cash per shish; wheat, not as widely used, was 1,200 cash,
while red beans could be had for 800.

At those prices, a peasant was not likely to get much more than rice or
millet. Certainly most fruit was well beyond his income: a single orange cost
50 cash, a peach or an apple 30, fresh grapes or cherries 60 per chin (1.33
pounds). Milk was also expensive—50 cash per chin, or about 80 cash a quart;
but butter was worse—180 cash a chin. That can be explained by the fact that
in an already overpopulated China, cattle was growing scarce; but sugar was up
to 100 cash a chin. At least soy was cheap—12 cash—and so was vinegar—
8 cash.

Naturally, meat was only for the well-to-do. A pig cost 2,500 cash—fifty
days' worth of a peasant's income; a pound of pork could be had for 50 cash, a
pound of mutton for 60. This was cheap compared to the price of a goose—520
cash; a duck—360; a chicken—120; or even an egg, at 3.5 cash. You could buy
venison strips for the huge sum of 120 cash a chin. Dried fish was even worse
at 300 cash. In contrast, it is interesting to note that under the Ch'ien-lung
Emperor, the imperial household needed 400,000 eggs a year (worth 1,400 taels,
but perhaps there was a discount for bulk); 750,000 shish of cereals (nearly
45,000 tons), which went to feed not only the court, but its schools, administration, and, of course, its horses; and only 1,000 chin of wine, about 750 quarts.

Presumably, that vast quantity of cereals included rice, millet, wheat,
and buckwheat; and the Household Department also bought (or sometimes
received from the badly run imperial farms) those other staples—yams, soy-
beans, mung beans, and peanuts, as well as ginger, garlic, onions, cinnamon,
and red pepper—that were all considered to be essential. The vegetables, however, were few: malva, amaranth, mustard greens, turnips, radishes, mush-
rooms, and, of course, Chinese cabbage. The rich—and that obviously included
the court—ate a fair amount of meat, including pork, dog, beef, mutton, venison, goose, duck, chicken, and pheasant. Fresh fish was an essential ingredient
of haute cuisine, and very expensive. And, of course, there were wide regional
variations: what grew well in the south often did not grow at all in the north,
food was spicier in the south, game more abundant on the borders.

Except among the poor and the peasants—who ate what they could,
when they could, and often went hungry—food was part of the vast and complex system that in the Chinese view, kept the universe in balance. Just as there
was yin and yang, so, it was held, meals must consist of both *fan* (starch and
grains) and *tsai* (vegetable and meat) dishes: in that sense, a dumpling was the
perfect food in that it combined *fan* and *tsai* in one mouthful. There was not
much you could do to make the flavor of *fan* exciting, even if it was an essential

staple; *tsai*, on the other hand, could offer a world of mixed flavors because many of its dishes were composed of several meats, vegetables, and spices. Dishes made with fresh ingredients were, however, never served alone: abundant and diverse preserves figured at every meal. Meats, fish, and vegetables could be salted, smoked, sugared, steeped in brine, pickled, dried, or soaked in soy sauce, and they added to the already broad range of flavors provided by the *tsai* dishes.

Just as in Paris, course followed course, with vast quantities of food served to guests who expected to spend several hours at table, so in China abundance and variety were the keynote of any formal meal. Barrow was impressed by the "vast variety of made dishes very neatly dressed and served in porcelain bowls. The best soup I ever tasted . . . was made here from an extract of beef seasoned with a preparation of soy and other ingredients," he noted—the soup coming, of course, at the end of the meal. "Their vermicelli is excellent," he continues, "and all their pastry is unusually light and white as snow. . . . Although they drink their tea and other beverages warm, they prefer all kinds of fruit when cooled on ice."[22] A normal, not ostentatious dinner party consisted of sixteen dishes, eight platters of fried foods, and four desserts; but many meals were far more abundant.

The setting was as important as the food: the idea was to please as many senses as possible. Sainte-Croix noticed it when he was invited to dinner by a merchant in Canton. There were in the garden, he wrote,

> several ponds partly enclosed by galleries and very clean, tastefully furnished, airy rooms which all looked out on the water . . .
>
> [The garden] was deliciously picturesque, with grottoes, rocks, vases, fountains, pots of flowers. . . . At five, we sat down to dinner . . . [warm rice was set on the table, then] we were served at least two hundred different dishes . . . all in little saucers. . . . Dessert, to the contrary of our custom, is served first.

And then, like the typical Frenchman he was, he added: "All these dishes seemed delicious to those who were used to them; but no European will ever like them."[23] Happily for all these highly skilled and well-paid Chinese cooks, there were several hundred million people who did appreciate their efforts.

Chief among them was the Ch'ien-lung Emperor. He expected to be served the best, most refined food; but even so, his everyday meals were hardly excessive. In Europe, every dish coming to the table contained a quantity of food; in China, each bowl would only hold barely two or three mouthfuls, so that when the emperor's dinner consisted (as it usually did) of seven main courses and three dishes of pastries, he was not in fact eating all that much. A typical dinner might consist of a dish of fat chicken, pot-boiled duck, and bean curd; a dish of swallows' nest with strips of smoked duck; a bowl of clear soup; a dish of strips of pot-boiled chicken; a dish of smoked fat chicken with Chinese cabbage; a dish of salted duck and pork; and a dish of court-style fried chicken. The pastries were bamboo-stuffed steamed dumplings, rice cakes, and rice cakes with honey, while the pickles consisted of Chinese cabbage pickled in wine, cucumbers preserved in soy, and pickled eggplant; and with it all there was boiled rice.

That was one of the emperor's private meals; but on the ceremonial occasions that occurred throughout the year, banquets were held, and like everything else, they were elaborately regulated. There were six classes of banquets. For a class one banquet, for instance, the cooks were expected to use 120 chin of white flour, 8 chin of bean flour, 150 hen's eggs, 18 chin of white sugar, 4 chin of white honey, 6 chins of sesame, and a variety of fresh and dried fruit. For a class six banquet, the quantity of flour dropped down to 20 chin, that of sugar to 2.8 chin, and there were no eggs. Because these were Manchu-style banquets, the food was strictly vegetarian, a practice the Chinese thought odd and annoying. On less formal occasions, though, the court indulged in standard, Chinese-style banquets.

The food was naturally not the main attraction at an imperial banquet: just being there, and being close to the emperor, mattered far more. At the other end of the scale, though, there were places where anyone with money could be sure of a welcome: already by 1800, restaurants were numerous, good, and popular. They also tended to be expensive. Thus a dinner consisting of nine standard dishes might cost 900 cash per person, or 1,080 if those were large dishes. A more generous host would order eleven dishes, which might comprise mixed cut meats, pig's trotters, venison, dumplings, mussels, shark's fins, several fresh fish dishes, chicken, and preserved eggs; for six people that would mean spending about 8 taels, a very large sum—the equivalent, for a peasant, of 160 days of work.

Significantly, this menu does not include swallows' nest, the greatest and most costly delicacy of all, or sea slug; but shark's fin was itself considered a rare treat. Still, for a true gourmet, it was quality, not cost, that really mattered. Yüan Mei made that very clear in his *Book of Cookery*. Published in 1824, it addressed all the great issues of Chinese cuisine and vigorously denounced vulgar lavishness.

> A good cook cannot with the utmost application produce more than four successful dishes in one day, and even then it is hard for him to give proper attention to detail; and he certainly won't get through unless everything is in the right place, and he is on his feet the whole time. It is no use to give him a lot of assistants: each will have his own ideas and there will be no proper discipline. The more help he gets, the worse the results will be. I once dined with a merchant. There were three successive sets of dishes and sixteen different sweets. Altogether more than forty kinds of food were served. My host regarded the dinner as an enormous success. But when I got home, I was so hungry that I ordered a bowl of plain rice-gruel. From this it may be imagined how little there was, despite the profusion of dishes, that was at all fit to eat.[24]

That it should have been a merchant who gave this dinner is significant: the newly rich traders, always denounced as uncouth for all their success, were generally despised by more sophisticated persons. Happily, however, Yüan Mei went on to instruct the reader in the proper principles:

> I always say that chicken, pork, fish and duck are the original geniuses of the board, each with a flavor of its own, each with its distinctive style; whereas sea-slug and swallows' nest (despite their costliness) are commonplace fellows with no character—in fact, mere hangers on. I was once asked to a party given by a certain governor, who gave us plain boiled swallows' nest, served in enormous vases, like flower pots. It had no taste at all. The other guests were obsequious in their praise of it, but I said: "We are here to eat swallows' nest, not to take delivery of it wholesale." If our host's object was simply to impress, it would have been better to put a hundred pearls in each bowl. Then we should have known that the meal had cost him tens of thousands, without the unpleasantness of being expected to eat what was uneatable.[25]

Yüan Mei was obviously a true gourmet. Even so, his argument is convincing: ostentation was beginning to replace culinary refinement, quantity mattering more than quality, and expense more than taste. It is also telling that his host should have been a governor. All those swallows' nests had almost certainly been paid for with money received in bribes or stolen from tax receipts. The deterioration in gastronomy was yet another sign of the breakdown in the government resulting from Ho-shen's tenure.

THE NUMBERS OF POWER

Great civilizations do not collapse quickly. Although rotting at the core, the empire still looked strong and prosperous. The very size of its population—more than 300 million—seemed to confirm that it was indeed mighty. The emperor might know that all was not well, but he still thought of his country as incomparably the greatest on earth; and the few foreigners who saw anything of China understood little or nothing about the decay of its government. What they saw, instead, was a vast population manifesting its willing and perfect obedience to the emperor's government. All, apparently, was in perfect order.

The very life of the two cities visited by foreigners, Canton and Peking, offered abundant proof of civil peace and prosperity. "The police of the Capital," Barrow noted,

> is so well regulated, that the safety and tranquillity of the inhabitants is seldom disturbed. At the end of every cross street, and at certain distances in it, are a kind of cross-bars with sentry-boxes at each of which is placed a soldier, and few of these streets are without a guard-house. Besides, the proprietor or inhabitant of every tenth house takes in turn to keep the peace . . . If any

riotous company should assemble, or any disturbances happen within his district, he is to give immediate information thereof to the nearest guard-house. . . . The soldiers also go their rounds and . . . strike upon a short tube of bamboo which gives a dull, hollow sound.[26]

This quiet and peaceful city must have seemed like a dream to an Englishman. London, in 1800, was dangerous, dirty, and seldom quiet. Violent riots were always possible; and there were no police; thus, in comparison, Peking seemed a very paradise.

Not only were the cities well policed, they were also clean. Night soil was removed daily for use as a fertilizer, so there was none of the stink pervading most European cities. Cheap prostitution, so visible in every Western capital, here seemed absent—and so did venereal diseases. There were courtesans, of course, some of whom were at the top of their profession (just like in Europe), and cheaper women; but even these last seemed to maintain a high degree of decorum. Commenting on the houseboats moored in the river at Canton, Sainte-Croix noticed those of the prostitutes. "Some of them are very elegant," he wrote, "with rooms better adorned than those of the richest houses [Sainte-Croix had never visited a great noble household]. Prices vary according to the women's beauty and talent; they sing and play musical instruments."[27] He adds, with an almost audible sigh of regret, that they are not allowed to entertain any European clients.

All that was impressive enough; but it was the animation, the visible prosperity of the great cities that amazed the foreigners. The streets, in Peking, were wide and clean. They were lined with shops whose goods were set out at the edge of the sidewalk, with great pillars and gilt inscriptions describing the wares and praising the reputation of the merchant; and the whole scene was not just animated but literally colorful. "To attract more notice," Barrow wrote, "[the shops] were generally hung with various coloured flags and streamers and ribbands from top to bottom, exhibiting the appearance of a line of shipping dressed, as we sometimes see them, in the colours of all the different nations in Europe. The sides of the houses were not less brilliant in the several colours with which they were painted, consisting generally of a blue or a green mixed with gold."[28] All that was proof enough of prosperity—indeed, there were few shops in London that could rival these—but that was not all: there were also the people.

Only established merchants had shops; but the streets were also lined with the movable workshops of tinkers, barbers, and blacksmiths, all busily plying their trade. Tents and booths were set up to serve tea, fruit, and the equivalent of fast food. Then, in the middle of the streets, was the crowd: thousands of people, some singly; others, who carried flags and umbrellas, as part of the retinue of an important person. Carts rumbled through, sedan chairs were carried along. Dromedaries brought in coal, wheelbarrows and handcarts took vegetables to the markets. As Barrow noted,

> the sides of the streets were filled with an immense concourse of people buying and selling and bartering their different commodities. The buzz and confused noise of this mixed multitude, proceeding from the loud bawling of those who were crying their wares, the wrangling of others, with every now and then a strange twanging noise . . . , the barbers' signal made by his tweezers, the mirth and the laughter that prevailed in every group could scarcely be exceeded. . . . Peddlers with their packs, and jugglers, and conjurers, and fortune tellers, mountebanks and quack doctors, left no space unoccupied.[29]

Here was prosperity made visible to all. You hardly needed to speak Chinese: the animation of the streets, the prosperity of the shops, the sheer number of the people, all kept in perfect order, proved that Peking was the heart of a mighty, rock-solid empire. The Chinese knew that their civilization had lasted almost twenty-five hundred years; the Westerners were aware that there had always been an empire of China; and though the country was largely closed to them, enough of them made it into Canton or Peking to let the rest of the world know that this was not just a faraway, exotic land, but one of the greatest powers anywhere. China, in 1800, had lost none of its exotic fascination for the West; now it was also seen as a country that mattered.

CHAPTER FIFTEEN

Splendid Japan

CHINA WAS HUGE, Japan was small. China had a population of 300 million, Japan's was about 28 million. When China failed to pay attention to the rest of the world, it was out of a sense of superiority; when the Japanese government decreed the closing of Japan, it was out of fear that Japan's very identity might be lost. Of course, that closing could never be complete, nor could the country remain exactly as it had been in 1600 when the shogunate was established; but still Japan looked firmly inward.

Even then, it was not completely cut off from the rest of the world. It sold luxury goods to the West and copper to China. Chinese and Dutch ships entered the one permitted harbor at Nagasaki; but no one in Japan felt connected to any other country. The rest of the world might be one; Japan stood alone.

A CLOSED EMPIRE

Japan, in 1800, was a country apart. Naturally, its language, history, and culture were different from those of China or the rest of East Asia; less naturally, its government relied on a complex system of power relationships, set up 200 years earlier, and held to be a model of unchanging perfection. The most startling characteristic of all, though, was that, for 165 years, the Japanese islands had, deliberately and almost completely, been insulated from the outside world.

The Edict of Closing, which was promulgated in 1635, was specific and thorough. "Japanese ships," it declared, "are strictly forbidden to leave for foreign countries. No Japanese is permitted to go abroad. If any Japanese returns from overseas after residing there, he must be put to death."[1] It went on to restrict all trade and diplomacy to the port of Nagasaki. Even there, activities were largely restricted to trade with China—although an occasional Portu-

Hokusai, *Mount Fuji*. A new, radically simplified kind of landscape view of Japan's most admired mountain is typical of the work of this great artist. (*Print Collection, Miriam and Ira D. Wallach Division of Art, Prints and Photographs, The New York Public Library, Astor, Lenox and Tilden Foundations*)

guese ship was allowed in. The only diplomats ever seen there were Chinese, and they came rarely. As for trade, which was most often discouraged by the government, it was carried out by Chinese and Dutch merchants. The former bought copper; the latter came mostly to buy lacquerwork, bronzes, silks, and porcelain. More trade came through the Ryukyu Islands, the property of the Satsuma clan, but that was largely ignored by the government.

There were three main reasons for this extraordinary state of affairs. One was to prevent any outflow of gold and silver—always in short supply within the empire. If nothing were known of the outside, if no traders were permitted outside Nagasaki, then there would be no imports. The sale of luxury goods, on the other hand, brought in precious metals, and so it was allowed. The second, and even more important reason, was to prevent missionaries from entering Japan. The Jesuits had come first, in the sixteenth century, and displayed their usual understanding of foreign cultures; but then, some four decades later, the Franciscans, who were both more simple-minded and more zealous, followed them.

This was when the government really began to object. The culture and government of Japan were based on religion; if the gods suddenly were mere pagan idols, as the missionaries claimed, then the whole structure of the country was likely to be destroyed. The government therefore banned Christianity. The converts resisted in a number of places, particularly the samurai and peasants at Shimabara in southern Kyushu, adding civil unrest to the threat presented by a new religion. Political fighting, now revived, was the very problem which the rulers had taken pride in solving. Even worse, the Franciscans in Manila, their headquarters in the Far East, let it be known that they would ask the king of Spain to intervene: thus, to actual civil unrest, Christianity added the threat of foreign invasion. That was clearly intolerable. Just as alarming, the Christians in Shimabara defended themselves so efficaciously that their fortress could be taken only with the help of Dutch warships. The Dutch, being Protestant, were naturally delighted to help put down Catholic converts.

As for Western religious publications, the government made very sure they could not be accidentally brought in. When, in the 1770s, a Dutch trading ship came into the harbor at Nagasaki, "all the Prayer-Books and Bibles belonging to the sailors were collected, and put into a chest, which was nailed down . . . [and] left under the care of the Japanese till the time of our departure,"[2] one of the officers, Carl Peter Thunberg, noted.

The third reason for the closure was just as cogent. The Japanese ruling class prized its culture; it had no wish to see it Westernized. The best way to defend it from all intrusions, it decided, was physically to prevent all non-Japanese ideas and artifacts from reaching the people. These were all strong and clearly stated motivations. Just as important, however, was the essential justification of Japan's peculiar system of government: that it must preserve, unaltered, the settlement reached in 1600 by the first shogun of the Tokugawa family; and that the best way to do that was to prevent any change of any kind. By 1800, this political and economic system was already two centuries old; changes had occurred; the economy had grown and prospered. Yet, as the ruling class saw it, everything else was supposed to remain the same.

This was an astonishing goal, especially because the system in question was both illogical and complex. There was, of course, an emperor, whose person was sacred and who, alone, was able to perform the most essential rites of Shintoism, Japan's state religion. He resided in Kyoto, where he had become a virtual prisoner in his palace compound. Courtiers who lived in palaces around the emperor surrounded him; but neither the ruler nor the court had any power or, indeed, money: they lived on the very small subsidy paid them by the government.

That government was under the absolute control of the shogun, a sort of regent to whom all the emperor's nonreligious powers had passed, and it was established in Edo, today's Tokyo. In theory, the emperor appointed the shogun. In fact, the shogun was, after 1600, always a member of the Tokugawa family, most often the son of the previous shogun, whose succession the emperor invariably confirmed. It was the shogun, on the other hand, who chose the emperor: when the emperor had several sons, it was the shogun who selected his successor. Thus, while the shoguns always claimed to rule in the emperor's name, it was the supposed sovereign who was wholly dependent on the shogun. This was made particularly obvious on those occasions when a shogun forced the emperor to retire in order to replace him with a more obedient successor.

A Transformed Society

The shogun ruled absolutely, but his power was limited by a rigid class system based on four principal castes. At the top were the nobles; next came the peasants; lower still were the artisans; and at the bottom were the merchants, because, unlike the peasants and the artisans, they produced nothing. Outside this grid, three more categories existed: the emperor's courtiers; the priests and monks, who had, in earlier centuries, been so powerful as to challenge the emperor himself, but then had lost all their former power to the shoguns; and a small number of outcastes, mostly those who had lost their native status.

The peasants worked extremely hard and paid almost all the taxes; that struck everyone as normal. The merchants, though, presented the government with a serious problem. Instead of remaining at the bottom of the social order, they had prospered. Starting in the mid seventeenth century, Japan had shifted from barter to a money economy, and the merchants had stopped being merely retail distributors of rice and other foods. Many had made sizable fortunes, and they lived luxuriously—far better, in fact, than many half-ruined nobles. Even worse, by lending money to the nobles at a high rate of interest, they enriched themselves while impoverishing the borrowers; and this new state of affairs gravely upset all those who sought to ensure that nothing ever changed.

Even in the countryside, although there were major exceptions, the Tokugawa era was marked by great prosperity—for those who owned the land, at least. This was less the result of an enlightened economic policy than a dividend of peace. Before 1600, the endless civil wars had devastated the fields at regular intervals. Peace, that greatest achievement of the shoguns, had allowed people to prosper; and this new well-being was reflected in the growing number of temple schools and the progress of education. By 1800, a large part of the population was literate.

Still, in theory at least, you could always tell the class to which a person belonged: each had its specific costume, way of speaking, and rules of politeness. In reality, it was often impossible to know who was what in the cities. All through the eighteenth century, there was a marked population movement into the towns; and there the former peasants became traders or artisans, and dressed accordingly.

Far worse, from a traditional point of view, was the position of many nobles. All members of the nobility shared certain privileges: they could kill any commoner who was not properly respectful to them, and they did not have to pay taxes. They were immediately recognizable because they wore two swords and a distinctive hairstyle in which the center of the head was shaved in front, with the side hair lifted up and back. But here, too, things were often not as they were supposed to be.

At the top of the aristocracy were the daimyo. They were great feudal lords who controlled extensive domains. Before 1600, they had ruled Japan and fought endless civil wars; and it was a part of the Tokugawa settlement that as the daimyo lost any share in the government, they were allowed great autonomy within their domains. This was particularly true of the economy: a significant part of the Tokugawa prosperity was due to the expansion of crops and trade within these semiautonomous areas.

Still, the daimyo were subject to the shoguns, and perhaps the most visible manifestation of this was their obligation to reside part of the year in Edo. That proved to be costly for them: away from their domains, they had to buy food and other necessities of life. Because many more luxuries were available in the capital, they often found themselves in debt. The size of their resources was such, however, that they could usually pay their creditors by cutting their expenses. The case of the samurai, unfortunately for them, was very different.

Originally, the samurai had been rural, frequently illiterate warriors in the service of a daimyo; they fought for him, led his troops, and, in return, were given enough land to sustain them decently. Bravery, therefore, was their most important quality. Yamamoto Tsunetomo explained it all in a book written in 1716: "The way of the warrior," he wrote, "is to find a way to die. If a choice is given between life and death, the samurai must chose death. There is no more meaning beyond this. . . . If you make a conscious effort to think of death and resolve to pursue it, and if you are ready to discard life at a moment's notice, you and the bushido [the Samurai code of honor] will become one."[3]

Even when that was written, however, it had ceased to be relevant. The Samurai had been needed because there were constant civil wars; but that had all stopped with the Tokugawa takeover in 1600; nor were there any foreign wars. Even worse, the samurai had been forced to exchange their land for an income paid to them (usually a certain quantity of rice) by the daimyo they served: the samurai had, in fact, become civil servants. "Nowadays," one of them complained in the 1730s, "samurai are forced to live in castle towns in discharge of their duties. They must sell rice [from their stipends] for cash and purchase their daily needs from merchants. In this way merchants become masters while samurai are relegated to the position of customer, unable to determine prices fixed on different commodities."[4] Under the cover of apparent stability, Japan had ceased being a military society. This was, in fact, yet another instance of transformation hidden by the pretense of immobility. Neither the laws nor the principles of government had changed—but the reality in 1800 was utterly different from what it had been two centuries earlier.

Being an impoverished noble was no fun. To keep up a warlike spirit when the last war was two hundred years ago, especially if you are wondering how you will manage at the end of the month, is no easy task. Some samurai, sensibly going where the money was, courted a rich merchant. Some adopted the son of a merchant, married him to a daughter, and thus got a badly needed infusion of capital. Another possibility was for the son of a samurai to marry a merchant's daughter. The consequence of these ties was to make it much harder to tell at one glance what someone's status might be. A proper-looking samurai might well have come from the lowest caste of all, while an impoverished (and thoroughly authentic) samurai who was reduced to hoping for dinner invitations from a merchant was hardly in a superior position. And then there was that special category outside the norms, the *ronin*. These were samurai who left the service of their lord because they were desperate for money, and so automatically lost their status. Thus someone who looked like a commoner, and was legally a commoner, might have been born a noble. Finally, to confuse the issue further, it had become possible to buy the title of samurai from the government at those times when the treasury was particularly depleted.

This reversal of the proper order of things had yet another consequence. As the decades passed, with prices rising and the stipends remaining fixed, samurai families shrank in size. Younger children were forced to remain single; sometimes they were adopted by a merchant, who could then refer complacently to his son, the samurai. The only thing now left to this once-fierce warrior class was, ironically, the civil service: staffed exclusively by samurai-educated bureaucrats who lived in Edo or one of the administrative capitals—it worked according to fixed, complex rules and generated immense quantities of paperwork. Originally, the samurai had been both fierce and illiterate. In 1800, many of them were well-educated paper pushers.

Unchanging Appearances

These economic changes were, in the nature of things, unstoppable. Everything else was as tightly controlled as possible: the shoguns were intent only on ensuring the status quo, and they did it by forbidding anything that might eventually provoke visible change. There were all kinds of things people might not do. The emperor's courtiers, for instance, were "strictly forbidden, whether by day or by night, to go sauntering through the streets or lanes in places where they have no business to be."[5] The message was clear: courtiers who wandered around might be plotting a restoration of their master's power, so they must be stopped from even trying. They, however, were not dangerous, but the 260 daimyo had been, and might be again.

As a result, the rules governing their behavior were both numerous and detailed. They were forbidden to move troops outside their own domains, to form political alliances among themselves, to maintain more than one castle on their lands (to avoid the building of fortresses), to marry without the shogun's approval, to coin money, to have direct relations with the imperial court or with foreigners, and to build warships. If they disobeyed, they were promptly punished by a reprimand, dismissal in favor of their heir, or even outright confiscation. They were also subject to forced contributions for road building and land reclamation.

There were, of course, strict rules about trade—that was part of the closure of the empire. They failed to prevent economic development because the government never realized what the shift to a money economy meant, and was unable to control the mercantile activities in the cities; but they froze technology and had one dire effect: with a population of some 28 million in 1780, Japan could feed itself only if the harvest was good. Any bad weather, any crop failure, invariably caused a famine. That happened several times in the late 1780s; and by 1796 there were nearly 2 million fewer Japanese, the result of starvation and disease. Those most affected were, of course, the peasants: heavily and ruthlessly taxed, one bad crop could reduce them to despair; and then, not infrequently, they rebelled against the landlords—usually daimyo—and the government.

Looking Back to Greatness

That might not have really alarmed Edo; but there were also riots in the towns where the price of rice had, in the summer of 1787, risen to six times its normal level. At the same time, the treasury was found to be empty, in part because of overspending, but even more because the tax system was highly inefficient. From 1600 on, the government had depended almost exclusively on a land tax, which was reasonably productive in good years and the reverse when the crops failed. No other tax had been imposed in almost two centuries: that was a part of the initial agreement between the first Tokugawa shogun and the daimyo. Here, obviously, was a crisis. Logically, it was met not by changing or rethinking the system, but by looking backward to the prosperous times under the Kyoho government in the 1720s.

This attempted return to a happier past, the so-called Kansei reforms, was based entirely on the notion that there must have been changes, that change was negative, and that a return to an earlier age of greatness must therefore be the solution. The new policy was in fact a reaction, not a reform. It was also essentially the work of an austere, intelligent member of a younger branch of the Tokugawa family. Matsudaira Sadanobu, a distant relative, had been adopted into that branch of the family, and had thus become the daimyo of a large fief. It was noticed that, uniquely, he had managed to feed all his peasants during the famine of 1783. Clearly, that was a talent, which the government now needed badly. Just as important, Matsudaira was well able to make his views prevail. Highly eloquent, notably pious, he was learned, hardworking, and earnest. That he was also humorless, narrow-minded, and frequently intolerant hardly seemed to matter.

As a member, by birth, of the Tokugawa clan, Matsudaira was already part of the Edo government. At the death of the shogun Ieharu in 1786, he had been instrumental in ensuring the succession of the fourteen-year-old Ienari. Then, in 1787, the Council of Elders appointed him adviser to the shogun: he had in fact become regent, and was thus able to carry through the measures necessary to bring back the peace and prosperity of the 1720s. Some of his ideas were unquestionably good: he tried hard to end the corruption prevalent throughout the civil service, and often succeeded. He balanced the budget by cutting unnecessary expenditure and creating new taxes on trade and on the profits made by the guilds—less a return to the past than a marked advance in fiscal efficiency. When extraordinary expenses came along, like the rebuilding of the Kyoto palaces after a fire, he raised the money through forced loans on the rich, an early form of income tax. He also made more stringent rules, which ensured that the daimyo would pay the treasury the full amount they owed— and it all worked. Helped also by luck (the harvests of 1788 and 1789 were excellent), the treasury enjoyed a surplus in 1790.

Making the state more efficient mattered, but it did nothing to solve the underlying causes of the distress, so Matsudaira tackled these next. Once again, that meant an effort at going back to a more successful time at the beginning of the century. Certain measures were relatively harmless: he for-bade the continuation of loans to the samurai and reduced the rate of interest on existing debt. That helped at least a few of the samurai; but it was their con-version from warriors to civil servants that had caused the trouble in the first place, and that was not reversible.

In the same way, lowering food prices by decree lessened the general dis-tress in the short term. In the long term, had the shortages continued, these measures would merely have led to the creation of a black market; but then those abundant harvests came in, and the prices dropped naturally. The next measures, though, were totally unrealistic: the adviser tried to limit the money

economy and grow more food by reclaiming land through drainage and irriga-
tion, and ordering the peasants to leave the cities and return to the countryside—where the tax load was as heavy as before. Naturally, the peasants stayed
where they were.

Nor was the attempt at controlling the uncontrollable limited to econom-
ics. Strict (and ridiculous) sumptuary laws were published. Henceforth, it was
forbidden to wear luxurious clothing and use the services of a barber or hair-
dresser. Betting and gambling were forbidden. Bathhouses, those mainstays of
Japanese city life, were now divided according to gender. They had been one of
the few places where men and women could meet easily—to talk, not to have
sex—and the closure was much resented. Censorship, too, was severely tightened: no book criticizing the government could be published any longer, and
erotic publications were banned, although they were an old and valued part of
the culture. At the same time, a rigid control of all teaching was put in place.
Even worse, spies were hired to denounce any infractions; and arrests were
multiplied. By 1794, the government's unpopularity was such that Matsudaira
had to resign. By 1800, the young shogun had begun to rule; but he paid more
attention to his pleasures than to the problems of Japan, and the government
just drifted along, hoping that nothing much would ever happen.

The Dazzle of Japan

For all its difficulties, however, and with the help of an expanding economy,
Japan still presented a splendid image. On very rare occasions—two or three
times in a century—a Westerner would be allowed in, and what he saw invariably dazzled him. One of these, Aland Churchill, watched as the shogun went
past. "Nothing is so surprising," he noted,

> as to see so many brave chosen fellows, as attend [the shogun] when he goes
> abroad [i.e., out of his palace] . . . all clad in black silk, to keep their ranks to an
> admiration; and neither they, nor his halberdiers, who surround his person,
> speak one word . . . The streets are very well cleansed and covered with sand;
> nobody dares so much as open a window, much less stand at his shop or
> house-door, as [the shogun] passes by, but must remain at home or else kneel
> down in the street. His nobles, generals and colonels follow him at the head of
> several thousand men, horse and foot, but they must keep at a distance and
> not come within his sight.[6]

That sort of order was impressive. In Kyoto, where no such processions
took place, there were other things to admire. "There is scarce a house in this
large capital where there is not something made or sold," another traveler
reported. "Here, they refine copper, coin money, print books, weave the richest
stuffs with gold and silver flowers. The best and scarcest dies, the most artful

carvings, all sorts of musical instruments, pictures, japan'd cabinets, all sorts of things wrought in gold and other metals, particularly in steel, as the best-tempered blades and other arms, are made here in the utmost perfection, as also the richest dresses, and after the best fashion."[7]

The traveler was right. Japanese skill, allied to Japanese style, resulted in the creation of extraordinary objects and textiles. Refinement and an apparently impossible blend of austerity and splendor could be seen in the porcelain and lacquered objects, in the sword hilts and the costumes, in the delicately lacquered litters, that preferred mode of travel for the rich. Carl Peter Thunberg, who saw Japan in the 1770s, was duly impressed. The litters, he wrote, are "made of thin boards and bamboo canes in the form of an oblong square, with windows before and on each side. Over the roof runs a long edged pole, by which the vehicle is carried on the bearers' shoulders. It is so large that one may . . . even lie down in it. . . . It is . . . adorned in the most elegant manner, with the most costly silks and velvets."[8] Japan was not only orderly: it glittered.

Architecture in Stone and Silk

There were also many things the few foreign visitors never saw. The palaces in and around Kyoto and Edo were not only superb examples of that capacity for sparse elegance that distinguishes Japanese architecture: they were surrounded by gardens in which every rock, every bush, every pebble was carefully placed and shaped so as to create a balanced and harmonious whole. Some gardens were specialized, places to be visited when the iris were in bloom; others, made of carefully raked sand, a few bonsai, and some stones, had the timeless authority that came from centuries of refinement. And then there were the castles.

The first thing anyone would notice, when approaching a castle, was the extraordinary complexity of its silhouette. Layer upon layer of tiled roofs with curling corners topped the building; at Himeji, one very tall tower and four shorter ones formed a harmonious contrast; triangular pediments, disposed at a variety of angles, led the eye up toward the roof peak. The great achievement, though, was not just in the details, but also in the design, which seemed almost abstract in the way it balanced line and volume.

That blend of rich details and lines, so subtly complicated that they seemed more like pure design than a part of reality, characterized costume as well. Both men and women wore robes. "The rich have them of the finest silk," Thunberg noted, "and the poor of cotton. The women wear them reaching down to their feet, and the women of quality frequently with a train. Those of the men come down to their heels. . . . The men generally have them made of a plain silk of one color, but the silken stuffs worn by the women are flowered, and sometimes interwoven with gold flowers. . . . The men fasten to [their] belt their sabre, fan, tobacco pipe and pouch and their medecine box."[9] That sounds relatively simple. In fact, the belts were used to create the intricate effect of draperies; and when worn by the women, these obis became highly elaborate constructions, usually of a color or pattern contrasting with that of the dress. Then there were the immensely wide and long sleeves, again worn by the women, which added yards of fabric to the costume—so much so that it is hard, in retrospect, to see how they managed to move. Of course, when they did, it was in a series of small steps and small gestures: this, after all, was a place where sophistication was highly prized, and the natural look disdained.

Makeup was just as sophisticated, Thunberg recorded.

> The colour with which they paint themselves is kept in little round porcelain boxes. With this they paint . . . their lips. . . . If the paint is very thin, the lips appear red; but if it be laid on thick, they become of a violet hue, which here is considered as the greater beauty.
>
> That which chiefly distinguishes the married women from the single is their black teeth. . . . Some begin to make use of this ornament as soon as they are courted.[10]

Black teeth and purple lips: it would be hard to get farther away from nature.

Logically enough, hairdos were just as remarkable. "Their hair," Thunberg continued, "made smooth with oil and mucilaginous substances, is put up close to the head on all sides . . . standing out at the sides in the form of wings. After this the ends are fastened together round a knob at the crown of the head. Just before this knot, a broad comb is stuck . . . Besides this the rich wear several long ornaments of tortoise shell stuck through this knot, as also a few flowers."[11] The combs had tall, sculpted tops; the "ornaments" looked like very long pins placed at often startling angles; the hair seemed literally lacquered; and the total effect was more like an elaborate, hard-to-read sculpture than actual human hair.

Obviously, these fashions were worn only by upper-class ladies: the peasants in the fields wore the simplest shifts, longer for the women, shorter for the men, who sometimes stripped down to just a loincloth. And while the latter kept their hair plain and short, the nobles had a coiffure that looked, if anything, even more improbable than that of their consorts. Thunberg was fascinated. "The men shave the whole of their head, from the forehead down to the nape of the neck, and what is left near the temples and in the neck is well greased, turned up, and tied at the top of the head with several rounds of white string made of paper. The end of the hair that remains above the tie is cut off to about the length of one finger, and, after being well stiffened with oil, bent in such a manner, that the tip is brought to stand against the crown of the head."[12] The complexity of the costume, in fact, reflected that of the manners.

It was not just that each class had its own etiquette—simpler, of course, at the bottom of the scale. Within a class, the demands of politeness were such as to require a sort of elaborate ballet on many occasions. The appropriate number and depth of the bows, the necessary remarks, the phrasing of these remarks, even the grammar, all were strictly governed by convention. The emperor, for instance, spoke a distinct, old-fashioned Japanese; nobles another slightly less formal one. There were precise rules for the frequency and kinds of meetings, ways to address someone more (or less) important than oneself, subjects that were permissible while others were forbidden. Even everyday meals were formal: each of the guests had his own table (the ladies ate separately) on which would be placed many small dishes of porcelain or lacquered wood, each containing an individual portion. There was no vulgar passing of dishes, no sharing of anything.

In this enormously formal society, however, there were moments of total informality. Whether at the public baths or in the bathroom of private houses—and any reasonably prosperous family had a bathroom—men and women bathed nude together. Sex, like nudity, had no power to shock: considered a normal, but interesting, function, it was abundantly depicted in books of engravings, which, except during the Kansei reforms, were not considered pornographic in the slightest degree. Indeed, making the wrong number of bows was considered far more shocking than the depiction of sexual intercourse. Even here, however, there was an exception, a place where the usual rules no longer applied.

Pleasure Unleashed

The floating world—*ukiyo* in Japanese—was a poetic simile to describe the quarters, in all the larger cities, where brothels, theaters, teahouses, and public baths were clustered. Every sort of entertainment could be found there, from classical theater and music to cheap prostitutes, from an elaborate tea ritual and the attention of the beautiful and highly educated geishas to the most unchained orgies. These floating worlds served an essential function: they were the one place where men could escape the duties and obligations of family and function. Some of the visitors were content with a friendly gathering where their recently written poetry could be read to like-minded friends; others spent a great deal of money on more sensual pleasures. And here, indeed, was another reason why the *ukiyo* were so important: money counted for more than status, and personal achievement mattered more than inherited grandeur.

There was much to admire there as well. The money that was spent so freely bought, for the geishas and their less-educated colleagues, the most expensive, most spectacular clothes imaginable in the very newest patterns: here, in fact, was the cutting edge of fashion. The decor of many of the houses, including that of the best brothels, was both lavish and tasteful. Entertainments on the grandest scale were frequently given. A man could easily ruin himself in the *ukiyo*. He could also have the time of his life. Thus it is no wonder that the scene appealed to artists, and particularly to the great woodcut designers who flourished between 1770 and 1820.

There is no better way to know what an actor, or a geisha, or, indeed, an elegant room looked like than to leaf through the wood-block prints designed by Kitagawa Utamaro. We can see a geisha preparing for a carnival, with her two maids dressing her in an elaborate brocade robe, or a fete in a teahouse, where groups of seated men are served by geishas in an interior decorated with many screens. We can be present at an outing on the banks of the Sumida River in 1788, in which two elegantly tall women, one wearing an immense straw hat, the other sheltering beneath an equally huge parasol, stroll toward a bridge. The scene, however, is not just an account of the fashionable life: the patterns of the brocade dresses form an abstract design in sharp contrast to the highly realistic figures of a maid and manservant, and the composition thus created is literally fascinating.

For Utamaro, and now for us, all this was the stuff of life itself. Because he was a great artist, we are offered not only many vivid images of that aspect of Japanese society, but also compositions filled with bright, sophisticated colors in which passion, immediacy, and a sense of psychological nuance are combined to stunning effect. In *A Girl Rouging Her Lips*, for instance, the ground is a yellowish gray, the girl's tall black coiffure and black handheld mirror contrasting with the flesh tones of the long, graceful arms and fingers. The sitter's robe is gray and black, but then her dark-green and maroon obi adds just the right intensity. In Utamaro's work, tall, willowy, endlessly elegant women, in an almost infinite variety of positions, are presented to us. Animated or sad, cheerful or pensive, their moods are communicated to us even as we marvel at the intricacy of the composition. Line on line, pattern on pattern form a ground from which usually emerges the face and hands of the sitter: the human qualities, the directness of the image are all the more real because of their contrast with costume or landscape.

Some of Utamaro's prints show us the daily life of the streets of Edo—the shops, the shoppers, the crowds. There are elegant upper-class men wielding their fans, and dogfights, but in the end it is the women who matter. With their oval faces, the sweeping curve of their noses, and their small, petal-like lips, it is a whole world of beauties that is presented to the viewer. Sometimes the woman holds a fan, sometimes a letter she has just received, or a cup of tea, or a lipstick brush, or the edge of her sleeve. Some of the women are putting on makeup, or having their hair done by a maid, or dressing. Others are bathing in tall wooden tubs held together by green ropes, and as they get in or out of the

Utamaro, *Three Beauties.* For this great Japanese artist, feminine beauty, the world of the theater, and the charms of the courtesans had an endless appeal. (*Charles Stewart Smith Collection, Miriam and Ira D. Wallach Division of Art, Prints and Photographs, The New York Public Library, Astor, Lenox and Tilden Foundations*)

bath, they show us a form and position that helped, three-quarters of a century later, to inspire Degas.

Some of the women are seen in the intimacy of their toilette; others are shown in seductive half-length portraits. Their robes often fall open to reveal their breasts, but they remain remote, caught in their own thoughts, unaware of us. Far more erotic, although just as subtle, are the images of lovers. In *Lovers Kissing,* for instance, we see neither the lovers' faces nor the kiss itself: the woman, seen from behind, hides the man's face. She is fully dressed in an intricately patterned black, bronze, and white kimono, with an orange flowered obi; but her red petticoat is lifted up in back to reveal her naked body up to the waist, while his patterned brown and white robe, next to which his fan is open, partly covers her thigh. Nothing is visibly going on; but the suggestion is powerful, and the image has extraordinary intensity.

For all that, there is nothing here to shock us; but like most Japanese artists, Utamaro also produced prints in which sexual activity is directly shown. Although, certainly, the images are utterly frank, they are not obscene: they are not meant to make us into voyeurs. Rather, they celebrate sex as one of the normal pleasures of life, one that we need not hide. In these prints, the positions of the lovers are extremely complicated; all the color is in the carefully disarrayed clothes, while the genitals are rendered in great detail—but treated much like the depiction of an insect or a flower. What we see is pleasure, not passion; sophistication, not raw lust. Here, sexual intercourse is enlivened by a touch of irony, and seems as complicated—and in some ways as ruthlessly polite—as the tea ceremony.

As a result, there is far greater intensity in the entirely proper print that shows the viewing of the cherry blossoms at Yoshiwara, the floating world at Edo. The flowering cherry trees are in the foreground, with small, red-flowered bushes growing around them; the splendidly attired women, strolling or sitting, are dressed in brilliant red, blue, and yellow brocades, with the men in brown and dark green robes. In the background, an open pavilion is filled with figures dressed in more subdued colors—plum, dark blue, beige. The contrast of colors, the depth of the scene—we look straight into the pavilion's lower and upper story halls—all combine to give extraordinary vividness and power to an image of what is, after all, but a fleeting moment.

For an artist like Utamaro, life was easy. His work was popular; he was consequently prosperous and much respected. Even if the Kansei reforms made it temporarily impossible to depict the *ukiyo*, he still could focus on many different themes; and so, in 1788, he produced his *Insect Book,* in which the most precisely rendered insects sit on, or next to, big, brightly colored flowers, stems, and leaves. These are images of jewel-like beauty; and for sheer elegance, the lizard could shame most geishas.

Utamaro was the greatest artist of his generation, but there were many others; then, in the next generation, Hokusai took Japanese art in a new direction. Although trained in the depiction of the floating world, he soon began focusing on landscapes. Until then, the figures had been what mattered; now they shrank to an often tiny size, and the landscapes became the main subjects. Like Monet, but fifty years before him, Hokusai was fascinated by the changes of light over the same area. This exploration culminated in his celebrated images of Mount Fuji seen from different viewpoints and at different times of the year and the day. Stylized, yet intensely real, these images show us a Japan where the precise depiction of the moment takes on an eternal, mythic quality.

All these wood-block prints were in great demand, but they were hardly the only kind of art. There were screens, of course, often with a gold ground against which interior and exterior scenes, flowers and animals were depicted. And for sheer visual beauty, there was the Kabuki theater.

Originally, the Kabuki had simply been a facade for prostitution, so the government made it illegal for women or seductive youths to appear on stage. The result was the birth of an art form. Henceforth, women's roles were played by male actors who specialized in such parts: obviously, there was no attempt at verisimilitude. Instead, a highly stylized kind of acting was developed, which soon passed on to the men's roles. There was intricate dancing to the music of a large orchestra. Elaborate scenery, often mounted on turntables that allowed quick scene changes, sumptuous costumes, elaborate makeup, and formal poses added to the impression that the actual theme mattered less than the series of dazzling images that filled the stage. By the beginning of the eighteenth century, however, a new, extraordinarily talented author changed that. In Chikamatsu Monzaemon's plays, the spectacle remained splendid, but the content also mattered a great deal, and it was usually tragic. Characters who were rejected by their lovers committed suicide; his women were forceful personalities; his men were seen to grow in moral stature throughout the play. At the same time, however, there were humorous moments and a brilliant use of language. Still, Kabuki, which played in large, sumptuous theaters, was by definition a collaborative work. Another art form required nothing more than a brush, ink, and paper: the haiku.

That most Japanese form of poetry had been invented in the 1680s by Matsuo Bashō. The poems themselves were very short, apparently very simple and, at their best, extraordinarily evocative:

The summer grasses—
All that has survived from
Brave warriors' dreams.

It would be difficult to say more about the vanity of ambition in fewer words. Not all Bashō's poems were so melancholy, though. The love of nature also played an important role:

Such stillness—
The cicada's cries penetrate
The very rocks!

By the end of the eighteenth century, haiku writing had become a national pastime. Men met in teahouses to read what they had written to one another;

countless poets and would-be poets published their work. And here too, stylization prevailed.

That, in the end, seemed the most essential characteristic of Japan. Closed to the outside world, committed to reproducing a greatly admired past, it was not a country where grand military or political schemes could occupy the ambitious. Instead, more and more, the pleasures of a highly refined civilization seemed enough for most people: more than anything, Japan was a show that dazzled itself. It impressed the visitors as well. After giving high praise to the many qualities of the Japanese, Thunberg went on: "Their present mode of government, regulations for foreign commerce, their manufactures, the vast abundance, even to superfluity of all the necessaries of life give convincing proof of their sagacity."[13] Many of the Japanese themselves knew that all was not well; few could imagine any kind of change; and so the pageant continued.

CHAPTER SIXTEEN

India: The Invention of an Empire

INDIA, IN 1800, was at least six weeks away from Europe—a vast, hugely rich subcontinent whose emperors had been the stuff of legend. It was less mysterious than China because France, Portugal, and England had long owned a few ports on its coasts; it was also thoroughly disunited. Within ten years, the greater part of it had become British. It was not even like the former American colonies, which had always enjoyed a significant degree of autonomy. India, through a governor-general, was ruled directly from London.

One reason for this transformation was the war between France and Great Britain. It seemed preferable to conquer great swathes of India, if the choice was to sit back and watch an extension of French influence. Of course, these fears were groundless: the French were quite incapable of taking over any part of India, but the result remains: from Delhi to Calcutta to Varanasi—the holiest city in India—the subcontinent was conquered and became a mere dependency of Great Britain.

Trade also tightened these links. It was not just that India offered a growing market for British products. It grew opium, which could be exchanged for Chinese tea, and involved Great Britain further with that other vast empire. Here, once again, it was plain to see: the world, in 1800, was becoming a very small place.

THE BRITISH IN INDIA

India, in the eighteenth century, was an empire ready to be conquered. This vast continent, so rich in resources of every kind, was divided into many states, colonized on the edges, and constantly rent by war. By the 1730s, the Mogul Empire, which had once ruled two-thirds of its land area, had collapsed; new states had arisen in great numbers; older states, once subordinated to the empire, had recovered their full independence. And then there were the foreigners.

Some, like the Portuguese in Goa, really did not matter: they controlled a port and its immediate hinterland in order to trade—in spices, rice, ivory, precious stones, rare tropical woods, and silk—and that was the limit of their ambition. Others, like the French, had once hoped to have an empire in India, but Great Britain had defeated them during the Seven Years' War (1756–1763), and they had been left with a mere five ports. There remained the British, or rather that oddest of entities, the East India Company.

Two centuries earlier, the company's sole purpose had been to monopolize, as far as possible, the enormously profitable trade in tropical goods. Eventually, it acquired a series of ports. Bombay, Madras, and Calcutta, a little way up the Hooghly River, soon became the three largest, but as time passed, the very nature of the company changed. First, it began to be very much less profitable as it lost its monopoly: by the mid eighteenth century, all the commodities in which it traded were available elsewhere. That was just when it discovered a new source of income. By extending the area of its rule to the mainland beyond the ports, it could appropriate the vast riches that had, until then, been reserved for the local rulers. Still, this was an ad hoc process: conquest as such was never a goal; simply, whenever it seemed possible to make a great deal of money by despoiling a raja or exploiting the population, the company did so. By 1798, it ruled over the rich province of Bengal; a part of the coast to the south of Calcutta, in today's state of Orissa; a strip of territory along the Ganges, up to and including Varanasi; a small area along the southwest coast, in today's state of Kerala; Madras and a significant part of what is today Tamil Nadu; and Bombay.

In order to conquer, then hold, these possessions, an army was needed; in order to administer them, a civil service was required; and that, in turn, implied the existence of a body of law. Further, to rule the company's domains, a government was required: a business had thus created a state. That was an obvious anomaly, especially since the company's army was essentially British. Strictly speaking, those Indian territories belonged solely to the company; yet, as the Seven Years' War had proved, they were defended as part of the British Empire; and the company itself was, after all, an English corporation.

LONDON AND CALCUTTA

It had long been an exceptionally powerful corporation, though: its vast income allowed it to pay the election expenses of a number of members of Parliament, who then showed their gratitude by protecting the company from gov-

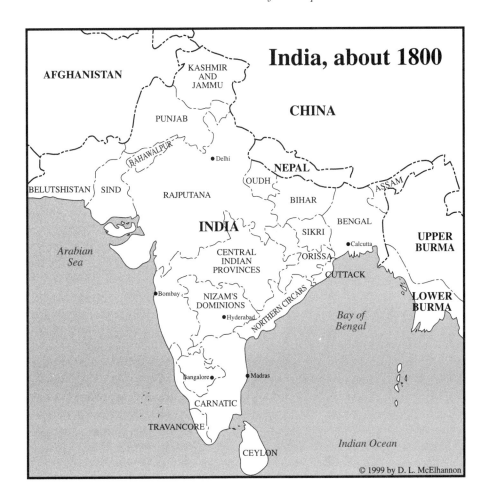

ernment interference. This might have gone on forever had it not been for
a startling development: by the early 1770s, the company, faced with competition from other European traders, was losing so much money that it found
itself forced to apply for a loan. The amount requested—£1.4 million at an
interest rate of 4 percent—was so immense a sum that only the government
could provide it. The result, in the India Acts of 1773, was the first assertion of
parliamentary control over the company. The company was given its loan; but
the workings of its Board of Directors were modified so as to make them more
businesslike; and a formal Indian government was created. Henceforth, there
would be a governor-general of Bengal, assisted by four councillors, and he
was given authority over the heretofore autonomous presidencies of Madras
and Bombay. Just as important, a Supreme Court was set up to act as a court of
final appeal; this was a brand-new assertion of the rule of law.

As it soon became obvious, this compromise between the company and Parliament was an inefficient solution. Eleven years later, William Pitt's India Act went a good deal further by creating a joint government of Crown and company. The Board of Directors remained; but it was now subject to a Board of Control, appointed by the Crown and composed of six privy councilors. Its first president was Henry Dundas, a close political ally of the prime minister's, who thus became, in effect, minister for India. The Board of Control itself had the power to "superintend, direct and control all acts, operations and concerns which in anywise relate to the civil or military government or the revenues of the British territorial possessions in the East Indies."[1] It also approved, modified, or rejected the directors' draft dispatches, but could send its own without the directors' consent. The directors appointed the governor-general, but the Crown could recall him; the role of the Governor's Council was reduced while his authority over Madras and Bombay was extended—in fact, he could, if he chose, override the council—he could also appoint himself commander in chief. Clearly, henceforth, it would be the governor-general who would rule British India. Even so, there was one major restriction. "To pursue schemes of conquest and extension of dominion in India are measures repugnant to the wish, honour and policy of this nation,"[2] the new act declared, and the Indian government was explicitly forbidden to declare war without authority from London. These restrictions were very clear, but they had an important flaw. In an age when it took at least six weeks for a dispatch to travel from London to Calcutta, the governor could always claim to be responding to an emergency, the consequence of which might well be war and an extension of territory.

The personality of the governor-general thus mattered a great deal, and the first one under the new act was chosen with great care. Since the directors appointed him, but the Board of Control could dismiss him, it was, in fact, that board whose power was the greatest. Dundas knew exactly the man he wanted, and the directors also approved of him. He was honest, intelligent, hardworking; he had already long been in the service of his country. It might perhaps have been held against him that his defeat at Yorktown three years before had lost the North American colonies, but apparently no one minded; and so Charles Cornwallis went off to general acclaim.

GOVERNOR-GENERAL CORNWALLIS

It was, in fact, an excellent choice. Before he arrived in Calcutta, corruption had been general. Commercial agents, whose income depended on the commissions they earned, were also administering the colony; nicknamed "nabobs," they enriched themselves while the company lost and the natives suffered. Cornwallis ended all that. He separated the commercial aspect of the company from the civil service, whose members were given generous salaries but were forbidden to trade. Suddenly, a civil servant's only way to improve his lot was to do a good job. At the same time, the Board of Revenue, which assessed and collected taxes, was reorganized so as to make it both fairer and more efficient. The revenue districts were reduced in number from thirty-five to twenty-three, which made the whole process cheaper and more easily controlled; and the collector of each district was given the powers of a magistrate, thus introducing the rule of law in distant areas where it had not existed before.

At the same time, new civil and criminal justice court systems were created. Soon every district had both a collector and a judge, a major step away from the arbitrariness that had prevailed until then. Even more important, all officers of government could henceforth be sued for the actions carried out in their official capacity. Here were the beginnings of accountability for the government, and civil liberty for its subjects.

It was all a remarkable achievement, and Cornwallis was duly reappointed to a second four-year term. Then, in 1793, Sir John Shore, who had been his chief aide, succeeded him. Shore was honest, hardworking, and efficient, but utterly devoid of initiative. When, in 1795, the nizam of Hyderabad, who ruled over one of the largest states in southern India, was attacked by the Mahrattas, whose power centers were on the west coast near Bombay, he promptly invoked his treaty of alliance with the company. Shore should unquestionably have come to his help, but he dithered and did nothing. The consequence was a severe defeat for the nizam, while the other states concluded that alliances with the British were a perfect waste of time.

Even so, Shore might have been reappointed, if only because he so took to heart the prohibition against making war without authorization from London; but when, in 1797, he gave in to a semi-mutiny of the Bengal officers, who were demanding a larger allowance, the Crown decided to recall him. It was then a question of whom to nominate. Reaching for safety, the directors decided to send Cornwallis back to India, while appointing the Earl of Mornington, an Irish peer who had been a member of the Board of Control, as governor of Madras. For a man of Mornington's ambition, Madras was not much—he wanted, of course, to be governor-general—but it was hinted that he might eventually succeed Cornwallis. Even more important, perhaps, Mornington was deeply in debt. Madras meant an immense salary, £20,000, of which he expected to save half every year; so he accepted the post.

It was, as it turned out, the cleverest thing he ever did. Cornwallis, who had been sworn in on February 1, 1797, delayed his departure. When, in August, the company gave in to the Bengal officers' demands, he resigned in disgust; and the company, which had just appointed Mornington to Madras, now made him governor-general and procured him a step up in the peerage. On November 9, the Marquis Wellesley, as he became, sailed for Calcutta.

THE CREATION OF AN EMPIRE

Had the British government really been intent on maintaining the status quo, it could hardly have made a worse choice. Lord Wellesley was brilliant, imperious, imaginative, energetic, and wildly ambitious. He meant to make a name for himself such as would be long remembered; and because he spent money on the vastest scale, he also needed to make a huge fortune. Further, he added to his own talents those of his brothers (whom, of course, he took with him). Arthur, the future Duke of Wellington, whose massive common sense was allied to just the right kind of daring, served as a colonel in the army; Charles, the future Lord Cowley, was a brilliant diplomat, a man who could disentangle the most complicated problems. This was not a team to sit back and do nothing, especially since Wellesley was quite clear about how British India should be ruled. "The mainspring of such a machine as the government of India can never safely be touched by any other hand than that of the principal mover,"[3] he wrote the directors in 1799.

In a more ordinary man, this imperiousness would have been the first step to disaster. In Wellesley, it began by inspiring all his subordinates. "His great mind pervaded the whole [empire], and a portion of his spirit was infused into every agent he employed," wrote Sir John Malcolm, who knew him well.

> His authority was as fully recognized in the remotest parts of British India as in Fort William [Government House in Calcutta]; all sought his praise; all dreaded his censure: his confidence in those he employed was unlimited; and they were urged to exertion by every motive that can stimulate a good and proud mind to action. . . . It was the habit of his mind to be slow in counsel but rapid in action; and he expected the greatest efforts from those he employed in the execution of his measures.[4]

Here was the very opposite of Sir John Shore. Success was what mattered, not the strict observance of bureaucratic procedures. And in 1798, with the war raging in Europe, success everywhere was measured in territory conquered. In principle, the governor-general was forbidden to expand the British dominion. In the event, Wellesley, who knew Pitt and Dundas well, had just the right lever: the French scare. With the French armies victorious in Europe, a single hint that they might be looking at India was enough: any measure taken to prevent that eventuality became justified. This was a line of reasoning which could be taken quite far: not only was it now necessary to defeat all potential allies of the French, it was just as important to end the "anarchy" (i.e., the disputes between various native princes) which might eventually encourage French intervention. The solution to this problem was obvious: the more land Wellesley conquered, the safer India would be from the Gallic ogre. That struck

Arthur Wellesley, Duke of Wellington, after the portrait by Lawrence. As a young man, he won many battles in India; a few years later, he defeated Napoléon at Waterloo.
(Portrait File, Miriam and Ira D. Wallach Division of Art, Prints and Photographs, The New York Public Library, Astor, Lenox and Tilden Foundations)

London as perfectly reasonable. As for Wellesley, who was perhaps not quite as worried about the French as he appeared, his motive was simple. British supremacy, he felt sure, was good for India.

On occasion, the British possessions could be extended by simple purchase: when the raja of Tanjore, a substantial state south of Madras, found himself involved in a complicated money dispute, Wellesley offered him an annual income of £40,000 in exchange for his territory. Forty thousand pounds was a huge sum: the raja accepted it, and Tanjore became British. Far subtler was the subsidiary treaty.

Because there were so many states in India, war was almost constant. Many of the weaker princes dreaded being swallowed up by a more powerful neighbor; and that was when Wellesley moved in. He offered to station troops in the threatened state, thus guaranteeing it from attack. These troops, in turn, were to be paid for by the local ruler—not directly, but either through an annual fee to the company, or by the cession of some territory. The result was simple: the ruler was paying for troops that were prepared to defend him, certainly, but whose very presence ensured that he remained henceforth a British client. That, of course, protected the people from invasion; but it also delivered them absolutely into the hands of often incompetent rulers. With British troops ensuring the status quo, there was no recourse against tyranny or profligacy.

The system could also be taken a step further. The often very large subsidy was due annually; not infrequently, the ruler was unable to pay. The company then took over the government, paid the ruler a pension, and ruled in his place. Thus, without risk, and at virtually no cost, British India grew by leaps and bounds.

These successes were no less than Wellesley expected, and they were greeted with approval in London. As for the governor-general himself, he behaved as if he were less a governor than a viceroy. "His Lordship's own establishment of servants, equipages, etc., were extravagant in the superlative degree, not only in point of number but splendour of dress, the whole being put to the account of the chaste managers of Leadenhall Street [the headquarters of the company],"[5] a contemporary reported. It was not only servants, carriages, silver, crystal, and porcelain: Wellesley built a vast and splendid Governor's Mansion, now the residence of the governor of West Bengal. Neoclassical in style, duly fronted with columns, it is as good architecturally as the best examples of the style in England itself; and today it stands as a reminder that in establishing an empire, Wellesley saw to it that he lived in the grandest of styles.

He also worked hard. "I rise early and go out before breakfast, which is always between eight and nine," he wrote. "From that hour until four (in the hot weather) I remain at work, unless I go to Council, or to Church on Sundays; at five I dine and drive out in the evening. No constitution here can bear the sun in the middle of the day at any season of the year, nor the labour of business in the evening."[6] The climate in Calcutta is hot at the coolest time of the year; in the summer, it is well nigh unbearable; and for the English, accustomed as they were to cool temperatures, it was a constant trial. Still, there were evening activities: Wellesley, for one, gave the grandest parties. At one ball, the illuminations alone cost £3,248, an almost unimaginable sum in an era when, in England, you could live very comfortably on £1,000 a year. All the more socially eminent members of the colony were invited to these receptions—but no Indian below the rank of ruler. Like most of his upper-class contemporaries, Wellesley was a thorough snob who despised those he considered his inferiors.

This semiregal pomp accompanied him everywhere, even when he was on campaign. Thomas Twining, who was traveling in India, visited him in camp.

> I went to the dining tent and found assembled there a party of military officers who formed H.E.'s [His Excellency's] suite. . . . The dinner being brought down from the cooking house by a long train of servants . . . The Governor-General arrived . . . and took his seat in the middle of the table which was of great length. . . . The Marquis was dressed in the splendid uniform of Captain-General. . . . The brilliancy and profusion of the dinner table surprised me. Costly chandeliers of cut glass were suspended over it, and it was covered with beautiful porcelain and glass-ware, and with dishes and wine as varied and abundant as at his Lordship's famed entertainments at the palace at Calcutta.[7]

Wellesley spent, and, reluctantly, the company paid. It had no choice, really. At a time when Britain was everywhere defeated, when, in Europe, she had lost her allies, the only good news came from India. "By your firmness and your decision," the future Duke of Wellington wrote his brother, "you have not only saved, but enlarged and secured the valuable empire entrusted to you at a time when everything else was a wreck and the existence even of Great Britain was problematical."[8] Wellington was not given to flattery; and here, as usual, he spoke the most exact truth.

THE FALL OF TIPU SULTAN

Some of Wellesley's conquests were entirely peaceful; others, like his takeover of the kingdom of Oudh, the area around Lucknow, and then of Delhi itself, required a mere show of force. The war with Mysore, on the other hand, was a full-fledged fight. South India, in 1798, counted four major powers: the British; Hyderabad—but the nizam and his army were invariably defeated; the Mahrattas, split among several rulers but still formidable; and Mysore. This last was an unusual place. The Hindu maharaja of this Hindu state had been displaced by a Muslim adventurer whose son, Tipu Sultan, now ruled the kingdom. From the very beginning, Tipu had understood that British expansion was a terrible danger; he had already fought the colonizers, winning the first war and losing the second. Now he seemed ready to start hostilities again, and with good reason.

He saw that if Wellesley and the British were not stopped soon they would seize all India. Other rulers—Madhva Rao Scindia of Gwalior, particularly—saw this as well. Unfortunately for them and for India, they were never able to form a united front against the British invaders.

As for Wellesley, he knew just what he wanted: a war to annihilate Tipu; so, on August 12, 1798, at a time when Tipu and he were still negotiating, he wrote, most untruthfully, to the directors: "[Tipu's] is a public, unqualified and unambiguous declaration of war, aggravated by an avowal that the object of the war is neither explanation, reparation nor security, but the total destruction of the British government in India."[9] After that, the Board of Control could hardly deny him his war, especially since it became known that Tipu and Bonaparte had been corresponding. Here, indeed, was the ever-useful French peril.

In 1797, in fact, Tipu had concluded an alliance, at Bonaparte's suggestion, with the French commander in Mauritius. Tipu then, comically enough, since he was an absolute ruler, planted a tree of liberty at Seringapatam, his capital. This was, of course, an imitation of the French revolutionary ceremony, though it was singularly inapposite in Mysore; then a few French troops—less than two hundred—arrived. They were soon followed by a letter from Egypt. "You have already been informed of my arrival on the borders of the Red Sea, with an innumerable and invincible army, full of the desire of delivering you from the iron yoke of England,"[10] General Bonaparte wrote. It is quite an amazing text: the contempt Bonaparte felt for all non-Europeans is clear; "innumerable" and "invincible" are hardly accurate descriptions of the French army in Egypt. As for the assumption that it was but a leap from the Red Sea to southeastern India, a look at a map will quickly show how absurd it is. Tipu knew, therefore, that he could not actually expect practical aid; but his—entirely reasonable—hatred of the British was so great that even this futile correspondence must have given him some satisfaction.

Tipu Sultan was, in fact, so remarkable that his very enemies could hardly help praising him. Of average height for the region (he was five feet seven), he was strong and athletic, with elegant, delicate hands. "When I saw him [in 1770, when he was almost twenty]," noted William Petrie, a member of the council in Madras, "he was remarkably fair for a Mussulman in India, thin, delicately made, with an interesting, mild countenance, of which large, animated black eyes were the most conspicuous features."[11] He usually wore a robe of fine white cloth, cut very tight, high-waisted, long-skirted, with sleeves drawn up in pleats, together with a gold embroidered belt and a turban made of about fifty yards of red, crimson, or green silk shot with gold threads—a remarkably simple outfit by local standards.

Tipu had, in fact, no time to think about his clothes. It was not just that he was erudite—his library, remarkably, numbered over two thousand volumes. He was also a hardworking, effective, and fair ruler whose subjects prospered greatly. "When a person traveling through a strange country finds it well cultivated, populous with industrious inhabitants, cities newly founded, commerce extending, towns increasing and everything flourishing so as to indicate happiness, he will naturally conclude it to be under a form of government congenial to the minds of the people. This is a picture of Tipu's country,"[12] Edward Moor, an English traveler, noted in 1794. Even Sir John Shore, Wellesley's predecessor and no friend of Tipu's, agreed. "We know by experience his abilities," he wrote. "He has confidants and advisers, but no ministers and inspects, superintends and regulates himself all the details of his government. . . . The peasantry of his dominions are protected and their labours encouraged and rewarded."[13] Mysore was, Shore concluded, the best run, most prosperous state in India.

Such was the man whom Wellesley had sworn to destroy. Of course, Tipu was not perfect. His hunger for innovation caused him to make many mistakes—the introduction of two wholly new calendars in less than ten years, for instance, made life in Mysore more confused, not more efficient. He was also a fierce warrior not much given to pity for the captured enemy. He had not refrained, on occasion, from attacking his neighbors; and having adopted the tiger as his emblem, he proudly displayed a startling automaton, which consisted of a roaring tiger rending an Englishman. Still, he was unquestionably the most prestigious, most admired ruler in India. Wellesley had, therefore, a correspondingly intense desire to be rid of him.

In 1789, as a result of crooked dealings by the company, Tipu had gone to war with Travancore, a state on the southwestern coast. Travancore was an ally of the company's; Cornwallis had intervened. At first, the war resulted in a stalemate; but then the superior resources of the British and Cornwallis's experience began to tell: the governor-general had apparently learned from his defeat by the American army. By 1792, Tipu had lost the war. The British annexed half his territory and made him pay the enormous sum of £3 million. Wanting more than just revenge, though, he was intent on preserving the rapidly disappearing independence of the Indian states. He also knew that the British could be defeated: he had himself routed their troops at Pollilur in 1780. And the well-known incompetence of the British administration in Madras led him to think he could repeat his earlier victory.

Tragically, however, by 1798, too much had already changed. The British army was larger, better armed, and better led than it had been eighteen years earlier; Wellesley understood just how to isolate Tipu; and Wellesley's younger brother Arthur was (something no one knew yet) a commander of genius.

Wellesley, upon arriving in India, decided to eliminate Tipu forthwith; but his brother Arthur's reports from Madras convinced him that preparations must first be made. These were of two kinds. On the diplomatic front, the nizam of Hyderabad was talked into signing a subsidiary treaty, which not only stationed British troops in his capital but also transferred the conduct of foreign policy to the company. Tipu could thus count on no support from his neighbor to the northeast. To the west, an agreement ensured the neutrality of the Mahrattas. Mysore was now completely isolated. At the same time, on the military front, the British army was resupplied and reorganized. Everything was now ready.

The war did not last long. British armies attacked from both west and east; the latter, ill-led originally, improved dramatically after Colonel Arthur Wellesley took over its chief component. Within days, Seringapatam was besieged; on May 6, 1799, Tipu was killed and the city fell. Having thus had his way, Wellesley went on to annex territory right and left. Only the center of the kingdom of Mysore was left semi-independent. The Hindu maharaja (at this point, a child of five) was restored to the throne, but the British reserved the right to intervene at any time "in the interest of good government." The rest—some two-thirds of the state—was simply annexed, as was a long strip of the southwest coast almost all the way up to Goa. A small section of northeast Mysore was given to Hyderabad (and taken back by the British soon afterward). Mysore was now an enclave in British-controlled territory; obviously it could never be a threat again.

FURTHER CONQUEST

These conquests might have pleased a lesser man—and they struck London as both unexpected and sufficient—but Wellesley already looked to the rest of India. The decay of the Mahrattas' power in the west provided him with the opportunity he wanted, and, once again, the disunity of the Indian princes gave the British their chance. All the way to the north, two maharajas, Scindia of Gwalior and Holkar of Indore, went to war because both wanted to control the weak Mahratta rulers. Under the pretext of protecting the populations from the "anarchy" unleashed by the two kings, Wellesley, in 1803, went back to war. This time, the recently promoted General Arthur Wellesley, who commanded the main army, was ordered by his brother to restore tranquillity in the Deccan. On August 12, after a siege of only four days, he took the supposedly impregnable fortress of Ahmednagar from Scindia.

That was only the beginning. On September 23, at Assaye, General Wellesley, with only seven thousand men, faced Scindia, whose army numbered about forty thousand. Scindia was protected by a river. The trick, for Wellesley, was to get his army across it, although he had been informed that there were neither bridges nor fords. And that is where his massive common sense, combined with an extraordinary military instinct, was first displayed. Twelve years later, these qualities enabled Wellington, as he had become, to win the battle of Waterloo. On that earlier day, in central India, he noticed that at one point, there were two villages exactly opposite each other on the two banks of the river. From this, he concluded that there must be a ford between the two. He went, he looked, he saw that he was right; and it enabled him to take a triangular piece of ground, bound by the two rivers, where the space was too narrow for Scindia to use his cavalry. Despite heavy cannon fire, Wellesley attacked. "The General," one of his aides wrote, "was in the thick of the action the whole time. . . . I never saw a man so cool and collected as he was, . . . though I can assure you, till our troops got the orders to advance, the fate of the day seemed doubtful."[14] Without Wellesley, in fact, the British would surely have been beaten. Scindia had imported French officers to train his army; his artillery was both abundant and modern; he was, himself, a brave, experienced, and effective general; but Wellesley was a genius, and it was on the field of Assaye that he first applied the method that defeated Napoléon twelve years later.

After that, there were more victories—at Parterly on November 25, at Gawilghur on December 15. By the end of the year, much of northern India was under British control—and while General Wellesley had been winning his battles, another general, Gerard Lake, had, at the governor-general's orders, taken Delhi.

THE IMPORTANCE OF DELHI

Of all Indian cities, and there were many, none had a deeper mythic resonance than Delhi. Built, rebuilt, rebuilt yet again—there are seven successive cities on the banks of the Yamuna River—Delhi had long been a center of Muslim power. The capital of a sultanate, it was conquered by Babur, the first of the great Moguls, in 1526, and it was as the imperial capital that it had been most famous. Shah Jahan built a new city there, complete with fort, palace, and mosque, in 1638. From Delhi, Aurangzeb had ruled with an iron hand; and then decay set in.

Faced with Mahratta raids and an Afghan invasion under Nader Shah in 1739, the Mogul Empire had soon begun to crumble. In the 1750s, it lost Bengal, its richest province, to the British, and, in 1753, a civil war between the emperor's chief ministers marked its final dissolution. All that was left of the mighty state which had once ruled two-thirds of the subcontinent was the kingdom of Delhi: the emperor still kept his title, and that title still had prestige, but the power—and the money—were gone. From then on, the decay accelerated. In 1783, Shah Alam II, the Emperor, surrendered to Madhva Rao

Scindia, maharaja of Gwalior, whose capital was some one hundred miles east of Delhi. In 1788, an invasion by the Afghans from the northwest took Delhi. Shah Alam was blinded, but survived, as did much of his immense family. They were hardly to be congratulated, though. An English envoy, who had visited him, wrote: "The poor old King has his eyes put out, wanted common necessaries and was often beaten by the abominable Golavur Khadir, who made the young Princes sing for his amusement, calling them . . . vile names. The women of the Harem were stripped, beaten and numbers died from hunger."[15]

All these punishments were inflicted on the imperial family because Shah Alam's letter, begging Scindia to save him, had been intercepted. Thus, when Scindia retook Delhi just a year later, he might have been expected to feel kindly to the old, blind emperor, but his degradation suited him too well for that. "It is very discreditable to Scindia to leave the [Emperor] and his family so long without any settled provision," he wrote the governor-general. "You can hardly imagine how indigent and degrading [his] position is."[16] Indigent and degrading it remained for the next fourteen years; and then the new paramount power intervened.

By 1803, Wellesley was intent on weakening Scindia so as to assert undisputed control over northern India. The defeat at Assaye helped, of course, but it was not enough. Already, because of their takeover of Varanasi and Oudh, the British had reached westward along and past the line of the Ganges. Now Scindia, between Oudh and Delhi, was not only the main geographical obstacle to the company's progression, but he was also the most dangerous enemy of the British army. That was when, impelled by his logic of perpetual conquest, Wellesley decided that the time had come to take Delhi. And it was not the city alone: if Shah Alam could be made to cooperate, that would further solidify the company's possession. The emperor might be powerless, but his endorsement of someone else's power still made a difference.

As for Shah Alam, he hoped, by pitting the Mahrattas, Scindia, and the British against one another, at least to regain some autonomy; so he put out secret feelers to Wellesley, who was naturally delighted. "If your Majesty should be disposed to accept the Asylum which . . . I have directed the Commander-in-Chief [General Lake] to offer, . . . your Majesty may be assured that every demonstration of respect and every degree of attention which can contribute to the ease and comfort of your Majesty and the Royal Family will be manifested on the part of the British Government, and that adequate provision will be made . . . for the support of your Majesty, your family and household,"[17] Wellesley wrote the emperor. It was obviously a tempting offer: respect and financial abundance, as opposed to scorn and poverty. Of course, Shah Alam would have preferred to be restored as the actual ruler of Delhi; but as he soon understood, that was not a possibility. On August 29, 1803, therefore, the blind emperor asked for British help, only to regret it immediately: three days later,

Scindia, having found out, forced Shah Alam to declare war on the British. That purely theoretical state of hostility lasted exactly ten days. On September 11, Lake defeated Scindia; and on the sixteenth, Shah Alam welcomed the British as his deliverers.

Wellesley, writing the emperor, congratulated him on "Your Majesty's restoration to a state of dignity and tranquillity under the powers of the British Crown."[18] It was a meaningful phrase: henceforth the emperor was a well-treated pensioner. He received £115,000 a year—a great sum, but not excessive given the size of the family, which ran into the hundreds. He ruled absolutely within the confines of the Red Fort, where his palace was situated; he was treated with the greatest respect; and he was absolutely powerless. From 1803 on, it was the British who ruled Delhi; almost as important, they were able to use the emperor's name to obtain a far more willing obedience in other parts of India.

Shah Alam's new status, besides the fact that it gave him a comfortable old age, had at least one wholly positive consequence. The palace in the Red Fort had been built by Shah Jahan and was one of the most spectacular tri-umphs of Mogul architecture. In the eighteenth century, it had endured one indignity after another—the Peacock Throne looted, the silver ceilings re-moved, the precious stones inlaid into the white marble prized out, the foun-tains dried up, the gardens reduced to dust. Now, with his newfound prosper-ity, Shah Alam began to clean up and restore the palace. Much was gone, but there was still much left to preserve; and today we may be grateful that the emperor saved the palace he could no longer see.

The addition of Delhi to the East India Company's territories was un-doubtedly a great success; but by 1804, the directors in London were begin-ning to feel that it was all too much. Wellesley was expensive, and so were his conquests. The company, although now under the tutelage of the Crown, still thought of itself as a profit-making entity. With Wellesley as governor-general, those profits served to pay for ever-expanding conquests. Of course, it was relatively difficult to fire Wellesley as long as he was successful—there was, after all, the prospect of milking the new possessions, and with a series of defeats in Europe, victories in India were popular. That all changed in 1804. In the course of the war against Holkar, the British troops were crushed. This time, Wellesley had gone too far, and both the directors and the Board of Con-trol decided they had had enough. A major war in India was the last thing the government wanted when it was busy trying to defeat Napoléon; and the directors thought it was time to make money, for a change. With both the directors and the board in agreement, therefore, Wellesley was recalled in 1805.

Naturally, Wellesley was outraged. Still, there were some consolations. He had, himself, saved a good deal of money. His younger brother Arthur had not only made a name for himself—Assaye was a celebrated victory—but also come away with £50,000, which made him very comfortable, indeed. And, most important of all, there was the new British Empire in India, stretching now from coast to coast and from Cape Comorin, the southernmost point of the subcontinent, to an area north of Delhi. In 1798, Great Britain had governed a few territories; in 1804, to all intents and purposes, it ruled India.

The brothers naturally took great pride in this transformation. "Our policy and our arms have reduced all the powers of India to the state of mere cyphers at the same time that their intriguing, discontented, rebellious followers still remain with increased causes of discontent,"[19] Arthur wrote Lord Wellesley in 1805. He was right, and it was, from the British point of view, a perfect situation: rulers who worried about their people had no choice but to rely on the British for protection, thus ensuring their own obedience to the paramount power.

A STRANGE COUNTRY

Although, on the whole, Wellesley was content with his position as governor-general, there remained, he felt, one respect in which it left much to be desired. In London, he moved in the most exalted society; in Calcutta, the capital of British India, most of his compatriots belonged to a class for which he felt nothing but contempt. "In the evening," he wrote, "I have no alternative but the society of my subjects or solitude. The former is so vulgar, ignorant, rude, familiar and stupid as to be disgusting and intolerable; especially the ladies, not one of whom . . . is even decently good-looking."[20] The degree to which Wellesley thought of himself as a sovereign is betrayed by his use of the word "subjects"—many of the Englishmen in India were his subordinates, but their wives, and the other ladies, owed him nothing, and no one was his subject. When it comes to that list of unappealing characteristics, though, many people agreed with Wellesley. In England, the manners, and lack of culture, of the returning nabobs were often denounced: the fat and vulgar Joseph Sedley, in William Makepeace Thackeray's *Vanity Fair*, is a perfect example of this.

Many of the English who went out to India did so because they felt they had no choice. Younger sons desperate for money, crooks of various kinds who hoped to be (and often were) more successful preying on the Indians than they had been at home, men so tainted by fault or scandal that they could no longer remain in England, lawyers, doctors, and other professionals who hoped for faster, better rewarded success out East: most of the English in India did not reflect their country's elite. Of course there were also hardworking, intelligent, and honest men—but, as yet, not many.

Indeed, going to India involved more than just a very long trip—as much as three months, sometimes. India was a dangerous place, and many of the

English died there. Some of them, of course, were officers and soldiers—the battles against Tipu, Scindia, and Holkar resulted in significant casualties. Most of them, however, exposed to a variety of tropical diseases against which they had developed no immunity, simply sickened and died. Malaria, yellow fever, typhus, encephalitis, and venereal diseases made many victims. So did a mode of life utterly unsuited to the climate. Eating and drinking as if they were still at home, the English developed a variety of painful, sometimes fatal, intestinal disorders, ranging from jaundice to cirrhosis of the liver. Men and women alike, Westerners often died young; and of those who survived and went home, a significant proportion were in ill health, a sort of permanent hepatitis being the most common affliction.

There were also problems beside illness. The heat was often felt to be unbearable; by 1800, it had occurred to a few bright souls that houses needed to be both much more shaded and much more open than in England. The veranda (an Anglo-Indian word) appeared as a major architectural feature; doors and windows were oriented so as to catch the breezes, but in the climate of Calcutta, or Madras, none of that helped very much. Then, just before and during the yearly monsoon, the humidity rose to appalling levels. Mildew was everywhere, paper melted away, all glued objects (ladies' slippers, for instance) came undone. Finally, there were the insects; not just ordinary mosquitoes, but all kinds of biting creatures who often carried disease and against whom there was virtually no protection—as was true of the many species of snakes. On the very simplest level, therefore, life was dangerous, even in the big cities. Out in the countryside these dangers multiplied: cholera, several varieties of dysentery, and typhoid were all too common, and most often fatal.

It is no wonder, therefore, that the English in India were chiefly intent on two things: making money as fast as possible so that they could go home; and having as good a time as possible while they were there. For most of them, India itself, besides being a place where they could make a fortune, was of no interest. Unaware that they were in the midst of one of the world's oldest and richest civilizations, they simply stuck to their own habits, and took notice of the natives only when something disturbed them. The temple dancers were a case in point.

Many of the Hindu temples, in and around Madras, had temple dancers, especially those dedicated to Shiva as Lord of the Cosmic Dance. These dancers, often themselves the daughters of dancers, became part of the temple personnel at an early age, usually between six and eight. They were trained to perform the sacred dances that entertained the god, and were, in return, fed, housed, and dressed with part of the income from the temple properties. When, at the end of the eighteenth century, the British seized many of these properties, this income shrank accordingly. In order to survive, the dancers prostituted themselves; upon which the government banned temple dancing, thus ending a two-thousand-year-old tradition. This kind of reaction was typical: firmly ignoring both the local traditions and the consequences of their own actions, the British took notice only in order, arbitrarily, to suppress.

BRITISH INDIA

In many ways, the British tried to pretend that they were not in India. Although, unlike in England, houses had flat roofs, they were built in the neoclassical style fashionable at home. Just as in London, there were chic parts of town, and slums farther away—here, usually the native quarters. The three chief cities—Calcutta, Madras, and Bombay—were new, the creations of the British. So there was a park somewhere near the center, and the grandest mansions could be found along its sides—just like in London. The hours were English hours, except that people tried not to go out in the middle of the day. The organization of the households tried to copy what it was at home. The fashions, for both men and women, were English fashions. The main difference, in fact, was that most of the English in India lived far more luxurious lives than they ever could have at home.

In spite of all these efforts at pretending that Madras or Calcutta was just like London, though, it was immediately obvious to the new arrivals that India was a very different place indeed. First, if they had any sense, they arrived with a bundle of letters of introduction. There were no hotels; once you got off the ship, you desperately needed an invitation to stay somewhere until you could find your own quarters. Then there was the crowd milling on the quay, which was made of people of all nations, European and Indian, speaking a variety of languages. It was hot, it was loud, and there was a variety of exotic smells. Suddenly, brown men who spoke no English seized your luggage; you often were not quite sure where to go; and it was a considerable relief when the first people you visited read that letter of introduction and asked you to be their guests.

Still, for most of the English, there was no doubt that they had come to the right place. Sailing up the Hooghly to Calcutta, Eliza Fay, the wife of a lawyer, looked around with approval. "The banks of the river are . . . absolutely studded with elegant mansions," she wrote. "These houses are surrounded by groves and lawns which descend to the water's edge and present a succession of whatever can delight the eye. The noble appearance of the river also, which is much wider than the Thames at London Bridge, together with the amazing variety of vessels . . . add to the beauty of the scene."[21]

It might have been a water party in England—except that the groves noticed by Mrs. Fay were full of tropical trees and bushes. Calcutta, a city with a population of over 150,000, was also built to an English pattern. The grand houses along the Chowringhee Road, by the Esplanade, looked not unlike their counterparts in London. The Writers Building, where the clerical offices of the East India Company were placed, the governor-general's mansion, and all official buildings followed the pattern to be seen all over England. Once the traveler went indoors, though, what he or she saw looked new and strange. One major difference, of course, was the openness of the architecture. Inside, there were venetian blinds over the windows to keep out the sun. Outside, between the columns of the veranda, *tatties,* made of fine strips of bamboo, were hung to create shade. *Kus-kus,* a matting material wetted with water, was hung in the doorways as a primitive — and relatively effective — form of air-conditioning. Then, hanging from the ceilings, there were punkahs, vast fans moved by a cord and pulley. Servants soon learned how to work them: they tied the cord to their big toe and could keep the punkah flapping even when fast asleep.

Another great difference, which struck the visitor, was the relative lack of furniture. All the armchairs, stools, sofas, tables, consoles, and chests that were an essential part of the good life at home somehow lacked convenience in India. It was simply too hot for upholstered furniture or for crowded rooms, so fine Oriental carpets became the great luxury. The dining room, however, was an exception. Large mahogany tables, the requisite numbers of chairs, the appropriate sideboards, were all firmly in place.

Immediately outside, there were stables and servants' quarters. That was not so strange, but most houses also had a poultry yard and a piggery, as well, of course, as a garden with lawns and orange or lemon trees, all usually kept up by Chinese gardeners. Already in 1800, the East India was importing Company tea from China, and its ships often called on India on the way back. The most striking difference, though, was the number of servants. Grandees, at home, might have vast domestic staffs; but even a well-to-do family would make do with a mere five or six servants. Here, the domestics were legion. There were two good reasons for this. One was that they were cheap; the other was that each servant had his or her own job and would do nothing else. The sweeper would not make up the beds, the bearer would not clean boots, the man in charge of filling the hookah, the water pipe, would not wait at table. Poor Mrs. Fay found it all very difficult: "I am arranging my establishment," she wrote her sister, "which is no little trouble in a country where servants will not do a single thing, but that for which you expressly engage them."[22]

Thus, even a bachelor's household could be the size of a battalion. At its head there was the steward, who took a commission on everything that was bought for the house, but no salary. It was a firmly believed cliché that all stewards were thieves, and judging by the number of those who opted for an early and prosperous retirement, the cliché may often have been true. Since, however, it was the steward who controlled the other servants, he was indispensable. After the steward came the *munshi,* a clerk-interpreter, who was equally necessary since the English usually spoke only their own language, while the servants understood only Bengali.

At the next level down were the outdoor servants—gardeners, coachmen, stable boys, and, most important of all, the palanquin bearers (usually six or eight), headed by the *jummadar*, who walked beside the palanquin and was often his master's confidant. Preceding the palanquin were two *soontah-burdars*, who carried silver-tipped batons, or a *chobdar*, who carried a silver pole four-and-a-half feet long; or both. And at night, naturally, there were torchbearers: street lighting had not reached Calcutta.

Inside, there were many more servants. The doorkeeper and the watch-man were at the entrance; cleaners and servers abounded; the cook was usually Muslim; there was a *kitmagar*, whose principal job was to stand behind his master's chair at dinner and who went with him when he dined out. The hookah keeper took care of the water pipe, presented it to his master at the appropriate times, and kept it filled. The valet looked after his master's clothes. Then, to that already plethoric staff, were added the gardeners, the grass cut-ters, the water carrier, and the *dhobi*, the laundryman. As for the barber, he came by every day, while the tailor's visits were slightly less frequent.

Naturally, there were company employees—the simple clerks, for in-stance—who hardly lived on that scale; but, in a more modest way, they, too, were significantly better off than they ever could have been at home. As for the well-to-do Anglo-Indian, life was indeed easy, as one visitor noted.

> About the hour of 7 A.M., his door keeper opens the gate and the verandah is free to his cash keepers, footmen, messengers, constables, stewards and but-lers, writers [clerks] and solicitor. The head bearer and jemmadar enter the hall and his bedroom at eight o'clock. A lady quits his side and is conducted by a private staircase either to her own apartment or out of the yard. The moment the master throws his legs out of bed, the whole force is waiting to rush into his room; each making three salaams by bending the body and the head very low. . . . In about half an hour after undoing and taking off his long drawers, a clean shirt, stockings, breeches and slippers are put on . . . without any greater exertion on his part than if he was a statue. The barber enters, shaves him, cuts his nails and cleans his ears. The chillumgee [basin] and ewer are brought by a servant . . . who pours water upon his hands and face, and presents a towel. The superior then walks in state to his breakfasting parlour in his waistcoat; is seated; the consumah [table footman] makes and pours out his tea and presents him with a plate of bread or toast. The hairdresser comes behind and begins his operation, while the houccaburdar [pipe bearer] slips the upper end of the . . . tube of the houcca into his hand. While the hair-dresser is doing his duty, the gentleman is eating, sipping and smoking by turns. [Then come waiting solicitors until ten o'clock] . . . when attended by his cavalcade, he is conducted to his palanquin and preceded by eight or twelve [servants] . . . They move off at a quick amble. . . . [Then he does busi-

ness] until two o'clock when he and his company sit down perfectly *at ease* in point of dress and address to a good dinner, each attended by his own servant. . . . The moment the glasses are introduced, the houccaburdars enter. . . . As it is expected that [the guests] shall return to supper, at four o'clock they begin to withdraw without ceremony and step into their palanquins, so that in a few minutes the man is left to go into his bedroom where he is instantly undressed to his shirt, and his long drawers put on. . . . He sleeps till seven or eight o'clock. [Then, after the same dressing, tea and hairdressing ceremony as in the morning], he puts on a handsome coat, and pays visits of ceremony to the ladies; returns a little before ten o'clock, supper being served at ten. The company keeps together until twelve or one in the morning, preserving great sobriety or decency; when they depart, our hero is conducted to his bedroom where he finds a female companion to amuse him. . . . With no greater exertions than these do the company's servants amass the most splendid fortunes.[23]

Obviously, the tone of this description is sarcastic; but the day depicted here is real enough. There is also the interesting detail of the female companion. Just as in England, unmarried women were expected to remain chaste; and in this small society, it was more difficult for married women to have lovers than it would have been at home. Then, because many of the men had come to seek their fortune, they were usually single; so they had Indian concubines. Some of these Englishmen treated their companions relatively well, keeping them in comfort without, of course, ever acknowledging them socially. Others used them simply as prostitutes, changing them often and paying them little. As for the children who were not infrequently the outcome of these liaisons, they might be looked after by their father while he was still in India; but once he went home, they were usually left behind and forgotten. The lucky ones were educated and became clerks; the unlucky ones went on to earn a living however they could.

The social life in Calcutta, Bombay, and Madras simply imitated England. Just as in London, Mrs. Fay explained to her sister, "after tea, either cards or music fill up the space, 'till ten, when supper is generally announced. Five card loo is the usual game, and they play a rupee a fish, limited to ten. This will strike you as being enormously high but it is thought nothing of here. . . . Formal visits are paid in the evening; they are generally very short as each lady has a dozen to make and a party waiting at home besides."[24] And then there were grand evening parties, usually balls, with dancing until dawn, and a great deal to eat and drink.

The one element absolutely missing in all this socializing was culture. Little or no theater, no opera, no concerts (other than of that oxymoron, military music), no painting or sculpture exhibitions or collections, and very little reading: the Anglo-Indians were thorough philistines, and were promptly denounced as such when they returned home. Firmly ignoring Indian art,

literature, and music, utterly contemptuous of the Indians themselves, they
tried to create a series of little Englands on the subcontinent, with all the
shortcomings of home and none of its achievements.

One result was constant discomfort. To dress in India as if one were in
England was not advisable. The food, too, remained unchanged, except for the
often abundant use of hot pepper, in a country whose native cuisine was rich,
subtle, and endlessly varied. "I will give you our bill of fare," Mrs. Fay told her
sister. "A soup, a roast fowl, curry and rice, mutton pie, a forequarter of lamb, a
rice pudding, tarts, very good cheese, fresh churned butter, fine bread, excellent Madeira (that is expensive but the eatables are very cheap)."[25] They were
indeed. You could buy a whole sheep for two rupees (there were about ten
rupees to the British pound); a lamb, two pounds of butter, or six fowls for one
rupee; while claret, being imported, was sixty rupees for a dozen bottles.

And so the Anglo-Indians prospered. As for the Indians themselves, they
simply obeyed new masters within the East India Company's territories, and
old masters elsewhere. Their own artistic traditions were soon corrupted by
Western influences: 1800 is about the time when the Rajput schools of painting begin to import European motifs and techniques. The result, most often, is
a stiff, awkward image. Architecture, for a while longer, remained uninfluenced
by the Anglo-Indian neoclassical style; but not much was being built. In that
moment of transition, in fact, it was as if India held its breath. The past was
dead, the future was on the way. Only one thing was sure: in the long history of
Indian empires a new raj had been born, and it was British.

CHAPTER SEVENTEEN

The Middle East:
The Ottoman Empire

TURKEY, IN 1800, was right in the middle of the first reforming reign in its history. Convinced that the decay of his empire must be stopped, Sultan Selim III looked to western Europe for inspiration: a new army, a new navy, a more modern system of education were all meant to revive the Ottomans' fading glories. Unfortunately, it was not just a question of spending a great deal of money at a time when revenues were chronically insufficient: there was a large group of reactionaries to whom change was anathema.

It was, in many ways, a paradox. Turkey fascinated western Europeans because it was so exotic and so wealthy, because its women were hidden and its customs were so different. The greatest part of the Ottoman Empire was in Asia, but western Europe was a lodestar to Selim and the reformers because its armies were modern and its technology more advanced. The result was that for the first time since the fall of Byzantium to the Turks in 1453, these two very different worlds were coming closer together.

There was another, unacknowledged, link: slavery. Not all Turkish slaves were African: there were, for instance, Circassian or Armenian women in many harems. Still, most of the slaves came from Africa, and were sold to the Arab traders by the same people who were also selling them to English, French, or American buyers. Here, too, this vast, apparently self-sufficient empire was linked to the rest of the world.

A FASCINATING CITY

Riches beyond counting; an imperial court as splendid as it was mysterious; cloistered women and ferocious soldiers: Turkey, in 1800, seemed both exotic and fascinating to western Europeans. It was close enough to be better known than China; it had played a major role in war and politics as it conquered a significant part of the European continent. Indeed, for almost three centuries, its power had seemed irresistible. It had very nearly taken Vienna in 1683; then, in the mid eighteenth century, it had endured a series of defeats, but it still controlled an empire of extraordinary size.

From Bosnia and the edge of Hungary to the borders of Morocco, from the Crimea to the border of Persia, the Ottoman sultan reigned over a vast mosaic of states and peoples. Today's Bosnia, Serbia, Albania, Macedonia, Romania, Bulgaria, Greece; the entire shore of the Black Sea (including a good part of today's Ukraine); Georgia, Armenia, Tajikistan, Uzbekistan, today's Turkey, Iraq, Syria, Lebanon, Palestine, Egypt, and, less directly, Tunisia and Algeria—all the eastern shores of the Mediterranean, half the coast of the Adriatic, all that was part of the empire. The sultan, from his palace at Istanbul, ruled in Bucharest, Belgrade, Sophia, Athens, Baghdad, Damascus, Cairo. His subjects spoke a bewildering array of languages; most of them were Muslim, of course, but there were also large Christian and Jewish minorities. And from all the parts of the empire, people and goods flowed to Istanbul, his capital.

That city was, everyone agreed, vast, wealthy, and fascinating. It was also very beautiful. Lady Mary Wortley Montagu, who traveled there in the early eighteenth century, described "an agreeable mixture of gardens, pine and cypress trees, palaces, mosques and public buildings raised one above the other."[1] Indeed, Istanbul was an unusually green and open city, not least because each of the numerous mosques sat in a large garden, so that even the narrow, tortuous, and crowded streets at the center of the city led to these parklike spaces. As for Joseph Pitton de Tournefort, who visited Istanbul in 1715, he knew just how thrilling it was to see the city. "Constantinople, with its suburbs, is without question the greatest city in Europe," he wrote. "Its [geographical] position is the pleasantest and most advantageous in the world: it seems as if the straits of the Dardanelles, and those of the Black Sea have been created to bring here the riches of all the four parts of the world."[2] That, of course, was what made the difference; not just the size of the city, whose population was then a little over half a million—greater, therefore, than those of London or Paris—but its vast wealth. Then, the natural setting, the blue waters of the Bosporus and the Golden Horn, the hills along the crests of which a vast array of domes and minarets was silhouetted against the bright sky, the gardens and the imperial palace on Seraglio Point, all contributed to Istanbul's magic. "Discovering at one glance all the buildings . . . of the city is the most pleasant thing in the world," Tournefort went on. "Its covered markets, terraces, balconies and gardens form several amphitheaters varied by the caravanserais [combinations of warehouses and inns], the palaces and above all the mosques . . . whose principal domes are flanked by other smaller domes, all of them covered in lead or gilded . . . All that makes an enchanting spectacle."[3]

This was the view from just outside the city. Once inside, it soon became clear that each of its many sections was organized around a mosque, a church, or a synagogue. There were public markets: the old bazaar and the new bazaar were immense covered spaces whose many rows of small domes sheltered every kind of merchandise, from gold, jewels, and precious furs to spices and secondhand clothes. Buyers sometimes needed to bargain, but the prices of all commodities were strictly regulated, and the grand vizier himself, the sultan's prime minister, came through once a week to make sure that all was as it should be. Coffeehouses, everywhere, served the famously excellent Turkish coffee and provided their exclusively male customers with water pipes. The waters before the city were crowded and active. Warships, trading ships, and caïques—long slender rowboats, some of them brightly painted and shaded by silk canopies—were all part of the excitement, while the suburb of Eyup, at the top of the Golden Horn, was famous for its beauty, its quiet, and the excellence of its gardens.

The crowds, which filled the city, were also highly picturesque. Coming from all the corners of the Empire, there were people wearing all kinds of costumes. Mullahs, Greek Orthodox priests, and rabbis all passed one another peacefully. The rich and powerful, sumptuously dressed and lavishly bejeweled, rode through; closed carriages, sheltering invisible women, were everywhere. The main difference, in fact, between Istanbul and many other great cities was the virtual absence of all but the poorest women. "Most of the Turkish ladies," Tournefort noted with disapproval, "are forced to remain at home. The Greek, Jewish and Armenian women have more freedom, but they do not go out as often as women in France because they have slaves who take care of all outside business, such as going to the market or running errands."[4]

Indeed, to be a woman—especially one belonging to any but a poor family—meant being almost a prisoner. Restricted to a special section of the house, able to go out only in a closed carriage or so wrapped and veiled as to be utterly unrecognizable, respectable women were excluded from the life of the city. Of course, there were others who were anything but respectable: Istanbul had its brothels, clustering mostly around the harbor, and they were frequented mostly by sailors and workingmen. In a culture where divorce was instantaneous (if you were a man) and where a concubine could always be added to the household, there was really no reason for those who were better off to seek them.

Far more visible were the black slaves. For centuries, Arab traders had bought Africans for the empire—some 9 million men, women, and children since 1500. It was not surprising, therefore, to come across Africans in Istanbul or in the other Ottoman cities. There was a great difference between slavery here and slavery in the Americas, though: no child was born a slave; and so there were far fewer slaves, and slavery lasted a single generation. One of the results was a great variety of skin tones in the population; another was that Turkey, unlike the United States, was not dependent on its slaves.

These Africans were part of the ever-animated street scene: this was, after all, a great trading center, and merchandise passed to and fro, while businessmen moved from appointment to appointment. Then there were the shoppers, not only local, but men who came from all over the empire to buy what could be found only in those famous bazaars. Frequently, dignitaries, from the grand vizier and the chief mufti on down, came by, surrounded by a brilliant cortege. On feast days, processions of the guilds added to the city's glitter. There were street performers of all kinds, as well—musicians, acrobats, and, most of the year, puppeteers. Puppets, in fact, were immensely popular. A stage would be set up; elaborate sets, lit by oil lamps from the back, represented landscapes, cityscapes, palaces. The puppets were articulated and controlled by rods connected by strings to the articulations; the puppeteer could thus give his figures convincing movement while speaking the puppets' parts in a variety of voices. Often, a two-man band would add its music to the proceedings. Then, accompanied by many other figures, the two favorite puppets, Karagöz and Hajivat, would go at each other. Karagöz was a simple but cunning man of the street, the symbol of popular wisdom and resourcefulness; Hajivat was an educated fellow, who gave himself airs, and was often bested by his rival. Together they were so popular that what had started out as a distraction for Ramadan, the month of fasting, became a year-round entertainment.

Naturally, there was still much more, from the street vendors to the construction workers repairing the damage inflicted by one of the city's frequent fires. Most of the houses in Istanbul were made of wood, sometimes with a stone base, and they burned easily. Only the religious monuments, mosques, churches, and synagogues were entirely built of brick or stone—and they were busy as well, with a variety of services on different days of the week. "You would have to spend several years in Constantinople to be aware of all that goes on there,"[5] Tournefort sighed, and he was right.

At the Heart of All Splendor

Within the city, you could go anywhere. You could cross to Pera, see its walls and towers, many of which went back to the Byzantine Empire, visit the establishments of merchants from Genoa or Venice; but one place, in Istanbul itself, was separate and, to most people, inaccessible—the sultan's palace. There was, in fact, more than one palace: over the centuries, the sultans had built, usually on the edge of the water, less formal residences; but when you said "the Palace," everyone understood that it meant Topkapi. Built on the spit of land where the Byzantine emperors had also had their own palaces, Topkapi was a compound, a great many different buildings, some connected, some freestanding, set in the midst of a vast park that reached down the hill to the water. It was, of course, well defended, girt with stout walls, and reached through a formidable gate; but, by 1800, those ramparts no longer served any purpose. As for the enemy, it was already inside. The janissaries, those famous warriors who had once been the terror of Europe, were, some of them, encamped in the first of the palace courtyards; and they had, on occasion, risen against the reigning sultan, killed him, and replaced him with a prince of their choice.

That first courtyard was open to all. The janissaries, with their fierce mustaches, and their tall hats decorated with an extra flap of material and, often, a long feather set downward, were there, of course, but so were the merchants who supplied the court. The servants of the dignitaries who were attending the sultan waited there, together with their horses. In the buildings on either side were the imperial infirmary, the bakery, the mint, with its goldsmiths and gem setters, the silk weavers, the glovers, the upholsterers, the coppersmiths, the makers of musical instruments—all permanently employed by the imperial household. And over it all reigned the deepest silence. To speak loudly was considered an offense to the sultan and was punished instantly by a severe beating. It was, all the travelers agreed, eerie: so many people, so little noise.

Far fewer people entered the second courtyard—ministers, ambassadors, people who attended on the sultan or the grand vizier, the agas (military commanders), the pashas (governors of provinces), the great nobles. The way in was through the thoroughly warlike Ortokapi, the great gate flanked by two large, powerful towers with copper-covered conical tops, while inside there were reception rooms where the ambassadors waited to be called before the divan, the council of state, which met four times a week. The courtyard itself was surrounded by a colonnade. Fountains played, flowers were everywhere, and tame gazelles strolled elegantly. Straight ahead as you came in was the pavilion of the divan. Although the sultan was an absolute ruler, restrained only by the *sharia*, the Islamic law, most of the actual governing, under Selim III, was done by his ministers. There was a grated opening in the wall of the divan's meeting room, so that if he chose, the sultan could listen in to his ministers' deliberations. Selim must have done it often: he was, for most of his reign, a sultan who was trying to make changes.

The second court was also a great ceremonial space. Whether the occasion was a declaration of war, the accession of a sultan, the circumcision of a prince, or the reception of an ambassador, all the splendor of the empire was displayed there. On all those occasions, the janissaries lined the colonnade and the central path, which led to the sultan. On either side of this path, officials and courtiers, each wearing precisely the costume of his rank, formed a glittering parterre of brocades, velvets, and jewels. Then there were the turbans, of all shapes and sizes, made of a variety of sumptuous materials and further adorned with jeweled and feathered aigrettes. As for the sultan, a dazzling figure in gold-embroidered robes abundantly adorned with precious stones of enormous size, he sat cross-legged on gold cushions or on one of the gold thrones he owned, and watched it all.

The thrones themselves amazed everyone. Shaped like low platforms on short legs, with a tall back and sometimes a canopy, they were made of gold inset with precious stones. One was a replica of the Great Mogul's Peacock Throne; others varied slightly, but all glittered and proclaimed the sultan's immense wealth. The fact that these great ceremonies took place in the courtyard, not in some vast and ornate hall, also said something about the Turks. Originally a nomadic people, their architects still thought in terms of tents—only now the tents had become pavilions with walls covered in ceramic tiles; and these, too, seemed to deny the need for any permanent building. Adorned with flowers in red, blues, greens, the Iznik tiles were themselves like an unchanging garden. By 1800, they were no longer made; but so many of them had entered the imperial reserves in the sixteenth and seventeenth centuries that they could still be used as if nothing had changed.

Elsewhere in the compound, in the sultan's apartments or the pleasure kiosks, endless numbers of precious objects were used as the chief adornments. Aside from the built-in sofas, there was very little furniture: precious carpets, rich draperies, and plates, cups, goblets, clocks, boxes, and water pipes were made of gold and precious stones. "All," the traveler Jean-Claude Flachat reported in 1755, "is of unparalleled magnificence. The window openings and ceilings are inlaid with flowered porcelain of remarkable finish. Foliage carved in gold covers the stucco which joins the slabs of porcelain. The walls are covered with tapestry of cloth of gold. The sofa is of a material just as rich. The mirrors, clocks, caskets are all remarkable and what is extraordinary is that these masterpieces are the production of foreign artists."[6] Flachat was right: already by the mid eighteenth century, and to a still greater degree in 1800, it seemed as if the Turks had somehow lost faith in their own culture. The apartments of the Valideh, the sultan's mother, of that day have survived. Decorated with charming rococo motifs, they might just as well adorn an Italian interior.

THE MYSTERIES OF THE HAREM

Still deeper into the palace compound, the third court led to the key places in the Topkapi: the imperial apartments, the harem, and the relics pavilion, where hairs of the beard of the Prophet were piously preserved. Beyond that still was a park with pleasure pavilions and terraces. It was the harem, however, which was, in many ways, the center of the palace. The early sultans, although they had also had harems, spent much of their time away at war; but for some two centuries, most of them simply stayed in or around Istanbul; and then, as often as not, the women took over. It was, in fact, an extraordinary paradox. The oda-lisques, whose numbers varied from four hundred to over a thousand, were the sultan's slaves. They had no rights; their chief duty was to please him, should he choose one of them. For a few of them, that meant a single night spent with the sultan, and duly recorded in a register. After that, if they became pregnant, the sultan decided: if he wanted a child, the concubine was allowed to carry to term; if he did not, the resident abortionist was called in. Most of the oda-lisques, though, never saw the sultan's bed. They were simply given jobs—cler-ical work, sowing, waiting on one of the four *kadins*—the chief concubines—or the Sultana Valideh, the emperor's mother.

How then could they be so powerful? Most of them, of course, were not. But the *kadins*, the chief concubines whom the sultan saw often, had their chance: a strong-minded woman who knew how to please a lazy, or sometimes weak-minded, sultan could rule the empire through him. As for the Sultana Valideh, she had the best position of all: she was irreplaceable, and often beloved by the son whom she had protected in his youth. She ruled the harem officially, with her own treasurer and administration; she often chose her son's concubines, thus ensuring that he would hear no advice but her own; and so she was often the person who actually made policy. She was also happily unencumbered by a daughter-in-law: in order to save the immense expense involved in setting up the household of an actual wife, the sultans remained unmarried.

There was another good reason why the Valideh had so much power. Being an Ottoman prince was, at the best of times, unpleasant and dangerous. First, there was a significant risk of an early death: each mother wanted *her* son to become sultan, and most were quite prepared to arrange the death of those who stood in the way. Given the intrigues at court, this was often quite easy. A *kadin* could line up with a powerful minister, then make it look as if the heir presumptive was a tool of the opposite faction. The minister was then quite likely to convince the sultan that it was a good idea to get rid of a traitor. Killing princes in Turkey was, after all, quite commonplace. In the six-teenth century, sultans had normally had their brothers executed to prevent possible revolts. Now the princes were kept in the Cage, a tightly locked series of rooms next to the harem. Not infrequently, one or more of the inmates was killed. Some were surreptitiously poisoned. Eventually, at the sultan's death, the eldest one emerged to become sultan. When, for instance, Abdülhamid succeeded to the throne in 1774, he had spent forty-five years in the Cage. That system, obviously, did not make for well-educated, well-informed heirs: all too often, the new sultan barely knew where Turkey was. A clever and powerful *kadin* counted on this; and she also knew how to keep her son alive.

The situation was further complicated by the rules of succession. In Turkey, it was not the eldest son of the sultan who succeeded, but the eldest living prince, whose father was likely to have been an earlier sultan: when

Selim III came to the throne in 1789, he succeeded, not his father, but his uncle, Abdülhamid. In that case, the sultan, who was fond of Selim, had had him released from the Cage early and made sure that nothing happened to him. Far more often, however, the sultan felt no particular affection for the heir and did not at all mind having him strangled. Thus it was up to the potential Valideh to save her son; and when she succeeded, that son tended to be extremely grateful.

The harem itself was a vast warren of corridors, small rooms, baths, and small courtyards completely closed off from the world. No normal man ever entered it besides the sultan; but it was staffed with about six hundred black eunuchs whose castration had been so complete that they were left without any genitals at all. To ensure their obedience, bastinado boards were kept ready at hands. These were wooden boards with holes for either the feet or the hand, and the bastinado—an extremely painful punishment—consisted of beating either feet or hands with a rod.

The chief of the black eunuchs, the *kislar aga*, was a man of vast importance and, usually, equally vast proportions. He ran the harem—under the Sultana Valideh if there was one, alone if there was not. He was the only conduit between the ministers and other outsiders and the sultan, whom he could approach at any time. He also conveyed the sultan's orders to the outside world. Naturally, therefore, he was seen as the person most necessary to the success of any request, and was bribed in consequence. The sultans knew it and took it in good part: being, obviously, unmarried, the *kislar aga* always made the sultan his heir.

This physically diminished, but otherwise powerful, high officer of state had his own prescribed costume: a robe of flowered silk with, over it, a tunic of blue, red, or green material trimmed with sable; on his head, he wore a huge hat shaped like a sugarloaf. "He was so fat," the French writer Maxime du Camp wrote of the *kislar aga* of the 1840s, "that he seemed to have a human shape only because his overwhelming bulk was contained by his clothing. His yellow and flabby cheeks were crisscrossed by a thousand wrinkles. He had no beard; a child's down shadowed his thick lips. His amiable eyes moved slowly and seemed to open with difficulty. Behind him, a black boy was making coffee on a portable stove; he called him and his voice was thin, high and weak like that of a woman."[7] The amiability was mere appearance: *kislar agas* were notoriously tough. They arranged for the elimination of unwanted princes and disposed of any woman who had become tainted (perhaps because she had concealed her pregnancy and given birth to a forbidden child).

Almost as important in this enclosed world, where primping, gossip, and intrigues were the main activities, the *kislar aga* could control the distribution of clothes and jewels. Of course, a powerful *kadin* could demand, and get, what she wanted, but the others depended on him—and a well-dressed woman, whether in the sultan's harem or in that of a dignitary, could be quite a spectacular sight. When, in the 1740s, Lady Mary Wortley Montagu arrived in Istanbul, she promptly arranged to be given Turkish dress. "The first piece of my dress," she reported,

> is a pair of drawers, very full, that reach to my shoes, and conceal the legs more modestly than your petticoats. They are of thin, rose-coloured damask, brocaded with silver flowers, my shoes are of white kid leather, embroidered with gold. Over this hangs my smock, of fine white silk gauze edged with embroidery. The smock has wide sleeves, hanging half way down the arm, and is closed at the neck with a diamond button; but the colour and shape of the bosom very well to be distinguished through it. The *antery* is a waistcoat . . . , of white and gold damask, with very long sleeves falling back and fringed with deep gold fringe, and should have diamond or pearl buttons. My *caftan*, of the same stuff with my drawers, is a robe exactly fitted to my shape and reaching to my feet, with long straight falling sleeves. Over this is the girdle, about four fingers broad . . . entirely of diamonds or other precious stones . . . fastened before with a clasp of diamonds. . . . The headdress is composed of a cap . . . of fine velvet embroidered with pearls and diamonds. . . . This is fixed on one side of the head . . . [On the other side is] a large bouquet of jewels, made like natural flowers.[8]

Fashion did not change much in Turkey: in 1800, the women of the harem were dressed in just this way.

THE FRENCH SULTANA

The most important of these women, though, might have expected to wear a very different costume. She had been Abdülhamid's first *kadin*, and much loved by the sultan. Just as important, she had formed a close friendship with the heir, who, upon mounting the throne as Selim III, continued to rely on her; and she was the mother of the next heir but one. It was, apparently, a typical story. The difference was that the lady in question was neither Turkish, nor Circassian, nor Armenian, as was the norm; nor was she a black-haired, black-eyed beauty. Uniquely in the long history of the harem, she was blonde, blue-eyed, and French.

Aimée Dubucq de Rivery should never have been there if it had not been for a series of events that read more like an adventure novel than a true story. Born in Martinique of a family of rich French planters, she was the cousin of Joséphine de Beauharnais, who eventually became Napoléon's empress. At the age of twelve, she was sent to Nantes, where she continued her education in a fashionable convent. The American War of Independence delayed her return;

so it was not until 1784, at the age of twenty-one, that she set sail for home together with her faithful black nurse. And that is where the story begins.

In the Bay of Biscay, her ship ran into a terrible storm and had started to sink when a Spanish merchantman appeared in the very nick of time. Rescued, Aimée and the other passengers were informed that they were going to Palma de Mallorca, from where they could take another ship to their destination. For a few days, all went well; then, in sight of the harbor, the Spanish ship, its goods, and its passengers were seized by Barbary pirates. History does not record the fate of the other passengers or the crew; but it was clear to the pirates that Aimée, being so blonde and so beautiful, was much too good for them; so they decided to give her to their ruler, the dey of Algiers.

The dey, in turn, was stunned by the young woman's beauty. He wanted, at just this time, to earn the good graces of his sovereign, the sultan; and so, no doubt reluctantly, he sent him Aimée as a gift. It all must have been both odd and frightening to the young woman, but she had no choice. Dressed now in Oriental clothes, she sailed off to Istanbul in a luxuriously appointed ship; and upon arrival, she entered the harem. How this convent-educated girl coped with what came next is hard to imagine. She had to learn Turkish, of course; but, far worse, she had to discard everything she had been taught when it came to life and morality. In the convent, she had worn a chemise reaching down to her ankles on those rare occasions when she was allowed to take a bath; here, she bathed, every day, nude among other nude women. All the hair on her body was removed; she was taught how to make herself desirable, not just by the use of perfumes and cosmetics, but also through the techniques that were most likely to give the sultan pleasure. As the only blonde in a world of brunettes, she must have excited much envy, and suffered accordingly. Still, throughout it all, she must have been dazzled by the splendors that surrounded her; and she was protected by the one person who really mattered.

There was, in 1784, no Valideh, and the *kislar aga* thus reigned supreme over the harem. As luck would have it, he was allied with Prince Selim, a tall, sweet-tempered and scholarly young man, and with the reformers, those who wanted to Westernize Turkey, against the first *kadin*. The *kadin* was tied to the reactionaries who opposed all change because she wanted her son Mustafa to succeed instead of Selim. What the *kislar aga* saw right away was that Aimée was the perfect way to defeat the *kadin*; and he must soon have discovered that Aimée remained convinced of the superiority of the West. At a time when the reformers wanted to bring in European techniques and instructors, Naksh, "the beautiful one," as she was now called, could make all the difference. Finally, every odalisque's ambition was to become first *kadin*: Aimée thus had every reason to side with the *kislar aga* against the current holder of the position.

At the earliest possible opportunity, the *kislar aga* brought Aimée to the sultan; the results were everything he had hoped. Abdülhamid fell in love; the erstwhile first *kadin* was displaced; and a firm alliance was forged between Prince Selim, the *kislar aga,* and Aimée. When, on July 25, 1785, she gave birth to a son, there were spectacular celebrations, and the baby was given a ruby-studded cradle.

She was now the mother of the next heir after the princes Selim and Mustafa. Selim was her friend and ally. Already in 1786, she had convinced him to break all precedents by writing a letter of friendship to Louis XVI. Nothing came of it—the startled French foreign minister hardly knew how to react—but it was clear to both Aimée and Selim that Turkey, if it was to survive, must Westernize. That is just what they set out to do when the twenty-seven-year-old Selim succeeded to the throne in April 1789.

Reform was a long-term project, of course. In the meantime, there were premonitory signs. In the 1790s, for instance, hot air balloons were seen floating over the domes of Istanbul. In the harem, Aimée's apartment was redecorated in neoclassical style, while European objects of all kinds were imported, and a French troupe of musicians and dancers came to dance the minuet before a parterre of hidden odalisques. France, clearly, was in fashion at the Topkapi. In 1797, the first permanent Turkish ambassador was appointed to France (where he was extremely popular); and in 1806, the startled Joséphine received, from her long-disappeared cousin, a present of a hundred cashmere shawls.

A Declining Empire

The eighteenth century, for Turkey, had not been a happy time. At the very end of the seventeenth century, it had lost Hungary and Serbia. It regained Belgrade in the 1730s, but already it was clear that the empire's chief enemy was no longer Austria. Russia, woken from its slumbers by Peter the Great, was large, dangerous, and hungry. It also had an immense border with Turkey, and the will to expand toward the southeast. Nothing very much happened until the 1770s; but then Catherine the Great attacked, and in 1774, Turkey, for the first time ever, acknowledged a major loss of territory.

The Treaty of Kuchuk Kainarji not only gave Russia a foothold on the north shore of the Black Sea, it also gave the Tartars, who lived in the Crimea, their independence. That, as everyone understood, was just a first step; annexation by Russia would be next—which, indeed, occurred exactly ten years later. More menacing still were two other clauses. One gave Russia the right to protect the Christians of Moldavia and Walachia, today's Romania, thus legitimizing Russia's interference into the internal affairs of Turkey. The other, although vaguely worded, appeared to extend that right to all the Greek Orthodox

Christians living within the empire. There was more. Russia was now allowed to have a permanent ambassador in Istanbul; it gained a variety of commercial privileges, and its ships were given the right to pass through the Bosporus and the Dardanelles. Thus, although the loss of actual territory was relatively minor, the other clauses gave Russia a right of permanent interference: Turkey was now becoming the Sick Man of Europe.

For Catherine the Great, this was a mere beginning. In the late 1780s, she floated a plan to divide the Ottoman Empire; about half of it (including Istanbul) was to be a new Byzantine Empire ruled by her grandson Constantine, with the other half divided between Austria, France, and Venice. Britain and Prussia soon squelched the idea, but henceforth, Russian goals were clear.

In Istanbul, the sultan also understood what was happening. In 1787, in an attempt to roll back the annexation of the Crimea, he declared war on Russia; in response, Austria declared war on Turkey in February 1788. At first, from the Ottoman point of view, the war went relatively well. The early campaigns were short and indecisive, but victory at least seemed a possibility. Then reality asserted itself: the Russians and the Austrians were better armed, better trained, better supplied, better organized. In the spring of 1788, the Austrians occupied Bosnia; in October 1789, they took Belgrade, while at the same time the Russians occupied Bucharest. Turkey was now well on its way to another disastrous treaty, but it was partially saved by the French Revolution. By 1791, events in France had reached a point such as to alarm Austria; the last thing its government wanted was a war on two fronts, so it made peace on the basis of the status quo ante, receiving as a sop the right to protect the (very few) Roman Catholics in Turkey.

That left Russia. Its army won a major victory at Maç in April 1791; in January of the following year, the Treaty of Jassy acknowledged the annexation by Russia of the Crimea and Georgia. The Black Sea was now under Russian control.

SELIM THE REFORMER

Those were the circumstances when, in 1789, Selim III inherited the throne. As a very young man, under the reign of Mustafa III, his father, he had been allowed to watch the training, by French officers, of a new artillery corps. Aimée had helped to convince him that Western ways—in certain areas, at least—were best. In other areas, Selim felt that the Turkish institutions, although good in themselves, were not operating properly: major changes were needed, therefore, but they could not be carried out during the war. The Treaty of Jassy, humiliating as it was, gave him a chance to reverse the decay of the empire, and when it came, he was ready to start.

During the previous three years, he had built up a cadre of officers and administrators, young men who shared his views. Now he went to work on two closely linked goals: he tried to end abuses and corruption while creating a new, modern, and effective army. Neither task was easy. Corruption and bribes were a way of life: everyone expected to be paid for favors, in the civil administration as well as the army. Then, when it came to reforming the army, there was the Corps of the Janissaries, and they were fiercely opposed to any change at all.

Of all the peculiar institutions of the Ottoman Empire, the janissaries were probably the oddest. About sixty-thousand strong, they had originally been composed of specially drafted, unattached non-Muslims, who were taken away from their villages, converted to Islam, trained, and forbidden to marry, trade, or do anything but fight and train. As such, they had been the elite corps of the partly feudal Ottoman army, a group of warriors deeply devoted to the sultan and capable of spreading terror wherever they went into battle. In the centuries since the creation of the corps, however, a great deal had changed.

Weak sultans had allowed the janissaries to marry, thus giving them a good reason to want to survive; they had allowed them to trade, and earn money, over and above their pay, thus making them feel that Istanbul in comfort was greatly preferable to fighting a war. Finally, the janissaries, a large number of whom were encamped in the first courtyard of the Topkapi, were allowed to become the arbiters of government, making and unmaking sultans. Their revolts were feared, with reason; and they were not about to give up their privileged existence for the hard life of the camps.

Selim knew that, of course, and took it into account. It was almost impossible to reform the janissaries, but he tried. They had been paid irregularly; the sultan halved their number to thirty thousand and raised their pay. In return, he demanded more discipline and better trained soldiers—and in doing so excited furious resentments. It was even worse when he decided that, in order to avoid corruption, promotions would be by seniority. Having just been so soundly beaten by the Russians, the janissaries were not yet ready to revolt; but they watched and waited.

A strong sultan would have been planning for the day when they rose: Mahmud II, Aimée's son, did exactly that, and won. Selim, tragically, was too kind; he tried to convince rather than fight, and his enemies saw it as weakness. He was also too traditional. Although he carried out a number of reforms, he left the basic framework of the Ottoman government intact. The incredibly inefficient treasury, for instance, was allowed to continue as it was; reactionaries in positions of power remained in office. These were people eager to block change partly because they wanted the bribes to keep on coming, partly because they genuinely believed that Westernization could only weaken Turkey.

As it was, Selim did carry out a number of reforms. Administrative functions, within the army, were separated from the military command and given their own personnel. A new hierarchy was established, with a clear chain of command; officers were made to take an exam and were dismissed if they failed it. Barracks were enlarged and modernized, and wages paid on a monthly basis—all this was meant to make a military life more attractive. At the same time, regular drills and exercises were decreed: Selim wanted to have an enthusiastic, well-trained army. It was soon obvious, however, that the janissaries would never reach that degree of competence; and so Selim created the New Order infantry, a body of men organized, trained, and clothed like a European army, with European weapons, tactics, and discipline. Instructors were brought in from France, Britain, and Germany, with a special treasury created to finance this effort. By 1806, the New Order troops numbered twenty-two thousand men and sixteen hundred officers.

Nor was that all. Selim ordered the creation of new cannon foundries and rifle works. He founded the Naval Engineering School and tried to revive the defunct Turkish navy, giving it a treasury of its own and establishing an effective Naval Medical Service; and by 1806, Turkey could indeed deploy a small, but modern, war fleet.

All these reforms affected the military; but what Selim refused to see was that it was, in the end, impossible to have a modern military in a medieval state. The treasury, unreformed, was a complete shambles. There was no budget of any kind, no economic policy. As inflation raged, the government simply debased the currency and raised taxes. When there was a fiscal emergency—and this happened often—the answer was to take forced loans from the rich merchants, thus further slowing down the economy. Then there was the grand mufti, the chief religious leader who had, in theory, the right to annul the sultan's decrees. He did not usually dare to do so, but he could be an effective focus for the conservative opposition.

All that was bad enough. Even more seriously, the empire, under Selim, was rapidly, if undramatically, coming apart. Because the local leaders were so desperately needed during the war of 1787, they gained a great deal of power and became, essentially, autonomous. They obeyed the sultan's orders when they approved of them, and not otherwise. The New Order's officers were a typical case in point: outside of Istanbul, most of these leaders refused to allow enrollments. This was even worse in some places: Ali, pasha of Janina, ruled over Albania and northern Greece as a virtually independent sovereign; the same was true of Pasvanoglu Osman Pasha in Bulgaria, and of the Russophile princes appointed, under Russian pressure, to govern Moldavia and Walachia. In the same way, and with the help of Russian money, the section of Anatolia between the cities of Trabzon and Bursa virtually stopped obeying the sultan. Much of the Middle East now simply ignored Istanbul. As for Egypt, it was a problem of its own.

THE EGYPTIAN CAMPAIGN

In 1798, in one of his least inspired moments, General Bonaparte decided to conquer Egypt and Syria. The Directoire, delighted to be rid of him, gave him a fleet and an army, and on July 1, he arrived in Alexandria. Egypt, at this point, was governed as an autonomous state by the Mamlūks; their military strength was laughable, so Bonaparte defeated them at Rahmaniye on July 13, and at Giza eight days later. This enabled him to occupy Cairo; but then the conqueror found himself stymied. The Mamlūks had taken refuge in Upper Egypt. The French army was too small to hold the entire country, too ill-supplied for a lengthy campaign, too afflicted by the heat, and eventually a plague epidemic, to be a really effective fighting force. Nor was there any prospect of receiving supplies or reinforcements from France. On August 1, 1798, Nelson destroyed the French fleet at Aboukir.

Still Bonaparte persisted. In the spring of 1799, the French tried to conquer Syria. By the time they were defeated at Acre, Bonaparte had already left for home. On August 31, 1801, abandoned by their leader, bereft of supplies, the French army, under General Jacques Menou, finally surrendered to an Anglo-Ottoman force. Egypt, briefly wrenched from the sultan, now came back into his obedience. It was the single success of the reign.

REFORM ENDED, REFORM BEGUN

Recovering Egypt could hardly be enough to appease the reactionaries. They were frantic to end the reforms; they knew that the Sultan had been weakened by his failure to control the provinces; and they could count on the janissaries. All that was needed was a single spark: the grand mufti supplied it on May 29, 1807. Announcing that Selim's reforms were contrary to the laws of Islam, he issued a *fatwa* removing him from the throne. The next day, rather than face the janissaries, Selim abdicated and was imprisoned in the Cage. His successor, Mustafa III, was everything the reactionaries wanted. Unfortunately for them, he was also cruel and stupid; and so, in 1808, a rescue force led by a provincial pasha appeared at the gates of the Topkapi. Mustafa promptly had Selim murdered, but Mahmud, Aimée's son, managed to hide just long enough to be saved. Promptly acclaimed as the new sultan, he eventually succeeded in breaking up the janissaries and reforming the bureaucracy. Still, in 1800, and for most of the century that followed, as Turkey sank deeper into decadence and the empire kept shrinking, wars and poverty became the norm for part of eastern Europe and all of the Middle East. Turkey, the Sick Man of Europe, was rapidly moving toward its deathbed.

PART FIVE

Africa

CHAPTER EIGHTEEN

So Close, So Far

A Mysterious Continent

Africa, in 1800, was an apparently endless series of contradictions. For the Europeans and the Americans, it was both well known—as a place to buy spices, slaves, ivory, gold dust, and tropical goods—and completely unknown—because much of its geography and population remained a mystery. While trading ships had visited its coasts for over two hundred years, and the Portuguese had even conquered a thin slice of the interior, the costs, both of the conquest and of the maintenance of their new colony, had been great. Forts had to be built and manned; defensive, and sometimes offensive, expeditions mounted. There was disease, too, which killed off many of the officers and administrators: as profit-making propositions, these colonies rated very poorly. Then, the many African cultures had failed to spark interest among the Europeans. True, a few travelers—often missionaries—had ventured some distance into the continent and written about what they had seen, but it had all stopped there. Of all the continents, it was the most mysterious.

There were two good reasons for this. The less important was that the Africans were fully prepared to defend themselves against foreign invaders, and the traders knew it. War was endemic across the continent. Well-organized societies, fighting with one another, created and lost empires. Foreign aggression (albeit from fellow Africans) was no novelty. This knowledge of Africa's ability to defend itself was reinforced by the myth of the poisoned arrow, a weapon supposedly as effective as it was deadly.

That, alone, might have been enough to discourage would-be conquerors, or even explorers. Still, very few Europeans had actual experience of the African states' military potential. What they knew all too well—and it was their most important reason for staying away—was the virulence of the tropical diseases to be caught in Africa. Malaria and yellow fever, the most prevalent of them, killed Africans, too, of course, but many of them had developed at least partial immunity. Europeans, on the other hand, died in great numbers—more than a third of the traders and sailors who came to the African coast never returned from it, and any attempt at conquest was therefore seen as self-defeating.

ANOTHER CIVILIZATION

Although the Europeans thought of Africa as being mysterious, primitive, and utterly different from anything they knew, they were quite wrong. In fact, Africa had far more in common with Europe than could be imagined. Although technologically backward—the Africans, for instance, did not know how to make firearms, or gunpowder, or large metal objects such as cannons or even very big cooking pots—the continent was politically quite up to date. It, too, had different societies, with different economies and different systems of government. In some of the states, the equivalent of a constitution was in force. There were laws about property and family, marriage and inheritance. And, of course, the Africans could boast of that chief attribute of developed cultures—well-organized wars. There were wars for trade and wars for conquests. Long-established states, like Benin, sometimes won and sometimes lost, but their territorial extent remained largely stable. Other states, very much like France at that time, conquered a vast empire with startling rapidity. Here, too, there were many languages; here, too, people who spoke variants of the same language found themselves divided between various political entities. Far from being a vast and confused home of illiterate, but dangerous, tribes, as the Europeans supposed, Africa was, in many ways, just as sophisticated as Europe.

Benin (in the area of today's Nigeria) could look back to an already long and eminently successful past. It had reached the peak of its military power in the sixteenth century, and produced bronze sculptures of extraordinary beauty (but relatively small size) just when the Italian Renaissance was doing the same thing. It could also boast of a complex social system in which the power of the *oba* (king) was balanced by that of the merchants; and together, they decided what the main exports of the country would be: not slaves, but commodities such as pepper, ivory, and cotton. An embargo on the export of male slaves lasted until the early eighteenth century, and even then, slave trading remained a minor activity because prices were kept higher than elsewhere on the continent. By 1800, no more than a thousand slaves a year left Benin—a tiny proportion of the whole; and the elaborate religious and cultural rituals that bound the society together were still fully alive even though they were centuries old.

Benin was stable, able to defend itself, but no longer a conquering power. The Asante Empire (in the region of today's Ghana), on the other hand, was new, vast, and growing throughout the eighteenth century. Founded around 1680 by Osei Tutu, Asante had already become a major power by 1700. Unlike France under Napoléon, however, it was ruled not by one man, but by the Kotoko Council, a gathering of representatives of the different components of the empire. It developed new, empire-wide judicial institutions, and a new national identity. Each of the original smaller nations gathered into the empire had had its stool of office which symbolized the ties of kinship, that most basic of African political units. Now, a new golden stool represented the unity of the Asante people. Thus, a fictitious extension of kinship helped to create a permanent state that even included territories, conquered from, and still occupied by, different ethnic groups. This new entity proved highly resistant to challenge, because it had not only an effective political system, but also a powerful army. All through the eighteenth century, provinces that tried to secede were reincorporated by force, while non-kin neighboring states like Ganja and Dagomba were made to pay tribute. Others societies—the Ga, for instance—were dominated by the empire without being invited to become a part of it.

Like Benin, the Asante Empire found itself well able to shape its economy. Because of its position as a link between the interior and the coast, it chose to export gold dust and slaves, and thus became a chief supplier of that trade.

Slaves were important, but not essential, to the Asante economy. In nearby Dahomey, though, that trade was the principal support of the state. Dahomey, too, was a constitutional monarchy. The *oba*'s power was sharply limited. The several councils, some representing lineages, others professional groups, had the real authority. One of these councils chose the *oba* from among the royal lineage; another could order him to commit suicide. By the 1730s, though, the system had begun to break down. Its replacement by despotism did the country little good: Dahomey was soon forced by the inland Oyo kingdom into a tributary relationship. Then, in 1796, after the Oyo ruler had been condemned to commit suicide, that state declined into civil strife. By 1800, both Dahomey and Oyo were characterized by highly unstable political systems.

Farther south, in western equatorial Africa, a very different arrangement prevailed. The Luanda Commonwealth was just that, an alliance of many small kingdoms that recognized the supremacy of an emperor without giving him the power to govern more than a small area around the federal capital. The emperor had neither standing army, nor a rich treasury; but his prestige allowed him the power of confirming the subordinate kings in their (often greater) positions of power.

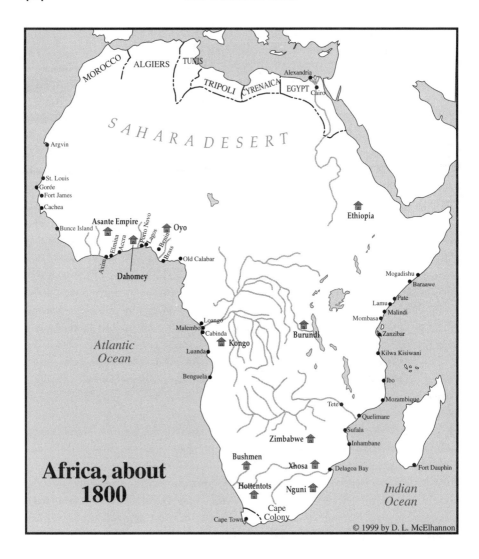

Africa, about 1800

© 1999 by D. L. McElhannon

AFRICA BY ITSELF

Indeed, in most of Africa, traditional power structures endured together with the rites and customs that expressed them. Before the arrival of the European traders, the Africans had lived in a nonscientific, preindustrial Iron Age society based on an economy of subsistence. The introductions of guns and other Western products changed that to some degree, but without radically modifying older customs. Just as before, African governments held sway and trading continued between the various parts of the continent. By the eighteenth century, in fact, the regions under direct colonial control were shrinking. That applied particularly to Portuguese East Africa, where cities like Mombasa regained their independence, and foreign control was limited to a few trading ports.

Some of the African societies were highly structured for greater efficiency. The Fulani in Sierra Leone, for instance, had specialized artisans: some tanned and worked leather into saddles, bridles, or sandals; others were highly competent blacksmiths who produced not only utilitarian objects, but also finely chased sword handles, or gold and silver jewelry. Their canoes, made from tree trunks, could carry up to ten tons; their fishing lines were as durable as any of those made in Europe. Here, in fact, was a people whose competence also allowed for the finest artistic expression.

In other areas, though, mighty states found their power eroded, from 1700 on, by three major factors: the slave trade, the technological innovations imported from Europe, and the work of the Christian missionaries. This was true, for instance, of the Loango kingdom, between the Zaire estuary and the Gabon forests. A major producer of cloth, which it used also as currency, Loango had prospered all through the seventeenth century. It exported its cloth, and also sold salt and copper to the rest of Africa; the Dutch bought copper and ivory from it; but then, as the supply of these commodities became exhausted, the Loango traders switched to slaves. By 1800, they were exchanging about ten thousand slaves a year for cloth, beads, iron or brass manufactured objects, alcohol, tobacco, and guns. This trade, on a societal level, was a commercial and political equivalent of AIDS: as economic and political structures felt the effect of the virus, they grew weaker and weaker until they finally collapsed.

Much the same thing happened to the once-powerful kingdom of Kongo, where, by 1800, a small, parasitic upper class lived principally from kidnapping people to sell them into slavery. As late as the 1760s, it was, according to Abbé Proyart, a Western traveler, a place where "the Kings . . . hold as a principle that it is their duty as well as their interest to occupy themselves with the care of rendering [their subjects] happy, and maintaining peace and justice among them. Every day, they pass several hours in deciding the processes of those who have appealed to them in their tribunals; they hold frequent councils."[1] Even the wars were mercifully brief: seldom lasting more than eight or ten days, they tended to be over when the army had eaten the provisions it had brought along, and run out of gunpowder and bullets.

Although, by 1800, Kongo was no longer a great power, appearances remained unaltered. The capital, Mbanza Kongo, was still a large city. "The sites were not laid out in straight lines," a traveler wrote. "There were no avenues bordered by palms or decorative trees. Narrow paths ran in all directions through the tall grass. The habitations of the important dignitaries were close to the King's enclosure. Distributed according to individual taste or whim, they sometimes occupied a considerable space. The houses were made of unadorned straw except for their interiors, where there were mats with designs. . . . They were surrounded by walls made of perennial trees."[2] The mats were more than the travelers understood: finely woven with intricate motifs, they were the equivalents of paintings in a European house.

Because rivalries were fierce, the houses of important people, the king first and foremost, were placed at the end of a maze: as visitors blundered through, there was time for the guards to get ready. Outside the royal enclosure, however, there was a vast open space where justice was dispensed and ceremonies took place. And everywhere, manners mattered a great deal. "Whenever they meet some person of quality on the road, they fall to their knees and greet him by clapping their hands," Laurent de Lucques reported. "If they are equal, they simply go on their way . . . In the gathering of chiefs, . . . the most important of the dignitaries grasps his own right wrist in his left hand, places the index finger of his right hand on the ground, carries it to his temples three times, opens the hand, presses the tips of the fingers to the ground and then, with closed fists, beats the hands together rhythmically. This last gesture is repeated by every person present."[3] Indeed, the etiquette of Kongo was worthy of a European court.

Although limited in its resources, this was a society in which subtleties mattered: its cuisine proved that. Manioc was the basic food. It could be made into flour, or steamed. Legumes, bananas, oranges, and lemons were widely available, but meat, fish, and chicken were rare, and eaten only by people of high rank—although insects, rats, and snakes also formed part of the diet. It was the sauces that made the difference, however. Made with palm oil, spices, peppers, onions, cucumber seeds, and hot pepper, they were as varied as in France: in Kongo, gastronomy was alive and well.

So was fashion. Cloth was woven in changing, but always complex, patterns, and it was very expensive. So was the copper jewelry incised with rich stylized designs, and made into armbands for the men, and bracelets, neck bands, and anklets for the women. Then there were more permanent adornments: tattoos reflected the village of origin, but were also highly decorative; and it was customary for both sexes to rub their skin daily with palm oil to make it softer and more lustrous.

TRADING BLACK FLESH

None of this was known by the Europeans. As for the Africans themselves, the rest of the world could be easily summed up. There were the caravans that came from the Arab countries, and the ships that came from Europe and America, and their principal purpose was the trade and purchase of slaves. This was not new: kingdoms might grow or shrink, but the essentials remained the same. In one respect, though, life had changed enormously. Coming from the outside, firearms revolutionized fighting, while alcohol (especially gin) and tobacco proved addictive and therefore highly desirable. All these commodities came from the European and American ships that called at the ports on both coasts; and they, in return, wanted slaves. Slavery was hardly new to Africa; the slave trade, on a large scale, was something altogether different. The kingdoms trading in slaves fought with their neighbors in order to make prisoners who could then be sold as slaves. In some cases, rulers rounded up some of their own subjects in order to sell them. The trade itself spread terror deep into the continent where gangs of kidnappers abducted women, adolescents, children, and anyone who was not in a position to defend himself. Thus the sale of slaves to foreigners had become a major fact of life—not so much for profit, but because the sale of slaves was the only way to acquire firearms and other desirable commodities. Even so, that was all most Africans knew about the people or the countries whose trade had so starkly redefined their lives.

Selling men, women, children: for countries who prided themselves on being Christian and believing, therefore, that all souls were equal in the eyes of God, it was surely a strange activity. And yet in British, Spanish, and French ships, over two centuries, some 9.5 million human beings were brought from Africa to the Americas and the West Indies. In a world where there were far fewer people than today, this was an enormous number—about the same as that of the entire population of Great Britain. In the three decades from 1781 to 1810, and for the United States only, 531,000 Africans were seized from their farms and villages, brought to the coast, and sent across the ocean in chains; and that figure does not include the unknown number of those who died on the trip, anywhere from 10 to 20 percent. In 1800 alone, almost 18,000 new slaves arrived in North America. That was less than in 1775 (over 21,000), the diminution being caused by the War of Independence; it was far more than in 1720 (9,000). Another cause for the slowdown of the slave trade was the French Revolution. From 1792 on, France was at war with Great Britain; French ships thus became designated prey for the British navy, and their trade came to a virtual halt.

Slaves came to the United States. Many were also sent to South America—about a quarter of a million of them between 1774 and 1807—and to the Caribbean. Because of the changes brought about by the French Revolution, though, the traffic was slowing down in that area also. In 1800, for instance, only 1,110 slaves were imported to Martinique, as opposed to 3,500 in 1787. In Guadeloupe, the numbers were similar; but then, slaves were also supplied to the British and Spanish islands. Thus, during the ten years from 1791 to 1800, the traders delivered very nearly half a million African slaves to their buyers. Some of them were taken as slaves for their skills, not just their labor: they knew how to grow rice, indigo, and other commodities. They were also far more resistant than European workers to the tropical diseases prevalent in the West Indies, the southern United States, and South America.

This highly profitable influx consisted of men in great numbers, women (sometimes pregnant), and children. Neither age nor gender offered any protection; and while it paid to ensure the survival of as much of the cargo as possible, the severest punishment was used to keep the human cattle properly cowed. Violent, prolonged, and repeated floggings were a usual part of the trip, but merely being chained in a suffocating hold was itself the source of acute suffering.

Adding to this bleak picture was the mental state of the captives: they were utterly terrified, and with good reason. They had lost their families, their homes, everything that had given life its meaning. Almost worse, because they knew nothing about the white men who kept them in chains, many of them expected to be eaten, right there and then on the ship. They also expected to be tortured, and often were; and since many of them had simply been kidnapped by other Africans, they knew that they owed this unimaginably awful fate to the very men who should have been their allies against the white traders if there had been any sense of African solidarity. "All that vast number of slaves whom the Calabar Blacks sell to the European nations are not their prisoners of war, the greater part of them being bought by these people from their inland neighbours,"[4] a traveler wrote in 1680. In 1800, that had not changed. Of course, there were occasions when trade was not productive enough; then the chiefs from the coastal areas mounted military kidnapping operations as a means of resupplying themselves.

In fact, not all African slaves were sold to traders who shipped them abroad. Those who stayed, often prisoners of war, served their conquerors. Those sold to the traders were exchanged for a variety of desirable goods. Chief among these were guns, powder, and bullets; and the Europeans saw to it that the guns were of poor quality so that they would frequently have to be replaced. These guns, in turn, made it easier to capture new slaves, who were themselves exchanged for new guns. As far as the white traders were concerned, guns were the perfect medium of exchange. They had other goods to offer, though: in order of desirability, these were liquor, tobacco, cloth, kettles, and glass beads.

It was naturally the rich and the powerful who did the trading. "The trade of slaves . . . is the business of kings, rich men and prime merchants, exclusive of the inferior sort of blacks," the English trader John Barbot reported at the end of the seventeenth century. "The Gold Coast, in times of war between the inland nations and those nearer the sea, will furnish great numbers of slaves of all sexes and ages. . . . I remember that in the year 1681, an English [trader] at Commendo got three hundred good slaves almost for nothing beside the trouble of receiving them at the beach in his boats . . . as the Commendo men . . . having obtained a victory over a neighbouring nation . . . [had] taken a great number of prisoners."[5]

All this was still true in 1800. For those various African nations which traded in slaves, the activity was seen as conducive to the greater well-being of the society. Each kingdom fitted the slave trade into its own policies of defense or expansion. Far from being understood as a monstrous crime perpetuated by Europeans against Africans, the slave trade was in fact only one element in an often complex set of policies. There were exceptions, though. The Nguni people of Zululand, Botswanaland, and Swaziland, whose upper classes frequently intermarried, were at peace with one another. The concept of enslavement was also foreign to them; and they were thus safe from the traders' temptations.

Certainly, there would not have been a slave trade on this massive scale without the demand from the Americas. Wars would have continued, but those taken into slavery would at least have remained in an environment they knew. Equally, not a single slave would have been shipped from Africa without the enthusiastic cooperation of the coastal Africans. Indeed, the chain of trade was well established; James Penny, a trader, described it in 1789.

> At Bonny [in the Niger delta] slaves are purchased by the king, who is the principal trader. . . . [His men] go up the river to a distance of about eighty miles from Bonny . . . in large canoes with two or three principal persons, and about forty men in each. The canoes go in a body all together to defend themselves if attacked. At the head of these two rivers there is a mart for trade, where the black traders purchase these slaves of other black traders, who bring them from the interior country.[6]

All these slaves were shipped west—and that trade has now been abundantly studied. Less often mentioned is the parallel trade into the Arab countries of the Ottoman Empire. For centuries, Arab traders had been buying slaves in Africa and shipping them home. The numbers, over a longer period, are roughly equal to those of the western trade; altogether, some 20 million Africans were sold into foreign bondage.

For many of the slaves sold to Turkey and the Arab countries, though, life could be less unpleasant than for those shipped to America. The trip itself was both less terrifying and less deadly; moreover, the children of slaves were eventually allowed to buy their freedom and merge into the society at large.

For an African sold to a European trader, though, the horror was unrelieved, especially since those who were captured often came from slaveholding families—the upper classes, that is. That was the case of Olandah Equiano, who ended up as a slave in the West Indies, and, in 1789, told his story.

"My father, besides many slaves, had a numerous family of which seven lived to grow up," he remembered. "I was trained from my earliest years in the arts of agriculture and war; my daily exercise was shooting and throwing javelins."[7] Equiano was, in other words, typical of the class that owned land and slaves. Its men were both farmers and warriors who, on not infrequent occasions, went to war against their neighbors. Naturally, the boy might have been expected to follow in his father's footsteps. Instead, he became yet another victim of the slave trade.

"One day, [at the age of eleven]," Equiano continued, "when all our people were gone out to their work, and only I and my dear sister were left to mind the house, two men and a woman got over our walls, and in a moment seized us both; and without giving us time to cry out, or make resistance, they stopped our mouths and ran off with us into the nearest wood. Here, they tied our hands, and continued to carry us as far as they could, till night came on, when we reached a small house where the robbers halted for refreshment and spent the night . . . The next morning, we left the house and continued traveling all the day . . . The next day, my sister and I . . . were separated while we lay clasped in each others' arms."[8]

Equiano naturally never saw his sister again; and for him, this was just the beginning. Passing from kidnapper to kidnapper on the way to the coast, he was eventually sold to a smith, and there set to working the bellows. That, however, lasted less than a year. Within the next few months, he was sold and resold until, finally, he reached the coast. There, he said, "a slave ship . . . was riding at anchor waiting for its cargo . . . When I was carried on board, I was immediately handled and tossed up, to see if I were sound, by some of the crew. . . . When I looked round the ship, and saw a large furnace, or copper boiling, and a multitude of black people of every description chained together, every one of their countenances expressing dejection and sorrow . . . , I asked if we were not to be eaten by those white men with horrible looks, red faces and long hair."[9]

Appearance and manner to the contrary, the crew were not cannibals; they were, however, capable of the greatest brutality. This was in part, no doubt, because the newly captured slaves were still strong. They were also more likely to revolt at a point when it was possible to swim ashore, and revolts were in fact numerous. What remains is that these are mere explanations: it is hard to feel sympathy with the apprehensions of the traders, or the difficulties they encountered, while buying and transporting enslaved Africans.

Bad as the arrival on board the ship undoubtedly was, things soon got worse. "I was soon put down under the deck. . . . With the loathsomeness of the stench and crying together, I became so low that I was not able to eat. . . . Two of the white men offered me eatables; and on my refusing, one of them held me fast by the hands, and laid me across, I think, the windlass, and tied my feet while the other flogged me severely. . . . I have seen some of these poor African prisoners . . . hourly whipped for not eating. This indeed was often the case with myself."[10] And, of course, there were similar punishments for the slaves who tried to jump into the ocean, because, for them, certain death was better than their captivity.

As for the conditions on the ship, they were as appalling as the treatment meted out to the cargo. "The stench of the hold," Equiano remembered, "was so intolerably loathsome that it was dangerous to remain there for any time. . . . The closeness of the place, and the heat of the climate, added to the numbers in the ship, which was so crowded that each had scarcely room to turn himself, almost suffocated us. This produced copious perspiration, so that the air soon became unfit for respiration, from a variety of loathsome smells, and brought on a sickness among the slaves, of which many died. . . . This wretched situation was again aggravated by the galling of the chains, now become unsupportable; and [so was] the filth of the necessary tubs, into which the children often fell, and were almost suffocated. The shrieks of the women and the groans of the dying rendered the whole a scene of horror almost inconceivable."[11]

It is no wonder that the percentage of the deaths was so high; and, of course, the longer the trip, the greater the numbers of those who died. Contrary winds meant larger losses for the traders, more agony for the slaves. There were, however, rare occasions on which the captives managed to free themselves from their chains. If they did, there were three possible outcomes: the crew realized what was happening and killed as many Africans as necessary to end the rebellion; the slaves killed the crew, found themselves unable to navigate the ship, and died of hunger and thirst or were shipwrecked; the ship was seized by another trading ship, and many of the slaves were massacred. In any event, the slaves were doomed. If they were lucky, they were sold to a relatively humane master; if not, they usually died within a very few years, and were then replaced by recent arrivals. Either way, the slave trade, unjustifiable in principle, also entailed the most shameful and continuous inhumanity. But in 1800, there were still very few people who thought that it should be stopped.

The Dutch in Africa

At least, unlike the Americas, Africa had not been conquered by a European power—or, at least, almost not. At the southern end of the continent, the Dutch East India Company ruled Cape Colony, a relatively small area with a fairly modest Dutch population, to which it had imported Malay slaves in the preceding century. In 1800, though, it was expanding rapidly, and the natives whose lands were seized were either pushed out or reduced to slavery.

In the rest of Africa, some of the older kingdoms were partly free of the slave trade—that was the case of Benin. In the southern hinterland, Swaziland, Zimbabwe, and Zululand were wholly closed to it. Their customs, their political structures, their ceremonies were apparently unaltered; and yet, in many places, the effect of the slave trade was both destabilizing and enervating. Geographical ignorance, tropical diseases, and the reputed fierceness of the African warriors had shielded its populations from European conquest. As Cape Colony was beginning to show, these were rapidly becoming illusory protections.

There was no mercy for those Africans who were taken away from their lands; there was equally none for those who stayed, but found themselves, as a result of events they usually did not understand, living on the territory of Cape Colony, at the very bottom of the continent. Here, too, they were slaves; here, too, they were treated worse than cattle. And, amazingly, the resident Europeans denied the Africans the right to live in their own ancestral lands.

Founded by the Dutch East India Company, Cape Colony was, in one way, not unlike India: the company ruled, but it deferred to its government. Like the British East India Company, this company found itself facing increasing financial difficulties as the eighteenth century progressed. In another way, though, the situation was very different. India was a great prize, and the British East India Company, in 1795, already ruled over millions of subjects. The Cape Colony was good only for fairly small amounts of grain, wine, and cattle; its population was a mere 73,000, half of European origin, and it mattered very little to the Dutch government, which had far more serious concerns at home — invasion by France being not the least of them. Finally, there was another key difference. The English who went to India did so in the hope of making a quick fortune and then coming home. The Dutch, who had settled at the Cape of Good Hope a hundred years earlier, considered themselves Africans first and Dutch second. The southern tip of Africa was, they felt, their country; they were the only ones who had a right to it. And as they claimed that right, they firmly ignored the previous right of the Hottentot populations.

Because they were fundamentalist Calvinists, these Boers (farmers), as they proudly called themselves, had developed a religious argument to bolster their claim: all Africans being descended from Ham, the biblical figure, they were so tainted as to be predestined to be the Boers' slaves. This was the result of a convoluted piece of reasoning: Ham, Noah's youngest son, had failed to cover his father's nakedness (Noah was drunk), but had merely called in his brothers. The next morning, Noah, whose temper had presumably not been improved by his hangover, cursed Ham and decreed that Ham's son would henceforth be the slave of his uncles. Because the Boers found it profitable to enslave the Africans, they reasoned that the Africans must, therefore, be the descendants of Ham's enslaved son. From that it also followed that the natives could not legitimately own land: anything the Boers chose to take became rightly theirs. Having devised this extraordinary justification, they proceeded to apply it on as large a scale as their small numbers allowed. In 1760, they crossed the Orange River and started moving deeper into Africa; in 1779, having progressed further, they fought their first major war with the Bantus over the Great Fish River; and in 1799, continuing their movement inward, they were involved in the so-called Third Kaffir War. Invariably, they won. The Bantus and the Hottentots fought by charging the enemy. The Boers developed the laager, a circle of tall carts whose interstices were blocked by spiny plants, with ox skins filling the space between the wheels. From these mobile fortresses, they shot at their assailants, whom they invariably defeated: it was to be many decades before the Africans could devise a more effective set of tactics.

"It is the practice of the Boer here, when one of them wants a farm, to proceed beyond the nominal boundary of the Colony, and take possession of the choicest situation he can find in the Bushmen country. . . . The great ambition, which all African colonists have, is to see their children settled upon . . . farms of six thousand acres in extent,"[12] a traveler reported in the 1790s. It was all very simple: the Boers had been chosen by God to take whatever land they wanted; and having done so, they need not give themselves much trouble cultivating it.

As a result, each farmer wanted to own a vast estate; as late as 1830, another observer, a Dr. Philip, could see it clearly:

> They still think that they cannot subsist unless a farm includes the same range of country as it did in the days of their ancestors. Their habits are pastoral, they seldom cultivate more ground than is necessary for their own use, and their wealth is in their cattle. Having extensive herds, they not only require much pasture, but are not satisfied if they have not different places to resort to at different times of the year . . . They must have game also and each farmer . . . must have a district for himself. . . . All they can see, they consider their own, and, when needed, the natives are obliged to [go].[13]

Coming from a people professing to be particularly worthy of God's favor, it was a singularly profligate way of life.

That the Boers were neither elegant, nor sophisticated, nor cultured, nor, in fact, good company, everyone agreed. Anders Sparrman, a Swedish physician who traveled extensively through the colony in the 1770s, liked them better than most visitors. They were, he wrote, "a set of hearty, honest fellows who, though they do not, indeed, differ in rank from our Swedish peasants, and make no better figure than the yeomen in our country, are yet for the most part extremely wealthy."[14] Most other travelers also found them rude, greedy, and avaricious.

As a result, the Boers, so smugly sure of their superiority, so full of disdain for all intellectual pursuits, were hardly appealing. Freshly back from China, John Barrow, Lord Macartney's aide, found life in Cape Town altogether dreary.

That portion of the day, not employed in the concerns of trade, is usually devoted to the gratification of the sensual appetites. Few have any taste for reading, and none for the cultivation of the fine arts. They have no idea of public amusements, except occasional balls; nor is there much social intercourse, but by family parties, which usually consist of card playing and dancing. Money matters and merchandise engross their whole conversation . . . The young men . . . are clumsy in their shape, awkward in their carriage and of an unsociable disposition.[15]

This was actually surprising. While, as a matter of course, life in a new colony tends to be rough and ready, the Dutch had been at the cape for over a hundred years. Back home, their compatriots were also devoted businessmen; but they sustained, through their commissions to painters, one of the most spectacular artistic developments in Europe. Their interest in architecture resulted in cities of harmonious beauty. Their printing presses produced books of great quality, while their authors reached the very first rank in Europe. None of that existed in Africa: the people who were so cheerfully annihilating the local culture had, in fact, none of their own.

These austere Calvinists were also thoroughly dependent on slaves; and they treated these Africans as if they were not human at all. "Among the upper ranks, it is the custom for every child to have its slave, whose employment is to humor its caprices," Barrow reported. "Even the lower class of people object to their children going out as servants, or being bound as apprentices to learn the useful trades, which, in their contracted ideas, would be condemning them to perform the work of slaves."[16]

That was going a good deal further than in the Americas, where white men still worked as craftsmen, servants, and farm laborers. At Cape Colony, however, the Boers had no hesitation about relying entirely on slaves. In their view, Africans were no better than cattle, and far easier to replace. Unlike the planters on the other side of the Atlantic, the Dutch were not forced to depend on the vagaries of the slave trade: there was a large pool of Hottentots ready for enslavement right there. All it took was a raid, and a large batch of newly enslaved men, women, and children could be brought to the market. "Not only do [the colonists] consider the capture of the Hottentots as a party of pleasure," Sparrman observed, "but in cold blood they destroy the bands which nature has knit between husbands and their wives and children. . . . They endeavour all they can, and that chiefly at night, to deprive [the mother] of her infants; for it has been observed that the mothers can seldom persuade themselves to flee from their tender offsprings."[17] Calves, after all, are taken away from their mothers, and bulls from the cows: as far as the Boers were concerned, the Hottentots deserved no better treatment.

This deliberate dehumanization had at least one curious consequence. Sparrman noticed it on one of his stops. "About ten o'clock," he wrote, "I took refuge from the rain in a farmhouse, where I found the female slaves singing psalms, while they were at their needle-work. Their master . . . had prevailed with them to adopt this godly custom; but with the spirit of economy that universally prevails among the colonists, he had not permitted them to be initiated into the community of Christians by baptism; since by that means, according to the laws of the land, they would have obtained their freedom."[18] Coming from fervent Christians, this was, to say the least, a remarkably unchristian kind of behavior; but then the Boers were past masters at using religion when it suited them and ignoring it whenever its practice might shrink their profits.

Not surprisingly, the Africans were eager to take revenge whenever possible. Some few slaves did occasionally manage to run away, and they were then likely to come back and murder their former owners. Thus, even those few Boers who actually treated their slaves humanely lived in constant terror of their life. A band of runaways would not make any distinction between one white man and another; and so doors were locked, loaded guns placed ready at hand, and all slaves confined at night. Nor was there any guarantee that even the better-treated slaves could not be convinced by runaways to turn against their master: even they, after all, had a good deal to resent. And so, in this society which was so thoroughly dependent on captive Africans, fear was part of everyday life.

This set of circumstances also curtailed profit. Breeding slaves was even more profitable than breeding horses, and was managed very much the same way; only, instead of behaving like the cattle they were supposed to be, the slaves actually displayed human emotions. A man whose wife was taken away to be bred with another man might actually show resentment; this might cause quarrels, fights, even murders in the slave quarters. How to avoid these disruptions, while still expanding the black population, was, the colonists considered, a real problem. Most of them were, however, entirely prepared to waste a little money under the right circumstances: punishments so violent as to end in death were by no means uncommon.

"I have known some colonists . . . deliberately and in cold blood, undertake themselves the low office . . . of not only flaying, for a trifling neglect, both the backs and limbs of their slaves by a peculiar slow lingering method, but . . . throw pepper and salt over the wounds," Sparrman related. "But what seemed to me more strange and horrible was to hear a colonist not only describe with great seeming satisfaction the whole process of this diabolical invention, but even pride himself on the practice of it."[19] This, obviously, goes well beyond what was practiced in the Americas; but such savagery, inflicted on so-called savages by supposedly civilized people, was by no means uncommon. There could be no doubt about it: in Cape Colony, in 1800, animals were incomparably better off than the African slaves.

BLACK AND CIVILIZED

The Boers had no interest in the local populations, except for their potential use as slaves. Travelers, however, noticed that the Hottentots were really quite interesting people. Tall, slender, elegant-looking, with small hands and feet, the native people seemed all the more appealing because they lacked the marks of hard labor usually seen in the European peasants. Indeed, theirs was a pastoral culture. They followed their flocks from pasture to pasture, and cattle raids were the normal form of warfare. Usually naked, except for a loincloth, they nevertheless did not lack for ornament. They wore metal necklaces, bracelets, and anklets; even more important, they painted their bodies in intricate patterns with fat mixed with soot, and they perfumed themselves with powdered herbs worn on both head and body.

As for their way of life, it was very simple, and adapted to their wandering life. The villages in which they lived were composed of huts, some rectangular, some round, about eighteen to twenty-four feet in diameter, and built with a single opening that served as door, window, and chimney. There was a fireplace in the center, and the ceiling was so low that a man could not stand up straight. Given the impermanence of these dwellings, however, this lack of comfort hardly seemed to matter: the village was here today, elsewhere tomorrow. In most ways, life was as simple as the huts: the men looked after their flocks, and engaged in the occasional intertribal war, in which the opposing forces, armed with spears, rushed headlong at each other, shouting deafeningly. The women looked after themselves, the men, and the children. Still, these were not simple people. Their myths and their rituals were old and complex, and were expressed through dance. Even a late-eighteenth-century traveler, for whom much remained incomprehensible, was impressed.

"With their feet employed in a kind of stamping and moderately slow movement, every one of them . . . made several small, gentle motions with a little stick which they held in their hands," Sparrman wrote. "The simplicity which prevailed in their dances was equally conspicuous in their singing . . . [with the same word] chanted repeatedly *piano* by an elderly matron, who was answered by the young men and maids, [singing] *staccato* by way of chorus. . . . It inspired a certain degree of joy and cheerfulness and was by no means disagreeable."[20] For someone whose standard of dance was the minuet, and who was unprepared for any non-European mode of musical expression, this is high praise. In fact, the Swede was clearly engaged by what he saw and heard, and that is a tribute both to him and to the communicativeness of the ceremony he attended.

"They had an other kind of dance," he continued,

> which consisted in taking each other by the hand, and dancing gently in a circle around one or more persons, who were placed in the center of the ring, and whose movements were brisker and quicker . . . Besides [these] pleasures,

they have, at their greater festivals, the more delightful enjoyment of voluptuous love which, at those times, the youths of both sexes have full opportunity given them to pursue. For it is said that the unmarried part of the company, in the very middle of the dance, withdraw to a private place in couples, successively and at different intervals without giving the least subject of offense or scandal.[21]

Of course, all that could happen only outside the boundaries of the colony. Only there were the Hottentots free; and even then, it was only a temporary freedom as, relentlessly, the Boers grabbed more land.

George Thompson, who visited the cape at this time, saw it clearly. "The same acts of rapacity and cruelty which marked the progress of the Spaniard in Mexico and Peru . . . have merely been acted over again by the Dutchman in South Africa," he noted. "The superior force, enterprise and address, and still more, the dissemination of the worst vices of their conquerors have produced their usual effects . . . till the numerous tribes . . . have been gradually driven . . . to the bush, or amalgamated with the general mass of the servile coloured population."[22]

There could hardly be any doubt: for Africa, the advent of the Europeans, either as slave traders or as settlers, had been an immense catastrophe.

A COLONY IN TROUBLE

Seen from the point of view of the dispossessed tribes, the Boers seemed powerful and purposeful, but a white observer, in 1795, looked at a very different situation. In much of the colony, people were contesting the rule of the Dutch East India Company. On the verge of bankruptcy, unable to meet its debts or obtain fresh credit, the company, always a tyrannical ruler, now seemed merely oppressive. Metallic currency had vanished; the new paper money was depreciating daily; internal trade had almost stopped, and was replaced by barter, that last resource of desperate economies. In this emergency, the company had suspended its prohibition on foreign trade, but that hardly helped, since trade, the world over, was suffering from the effects of the war between France and England. At the same time, the colony was at war with the Bushmen on its northern border, and with the Xhosas to the east.

This was all more than the Boers were willing to accept. Carefully differentiating between the company and the Dutch Estates-General, the burghers at Graaf-Reinet and at Swellendam, two of the colony's five provinces, set up their own governments in defiance of the company and called for the election of a national assembly. This was partly because they were fed up with the mess, partly because the French Revolution's ideas of self-government were beginning to reach South Africa.

These developments were soon interrupted, however—not by the company's fifteen-hundred-man army, but by the arrival of a British fleet. Cape Colony might be far away from Europe, and unimportant as a political or economic power; but it provided a port where all ships sailing between Great Britain and India called for water and provisions. It was essential, in London's view, that the Cape be protected from the French, whose own colony of Mauritius was relatively close. In Europe itself, French troops had occupied Holland, which had now become the Batavian Republic. The new Dutch government was no longer likely to favor Britain; the problem of the Cape had thus become pressing.

The British, typically, did not hesitate. On June 11, 1795, the fleet arrived and its admiral, Sir George Elphinstone, presented the Cape Town authorities with a letter from the prince of Orange ordering them to admit British troops. That was a little awkward: the prince, the former Stadtholder (head of government), was now a refugee in England; the republican Dutch government, on the other hand, had given no such order; and so the council in Cape Town refused to allow the disembarkation of the troops. On June 18, in an attempt at resolving the situation peacefully, James Henry Craig, the commander of the British troops, announced that he intended to protect the colony until the restoration of the former Dutch government, and that, in the meantime, he would make no changes in the established order. At just this time, official news came from Holland that the Stadtholderate had been abolished, and a republic declared; and so the council still refused to allow in the troops. After that, things happened quickly: on July 9, Elphinstone took three Dutch ships that were sailing into Simon's Bay; on the fourteenth, soldiers landed and occupied Simonstown. And then there was a pause.

That was broken by the arrival, on August 9, of a ship bringing 398 soldiers from India, together with some artillery. On September 4, a small fleet arrived with another 3,000 men. After that, there was no possible contest. On September 14, the soldiers marched toward Cape Town; the next day, the council capitulated. To all intents and purposes, the Cape Colony was now British.

Still, the new authorities were careful to respect the fiction of Dutch sovereignty. Nothing was changed, except that the economy began to perk up, the British having brought gold and silver with them. As for Britain's superiority in this part of the world, it was perfectly clear: a Dutch fleet sent to retake the colony was soundly defeated by them on August 17, 1796.

The next step was the installation of a British governor, and that came on May 5, 1797, when Lord Macartney, the former ambassador to China, arrived to take up his post: from Peking to Cape Town, Britain demonstrated that it was indeed a world power. Had Macartney behaved in South Africa with the tact he had shown in China, all would have been well. Instead, he set about exploiting the colony. First, he announced that his salary would amount to the immense sum of £12,000 a year; then he fired all the Dutch administrators and replaced them with well-paid Englishmen, so that the yearly cost of all salaries rose to £28,903, an awkward sum considering that the government's total income was only £23,123. At the same time, he ruled in the most narrow and oppressive manner, thus making himself—and his country—highly unpopular.

Before there could be any serious attempt at a revolt, though, Macartney was gone. At the end of 1798, the British force was greatly reduced, the troops being sent to India in case General Bonaparte decided to attack it; and much of the fleet was sent to Egypt, which the French did actually invade. Clearly, the position of governor had lost much of its attraction, so Macartney went home, leaving Major General Dundas in charge. He, in turn, was followed by the spectacularly incompetent Sir George Yonge, who reached Cape Town in early December 1799. Sixteen months later, having created new, unnecessary government jobs, raised taxes, and taken bribes on a large scale, he was re-called. Once again, Dundas was in charge, but at this point, it hardly mattered. In the Treaty of Amiens, Great Britain had agreed to give Cape Colony back to Holland, and so it was done in February 1803.

That, too, proved to be only a short-lived situation. As the war between France and England began again in 1804, the British government decided to retake the colony. By January 18, 1806, this was done. The British were back to stay. Cape Colony, as it turned out, had been no more than a detail in the global confrontation between France and Great Britain.

Afterword

CHANGE, TRANSFORMATION, and the withdrawing of boundaries: the world, in 1800, was hardly a quiet place, but it seemed possible to predict what might come next. In Europe, Russia was expected to remain involved in the politics of the continent—and so it did. In France, Napoléon, young and invariably victorious, seemed to be at the beginning of decades of rule; the country itself was clearly established as the major military power in Europe. All that, however, came to an end in 1814. The emperor, having been defeated, abdicated and went off into exile. More amazing still, a Bourbon restoration followed, and the new king, Louis XVIII, gave France a constitution that was among the most democratic in Europe.

Still, Napoléon had been right: there was no stopping the Revolution. It came back in 1830, pushing Charles X off his throne and replacing him with Louis Philippe, a distant cousin; then, in 1848, that king was gone also, and the Second Republic began.

Austria, too, went an unpredictable way. Greatly strengthened in 1814, it set itself up as the guarantor of the new, post-Bonaparte European settlement. Sending troops off to Italy to suppress risings, fiercely defending the counter-revolutionary status quo, Metternich, its chancellor, willed time to stand still, until it caught up with him in 1848. Vienna exploded, the imperial family fled, and, although the young new emperor, Francis Joseph, soon restored Habsburg rule, Austria began its long decline. As for Russia, under Nicholas I, who came to the throne in 1825, it, too, seemed frozen forever in a rigidly absolutist mold. Strict censorship, the continuation of serfdom, the most autocratic form of government: it all belonged more to the seventeenth than to the nineteenth century. Of course, there was a cost for this immobility: as the rest of Europe entered the industrial age, Russia stayed far behind, a country that produced commodities but no manufactured products.

In England, on the other hand, change came—slowly, with difficulty, but, in the end, irresistibly. The Catholics and the Dissenters were freed from all legal disabilities: they could now be elected to the House of Commons and hold office. The House of Commons itself was reformed so as to give a voice to a greater percentage of the (male) population; and the economy, fueled by the new industries, made Great Britain the most advanced and richest country on earth.

Elsewhere, too, a new order came into being. In Latin America, independence was irreversible, but the new republics were wracked by political and economic disorder. In the United States, after a further advance of democracy in the 1830s during the presidency of Andrew Jackson, the North and the South began the dispute that eventually brought on the Civil War.

For some years, China and Japan remained much as they were; so did India, ruled by the British. Africa, in the first half of the century, was still largely unexplored, but there were premonitory signs. Great Britain went to war with China to force it to buy the opium it produced in India; the United States became ever more eager to trade with Japan; and all over Europe, people began to think that Asia and Africa might be ripe for colonization.

No one, in 1800, could have predicted any of this. The future, as always, turned out to be a surprise, but looking back, it is possible to see that many later events flowed logically from what had happened at the turn of that century. Historians sometimes say that the nineteenth century began in 1789. For the hundred years that followed 1800, people thought that much of what was happening to them had begun in 1800.

Notes

Chapter 1. A Very Great Change

1. Prince de Talleyrand, *Mémoires* (Paris, 1891), 1:126.
2. Georges Lefebvre, *La France sous le Directoire* (Paris, 1977), 27.
3. Jean-Paul Garnier, *Barras, Roi du Directoire* (Paris, 1970), 126.
4. Lefebvre, *La France sous le Directoire*, 35.
5. Ibid., 89.
6. Garnier, *Barras*, 142.
7. Edmond de Goncourt and Jules de Goncourt, *Histoire de la Société française pendant le Directoire* (Paris, 1879), 2–4.
8. *Le Tribun du Peuple*, no. 35, December 10, 1795.
9. Napoléon Bonaparte, *Lettres de Napoléon à Joséphine* (Paris, n.d.), 4–5.
10. Ibid., 9.
11. Ibid., 18–19.
12. Ibid., 19.
13. Lefebvre, *La France sous le Directoire*, 242.
14. *La petite armée du grand Pichegru* (Paris, n.d.), 3.
15. Talleyrand, *Mémoires*, 1:254.
16. Lefebvre, *La France sous le Directoire*, 423.
17. Talleyrand, *Mémoires*, 1:257.
18. Lefebvre, *La France sous le Directoire*, 458.
19. *Le Conservateur*, December 3, 1797.
20. Talleyrand, *Mémoires*, 1:259.
21. Ibid., 1:259–260.

Chapter 2. All the Pleasures of Life

1. A. B. L. Grimod de la Reynière, *Almanach des Gourmands* (Paris, 1806), 91.
2. J. F. Reichardt, *Un Hiver à Paris sous le Consulat* (Paris, 1896), 427.
3. A. B. L. Grimod de la Reynière, *Manuel des Amphitryons* (Paris, 1808), 143–148.
4. Jean Robiquet, *La Vie Quotidienne au temps de Napoléon* (Paris, 1942), 117.
5. Grimod, *Manuel*, 25.
6. Ibid., 33.
7. Grimod, *Almanach*, 165.
8. Reichardt, *Un Hiver à Paris*, 223.
9. Grimod, *Manuel*, 130.
10. P. L. Roeder, *Autour de Bonaparte* (Paris, 1809), 107.
11. Reichardt, *Un Hiver à Paris*, 366.
12. Ibid., 87–89.
13. Pierre Barbaud, *Haydn* (Paris, 1957), 145–146.

14. Ludwig van Beethoven, *Beethoven's Letters,* ed. J. S. Shedlock (London, 1909), 1:31.
15. Ibid., 1:89.
16. Ibid., 2:35.
17. Ibid., 1:27.
18. J. Christopher Herold, *Mistress to an Age: A Life of Madame de Staël* (London, 1959), 217.
19. Ibid., 227.
20. Reichardt, *Un Hiver à Paris,* 212.

Chapter 3. Unbeatable Bonaparte

1. *Le Moniteur,* October 15, 1799.
2. Georges Lefebvre, *La France sous le Directoire* (Paris, 1977), 467.
3. Jean-Paul Garnier, *Barras, Roi du Directoire* (Paris, 1970), 286.
4. Prince de Talleyrand, *Mémoires* (Paris, 1891), 1:271.
5. Ibid., 1:272, n. 1.
6. Garnier, *Barras,* 295.
7. Jacques Godechot, *Les constitutions de la France depuis 1789* (Paris, 1979), 147.
8. José Cabanis, *Le Sacre de Napoléon* (Paris, 1970), 11.
9. *Mémoires de Constant* (Paris, 1830), 1:46.
10. P. L. Roederer, *Autour de Bonaparte* (Paris, 1809), 84.
11. Cabanis, *Le Sacre de Napoléon,* 109.
12. Comte Matthieu Louis Molé, *Le comte Molé, sa vie, ses mémoires* (Paris, 1922), 1:55–56.
13. Ibid., 1:67.
14. Ibid., 1:96.
15. Ibid., 1:79–80.
16. *Le Moniteur,* December 28, 1800.
17. Cabanis, *Le Sacre de Napoléon,* 27.
18. General Savary, duc de Rovigo, *Mémoires pour servir à l'histoire de l'Empereur Napoléon* (Paris, 1828), 1:451.
19. Molé, *Mémoires,* 1:76.
20. *Le Moniteur,* April 10, 1802.
21. Cabanis, *Le Sacre de Napoléon,* 168.
22. Ibid., 99.
23. Godechot, *Les constitutions de la France depuis 1789,* 167.
24. Claire Elisabeth, comtesse de Rémusat, *Mémoires de Madame de Rémusat* (Paris, 1881), 107.
25. Ibid., 102.
26. Ibid.
27. Reine Hortense, *Mémoires* (Paris, 1927), 1:166.
28. Molé, *Mémoires,* 1:143.
29. Talleyrand, *Mémoires,* 1:302.
30. Molé, *Mémoires,* 1:140.

Chapter 4. Great Britain and France

1. L. G. Mitchell, *Charles James Fox* (Oxford, U.K., 1992), 119.
2. Ibid., 137.
3. Ibid., 170.
4. *Le Moniteur,* June 8, 1806.

Chapter 5. Eastern Europe: Dealing with France

1. Friedrich Meinecke, *The Age of German Liberation, 1795–1815* (Berkeley, Calif., 1977), 36.
2. E. M. Almedingen, *The Emperor Alexander* (London, 1964), 37.

3. Ibid., 50.
4. Ibid., 63.
5. W. H. Zawadzki, *A Man of Honour: Adam Czartoryski* (Oxford, U.K., 1993), 65.
6. Ibid., 100.
7. John Holland Rose, ed., *Select Despatches from the British Foreign Office Archives* (London, 1904), 102.
8. Napoléon Bonaparte, *Lettres de Napoléon à Joséphine* (Paris, n.d.), 54.
9. Ibid., 61–62.
10. Prince de Talleyrand, *Mémoires* (Paris, 1891), 218.
11. Prince Adam Czartoryski, *Alexandre Ier et le Prince Czartoryski* (Paris, 1865), 7–10.
12. Ibid., 47.

Chapter 6. Inventing Politics

1. *Gazette of the United States,* New York, March 23, 1790.
2. John Adams, *Works,* ed. Charles Francis Adams (Boston, 1856), 8:493.
3. Thomas Jefferson, *Writings,* The Library of America (New York, 1984), 971–972.
4. Médéric Moreau de Saint-Méry, *Voyage aux Etats-Unis de l'Amérique, 1793–1798* (New Haven, 1913), 149.
5. François duc de la Rochefoucault-Liancourt, *Voyages dans les Etats-Unis d'Amérique faits en 1795, 1796 et 1797* (Paris, 1799), 7:149–150.
6. Ibid., 86.
7. Alexander Hamilton, *Works,* ed. Henry Cabot Lodge (New York, 1880–1886), 6:355.
8. Paul L. Ford, ed., *The Writings of Thomas Jefferson* (New York, 1892–1899), 6:109.
9. Ibid., 6:102.
10. Ibid., 9:296.
11. Ibid., 6:5.
12. John Adams, *Works,* 1:460.
13. Ford, *Writings of Thomas Jefferson,* 7:40.
14. Jefferson, *Writings* (Library of America), 1002.
15. Ford, *Writings of Thomas Jefferson,* 6:154.
16. Jefferson, *Writings* (Library of America), 1011.
17. Ford, *Writings of Thomas Jefferson,* 7:32–33.
18. Charles Francis Adams, ed., *Letters of John Adams Addressed to His Wife* (Boston, 1841), 2:195.
19. Ibid., 2:193.
20. John Adams, *Works,* 7:518.
21. *Philadelphia Aurora,* September 13, 1796.
22. Ford, *Writings of Thomas Jefferson,* 7:72 ff.
23. Ibid., 7:93–94.
24. John Adams and Thomas Jefferson, *The Adams-Jefferson Letters,* ed. Lester J. Cappon (Chapel Hill, N.C., 1959), 336.
25. Ford, *Writings of Thomas Jefferson,* 7:91–92.
26. Hamilton, *Works,* 10:238.
27. C. F. Adams, *Letters,* 2:235.
28. Ibid., 2:242–243.
29. Hamilton, *Works,* 10:233–234.
30. John Adams, *Works,* 8:522–523.

Chapter 7. Quasi-War and Dangerous Aliens

1. Charles Francis Adams, ed., *Letters of John Adams Addressed to His Wife* (Boston, 1841), 2:245.
2. John Adams, *Works,* ed. Charles Francis Adams (Boston, 1856), 9:108.
3. Ibid., 1:507.

4. C. F. Adams, *Letters*, 2:252.

5. Alexander Hamilton, *Works*, ed. Henry Cabot Lodge (New York, 1880–1886), 10:241–242.

6. Ibid., 10:255.

7. John Adams, *Works*, 9:575.

8. Ibid., 8:546–547.

9. Abigail Adams, "Letters to Mary Cranch," in *Proceedings of the American Antiquarian Society, 1945*, vol. 55, pt. 1 (Worcester, Mass., 1947), 200.

10. Ibid., 202.

11. Ibid., 202–203.

12. Ibid., 203.

13. Ibid., 208.

14. Ibid., 209.

15. Ibid., 203–204.

16. Ibid., 206.

17. Ibid., 305.

18. Ibid., 311.

19. Ibid., 210.

20. Paul L. Ford, *The Writings of Thomas Jefferson* (New York, 1892–1899), 7:154.

21. John Adams, *Works*, 7:547–548.

22. Stanley Elkins and Eric McKitrick, *The Age of Federalism* (New York, 1993), 582.

23. Hamilton, *Works*, 10:276.

24. Lowrier, Walter, ed., *American State Papers, Foreign Relations* (Washington, D.C., 1861), 2:152.

25. Hamilton, *Works*, 10:285.

26. John Adams, *Works*, 9:82.

27. Abigail Adams, "Letters," 345.

28. Ford, *Writings of Thomas Jefferson*, 7:2323.

29. John Adams, *Works*, 9:159.

30. Hamilton, *Works*, 10:287.

31. John Adams, *Works*, 8:574.

32. Hamilton, *Works*, 10:302.

33. John Adams, *Works*, 8:580.

34. Ibid., 8:588.

35. Ibid., 8:592.

36. Dumas Malone, *The Ordeal of Liberty* (Boston, 1967), 429.

37. John Adams, *Works*, 8:625–626.

38. James Madison, *Writings*, ed. Gaillard Hunt (New York, 1900–1910), 6:352.

39. Ford, *Writings of Thomas Jefferson*, 7:336.

40. Malone, *Ordeal*, 437.

41. John Adams, *Works*, 9:3.

42. Ibid, 9:5.

43. Herbert A. Johnson et al., eds., *The Papers of John Marshall* (Chapel Hill, N.C., 1974), 4:44.

44. Hamilton, *Works*, 10:318.

45. Abigail Adams, "Letters," 403.

Chapter 8. A Vast New Country

1. François duc de la Rochefoucault-Liancourt, *Voyages dans les Etats-Unis d'Amérique faits en 1795, 1796 et 1797* (Paris, 1799), xi.

2. Ibid., 7:132.

3. Médéric Moreau de Saint-Méry, *Voyage aux Etats-Unis de l'Amérique 1793–1798* (New Haven, 1913), 58–59.

4. Liancourt, *Voyages*, 4:9.

5. Ibid., 6:312.

6. Ibid., 6:327.

7. Ibid., 4:329.

8. Henry S. Randall, *Life of Thomas Jefferson* (New York, 1858), 2:191.

9. Thomas Jefferson, *Writings*, The Library of America (New York, 1984), 975–976.

10. William Seale, *The President's House* (Washington, D.C., 1896), 1:81.

11. Abigail Adams, "Letters to Mary Cranch," in *Proceedings of the American Antiquarian Society, 1945*, vol. 55, pt. 1 (Worcester, Mass., 1947), 434.

12. Ibid., 435–438.

Chapter 9. The Spirit of 1800

1. Thomas Jefferson, *Writings*, The Library of America (New York, 1984), 1062.

2. Stanley Elkins and Eric McKitrick, *The Age of Federalism* (New York, 1993), 680.

3. Jefferson, *Writings* (Library of America), 1075.

4. Alexander Hamilton, *Works*, ed. Henry Cabot Lodge (New York, 1880–1886), 10:375–376.

5. Elkins and McKitrick, *Age of Federalism*, 736.

6. Hamilton, *Works*, 10:383.

7. Dumas Malone, *The Ordeal of Liberty* (Boston, 1967), 481.

8. Ibid., 483.

9. Hamilton, *Works*, 10:377.

10. Ibid., 15:233 ff.

11. Ibid.

12. Ibid., 15:181–182.

13. John Adams, *Works*, ed. Charles Francis Adams (Boston, 1856), 9:577–578.

14. Malone, *Ordeal*, 496.

15. Hamilton, *Works*, 15:319–320.

16. Ibid., 15:271.

17. Jefferson, *Writings* (Library of America), 492–493.

18. Ibid., 494–495.

19. Dumas Malone, *Jefferson the President: First Term, 1801–1805* (Boston, 1970), 22.

20. Jefferson, *Writings* (Library of America), 1084.

21. Ibid., 1145–1146.

22. Paul L. Ford, *The Writings of Thomas Jefferson* (New York, 1892–1899), 8:67–70.

23. *New York Post*, July 7, 1802.

24. Ford, *Writings of Thomas Jefferson*, 8:176.

25. Jefferson, *Writings* (Library of America), 1089.

26. Ibid., 567.

27. Thomas Jefferson, *Writings*, ed. A. A. Lipscomb and A. E. Bergh (Washington, D.C., 1903), 10:255.

28. Hamilton, *Works*, 8:601.

29. Malone, *Jefferson the President*, 93.

30. Margaret Bayard Smith, *The First Forty Years of Washington Society* (New York, 1965), 29.

31. Ibid., 30–31.

32. Jefferson, *Writings* (Library of America), 1115.

33. Smith, *First Forty Years*, 13–14.

34. Abigail Adams, "Letters to Mary Cranch," in *Proceedings of the American Antiquarian Society, 1945*, vol. 55, pt. 1 (Worcester, Mass., 1947), 419–420.

35. Smith, *First Forty Years*, 46–47.

36. Ibid., 2–3.

37. Ibid., 11–12.

38. Ford, *Writings of Thomas Jefferson*, 8:149.

39. E. S. Corwin, *Court over Constitution* (New York, 1950), 66.

40. Malone, *Jefferson the President*, 258.

41. Ibid., 268.

42. Jefferson, *Writings* (Library of America), 1112.

43. Albert Gallatin, *Writings*, ed. Henry Adams (Philadelphia, 1879), 113–114.
44. Smith, *First Forty Years*, 39.
45. Ford, *Writings of Thomas Jefferson*, 8:244.
46. Malone, *Jefferson the President*, 321.
47. Jefferson, *Writings* (Library of America), 1147.

Chapter 10. New Spain, Old Habits

1. Alexander Freiherr von Humboldt, *Personal Narrative of Travels to the Equinoctial Regions of the New Continent, during the Years 1799–1804* (London, 1822), 1:214.
2. Ibid., 1:428–429.
3. Ibid., 1:381–382.
4. Frances Calderón de la Barca, *Life in Mexico* (Mexico City, n.d.),184.
5. Humboldt, *Personal Narrative*, 1:412–413.
6. Ibid., 1:221.
7. Cornelius de Pauw, *Recherches Philosophiques sur les Américains* (Berlin, 1768–1769), 2:164–165.
8. Humboldt, *Personal Narrative*, 2:2–3.
9. Calderón, *Life in Mexico*, 338.
10. Humboldt, *Personal Narrative*, 1:411.
11. Hugh H. Hamill Jr., *The Hidalgo Revolt: Prelude to American Independence* (Gainesville, Fla., 1966), 42.
12. Robert W. Patch, *The Bourbon Reforms, City Councils and the Struggle for Power in Yucatán, 1770–1796* (Lincoln, Nebr., 1981), 195.
13. Calderón, *Life in Mexico*, 257.
14. Ibid., 92.
15. Joel R. Poinsett, *Notes on Mexico Made in the Autumn of 1822* (Philadelphia, 1824), 64.
16. Ibid., 119.
17. Ibid., 12.
18. Ibid., 119.
19. Ibid.
20. Quoted in David A. Brading, *Church and State in Bourbon Mexico* (Cambridge, U.K., 1994), 168.
21. Calderón, *Life in Mexico*, 129.
22. Ibid., 132–133, 136–137.
23. Poinsett, *Notes on Mexico*, 49–50.
24. Humboldt, *Essai*, 1:261.
25. Calderón, *Life in Mexico*, 64–66.
26. Poinsett, *Notes on Mexico*, 58.
27. Ibid., 81.
28. Calderón, *Life in Mexico*, 90–91.
29. Ibid., 64.
30. Ibid., 88.

Chapter 11. Autonomy or Independence?

1. Alexander Freiherr von Humboldt, *Personal Narrative of Travels to the Equinoctial Regions of the New Continent, during the Years 1799–1804* (London, 1822), 363.
2. Ibid., 1:293–294.
3. Quoted in Doris M. Ladd, *The Mexican Nobility at Independence, 1780–1826* (Austin, 1976), 70.
4. Quoted in Hugh H. Hamill Jr., *The Hidalgo Revolt: Prelude to American Independence* (Gainesville, Fla., 1966), 3.
5. Joel R. Poinsett, *Notes on Mexico Made in the Autumn of 1822* (Philadelphia, 1824), 48.
6. Frances Calderón de la Barca, *Life in Mexico* (Mexico City, n.d.), 125.
7. Poinsett, *Notes on Mexico*, 23.
8. Ibid., 24.

9. Ibid., 70.

10. *Documentos Historicos Mexicanos* (Mexico City, 1985), 2:27.

11. Hamill, *The Hidalgo Revolt*, 32.

12. Ibid., 81.

13. Ibid., 121–122.

14. Ibid., 129.

Chapter 12. Peru and Brazil

1. Cited in Timothy E. Anna, *The Fall of the Royal Government in Peru* (Lincoln, Nebr., 1979), 5.

2. W. B. Stevenson, *Historical and Descriptive Narrative of Twenty Years' Residence in South America* (London, 1829), 2:76.

3. Cited in Leon G. Campbell, *The Military and Society in Colonial Peru, 1750–1810* (Phildelphia, 1978), 100.

4. Vassilii Mikhailovich Golovnin, *Around the World on the Kamtchatka, 1817–1819* (Honolulu, 1979), 67–68.

5. Ibid., 56.

6. Stevenson, *Twenty Years' Residence*, 1:213–214.

7. Ibid., 1:226–227.

8. Golovnin, *Around the World*, 61–62.

9. Stevenson, *Twenty Years' Residence*, 1:295.

10. Ibid., 1:212.

11. Ibid., 1:318.

12. Cited in Jean Descola, *La Vie Quotidienne au Pérou au temps des Espagnols, 1710–1820* (Paris, 1962), 155.

13. Gerhard Masur, *Simon Bolívar* (Albuquerque, 1948), 366.

14. Golovnin, *Around the World*, 61–62.

15. Stevenson, *Twenty Years' Residence*, 1:220–221.

16. Captain Basil Hall, *Extracts from a Journal Written on the Coasts of Chile, Peru and Mexico in the Years 1820, 1821, 1822* (London, 1824), 1:97–98.

17. Stevenson, *Twenty Years' Residence*, 1:223–224.

18. Hall, *Extracts from a Journal*, 1:107.

19. Stevenson, *Twenty Years' Residence*, 1:319–320.

20. Ibid., 1:402–404.

21. Timothy E. Anna, *Spain and the Loss of America* (Lincoln, Nebr., 1983), 37.

22. Bertita Harding, *Amazon Throne* (New York, 1941), 45.

Chapter 13. The Center of the World

1. J. L. Cranmer-Bying, ed., *An Embassy to China, Being the Journal Kept by Lord Macartney during His Embassy to the Emperor Ch'ien-lung, 1793–1794* (Hamden, Conn., 1963), 88.

2. Ibid., 77.

3. Ibid., 101–102.

4. Lo-shu Fu, ed., *A Documentary Chronicle of Sino-Western Relations, 1644–1820* (Tucson, 1966), 1:323.

5. Ibid., 1:325.

6. Cranmer-Bying, *An Embassy to China*, 33.

7. Ibid., 122.

8. Ibid., 123.

9. Ibid., 124.

10. Susan Mann Jones, *Decline and the Roots of Rebellion*, Cambridge History of China, vol. 10, pt. 1 (Cambridge, U.K., 1978), 115.

11. Edmund Backhouse and J. O. P. Bland, *Annals and Memoirs of the Court of Peking* (New York, 1970), 364–367.

12. Ibid., 347–349.

Chapter 14. A Civilized Empire

1. Hope Danby, *The Garden of Perfect Brightness* (London, 1950), 44.
2. Harold L. Kahn, *Monarchy in the Emperor's Eye: Image and Reality in the Ch'ien-lung Reign* (Cambridge, Mass., 1971), 132–133.
3. Luther Carrington Goodrich, *The Literary Inquisition of Ch'ien-lung* (Baltimore, 1935), 32.
4. Ibid., 33.
5. Ibid., 39.
6. Edmund Backhouse and J. O. P. Bland, *Annals and Memoirs of the Court of Peking* (New York, 1970), 325.
7. Ibid., 320–321.
8. Kahn, *Monarchy in the Emperor's Eye*, 198.
9. Backhouse and Bland, *Annals and Memoirs*, 353–354.
10. John Barrow, *Travels in China* (London, 1804), 193.
11. Ibid., 123.
12. Ibid., 124.
13. Ibid., 206.
14. Ibid., 124–125.
15. J. L. Cranmer-Byng, ed., *An Embassy to China, Being the Journal Kept by Lord Macartney during His Embassy to the Emperor Ch'ien-lung, 1793–1794* (Hamden, Conn., 1963), 95.
16. Lo-shu Fu, ed., *A Documentary Chronicle of Sino-Western Relations, 1644–1820* (Tucson, 1966), 1:292–293.
17. Ibid., 1:299.
18. Cranmer-Byng, *An Embassy to China*, 73.
19. Howard S. Levy, *The Lotus Lovers* (Buffalo, 1991), 34.
20. Félix Renouard de Sainte-Croix, *Voyage commercial et politique aux Indes orientales, aux îles Philippines, á la Chine, avec des notions sur la Cochinchine et le Tonkin, pendant les années 1803, 1804, 1805, 1806 et 1809* (Paris, 1810), 2:164 ff.
21. Ibid., 3:163.
22. Barrow, *Travels in China*, 109.
23. Sainte-Croix, *Voyage commercial et politique*, 3:156 ff.
24. K. C. Chang, ed., *Food in Chinese Culture* (New Haven, 1977), 273.
25. Ibid.
26. Barrow, *Travels in China*, 100.
27. Sainte-Croix, *Voyage commercial et politique*, 3:90.
28. Barrow, *Travels in China*, 44–45.
29. Ibid., 95–96.

Chapter 15. Splendid Japan

1. David J. Lu, *Japan: A Documentary History* (London, 1984), 221.
2. Carl Peter Thunberg, *Travels in Europe, Africa and Asia Performed between the Years 1770 and 1779* (London, 1793), 3:11–12.
3. Quoted in ibid., 3:262.
4. Quoted in ibid., 3:229.
5. R. H. P. Mason, *A History of Japan* (New York, 1974), 161.
6. Aland Churchill, *A Collection of Voyages and Travels* (London, 1744), 1:416–417.
7. Mason, *History of Japan*, 190–191.
8. Thunberg, *Travels*, 97–98.
9. Ibid., 3:267–268.
10. Ibid., 3:77–78.
11. Ibid., 3:275–276.
12. Ibid., 3:274–275.
13. Ibid., 3:252.

Chapter 16. India: The Invention of an Empire

1. Percival Spear, *The Oxford History of Modern India* (Oxford, U.K., 1978), 78.
2. Ibid., 79.
3. M. Martin, *Despatches, Minutes and Correspondence of the Marquis Wellesley* (London, 1836), 1:528.
4. Sir John Malcolm, *The Political History of India* (London, 1826), 1:331–332.
5. Dennis Kincaid, *British Social Life in India* (London, 1938), 117.
6. Percival Spear, *The Nabobs* (London, 1932), 96.
7. Thomas Twining, *Travels in India* (London, 1893), 483–484.
8. Sidney Owen, ed., *A Selection from the Despatches of the Duke of Wellington* (Oxford, U.K., 1879), 566–567.
9. Martin, *Despatches,* 1:159.
10. Paul Ernest Roberts, *India under Wellesley* (London, 1929), 50–51.
11. Denys Forest, *Tiger of Mysore* (London, 1970), 205.
12. Roberts, *India under Wellesley,* 59–60.
13. Ibid., 59.
14. Elizabeth Longford, *Wellington: The Years of the Sword* (London, 1969), 1:93.
15. Percival Spear, *Twilight of the Moghuls* (Cambridge, U.K., 1951), 27–28.
16. Ibid., 29.
17. Ibid., 35.
18. Ibid., 36.
19. Owen, *Despatches of the Duke of Wellington,* 471.
20. Kincaid, *British Social Life in India,* 117.
21. Eliza Fay, *Original Letters from India* (London, 1925), 181.
22. Ibid., 187.
23. Spear, *Nabobs,* 53–55.
24. Fay, *Original Letters,* 199–200.
25. Ibid., 191.

Chapter 17. The Middle East: The Ottoman Empire

1. Jason Goodwin, *Lords of the Horizon* (London, 1998), 216.
2. Joseph Pitton de Tournefort, *Relation d'un voyage du Levant* (Lyon, 1717), 2:173.
3. Ibid., 2:179.
4. Ibid., 2:184.
5. Ibid., 2:234.
6. Jean-Claude Flachat, *Observations sur le commerce et sur les arts d'une partie de l'Europe, de l'Asie, de l'Afrique et même des Indes Orientales* (Lyon, 1766), 2:198 ff.
7. Maxime du Camp, *Souvenirs et Paysages d'Orient* (Paris, 1848), 197.
8. N. M. Penzer, *The Harem* (London, 1965), 167–168.

Chapter 18. So Close, So Far

1. Cited in Basil Davidson, *Africa: History of a Continent* (New York, 1966), 234.
2. Basil Davidson, *The African Past* (Boston, 1964), 212.
3. Ibid., 227–228.
4. Philip D. Curtin, *Africa Remembered* (Madison, Wis., 1986), 84.
5. Ibid., 85.
6. Ibid., 90–92.
7. Ibid., 93.
8. Ibid., 95.
9. Ibid., 96 ff.
10. Ibid., 98.
11. Ibid., 99.

12. George Thompson, *Travels and Adventures in Southern Africa* (Cape Town, 1972), 57.
13. Gideon S. Were, *A History of South Africa* (New York, 1974), 233.
14. Anders Sparrman, *A Voyage to the Cape of Good Hope* (London, 1785), 1:50.
15. John Barrow, *An Account of Travels into the Interior of Southern Africa* (London, 1801), 1:49–51.
16. Ibid., 1:47.
17. Sparrman, *Voyage to the Cape of Good Hope,* 1:205–206.
18. Ibid., 1:58.
19. Ibid., 2:329.
20. Ibid., 2:29.
21. Ibid., 2:30.
22. Thompson, *Travels and Adventures,* 380.

Bibliography

Abrantès, duchesse d'. *Mémoires*. Paris, 1835.

Adams, Abigail. "Letters to Mary Cranch," in *Proceedings of the American Antiquarian Society, 1945*. Vol. 55, pt. 1. Worcester, Mass., 1947.

Adams, Charles Francis, ed. *Letters of John Adams Addressed to His Wife*. Boston, 1841.

Adams, John. *Works*. Edited by Charles Francis Adams. Boston, 1856.

Adams, John, and Thomas Jefferson. *The Adams-Jefferson Letters*. Edited by Lester J. Cappon. Chapel Hill, N.C., 1959.

Almedingen, E. M. *The Emperor Alexander I*. London, 1964.

Anna, Timothy E. *The Fall of the Royal Government in Peru*. Lincoln, Nebr., 1979.

———. *Spain and the Loss of America*. Lincoln, Nebr., 1983.

Backhouse, Edmund, and J. O. P. Bland. *Annals and Memoirs of the Court of Peking*. New York, 1970.

Balandier, Georges. *Daily Life in the Kingdom of the Kongo*. New York, 1968.

Barbaud, Pierre. *Haydn*. Paris, 1957.

Barrow, John. *An Account of Travels into the Interior of Southern Africa*. London, 1801.

———. *Travels in China*. London, 1804.

Bausset, L. F. J. de. *Mémoires anecdotiques sur l'intérieur du Palais impérial*. Paris, 1877.

Beethoven, Ludwig van. *Beethoven's Letters*. Edited by J. S. Shedlock. London, 1909.

Bonaparte, Napoléon. *Lettres de Napoléon à Joséphine*. Paris, n.d.

Brading, David A. *Church and State in Bourbon Mexico*. Cambridge, U.K., 1994.

Cabanis, José. *Le Sacre de Napoléon*. Paris, 1970.

Calderón de la Barca, Frances. *Life in Mexico*. Mexico City, n.d.

Camp, Maxime du. *Souvenirs et Paysages d'Orient*. Paris, 1848.

Campbell, Leon G. *The Military and Society in Colonial Peru, 1750-1810*. Philadelphia, 1978.

Chang, K. C., ed. *Food in Chinese Culture*. Yale University Press, 1977.

Churchill, Aland. *A Collection of Voyages and Travels*. London, 1744.

Corwin, E. S. *Court over Constitution*. New York, 1950.

Cranmer-Bying, J. L., ed. *An Embassy to China, Being the Journal Kept by Lord Macartney during His Embassy to the Emperor Ch'ien-lung, 1793–1794*. Hamden, Conn., 1963.

Curtin, Philip D. *Africa Remembered*. Madison, Wis., 1986.

Czartoryski, Prince Adam. *Alexandre Ier et le Prince Czartoryski*. Paris, 1865.

Danby, Hope. *The Garden of Perfect Brightness*. London, 1950.

Davidson, Basil. *Africa: History of a Continent*. New York, 1966.

———. *The African Past*. Boston, 1964.

Descola, Jean. *La Vie Quotidienne au Pérou au temps des Espagnols, 1710-1820*. Paris, 1962.

Documentos historicos Mexicanos. Mexico City, 1985.

Elkins, Stanley, and Eric McKitrick. *The Age of Federalism*. New York, 1993.

Fay, Eliza. *Original Letters from India*. London, 1925.

Flachat, Jean-Claude. *Observations sur le commerce et sur les arts d'une partie de l'Europe, de l'Asie, de l'Afrique et même des Indes Orientales*. Lyon, 1766.

Ford, Paul L., ed. *The Writings of Thomas Jefferson.* New York, 1892–1899.

Forest, Denys. *Tiger of Mysore.* London, 1970.

Fu, Lo-shu, ed. *A Documentary Chronicle of Sino-Western Relations (1644–1820).* Tucson, 1966.

Gallatin, Albert. *Writings.* Edited by Henry Adams. Philadelphia, 1879.

Garnier, Jean-Paul. *Barras, Roi du Directoire.* Paris, 1970.

Godechot, Jacques. *Les constitutions de la France depuis 1789.* Paris, 1979.

Golovnin, Vassilii Mikhailovich. *Around the World on the Kamtchatka, 1817–1819.* Honolulu, 1979.

Goncourt, Edmond de, and Jules de Goncourt. *Histoire de la Société française pendant le Directoire.* Paris, 1879.

Goodrich, Luther Carrington. *The Literary Inquisition of Ch'ien-lung.* Baltimore, 1935.

Goodwin, Jason. *Lords of the Horizons.* London, 1998.

Hall, Captain Basil. *Extracts from a Journal Written on the Coasts of Chile, Peru and Mexico in the Years 1820, 1821, 1822.* London, 1824.

Hamill, Hugh H. Jr. *The Hidalgo Revolt: Prelude to American Independence.* Gainesville, Fla., 1966.

Hamilton, Alexander. *Works.* Edited by Henry Cabot Lodge. New York, 1880–1886.

Harding, Bertita. *Amazon Throne.* New York, 1941.

Herold, J. Christopher. *Mistress to an Age: A Life of Madame de Staël.* London, 1959.

Hortense, Reine. *Mémoires.* Paris, 1927.

Humboldt, Alexander Freiherr von. *Personal Narrative of Travels to the Equinoctial Regions of the New Continent, during the Years 1799–1804.* London, 1822.

Jefferson, Thomas. *Writings.* The Library of America. New York, 1984.

———. *Writings.* Edited by A. A. Lipscomb and A. E. Bergh. Washington, D.C., 1903.

Johnson, Herbert A, et al., eds. *The Papers of John Marshall.* Chapel Hill, N.C., 1974.

Jones, Susan Mann. *Decline and the Roots of Rebellion.* Cambridge History of China, vol. 10, pt. 1. Cambridge, U.K., 1978.

Kahn, Harold L. *Monarchy in the Emperor's Eyes: Image and Reality in the Ch'ien-lung Reign.* Cambridge, Mass., 1971.

Kincaid, Dennis. *British Social Life in India.* London, 1938.

Ladd, Doris M. *The Mexican Nobility at Independence, 1780–1826.* Austin, 1976.

La petite armée du grand Pichegru. Paris, n.d.

Lefebvre, Georges. *La France sous le Directoire.* Paris, 1977.

Levy, Howard S. *The Lotus Lovers.* Buffalo, 1991.

Liancourt, François duc de la Rochefoucault. *Voyages dans les Etats-Unis d'Amérique faits en 1795, 1796 et 1797.* Paris, 1799.

Longford, Elizabeth. *Wellington: The Years of the Sword.* London, 1969.

Lowrie, Walter, ed. *American State Papers, Foreign Relations.* Washington, D.C., 1861.

Lu, David J. *Japan: A Documentary History.* London, 1984.

Madison, James. *Writings.* Edited by Gaillard Hunt. New York, 1900–1910.

Malcolm, Sir John. *The Political History of India.* London, 1826.

Malone, Dumas. *Jefferson the President: First Term, 1801–1805.* Boston, 1970.

———. *The Ordeal of Liberty.* Boston, 1967.

Martin, M. *Despatches, Minutes and Correspondence of the Marquis Wellesley.* London, 1836.

Mason, R. H. P. *A History of Japan.* New York, 1974.

Masur, Gerhard. *Simon Bolívar.* Albuquerque, 1948.

Meinecke, Friedrich. *The Age of German Liberation, 1795–1815.* Berkeley, Calif., 1977.

Mémoires de Constant. Paris, 1830.

Mitchell, L. G.. *Charles James Fox.* Oxford, U.K., 1992.

Molé, Matthieu Louis, comte. *Le comte Molé, sa vie, ses mémoires.* Paris, 1922.

Owen, Sidney, ed. *A Selection from the Despatches of the Duke of Wellington.* Oxford, U.K., 1879.

Patch, Robert W. *The Bourbon Reforms, City Councils and the Struggle for Power in Yucatán, 1770–1796.* Lincoln, Nebr., 1981.

Pauw, Cornelius de. *Recherches Philosophiques sur les Américains.* Berlin, 1768–1769.

Penzer, N. M. *The Harem*. London, 1965.

Poinsett, Joel R. *Notes on Mexico Made in the Autumn of 1822*. Philadelphia, 1824.

Preston, M. Torbert. *The Ch'ing Imperial Household Department: A Study of Its Organization and Principal Functions, 1662–1796*. Cambridge, Mass., 1977.

Randall, Henry S. *Life of Thomas Jefferson*. New York, 1858.

Reichardt, J. F. *Un Hiver à Paris sous le Consulat*. Paris, 1896.

Rémusat, Claire Elisabeth comtesse de. *Mémoires de Madame de Rémusat*. Paris, 1881.

Reynière, A. B. L. Grimod de la. *Almanach des Gourmands*. Paris, 1806.

———. *Manuel des Amphitryons*. Paris, 1808.

Roberts, Paul Ernest. *India under Wellesley*. London, 1929.

Robiquet, Jean. *La Vie Quotidienne au temps de Napoléon*. Paris, 1942.

Roeder, P. L., comte. *Autour de Bonaparte*. Paris, 1809.

Rose, John Holland, ed. *Select Dispatches from the British Foreign Office Archives*. London, 1904.

Rovigo, General Savary, duc de. *Mémoires pour servir à l'histoire de l'Empereur Napoléon*. Paris, 1828.

Sainte-Croix, Félix Renouard de. *Voyage commercial et politique aux Indes orientales, aux iles Philippines, à la Chine, avec des notions sur la Cochinchine et le Tonkin, pendant les années 1803, 1804, 1805, 1806 et 1809*. Paris, 1810.

Saint-Méry, Médéric Moreau de. *Voyage aux Etats-Unis de l'Amerique, 1793–1798*. New Haven, Conn., 1913.

Seale, William. *The President's House*. Washington, D.C., 1896.

Smith, Margaret Bayard. *The First Forty Years of Washington Society*. New York, 1965.

Sparrman, Anders. *A Voyage to the Cape of Good Hope*. London, 1785.

Spear, Percival. *The Nabobs*. London, 1932.

———. *The Oxford History of Modern India*. Oxford, U.K., 1978.

———. *Twilight of the Moghuls*. Cambridge, U.K., 1951.

Stevenson, W. B. *Historical and Descriptive Narrative of Twenty Years' Residence in South America*. London, 1829.

Talleyrand, Prince de. *Mémoires*. Paris, 1891.

Thompson, George. *Travels and Adventures in Southern Africa*. Cape Town, 1972.

Thunberg, Carl Peter. *Travels in Europe, Africa and Asia Performed between the Years 1770 and 1779*. London, 1793.

Tournefort, Joseph Pitton de. *Relation d'un voyage du Levant*. Lyon, 1717.

Twining, Thomas. *Travels in India*. London, 1893.

Were, Gideon S. *A History of South Africa*. New York, 1974.

Zawadzki, W. H. *A Man of Honour: Adam Czartoryski*. Oxford, U.K., 1993.

Index